WORLD OF LANGUAGE

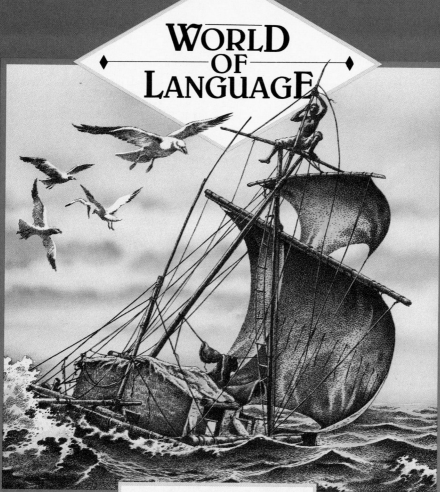

SILVER BURDETT & GINN

Betty G. Gray   Marian Davies Toth   Nancy Nickell Ragno

Contributing Author — Primary   Elfrieda Hiebert
Contributing Author — Vocabulary   Richard E. Hodges
Contributing Author — Poetry   Myra Cohn Livingston

Consulting Author — Thinking Skills   David N. Perkins

SILVER BURDETT & GINN
MORRISTOWN, NJ   NEEDHAM, MA

Atlanta, GA   Cincinnati, OH   Dallas, TX   Menlo Park, CA   Deerfield, IL

Acknowledgments

Cover: Isidre Mones

Contributing Writers: Sandra Breuer, Judy Brim, Gary Davis, Wendy Davis, Jack Dempsey, Anne Maley, Margarete Wright Pruce, Duncan Searl, Diana Sergis, Gerry Tomlinson

Contributing artists: Bradley Clark, Suzanne Clee, Rick Cooley, Patricia A. Courtney, Allen Davis, John Dyess, Len Ebert, Michele Epstein, Gabriel, Grace Goldberg, Denman Hampson, Langaron, Fred Marvin, Rebecca Merrilees, Joseph Miralles, Isidre Mones, Dennis O'Brien, Laughran O'Connor, Taylor Oughton, Eileen Rosen, Sally Schaedler, Wayne A. Still, Phyllis Tarlow, Gonzallez Vicente, Lane Yerkes.

Handwriting models: Michele Epstein

Picture credits: All photographs by Silver Burdett & Ginn (SB&G) unless otherwise noted. **Unit 1** 5: The Granger Collection. 7: Steve Hanson/Stock, Boston. 8: UPI/Bettmann Newsphotos. 13: North Wind Picture Archives. 21: The Granger Collection. 26: © 1937 Estate of Norman Rockwell. 44: Illustration by Cheryl Harness from *Constance: A Story of Early Plymouth* by Patricia Clapp. Copyright © 1968 by The Viking Press, Inc. All rights reserved. Reprinted by permission of Viking Penguin, a division of Penguin Books, USA, Inc. **Unit 2** 56: Thor Heyerdahl/Courtesy Yvonne Heyerdahl. 61: Everett Johnson/Leo deWys, Inc. 63: The Granger Collection. 64: AP/Wide World Photos. 67: National Maritime Museum, London. 71: Peter Menzel/Stock, Boston. 74: Bridgeman Art Library/Art Resource, *Forbes* Magazine Collection, New York. 81: Thor Heyerdahl/Courtesy Yvonne Heyerdahl. 87: UPI/Bettmann Newsphotos. 89: ZEFA/H. Armstrong Roberts. 91: H. Armstrong Roberts. 92: © 1990 Shelly Grossman/Woodfin Camp & Associates. 93: Detail, *Lewis and Clark at Three Forks,* painting by E.S. Paxson. Courtesy of the Montana Historical Society. 95–97: NASA. 104: Dan De Wilde for SB&G. 108: Graham/FPG International. 109: Book jacket from *Carry On, Mr. Bowditch* by Jean Lee Latham. Reprinted with permission of Houghton Mifflin Co. **Unit 3** 128: Michael Radigan/The Stock Market of NY. 133: Dan Cornish/Esto Photographics. 135: UPI/Bettmann Newsphotos. 137: Andree Abecassis/The Stock Market of NY. 140: *Detroit Industry,* 1932–1933, Fresco, Diego M. Rivera, Mexican 1886–1957. The Detroit Institute of Arts, Founders Society Purchase, Edsel B. Ford Fund and Gift of Edsel B. Ford. (33.10.N.) 162: Dan De Wilde for SB&G. 167: Jacket illustration from *Immigrant Kids* by Russell Freedman. Published by Dutton, 1980. **Unit 4:** 178: S. Sylvester/FPG International. 181: Richard Clement/Nawrocki Stock Photos. 184: UPI/Bettmann Newsphotos. 189: Dave Brown/The Stock Market of NY. 193: The Granger Collection. 195: R. Rathe/FPG International. 202: Jointly owned by The Cleveland Museum of Art and an anonymous collector. 203: S. Sylvester/FPG International. 206: The New York Times Syndication Sales Corporation. 208: S. Sylvester/FPG International. 217: Grant Heilman/Grant Heilman Photography. 224: Dan De Wilde for SB&G. 228: *l.* Bill Bene/Nawrocki Stock Photos; *m.* Manuel Dos Passos/Bruce Coleman; *r.* Marmel Studio/The Stock Market of NY. 229: Jacket illustration by Symeon Shimin from *Onion John* by Joseph Krumgold (Thomas Y. Crowell). Jacket © 1959 by Symeon Shimin. Reprinted by permission of Harper & Row, Publishers, Inc. **Unit 5** 244–246: The Granger Collection. 247: Culver Pictures. 249: The Granger Collection. 257: Shooting Star. 260: Historical Pictures Service, Chicago. 264: The New York Public Library, Astor, Lenox & Tilden Foundations. 273: Gabe Palmer/The Stock Market of NY. 284: Dan De Wilde for SB&G. 288: *t.l.* Art Resource; *b.l., t.m.* The Granger Collection; *b.m.* Chris Brown/Stock, Boston; *t.r.* Ray C. Moore/Shostal Associates; *b.r.* The Bettmann Archive. 289: Book jacket from *I'm Nobody! Who Are You?* by Edna Barth. Reprinted by permission of Houghton Mifflin Co. **Unit 6** 300: AP/Wide World Photos. 305: The Granger Collection. 306: TSW–Click/Chicago. 310: Charles Palek/Tom Stack & Associates. 311: Adolf Schmidecker/FPG International. 318: Lindbergh Picture Collection, Yale University Library. 314: Bill Ray. 323: *Royal-Tide Dawn,* 1960. Louise Nevelson. Wood painted gold, 91″ x 63″ x 10⅝″. Photograph courtesy The Pace Gallery. 325: Alon Reininger/Leo deWys, Inc. 330: AP/Wide World Photos. 334: Dan De Wilde for SB&G. 339: Jacket illustration from *The Second Mrs. Giaconda* by E.L. Konigsburg. Published by Atheneum, 1975. **Unit 7** 352: Hong Kong Man Hai Language Publications. 355: Eric Carle/Shostal Associates. 357: Kent Thompson/Nawrocki Stock Photos. 361: Natural History Museum of Los Angeles County. 363: Tronick/Anthro-Photo File. 368: Torino Museo Egizio/Art Resource. 372, 375: Hong Kong Man Hai Language Publications. 379: Robert Frerck/Odyssey Productions. 383: Art Resource. 389: Shostal Associates. 391: The Granger Collection. 392: Hong Kong Man Hai Language Publications. 396: Dan De Wilde for SB&G. 400: The Phillips Collection, Washington D.C. Acquired 1949. Acc. #1741. 401: Jacket illustration from *Art and Archaeology* by Shirley Glubok. Copyright © 1966 by Shirley Glubok. Reprinted by

Acknowledgments continued on page 582

CONTENTS

INTRODUCTORY UNIT

UNIT 1

EXPRESSING YOURSELF AS A WRITER

PART ONE
LANGUAGE AWARENESS ♦ SENTENCES

UNIT THEME

Personal Writing

PART TWO
COMPOSITION ♦ PERSONAL WRITING

LITERATURE

Constance: A Story of Early Plymouth

by

Patricia Clapp

UNIT 2

USING LANGUAGE TO INFORM

UNIT THEME

Voyagers Across the Ages

LITERATURE

"Westward Voyage," "Word from a Raft," "From Raft to Reef"

PART ONE
LANGUAGE AWARENESS ♦ NOUNS

PART TWO
A REASON FOR WRITING ♦ INFORMING

UNIT 3

USING LANGUAGE TO NARRATE

━━━━━━ **PART ONE** ━━━━━━
LANGUAGE AWARENESS ♦ VERBS

━━━━━━ **PART TWO** ━━━━━━
A REASON FOR WRITING ♦ NARRATING

UNIT THEME

America Grows

LITERATURE

Barrio Boy
by
Ernesto Galarza

UNIT 4

USING LANGUAGE TO PERSUADE

UNIT THEME

Environments Around the World

LITERATURE

"Vaccination drives for kids" by Coretta Scott King

PART ONE
LANGUAGE AWARENESS ♦ VERB FORMS

PART TWO
A REASON FOR WRITING ♦ PERSUADING

UNIT 5

USING LANGUAGE TO CREATE

PART ONE

LANGUAGE AWARENESS ♦ PRONOUNS

UNIT THEME

Famous American Poets

PART TWO

A REASON FOR WRITING ♦ CREATING

LITERATURE

Poetry

UNIT 6

USING LANGUAGE TO DESCRIBE

PART ONE

LANGUAGE AWARENESS ♦ ADJECTIVES

UNIT THEME

Early Air Travel

PART TWO

A REASON FOR WRITING ♦ DESCRIBING

LITERATURE

North to the Orient

by

Anne Morrow Lindbergh

UNIT 7

USING LANGUAGE TO RESEARCH

UNIT THEME

Interpreting Clues to the Past

LITERATURE

"The Great Underground Army"

by Marjorie Jackson

UNIT 8

USING LANGUAGE TO CLASSIFY

PART ONE
LANGUAGE AWARENESS ♦ PREPOSITIONS, CONJUNCTIONS, AND INTERJECTIONS

UNIT THEME

The Arts in America

PART TWO
A REASON FOR WRITING ♦ CLASSIFYING

LITERATURE

"Two Artists of the Old West"

by

Elisabeth Godolphin

UNIT 9

USING LANGUAGE TO IMAGINE

UNIT 10

MYTHOLOGY

UNIT THEME

Mythology

LITERATURE

"Athene's City"

by

Olivia Coolidge

WRITER'S REFERENCE BOOK

AWARD · LITERATURE · WINNING

Constance: A Story of Early Plymouth
by Patricia Clapp

The Hobbit
by J. R. R. Tolkien

"Athene's City"
from *Greek Myths*
by Olivia Coolidge

From Raft to Reef

from *Newsweek* magazine, August 25, 1947

For almost fifteen weeks, starting April 28, six young men from
Norway and Sweden survived the battering of Pacific storms and
poisonous eels as they drifted on a raft

The morns are meeker than they were,
The nuts are getting brown;
The berry's cheek is plumper,
The rose is out of town.

The maple wears a gayer scarf,
The field a scarlet gown.
Lest I should be old-fashioned,
I'll put a trinket on.

— *Emily Dickinson*

When I

When I hea
When the
me,
When I
me
When

Ho
Ti

LITERATURE: Mythology

from
Athene's City
by Olivia Coolidge

AWARD
WINNING
AUTHOR

WORLD OF LANGUAGE

Introductory Unit

Literature in Your World

In the *World of Language,* literature plays a key role. Literature unlocks your imagination. It opens your mind to the world of ideas. Through literature you can enter any time and any place. You can experience many different adventures, meet people you would never meet, share ideas with the greatest minds. Literature is indeed a key to expanding your world and to enriching your world of language.

Writing in Your World

When you read literature, you enter the world of the writer. You bring to that world your knowledge and experiences. Often you respond to literature by writing. That is natural, for writing and reading are a team. They enhance each other although they are distinctly different.

Writing is a way of connecting yourself to the outside world and to your inner world of thoughts and dreams. Writing is talk written down, but it is more. Unlike spoken words, written words can be changed. They can be shaped and improved. Writing is thinking. Writing helps you understand your world, and it can help you change it! That is a powerful thought, but writing is powerful. It deserves a special place in your world and in the world of language.

What Is a Writer?

A writer is anyone who writes. You write when you dash off a note to a friend or complete a research report. You write for others — your readers. Sometimes, though, you write just for yourself. Here are three kinds of writing you will try.

Writing to Inform ✦ Writing can help you get something done in the world. You might write a business letter, for example, to let someone know about a particular problem.

Writing to Create ✦ You can use your imagination to write a poem, a play, or a story.

Expressive Writing ✦ You can use writing to express what you think or feel, or to explore your ideas. The writing you do for yourself is valuable. Because it is not ''school'' writing, you may not have studied it. This year you will learn different uses for personal writing.

Many writers keep a journal when they write just for themselves. If you form the habit of writing in a journal every day, you will soon have your own sourcebook of ideas for writing.

Journal Writing

A journal is a writer's best friend. Carry one with you and you're always prepared to

- capture an idea by jotting it down
- practice and experiment with all kinds of writing
- think things through and explain things to yourself
- note what you think about books, movies, music
- record your impressions and your experiences

A journal can be a special notebook, a section of another notebook, or a notebook made by stapling paper into a folder. Once you have your journal, use it as a writer. You will find many ideas for journal writing throughout this book.

Introducing the Writing Process

Sometimes you want to write something, make it really good, polish it, then share it. The best way to do this is to focus on the *process of writing*. Take time to think, plan, get ideas, make changes. Do not expect to write a perfect product the first time. Take time to go through the writing process.

THINKING

The writing process breaks writing into steps. For each step, there are *strategies* — ways of working — that you can learn. There are ways to get ideas and ways to organize ideas. There are hints for how to get started and how to keep going. There are strategies for improving your writing and sharing it.

At the end of each unit, you will use the writing process to produce and "publish" a composition. In each unit the following lessons lead up to the writing process lesson.

READING

- A **Thinking Skills** lesson gives you a thinking strategy to use in reading and writing.
- A **Literature** lesson gives you a model for the kind of writing you will do.
- A **Speaking and Listening** lesson helps you develop skills for using language orally.
- The **Writing** lessons focus on the kind of writing you will be doing as you use the writing process.
- The **Connection** lessons help you apply to writing what you learned in grammar and literature lessons.

SPEAKING

WRITING

Using the Writing Process

WRITER'S HINT

As you write, keep these two guidelines in mind:

1. Purpose Why are you writing? To tell a story? To persuade your readers? To give information?

2. Audience Who will read what you write? Someone your own age? Someone younger? An adult?

Write a Description

On the next four pages you will have a preview of the five stages of the writing process: *prewriting, writing, revising, proofreading,* and *publishing*. You can try each one.

Writers often start with prewriting and end by publishing. They may, however, go back and forth among the other stages or do two or more stages at once. With each stage there is an activity. When you have completed all five activities, you will have written a description.

Read the Writer's Hint now. For your description your *purpose* is to describe something you are wearing so accurately your audience can visualize it. Your *audience* is your classmates.

1 Prewriting ♦ Getting ready to write

Have you ever said, "I don't know what to write about"? If so, you are not alone. Most writers feel that way before they start writing. However there are lots of ways you can get ideas. Here are just a few prewriting strategies for getting ideas for writing: brainstorm, make a cluster map, keep a writer's journal, or conduct an interview.

PREWRITING IDEA

Using Your Senses

Clothes are one of the ways we tell others who we are. For that reason, clothes make a fascinating subject for description.

Choose something you are wearing, something that expresses your individuality. Study it carefully for several minutes. Use your senses as you observe and write down details that make the item unique. What does it look like? Does it make a sound when you move? What does it feel like? Does it have a smell? The notes you make about your observations can just be words.

2 Writing ◆ Putting your ideas on paper

You have chosen an item of clothing to describe. You have observed it carefully and have taken notes. You have gathered some ideas. It's time to start writing—but you may have trouble getting started. Or once you start, you may not know how to keep going.

The important thing is just to start writing. Don't worry if your ideas are out of order or if you make spelling errors. You will be able to make changes to improve your writing when you revise and proofread.

WRITING IDEA

Starting with a Question

Put your prewriting notes in front of you before you begin writing your description. How can you begin? You might start with a question, such as, "What does my jeans jacket tell the observer about me, its owner?" As you write, use your notes to give details that tell exactly what makes the item unique. Do not use every detail you noted, however. Instead be selective. Choose those details that suit your writing purpose. You may wish to end your description with a concluding sentence, such as, "To a careful observer my jeans jacket reveals much about who I am."

3 Revising ♦ Making changes to improve your writing

Reading to yourself is the first part of the revising strategy. As you read, think about your purpose. Did you stick to your purpose of describing something you are wearing? Also think about your audience. Were you writing for your classmates? Will they understand your writing?

The second part of the revising strategy is sharing with a partner. Read your writing aloud. Ask your partner to make suggestions. Think about your partner's suggestions. Then make only the changes you feel are important.

REVISING IDEA

Reading to Yourself and Reading to a Partner

First read your description to yourself. Think about your purpose and audience. Did you really write a description? Will your classmates be able to visualize what was described? Make changes to improve your description. You can cross out words, write in new words, and draw arrows to show where to move words or sentences. Your writing may look messy at this point. That is all right.

Next read your description to a partner. Ask, "What part did you like best? Is there any part that needs more details?" Listen to your partner's suggestions. Make changes you think will improve your description.

4 Proofreading ♦ Looking for and fixing errors

After you have made sure your writing says what you want it to say, proofread for correctness. Check for capital letters and punctuation, indenting, and spelling. Then make a clean copy in your best handwriting. A correct copy is a courtesy to your reader.

5 Publishing ♦ Sharing your writing with others

There are many ways to share your writing. You may read it aloud to others. You may record it with a tape recorder, or you may post it on a bulletin board. One of the best parts of writing is hearing or seeing how your audience responds.

UNIT ONE

EXPRESSING YOURSELF
AS A

WRITER

PART ONE

Unit Theme   *Personal Writing*

Language Awareness   Sentences

PART TWO

Literature   *Constance: A Story of Early Plymouth*
by Patricia Clapp

Composition   Personal Writing

Writing
IN YOUR JOURNAL

WRITER'S WARM-UP ◆ Personal
writing tends to capture everyday
events that seem ordinary now but
might turn out to be important in the
future. How might journals written today be of
value in the future? Write about journal writing.
Tell how you might use in the future a notebook
of personal writing that you kept in the past.

How does the meaning of each of these sentences change? *I'm happy.*
I'm happy? I'm happy! Make up sentences that change meaning
according to how you say them.

1 Writing Four Kinds of Sentences

Sentences express complete thoughts in four ways. The chart below will help you recognize and write each kind of sentence.

Kind of Sentence	Purpose	End Mark	Examples
Declarative	makes a statement	.	It is an old letter. The paper has yellowed.
Interrogative	asks a question	?	Can you read it? Who signed the letter?
Imperative	gives a command or makes a request	.	Look at its date. Please do not fold it.
Exclamatory	expresses strong feeling	!	How exciting this is!

If a statement, question, or command expresses strong feeling, it
becomes an exclamatory sentence and ends with an exclamation mark.

■ **This letter is old! Look who signed it! Can you believe it!**

Summary ◆ A **sentence** is a group of words that expresses
a complete thought. The four kinds of sentences are **declarative**, **interrogative**, **imperative**, and **exclamatory**. When you
write, capitalize the first word in a sentence and use end punctuation carefully.

Guided Practice

Tell which kind of sentence each of the following is.

1. Why is America named for Amerigo Vespucci and not Columbus?
2. The secret is in a letter that Amerigo Vespucci wrote.
3. Can it be true!
4. Read on to find out.

Practice

A. Write whether each sentence is declarative, interrogative, exclamatory, or imperative. Then write the correct end punctuation mark.

5. Did Amerigo Vespucci really discover continental America

6. He claimed to have reached it in 1497

7. Wasn't Christopher Columbus there first

8. Read this letter

9. It was written by Columbus in 1493

10. What does Columbus say he found

11. He thought he had found islands near India

12. What a mistake that was

13. Now look at Vespucci's letter

14. Vespucci describes the discovery of a new continent

B. Rewrite each sentence, changing it into the kind of sentence indicated in parentheses.

EXAMPLE: Some do not believe Vespucci's letter. (imperative)

ANSWER: Do not believe Vespucci's letter.

15. Vespucci claimed to have touched a continent months before Columbus. (exclamatory)

16. He really did explore the coast of South America in 1499. (interrogative)

17. Will the truth ever be known? (exclamatory)

18. Should we rename the American continents? (declarative)

19. We might even name them for Leif Eriksson! (imperative)

C. Use the bank of words below to write five sentences. Include each of the four kinds of sentences.

20–24. is Vespucci's correct date in the letter not

Apply ✦ Think and Write

From Your Writing ✦ Tally how many of each kind of sentence you used in the Writer's Warm-up. Were they mostly declarative? Try using other kinds of sentences for variety or emphasis.

✎ **Remember** to use different kinds of sentences.

GETTING STARTED

Think of ways to use the same word in different ways. Follow this model: *Spring* bulbs *spring* up in *spring*.

2 Parts of Speech in Sentences

A tool is useful only if you know how to use it. Words are the tools we use to express our thoughts and feelings. That is why we study all eight kinds of words—which are called the eight parts of speech. The chart below is an essential toolbox for writers.

Nouns name persons, places, things, or ideas.
<u>Sue</u> and I record <u>observations</u> of <u>plants</u> in our <u>journals</u>.

Pronouns take the place of nouns.
This <u>entry</u> is <u>theirs</u>, but <u>they</u> will share <u>it</u> with <u>us</u>.

Adjectives describe or modify nouns or pronouns.
<u>Many</u> people put <u>important</u> data in <u>a</u> <u>special</u> notebook.

Verbs express action or being.
Sue <u>wrote</u>, "This plant <u>is</u> common, but still it <u>interests</u> and <u>puzzles</u> me."

Adverbs modify verbs, adjectives, or adverbs.
<u>Very</u> <u>often</u> observers must search <u>carefully</u> for a certain species.

Conjunctions join words or groups of words.
Sue <u>and</u> I do not have all the data, <u>but</u> we will continue the search.

Prepositions relate nouns or pronouns to other words in a sentence.
Naturalist Henry David Thoreau lived <u>in</u> the woods and filled journals <u>with</u> material <u>for</u> his books.

Interjections express emotion or feeling.
<u>Oh</u>, how we admire Thoreau's brilliant descriptions!

Summary ◆ How a word is used in a sentence determines its part of speech. Understanding how words function helps you use them to communicate your ideas clearly.

Guided Practice

Tell the part of speech of each underlined word.

1. A <u>famous</u> naturalist wrote <u>about</u> nature <u>and</u> civil rights.
2. <u>He</u> was <u>Henry David Thoreau</u>.
3. His writing <u>greatly</u> <u>influenced</u> Martin Luther King, Jr.

Practice

A. Use the words below to complete this excerpt from Thoreau's journal entry for December 15, 1841. Write the excerpt.

> I   trees   to   familiar   is   calmly   and

The (**4. noun**) have come down (**5. preposition**) the bank to see the river go by. This old, (**6. adjective**) river is renewed each instant; only the channel (**7. verb**) the same. The water which so (**8. adverb**) reflects the fleeting clouds (**9. conjunction**) the primeval trees (**10. pronoun**) have never seen before.

B. Use your own observations of nature to complete each sentence. Use the indicated parts of speech.

11. The ____ has ____ on its ____ . (nouns)
12. Our world is ____ and ____ . (pronouns)
13. The ____ tree is ____ but ____ . (adjectives)
14. Rivers ____ and ____ as they ____ . (verbs)
15. Very ____ turtles climb ____ onto rocks. (adverbs)
16. Fish ____ turtles live in ponds, ____ turtles can live on land ____ in water. (conjunctions)
17. Wildflowers grow ____ trees, ____ fields, and ____ rivers. (prepositions)
18. ____ The lake has become a mirror. (interjection)

Apply ◆ Think and Write

A Journal Entry ◆ Write a journal entry about an experience you had or an observation you made in the past week. Include things that perplexed you or made an impression on you. Make it more lively by using as many of the eight parts of speech as possible.

✎ **Remember** to use the parts of speech carefully to communicate your ideas clearly.

Make up tongue twisters. Name someone or something, such as *Sam's song*. Then tell what that person or thing is or does. For example: *Sam's song sounded simply stupendous.*

3 Complete Subjects and Predicates

A sentence has two parts, a subject and a predicate. The subject part names someone or something. The predicate part tells what the subject is or does. Together, all the words in the subject part of a sentence make up the complete subject. Similarly, all the words in the predicate part make up the complete predicate. In the sentences below, the complete subject is tinted blue, and the complete predicate is tinted green.

> Lorraine Hansberry   was a talented writer.
> Her first play   received great praise.
> It   was the first Broadway play by a black woman.
> Her circle of admirers   grew.

Notice that a complete subject can be several words or one word. A complete predicate can also be one word or many words.

Summary ✦ The **complete subject** is all the words in the subject part of a sentence. It names someone or something. The **complete predicate** is all the words in the predicate part of a sentence. It tells what the subject is or does. When you write, use complete subjects and complete predicates to express your ideas clearly.

Guided Practice

Identify the complete subjects and the complete predicates.

1. Lorraine Hansberry died in 1965.
2. The husband of this woman kept her diaries and journals.
3. He developed them into a two-act drama.
4. This famous drama is called *To Be Young, Gifted, and Black.*
5. It tells of her childhood and private life.

Practice

A. Write each sentence. Underline the complete subject once and the complete predicate twice.

6. Lorraine Hansberry's journals were about her memories.
7. She was born on the south side of Chicago in 1930.
8. Her interest in the theater developed during her childhood.
9. Mr. and Mrs. Hansberry taught Lorraine about self-worth.
10. They often told her about their childhood in the South.
11. The University of Wisconsin accepted her as a student.
12. Her interest in plays grew at the university.
13. The future playwright moved to New York City in 1950.
14. *Freedom* magazine hired her there.
15. People seemed funny and beautiful to Lorraine Hansberry.

B. Match each complete subject with a complete predicate. Write the sentence.

Complete Subjects	Complete Predicates
16. Lorraine Hansberry	was stressed in her family.
17. Her family	kept journals.
18. The importance of education	studied African history.
19. She	made her feel important.
20. *A Raisin in the Sun*	is one of her plays.

C. Use the facts in this lesson to complete each sentence. Supply a complete subject or a complete predicate. Label the part you supply.

21. Lorraine Hansberry ＿＿ .
22. ＿＿ used her journals in *To Be Young, Gifted, and Black*.
23. ＿＿ died at the age of thirty-five.
24. Her family ＿＿ .
25. Hansberry's interest in the theater ＿＿ .

Apply • Think and Write

Comparing Sentences ◆ Write some sentences about a play or movie you have seen. On another sheet of paper, copy only the complete subjects. Exchange papers with a partner and complete the sentences. Compare versions.

> ✎ **Remember**
> to make sure every sentence has a complete subject and a complete predicate.

4 Simple Subjects and Predicates

Simple Subject, or Subject   The simple subject is the main word or words in the complete subject. It is usually a noun or pronoun. In the sentences below, the simple subject is dark blue.

1. Two women from opposite sides kept journals.
2. One was the Southerner, Mary Boykin Chesnut.
3. Louisa May Alcott was the Northerner.

In sentence **2**, the complete subject is just one word. It is also the simple subject. In sentence **3**, the simple subject is three words because it is a name.

Simple Predicate, or Verb   The simple predicate is the main word or words in the complete predicate. The simple predicate is always a verb. In the sentences below, the simple predicate is dark green.

4. The war experiences of the two women differed.
5. Alcott had become a nurse in Washington, D.C.
6. Chesnut had often dined with the Confederate president.

In sentence **4**, the simple predicate, or verb, is one word. In sentence **5**, the verb is two words. In sentence **6**, the two-word verb is interrupted by the word *often*.

> **Summary** ◆ The **simple subject** is the main word or words in the complete subject. The **simple predicate** is the main word or words in the complete predicate. It is always a verb.

Guided Practice

Name the subject and the verb in each sentence.

1. The Civil War began in early 1861.
2. It would not end until the spring of 1865.
3. More Americans died from disease than in battle.

Practice

A. Write and label the subject and verb of each sentence.

4. Louisa May Alcott left home in 1862.
5. She was thirty years old at that time.
6. A hospital in Washington, D.C., accepted her as a nurse.
7. Her journal tells about hard work and long hours.
8. Many wounded soldiers were brought to the hospital.
9. Several soldiers caught pneumonia or other diseases also.
10. Even some nurses at the hospital died.
11. Hard-working Alcott caught pneumonia, too.
12. Her entry for January 16, 1863, mentions a visitor.
13. Her father had finally come for her.

B. Each sentence in this paragraph about Mary Chesnut's journal is missing either a subject or a verb. Choose a word or words from below to complete each sentence. Write the paragraph.

ends   **C. Vann Woodward**   **won**   **journal**   **is called**

Mary Chesnut's (**14.** ___) begins with an entry for February 18, 1861. It (**15.** ___) on July 26, 1865. (**16.** ___) had edited her lengthy journal. His edited version (**17.** ___) *Mary Chesnut's Civil War*. The book (**18.** ___) the 1982 Pulitzer Prize in history.

C. Expand the following subjects and verbs into sentences. Write each sentence.

19. Civil War/was
20. Louisa May Alcott/wanted
21. hospitals/had become
22. Mary Chesnut/wrote
23. C. Vann Woodward/edited

Apply ◆ Think and Write

Dictionary of Knowledge ◆ Like Louisa May Alcott, Mary Chesnut worked in hospitals during the war. Another woman who helped wounded Civil War soldiers was Clara Barton. Read about her in the Dictionary of Knowledge. Write several sentences telling what she is known for. Underline the subjects and verbs in your sentences.

✎ **Remember** that every sentence needs a subject and a verb.

GETTING STARTED

Play a game of backward sentences. One person says a sentence, and another turns it around: *The fog crept silently. Silently crept the fog.* Now try this one: *The sun set swiftly.*

5 Locating the Subject

The subject often begins a sentence. In many sentences, however, the subject appears in different places, thus adding variety to writing.

Subjects in Declarative Sentences   In most declarative sentences the subject comes before the verb. This order is called **normal word order**.

■ Old diaries tell us about life in Colonial America.

Subjects in Interrogative Sentences   In interrogative sentences the subject often follows the verb or comes between the parts of the verb. Such interrogative sentences usually begin with a verb, a *wh-* word, or *how*. To find the subject of an interrogative sentence, just reword it as a declarative sentence.

Do you keep a diary?	You do keep a diary.
How would I start a diary?	I would start a diary how.
Is this diary yours?	This diary is yours.

Subjects in Imperative Sentences   The subject of an imperative sentence is always the pronoun *you*, but it is usually understood rather than stated.

■ (You) Do not read my diary.

An imperative sentence may include the name of the person being spoken to. A name used in this way is set off from the sentence by commas. The subject is still *you*, even though the name of the person is included.

■ Gloria, (you) put down your pen for a moment.

Inverted Sentences   In sentences in inverted word order, the subject comes after the verb. To find the subject of an inverted sentence, simply reword it in normal word order.

Into his diary **went** the **details** of his life.
The **details** of his life **went** into his diary.

Did you notice that inverted word order gives a dramatic touch to an ordinary sentence?

Sentences Beginning with *Here* and *There* The words *here* and *there* often begin sentences, but they are never subjects. In such a sentence, look for the subject after the verb.

Here **is** the lost **diary.**   The lost **diary** **is** here.
There **are** the missing **pages.**   The missing **pages** **are** there.

Sometimes a sentence cannot be reworded in normal word order. To locate the subject, find the verb and ask *who?* or *what?* about it.

There **is** no **reason** for it. (What is? <u>Reason</u> is.)

Sentences Beginning with Other Words Words other than the subject are often used to begin sentences in normal word order. These words are usually part of the predicate. Again, to locate the subject, find the verb and ask *who?* or *what?* about it.

Mysteriously the **diaries** of William Byrd **disappeared.**
In 1941 some **diaries** **were found** in a library.

Summary ✦ A subject may precede or follow a verb. It may come between the parts of a verb or be understood. Varying the placement of subjects in your sentences will make your writing more interesting.

Guided Practice

Name the subject of each sentence. Say *you* when the subject is understood.

1. How do we know about life in the American colonies?
2. From old diaries many important facts about Colonial life are learned.
3. Here is a diary of William Byrd.
4. Everyone, look at the writing in his diary.
5. Out of a forgotten shorthand came his secret code.

Practice

A. Write the subject of each sentence. Write (*you*) if the subject is understood. Then write whether the sentence is declarative, interrogative, or imperative.

6. Why did William Byrd use a secret shorthand in his diaries?
7. Here is my guess.
8. In his diaries the Colonial gentleman wrote about his private life in Virginia.
9. How did modern editors figure out his secret code?
10. From a translation of French in Byrd's handwriting came some coded words.
11. Carefully the editors compared these shorthand scribbles with the original wording.
12. Over time they built up a shorthand alphabet like Byrd's.
13. Have all Byrd's diaries been found?
14. No, somewhere are several secret notebooks.
15. Historians, help us find the missing diaries.

B. Write the subject and verb of each sentence in this paragraph about another Colonial diarist. Underline each subject.

EXAMPLE: On October 2, 1704, Sarah Kemble Knight began her journey on horseback from Boston to New York City.
ANSWER: <u>Sarah Kemble Knight</u>, began

16. In the journal of this Boston businesswoman is the record of a daring journey. 17. With humor and even some poetry, she tells of a two-hundred-mile horseback ride. 18. Why did this woman travel by horse? 19. Here is a surprising fact. 20. In the early eighteenth century, stagecoach travel was still in its infancy. 21. People traveled mostly by horse, by foot, and by boat. 22. Quite often travelers never reached their destination. 23. For this reason the tongues of innkeepers wagged at Madam Knight about the dangers of the journey. 24. Into her journal went their colorful comments. 25. Through her words modern readers can visit Colonial New England and old New York.

C. Enliven this paragraph about John Woolman by varying the placement of subjects in the sentences. Write the new paragraph.

EXAMPLE: Woolman began his journal at age thirty-six.
ANSWER: At age thirty-six Woolman began his journal.

26. John Woolman worked in a store in New Jersey in 1742. **27.** A female slave was sold at the store one day. **28.** Woolman was very upset about the sale for a long time. **29.** He soon began a crusade against slavery. **30.** He had been a devout member of the Society of Friends since childhood. **31.** His focus of attention during his campaign was this Society, the Quakers. **32.** He argued against slavery from then until his death in 1772. **33.** The practice of slavery ended in the Society within twenty years after the death of John Woolman. **34.** Woolman humbly tells of his crusade in simple words in his journal. **35.** His journal was published after his death.

D. Only the beginnings of sentences are given below. Use each to write a complete sentence. Underline the subjects. Write (*you*) if the subject is understood.

36. Here are . . .
37. Write . . .
38. In her journal . . .
39. Diarists, please . . .
40. Why did . . .

41. After that incident . . .
42. Suddenly . . .
43. Where did . . .
44. This is . . .
45. In a secret code was . . .

Apply ◆ Think and Write

Writing for the Future ◆ William Byrd, Sarah Kemble Knight, and John Woolman have given twentieth-century readers a valuable picture of life in Colonial America. Imagine that you are writing a diary that will not be found until the twenty-third century. Write an entry for a day in your life. Record the day so vividly that some future reader would see a "snapshot" of life in late twentieth-century America. Make the entry more interesting by varying the location of subjects in your sentences.

Remember to vary the placement of subjects in your sentences to make your writing more interesting.

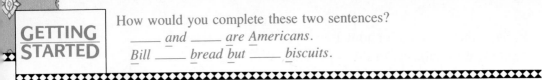

How would you complete these two sentences?
_____ and _____ are Americans.
Bill _____ bread but _____ biscuits.

6 Compound Subjects and Verbs

Two or more simple subjects that share the same verb are called a compound subject. The parts of a compound subject are connected by a conjunction, such as *and*, *but*, *or*, or *nor*.

■ Meriwether Lewis and William Clark explored the West.
■ No atlas, map, or road aided them on their journey.

Two or more verbs that share the same subject are called a compound verb. They are also connected by a conjunction.

■ They kept journals, made maps, and often drew pictures.

A sentence may have a compound subject and a compound verb.

■ Years later travelers and settlers read and used the maps.

You can improve your writing by putting repeated ideas in one sentence with a compound subject or compound verb.

■ Men traveled west. Women traveled west. Children traveled west.
■ Men, women, and children traveled west.
■ The pioneers worked hard. The pioneers often played, too.
■ The pioneers worked hard but often played, too.

> **Summary** ♦ A **compound subject** is two or more simple subjects that have the same verb. A **compound verb** is two or more verbs that have the same subject. Using compound subjects and compound verbs can make your writing smoother.

Guided Practice

Name each compound subject and each compound verb.

1. President Jefferson ordered and financed the expedition.
2. Lewis, Clark, and five other people kept journals.
3. The artist and mapmaker was William Clark.

Practice

A. Write and label each compound subject and compound verb.

    4. Mollie Dorsey and her family settled in the Nebraska Territory in 1857. **5.** Her diary records the move and mentions a Byron N. Sanford. **6.** Later Mollie and Byron married and followed the gold rush to Colorado. **7.** In her diary Mollie describes the journey and tells about Denver. **8.** The Sanfords' hardships and success represent and reflect life in the West.

B. Write each set of sentences as one sentence with a compound subject or a compound verb.

    9. Elinore Pruitt Stewart lived in the early 1900s. Elinore Pruitt Stewart recorded her life in letters.

    10. Her husband died. Her husband left her penniless.

    11. She was caring for her baby. She needed employment.

    12. Elinore went to Denver. Her baby went to Denver.

    13. She cleaned houses. She did laundry.

    14. In 1909 the mother went to Wyoming. In 1909 the baby went to Wyoming.

    15. Elinore went as a maid. Elinore became a rancher.

    16. Her letters were published in a book. Her letters were made into a movie.

    17. Read *Letters of a Woman Homesteader*. Enjoy *Letters of a Woman Homesteader*.

    18. Did you read the book? Did you see the movie?

C. Use each of the following compound subjects or compound verbs in sentences.

    19. settlers and prospectors   **22.** the Great Plains, the Rocky
    20. sought and found   Mountains, and the desert
    21. did not lose but won   **23.** bravery or foolishness

Apply • Think and Write

A Picture in Words • Write about an area you have explored or visited—a park, desert, forest, or mountain. Describe its outstanding features. Use compounds to combine your ideas.

Remember that compound subjects and verbs make your sentences less repetitious.

7 Simple and Compound Sentences

A simple sentence expresses one complete thought. It has at least one subject and one verb.

The great Thomas Jefferson wrote hundreds of letters.
His journals and notes still attract and influence readers.

When simple sentences with related ideas are joined, they form a compound sentence. Join simple sentences with the conjunction *and*, *or*, *but*, or *nor* or with a semicolon.

MECHANICS ";?!"
Put a comma before the conjunction in a compound sentence unless the sentence is very short. A semicolon may be used in place of the comma and conjunction.

Jefferson ran for President in 1796, but John Adams won the election.
Adams and Jefferson were good friends; Jefferson happily became Adams's Vice President.
Adams tried and he succeeded.
(no comma)

Do not confuse a simple sentence containing a compound subject or verb with a compound sentence.

Simple: Jefferson ran again in 1800 and won.
Compound: Jefferson ran again in 1800, and he won the election.

> **Summary** ♦ A **simple sentence** has one subject and one verb, either or both of which may be compound. A **compound sentence** consists of two or more simple sentences.

Guided Practice

Identify the two simple sentences within each compound sentence.

1. Jefferson wrote many things, and he studied law.
2. He lived awhile in Paris; there he kept a journal.
3. He was always busy, but he wrote letters home weekly.

Practice

A. Write the sentences. Underline each subject once and each verb twice. Then label each sentence *simple* or *compound*.

4. Abigail Adams was the wife of one President and the mother of another. **5.** She had little formal education, but she was one of the most powerful women of her time. **6.** Abigail was separated from her husband for long periods of time during and after the American Revolution, but they kept close through letters. **7.** Their letters were published by their grandson in 1876. **8.** Abigail's letters show her wisdom and kindness and tell about her social and political life.

B. Write a compound sentence from each pair of simple sentences.

    9. The Adamses and Jefferson were friends. They quarreled.
10. Adams had become unpopular by 1800. Jefferson was elected.
11. Then Jefferson fired their son. The Adamses were angry.
12. Jefferson wrote a letter of apology. They did not reply.
13. Years later they did write back. Their friendship survived.

C. Improve the following article by joining some of the sentences as compounds. Write the new, smoother article.

14. J. Hector St. John became famous for his *Letters from an American Farmer*. **15.** His real name was Michel-Guillaume Jean de Crèvecoeur. **16.** He had gone to Canada from France at the age of nineteen. **17.** He had fought in the French and Indian War. **18.** In Canada he also served as a mapmaker. **19.** That gave him experience in a job. **20.** After the war he went to the colonies of New York and Vermont. **21.** There he worked as a surveyor. **22.** Crèvecoeur became a citizen of New York in 1765. **23.** He married an American soon afterward.

Apply ✦ Think and Write

A Reader's Response ✦ Read a letter to the editor in a newspaper. Write some sentences expressing your opinion about the letter. Include some compound sentences to join related ideas.

✎ **Remember**
to use compound
sentences to make
your writing
smoother.

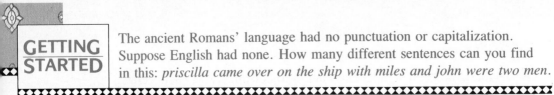

GETTING STARTED

The ancient Romans' language had no punctuation or capitalization. Suppose English had none. How many different sentences can you find in this: *priscilla came over on the ship with miles and john were two men.*

8 Avoiding Sentence Errors

A **run-on sentence** is two or more sentences separated by just a comma or no punctuation. To correct a run-on sentence, make separate sentences or add a comma and a conjunction.

Run-on: The *Mayflower* landed in 1620 it had 102 passengers.
Run-on: The *Mayflower* landed in 1620, it had 102 passengers.
Correct: The *Mayflower* landed in 1620. It had 102 passengers.
Correct: The *Mayflower* landed in 1620, and it had 102 passengers.

A **sentence fragment** is part of a sentence written as if it were a sentence. To avoid this sentence error, make sure that every sentence contains a subject and a verb and expresses a complete thought.

Fragment: <u>Including John Alden, William Bradford, and Miles Standish.</u> Forty-one people signed the Mayflower Compact.
Correct: Forty-one people, including John Alden, William Bradford, and Miles Standish, signed the Mayflower Compact.
Fragment: John Alden was the first. <u>To set foot on land.</u>
Correct: John Alden was the first to set foot on land.

> **Summary** ♦ Run-on sentences and sentence fragments are errors. Avoid them in your writing.

Guided Practice

Tell whether each group of words is a sentence, a run-on sentence, or a sentence fragment.

1. Agreed with the provisions of the Mayflower Compact.
2. Miles Standish was the Pilgrims' military leader in the Plymouth Colony he had come over with his wife, Rose.
3. William Bradford wrote the history of the Plymouth Colony.

Practice

A. 4–15. There are six run-on sentences in this entry from a reader's journal. Rewrite the entry correctly by making twelve sentences.

Today I read a poem about people in the Plymouth Colony by Henry Wadsworth Longfellow it is called *The Courtship of Miles Standish*. Captain Standish's wife, Rose, was the first of the colonists from the *Mayflower* to die this left him very lonely. Eventually he thought of marrying a beautiful girl named Priscilla her family had died recently, and she lived alone. Miles could not get up the courage to ask her finally he asked his friend John Alden to propose for him. Unfortunately for Miles, John was in love with Priscilla, too nevertheless he proposed for his friend Miles. Priscilla listened to John speak for Miles then she said, "Why don't you speak for yourself, John?"

B. Add words to make each fragment into a complete sentence. Write the new sentence that results.

16. Wrote in a journal about those events.
17. The best of the entries.
18. Became a careful observer.
19. To find out about it.
20. Including the three of them.
21. For your friend and mine.
22. Enough time to finish it.
23. The one with the leather binding.

Apply ♦ Think and Write

Pilgrim Punctuation ♦ Write a true or made-up story about the Pilgrims. Then copy your sentences onto another paper but leave out all beginning capital letters and end punctuation. Exchange papers with a partner and supply capitals and end punctuation. Compare your partner's paper with the original. Were any sentences marked differently from yours but still correct?

✎ **Remember**
to avoid run-on sentences and sentence fragments.

GETTING STARTED

What adjectives besides *big*, *heavy*, and *powerful* might you use to give a description of a rhinocerous?

VOCABULARY ◆
Using the Thesaurus

A **thesaurus** is a book that contains lists of synonyms, or words that have similar meanings. The words listed in a thesaurus are often arranged in alphabetical order. A thesaurus entry usually also includes a list of antonyms, or words that have opposite meanings. With a thesaurus, you can find the words that best express your intended meaning.

Below is part of the entry for *copy* found in the Thesaurus that begins on page 612.

	Part of Speech	**Definition**

Entry word —— **copy** (n)—a reproduction or imitation of an original work (as a painting or a dress).

Example sentence —— Send me a copy of that map of Glacier National Park.

duplicate—either of two things that exactly resemble each other. Where is the duplicate of the license?

replica—any close reproduction of something, such as a work of art. That is a replica of the Eiffel Tower.

Informal Synonyms —— *ditto* [informal]—a copy of something. Our science teacher gave us a ditto of the solar system.

Slang —— *phony* [slang]—something not real or genuine; one that tries to deceive or mislead. As soon as he showed me the emerald, I knew it was a phony.

Idiom —— *dead ringer* [idiom]—an exact likeness. She is a dead ringer for my aunt Jane.

Specific field of knowledge —— *tenor* [law]—an exact copy of a document. The trial will not proceed until the judge receives a tenor of the deed.

Cross-reference —— See also *picture* (n).

Antonyms —— ANTONYMS: archetype, the genuine article, original (n), paradigm, prototype, the real McCoy, the real thing

Building Your Vocabulary

Change the following sentences, using synonyms of *copy* in place of the underlined words. Follow the directions in parentheses.

1. He <u>looks just like</u> Abraham Lincoln. (Use an idiom.)
2. That painting is <u>very much like</u> the original. (Fit the meaning.)
3. The twenty-dollar bill looked real but was a <u>counterfeit</u>. (Use slang.)
4. Dina received a <u>copy</u> of her lost library card. (Fit the meaning.)

Practice

A. Pretend the sentences below describe you. Find synonyms in the Thesaurus to replace the underlined words. Notice how much more interesting you become!

1. Why just be <u>great</u> when you can be _____ ?
2. Why just be <u>nice</u> when you can be _____ ?
3. Why just be <u>interesting</u> when you can be _____ ?
4. Why just be <u>bright</u> when you can be _____ ?
5. Why just be <u>good</u> when you can be _____ ?

B. The following paragraph describes the voyage to America of a group of early Pilgrims. Use the Thesaurus to find synonyms to replace the underlined words. Rewrite the paragraph, using the synonyms.

The (**6.** trip) across the Atlantic was dangerous and (**7.** slow). The Pilgrims often (**8.** saw) (**9.** great) storms appear (**10.** suddenly) on the horizon. To (**11.** keep) from possible harm, they would sometimes (**12.** change) their direction when a storm (**13.** moved) toward them. They knew what they must (**14.** do) if they hoped to (**15.** live) through the (**16.** trip) to the new land.

LANGUAGE CORNER ◆ Borrowed Words

English has many synonyms, partly because words with similar meanings have been borrowed from more than one language. *Funny* is an Old English word, *humorous* is from Latin, and *comical* is from Greek. Which words in these synonym "trios" come from English? Latin? Greek?

dialogue, conversation, talk   **top, summit, acme**

smell, aroma, scent   **tutor, teacher, mentor**

How to Combine Sentence Parts

Sometimes two sentences contain repeated information or related ideas. Notice how the sentence in example **2** combines the information from example **1** to form a single, strong sentence.

1. **Many famous Americans kept diaries. Many famous Americans kept journals.**
2. **Many famous Americans kept diaries and journals.**

By combining sentences that repeat information, you can make your writing more effective and less repetitious. Notice how different parts of sentences are combined to form the sentences in examples **4** and **6**. Can you identify the combined parts?

3. **Students read the diaries. Historians read the diaries.**
4. **Students and historians read the diaries.**

5. **George Washington was a soldier. He was a politician. He was a writer.**
6. **George Washington was a soldier, a politician, and a writer.**

As you know, simple sentences with related ideas can also be combined to form compound sentences. Such sentences can be combined by using a comma and a conjunction. Notice how example **8** better shows the relationship between the sentences above it.

7. **Was Washington born in Wakefield, Virginia? Was he born in Richmond?**
8. **Was Washington born in Wakefield, Virginia, or was he born in Richmond?**

The Grammar Game ◆ Create your own examples! Write at least four pairs of sentences that can be combined by using conjunctions or by joining parts of sentences. Then exchange papers with a classmate and combine each other's sentences.

Working Together

As your group works on activities **A** and **B**, notice that combining sentences helps you write stronger, more effective sentences.

In Your Group
♦ Contribute your own ideas.   ♦ Encourage everyone to participate. ♦ Don't interrupt each other.   ♦ Help the group finish on time.

A. Imagine that your group was part of General George Washington's army during the American Revolution. Describe your experiences in five sentences by combining pairs of sentences below. Then arrange the new sentences to form a paragraph.

Our group reached the river.   Washington made plans.
Our army marched until dusk.   Our army set out at dawn.
The officers were exhausted.   The march was difficult.
The march was dangerous.   We did not see the enemy.
Washington's officers made plans. Soldiers were exhausted.

B. Combine sentences to make the paragraph below less repetitious.

    The Adams family was from Massachusetts. The Adams family contributed many leaders to our country. John Adams was a leader of the American Revolution. John Adams was the first Vice President and the second President of our country. His diaries give a firsthand look at the politics of his time. His diaries make remarkable reading today. His son, John Quincy Adams, became President in 1825. John Quincy Adams served in Congress for many years.

WRITERS' CORNER ♦ Sentence Variety

    Add variety to your writing. Whenever possible, use different kinds of sentences in a piece of writing. Varying the kinds of sentences you use can improve your writing by making it more interesting to read. It really works! Can you identify the four kinds of sentences used in this paragraph?

Read what you wrote for the Writer's Warm-up. Can you improve any of your paragraphs by using different kinds of sentences?

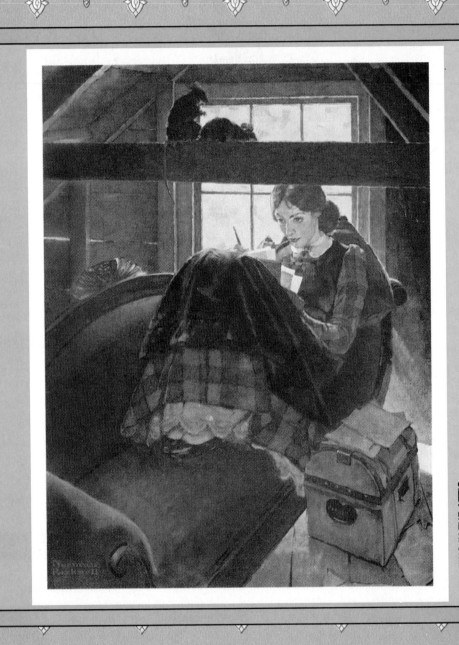

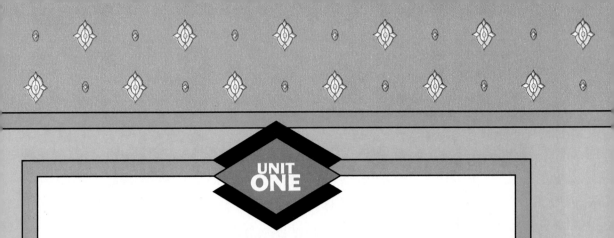

UNIT ONE

EXPRESSING YOURSELF AS A
WRITER

==== PART TWO ====

Literature *Constance: A Story of Early Plymouth*
by Patricia Clapp

Composition Personal Writing

CREATIVE *Writing*

FINE ARTS ◆ Louisa May Alcott wrote *Little Women* and other classic novels at a time when it was not acceptable for women to be published writers. What do you imagine Miss Alcott's life as a writer was like? What questions would you like to ask her? Write a dialogue between yourself and Miss Alcott. Include a description of the setting where the conversation took place.

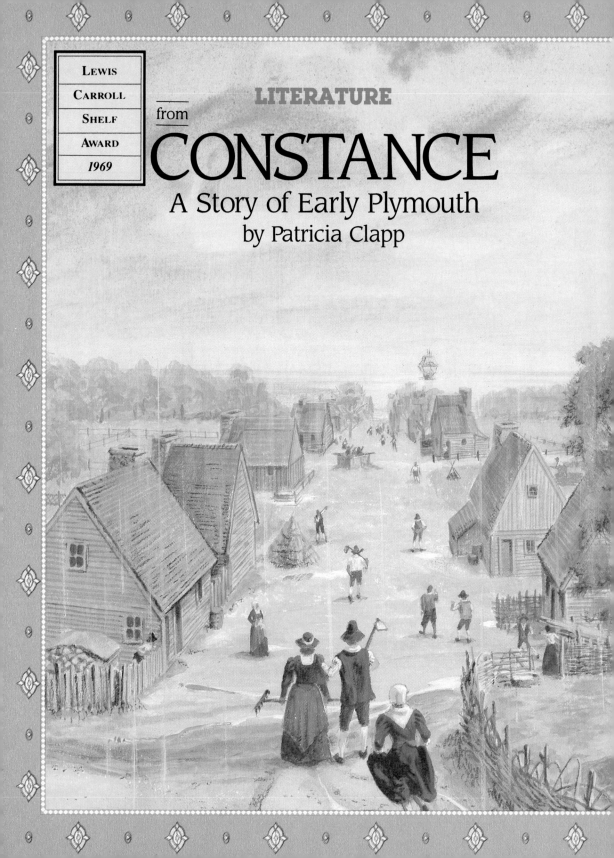

LITERATURE

from

CONSTANCE
A Story of Early Plymouth
by Patricia Clapp

Constance Hopkins was fourteen when she sailed to America with a group of English settlers on the Mayflower. Constance and her family helped establish the first English colony of Plymouth in 1620. More than three hundred years later, author Patricia Clapp—a descendant of Constance by marriage—decided to tell this young girl's story through an imaginary journal. In it, many real people of early Plymouth come to life.

Constance's stepmother, Elizabeth, gave her the journal to record their "strange adventure"—one marked by hunger and hardship. Of the four Hopkins children who came to America, only Constance and her younger brother Giles survived the first two years. But in August 1623, Constance has news "of a pleasurable nature" to write about. A long-needed rain has saved the settlers' crops and assured an adequate food supply. A long-awaited ship has brought more family members and two intended brides.

August 1623

There has been such a pother of excitement these past several days that I hardly know where to start noting it here in my journal! So much has passed, and all of a pleasurable nature, that—but let me try to put it down in orderly fashion! . . .

It must have been close to the noon hour, or so my stomach told me, when the first cry went up.

"A ship! A ship! There's a ship entering the harbor!" And then, a moment later, "She flies the English flag!"

Hoes were dropped, spades forgotten. From the fields, from the houses, down the Street, came the people of Plymouth, patched, soaked, muddied—and breathless with excitement.

"What ship? Who comes? Is it more of Weston's men? Is it our families? Are they for Virginia or Plymouth?" None could tell. I saw the Governor [William Bradford] and the Captain [Miles Standish] in a hurried conversation, and then they both breasted the tide of those hurrying down the Street, and proceeded to run up it to their homes. I was puzzled and somewhat frightened. Always these two are among the first to greet any visitors, yet now they did not even join us! I spoke of it to Father as we stood watching the ship slowly move into the bay.

"Think you it means trouble?" I asked. "Have they gone to arm themselves?"

Father bit his lip as he sometimes does when he is trying to hide his grin. "If 'tis as I imagine," he said, "it may be trouble, but firearms will be of no help."

I could not understand him, but he would say no more. Giles eeled his way through the gathering crowd standing on the beach, and I pushed after him to a spot where I could see clearly. Just as a little shallop was being lowered from the now-anchored ship, Will Bradford and the Captain shouldered through to the forefront of the people, and I gaped in amazement. The Governor was clean and dressed in the blue suit he keeps for the most state occasions. His broad collar was freshly white, his shoes shone, his hat had been brushed almost dry. Beside him, the little Captain stood in splendor. His breastplate and helmet were polished, his breeches were his most beautiful scarlet ones, his beard had been combed. Together they made a truly impressive sight, putting the rest of us to utter shame! I could not help but wonder what important personages they expected, to have thus arrayed themselves in their rarely worn best apparel. For their sakes I was glad that the rain chose this moment to slacken, so that it fell in only the softest possible misty shower.

The shallop was loaded now, and coming in toward the shore, and suddenly I heard John Cooke's voice shouting, joined a second later by that of Mistress Brewster.

"It's Mother," John bellowed. "Father, Mother has come . . . and . . . yes . . . I see Jacob, and Jane . . . and little Hester."

And then Mistress Brewster's voice, "William, our daughters! Patience and Fear—both of them! Oh, thank the Lord!"

Never have I seen such happy tears, or heard such joyous commotion. Good Dr. Fuller spied his wife in the approaching boat, and then Robert Hicks and William Palmer, both of whom had come on the "Fortune," saw theirs. The men ran to the very edge of the water, reaching out to pull the boat ashore, lifting the women bodily from the shallop and carrying them the few feet to the sandy beach. There was such laughing and crying as affected us all, and the sight of men holding close to them women they must sometimes have feared never to see again was a beautiful thing. The questions rose all about us.

"What ship is she?"

"Is my wife aboard?"

"Are all well?"

"Who else has come?"

The ship was the "Anne," this much I learned. With another, the "Little James," they had left England some weeks before, but since a storm many days back they had seen nothing of the "Little James." In the midst of the joy this brought fear to many, as the newcomers were asked repeatedly who had sailed on which ship. On the faces of some shone relief as they were assured their friends or families were safe on the "Anne"; others turned away in despair, praying for the safety of the "Little James."

As the shallop started back to bring more passengers from the "Anne," I looked at those who had landed, and felt an unexpected shock. Without exception these people were well dressed and well fed. Beside the Plymouth residents, all of whom were thin and drawn from lack of food, and all of whom, with the notable exception of the Governor and Captain Standish, were ragged, patched, and muddied, the newcomers with their sleek skin, their fresh and well fitting clothes, made us look a sorry sight indeed! They saw it too, I know, for Fear and Patience Brewster, both very fair young women, were weeping in their mother's arms with sorrow for the condition in which they found her. I could see that we must look a discouraging sight at best to people who were about to make their lives here!

The little boat was coming back with its second load, and I watched eagerly as the Governor strode to the side of the shallop and extended his hand with the greatest ceremony to a most handsome woman.

"Mistress Southworth," I heard him say as he handed her from the boat and bowed with a gallantry I had not seen in any man since we left London. I glanced quickly around the crowd for Priscilla [Alden], and seeing her, she and I smirked at each other with our pleasant secret knowledge. A second woman, greatly resembling the first, was handed out, and then a man who embraced the Governor affectionately. Prissy, by this time, had pushed near enough to me so that we might whisper together.

"That must be George Morton," she said, "and his wife Juliana, who is Mistress Southworth's sister. And see, there are their children, hopping out now."

"Do you think they will truly wed?" I asked softly. "The Governor and Mistress Southworth?"

"Surely she would not have come all this way did she not intend to marry him," Prissy answered. "What a fine-looking woman she is!"

"And note her gown," I murmured. "That soft green becomes her well. And the fit of it!"

"You could sew as well had you something to work with," Prissy said loyally.

"Perhaps they have brought fabrics with them on the ship," I dreamed aloud. "Oh, Pris, I do hope they have!"

As the shallop went back and forth, discharging each load, and being aided by our own shallop which some of the men took out to speed the landing, I saw Captain Standish move away from the group and walk slowly up the Street toward his house. Something in his dragging step and his drooping head made my heart ache for him. Quite surely, if it were true that he, too, had hoped for a bride, she was not on the "Anne." Whatever his faults of belligerence and hotheadedness, I could not but be sorry for him now.

We gathered in the Fort, which we now use as a meeting place, where Elder Brewster offered a prayer for the safe arrival of so many loved ones, and for the deliverance of the "Little James" from whatever trouble it may have seen. Then the company, so many of them filled with thanksgiving at being reunited with their families, and so many others yearning for news of the second ship, dispersed to the various homes along the Street. There could be no toasts, since there was naught but spring water to drink, and there could be no breaking of bread, for bread we do not have. But of lobsters and other fish there was a plenty, and it would have to do for these new residents of Plymouth as it has done for the old.

Library Link ♦ *Read more about Constance's life in the New World in* Constance: A Story of Early Plymouth *by Patricia Clapp.*

 Reader's Response

Constance faced the frontier of a new continent. Today, we face the frontier of outer space. Which would you rather face? Why?

CONSTANCE

A Story of Early Plymouth

 ## Responding to Literature

1. Why is the arrival of the ship *Anne* an important event for the Plymouth colonists? If you were one of the colonists, how might your life be changed as a result of the *Anne's* successful crossing?

2. Constance's journal allows you to look into another time. By reading the journal, what have you learned about the colonists that you did not know previously?

3. Remember the last time you waited to greet people arriving from a distant place. How did your experience differ from Constance's description of meeting the *Anne?*

 ## Writing to Learn

Think and Respond ◆ Often a particular passage in literature makes us want to respond or question. Read Constance's journal again and find a passage that interests you. In your own journal, copy the passage.

> ... I looked at those who had landed, and felt an unexpected shock. Without exception these people were well dressed and well fed.

> Constance must feel hungry every day. She can't even buy new shoes, since there are no stores.

Write ◆ Beside the passage, express your ideas and views about it. Keep writing until you have explored all your thoughts.

Imagine that you are part of an expedition exploring Mars. What is your special contribution to the team's success?

SPEAKING and LISTENING ◆
Working in Groups

You can make a valuable contribution to any group effort—from an informal discussion with classmates to a formal committee meeting or panel discussion. An informal group meeting to share ideas or solve problems does not require organization, and the participants seldom have to prepare.

On the other hand, a formal discussion group requires preparation by its members. Usually a chairperson is appointed to lead the group. Special responsibilities of a chairperson include the following.

◆ Preparing thoroughly, having pertinent facts and necessary materials at hand, and assigning research to group members if it is necessary
◆ Stating the topic or purpose of the discussion
◆ Calling on speakers and keeping them on the topic
◆ Resolving disagreements and summarizing information as needed

Follow these guidelines to make your group work more successful.

	Guidelines for Working in Groups
As a Speaker	1. Be prepared so that you can present your facts and ideas confidently. 2. Keep to the topic. 3. Cooperate with the chairperson. 4. Compliment other members' contributions. 5. Ask questions and make helpful suggestions. 6. If you disagree with a speaker, explain why politely.
As a Listener	1. Make certain you understand the purpose of the discussion. 2. Listen politely without interrupting other speakers. 3. Listen critically. Evaluate suggestions by group members carefully in order to arrive at the best decision.

Summary ◆ Working in groups provides opportunities to share ideas and solve problems.

Guided Practice

Tell why you agree or disagree with each statement about group discussions.

1. The best role in a group discussion is the chairperson's.
2. The chairperson must help group members to work well together.
3. If I feel the speaker is wrong, I should interrupt.

Practice

A. Write *agree* or *disagree* for each attitude expressed below. Then write a sentence explaining your reason.

4. "I want no criticism," Eva blurted. "I researched that data for a week before the meeting."
5. "You scheduled me fourth, but I really must speak first," Carl pleaded with the chairperson.
6. "If I make some assignments before the meeting, we will be more able to make an informed decision," thought chairperson Lee.
7. "There is a great book at the library that can help us, but I've forgotten the title and lost my notes," Sasha said.
8. "Well, here we are," said chairperson Kim. "Who wants to go first? What's the situation, anyway?"

B. With four to six classmates, hold a group discussion. First select a topic or use one of the topics below. Elect a chairperson and decide what information each participant should research. Allot time for preparation. Then, following the guidelines in this lesson, conduct your discussion.

> Creating a literary magazine
> Planning an art show
> Raising money for new band instruments

Apply • Think and Write

Evaluating a Discussion • Watch an in-depth television program on which representatives from more than one side of an issue are interviewed. Discuss with a group of classmates whether the participants spoke and listened well.

✎ Remember to be prepared and to contribute to a group discussion.

WRITING ♦
Identifying Purpose and Audience

Know Your Purpose   Purpose is your reason for writing. Some of the main reasons are to persuade, entertain, inform, and express ideas. For example, if you want to share an amusing story with others, your purpose is to entertain. If you want your readers to do something or believe something, your purpose is to persuade. In the early stages of writing, you should establish your reason for writing.

What is the purpose of each of these writing forms?

cookbook   letter to the editor   journal entry

The cookbook writer's purpose is to inform; the letter writer's, to persuade; and the journal writer's, to express thoughts and ideas.

Know Your Audience   Your readers are your audience, and your writing must be shaped specifically for them. Suppose again that your purpose is to entertain with a story. Now you must ask who will understand and appreciate it. What kinds of sentences, vocabulary, and writing form are appropriate? Writing a story for a friend is quite different from writing a story to enter in a contest.

Finding answers to the questions below will help you communicate with your audience more effectively.

♦ Who will read this material?
♦ How old are they?
♦ How can I capture their interest?
♦ What main ideas do I want to tell them?
♦ How much do they already know about this subject?
♦ What reasons or examples can I use that will be appropriate for this audience?

Summary ♦ Know your purpose for writing and know your audience. Then you can make effective writing choices.

Guided Practice

Identify a purpose and a possible audience for each writing form.

1. advertisement for toys
2. science textbook
3. political comic strip
4. science-fiction story
5. historical novel
6. book about the solar system
7. catalog for sports equipment
8. movie review

Practice

A. For each writing idea, write a purpose and a possible audience.

9. an article on microwave-oven recipes.
10. a story about the misadventures of a young genius who likes to solve algebra equations for fun but is absentminded
11. an editorial on how to spend tax dollars most effectively
12. a journal entry describing the first day in a new school
13. a brochure outlining the many things senior citizens can do to be involved in community affairs after retirement

B. The purpose of the editorial below is unclear. Rewrite it so that an audience of your choice can easily see what its purpose is.

Have you noticed lately how many swimmers, wind-surfers, and boaters are making use of Ell Pond? I love to go there and watch the whole community having a good time. I saw a very strange thing happen there yesterday that started me thinking. It does bother me that the pond is getting a bit polluted. We're going to have to be more careful or <u>my</u> children, for example, won't be able to enjoy it as I do. Shouldn't speedboats be regulated? Oh, yes, the other day I was watching a talented water-skier streak by. I happened to notice some large pieces of debris floating nearby, too.

Apply • Think and Write

Identifying Purpose and Audience • Look again at the editorial you rewrote in **Practice B**. Write a brief explanation of its purpose. Then explain the characteristics of the audience you chose and why you chose that particular group.

✏️ **Remember**
to set a purpose and identify an audience for your writing.

GETTING STARTED Think about all the different forms of writing you have come across this week. Name as many as you can.

WRITING ◆
Choosing an Appropriate Form

After you set your purpose for writing and identify your audience, you need to select a form that is most appropriate or natural. At times you may use or adapt a form you have seen other writers use well. At other times you may create a writing form of your own.

A writing form provides a frame for your material. It gives writing structure and helps organize ideas. As you try to select a form, ask yourself these questions: What is my purpose? Who is my audience? Which form will be most effective? For example, would a poem or a personal narrative be better for the ideas I want to express?

The more forms of writing you are familiar with, the more creative you can be in adapting them to meet your needs. The chart below lists a few basic forms and their uses. With imagination, skill, and a willingness to experiment, you can adapt or combine these forms creatively to fit your needs.

Form of Writing	Appropriate Use
Journal; Notebook	personal insights; writing ideas
Diary	personal entries
News Article; Editorial	to inform; to persuade
Feature Story	to inform, persuade, entertain
Personal or Formal Essay	to entertain, to inform
Fiction; Poetry; Song	to entertain; to express thoughts
Report; Critical Review	to inform; to evaluate
Sticker; Poster; Flier	to advertise, persuade, entertain

Summary ◆ Choose the writing form that is most appropriate for your idea, your purpose, and your audience.

Guided Practice

Name the form you would use for each writing situation.

1. promotional information for your own video
2. your view of how students should vote in the class election
3. why you are disappointed with an exhibition of paintings

Practice

A. Write the name of the form you think would be most appropriate for each writing situation. Then identify an appropriate audience.

4. a personal description of the best day of your life
5. a profile of the life and work of scientist Margaret Mead
6. what visitors should see on the island of Bali
7. your evaluation of a popular new movie
8. why you believe recycling should be mandatory

B. Write a sentence to explain what is inappropriate about the form for each writing situation.

9. a news article, written for fifth graders, that contains long sentences and difficult words
10. a research report that states an opinion without evidence
11. a short comic novel aimed at proving a scientific theory
12. an advertisement written up as a lengthy research report

C. Choose one of the following writing forms or select one of your own. Set your purpose for writing and identify an appropriate audience. Then write in that form for your chosen audience.

a bumper sticker   **a simple lullaby**   **a flier for a car wash**

Apply • Think and Write

Dictionary of Knowledge ◆ American anthropologist Margaret Mead used many writing forms to tell of her expeditions and research. Read about her in the Dictionary of Knowledge. Choose any form you wish and write your impression of this woman and her work.

✎ **Remember**
to select a writing form that is appropriate for your purpose and audience.

Focus on Journals

You probably keep notebooks for a number of school subjects. These notebooks are useful for study and review. A writer's notebook is somewhat different. Often called a journal, it serves a variety of purposes:

- To record facts, phrases, descriptive details, or insights
- To give form to your thoughts so that you can examine them
- To become a source of writing ideas that you can draw upon later

The idea of keeping a journal has been around for a long time. Many early American colonists kept detailed records of what they saw, felt, and believed. They weren't trying to create art. They were simply trying to understand themselves and their experiences.

In *Constance: A Story of Early Plymouth,* the Puritan girl who is the narrator mentions one of the challenges in keeping a journal:

There has been such a pother of excitement these past several days that I hardly know where to start noting it here in my journal! So much has passed, and all of a pleasurable nature, that—but let me try to put it down in orderly fashion!

It *is* hard to record items in a journal when life around you is a "pother of excitement." Yet it is well worth doing. Writing and reviewing entries (on people, events, dialogues, scenes, and so on) will allow you to build on your experiences. Entries that began as personal observations can form the basis of stories, essays, and poems. Or they may just give you the right word or phrase or remind you of a significant detail.

The Writer's Voice ♦ What familiar, unimportant event in your life or in the news might serve as the opening of a story?

Working Together

See how a journal can provide an ever-growing supply of ideas and details as your group works on activities **A** and **B**.

In Your Group

- Encourage everyone to participate.
- Keep a list of members' ideas.

- Show appreciation for ideas.
- Help the group to reach agreement.

A. When Constance describes the arrival of a ship in Plymouth, she records the mixed emotions of the people on shore. What are the mixed emotions? What accounts for them? Discuss whether this paragraph seems to be a journal entry or a finished piece of writing. Is there a difference between the two?

> The ship was the "Anne," this much I learned. With another, the "Little James," they had left England some weeks before, but since a storm many days back they had seen nothing of the "Little James." In the midst of the joy this brought fear to many, as the newcomers were asked repeatedly who had sailed on which ship. . . .

B. Discuss an event that you recently experienced. Notice the reaction to it among the members of your group. Then write a brief journal entry about it and read the entry aloud. Is your entry an improvement on the discussion? If so, why?

THESAURUS CORNER ♦ Word Choice

Sometimes a journal will contain superb examples of word choice. English contains many synonyms for some words, and a writer must use care in choosing the most precise synonym. Write an original sentence containing each word below. Then look in the Thesaurus to see if you can find a more exact synonym. If you can, cross out the word below and use the synonym. If not, leave the original word in place.

bright	change	get
interesting	pleasure	vacation

Writing Across the Curriculum Social Studies

Historians continually make notes of their responses to historic events. Recording your responses while they are forming helps you develop and reflect on your ideas. The habit of recording personal responses in your journal can help as you study history.

Writing to Learn

Think and Respond ◆ Make two columns. In the left column, list the historical objects that you see in the picture below.

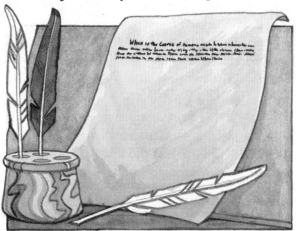

Write ◆ In the right column, express your ideas about the items in the picture. Consider "Is the pen mightier than the sword?" and "Can personal writing influence history?" Consider the items' owner. Record your ideas as rapidly as they enter your mind.

Writing in Your Journal

You began this unit by writing in your journal. Then throughout the unit, you read about the personal journals of people such as Thomas Jefferson, Mary Chesnut, and Lorraine Hansberry. Now in your journal write about how *you* use writing as a way of discovering what you think and what you know.

BOOKS TO ENJOY

Read More About It

Constance: A Story of Early Plymouth
by Patricia Clapp

If one entry from Constance's journal has whetted your appetite, read on. The journal begins with the fifteen-year-old's voyage from London and concludes with her marriage in 1626.

Thomas Jefferson: The Complete Man
by James A. Eichner

Farmer, naturalist, inventor, musician, writer, diplomat, President Thomas Jefferson was an amazing man, indeed. This spirited biography explores our third President's many facets.

Invincible Louisa: The Story of the Author of Little Women   *by Cornelia Meigs*

The author used the personal writing of Louisa May Alcott when writing this perceptive biography. We also see a broad view of the period and people in the author's life.

Newbery Award

Book Report Idea   An Invitation to a Reader

Who's the most inviting character that you've met in a book recently? Choose a character that you would like your friends and classmates to meet, too. Then when it's time to give your next book report, present it as an invitation in note or letter form. The invitation to read the book should appear to be written by the character. Add some intriguing details about the plot to make readers accept the invitation. Be sure to give the title and author.

Dear Reader:
    You're invited to a twenty-first century adventure in a land once called "Switzerland." Tripods, dreadful machine creatures, control most people by placing steel caps in their skulls. Can Will, Henry, and I remain free? Or will we be capped too? Find out in *The White Mountains* by John Christopher.

Sincerely,
Beanpole

UNIT REVIEW

Unit 1
Sentences   *pages 4–21*

A. Write the sentences, using correct end punctuation. After each sentence write *declarative, interrogative, imperative,* or *exclamatory.*

1. Where are the Olympics tryouts
2. Get into shape now
3. The competition is keen
4. How sweet victory is

B. Write each underlined word and its part of speech.

5. <u>John Jay was</u> the first Chief Justice of the United States Supreme Court.
6. Did <u>he</u> advocate a strong <u>or</u> weak central government?
7. This <u>eminent</u> statesman <u>from</u> New York was trained as a lawyer.
8. <u>Oh,</u> who is the Chief Justice <u>today</u>?

C. Write each complete subject. Underline each simple subject.

9. Queen Victoria of Great Britain ruled during the greater part of the nineteenth century.
10. Her reign was the longest in English history.
11. Her nine children married into other royal houses.
12. This enormously popular queen was also the empress of India.

D. Write each complete predicate. Underline each verb.

13. The soybean is a tropical plant of Asia.
14. It has been a principal crop for thousands of years.
15. Many varieties of this plant produce high-protein beans.
16. Soybeans are used for oil, milk, and even soap.

E. Write the subject of each sentence.

17. Here are your gloves.
18. Remember your manners.
19. Did Carol thank her host?
20. In time she will forget.

F. Write the compound subject or compound verb in each sentence.

  21. Veterinarians and breeders know dogs' nutritional needs.
  22. Dogs like and need quality sources of protein.
  23. Dog foods may contain grain but lack essential nutrients.

G. Write *simple* or *compound* for each sentence.

  24. This movie star's homeland is Puerto Rico.
  25. He can afford a hotel, but he prefers a country inn.
  26. Do you prefer an old inn or a newer one?

H. Add words to each fragment to make a complete sentence. Rewrite each run-on sentence as two correct sentences.

  27. Anita solved the mystery she is a born detective.
  28. To gather the necessary facts of the case.
  29. She recovered the lost wallet her friends were amazed.

Thesaurus *pages 22–23*

I. Use the Thesaurus entry for answers to questions **30–35**.

fast (adj) — moving, doing, or acting with speed. The <u>fast</u> train whizzed by.	**30.** What part of speech is *fast*?
expeditious — efficient.	**31.** Which words are synonyms of *fast*?
fleet — swiftly moving; rapid.	**32.** How many antonyms are listed for *fast*?
hasty — done or made in a hurry.	**33.** What phrase is an idiom for *fast*?
quick as lightning [idiom] — extremely fast.	**34.** Which synonym means "efficient"?
ANTONYMS: **deliberate (adj), languorous, slow (adj)**	**35.** Which synonym means "rapid"?

J. Write an appropriate synonym to replace the word *fast* in each sentence.

  36. The fast runner took off quickly at the starting line.
  37. This fast method will get the job done promptly.
  38. Think the problem through to avoid making a fast decision.

Sentence Ciphers

Study the example. Then try to decipher the five sentences. Capitalize and punctuate to make the messages read correctly.

vevibgsrmtrhyzxpdziw = Everything is backward.

1. xzmblfyivzpgsrhxlwv
2. dirgvgsvzokszyvgyzxpdziw
3. xlwvhzmwxrksvihzivhvxivghbhgvnh
4. xibkgzmzobhghhgfwbzmwyivzpxlwvh
5. xibkgzmzobhrhrhvcxrgrmt

An Explorer Chain

The clue to this explorer puzzle is a chain of letters. The last letter of each simple subject is the first letter of the verb in the following sentence. The subject in the last sentence gives the clue for the verb in the first sentence. (Hint: Remember that *You* is the understood subject of an imperative sentence.)

1. The Vikings _ _ _ _ the North Star, not maps.
2. Captain Cook _ _ _ _ _ _ around Australia.
3. What Italian _ _ _ _ a travel journal in 1492?
4. The French _ _ _ _ _ _ canoes to explore the Great Lakes.
5. Hernando de Soto of Spain _ _ _ _ _ _ an expedition to the Mississippi.
6. Marco Polo's father _ _ _ _ _ _ _ _ _ _ a trip to China in 1271.
7. _ _ _ _ more about explorers in your library.

Unit 1 Extra Practice

1 Writing Four Kinds of Sentences

p. 4

A. Write whether each sentence is declarative, interrogative, or imperative. Then write the correct end punctuation mark in parentheses.

1. The original Parthenon in ancient Greece was built to honor the goddess Athena
2. Was she the goddess of wisdom
3. Unfortunately, an explosion in the year 1687 destroyed much of the Parthenon
4. Now look over here, please
5. The people of Nashville, Tennessee, completed this full-scale replica of the Parthenon in 1931
6. Please show it to us
7. Do many people visit this building each year
8. Over one million visitors come annually
9. Look at these massive bronze doors
10. Are these doors really the largest bronze doors in the world
11. Notice the beautiful marble floors
12. The ceiling is built from red cypress
13. Why is the Parthenon an impressive structure
14. It is a perfectly proportioned building
15. Photograph us beside these extraordinary columns

B. Rewrite each sentence, changing it into the kind of sentence indicated in parentheses.

EXAMPLE: Will you visit it again? (imperative)
ANSWER: Visit it again.

16. Admission to the Parthenon is free. (exclamatory)
17. Souvenirs are available. (interrogative)
18. Do you want to buy a picture of it? (imperative)
19. Does each door weigh many tons? (declarative)
20. The Parthenon is a great treasure. (exclamatory)
21. Is the Parthenon being restored? (declarative)

2 Parts of Speech in Sentences

A. Write the part of speech of each underlined word.

1. "Gee! That painting is really good!"
2. Justin was admiring Sharon's work.
3. They were at the museum together.
4. Sharon was copying a masterpiece on the wall.
5. She put down her brush and smiled.
6. "Maybe someday mine will hang here," she said.
7. Justin and Sharon wandered through the museum.
8. They had to ask the guards for directions occasionally.
9. They spent a long time looking at the French paintings.
10. The two friends admired the soft colors in these works.
11. Many of the paintings showed country scenes.
12. Other paintings portrayed children or animals.
13. Just then Sharon cried, "Wow! Look at the size of that!"
14. They had arrived in the gallery of Roman statues.

B. Two words in each sentence of the following paragraphs are underlined. Write the part of speech of each underlined word.

15. Have you ever heard about the Roaring Twenties? 16. The 1920s seemed like a decade of celebration. 17. Booming businesses created new jobs and products. 18. Lifestyles and fashions were constantly changing. 19. American life appeared bright after World War I.

20. The automobile almost certainly affected everyone. 21. At $500, cars were truly inexpensive. 22. Roads and filling stations appeared everywhere. 23. Billboards and diners also became common. 24. Soon thousands of new jobs were created.

25. The heroes of the decade received much acclaim. 26. Mary Pickford was a great star of the movies. 27. Charles Lindbergh flew from New York to Paris. 28. Gertrude Ederle swam across the English Channel. 29. The importance of sports and entertainment in the lives of people grew throughout the decade.

30. The decade's prosperity was not felt by farmers. 31. Droughts and low prices ruined many of them. 32. In the late 1920s a business slowdown occurred. 33. Many banks could not collect on loans and failed. 34. The crash of the stock market in 1929 ended the decade with a tremendous roar!

3 Complete Subjects and Predicates   *p. 8*

A. Write each sentence. Underline the complete subject once and the complete predicate twice.

1. The swampy Everglades is Florida's treasure.
2. Many wonderful trails await visitors there.
3. The wonders of Anhinga Trail in the national park include such animals as alligators and turtles.
4. The green jungle of the Gumbo-Limbo Trail contains extraordinary plants and trees.
5. The ponds north of Flamingo are noted for birds.
6. Many kinds of birds have been spotted.
7. Different species of herons, egrets, pelicans, spoonbills, and flamingos find a haven in the park.
8. Wooden trails reach out to hammocks—clumps of fertile land with many kinds of trees.
9. The famous alligators of the park dig gator holes.
10. These wide and deep holes hold life-giving water for the reptiles during dry winter months.
11. Numerous species of snakes live in the park.
12. Very few of these are poisonous.
13. The prop roots of red mangrove trees trap shells, grasses, and leaves in the water.
14. Large areas of land are created in this way.
15. The yard-wide webs of the golden orb weaver spiders are a common and lovely sight.

B. Write each sentence. Underline the complete subject.

16. Thousands of animals no longer exist on Earth.
17. Most of these creatures died off naturally.
18. People should not be blamed for their disappearance.
19. Thoughtless human actions have caused the death of many creatures, however.
20. All the odds seem to be against wildlife.
21. Even the largest animals are no match for humans.
22. The oceans were once full of enormous blue whales.
23. Few of them remain.
24. Many whale species are now protected by international agreement.

C. Write the sentence. Underline the complete predicate.

25. Reptiles appeared on land about 300 million years ago.

26. They were egg-laying animals.

27. These reptiles had firm backbones and jointed wrists and ankles.

28. Some of these creatures could stand on their hind legs.

29. They were the ancestors of dinosaurs.

30. Most dinosaurs were not small.

31. Some dinosaurs were fierce meat eaters.

32. These dinosaurs ranged in size from small to enormous.

33. Other dinosaurs appeared as huge, long-necked plant eaters.

34. They walked on two or four feet.

35. Many dinosaurs had short front legs for grasping things.

36. Some dinosaurs were the ancestors of modern birds.

37. The arrangement of their hip bones resembled that of birds.

4 Simple Subjects and Predicates   *p. 10*

A. Each word group is a complete subject. Write only the simple subject.

1. Two large alligators

2. An hour in the park

3. Many kinds of snakes

4. Plants of interest

5. Everyone but you

6. Some of the reasons

7. A photo of the bay

8. Late August weather

9. The mangroves nearby

10. Webs of rare spiders

B. Underline the simple predicate in each sentence of this article about the Outer Banks of North Carolina.

11. Several natural features such as sand bars, sand dunes, and islands have formed an unusual arc beyond the coastline of North Carolina. **12.** This arc is called the Outer Banks. **13.** The Outer Banks were doubtlessly connected to the mainland in the distant past. **14.** Huge glaciers melted during the last ice age. **15.** The lower land between the Outer Banks and the present inner shore was flooded by the glacial waters. **16.** Only this thin arc of sandy shore remained above the water. **17.** The sea, however, is still causing gradual erosion of the land. **18.** The relentless sea may in time win its battle with the Outer Banks. **19.** The stubborn land might persist, on the other hand. **20.** Only time will tell.

C. Write the complete predicate of each sentence. Then underline the verb.

21. Geographers have divided North Carolina into three regions.
22. The coastal plain stretches from the Atlantic coast far inland.
23. About half of the state's 52,586 square miles are located on the plain. **24.** This seemingly level low country does gradually rise into the plateau region. **25.** The Piedmont Plateau sweeps across much of the central part of the state. **26.** It ascends to an elevation of about 1,500 feet above sea level at its western edge. **27.** The mountain region then begins. **28.** This region includes the Blue Ridge Mountains and a number of other mountain ranges. **29.** The highest peak east of the Mississippi River is Mount Mitchell in western North Carolina.

D. Write the sentences. Underline the simple subject once and the verb twice.

30. The Petrified Forest in Arizona contains logs of stone. **31.** These stone logs were once trees of the pine family. **32.** This area of Arizona was a wet lowland then. **33.** Many trees fell into the muddy swamps. **34.** Heavy deposits of sand soon covered the trees.

35. Minerals from the swampy water gradually penetrated the wood. **36.** The logs became almost completely stone in time. **37.** The various colors of the logs were caused by forms of manganese and iron.

5 Locating the Subject

p. 12

A. Write the subject of each sentence. Write *(You)* when the subject is understood. Then label each sentence *declarative*, *interrogative*, or *imperative*.

1. What does *Alamo* mean in Spanish?
2. Here comes a guide now.
3. Will you ask him your question?
4. Sir, tell us the meaning of *Alamo*, please.
5. In the Spanish language, *Alamo* means "cottonwood."
6. Around this mission grew many cottonwood trees.
7. They gave their name to the historic site.
8. Give us more information about the Alamo.
9. Why do people call the Alamo the "Cradle of Texas Liberty"?

B. Write the subject and verb of each sentence in this article about the Alamo. Underline the subject once and the verb twice.

EXAMPLE: **At San Antonio, Padre Olivares established a mission about 1718.**
ANSWER: Padre Olivares established

10. Within a fairly sizable walled-in area sat the historic Alamo mission. **11.** Originally the name of the mission was San Antonio de Valero. **12.** There was a large compound with a monastery and a church. **13.** Today there stands only the familiar chapel.

14. By 1835 there were nearly 30,000 people in Texas. **15.** During the winter of 1835-1836, these Texans severed relations with their rulers, the Mexican government. **16.** General Antonio Lopez de Santa Anna formed a Mexican army of about 5,000 soldiers. **17.** With lightning speed Santa Anna marched on the Texans in San Antonio. **18.** In that city were only some 150 Texan soldiers. **19.** Yet there was no thought of surrender in their minds. **20.** To the Alamo mission retreated the courageous little band. **21.** With stirring bravery fought the outnumbered Texans. **22.** There could not have been any question about the eventual outcome though. **23.** Not one of the defenders of the Alamo survived the battle of March 6, 1836. **24.** Because of this loss, Texans by the thousands fought even harder for their independence.

C. Write each sentence below in normal word order. Then underline the simple subject.

EXAMPLE: **On this site in March of 1836 stood the embattled Texans.**
ANSWER: **The embattled Texans stood on this site in March of 1836.**

25. On the walls of the Alamo fought Davy Crockett.
26. Everywhere was the clamor of this fierce battle.
27. At the same time in another part of the state gathered a group of Texas patriots.
28. At the town of Washington-on-the-Brazos was issued a Texan declaration of independence.
29. Under Sam Houston's direction was formed a well-disciplined army of Texans.
30. Defeated and captured by Houston's band of fierce fighters was Santa Anna.

6 Compound Subjects and Verbs

p. 16

A. Write and label the compound subject or compound verb in each sentence.

1. No map or atlas lists the prosperous Silicon Valley of California. **2.** Technological advances and great fortunes are being made in this valley all the time. **3.** Hundreds of computer engineers live and work here. **4.** The silicon chip was invented and is being further perfected in this area south of San Francisco.

5. Palo Alto and San Jose mark the two end points of Silicon Valley. **6.** Thirty years ago farmers grew and harvested much fruit in this very fertile valley. **7.** Today offices and industrial plants have replaced the orchards. **8.** Inside the buildings workers design and assemble tiny integrated circuits for computers. **9.** Switches and wires by the thousands are etched onto each tiny chip of silicon.

B. Write the subject and the verb of each sentence. Underline the subject. If either the subject or the verb is compound, write *compound* after it.

> **EXAMPLE:** New computer companies grow and prosper in the Silicon Valley.
>
> **ANSWER:** <u>companies</u> grow, prosper (compound verb)

10. Many new discoveries were born and flourished in the state of California. **11.** The invention and success of the computer chip in Silicon Valley is an example of this. **12** Digital watches, video games, and dozens of other products all utilize the microscopic computer chip. **13.** As a result of the chip, personal computers are finding their way into many of the nation's homes, schools, and offices. **14.** A better-educated nation and higher industrial productivity may be important results.

15. Computers are rapidly and irreversibly changing our lives. **16.** Silicon Valley and its people may well be a glimpse into our future of advanced computer technology. **17.** With intelligence and hard work, computer scientists in the valley confronted and solved many complex problems. **18.** New breakthroughs will further increase our knowledge and will improve our lifestyles. **19.** For the foreseeable future, Silicon Valley will probably remain the center of computer research and innovation.

7 Simple and Compound Sentences *p. 18*

A. Write each pair of simple sentences as one compound sentence. Join each pair with a comma and a conjunction—*and, but,* or *or.*

1. I call them comics. You call them funnies.
2. Some people laugh silently. Others laugh out loud.
3. Lisa draws colorful cartoons. She writes very funny captions for them.
4. Full-color comics first appeared in the 1890s. They became an immediate success.
5. Are these drawings good? Do they need work?

B. Write each sentence, underlining the subject(s) once and the verb(s) twice. Write (You) when the subject is understood. Then label the sentence either *simple* or *compound.*

6. *The Katzenjammer Kids* began in the late nineteenth century and remained a popular comic strip long afterward. **7.** The heroes were young Hans and Fritz Katzenjammer, and Americans laughed at their mischief. **8.** The kids' favorite sport was playing tricks on adults; no one could get into trouble faster. **9.** With *The Katzenjammer Kids,* the "slam-bang-pow" school of comics was born and passed through childhood. **10.** In 1897, Rudolph Dirks was a young artist on the staff of an American publication. **11.** Rudolph Dirks created *The Katzenjammer Kids,* and his work is important to the whole field of comics. **12.** Most cartoonists at that time changed their characters for each cartoon, but Dirks kept the same cast of characters. **13.** Many cartoonists did one large drawing, but Dirks preferred a sequence of panels, or pictures. **14.** Dirks's readers loved his imaginative ideas, or they admired his expressive drawings. **15.** Find some *Katzenjammer Kids* cartoons in the library.

C. Write each sentence and label it *simple* or *compound.*

16. Political cartoons, by contrast, are not primarily humorous. **17.** Instead, they show serious issues facing the nation and the world. **18.** These cartoons state opinions and are most likely found on editorial pages. **19.** A political cartoonist has artistic skills and knows current events. **20.** Most political cartoonists simplify the news, and they express basic ideas easily and clearly. **21.** Two famous political cartoonists are Herblock and Bill Mauldin.

8 Avoiding Sentence Errors

p. 20

A. Write each run-on sentence as two correct sentences.

1. Charles Schulz began the comic strip *Peanuts* in 1950 now it is read by millions every day.
2. Everything bad happens to Charlie Brown his life is a constant struggle.
3. However, Charlie Brown never loses faith soon things in his life are sure to get better.
4. Snoopy is one of the world's smartest dogs he is more imaginative than most people.
5. This famous beagle can't talk it is his thoughts that people love so much.

B. This article about *Peanuts* has eleven sentences. Write each sentence. Capitalize the first word and put a period at the end. Underline the word in italics.

most people have a favorite *Peanuts* character although the characters are all special, Lucy is always complaining or causing trouble for example, she has been holding Charlie Brown's football for years however, she always yanks it away at the last minute so that Charlie falls on his back Lucy isn't mean she just can't control herself being Lucy's brother isn't easy for Linus he at least has his famous security blanket for comfort although Lucy does seem to love Schroeder, that musician cares only for his music now and then, Pig-Pen, Franklin, Peppermint Patty, and Marcie join in the fun too although there had been birds in Schulz's earlier work, Woodstock joined the comic strip only in 1970

C. Write the paragraph, correcting run-on sentences and sentence fragments. Underline the words in italics.

The setting can give a comic strip its special appeal the strip *B.C.* is set in prehistoric times its characters act surprisingly like people today. Read the comic strip *Beetle Bailey*. If you want a light look at army life. The *Wizard of Id* is set in the Middle Ages. Thoroughly modern characters in some ways. In *Dennis the Menace* the hero merely walks down the street a typical suburban neighborhood falls to pieces.

UNIT TWO

USING LANGUAGE
TO

INFORM

Writing

IN YOUR JOURNAL

WRITER'S WARM-UP ◆ How do historians "travel" back in time? What sources do they rely on for information? How might a successful archaeological dig be like a voyage across time? If you could live at any time in history, what time would you choose? What would you do there? Write about that time in your journal. Tell about your voyage to another period of history.

Think of a person. Say words that name places or things associated with that person. How many words do you have to say before a friend guesses the person? Example: *island, sand, book—Robinson Crusoe*

1 Writing with Nouns

Every person, place, and thing has a name. *Explorer*, *sea*, and *boat* are names. An idea—something that cannot be seen, heard, or touched, such as *courage*—also has a name. All these names are nouns. A noun such as *Santa Maria* is more than one word.

Examples of Nouns	
Persons Columbus was an explorer. His crew were sailors.	**Places** The Atlantic Ocean was crossed. Many islands were discovered.
Things Three ships sailed. The journey was long.	**Ideas** He had courage and hope. Fame and honor came to him.

Most nouns have a singular and a plural form. A word, such as *voyage*, that refers to one is singular. A word, such as *voyages*, that refers to more than one is plural.

Effective writing is specific and informative, not general or vague. Which sentence below do you think is more effective?

The person gave people their first glimpse of a place.
Columbus gave Europeans their first glimpse of a new world.

Summary ✦ A **noun** names a person, place, thing, or idea. Use exact nouns that provide details to make your writing informative and interesting to the reader.

Guided Practice

Name the nouns in each sentence.

1. Europeans brought gold, gems, and spices from the Orient.
2. Columbus searched for shorter routes to such riches.
3. Americans are reminded of his bravery on Columbus Day.

Practice

A. Twenty words are underlined below; ten are nouns. Write the sentence numbers and the nouns.

4. <u>Across</u> the ages, sailors have <u>made</u> great <u>discoveries</u>. **5.** <u>Commerce</u> <u>encouraged</u> many <u>sailors</u> to explore. **6.** In the process, they <u>discovered</u> <u>new</u> <u>lands</u> and oceans. **7.** <u>Magellan</u>, for example, <u>found</u> a water <u>passage</u> around South America and <u>also</u> discovered an ocean that he called the <u>Pacific Ocean</u>. **8.** <u>Thus</u> many explorers <u>brought</u> home <u>glory</u> as well as <u>great</u> <u>riches</u>.

B. Write the nouns in each sentence. Write whether each noun names a person, place, thing, or idea.

   9. A successful journey needs more than luck.
   10. Travelers benefited from the work of scientists.
   11. Copernicus studied the movement of the planets.
   12. Galileo built a telescope that was used at sea.
   13. Navigators also used maps made by mapmakers.

C. Complete the paragraph using the nouns below.

North Pole	courage	space	Nile	explorers
Robert Peary	centuries	astronauts	Africa	land

  (**14.** person) of more recent (**15.** thing) made discoveries on (**16.** place) and on water. They, too, had (**17.** idea). They explored the continent of (**18.** place) and the waters of the (**19.** place). The polar explorer, (**20.** person), reached the (**21.** place). Today (**22.** person) make voyages in (**23.** place).

D. Use the model below to write four sentences. The first time, complete the sentence using two nouns that name persons, and then do the same for places, things, and ideas.

   24–27. _____ is an interesting _____ .

Apply • Think and Write

From Your Writing ♦ For each general noun you used in the Writer's Warm-up, can you list three nouns that are more specific in meaning?

✎ **Remember**
that precise nouns add interesting and meaningful details to your writing.

Tell what you would do if you could spend some time with famous people all over the world. Give a person's name and a place.

EXAMPLE: *I would solve crimes with Sherlock Holmes in London.*

2 Common and Proper Nouns

Nouns can be divided into two groups—common nouns and proper nouns. The word *explorer* is a common noun. It is the general term for anyone who searches. The word *Magellan* is a proper noun. It is the name of a particular explorer. Every noun is either a common noun or a proper noun.

MECHANICS ";?!"

A proper noun begins with a capital letter. When a proper noun is made up of two or more words, only the important words begin with capital letters. For more information about capitalization, see pages 636–645.

Common Noun	Proper Noun
language	French
scientist	Marie Curie
book	*West from Home*
nationality	Norwegian
region	the West Coast
mountain	Mount Everest
city	Charlotte
street	Tryon Street

When you write, use common nouns to give general information and use proper nouns to give specific information.

Summary ♦ A **common noun** is the general name of a person, place, or thing. A **proper noun** names a particular person, place, or thing. Use proper nouns to add specific details to your writing.

Guided Practice

Name the common and proper nouns in these sentences.

1. Thor Heyerdahl was born in the country of Norway.
2. His fame as an explorer and scientist is widespread.
3. Could early South Americans have sailed to Tahiti?
4. Heyerdahl went on an oceanic expedition seeking the answer.
5. His book *Kon-Tiki* describes that journey.

Practice

A. Find the proper nouns in each set of words. Then write and capitalize them correctly.

6. nationality   african   people   norwegian
7. hawke bay   bay   asia   continent
8. ship   *niña*   boat   *mayflower*
9. month   august   friday   date
10. sea   red sea   lake   lake erie

B. The nouns in the sentences below give general and specific information about two of Heyerdahl's voyages. Write the nouns in each sentence. Then label each noun *common* or *proper*.

11. Would his boat survive the trip across the Pacific?
12. The raft was made of logs from the jungles of Ecuador.
13. Its name was *Kon-Tiki*, after a legendary god of Peru.
14. Ancient Peruvians had built similar models.
15. The *Kon-Tiki* is now preserved in a museum in Oslo, Norway.
16. Heyerdahl used a raft made of papyrus on a later trip.
17. Early boats were often made of bundles of reeds, or papyrus.
18. Heyerdahl had a copy made of an ancient boat of Egypt.
19. The boatbuilders were from Lake Chad in Africa.
20. On this trip, the explorer set out to prove the possibility of contact between the early peoples of Africa and South America.

C. Write a proper noun for each common noun below. Then use each proper noun in a sentence.

21. language   **24.** book   **27.** month   **30.** state
22. city   **25.** country   **28.** ocean
23. singer   **26.** street   **29.** leader

Apply • Think and Write

A Voyager's Writing • Thor Heyerdahl wrote books about his various expeditions. List some common and some proper nouns that he may have used in his writing.

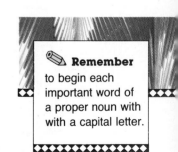

> ✏ **Remember**
> to begin each important word of a proper noun with with a capital letter.

You are about to be shipwrecked on a desert island. What supplies would you want to take with you? Name things that you would want at least two of. For example: *matches*, *shirts*, *ropes*, *nails*.

3 Making Nouns Plural

The singular form of a noun refers to one person, place, thing, or idea. The plural form of a noun refers to more than one person, place, thing, or idea. Here are a few basic rules for spelling plural nouns.

Add -*s* to most singular nouns.
voyage, voyages   **taxi, taxis**   **sailor, sailors**
Add -*es* to nouns ending in *ch, s, sh, ss, x,* or *z*.
arch, arches   **tax, taxes**   **dish, dishes**   **moss, mosses**
Add -*s* to nouns ending in a vowel and *y*. Change *y* to *i* and add -*es* to nouns ending in a consonant and *y*.
delay, delays   **ferry, ferries**   **lady, ladies**
Add -*s* to nouns ending in a vowel and *o* and to musical terms ending in *o*.
studio, studios   **ratio, ratios**   **trio, trios**   **alto, altos**
The spelling of nouns ending in a consonant and *o* varies. Many such nouns have two acceptable spellings. Check your dictionary.
auto   **halo**   **tornado**   **photo**   **autos**   **halos, haloes**   **tornados, tornadoes**   **photos**

Summary ◆ Most nouns are made plural by adding -*s* or -*es* to the singular form. Pay special attention to the spelling of plural nouns when you proofread your writing.

Guided Practice

Spell the plural form of each noun. Explain its formation.

1. photo   **4.** bus   **7.** trace   **10.** tattoo

2. quantity   **5.** alley   **8.** approach   **11.** discovery

3. piano   **6.** crash   **9.** auto   **12.** mile

Practice

A. Write each noun. Then write its plural form.

13. waltz
14. stereo
15. halo
16. idea
17. journey

18. donkey
19. wish
20. cello
21. speech
22. house

23. traveler
24. community
25. tray
26. mass
27. concerto

B. One plural form in each numbered line is misspelled.
Write the misspelled word correctly.

28. boxs   churches   boys   taxis
29. toys   bookes   armies   birches
30. tides   babys   attorneys   computers
31. soloes   tornados   crashes   autos
32. seas   sandwiches   photoes   kisses

C. One noun in each sentence should be made plural.
Find that noun and write the sentence correctly.

33. The science of navigation has evolved over many century.
34. Heavenly body, such as stars, guided ancient sailors.
35. Later, simple compass were also used.
36. Early map and charts were often inaccurate and distorted.
37. On land the first lighthouses used torch to warn sailors.

D. Write each sentence using the plural form of a noun below.

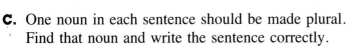

radio   approach   method   station   buoy

38. The _____ and instruments of navigation continue to improve.
39. _____ to ports and harbors can be dangerous to watercraft.
40. Floating markers, called _____, show safe channels to shore.
41. _____ broadcast signals to aid in locating ships.
42. Radio _____ help navigators around the world.

Apply ◆ Think and Write

Instruments That Inform ◆ List singular and plural
nouns that name instruments of communication. Everything
from a weather satellite to pencils can be included!

✎ **Remember**
to proofread your
work for correct
plural spellings.

When is a letter not a letter? When it is used as a word.
Mind your p's and q's. Dot your i's and cross your t's.
Can you think of more examples?

4 Nouns with Special Plural Forms

Not all nouns form their plurals according to the basic rules.
Use the guidelines below to spell nouns with special plural forms.

Add -*s* to many nouns ending in *f*, *fe*, or *ff*.
roof, roofs   **safe, safes**   **cliff, cliffs**   **gulf, gulfs**

Drop the *f* or *fe* and add -*ves* to some nouns.
wolf, wolves   **leaf, leaves**   **wife, wives**   **half, halves**

A few nouns have irregular plural forms.
man, men   **foot, feet**   **goose, geese**   **child, children** **ox, oxen**   **crisis, crises**   **datum, data**   **alumnus, alumni**

Some nouns have identical singular and plural forms.
sheep, sheep   **series, series**   **Chinese, Chinese**

For nouns formed from two or more words, make the most important word plural.
son-in-law, sons-in-law   **houseware, housewares**

Add -*s* to nouns ending in *ful*.
handful, handfuls   **tankful, tankfuls**   **cupful, cupfuls**

Add an apostrophe and *s* ('*s*) to form the plural of letters, numerals, and words used as words.
s, s's   **l, l's**   **4, 4's**   **why, why's**   **30, 30's**

Summary ♦ Some nouns have special plural forms. If you are uncertain about the spelling of a plural noun, use a dictionary.

Guided Practice

Spell the plural form of each noun. Explain its formation.

1. brother-in-law **3.** *if*   **5.** cliff **7.** half   **9.** doorstep
2. goose   **4.** cupful **6.** wolf **8.** *o*   **10.** grandfather

Practice

A. Thor Heyerdahl is an anthropologist. The sentences below tell of another famous anthropologist, the American Margaret Mead. Write the plural forms of the nouns in parentheses.

11. Anthropology is the study of men and (woman) in society.
12. Anthropologists seek to answer the (*why*) of human behavior.
13. In her early (*20*), Mead journeyed to Samoa to begin her work.
14. Samoa consists of islands ringed by coral reefs or (cliff).
15. Mead enjoyed the hospitality of local (chief).
16. The (wife) were friendly to her.
17. Youngsters would rush to greet her in their bare (foot).
18. She stayed in village huts with thatched (roof).
19. The huts were thatched with sugarcane (leaf).
20. Mead observed the customs of the Samoan (countryman).

B. One plural noun in each sentence is misspelled. Write the misspelled word correctly.

21. Family houseshold and activities were noted.
22. She studied Samoan parents raising their childs.
23. Grandsmother usually helped care for youngsters.
24. Mead's work focused on teenagers and their lifes.
25. Mother-in-laws welcomed brides into their families.
26. Believes about child-rearing practices interested Mead.
27. No major crisises seemed to occur within Samoan families.
28. Mead wrote boxesful of notes that later became a book.
29. She relied on observations rather than on numerical datas.
30. Mead's findings and point of views are sometimes challenged.

C. Write a sentence using the plural form of each noun below.

31. wolf	**33.** Japanese	**35.** series	**37.** *3*
32. capful	**34.** sister-in-law	**36.** suitcase	**38.** *how*

Apply • Think and Write

Informational Paragraph • Write a paragraph about your observations of family life in America. Think of sentences that allow you to use special plural noun forms.

> ✎ **Remember**
> that some nouns have special plural forms.

GETTING
STARTED

Some people, places, events, and things are connected historically.
EXAMPLE: *Audubon's birds*   *Boston's tea party*   *Columbus's ships*
How far through the alphabet can you go with this game?

5 Possessive Nouns

Nouns that tell whom or what something belongs to are possessive nouns. They have special endings and are usually followed by the name of the thing owned or possessed.

■ **The sailor's hat is red.** (The sailor owns or possesses the hat.)

Use these rules to help you write the possessive forms of nouns.

To write the possessive form of a singular noun, add an apostrophe and *s* (*'s*).
the journey's end   **Maine's coastline**   **the boss's office**   **Eva's courage**
To write the possessive form of a plural noun that ends in *s*, add only an apostrophe (*'*).
the two sisters' plans   **the Smiths' trip**   **many buses' motors**   **the ladies' concerns**
To write the possessive form of a plural noun that does not end in *s*, add an apostrophe and *s* (*'s*).
the women's team   **the oxen's slow pace**   **the mice's tails**   **the children's games**
To write the singular and plural possessive forms of nouns made of two or more words, follow the rules given above.
a backpacker's tent   **one sister-in-law's garden**   **many backpackers' tents**   **four sisters-in-law's gardens**

Do not confuse the possessive and the plural forms of nouns. Possessive nouns always show ownership and always have an apostrophe. Plural nouns rarely have an apostrophe.

> **Summary** ♦ A **possessive noun** shows ownership. Use possessive nouns to show the reader who or what possesses something.

Guided Practice

Name the possessive noun in each sentence. Identify it as singular or plural in form.

1. In 1768, few countries' ships had explored the South Pacific.
2. England's hope was to find an unknown continent there.
3. Previous seamen's attempts at discovery had been unsuccessful.

Practice

A. Write the singular and plural possessive forms of each noun.

4. man	**9.** wife	**14.** shoemaker
5. ferry	**10.** coach	**15.** theory
6. circus	**11.** trip	**16.** box
7. sheep	**12.** woman	**17.** deckhand
8. class	**13.** Brown	**18.** son-in-law

B. Write the correct possessive form for the sentence.

19. Captain James Cook was one of the (world) great explorers.
20. This admired (navigator) qualities were courage and leadership.
21. Most (child) studies often include learning about Cook.
22. He expanded many (countryman) knowledge of the world.
23. On the (Captain) first voyage, he visited New Zealand.

C. Find the incorrectly written possessive in each sentence. Then write each sentence correctly.

24. Cook also explored Australias' unknown areas.
25. Many of his sailor's shipmates were scientists and naturalists.
26. Joseph Banks, a botanist, studied plant's leaves and seeds.
27. Several scientist's interests centered on the planet Venus.
28. England gave Cook a heros welcome on his return home.

Apply • Think and Write

Dictionary of Knowledge • Read about Aborigines, the first people to live in Australia, in the Dictionary of Knowledge. Imagine yourself as a scientist. Write a paragraph about the Aborigines. Use some possessive nouns in your writing.

> ✎ **Remember**
> to use apostrophes correctly with possessive nouns.

GETTING STARTED

Play this matching game. Name a well-known person, place, or thing. Your partner must match the name with a phrase that tells about it.

EXAMPLES: *Hollywood—home of the stars; J.S. Bach—famous composer*

6 Appositives

An appositive is a word or group of words that gives more information about the noun or pronoun that directly precedes it. Most appositives are nouns or nouns with their modifiers. Appositives often include prepositional phrases. Appositives that are not essential to the meaning of the sentence are set off by commas.

> Alan Shepard was a test pilot.
> Alan Shepard, <u>the first American in space</u>, was a test pilot.

Notice that the second sentence gives extra information about Alan Shepard. The appositive *the first American in space* helps identify the preceding noun *Alan Shepard*.

Do not use commas with an appositive when it is part of a proper name or when it is needed to identify the noun it follows. Look at the examples below. Notice that the appositives are needed to give the sentences meaning.

> ■ This is our son José. Alexander the Great lived long ago.

When you write, use appositives to help combine sentences.

> V. Tereshkova was the first woman in space. She was a cosmonaut.
> V. Tereshkova, a cosmonaut, was the first woman in space.

> **Summary** ♦ An **appositive** is a word or group of words that follows a noun or pronoun and identifies or explains it. Using appositives in your writing can make your meaning clearer.

Guided Practice

Name the appositive in each sentence. Then tell which noun the appositive explains or identifies.

1. Neil Armstrong, an American, was the first moonwalker.
2. Armstrong was commander of Apollo II, the lunar-landing mission.
3. Edwin Aldrin, the lunar-module pilot, was the second moonwalker.

Practice

A. Write the appositive in each sentence about space travel. Then write the noun that each appositive explains.

   4. Astronauts, sailors of the stars, are today's voyagers.
   5. Sputnik I, a Soviet space satellite, was launched in 1957.
   6. Explorer I, an American satellite, then entered the race.
   7. Yuri Gagarin, a Soviet pilot, was the first person in space.
   8. John Glenn, the first American in orbit, circled the earth.
   9. Glenn's flight, a historic moment, took place in 1962.
   10. Sally Ride, America's first woman in space, traveled later.
   11. Edward White, an astronaut, was the first to walk in space.
   12. Skylab, an experimental space station, was launched in 1973.
   13. Pete Conrad, commander of a Skylab mission, had many flights.

B. Write each sentence, adding commas where necessary. If a sentence does not need a comma, write *correct* after it.

   14. Kennedy Space Center a launch facility is in Florida.
   15. Space probes vehicles without passengers explore space.
   16. Space shuttles reusable transports can return to earth.
   17. Space stations satellites for research are habitable.
   18. The space program Mercury began America's manned flights.

C. Use an appositive to combine each pair of sentences. Write your new sentence.

   19. Sir Isaac Newton wrote about artificial satellites in 1687. He was an English mathematician.
   20. Robert Goddard launched the first liquid-fueled rocket. He was an American rocket expert.
   21. Viking I returned photographs from the Martian surface. It was the first successful Mars lander.
   22. Voyager I sought facts about Jupiter. It was a space probe.
   23. Spacelabs gather data. They are orbital workshops.

Apply ⬧ Think and Write

Voyagers' Who's Who ⬧ Create a Who's Who of voyagers throughout history. Write sentences about five outstanding men and women. Use an appositive to identify or explain something about each person.

Remember
that you can use appositives to combine ideas in sentences.

Be a shipbuilder. Build as many "ships" as you can by connecting the word *ship* to the beginning or end of these words: *yard, wreck, shape, board, mate, air, battle, flag, space, war*.

VOCABULARY ◆
Compounds

Thousands of English words have been formed by connecting two or more smaller words. The combined words are called **compounds**. A compound may be written as a single word (shipbuilder), as separate words (ice cream), or with a hyphen (clean-cut). They can be any part of speech—*sunbelt*, noun; *anyone*, pronoun; *outgrow*, verb; *well-known*, adjective; *inside*, adverb; *throughout*, preposition; *whenever*, conjunction; *fiddlesticks*, interjection.

What is the part of speech of each compound in the sentence below?

As the <u>countdown</u> for the <u>moonshot</u> continued, a <u>hand-picked</u>, <u>well-prepared</u> crew <u>undertook</u> <u>last-minute</u> preparations for the <u>blastoff</u> of the <u>spacecraft</u> from the <u>launch pad</u>.

Building Your Vocabulary

These four words—*up, down, over, under*—are used in hundreds of compounds. Below are a few examples.

uphold	downhill	overboard	undertow
backup	splashdown	turnover	thereunder

How many other compounds can you think of that begin with *up, down, over, under*? How many compounds can you think of that <u>end</u> with these words? How is each of these compounds spelled—as one word, hyphenated, or as separate words? (You may use a dictionary to find out.)

Form as many compounds as you can by combining the words below. Compare lists with a classmate.

work	day	house	paper
time	some	dream	back
place	mate	play	ground

Practice

A. Many sports terms are compounds. Add the words below to *back*, *time*, or *down* to form compounds needed to complete the sentences. Write the sentences.

touch	show	stop	pack	out
hand	stroke	over	knock	field

1. Many swimmers do the back _____ .
2. The tennis player had an excellent back _____ .
3. The catcher missed the pitch, and the ball hit the back _____ .
4. The football player's position was in the back _____ .
5. Wilderness hikers carry equipment in a back _____ .
6. A time-_____ was called; the coach needed time to think.
7. The clock ran down and the game went into _____ time.
8. The boxer fell but got up quickly. It was only a _____ down.
9. The quarterback scored his ninth _____ down.
10. The skater faced his rival in a _____ down for the championship.

Find more compounds related to sports on the sports page of your newspaper.

B. Use each word below to form as many compounds as you can.

    foot   hand   off   stone   turn   up

C. Many compounds are associated with bodies of water—*seashell*, *whitecap*, *lake front*, *deep sea*. Write a brief description about a real or imaginary day you spent on the waterfront, using as many compounds as you can.

How to Revise Sentences with Nouns

You have been working with nouns in this unit to name people, places, things, and even ideas. When you write, it is important to choose nouns that make your writing as clear and exact as possible. Specific nouns can give important information to a reader. For example, which sentence below gives you more information?

1. **The man explores the water.**
2. **Jacques Cousteau explores the sea.**

Sentence **1** tells what the man does, but it is not very clear or informative. Sentence **2** replaces the vague noun *man* with the proper noun *Jacques Cousteau* to indicate exactly *who* is doing the exploring. It also replaces the vague noun *water* with the more specific noun *sea* to indicate more precisely *what* is being explored.

Notice how proper nouns and more exact common nouns are used to give clarity and information to the sentences in examples **4** and **6**.

3. **Cousteau helped design things and invent equipment.**
4. **Cousteau helped design boats and invent the aqualung.**

5. **The people arrived and boarded the boat.**
6. **The divers arrived and boarded the *Calypso*.**

By using the most specific nouns possible, you can improve your writing and make it more interesting to read. Look for opportunities to use specific nouns and proper nouns in all of your writing.

The Grammar Game ♦ Check your noun knowledge!
Quickly write as many proper nouns and specific common nouns as you can for each noun below. Then compare lists with a classmate. Did you write the same nouns?

fish	person	boat	storm
invention	equipment	place	tool

Working Together

Use specific nouns to make your group's writing clear and informative as you work on activities **A** and **B**.

In Your Group
♦ Be sure everyone understands the task.   ♦ Address people by name.   ♦ Respond positively to others' ideas.   ♦ Record all suggestions.

A. Write five sentences, each using one of the nouns below. Then write each sentence again at least twice, each time replacing the original noun with a more exact noun.

> **EXAMPLE:** I jumped into the <u>water</u>.
> I jumped into the <u>lake</u>. I jumped into <u>Lake Superior</u>.
> I jumped into the <u>sea</u>. I jumped into the <u>Black Sea</u>.

1. location   **2.** creature   **3.** building   **4.** shoe   **5.** vehicle

B. Changing the nouns you use can sometimes change the meaning of a sentence. How many ways can your group write this paragraph?

The person slipped beneath the surface of the water. As the person saw the ground, the shape below became clearer. Soon the person could make out the thing. It was large and covered with stuff. It must have been there for ages! The person carefully focused the instrument as animals calmly swam by.

WRITERS' CORNER ♦ Exact Information

When you choose nouns for sentences, think about what you want your reader to know. Sometimes you may want to give only general information. If more exact information is necessary, how exact do you want it to be?

> **GENERAL:** An American woman studied life in Samoa.
> **EXACT:** Margaret Mead studied life in Samoa.
> **MORE EXACT:** Margaret Mead, an American anthropologist, studied life in Samoa.

Read what you wrote for the Writer's Warm-up. Do the nouns you used give the information you intended? If they do not, change them.

THE RETURN OF ULYSSES
painting by John Linnell
Bridgeman Art Library/Art Resource. Forbes Magazine Coll., New York.

UNIT TWO

USING LANGUAGE
TO

INFOR**M**

=== **PART TWO** ===

Literature "Westward Voyage," Word from a Raft,"
"From Raft to Reef"

A Reason for Writing Informing

CREATIVE
Writing

FINE ARTS ◆ Ulysses returned home after being away for many years. How might that feel? Try to imagine the anxiety, the happiness, and the excitement of walking into your house and wondering if anyone would recognize you. Become Ulysses and write a page in his journal. Tell how it feels to be a wanderer who has finally come home.

CREATIVE THINKING ◆
A Strategy for Informing

A QUESTION WHEEL

One reason for writing is to give information, as in a news story. Examples that you will read after this lesson are three 1947 newsmagazine articles about the seagoing raft *Kon-Tiki*.

A newswriter often tries to anticipate and answer the reader's questions. Thor Heyerdahl, leader of the *Kon-Tiki* expedition, was trying to sail a primitive raft from Peru to Polynesia. Why? To prove that ancient Peruvians could have made the same amazing journey. The writer of the following passage may have anticipated the reader's next question: What made Heyerdahl think that the Peruvians had reached Polynesia?

> [Heyerdahl] was struck by resemblances between the cultures of Polynesia and South America. Both regions have "stepped" pyramids . . . . Both cultivate sweet potatoes and call them by names which closely resemble their ancient Peruvian name: *kumara*.

Wondering about things and asking questions can lead to learning and discovery. How do you think wondering and asking questions contributed to Thor Heyerdahl's accomplishments? What part do wondering and questioning play in a newswriter's job?

Learning the Strategy

Wondering is a form of curiosity. If you are curious about another country, you might ask, "What is school like there?" or "What kind of government do they have?" If you saw an article titled "High-Speed Trains—Transportation of the Future," what questions would come to mind? Suppose you are your school newspaper's consumer reporter. Your assignment: to write about a new magnetic tape that works in both audiocassette players and videocassette recorders. What questions would you research for your article?

A person who accepts information passively and never asks questions may be mentally lazy. Generating questions requires some effort. However, curiosity is a habit that can be developed almost like a mental muscle.

Making a question wheel is one way to prompt yourself to generate questions. Write the topic in the hub of the wheel. Then write questions on the spokes. The more spokes, the more questions, the better. Here is an example about the new audio/video tape. What questions might you add to this wheel?

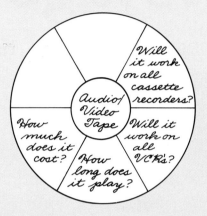

 ## Using the Strategy

A. Choose a partner. Write your partner's name in the hub of a question wheel. Then think of questions you could ask your partner; for example "What is your favorite TV show?" or "Where were you born?" Write questions on spokes of your question wheel until there isn't room for any more question spokes. Then you and your partner take turns asking each other the questions. When your teacher calls time, tell the class one new thing you learned about your partner.

B. Write *Kon-Tiki* in the hub of a question wheel. Then reread the passage on the opposite page. What additional questions come to mind? Write as many questions as you can think of on the spokes of your wheel. Then read the articles about *Kon-Tiki* and see which of your questions the articles answer.

 ## Applying the Strategy

◆ How did you think up your questions about the *Kon-Tiki*?
◆ Think of an example of how being curious or not being curious would make a difference in your life.

Westward Voyage

from *Time* magazine, April 21, 1947

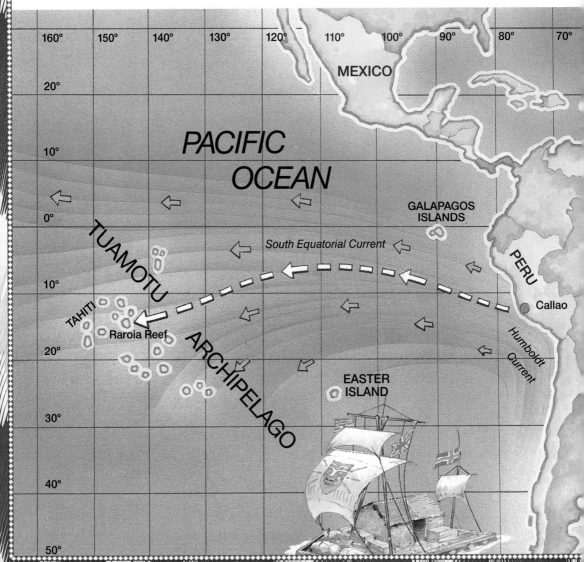

Anthropologists will put themselves to a lot of trouble to prove a pet theory. Last week, five Norwegians and a Swede were making plans to sail westward from Callao, Peru, on a seagoing raft. They were taking many of the same chances as their theoretical primitives: the raft was modeled after the *balsas* of the ancient Peruvians. They hoped to prove that the South Pacific islands had been visited—perhaps partly peopled—by civilized Indians from South America.

The leader of the expedition, Thor Heyerdahl, 32, had been to Tahiti in 1937 to finish a doctorate thesis in zoology. Like other scholars before him, he was struck by resemblances between the cultures of Polynesia and South America. Both regions have "stepped" pyramids, "megalithic" structures, elaborate featherwork. Both cultivate sweet potatoes and call them by names which closely resemble their ancient Peruvian name: *kumara*. The strange stone heads on Easter Island look a great deal like some sculpture in Peru.

Civilizing Trickle. One common explanation of these likenesses: a thin trickle of Polynesian canoemen might have brought such cultural bits from the South Seas to the Americas. But Heyerdahl decided that the trickle must have moved in the opposite direction. Ancient Peru, even during the Tiahuanaco period (about 1,000 A.D., before the start of the Inca Empire), was far more civilized than Polynesia. The Peruvians built large rafts of balsa wood which were probably capable of voyaging as far as the South Seas. The prevailing winds and the ocean currents (both moving from east to west) would help them make the one-way trip.

There is fair historical evidence of at least one such voyage. According to Peruvian tradition, the Inca Tupac Yupanqui sailed a large fleet of *balsas* into the Pacific, about 1470 A.D. Gone nearly a year, he returned with news of two islands he had discovered.

Kon-Tiki. After the war, Heyerdahl gathered around him a group of his countrymen, most of them veterans of Norway's underground, and led them to Peru. There they were joined by a Swedish anthropologist. Their daring plan: to sail to Tahiti, 5,000 miles from Callao. If they make Tahiti safely, the world's anthropologists will have to admit that ancient Peruvians could have done it.

Last week, the *balsa* was almost ready to sail. Named the *Kon-Tiki* after a Peruvian god, she is 40 ft. long, 18 ft. wide, built of buoyant balsa wood logs cut in the jungles of Ecuador. There is no metal in her; all parts are lashed together with ropes, as the ancient Peruvians did it.

The *Kon-Tiki* has a bamboo deck and a small bamboo cabin. Two masts support a primitive square sail. Modern conveniences are iron rations, U.S. Army suncream, anti-exposure suits. A radio will send daily weather reports to the U.S. Weather Bureau.

The voyage to Tahiti, Heyerdahl estimates, will take about 140 days. The Peru current will carry the *balsa* northward up the coast. Then the east wind and the "south equatorial current" will waft it across the Pacific. For entertainment while they drift, the Norwegians are taking along a guitar.

Word from a Raft

from *Time* magazine, July 7, 1947

The seagoing raft *Kon-Tiki,* modeled after an ancient Peruvian *balsa,* is carrying six Scandinavian adventurer-anthropologists on a voyage of historical induction (Time, April 21). After four days of radio silence, the raft was heard from again last week. Present position: about 1,300 miles east of the Marquesas. For a fortnight after the *Kon-Tiki* left Callao, Peru, the Peru current carried it northwest nearly to the equator. Then the south equatorial current and the southeast trade wind took over and pushed the raft due west across the Pacific. Drifting 40 to 50 miles a day, it was now well ahead of schedule and had covered more than half of the distance (5,000 miles) between Callao and its goal, Tahiti.

According to reports from its feeble radio, often picked up by "hams," the *Kon-Tiki's* voyage had been reasonably uneventful. There had been one moderate storm, which did not endanger the buoyant raft. Whales, dolphins and sharks had played around her slowly drifting hulk, and the crew caught lots of fish.

If the *Kon-Tiki* reaches Tahiti or the Marquesas, leader Thor Heyerdahl will claim to have proved his favorite anthropological theory: that ancient Peruvians in original-model *balsas* may have covered the same route many centuries ago.

LITERATURE: Article

From Raft to Reef

from *Newsweek* magazine, August 25, 1947

For almost fifteen weeks, starting April 28, six young men from Norway and Sweden survived the battering of Pacific storms and the attacks of sharks and poisonous eels as they drifted on a raft westward from Peru (NEWSWEEK, May 12). Now they are stranded on a tiny South Seas island, their raft shattered on the reef, with perhaps a long wait until a vessel can be chartered in Tahiti to pick them up.

Self-marooned, Thor Heyerdahl and his companions had accomplished their purpose. Heyerdahl had theorized that the South Seas islands had been settled not from Asia but from South America. He reasoned that prevailing winds and currents would carry a raft 4,000 miles from Peru to the neighborhood of Tahiti—and precisely that happened in his trip.

The frail balsa craft cracked up Aug. 7 on the coral reef of Raroia Atoll, in Tuamotu Archipelago, some 250 miles from Tahiti. The young explorers got ashore safely, taking along their supply of food and water, plus their radio transmitter, which last week was their only link with civilization.

After the men return to the United States, Heyerdahl plans to publish a book on the trip and carry out a lecture tour.

Library Link ♦ *Read other news articles in news magazines such as* Time *and* Newsweek.

Reader's Response

If you had been invited to join the *Kon-Tiki* crew, what would you have done? Explain.

Westward Voyage

Responding to Literature

1. Stories of bravery and courage touch our lives. How do these accounts of Thor Heyerdahl's belief in his own convictions affect you?

2. Imagine that you were on the *Kon-Tiki* the day before it was finally thrown ashore on the tiny South Sea island. Write a journal entry about what you might have felt and thought after weeks of being tossed on stormy seas. Read your journal entry to the class. What thoughts did your classmates have that you did not have?

3. Often true stories, like the account of the *Kon-Tiki,* are more interesting than fiction. Make a bulletin board of news clippings that detail interesting true stories. Decorate the bulletin board to attract attention to it.

Writing to Learn

Think and Question ♦ Create questions that you would like to ask members of the *Kon-Tiki* crew. Formulate five different questions, including *how* and *why* questions.

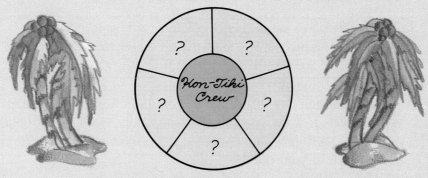

Question Wheel

Write ♦ With a partner, select the most interesting question on both lists and compose an answer to it. Use facts and your imagination to write the answer.

GETTING STARTED

Suppose that you could ask a famous explorer just one question. How would you word the question to obtain the most detailed description of your explorer's achievements?

SPEAKING and LISTENING ♦
Interviews

Interviewing is an important way of gathering firsthand information. An interview, a carefully planned conversation, can provide powerful supporting facts from an expert or eyewitness for your writing.

As you prepare for an interview, first determine your purpose. Then select a person who has special information about your topic and schedule an appointment. Do some research in order to ask appropriate questions. Write questions, such as *Why. . . ?* and *How. . . ?*, that require in-depth answers. Avoid questions that encourage only *yes* or *no* responses.

Follow these guidelines for a successful interview.

Conducting the Interview	1. Put the person you are interviewing at ease and state your purpose clearly. 2. Ask the questions you have prepared in advance. 3. Say "Please explain" to clarify a response or explore a point. 4. Keep the interview on the topic. 5. Ask additional questions if a response raises an unexpected point.
Listening Critically	1. Listen actively to each response. 2. Take accurate notes of specific facts, or tape-record the interview with the person's permission. 3. Notice not only what is said but how it is said, such as tone of voice and facial expressions.

After the interview thank the person and offer to send a copy of your project. Review your notes immediately, verify facts obtained during the interview, and complete the project while the information is fresh in your mind.

Summary ♦ An **interview** is a planned meeting for obtaining information.

Guided Practice

Tell how you would correct each interviewer's mistake.

1. "I've got some fast questions," Theo says. "Please be brief, sir."
2. Maya misquotes the mayor in her written report.
3. The person Bill interviews sneers as she agrees with a popular idea. Bill does not tell his readers about the sneer.

Practice

A. Write how you would correct each interviewer's mistake.

4. Gina just "drops in" on the judge she wants to interview.
5. Jed waits a week after the interview to write his report.
6. Not wanting to seem rude, Ellen lets the person she is interviewing ramble on about an unrelated topic.
7. After the interview, Rhea says "That's all" and walks out.
8. Arlo has all his questions ready in his head.

B. Rewrite each interview question for a would-be astronaut so that it requires more than a *yes* or *no* response.

9. Do your neighbors approve of the launch pad you have built?
10. Is your launch date absolutely essential to your success?
11. Are you sure that you really want to make this voyage?
12. Did you build this spacecraft by yourself?
13. Has NASA shown any interest in your private project?

C. Select someone in your area or school that you would like to interview. Choose a topic and determine your purpose. Then prepare at least five questions. Following the guidelines in this lesson, conduct the interview. Take notes or tape-record the interview.

Apply ✦ **Think and Write**

Summarizing an Interview ✦ Review the notes you took during your interview for **Practice C**. Summarize briefly the most important facts you learned. Then tell a small group of classmates about the person you interviewed, giving reasons why this person is an expert on your topic.

Remember that interviews require preparation and accurate reporting.

GETTING STARTED | Without naming the person, give three reasons why you think _____ is the greatest explorer of all. See if classmates can guess whom you mean.

WRITING ♦
Paragraphs

A paragraph is a group of related sentences that develops one main idea. The first line of each paragraph is indented about five spaces from the left margin. Indenting signals a new paragraph and tells readers that another main idea is beginning.

The **topic sentence** states the main idea. The topic sentence is usually the first sentence but may appear anywhere in the paragraph—in the middle or at the end. This sentence controls the paragraph because the other sentences relate to it. Not all paragraphs have a topic sentence if the main idea is clear without it.

Supporting sentences are also important. They provide specific details, facts, examples, and reasons that support the main idea. Include as many supporting sentences as are needed to develop the main idea completely. Each sentence should be written with the main idea clearly in mind. This will ensure a unified paragraph.

A paragraph may end with a **clincher sentence**. A clincher sentence summarizes or restates the main idea of the paragraph.

What is the main idea in the paragraph from "Westward Voyage" below? Notice how the sentences develop and support that main idea.

Anthropologists will put themselves to a lot of trouble to prove a pet theory. Last week, five Norwegians and a Swede were making plans to sail westward from Callao, Peru, on a seagoing raft. They were taking many of the same chances as their theoretical primitives: the raft was modeled after the *balsas* of the ancient Peruvians. They hoped to prove that the South Pacific islands had been visited—perhaps partly peopled—by civilized Indians from South America.

Summary ♦ A **paragraph** is a group of related sentences about one main idea. Write as many sentences as you need to support or explain your main idea.

Guided Practice

Answer each question about the example paragraph on page 86.

1. Which sentence states the main idea of the paragraph?
2. Which sentence summarizes the main idea?
3. Do any sentences *not* support the main idea?

Practice

A. For each group of sentences, write whether each sentence states a main idea, gives a supporting detail, or is an unrelated statement.

4. They often continue a quest despite what critics say.
   The first colony on Mars will be quite a place.
   Great explorers usually possess enormous self-confidence.
5. Humans seem to have a need to explore the unknown.
   Almost every known culture has its heroes of exploration.
   I am reading a biography of aviator Beryl Markham.
6. Explorers don't always find what they are seeking.
   Queens and kings often financed journeys of exploration.
   Ponce de León found Florida instead of eternal youth.

B. Rewrite the paragraph in correct paragraph form. Omit any unnecessary sentences and create a clincher sentence.

Many a great archaeologist's journey began in childhood, and this is true of Heinrich Schliemann, discoverer of the ancient city of Troy. Many other ancient cities still wait to be excavated. Schliemann's father often read to him from Homer's epic poem, the *Iliad*. Young Heinrich, unlike most people, believed that the poem told a true story. So he began to travel in search of the place where Greek and Trojan heroes had met in battle. His wife, a Greek woman, was named Sophia. After years of incredible frustration, Schliemann proved that he had been right.

Apply ◆ Think and Write

Writing a Paragraph ◆ Write several sentences that tell the qualities you think explorers must have. Then turn these sentences into a paragraph that includes a topic sentence and a clincher sentence.

> ✎ **Remember**
> to make each supporting sentence relate to your main idea.

GETTING STARTED

Tell classmates how to do something you can do well. As you give your explanation, leave out the most important step. Ask them to tell what is missing.

WRITING ♦
An Explanatory Paragraph

In an explanatory paragraph, the supporting sentences explain or give information about the topic sentence. For example, if your main idea is to tell how something works or how to do something, then your supporting sentences will explain the process in order in clear, detailed steps. Always include all the necessary information.

If, on the other hand, your purpose is to prove a point, then your supporting sentences will explain why the main idea is true. They will present detailed information to build evidence for the topic sentence. Add enough supporting details to explain your main idea.

Here are two examples of explanatory paragraphs. The first one explains how in a clear order. The second one proves a point.

> The voyage to Tahiti, Heyerdahl estimates, will take about 140 days. The Peru current will carry the *balsa* northward up the coast. Then the east wind and the "south equatorial current" will waft it across the Pacific. . . .

> Self-marooned, Thor Heyerdahl and his companions had accomplished their purpose. Heyerdahl had theorized that the South Sea Islands had been settled not from Asia but from South America. He reasoned that prevailing winds and currents would carry a raft 4,000 miles from Peru to the neighborhood of Tahiti—and precisely that happened in his trip.

Notice that both paragraphs list only facts that relate to the main idea. The first paragraph tells how the raft will travel from point to point in about 140 days. The second paragraph proves that Heyerdahl's group accomplished what they had set out to do.

> **Summary** ♦ An **explanatory paragraph** explains something or proves a point. Make the details in each supporting sentence clearly explain your main idea.

Guided Practice

Tell which of the sentences explain this main idea: *Our class is creating an exhibit about the* Kon-Tiki *expedition.*

1. Kimberly is painting a large map showing the *Kon-Tiki's* route.
2. Tyler is researching a later voyage on *Ra*, a papyrus reed boat.
3. Others are making posters and models of the raft.

Practice

A. Write only the sentences below that you could use to explain this main idea: *We may never know the truth about ancient cultures.*

   4. The work of plunderers tends to destroy scientific evidence.
   5. Modern science can determine the truth with little evidence.
   6. Time, weather, and later cultures help to bury clues.
   7. Few ancient cultures left written records of their history.

B. The notes below explain how Thor Heyerdahl's scientists built a statue on Easter Island using only primitive tools. Put the notes in proper order and use them to write an explanatory paragraph. Add a topic sentence and leave out two unnecessary notes.

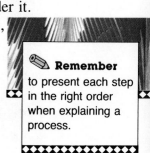

   8. First, they found bedrock of the type they wanted.
   9. After days of hard labor, the statue took shape.
  10. They chipped away under the statue, wedging chunks of wood beneath it as they worked.
  11. Maybe the statues had some purpose in ancient calendars.
  12. Second, the team made sharp stone hammers and tools.
  13. At last the rock between statue and bedrock could be cracked.
  14. With these hammers they began forming the statue's outline.
  15. Some people say that alien beings built the colossal statues.
  16. Next, they had to free the statue from the bedrock under it.
  17. The team finally drove wooden levers under the statue, heaved, and broke it loose from the rocky earth.

Apply ◆ Think and Write

An Explanatory Paragraph ◆ Write a paragraph that explains clearly step by step how to play your favorite game. Make sure you include all the necessary information.

> ✎ **Remember**
> to present each step in the right order when explaining a process.

What facts or examples can you list to support this topic sentence?
There are still many frontiers to be explored.

WRITING ◆
Paragraphs with Facts and Examples

Writers often build the supporting sentences of a paragraph from facts. A fact is a statement that can be checked and verified in a reference book or by firsthand observation. Many paragraphs you write will be developed by facts, such as reports in social studies and science. News stories are also built from facts. Notice how facts are used to develop the following paragraph.

> According to reports from its feeble radio, often picked up by "hams," the *Kon-Tiki*'s voyage had been reasonably uneventful. There had been one moderate storm, which did not endanger the buoyant raft. Whales, dolphins, and sharks had played around her slowly drifting hulk, and the crew caught lots of fish.

Another effective way to develop a paragraph's main idea is by examples. A concrete example that creates word pictures shows readers what you mean and helps them understand the main idea. A paragraph usually requires at least two examples to convince readers. Sometimes, however, one very good example is enough.

> Today boats are made from a variety of materials. There are wooden sailboats and metal canoes. There are motorboats with hulls made of aluminum. Speedboats are often constructed of fiberglass. Aluminum and fiberglass are especially durable and need less care than wood.

Whether you use facts or examples or both to develop your paragraphs, be sure to give readers enough information so that they can fully understand the main idea. However, include only what is actually essential.

Summary ◆ Use facts and examples to develop the main idea of a paragraph.

Guided Practice

Think about how you would develop the topic sentence below into a paragraph. Then tell how to correct each student's error.

Thor Heyerdahl has shed light on many ancient mysteries.

1. Fred writes only one fact and a long clincher sentence.
2. Helen uses one example with vague details.
3. Leo expresses strong opinions but supplies no facts.
4. Tia's not sure her statements can be verified.
5. Maya's example contains nonessential but colorful details.

Practice

A. Write two facts or examples to develop each topic sentence.

6. My first day at the new school was easier than I expected.
7. Driver education should be available to all students.
8. Our basketball team is making real progress this year.

B. Rewrite the paragraph correctly. Leave out the unproved personal opinions and facts that do not support the main idea.

Mary Austin was among the first American authors to investigate Native American cultures seriously. In her 1923 book, *The American Rhythm*, Austin celebrated the meanings of Native American dances and rituals, which were then generally little known. Robert Louis Stevenson was traveling in the West at this time, too. He would have applauded Austin's original insights. In later books, Austin detailed the links between the land and the lives of the first Americans. Her untraditional point of view made her a leader in these investigations. That was quite an achievement for that time, I think.

Apply • Think and Write

Imagining • Think of a frontier—past, present, or future—that fascinates you. Write a paragraph telling what your life might be like on that frontier. Develop your paragraph with facts or examples or both.

> ✎ **Remember**
> to use facts and examples to make your main idea convincing.

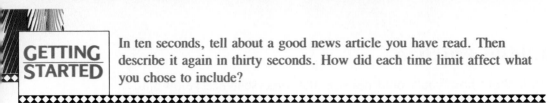

In ten seconds, tell about a good news article you have read. Then describe it again in thirty seconds. How did each time limit affect what you chose to include?

WRITING ◆
Order of Importance

There are many ways to organize ideas in your writing. Facts in a news story are arranged in order of importance. Read this news story of July 1914.

A French count and his three sons discovered a vast cave in the Pyrenees Mountains today. In the cave they found works of prehistoric art which may be 10,000 years old. The cave walls, they reported, are almost covered with paintings of bison, deer, and other animals. The father, Count Henri Bégouën, wants to name the cave "Trois Frères," for his sons.

The most important fact is given first. Then the other facts are presented in descending order of importance—from more important to least important.

The most important fact is the discovery of the cave. Next in importance are the details about the prehistoric paintings and what they look like. Of least importance is the possible naming of the cave for its discoverers.

To help you organize your paragraphs in order of importance, study the inverted pyramid below. The diagram shows the simple structure of this pattern of organization.

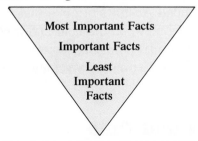

Most Important Facts

Important Facts

Least
Important
Facts

Summary ◆ When you organize a paragraph in order of importance, give the most important fact first. Then arrange the other facts in descending order of importance.

Guided Practice

Arrange the three facts below in order of importance. Tell which fact is most important and which one is least important.

1. A power failure caused a brief delay in the opening ceremony.
2. An exhibit on early air travel opened at the library today.
3. There are many models, photos, sketches, and paintings.

Practice

A. For each group of notes, write and label the fact that is most important and the fact that is least important.

4. **(a)** Amelia Earhart's plane disappeared **(b)** Earhart was attempting round-the-world flight **(c)** aviator set previous flight records
5. **(a)** boy may try other language next **(b)** scholars praised his new book **(c)** French boy Champollion solved ancient puzzle
6. **(a)** Jane Goodall returns after years in African jungle **(b)** scientist plans lecture tour **(c)** has stunning data on chimps, gorillas

B. Rewrite the paragraph. Organize it by order of importance.

Expedition members hope to return east with her continued assistance. When their food supplies ran out, Sacajawea showed the men various sources of nourishment. Her knowledge of Native American languages, they added, helped in their meetings with peoples of the western wilderness. They said she showed them the safest passages through the Rocky Mountains. According to expedition members, Sacajawea's guidance was crucial to their survival and success. The report says the group has reached the Pacific Ocean with help from Sacajawea, a Shoshoni woman. A report from the Lewis and Clark Expedition reached Washington recently.

Detail from **LEWIS AND CLARK AT THREE FORKS** by E. S. Paxson. Courtesy of the Montana Historical Society.

Apply • Think and Write

Notes for a News Story • Write notes for a news story about an adventure or a discovery. Think about readers of the time period you choose. Include facts they would want to know first, next, and last.

✎ **Remember**
to put the most important fact first in a news story.

Make up a topic sentence. Then every ten seconds call on a classmate to give a sentence that supports your topic sentence. Say *in* or *out* for each sentence you would use or not use.

WRITING ♦
Unity and Coherence

A clear, effective paragraph depends on the unity of all its parts. Each part—from the statement of the main idea in the topic sentence to the details in supporting sentences—should work together to express the message clearly. A paragraph has **unity** if all the sentences are directly related to the main idea.

To achieve unity, first determine your purpose for writing and state your main idea clearly in a topic sentence. This sentence is vital to a paragraph's unity because it determines what details, facts, reasons, or examples to use in your supporting sentences. Notice how this topic sentence controls the content of the paragraph.

> A ride on the lunar rover looked like fun, but it was also dangerous. In 1971, as two American astronauts drove this strange-looking vehicle on the moon, they seemed to enjoy the almost weightless, dusty ride over rough lunar terrain. They drove, however, frighteningly far from the safety of their main spacecraft. It was fortunate that the lunar rover worked flawlessly.

You might be tempted to include other mission details, such as how long the astronauts stayed on the moon. Such details, however, do not belong in this paragraph and would destroy its unity.

Effective writing must also be coherent. A paragraph is **coherent** when the sentences are arranged in a clear order and ideas flow smoothly from one to the other. A reader should be able to follow the thought without difficulty, and the transition from sentence to sentence should be easy and natural.

In addition to logical arrangement of ideas, the use of transitional words and phrases will help you achieve coherence. Transitional words are like bridges, connecting ideas within paragraphs or between paragraphs. Common transitional words and phrases are listed in the chart on the next page.

Transitional Words and Phrases			
Space	**Time**	**Logical**	**Comparison/Contrast**
above	after	as a result	although
behind	before	because	different from
below	during	consequently	however
beyond	earlier	due to	instead of
inside	finally	however	just as
outside	first	so	like
through	later	therefore	on the other hand
under	next	thus	similarly

Notice in the paragraphs below how transitional expressions make connections between sentences clear. They also indicate to the reader how the ideas are organized.

First, Commander Ed White checked his space suit thoroughly. At the same time, *Gemini* copilot James McDivitt adjusted the oxygen system. Then both astronauts shared a thumbs-up, and at last they opened the hatch for White's walk in outer space. (time order)

Astronaut White began his 1965 space walk carefully and calmly. However, after a few minutes, he began to feel excitement and awe. His training had prepared him for emergencies. Such training, on the other hand, could not have prepared him for the pure thrill of walking in space. (comparison/contrast)

Because Ed White so enjoyed his walk in space, he wanted to make it longer than NASA had planned. Outside the *Gemini* capsule, White felt almost gleeful, as a result of the spectacular view of Earth below contrasted with the ship's cramped interior. Consequently, NASA's Mission Control gave White a few extra minutes, and the world watched his graceful maneuvers. (logical order)

Summary ◆ In a unified, coherent paragraph, all details work together to support and develop the main idea clearly and smoothly.

Guided Practice

Tell which details below could be used to develop this topic sentence into a unified paragraph.

Crews on early space flights ate mostly freeze-dried food.

1. Their food was packaged in plastic bags shaped like tubes.
2. The crew had to carry out a variety of complicated experiments.
3. Astronauts had to inject hot water into the bags to mix with the food before a meal.

Practice

A. Write only the details below that could be used to develop this topic sentence into a unified paragraph.

Every adventure had its moment of crisis.

4. The 1970 flight of *Apollo 13* had a very critical period.
5. After fifty-six hours an oxygen tank exploded.
6. Many people take part in a space flight.
7. The explosion destroyed the command module's life-support and electrical systems.
8. I wished that NASA had invented a rescue vehicle.
9. The intended landing on the moon would no longer be possible.
10. The only mission of the crew now was to get back to Earth.
11. Every part of the ship is tested repeatedly before launch.
12. The crew tried switching to the lunar module's systems, which worked perfectly, and used them to return to Earth safely.

B. Rewrite these paragraphs to make them more unified and coherent. Add transitional words or phrases and remove unrelated details. If necessary, add clincher sentences and change the order of sentences. Change whatever you feel is necessary to make each paragraph as clear as you can.

The appearance of a space suit is less important than its safety. Each astronaut's suit must be tailored exactly for the individual. I'd like to have a space suit. The future space traveler dons the completed suit and practices various movements in a swimming pool, which simulates a weightless environment. In dozens of fittings, many technicians check every detail of the space suit.

One method for teaching astronauts about weightlessness involves a trip in a specially designed airplane. The plane climbs until it reaches the proper altitude. The trainees get ready in the plane's huge midsection. The plane makes a very steep, long dive so that it outruns the pull of gravity. Just thinking about it makes me nervous. The trainees become weightless during the dive.

Some experts say that space stations will serve as humanity's stepping-stones into the universe. With each station we build, we gain more experience in space and become more prepared for interplanetary journeys. Who wouldn't want to try living in a space station? Some experts disagree with this vision. In their view, direct flights to other worlds from Earth would be cheaper and faster. Both groups admit that we'll probably need at least one more orbiting laboratory. It would make a great place for a vacation.

Apply • Think and Write

Dictionary of Knowledge • Read in the Dictionary of Knowledge about the courageous aviation pioneer Charles Yeager, first person to break the sound barrier. Then list all the transitional words and phrases that help give the entry coherence.

Remember to include only those ideas that are related to the main idea.

Focus on the Elements of a News Story

A **news headline** is a phrase or sentence that states the main idea of the news story below it—and captures the reader's attention.

Headline: Seagoing Raft
Bound from Peru
To Prove Theory

A news reporter's purpose is to give significant facts about a subject quickly and efficiently. In the **lead,** or opening, of each story, the reporter tells the reader the most important facts first— the *who, what, when,* and *where* of the matter.

When: Last week. . .
Who: five Norwegians and a Swede. . .
What: were making plans to sail. . .
Where: westward from Callao, Peru,. . .

In the news story's lead, information is arranged in order of importance. Readers get the most important facts first. Then reporters add paragraphs about less important details. *How* and *why* the event happened are usually treated in paragraphs following the lead.

How: . . .prevailing winds and ocean currents (both moving from east to west) would help them make the one-way trip.
Why: . . .the world's anthropologists will have to admit that ancient Peruvians could have done it.

The Writer's Voice ◆ Look again at the *Time* story entitled ''Westward Voyage'' on page 78. It is the basis for the headline ''Seagoing Raft/Bound from Peru/To Prove Theory.'' Headlines are written to a ''character count''—in this case, 15 characters (letters plus spaces) on each of three lines. Write a new headline for the same story. Use a maximum character count of 24 (minimum 20) and fit the headline on two lines.

Working Together

A headline appears above a news story. The news story itself consists of a lead followed by the rest of the story. Information is arranged from most important to least important. Keep these things in mind as your group does activities **A** and **B**.

In Your Group
♦ Contribute your own ideas. ♦ Record the group's ideas.
♦ Invite others to talk. ♦ Agree or disagree in a pleasant way.

A. Here are notes for a news story. Decide whether each tells *who, what, when, where, how,* or *why.* Note that *what* has two meanings: (a) a subject that is not a person, (b) an action.

1. *U.S.S. Nautilus,* first nuclear-powered submarine
2. intent was to explore . . . and to test
3. completed its journey . . .
4. . . . on August 3, 1958
5. Commander William R. Anderson and several hundred crew members
6. hundreds of miles beneath ice of Arctic Circle
7. made possible by improved air-supply system and nuclear power

B. With your group, write and edit a good lead paragraph for the facts given in activity **A.**

THESAURUS CORNER ♦ Word Choice

Six of the main entry words in the Thesaurus are nouns. List them. Then write a news story based on one of the nouns. For instance, you might write on "A *Plan* That Went Awry" or "An Unexpected *Trip.*" In your news story, try to use at least three synonyms for the noun you have chosen. Make sure your story has a good lead and that the rest of the paragraphs are arranged in order from most important to least important. Write a headline for your story.

THE DAILY MESSENGER

CITY ANNOUNCES
PLAN FOR NEW
ARTS CENTER

WRITING PROCESS
INFORMING

Writing a News Story

The 1947 voyage of the *Kon-Tiki* was reported in *Time* and *Newsweek* magazines. The three articles you read earlier in this unit are model examples of a news story. A news story presents facts about people and events. A news story does *not* contain the writer's opinion.

Know Your Purpose and Audience

In this lesson you will identify sources, get information, and then write a news story on a topic you choose. Your purpose will be to inform.

Students in your school will be your audience.

1 Prewriting

Prewriting is getting ready to write. First you have to choose a topic. Then you need to gather information about your topic.

Choose Your Topic ✦ Start by listing categories such as School Events, Community Events, or Newsworthy People. Then list specific topics under each category. Under School Events you might list the science fair. Consider each listing, then choose the one that interests you the most.

Think About It	Talk About It
How can you research each topic? Will that person be available to interview? What sources of information are available to you? Cross out the ones that will be too hard to research.	Brainstorm possible topics with your class. Take time to evaluate and explore the topics that seem most interesting to class members. Choose a topic that others seem to show interest in.

Topic Ideas

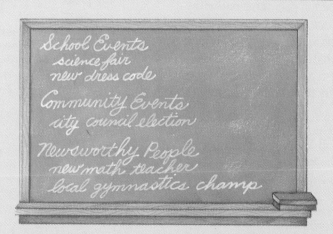

School Events
science fair
new dress code

Community Events
city council election

Newsworthy People
new math teacher
local gymnastics champ

Choose Your Strategy ♦ Following are two information-gathering strategies. Use the idea you find more useful.

PREWRITING IDEAS

CHOICE ONE

A Source Chart

One sign of a great reporter is the ability to find sources of information. A source chart can help. Write your topic at the top. List information sources at the left. Use your brainpower to think of as many sources as you can, such as people, public records, books, old newspaper files, and organizations. At the right, note what you need to do to tap, or get information from, each source. Leave some blank space, since one source often leads to another.

Model

Topic: Camera Club

Sources	How to Tap Sources
Principal	Make appointment for interview
Mr. Stein	Go to Art Room during lunch
Library	Look up school budget

CHOICE TWO

A Question Wheel

Every reporter gets information by asking questions. The Reporter's Formula is a list of six questions, five W's and an H: Who, What, When, Where, Why, and How. Make a question wheel. Write your topic in the hub and the Reporter's Formula on six spokes. Then write at least one good question related to your topic for each W or H category. Finally, figure out the best source to look up or interview to find the answer for each question.

Model

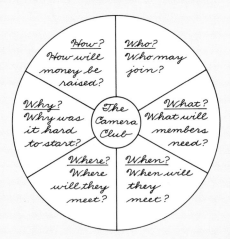

2 Writing

Writing is putting your ideas on paper. As you begin your news story, look at the information and answers you got from your pre-writing sources and questions. Take time to write a strong, attention-catching lead, or first paragraph. As you write your news story, follow the inverted pyramid formula: start with the most important information and end with the least important.

Sample First Draft ✦

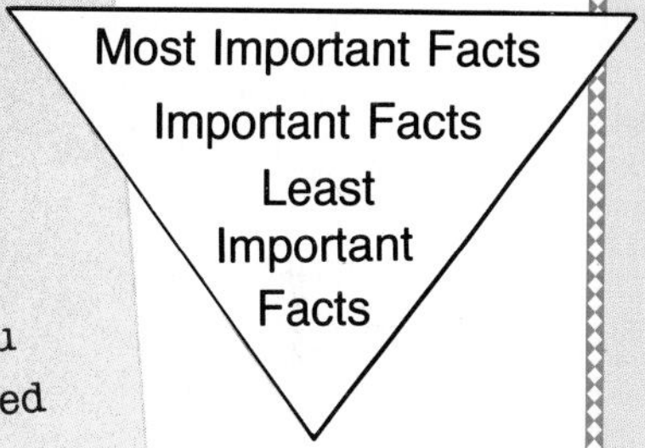

Focus on new Camera Club

The newly formed Camera Club will hold its first meeting in the art room after school. All intrested students are urged to attend this first session, which should take about an hour. If you own a Camera, bring it. However, you do not need to own a camera to join.

The first meeting will be on Thursday, April 19. Members will learn about different types of cameras and film they will also learn to develop and print their own black and white pictures. Guest speakers will appear frequently.

Last year mr Stein tried to form a camera club. He knew of eleven interested students. However, the school budget had no money for equipment. Early this year students raised some funds for the club. Then, late last month, two local businesses made generous donations of needed equipment.

Most Important Facts
Important Facts
Least
Important
Facts

3 Revising

Revising is making changes to improve your writing. Here is an idea that can help you revise your news story.

REVISING IDEA

FIRST   Read to Yourself

Read your story aloud to yourself and listen to the sound of your words. Are you adding words or hesitating as you read? You may need to make changes. Think about your purpose. Did you write a news story? Think of your audience. Will your classmates understand your story?

Focus: Have you followed the Reporter's Formula? Does your story answer the five W's and an H?

THEN   Share with a Partner

Choose a partner to be your audience. Read your story and ask him or her to respond. Below are some guidelines.

The Writer

Guidelines: Read aloud slowly and clearly. Listen to your partner's feedback. Make only changes you think are necessary.

Sample questions:
- Does my lead contain the most important information?
- **Focus question:** Have I answered all the questions in the Reporter's Formula?

The Writer's Partner

Guidelines: Be honest, be specific, and be courteous. Work with the writer in a helpful spirit.

Sample responses:
- What I liked most about your writing was _____.
- Your lead could include information about _____.

Revising Model ♦ As the model below shows, a revised draft doesn't have to look neat. The blue marks show the writer's changes.

Revising Marks

delete	ـe
add	∧
move	⟳

This information belongs in the lead.

The word *photographs* is more exact than the word *pictures*.

The writer realized that not everyone would know Mr. Stein.

The writer's partner wanted to know these details.

Focus on new Camera Club

The newly formed Camera Club will hold its first meeting in the art room after school. All intrested students are urged to attend this first session, which should take about an hour. If you own a Camera, bring it. However, you do not need to own a camera to join.

The first meeting will be on Thursday, April 19. Members will learn about different types of cameras and film they will also learn to develop and print their own black and white pictures. *photographs*
Guest speakers will appear frequently.

Last year *the art teacher* mr Stein tried to form a camera club. He knew of eleven interested students. However, the school budget had no money for equipment. Early this year students raised some funds for the club. Then, late last month, two local businesses made generous donations of needed equipment. *Camera City donated two cameras and an enlarger. Picture Perfect donated development equipment and chemicals.*

Read the news story above with the writer's changes. Then revise your own news story.

Grammar Check ♦ An appositive noun can be a short, simple way to add information to a story.

Word Choice ♦ Do you want to use a more exact word for a word such as *picture*? A thesaurus is a good source of synonyms.

Revising Checklist

☐ **Purpose:** Did I write to inform? Did I write a news story based on facts, not opinions?

☐ **Audience:** Will students in my school understand my news story?

☐ **Focus:** Did I answer all the questions in the Reporter's Formula: who, what, when, where, why, and how?

4 Proofreading

Proofreading is looking for and fixing surface errors. A correct copy is a courtesy to your readers.

Proofreading Model ◆ Below is the draft of the news story about the camera club. Proofreading changes in red have been added.

<table>
<tr><th colspan="2">Proofreading Marks</th></tr>
<tr><td>capital letter</td><td>=</td></tr>
<tr><td>small letter</td><td>/</td></tr>
<tr><td>add comma</td><td>⋀</td></tr>
<tr><td>add period</td><td>⊙</td></tr>
<tr><td>indent paragraph</td><td>¶</td></tr>
<tr><td>check spelling</td><td>◯</td></tr>
</table>

Focus on new Camera Club

→ The newly formed Camera Club will hold its first meeting in the art room after school. All *interested* (intrested) students are urged to attend this first session, which should take about an hour. If you own a ¢amera, bring it. However, you do not need to own a camera to join.

The first meeting will be on Thursday, April 19.
¶Members will learn about different types of cameras and film⊙they will also learn to develop and print their own black and white ~~pictures.~~ *photographs*
Guest speakers will appear frequently.
Last year mr⊙Stein tried to form a camera *the art teacher* club. He knew of eleven interested students. However, the school budget had no money for equipment.
¶Early this year students raised some funds for the club. Then, late last month, two local businesses made generous donations of needed equipment. *Camera City donated two cameras and an enlarger. Picture Perfect donated development equipment and chemicals.*

Proofreading Checklist

- ☐ Did I spell words correctly?
- ☐ Did I indent paragraphs?
- ☐ Did I use correct capitalization?
- ☐ Did I use correct punctuation?
- ☐ Did I type neatly or use my best handwriting?

PROOFREADING IDEA

One Thing at a Time

Check your work for one kind of error. Then read it a second and third time to look for different kinds of mistakes. For example, first look for spelling errors. Then look for capitalization and punctuation mistakes.

Now proofread your news story, add a title, and make a neat copy.

5 Publishing

Publishing is sharing your writing with others. Try one of the ideas below for sharing your news story.

Focus on New Camera Club

On Thursday, April 19, the newly formed Camera Club will hold its first meeting in the art room after school. All interested students are urged to attend this first session, which should take about an hour. If you own a camera, bring it. However, you do not need to own a camera to join.

Members will learn about different types of cameras and film. They will also learn to develop and print their own black and white photographs. Guest speakers will appear frequently.

Last year Mr. Stein, the art teacher, tried to form a camera club. He knew of eleven interested students. However, the school budget had no money for equipment.

Early this year students raised some funds for the club. Then, late last month, two local businesses made generous donations of needed equipment. Camera City donated two cameras and an enlarger. Picture Perfect donated development equipment and chemicals.

PUBLISHING IDEAS

Share Aloud	Share in Writing
Work with a group to put on a mock TV news show for your own class, another class, or a school assembly. Have one or two news anchors who call on various reporters for their stories. Add humorous commercials if you like. Ask the audience to offer comments and questions.	Submit your story to the school newspaper. Ask readers to write responses. Replies may be displayed on a ''Dear Editor'' bulletin board.

CURRICULUM CONNECTION

Writing Across the Curriculum   Science

In this unit you asked questions to get information for a news story. Scientists also get information by asking questions. It is a strategy you can use to help you learn more in science class.

Writing to Learn

Think and Question ◆ Look at the picture below. What do you want to know about it? Make a question wheel. Write a picture label in the center. Fill the wheel with questions about the picture.

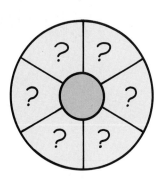

Question Wheel

Write ◆ Take your question wheel to the library. Research one of your questions. Write a summary of the answers you find.

Writing in Your Journal

In the Writer's Warm-up you wrote about traveling back in time. During the unit you learned about voyages across the ages by explorers, anthropologists, archaeologists, and astronauts. Should we continue to explore the universe? To study our own planet's past? In your journal express your ideas about our nation's commitment to exploring space and exploring history.

BOOKS TO ENJOY

Read More About It

Carry On, Mr. Bowditch   *by Jean Lee Latham*
Born in 1773 in Massachusetts, Nathaniel Bowditch went
to sea at age twelve. Self-taught, he became an outstanding
mathematician and astronomer who helped bring about the
age of modern navigation. This biography details his life,
focusing on his many adventurous voyages.

Newbery Award

Ishi, Last of His Tribe   *by Theodora Kroeber*
Ishi was the last of California's Yahi Indians. When the
other members of his tribe had all died, Ishi came out of
hiding, leaving his primitive life-style to enter modern-day
society. Eventually he came to live with the Kroebers, anthropologists who tell this true story from Ishi's point of view.

**A Day of Pleasure: Stories of a Boy Growing Up
in Warsaw**   *by Isaac Bashevis Singer*
Isaac Bashevis Singer is a modern American author and
Nobel Prize winner. In these biographical sketches, he looks
back at his traditional old-world boyhood in Warsaw, Poland.

National Book Award

Book Report Idea   News Story

A news story is an interesting format
in which to present facts about a
book. Use what you've learned about
writing news stories the next time
you have to give a book report. State
the main idea of the book in a headline. In subsequent paragraphs, tell
about the plot and characters. Be sure
to list the full title and author of the
book somewhere in the news story.

> *Eerie Hound Suspected
> in Baskerville Death*
> A ghostly and gigantic hound is
> thought to have played a role in the
> recent death of Sir Charles Baskerville.
> Two well-known London detectives,
> Mr. Sherlock Holmes and Dr. Watson,
> are in Devon to investigate. Oddly
> enough, local legends have long
> claimed that the Baskerville
> family lives under the curse of an
> evil and deadly hound....
> *The Hound of the Baskervilles
> by Sir Arthur Conan Doyle*

UNIT REVIEW

Unit 2

Nouns   *pages 58–69*

A. Write the nouns in each sentence. Then write whether each noun names a person, place, thing, or idea.

1. A landslide blocked the road in Mayville.
2. Hikers ran for safety to a higher elevation.
3. There was no damage to property or loss of life.
4. Geologists are studying erosion in the area.

B. Write the nouns and label each one *common* or *proper*.

5. The Mesa Verde National Park is in Colorado.
6. Visitors enjoy the prehistoric dwellings in the cliffs.
7. The discovery of gold brought many settlers to the state.
8. Cities sprang up rapidly during and after World War II.

C. Write the plural form of each noun.

9. trio
10. bunch
11. magazine
12. hospital
13. flurry
14. halo
15. crash
16. valley

D. Write the correct plural form in parentheses.

17. 10 (10s, 10's)
18. sheaf (sheafs, sheaves)
19. goose (gooses, geese)
20. fistful (fistfuls, fistsful)

E. Write the singular and plural possessive form of each noun.

21. century
22. patch
23. donkey
24. article
25. father-in-law
26. mouse

F. Write the appositive in each sentence.

27. Mount Rushmore, a gigantic sculpture, is in South Dakota.
28. Crater Lake, a deep lake in Oregon, has lava walls.
29. Carlsbad Caverns, a series of caves, aren't all explored.
30. Who designed the Stars and Stripes, the United States flag?

G. Write each sentence. Add commas where necessary. If a sentence does not need a comma, write *correct* after it.

31. The lemming a mouselike rodent is found in many arctic regions.
32. The Kremlin a large fortress is in Moscow.
33. Surrounding the South Pole is the continent Antarctica.
34. Admiral Richard E. Byrd the famous explorer led five expeditions to the continent.

Compounds *pages 70–71*

H. Write a compound that begins with each of the words below.

35. out	**37.** under	**39.** head	**41.** tooth
36. hand	**38.** over	**40.** space	**42.** door

Paragraphs *pages 86–87, 92–93*

I. Read each exercise. Write whether each sentence states a main idea, gives a supporting detail, or is an unrelated statement.

43. a. Thomas Jefferson was a man of many talents.
  b. He was tall and had red hair.
  c. He was an inventor, a naturalist, and a writer.
44. a. She excelled in golf, track, baseball, and basketball.
  b. Golf is a sport enjoyed by both amateur and professional players.
  c. Babe Didrickson was one of the greatest female athletes.
45. a. It can take years for a case to be heard in court.
  b. The judicial system is bogged down in red tape.
  c. Some lawyers don't charge their clients a fee.

J. Read each group of notes. For each group, write and label the fact that is most important and the fact that is least important.

46. (a) Mickey Mantle was born in Oklahoma **(b)** played center field for the New York Yankees **(c)** hit 536 home runs during his career
47. (a) U.S. Postal Service was reorganized in 1970 **(b)** is now an independent U.S. agency **(c)** hires part-time workers
48. (a) President McKinley was assassinated **(b)** happened six months after his second inauguration **(c)** Theodore Roosevelt became the next President

CUMULATIVE REVIEW

UNIT 1: **Sentences** *pages 4–21*

A. Write the sentences, using correct end punctuation. After each sentence write *declarative, interrogative, imperative,* or *exclamatory.*

1. What a bargain this is
2. It is below market price
3. Keep the change
4. What else do you want

B. Write each complete subject. Underline each simple subject.

5. The former queen of Sikkim lives in New York now.
6. She is a tour guide for one of the city's museums.
7. This graduate of Sarah Lawrence College knows the city well.
8. Her most important purchase was comfortable shoes.

C. Write each complete predicate. Underline each verb.

9. Jason was a hero in Greek legends.
10. This brave person led the expedition of the Argonauts.
11. He secured the Golden Fleece.
12. The Golden Fleece was under the watchful eye of a dragon.

D. Write the compound subject or compound verb in each sentence.

13. A mackinaw and a mackintosh are types of coats.
14. A short coat and a thick blanket are meanings for *mackinaw.*
15. The mackintosh is waterproof but is not thick.
16. It is a raincoat and was named for its Scottish inventor.

E. Write *simple* or *compound* for each sentence.

17. A magazine can be a room or building for military supplies.
18. The word came into English from the French, but it can be traced back to Arabic.
19. A magazine can also be a place for a roll of film in a camera.
20. It can hold cartridges in a gun, or it can contain articles.

Unit 2: Nouns *pages 58–69*

F. Write the nouns in each sentence. Then write whether each noun names a person, place, thing, or idea.

   21. The potential for success is in every child.
   22. Graduates today face stiff competition in every field.
   23. A winner seizes every opportunity.
   24. That counselor advised May to talk about her talents and accomplishments in an interview.

G. Write each noun and label it *common* or *proper*.

   25. The Library of Congress is a depository of valuable items, such as books, maps, manuscripts, and photographs.
   26. Located in Washington, D.C., this facility serves as the national library.
   27. Its system of classification is widely used.
   28. Printed works are housed in three buildings next to the Capitol.

H. Write the plural form of each noun.

   29. banjo   **31.** injury   **33.** hinge   **35.** jinx
   30. bonus   **32.** essay   **34.** warranty   **36.** rodeo

I. Write the correct plural form in parentheses.

   37. wolf (wolfs, wolves)   **39.** seaman (seasman, seamen)
   38. X (Xs, X's)   **40.** deer (deer, deers)

J. Write the singular and plural possessive form of each noun.

   41. sandwich   **43.** activity   **45.** sister-in-law
   42. umbrella   **44.** tortoise   **46.** goose

K. Write the appositive in each sentence.

   47. August, the eighth month of the year, has thirty-one days.
   48. Augustus, the first emperor of Rome, was the grandnephew of Julius Caesar.
   49. Where is Augusta, the capital of Maine?
   50. Augusta, a city in Georgia, is not the state capital.

Plurals Potion

The gods and goddesses on Mount Olympus decided to make a magic potion for Hercules. Write the total amounts of each ingredient they used.

Aphrodite added a bucketful of stardust, half of a mosquito, a magic number 8, a golden tooth, and a silver potato.

Eros added half of a mosquito, an armful of moonbeams, a bunch of deer antlers, and a louse.

Apollo added a box of rainbows, a loaf of sunshine, a magic number 8, a capful of lightning, and an armful of moonbeams.

Zeus added a golden tooth, a box of rainbows, a bunch of deer antlers, a capful of lightning, a louse, and a silver potato.

Artemis added a loaf of sunshine, a bucketful of stardust, a bunch of deer antlers, a silver potato, and half of a mosquito.

Hidden Nouns

Can you find thirty nouns in this puzzle? Use letters that touch each other consecutively in any direction, as the noun *sheep* is shown here. Write the plural possessive form of each noun you find.

i	s	t	s	u	n	m	u	l	a	s
s	y	e	l	l	a	v	b	c	u	s
i	r	c	p	e	h	x	o	o	t	l
e	r	o	g	n	e	s	s	a	p	a
s	e	f	i	w	o	p	o	c	o	r
z	c	o	u	n	t	r	y	h	o	v
s	i	x	a	s	u	c	t	o	f	a

Unit 2 Extra Practice

1 Writing with Nouns

p. 58

A. Write the nouns in each sentence.

   1. Henry Wadsworth Longfellow was a very popular poet in the nineteenth century.
   2. His work has been translated into many languages.
   3. Longfellow taught languages at Harvard University.
   4. People gathered at his home in Massachusetts.
   5. Events from history inspired this writer.
   6. "Paul Revere's Ride" is one well-known example.
   7. If Longfellow had not written this poem, Revere might be only a footnote in history books.

B. Write the nouns in each sentence. Then write whether the noun names a person, place, thing, or idea.

   8. Writers work hard.
   9. The workroom is quiet.
   10. Is a typewriter needed?
   11. Paper is essential.
   12. Is creativity necessary?
   13. Patience is necessary.
   14. Visit a big library.
   15. Authors work there.
   16. Librarians help authors.
   17. Does Ann write poems?

C. In this article about the poet Emily Dickinson, twenty words are underlined. Ten are nouns. Write each noun after its sentence number. Write *none* if the sentence has no underlined noun.

   18. Emily Dickinson was <u>born</u> in 1830 in <u>Amherst</u>, Massachusetts. **19.** She lived her <u>entire</u> life in the same <u>house</u>. **20.** As an <u>adult</u> she rarely <u>traveled</u> farther than her own garden. **21.** Few <u>people</u> knew she was a <u>poet</u>. **22.** <u>After</u> she died, Emily's sister found bundles of poetry <u>in</u> her room. **23.** This <u>poetry</u> is some of the greatest ever produced in <u>America</u>. **24.** Emily Dickinson lacked <u>experience</u> in a world larger than her own village. **25.** <u>However</u>, she had an <u>intense</u> inner life. **26.** In her <u>imagination</u>, an ordinary object <u>became</u> a sign of something great. **27.** For example, a tiny <u>flower</u> <u>held</u> the secrets of <u>the</u> universe.

2 Common and Proper Nouns

p. 60

A. Find the proper noun or proper nouns in each set of words. Then write and capitalize them correctly.

1. city town denver village suburb
2. vacation holiday memorial day feast july
3. country france nation state wyoming
4. youngster roger parent sister brother-in-law
5. planets neptune star comet galaxy

B. Write the nouns in each sentence. Then label each noun *common* or *proper*.

6. The literature of America began in colonial days.
7. Captain John Smith wrote about Jamestown.
8. Most writers in New England wrote about religion.
9. Anne Bradstreet of Massachusetts was a fine poet.
10. Phillis Wheatley was an important black poet.
11. Wheatley arrived in Boston from Africa.
12. Many patriots of this period were also writers.
13. Thomas Jefferson was also an author and architect.
14. Abigail Adams is remembered for her letters.
15. Benjamin Franklin wrote a popular autobiography.

C. In this article, eighteen of the underlined words are nouns. Write each noun after its sentence number. Label each proper noun.

16. Some great writers enjoy little fame while they are living.
17. Walt Whitman, for example, is often considered one of America's greatest poets. 18. His poems celebrate the American people and democracy. 19. However, few people bought or read his book of poems, *Leaves of Grass*, which he published at his own expense in 1855. 20. Whitman's poems rarely had rhyme, and lines were of unequal length. 21. The subjects of his poems were unusual for that period, too. 22. Despite being ignored or criticized, Whitman continued to write many poems until his death in 1892. 23. In time, younger poets came to admire Whitman's work more and more and patterned their poems after his. 24. Indeed, Whitman has had a tremendous effect on almost all western literature of the twentieth century. 25. He has inspired authors to experiment with the form and style of their writings.

D. Write the proper nouns in these sentences correctly. If a sentence has no proper noun, write *none*.

26. My sister manages a travel agency in fort worth, texas. **27.** Her office is lined with posters from hawaii, tahiti, and other exotic places. **28.** Many customers visit lake of the woods, a resort area in minnesota. **29.** She advises travelers in the southwest to use route 66. **30.** Vacationers in the northeast often choose the berkshire hills. **31.** Those visiting arizona usually stop to see the painted desert. **32.** One way to see canada, she says, is to cross the peace bridge at buffalo, new york. **33.** My sister also receives requests to see bourbon street in new orleans. **34.** One tourist actually asked who owned the brooklyn bridge. **35.** He also wondered who was buried in grant's tomb on riverside drive. **36.** She showed me pictures of newcastle-upon-tyne, a town in england. **37.** I also loved her photographs of mount fuji, a volcanic mountain in japan. **38.** She, herself, plans to visit the great pyramid of cheops in egypt. **39.** I hope I see australia with her. **40.** Travel agents know how to travel.

E. Write the proper nouns in these sentences correctly. Underline words in italics.

41. Harry houdini died on halloween day in 1926.
42. My office is on east main street in newark, delaware.
43. The civil war lasted from 1861 to 1865.
44. The painter el greco died on april 7 in 1614.
45. Read that article in *road and track*.
46. We will visit montreal, canada, this summer.
47. Last summer we toured yellowstone national park.
48. Some day we will drive across the golden gate bridge.
49. Do you think we could visit alaska and hawaii?

3 Making Nouns Plural

p. 62

A. Write the plural form of each noun.

1. tractor	**6.** address	**11.** degree
2. clutch	**7.** soprano	**12.** cargo
3. wax	**8.** highway	**13.** trolley
4. license	**9.** industry	**14.** Simmons
5. entry	**10.** area	**15.** ghetto

B. One noun in each sentence should be made plural. Find that noun and write the sentence correctly.

16. You will go over two bridges and two overpass.
17. Major towns and city are connected by turnpikes.
18. Those stereo were loaded into the trucks.
19. We played domino at tables in empty parking lots.
20. A good driver has quick reactions and reflex.
21. The hitching posts are for horse-drawn carriage.
22. All buses were equipped with emergency tool box.
23. Several flutes and oboe were left on the plane.
24. Many cars have been demolished by tornado.
25. Surrey were carriages used for pleasure riding.

C. One plural form in each sentence is misspelled. Write the misspelled word correctly.

26. Plantings of trees and bushs beautify highways.
27. Special dummies are used to test seat beltes.
28. Deep ditchs along shoulders of roads are unsafe.
29. The mashed potatos were extremely fluffy.
30. Tape deckes and radios are optional features.
31. Neither buses nor subwayes were running.
32. Participants in rodeoes sometimes ride horses.
33. Those railroad tracks have numerous switchs.
34. Kitchens on ships are called gallies.
35. Do driving tests ever include essaies?

D. Write each sentence. Change nouns as necessary to make each sentence correct.

36. Bike propelled by pushing on pedal date from the 1860s.
37. Vehicle similar to bikes were developed in a few European country.
38. In 1861 two French brother introduced machine called velocipede.
39. An English bike of 1871 had a large front wheel to suit the rider's leg.
40. The wheel measured from thirty-nine to fifty-nine inch across.
41. Bicycle wheel driven by chain were used in England in 1879.
42. Pedal are now standard feature, even on motor-driven bicycle.

4 Nouns with Special Plural Forms *p. 64*

A. Write the plural form of each noun.

1. series	**8.** sister-in-law	**15.** *s*
2. *100*	**9.** *i*	**16.** belief
3. yourself	**10.** board of health	**17.** *if*
4. woman	**11.** Swiss	**18.** armful
5. capful	**12.** chief of staff	**19.** elf
6. roof	**13.** larva	**20.** axis
7. deer	**14.** sweepstakes	**21.** bison

B. One plural form in each sentence is misspelled. Write the misspelled word correctly.

22. Pour two bucketsful of water on each of the shrubs.
23. Do you know your times tables through the *12*s?
24. Can mothers-in-law and daughter-in-laws get along?
25. Three of her tooths had cavities in them.
26. The Germans and the Japaneses both export cars.
27. Do mooses and wolves live together peacefully?
28. The chefs all had their favorite knifes.
29. The two cities' postmaster generals consulted.
30. In algebra *x*s and *y*'s represent amounts that vary.
31. Cut the longer loafs into halves.
32. The *ands* and *but*'s on the sign are painted in red.
33. The childs formed two large circles.
34. Were there two *M*s or two *N*'s on the license plate?
35. Does nonpayment of tariffs make people thiefs?
36. Both fleas and louses are considered vermin.
37. Mark's sister-in-law are editors of the town newspaper.
38. These two woman have been running the paper for years.
39. Their shelfs are crowded with books and papers.
40. They are often seen carrying sheafs of paper by the armfuls.
41. They try to keep crisis from occurring at the last minute.
42. The paper features the men and woman running for office.

C. Write a sentence using the plural of each item.

43. *8*	**46.** stepchild	**49.** crisis
44. die	**47.** right-of-way	**50.** aircraft
45. tankful	**48.** maid of honor	**51.** *and*

5 Possessive Nouns

p. 66

A. Label two columns *Singular Possessive* and *Plural Possessive*. Then write both forms of each word below.

EXAMPLE: trailer
ANSWER: Singular Possessive   Plural Possessive
      trailer's   trailers'

1. auto	**6.** wife	**11.** box
2. coach	**7.** valley	**12.** country
3. passenger	**8.** Roosevelt	**13.** circus
4. ferry	**9.** fox	**14.** sheep
5. boss	**10.** class	**15.** alumnus

B. In each sentence of the article below, one word is incorrectly written. It should be a possessive form. Rewrite the article, using the correct possessive forms.

16. Both my twin brothers passion has always been racing. **17.** It began when as toddlers they would swipe Sallys and my toy carriages to race. **18.** The Steins driveway was very long and smoothly paved. **19.** James and Frank spent hours pushing their two sisters hijacked carriages up and down this runway. **20.** Later Jameses skateboards and scooters took up almost half the garage. **21.** Our two neighbors kids were challenged at least weekly to a scooter or skateboard contest. **22.** Franks preference was for bicycle races. **23.** He felt winning a bicycle race was more of a testimony to a persons strength than was a skateboard victory. **24.** By high school the twins were the towns most renowned racers. **25.** I don't think anyone elses passion for racing can match that of my two brothers.

C. Write each underlined noun in its plural form or in one of its possessive forms as needed.

26. two <u>cousin</u> trips	**32.** three <u>fox</u>
27. a <u>chief</u> uniform	**33.** all <u>driver</u> seat belts
28. <u>Thomas</u> sweater	**34.** six <u>tablespoonful</u>
29. a <u>horse</u> gait	**35.** two <u>sister-in-law</u>
30. the <u>people</u> rights	**36.** a <u>sheriff</u> duties
31. two <u>tourist</u> cameras	**37.** many <u>woman</u> purses

Practice ◆ Practice ◆ Practice ◆ Practice ◆ Practice ◆ Practice ◆ Practice ◆ Practice

6 Appositives

p. 68

A. Write each sentence, adding commas where necessary.

1. Marge one of my dearest friends works for them.
2. *Clipper* an airline magazine has good articles.
3. Greg the hardest worker in our family has two jobs.
4. Hank the starting pitcher stepped up to the mound.
5. Rachel my friend wants to settle in Israel.
6. Leonardo da Vinci the artist was an inventor.
7. Ms. Ruiz my teacher comes from Puerto Rico.
8. Carole ate spaghetti one of her favorite dishes.

B. Write the paragraph, adding commas where necessary. Underline each appositive. If a sentence has no appositive, write *none*.

9. Alexander Graham Bell the inventor of the telephone became world-famous. **10.** Before he became an inventor, he taught deaf-mutes people who cannot hear or speak. **11.** He was born in Edinburgh the capital of Scotland. **12.** He came to the United States in 1871 and taught at Boston University. **13.** Joseph Henry the man who helped Morse encouraged Bell to develop his invention. **14.** Bell followed his advice. **15.** In March of 1876 he spoke to his assistant Mr. Watson over the wires. **16.** History has recorded those famous first words "Mr. Watson, please come here. I want you." **17.** Bell also invented other things. **18.** He will always be remembered for the telephone the first device to successfully transmit speech over a wire.

C. Use an appositive to combine each pair of sentences. Write the new sentences.

19. The people in this book deserve special respect. They are all handicapped heroes.
20. James Thurber was nearly blind since childhood. He was a world-famous cartoonist and humorist.
21. Wilma Rudolph wore a brace on her leg as a child. She was the first woman to win three Olympic gold medals in track.
22. Alexander de Seversky lost his leg on his first bomber mission. He was a great inventor in early aviation.
23. Leo "Bud" Daley was born with a deformed right arm. He was a star pitcher for the New York Yankees.

UNIT THREE

USING LANGUAGE
TO

NARRATE

=== **PART ONE** ===

Unit Theme *America Grows*

Language Awareness Verbs

=== **PART TWO** ===

Literature *Barrio Boy* by Ernesto Galarza

A Reason for Writing Narrating

IN YOUR JOURNAL

WRITER'S WARM-UP ◆ How is America today different from America 100 or 200 years ago? How did immigrants help America grow? All Americans, at one time or another, came here from other lands. In doing so, they helped America grow. Write what you know about the experiences of immigrants. You might write about someone you know who was an immigrant. Write about the person's contributions to the new homeland.

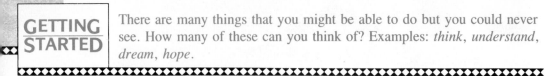

GETTING
STARTED

There are many things that you might be able to do but you could never see. How many of these can you think of? Examples: *think*, *understand*, *dream*, *hope*.

1 Writing with Verbs

Every sentence has a verb, and many verbs show action. *Run*, *talk*, *like*, and *use* all are **action verbs**. A verb may show an action that is visible or invisible.

Visible Action	**Invisible Action**
The ship <u>docked</u>.	People <u>thought</u> about the future.
People <u>went</u> ashore.	The immigrants <u>worried</u>.

Other verbs express being instead of action. These verbs state that someone or something exists. They are called **state-of-being verbs**. Information about a person or thing often follows these verbs in sentences. Forms of the verb *be* and words that can replace them are the most common state-of-being verbs.

remain   look
■ Passengers **are** on the deck of the ship. They **are** happy.

Forms of *Be*		Other State-of-Being Verbs		
am	is	appear	look	sound
are	was	become	remain	stay
been	were	feel	seem	taste
being		grow	smell	turn

Summary ♦ A **verb** expresses action or being. Use vivid verbs in your writing to appeal to the imagination.

Guided Practice

Name the verb in each sentence.

1. Immigrants came to this country from many lands.
2. They left their homelands for many different reasons.
3. Most Americans are descendants of immigrants.
4. Even today people enter this country in search of a new life.

Practice

A. Write the verb in each sentence.

   5. Millions of people immigrated to the United States.
   6. The cities attracted the greatest numbers of immigrants.
   7. In the 1840s and 1850s, many Irish came.
   8. Immigration climbed rapidly between 1860 and 1890.
   9. At first most newcomers were from northern Europe.
  10. In time the homelands of our immigrants shifted to southern and eastern Europe.

B. Write each verb and label it *action* or *state-of-being*.

  11. Some native-born Americans resented the new arrivals.
  12. Sentiment for restrictions became stronger in the 1880s.
  13. In 1882, Congress restricted immigration into the country.
  14. In 1924, Congress severely limited immigration.
  15. It set limits for the number of immigrants per year.
  16. Each country even had a quota for its immigrants.
  17. This policy was painful to people from many countries.
  18. The quotas for some countries seemed too low.
  19. Thousands of people waited for years for their immigration visas.
  20. Finally, in 1952, Congress changed these laws.

C. The writer of these sentences used forms of the verb *be* too often. Replace each verb with another state-of-being verb.

  21. Immigrants are in every part of the United States.
  22. At first many immigrants are uncomfortable in America.
  23. In their eyes they are different from the other Americans.
  24. In time, however, they are familiar with America, its people, and its customs.
  25. Eventually they are at home in their new country.

Apply ♦ Think and Write

From Your Writing ♦ Read what you wrote for the Writer's Warm-up. Working with a partner, add or change some verbs to express your ideas more precisely.

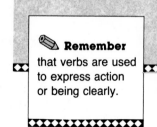

✎ **Remember**
that verbs are used
to express action
or being clearly.

2 Verb Phrases

A verb is often made up of more than one word. When a verb has two or more words, it is called a **verb phrase**.

■ People <u>had been coming</u> to North America long before Columbus.

The most important verb in a verb phrase is called the **main verb**. The other verbs are called **helping verbs**. In the example, *coming* is the main verb, and *had* and *been* are helping verbs. Common helping verbs are listed below.

am	were	have	could	shall	may
is	be	has	do	should	might
are	being	had	does	will	must
was	been	can	did	would	

Some verbs can be used as both helping verbs and main verbs.

They <u>were</u> from the mainland of Asia. (main verb)
They <u>were</u> searching for food. (helping verb)

Sometimes other words interrupt a verb phrase. Notice that *n't* and *ever* are not part of the verb phrase in this sentence.

■ <u>Haven't</u> you ever <u>studied</u> an ancient map?

> **Summary ◆** A **verb phrase** is made up of a main verb and one or more helping verbs. Use verb phrases to express action or being when you speak and write.

Guided Practice

Identify the main verbs and helping verbs.

1. These Asian hunters had been following game.
2. At that time Siberia and Alaska were not completely separated by a body of water.
3. The hunters must have walked across the land to America.

Practice

A. Write each verb phrase. Underline the main verb.

4. People must have been living in America for thousands of years. **5.** The first inhabitants had probably come from Asia. **6.** Water has not always separated Asia and North America. **7.** In fact, the two continents were joined by a bridge of land and ice. **8.** The ancestors of today's Native Americans may have crossed this land bridge during a hunt.

B. Write each verb or verb phrase. Underline any helping verbs.

9. These people were soon making their way throughout North and South America. **10.** By the time of Columbus, they were in almost every land area. **11.** Each group had its own way of life. **12.** Over the centuries some groups had developed great cities and civilizations. **13.** People in other groups were living a simpler life.

C. Write helping verbs to complete the sentences.

14. In Central America the Aztecs and Mayans _____created magnificent cities.

15. Astronomy and writing _____developed quite early by them.

16. _____ the Pueblos in southwestern North America also live in well-built cities?

17. By A.D. 500 an unusual civilization _____flourishing in the Mississippi River valley.

18. Today you _____visit the sites of several huge burial mounds of the Mound Builders.

D. Write original sentences, using the verbs as indicated.

19. is (main verb)   **22.** could (helping verb)
20. might (helping verb)   **23.** would (helping verb)
21. have (main verb)

Apply ◆ Think and Write

Dictionary of Knowledge ◆ Read more about the Mound Builders in the Dictionary of Knowledge. Write a description of their way of life. Underline the helping verbs in your description.

✎ **Remember**
to use appropriate helping verbs in verb phrases to express ideas exactly.

3 Verbs with Direct Objects

Every sentence has a subject and a verb. Some sentences also have a direct object. The direct object receives the action of the verb and answers the question *Whom?* or *What?* It is usually a noun or pronoun.

The   class   visited   Ellis Island in New York Harbor.
We   toured   the buildings and the grounds.

The direct object usually follows the verb in a sentence, even though other words may come between the verb and the direct object.

■ The   students   examined   in great detail the old facility.

To identify the direct object, look for the word or words that answer the question *Whom?* or *What?* after the verb.

■ Ellis Island   received   immigrants from many countries.
  (received whom? immigrants.)

Summary ♦ The **direct object** receives the action of the verb. When you write, use direct objects to help you express complete thoughts.

Guided Practice

Name the direct objects in the sentences.

1. America welcomed immigrants from various lands.
2. Many of them first encountered America at Ellis Island.
3. For over sixty years, officials there processed immigrants.
4. Today tourists from many areas eagerly visit the buildings and grounds of this historic island.

Practice

A. Write each sentence. Label the subject *S*, the verb *V*, and the direct object *DO*.

5. In 1808 the United States government acquired Ellis Island.
6. Many years later officials discovered its value.
7. In 1892 the government turned the tiny island into a reception center for immigrants.
8. For thirty years, Ellis Island greeted newcomers to America.
9. Over twelve million people entered America at Ellis Island.

B. Write the direct objects. Beside each, write *whom* or *what* to show what question it answers. If a sentence has no direct object, write *none*.

10. The facility often contained a thousand people at once.
11. They carried their belongings and papers with them.
12. Officials questioned immigrants about their background.
13. Several hours later the immigrants received permission for entry into their new homeland.
14. After 1924, Ellis Island's role in immigration declined.

C. Supply a direct object to complete each sentence.

15. Across the harbor we visited _____.
16. The Statue of Liberty impressed _____.
17. The French sculptor Frédéric A. Bartholdi designed _____.
18. We climbed _____.
19. From the crown we saw _____.
20. Did you notice _____?
21. We especially liked _____.
22. On the way down Marie lost _____.
23. At the gift shop I bought _____.
24. For lunch we ate _____.

Apply ◆ Think and Write

Narrative Writing ◆ How do you think immigrants felt as they passed through Ellis Island? Write a paragraph that tells about their feelings. Underline the direct objects that you use.

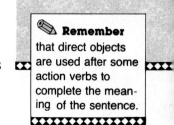

> **✎ Remember**
> that direct objects are used after some action verbs to complete the meaning of the sentence.

4 Verbs with Indirect Objects

Some verbs have more than one kind of object. Remember that a direct object usually follows the verb and tells who or what receives the action of the verb. An indirect object comes before the direct object and tells to whom or for whom the action is done. It does not receive the action of the verb.

■ **Immigrants have given <u>America</u> many wonderful gifts.**

In the example, *America* tells to whom and is the indirect object; *gifts* tells what and is the direct object. An indirect object is usually a noun or pronoun. Only verbs that have direct objects can have indirect objects. Although an indirect object tells to whom or for whom, it is not preceded by the word *to* or *for*.

America offers <u>men</u> and <u>women</u> a new home. (indirect objects)
America offers a new home to men and women. (no indirect object)

These verbs often have indirect objects: *bring, buy, give, lend, offer, owe, sell, send, show, teach, tell,* and *write.*

> **Summary ♦** The **indirect object** comes before the direct object. It tells to whom or for whom the action of the verb is done. Use indirect objects when you write sentences to complete the meaning of the predicate.

Guided Practice

Name the indirect objects in the sentences.

1. America gave many scientists and inventors new opportunities for advancement.
2. It has provided artists, musicians, and writers freedom of expression.
3. New citizens have given their fellow Americans many gifts in return.

Practice

A. Write the sentences and underline the indirect objects.

4. America provided Albert Einstein and Enrico Fermi safety during the troubled 1930s.

5. These scientists gave their new homeland many achievements in mathematics and physics.

6. A century ago America supplied Alexander Graham Bell a place for his experiments with sound.

7. North America's forests offered John J. Audubon the inspiration for his studies of American wildlife.

8. Louis Agassiz taught Americans facts about nature.

B. Write and label each verb, direct object, and indirect object. Some sentences do not contain indirect objects.

9. Andrew Carnegie and E. I. Du Pont provided jobs for Americans in dynamic new industries.

10. David Sarnoff brought American homes the first radio and television networks.

11. Many immigrant financiers left to their fellow citizens wealthy foundations and charitable organizations.

12. Other naturalized Americans have given presidents advice.

13. Immigrants Samuel Gompers and David Dubinsky left American laborers some early unions.

C. Add an indirect object to each sentence. Write the sentences.

EXAMPLE: Did you tell the story?
ANSWER: Did you tell Ms. Anjou the story?

14. Find a book about it.
15. She will lend her copy.
16. Will you read this part?

17. It provided a good laugh.
18. I told the story later.

Apply • Think and Write

Interview Questions • Imagine that you are preparing a feature story for the school newspaper about a new student who recently came to this country. Write several questions you would like to ask the student. Use direct and indirect objects in some of your questions.

✎ **Remember**
that you can use indirect objects to tell to whom or for whom something is done.

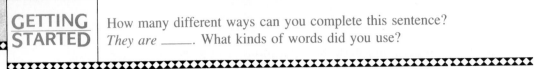

GETTING STARTED How many different ways can you complete this sentence? *They are _____.* What kinds of words did you use?

5 Predicate Nominatives and Predicate Adjectives

As you know, some verbs do not show action but express a state of being. These verbs are often used as linking verbs. (For a list of state-of-being, or linking, verbs, see page 124.) A **linking verb** links the subject of a sentence with a word in the predicate. If that word is a noun or pronoun, it is called a predicate nominative. It renames or identifies the subject.

> **Emma Lazarus was a poet.** (*Poet* identifies the subject.)
> **The author of this poem is she.** (*She* renames the subject.)

If the word linked to the subject describes the subject, it is a predicate adjective.

> ■ **Her poetry is famous.** (*Famous* describes the subject.)

You may use compound predicate nominatives and predicate adjectives in your speaking and writing.

> **This poem is a tribute and a memorial to America's immigrants.**
> **It is dramatic and stirring.**

Summary ✦ A **predicate nominative** is a noun or pronoun that follows a linking verb and renames or identifies the subject of the sentence. A **predicate adjective** follows a linking verb and describes the subject of the sentence.

Guided Practice

Identify each predicate nominative or predicate adjective.

1. The Statue of Liberty was a gift from France to all the people in the United States.
2. The statue's dedication in 1886 was highly successful.
3. The statue quickly became a major figure in American life.

Practice

A. Write the sentences. Underline each linking verb and label each predicate nominative and predicate adjective.

4. The Statue of Liberty seemed especially important for immigrants to America.
5. The statue was the first sight of America for many of them.
6. Over the years it became a symbol of freedom and hope.
7. The statue looked beautiful to Emma Lazarus, the daughter of Russian Jewish immigrants.
8. "The New Colossus" was her poem to the statue.

B. Write and label each predicate nominative, predicate adjective, or direct object.

9. Lazarus wrote "The New Colossus" as a tribute.
10. The poem is an expression of hope for America's future.
11. Americans admired the poem's sentiments from the very first.
12. In time "The New Colossus" grew famous, just like the Statue of Liberty itself.
13. In 1903 officials inscribed the poem on the base of the Statue of Liberty.

C. Complete each sentence with a predicate nominative or a predicate adjective.

14. This statue is ＿＿.
15. It seems ＿＿.
16. At night it looks ＿＿.
17. It appears ＿＿.
18. The statue remains ＿＿.
19. It grows ＿＿.
20. Its sculptor was ＿＿.
21. She soon became ＿＿.
22. Are you also ＿＿?
23. I am ＿＿.

Apply ◆ Think and Write

Descriptive Writing ◆ How would you describe a statue that you have seen? Write a brief description of it and underline the predicate nominatives and predicate adjectives you use.

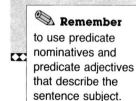

✎ **Remember**
to use predicate nominatives and predicate adjectives that describe the sentence subject.

GETTING STARTED

Some verbs get lonely by themselves: *He crushed. He crushed the box.*
Some verbs, on the other hand, do quite well alone: *The dolphin swam.*
Think of some more verbs that do well alone.

6 Transitive and Intransitive Verbs

A verb that expresses action often transfers this action to a direct object. A verb that transfers action to a direct object is called a transitive verb.

■ America <u>welcomes</u> many new citizens each year.

An intransitive verb does not have a direct object.

■ Thousands of immigrants <u>arrive</u> annually.

Many action verbs can be either transitive or intransitive, depending on their use in a sentence.

Transitive Verb   **Intransitive Verb**

They <u>asked</u> questions. They <u>asked</u> about their friends.

Since linking verbs do not express action, they do not have direct objects. A linking verb links the subject with a word in the predicate. A linking verb is always intransitive.

Over 100,000 immigrants <u>become</u> citizens of the United States each year.

Summary ♦ A verb that has a direct object is a **transitive verb**. A verb that does not have a direct object is an **intransitive verb**.

Guided Practice

Tell whether each verb is transitive or intransitive.

1. United States citizens have certain special rights and certain responsibilities.
2. Not all immigrants become citizens.
3. New citizens work hard for their citizenship.

Practice

A. Write the transitive verb in each sentence. Then write its direct object.

   4. New citizens take an oath of allegiance to this country.

   5. They study American history.

   6. They must demonstrate a knowledge of English.

   7. Citizenship also requires a residence of five years.

   8. New, or naturalized, citizens have nearly the same rights of native-born American citizens.

B. Write each verb and label it *transitive* or *intransitive*. If it is transitive, write its direct object.

   9. New citizens undergo a process of naturalization.

  10. They must pledge loyalty to the United States.

  11. Naturalized citizens become full American citizens.

  12. Naturalized citizens can vote in all elections.

  13. They may serve their country in almost every possible way.

  14. They can join police forces and fire departments.

  15. They may also serve in the United States armed forces.

  16. They have held important public offices.

  17. They have been governors, members of Congress, and advisors to Presidents.

  18. Naturalized citizens, however, cannot become President or Vice President of the United States.

C. Write two sentences using each of these verbs. Use the verb as a transitive verb in the first sentence and as an intransitive verb in the second sentence.

  19. learn   **21.** move   **23.** watch

  20. start   **22.** remember

Apply • Think and Write

Narrative Writing • What do you think it feels like to become a new citizen of a country? Write a paragraph telling how a young person might react and feel. Underline each transitive verb that you use.

>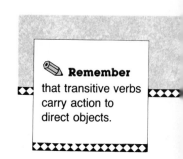
> ✎ **Remember**
> that transitive verbs carry action to direct objects.

Pretend you are a newspaper reporter. You have just written a headline: *STRANGE SOUNDS HEARD IN BOWLING ALLEY*. Your editor doesn't like the word *strange*. How many words can you think of to replace *strange*?

VOCABULARY ♦
Shades of Meaning

Skilled writers choose their words carefully. Many words have the same basic meaning but carry different **shades of meaning**. That is, many closely related words, or **synonyms**, are slightly different in meaning. For example, *decide* and *rule* (used as verbs) both have the same basic meaning, but notice the difference in the sentences below.

> Mr. Smith <u>decided</u> his family would go to Maine for the summer.
> The judge <u>ruled</u> that Mrs. Jones was guilty of speeding.

Both *decide* and *rule* mean "to come to a conclusion," but *rule* implies the official decision of a judge or some other person of authority.

The precise choice of words is one of the writer's most important abilities; skilled writers are masters of words.

The word web to the right shows synonyms for *argue*. How do these words differ in meaning?

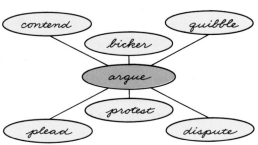

Building Your Vocabulary

For each sentence below, replace the underlined word with each of the synonyms in parentheses. Notice the difference in meaning that each of these synonyms causes. You may use a dictionary if you are unsure how these words differ from each other.

> What caused Fred to <u>fall</u>? (collapse, slip, stumble, topple)
> Sara <u>scolded</u> her little brother. (admonished, chided, berated, rebuked)
> Thane <u>threw</u> the ball to home plate. (flipped, hurled, lobbed, heaved)

Practice

A. For each sentence below, write the word in parentheses that fits the meaning of the sentence better.

1. They (chased, tracked) the animal through the forest, relying on footprints and broken branches.
2. The two presidents met to (discuss, negotiate) the agreement.
3. The climb up the steep face of the mountain was (perilous, risky); danger faced them every step of the way.
4. The king (ordered, decreed) the thirteenth of May a holiday.
5. The groundhog (dug, burrowed) his way underneath our fence.
6. The weary travelers (trudged, ambled) down the road.
7. He was (famous, notorious) for his brilliant work in chemistry.
8. The crash was a (misfortune, tragedy) that affected us all.
9. The lion (bellowed, shrieked) as we took the thorn from its paw.
10. The protesters (glared, glanced) menacingly at us.

B. Rewrite the sentences below, using the synonyms for *unusual* that best express the meaning indicated in parentheses.

> rare   peculiar   remarkable   exceptional   bizarre

11. Venice is a truly <u>unusual</u> city. (worthy of notice)
12. Tornados are <u>unusual</u> in this part of the country. (uncommon)
13. Velásquez was an <u>unusual</u> painter. (better than average)
14. Somehow, that house looks <u>unusual</u>. (odd, curious)
15. The circus sideshow was somewhat <u>unusual</u>. (very strange)

LANGUAGE CORNER ◆ Doublets

Did you know that *union* and *onion* are closely related? They both come from a Latin word meaning "one." *Lace* and *lasso* both come from a Latin word meaning "snare" or "noose." Two words derived from the same source are called **doublets**. Find the sources of these doublets.

card, chart   ride, road   tree, trust

Clues: You can make both a *chart* and a *card* from a leaf of _____ . A long *ride* on a *road* might be called a jou _ _ _ _ . A *tree* planted in the earth is _____, or stable.

How to Revise Sentences with Verbs

You know that verbs can express actions and states of being. A sentence can often be written with either an action verb or a linking verb. Which sentences below contain action verbs?

1. Many famous Americans were immigrants from other countries.
2. Many famous Americans immigrated to this country.

3. Igor Sikorsky of Russia was the inventor of the helicopter.
4. Igor Sikorsky of Russia invented the helicopter.

Choosing the best verb for a sentence usually involves finding a precise verb to give your reader the most complete information possible. Sometimes this could be a matter of deciding whether to use an action verb or a linking verb. The sentences in each pair of examples above give the same information, but the action verbs *immigrated* in sentence 2 and *invented* in sentence 4 express the information more directly. An action verb can often express an idea more clearly and directly than a linking verb. Look for opportunities to use action verbs rather than linking verbs in your writing.

By choosing vivid, colorful verbs for a sentence, you can also express an idea more clearly and make your writing come alive for your reader. Notice how changing the verb to *captured* in sentence 6 changes the tone and the impact of the sentence.

5. John J. Audubon put American wildlife in his paintings.
6. John J. Audubon captured American wildlife in his paintings.

The Grammar Game ♦ Concentrate on verbs! Replace the verbs in the sentences below with more vivid verbs. How many new sentences can you write?

Lisa hit the ball.   Tim looked at the pictures.
We smiled at them.   They came into the room.
I cooked potatoes.   My brother hurt his hand.

Working Together

Work with your group on activities **A** and **B** to discover how action verbs and vivid verbs can enliven your writing.

In Your Group
♦ Listen carefully to each other. ♦ Agree or disagree pleasantly. ♦ Show appreciation to others. ♦ Help the group reach agreement.

A. Rewrite the sentences below, substituting action verbs for linking verbs. Make any additional changes that are needed in the sentences. Then arrange the sentences to form a paragraph.

1. Albert Einstein was the developer and teacher of new theories in mathematics and physics.
2. Immigrants were seekers of a new and better life in America.
3. Many were constructors of businesses and creators of art, music, and film.
4. Many immigrants were contributors to the growth of our nation.
5. For example, Éleuthère Du Pont and John Astor were founders of important business empires.

B. Imagine that you are an immigrant traveling to a new land. With your group, write a paragraph or two about your experiences or feelings. Use action verbs rather than linking verbs whenever possible and choose vivid verbs to give life to your writing.

WRITERS' CORNER ♦ Stringy Sentences

Avoid using long, stringy sentences in your writing. Such sentences can be ineffective and difficult to read.

Meyer Guggenheim came to America from Switzerland in 1848, worked as a peddler, became wealthy importing Swiss lace, turned to the mining industry, amassed a vast fortune, which his sons later used to found the New York School of Aeronautics, and museums and fellowships for artists, and free dental clinics.

Can you break the sentence above into shorter, clearer sentences? Read what you wrote for the Writer's Warm-up. Did you write any stringy sentences? If you did, improve them now.

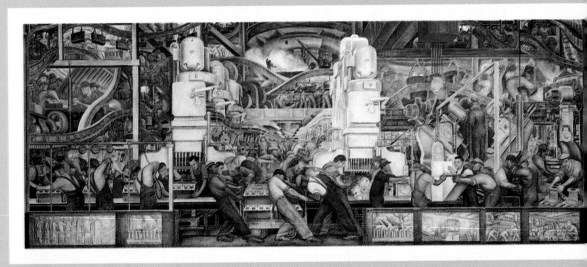

DETROIT INDUSTRY, 1932–1933
fresco by Diego M. Rivera, Mexican 1886–1957.
The Detroit Institute of Arts, Founders Society Purchase, Edsel B. Ford Fund and Gift of Edsel B. Ford.
(33.10.N.)

UNIT
THREE

USING LANGUAGE
TO

NARRATE

=== **PART TWO** ===

Literature *Barrio Boy* by Ernesto Galarza

A Reason for Writing Narrating

CREATIVE

Writing

FINE ARTS ◆ How must machines feel when they are required to churn the molten steel, stamp the trademark, or package the finished product day after endless day? Imagine that one of the machines in Diego Rivera's painting decided to speak out. Write the speech the machine would give.

CRITICAL THINKING ♦
A Strategy for Narrating

AN ORDER CIRCLE

Telling a story is often called narrating. In a personal narrative, a writer describes events in his or her own life, using the words *I* and *me*. After this lesson, you will read part of *Barrio Boy*, a personal narrative by Ernesto Galarza. Later you will write your own personal narrative.

In a story it is important to give information in an orderly way. This helps readers understand and remember what you have written. See if you can tell what kind of order the author is using in this passage from *Barrio Boy*.

> Like Ito and several other first graders who did not know English, I received private lessons from Miss Ryan in the closet, a narrow hall off the classroom with a door at each end. Next to one of these doors Miss Ryan placed a large chair for herself and a small one for me. Keeping an eye on the class through the open door she read with me. . . .

Space order is one way to organize information. In this passage, the author helped the reader move mentally about the classroom and the little closet to get a spatial understanding of the scene.

Learning the Strategy

There are lots of ways to put things in order. To organize your clothes closet, you might hang your clothes according to color. How many other ways can you think of to organize a closet? Imagine you have purchased a new address book. In what order might you arrange the names, addresses, and phone numbers of your friends and relatives? Suppose you had to write a report about the founding of your town or city. How would you organize the events? Is there another way of organizing the events that might make the report even more interesting?

Most of us need to do some organizing every day. An order circle can help you determine the kind of order that works best for each situation. Inside a circle write what you want to put in order. On arrows write some kinds of order. Study the order circle. Then decide which kind of order works best for what you plan to organize.

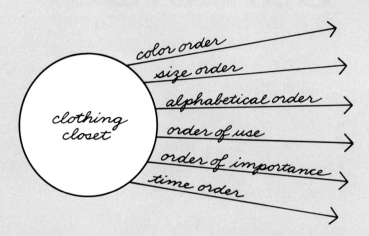

Using the Strategy

A. Write the topic *How to Clean My Room* inside an order circle. Write some kinds of order on the arrows. Think of your room or the room you share with someone at home. Make a list of all the chores that are needed to get that room clean. Decide what kind of order would be best for organizing the chores.

B. Write *Barrio Boy* in an order circle. Write some kinds of order on the arrows. Decide the kind of order you think the author will use most in his personal narrative. As you read the story, check to see if you were right. Note whether the author used other kinds of order as well.

Applying the Strategy

♦ How did using the order circle help you organize the way you might clean your room?
♦ When might it be useful to know how to choose a kind of order?

from Barrio Boy

by Ernesto Galarza

In 1905, Ernesto Galarza was born in the mountain village of Jalcocotán in western Mexico. He lived there until the Mexican Revolution began in 1910. Then Ernesto and his family were forced to leave their village and seek safety in the city of Mazatlán. When the turmoil grew worse, they fled from Mexico and finally settled in Sacramento, California.

Ernesto Galarza was one of many Mexican children who came to live in America's barrios—the neighborhoods or parts of cities where Spanish-speaking people live. Yet even in a barrio, life in an American city was different from that in a Mexican village. In this excerpt from his autobiography, Ernesto recalls some of his adjustments to American life and culture. He also tells the story of his American education at Lincoln School.

America was all around us, in and out of the *barrio.* Abruptly we had to forget the ways of shopping in a *mercado* and learn those of shopping in a corner grocery or in a department store. The Americans paid no attention to the Sixteenth of September, but they made a great commotion about the Fourth of July. In Mazatlán Don Salvador had told us, saluting and marching as he talked to our class, that the *Cinco de Mayo* was the most glorious date in human history. The Americans had not even heard about it.

In Tucson, when I had asked my mother again if the Americans were having a revolution, the answer was: "No, but they have good schools, and you are going to one of them." We were by now settled at 418 L Street and the time had come for me to exchange a revolution for an American education.

The two of us walked south on Fifth Street one morning to the corner of Q Street and turned right. Half of the block was occupied by the Lincoln School. It was a three-story wooden building, with two wings that gave it the shape of a double-T connected by a central hall. It was a new building, painted yellow, with a shingled roof that was not like the red tile of the school in Mazatlán. I noticed other differences, none of them very reassuring.

We walked up the wide staircase hand in hand and through the door, which closed by itself. A mechanical contraption screwed to the top shut it behind us quietly.

Up to this point the adventure of enrolling me in the school had been carefully rehearsed. Mrs. Dodson had told us how to find it and we had circled it several times on our walks. Friends in the *barrio* explained that the director was called a principal, and that it was a lady and not a man. They assured us that there was always a person at the school who could speak Spanish.

Exactly as we had been told, there was a sign on the door in both Spanish and English: "Principal." We crossed the hall and entered the office of Miss Nettie Hopley.

Miss Hopley was at a roll-top desk to one side, sitting in a swivel chair that moved on wheels. There was a sofa against the opposite wall, flanked by two windows and a door that opened on a small balcony. Chairs were set around a table and framed pictures hung on the walls of a man with long white hair and another with a sad face and a black beard.

The principal half turned in the swivel chair to look at us over the pinch glasses crossed on the ridge of her nose. To do this she had to duck her head slightly as if she were about to step through a low doorway.

What Miss Hopley said to us we did not know but we saw in her eyes a warm welcome and when she took off her glasses and straightened up she smiled wholeheartedly, like Mrs. Dodson. We were, of course, saying nothing, only catching the friendliness of her voice and the sparkle in her eyes while she said words we did not understand. She signaled us to the table. Almost tiptoeing across the office, I maneuvered myself to keep my mother between me and the gringo lady. In a matter of seconds I had to decide whether she was a possible friend or a menace. We sat down.

Then Miss Hopley did a formidable thing. She stood up. Had she been standing when we entered she would have seemed tall. But rising from her chair she soared. And what she carried up and up with her was a buxom superstructure, firm shoulders, a straight sharp nose, full cheeks slightly molded by a curved line along the nostrils, thin lips that moved like steel springs, and a high forehead topped by hair gathered in a bun. Miss Hopley was not a giant in body but when she mobilized it to a standing position she seemed a match for giants. I decided I liked her.

She strode to a door in the far corner of the office, opened it and called a name. A boy of about ten years appeared in the doorway. He sat down at one end of the table. He was brown like us, a plump kid with shiny black hair combed straight back, neat, cool, and faintly obnoxious.

Miss Hopley joined us with a large book and some papers in her hand. She, too, sat down and the questions and answers began by way of our interpreter. My name was Ernesto. My mother's name was Henriqueta. My birth certificate was in San Blas. Here was my last report card from the Escuela Municipal Numero 3 para Varones of Mazatlán, and so forth. Miss Hopley put things down in the book and my mother signed a card.

As long as the questions continued, Doña Henriqueta could stay and I was secure. Now that they were over, Miss Hopley saw her to the door, dismissed our interpreter and without further ado took me by the hand and strode down the hall to Miss Ryan's first grade.

Miss Ryan took me to a seat at the front of the room, into which I shrank—the better to survey her. She was, to skinny, somewhat runty me, of a withering height when she patrolled the class. And when I least expected it, there she was, crouching by my desk, her blond radiant face level with mine, her voice patiently maneuvering me over the awful idiocies of the English language.

During the next few weeks Miss Ryan overcame my fears of tall, energetic teachers as she bent over my desk to help me with a word in the pre-primer. Step by step, she loosened me and my classmates from the safe anchorage of the desks for recitations at the blackboard and consultations at her desk. Frequently she burst into happy announcements to the whole class. "Ito can read a sentence," and small Japanese Ito . . . slowly read aloud while the class listened in wonder: "Come, Skipper, come. Come and run." The Korean, Portuguese, Italian, and Polish first graders had similar moments of glory, no less shining than mine the day I conquered "butterfly," which I had been persistently pronouncing in standard Spanish as boo-ter-flee. "Children," Miss Ryan called for attention. "Ernesto has learned how to pronounce *butterfly!*" And I proved it with a perfect imitation of Miss Ryan. From that celebrated success, I was soon able to match Ito's progress as a sentence reader with "Come, butterfly, come fly with me."

Like Ito and several other first graders who did not know English, I received private lessons from Miss Ryan in the closet, a narrow hall off the classroom with a door at each end. Next to one of these doors Miss Ryan placed a large chair for herself and a small one for me. Keeping an eye on the class through the open door she read with me about sheep in the meadow and a frightened chicken going to see the king, coaching me out of my phonetic ruts in words like *pasture, bow-wow-wow, hay,* and *pretty,* which to my Mexican ear and eye had so many unnecessary sounds and letters. She made me watch her lips and then close my eyes as she repeated words I found hard to read. When we came to know each other better, I tried interrupting to tell Miss Ryan how we said it in Spanish. It didn't work. She only said "oh" and went on with *pasture, bow-wow-wow,* and *pretty.* It was as if in that closet we were both discovering together the secrets of the English language and grieving together over the tragedies of Bo-Peep. The main reason I was graduated with honors from the first grade was that I had fallen in love with Miss Ryan. Her radiant, no-nonsense character made us either afraid not to love her or love her so we would not be afraid, I am not sure which. It was not only that we sensed she was with it, but also that she was with us.

Ernesto Galarza's classes at Lincoln School were just the beginning of his American education. He went on to complete his doctorate and become a well-known teacher and writer.

Library Link ◆ *To learn more about Ernesto Galarza's life, read the rest of his autobiography,* Barrio Boy.

 ## Reader's Response

Were you able to identify with Ernesto's first day of school? Why or why not?

Barrio Boy

Responding to Literature

1. Why is the first day of school a memorable event in anyone's life? Explain.

2. If your family moved to a new country and you had to attend school there, how would you prepare for the experience?

3. Make a class memory poster. At the top of a poster board, print *I will never forget my first day of school because. . . .* Ask classmates to write what they remember about that day. These memories may be anonymous or initialed. Mount your poster in the classroom.

4. Ernesto had great admiration for his first-grade teacher. If you had been in that class, how might you have felt about her as a teacher?

Writing to Learn

Think and Plan ✦ Organize information about your first memories of school. Use an order circle like the one below. Decide whether you will use time order, order of importance, space order, or some other kind of order.

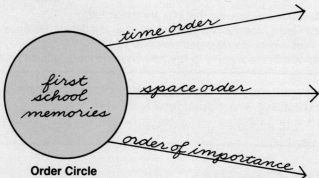

Order Circle

Write ✦ Apply the order you chose as you write a paragraph about your first memories of school.

Use a gesture, facial expression, or tone of voice to make this story opener mean just the opposite of what it says.

I'm so sorry to see that grand old building torn down.

SPEAKING and LISTENING ♦
Telling an Anecdote

Almost everyone enjoys telling or listening to an anecdote, a short entertaining or dramatic account of some happening. You can improve your telling of anecdotes by practicing a few helpful techniques. For example, nonverbal communication—such as gestures, body movements, posture, and facial expressions—can add liveliness and clarify meaning.

As you prepare, remember to choose an anecdote you really like or want to tell. Then practice telling the story several different ways to find the best way and to gain confidence. Follow these guidelines when you tell or listen to an anecdote.

Telling an Anecdote	1. Make the basic facts about what happened clear. Tell *who, what,* and *where.* 2. Describe the event vividly but do not include trivial or uninteresting details. 3. To create humor or add emphasis, shift your posture or change your facial expression and tone of voice. 4. Use dialogue and let the characters speak through you. 5. Tell your anecdote in logical order. Use transitional words such as *then, next,* and *consequently.* 6. Speak clearly and confidently, making eye contact with your audience.
Being an Active Listener	1. Show the speaker that you are interested. 2. Listen critically. Ask yourself whether the details, dialogue, and order of events are clear and effective. 3. Watch the speaker to see how body language affects the meaning.

> **Summary** ♦ An **anecdote** is a brief, interesting story. A well-told anecdote gives pleasure to listeners.

Guided Practice

Read each sentence from *Barrio Boy* on page 151 aloud three times. Use your voice and body language to change the emphasis each time.

1. . . . I tried interrupting to tell Miss Ryan how we said it in Spanish.
2. It didn't work.
3. She only said "oh" and went on with *pasture, bow-wow-wow,* and *pretty.*

Practice

A. Working with a partner, read aloud each part of an anecdote. Use tone of voice, facial expressions, or gestures to add to its effectiveness or change its meaning.

4. Dia could not believe her eyes. There, at the far end of the pier, was her father!
5. "No way," Rico said. "Absolutely, positively, no," he added.
6. "I have a secret I must tell you," Jenny whispered to Leo. "Hurry, let's go over there by the tree."

B. What is inappropriate in each student's telling of an anecdote? Write your answers.

7. Terry droned on monotonously, looking at the floor as he said, "So Michele opened the envelope. And what did she find? She'd won a four-year scholarship!"
8. "Well," said Gene, moving his eyebrows up and down and with a little snicker, "it looks like our candidate just lost."
9. "The football team had one play left. They were on the goal line," said Lena. "Last year our star player caught measles."

C. Tell an anecdote that you like to a small group of classmates. Use as much dialogue as possible. Arrange the events in proper order. Have the members of your group evaluate your telling of the anecdote according to the guidelines in this lesson.

Apply • Think and Write

Evaluating an Anecdote ♦ Listen to an anecdote told by your favorite character in a TV situation comedy or by a talk-show guest. Take notes on the techniques used, including body language. Then label each technique *effective* or *distracting*.

Remember to use dialogue and gestures when telling an anecdote.

GETTING
STARTED

Think of an amusing incident. Describe it first as if you had seen it from a distance. Tell what *he, she,* or *they* did. Then tell it as if you had taken part, using *I*. Which method do you prefer?

WRITING ◆
Point of View

Every narrative, or story, is told by someone. When you plan a narrative, you must choose a point of view—that is, you must decide who will tell the story. By this choice of point of view, you can control what information will be included.

If you write about something that happened to you and use the pronouns *I, me,* and *mine,* you are using **first-person point of view.** Ernesto Galarza used first-person point of view in *Barrio Boy* to tell about how he began school in a new country.

> Miss Ryan took <u>me</u> to a seat at the front of the room, into which I shrank. . . . She was, to skinny, somewhat runty <u>me</u>, of a withering height when she patrolled the class.

You may also use first-person point of view to tell a fictional story. The main character would then be the narrator, the "I" in the story. You can show what the "I" character thinks and feels. By using the first-person point of view, a writer can create suspense or help the reader experience the events with the character who tells the story.

If you write about something that happened to someone else—or to fictional characters—and use the pronouns *he, she,* and *they,* you are using **third-person point of view.** If you wish, you can show what each character thinks and feels.

> "I'm glad I moved to this town," Susan told <u>her</u> guests. "You all make me feel so at home," <u>she</u> added, hoping that Ken, in the back of the group, could hear <u>her</u>.
> "She looks so happy," Ken thought as <u>he</u> watched her speak.

> **Summary** ◆ **Point of view** is the way a story gets told—either in the first person or the third person.

Guided Practice

Tell whether each sentence is first- or third-person point of view.

1. Her family had come to America from Italy before World War I.
2. "I remember our arrival at Ellis Island in New York," she said.
3. "I would have been intimidated by New York," I told her.

Practice

A. 4–6. Rewrite each sentence in the **Guided Practice,** changing the point of view.

B. Find the error in the point of view of one of these passages. Which one contains a fact the storyteller could not realistically know? Write and explain your answer.

7. She loved to tell her grandchildren of the adventures she'd had when she came to America. The country had seemed so huge, strange, and fast-paced to her—very different from the life she'd known.
8. I loved telling all my grandchildren of my adventures. My oldest grandchild, Rikki, would listen and think to herself, "Grandmother has helped build and change America."

C. Adapt these notes to create a scene for a story that includes dialogue. Be sure to use one point of view consistently.

A bicyclist is on a tour of an unfamiliar area. Eventually he gets lost on one of the back roads. His map doesn't show which fork in the road leads back to town, but he has a feeling that both forks will lead him there. Suddenly he sees a local resident by the roadside. He asks the lanky farmer if it matters which fork in the road he takes. The farmer answers that it doesn't matter—to him.

Apply • Think and Write

Changing Point of View • Write the opening paragraph for a story, using first-person point of view. Then rewrite it, using third person. Notice how the point of view affects the way you write about the characters.

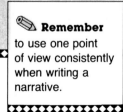

> ✎ **Remember**
> to use one point of view consistently when writing a narrative.

GETTING STARTED

Restate a conversation from a movie, TV program, or book. Use "he said" or "she said." Then just tell what was said without using direct conversation. Which is more vivid?

WRITING ◆
Using Dialogue

Dialogue, or conversation between characters in a story, reveals dramatically what characters feel and believe. As in real life, you learn more about people by watching and listening to them than by being told facts about them.

Writers listen to people and note what they say and how they say it. They use their observations to create realistic dialogue for their stories. What does this dialogue reveal about each character?

> "I found it!" cried Alfredo as he burst into his family's cramped apartment in the city. "I found a farm we can afford. Now we can move out of here. Wait till you see it!"
>
> "Where is it?" said his mother with cautious curiosity. "You thought the farm you found last week was perfect for us, too."
>
> "But that was different," he said. "You'll love this farm."
>
> "Now calm down, son," said his father. "We can't rush into this just because we don't like these tiny rooms."
>
> "Please," Alfredo urged, "just come and take a look!"

The dialogue shows that the family wants to move and that Alfredo's parents are more cautious about moving than he is. Dialogue reveals more about a situation and makes a story more lively.

Use these guidelines to help you write dialogue correctly. To review other rules for writing quotations, see pages 658–661.

◆ Begin a new paragraph each time a different person speaks.
◆ Capitalize the first word of each direct quotation.
◆ Enclose a speaker's exact words in quotation marks.
◆ Use commas to separate words such as *he said* or *she said* from the exact words of a speaker.

Summary ◆ **Dialogue,** the conversation between characters in a story, is written in a special way.

Guided Practice

Tell what you think each quotation reveals about its speaker.

1. "I'm not scared," little Mike said as he entered the dark room. "Not at all. I'll find the switch, yes sir. I'm not scared."
2. "I may not be able to go with you," Irene told her friend coolly. "Call me before you go. Don't forget. Do you have my number?"
3. "I can quit smoking any time I please. I've done it dozens of times," Mark Twain once said.

Practice

A. Write a brief dialogue for the characters in each situation.

4. Paul returns a shirt to the department store. He tells the salesclerk the shirt fell apart the first time it was washed.
5. Elise tells Joe about the Drama Club's next performance.
6. Diane asks her mother's permission to vacation with her friend Marie for a week at the shore.

B. Turn this description of a conversation into a dialogue. Add to it creatively as you write.

Alfredo and his parents go out to look over the old farmhouse and its fields. Then they go into the old barn and meet the farm owner. She greets Alfredo warmly and tells his parents that he was the only one who came to look at the farm. His parents ask the woman why she's selling the farm. The owner explains that it's too much work for one person, but that perhaps a family could manage it. Alfredo suggests that his is the family for the job. His parents aren't sure. He helps the owner point out the attractions of the farm.

Apply ◆ Think and Write

Dictionary of Knowledge ◆ Read about the Statue of Liberty in the Dictionary of Knowledge. Make up an imaginary dialogue between two immigrants who see the statue as they enter the United States.

✎ **Remember**
that dialogue helps your readers experience your story.

Focus on the Writer's Voice

Some writers create a **voice** that they use in story after story. Others change their voice depending on their material. Many factors can affect the voice you create: your current ideas, feelings, and experiences; your subject matter; your knowledge of literature and language. Here are some general methods for finding the voice that best suits you. Ask yourself these questions.

1. *What am I writing about?* Will first person ("I") or third person ("he/she") help me tell the story most honestly, realistically, and effectively?
2. *What is my attitude toward this material?* Do I like or dislike each character? Are the events humorous or serious? What mood or general feeling do I want to suggest?
3. *How can my telling of the story best reveal its meaning?* Look at this passage from Ernesto Galarza's *Barrio Boy* (page 147).

[Miss Ryan] was, to skinny, somewhat runty me, of a withering height when she patrolled the class. And when I least expected it, there she was, crouching by my desk, her blond radiant face level with mine, her voice patiently maneuvering me over the awful idiocies of the English language.

◆ Galarza writes in the first person ("I"). This helps him to recapture the significant events of his boyhood and also to involve the reader in the boy's adventures.
◆ He tells his story in a voice that mixes seriousness with humor. We share the boy's fears, but the humor provides emotional distance.

The Writer's Voice ◆ Think about a story that made a deep impression on you. How would you describe the writer's voice? Be as specific and detailed as you can.

Working Together

The writer's voice can reveal a great deal about the writer's attitude toward his or her subject. It can be first person or third person. As a group, complete activities **A** and **B**.

In Your Group
♦ **Contribute ideas.**   ♦ **Keep a record of the ideas discussed.** ♦ **Invite others to talk.**   ♦ **Express appreciation for others' ideas.**

A. Working together, decide upon one or two sentences that convey each of the following moods or attitudes: (1) enthusiasm, (2) fear, (3) dislike, (4) shyness, (5) admiration. Make some sentences first person and some third person. Use dialogue if appropriate.

B. Here are two different possibilities for a scene. As a group, choose one of them and write a script for it. Create characters, use dialogue, and give stage directions.

1. Dan, a lovable joker, is invited to a friend's wedding. He comes to the wedding dressed all in black. He gives the bride and groom a sympathy card. They are amused.
2. Dan, a joker with a strange sense of humor, comes to his friend's wedding dressed in black. When the bride and groom see him and receive his sympathy card, they are appalled.

THESAURUS CORNER ♦ Word Choice

The five words in dark type are *antonyms* of the words that the content of the paragraph requires. Rewrite the paragraph. Choose verbs from the Thesaurus that are appropriate. Use the Thesaurus Index to find the main entry you need.

From 1880 to 1900, the population of the United States not only grew, it also **held.** The abundance of new jobs in the United States **hindered** immigration. Most immigrants **detested** their new land. They found they could **wreck** a better living here than in Europe. Concerned about their own jobs, however, some less recent arrivals in America wished they could **expedite** the tide of immigration.

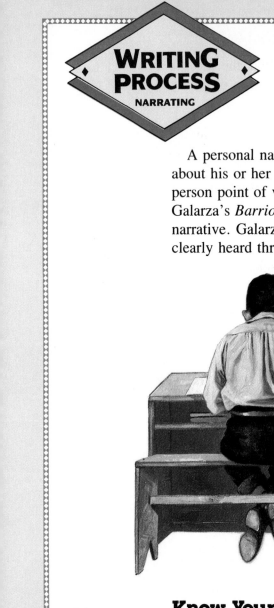

WRITING PROCESS
NARRATING

Writing a
Personal Narrative

A personal narrative is a true story that a writer tells about his or her own experiences. It is told from the first-person point of view, using the words *I* and *me*. Ernesto Galarza's *Barrio Boy* is an excellent example of personal narrative. Galarza's voice—his attitude and personality—is clearly heard throughout his story.

Know Your Purpose and Audience

In this lesson you will write your own personal narrative. Your purpose will be to entertain your audience with a story about an important event in your life. You will try to let your own voice, your own personality, come through.

Your audience will be your classmates. Later you might take part in a class read-around. You might also begin a collection of personal anecdotes.

What's
MY PURPOSE

Who's
MY AUDIENCE

1 Prewriting

Before beginning to write, choose a topic—an event to write about. Then explore and discover ideas about your topic.

Choose Your Topic ♦ In this unit, you learned about some ways writers find ideas. If you keep a journal, it can be a wonderful source of details and observations from your own life. Choose a topic that means most to you, then it will be of interest to your readers.

Think About It	Talk About It
Let your mind's camera roll back over the past few years of your life. What events appear? Ordinary events often make the best writing material. Decide what event you would like to share.	Discuss possible topics with a partner. Which events seem to interest your partner the most? Which topics spark the most questions?

Topic Ideas

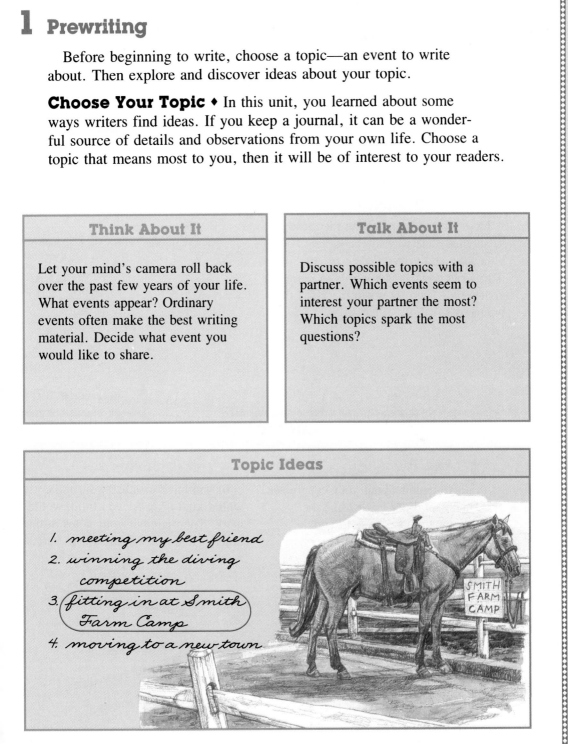

1. meeting my best friend
2. winning the diving competition
3. fitting in at Smith Farm Camp
4. moving to a new town

SMITH FARM CAMP

Choose Your Strategy ♦ Here are two strategies to help you explore and discover ideas. Read them both and use the idea you find more helpful.

PREWRITING IDEAS

CHOICE ONE

Branching

Ideas tend to branch, one idea leading to another. One way to encourage branching and to keep track of your ideas is to write down a few words to represent your topic. Then jot down the ideas that branch off.

Model

Events at Smith Farm
when I arrived
felt shy
didn't fit in
pig pen incident
birth of pigs
feelings of
success and
belonging
Becky's announcement
talk with Becky

CHOICE TWO

An Order Circle

Jot down details about your experience. Then make an order circle, like the example shown here, to help you organize them. Rotate the smaller part until you have matched your topic with a kind of order you think would work. Then number your notes in that order. Time order is illustrated here.

Topic: The day I delivered pigs at Smith Farm Camp

2 Mother pig ready to have babies

3 Becky and I were assigned to help

1 Background: how I felt when I got to farm

5 The birth of the pigs

4 The talk Becky and I had that morning

6 Becky's talk at lunch

Model

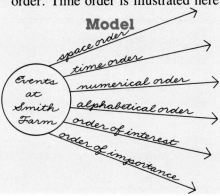

space order
time order
Events at Smith Farm
numerical order
alphabetical order
order of interest
order of importance

2 Writing

Use your prewriting notes for help in writing your narrative. Be sure to use first-person point of view. Including dialogue can add vitality to your narrative. Above all, let your own feelings and personality—your own voice—come across. Let your audience know why this event was significant for you.

Sample First Draft ◆

When I got to Smith Farm Camp, I didn't fit in. I'm from the City. I'd never seen a pig.

A week passed, and a pig was ready to have babies. Becky, a second-year farmer, was my partner. The farm leader, Sue, asked us to take turns caring for it. Becky talked, but I didn't say much. Finally she said, "Eric, don't you ever talk?"

I told her how I felt.

Her questions pulled out shy feelings buryed inside me. I talked on and on. She listened. Then she said "I was shy, but the farm helped me it can help you, too."

The pig started to have her first family. Becky ran to get sue. Before they got back, however, I greeted six piglets. At lunch Becky announces, "Eric delivered six baby pigs!" People crowded around me for the story.

I felt so good! Now I was a farmer. I had begun

3 Revising

You have drafted your personal narrative. Now it's time to consider changes that will strengthen its effectiveness. How can you know what needs to be changed? This strategy may help.

REVISING IDEA

FIRST Read to Yourself

As you read, review your purpose. Did you tell a story about something that really happened? Consider your audience. Will your classmates like it? Put a pencil check in the margin beside any part that you feel needs improvement.

Focus: Have you told your story in the first person? Do your own feelings and personality—your own voice—come through?

THEN Share with a Partner

Read your narrative aloud to a partner. Watch for your listener's nonverbal responses. Then ask for verbal responses. These guidelines may help you.

The Writer

Guidelines: Read clearly. Watch and listen for feedback. Make changes you feel are important.

Sample questions:
- What one word would you use to summarize the main point of this event?
- **Focus question:** Could you hear my voice in my writing?

The Writer's Partner

Guidelines: Listen thoughtfully. Then give honest, specific feedback.

Sample responses:
- I think your main point is that _____.
- Maybe you could add some dialogue when _____.
- I could really hear your sense of humor when _____.

Revising Model ♦ The draft narrative below looks messy because the writer is making changes to improve the writing.

Revising Marks

delete   _e_

add   ∧

move   ⟲

This event was out of time order.

The writer added dialogue to bring the event to life.

The writer's partner noticed this verb in the wrong tense.

The word *adept* is more precise than *good*.

When I got to Smith Farm Camp, I didn't fit in. I'm from the City. I'd never seen a pig.

A week passed, and a pig was ready to have babies. Becky, a second-year farmer, was my partner. The farm leader, Sue, asked us to take turns caring for it. Becky talked, but I didn't say much. Finally she said, "Eric, don't you ever talk?" *"I feel so awkward," I said. "I don't* I told her how I felt. *fit in here."*

Her questions pulled out shy feelings buried inside me. I talked on and on. She listened. Then she said "I was shy, but the farm helped me it can help you, too."

The pig started to have her first family. Becky ran to get sue. Before they got back, however, I greeted six piglets. At lunch Becky announces, *announced,* "Eric delivered six baby pigs!" People crowded around me for the story.

I felt so good! *adept* Now I was a farmer. I had begun

Revising Checklist

☐ **Purpose:** Have I written a personal narrative about a significant event in my life?

☐ **Audience:** Will my classmates understand and be entertained by my narrative?

☐ **Focus:** Have I used the first-person point of view and allowed my own personality, my own voice, to come across?

Read the personal narrative above the way the writer has decided it *should* be. Then revise your own narrative.

Grammar Check ♦ For clarity, keep all your verbs in the same tense.

Word Choice ♦ Some words, like *good*, are vague and often overused. A thesaurus is a good source of precise synonyms.

4 Proofreading

Correcting surface-level errors in spelling, capitalization, punctuation, and indentation makes your writing easier to read.

Proofreading Model ♦ Here is the draft of the narrative about the farm camp. Proofreading corrections appear in red.

When I got to Smith Farm Camp, I didn't fit in. I'm from the City. I'd never seen a pig.

A week passed, and a pig was ready to have babies. Becky, a second-year farmer, was my partner. The farm leader, Sue, asked us to take turns caring for it. Becky talked, but I didn't say much. Finally she said, "Eric, don't you ever talk?" I told her how I felt. *"I feel so awkward," I said. "I don't fit in here."*

Her questions pulled out shy feelings *buryed* inside me. I talked on and on. She listened. Then she said "I was shy, but the farm helped me it can help you, too."

The pig started to have her first family. Becky ran to get sue. Before they got back, however, I greeted six piglets. At lunch Becky *announced,* announces, "Eric delivered six baby pigs!" People crowded around me for the story.

I felt so good. *adept* Now I was a farmer. I had begun

PROOFREADING IDEA

Spelling Check

Here is a trick to help you focus on finding errors instead of reading for meaning. Place a ruler under one line to block out others. Read one line at a time.

Now proofread your personal narrative, add a title, and make a neat copy.

5 Publishing

Now that you have written and polished your personal narrative, here are two ways to share it with your classmates.

The Day I Delivered Pigs

When I got to Smith Farm Camp, I didn't fit in. I'm from the city. I'd never seen a pig.

A week passed, and a pig was ready to have babies. The farm leader, Sue, asked us to take turns caring for it. Becky, a second-year farmer, was my partner.

Becky talked, but I didn't say much. Finally she said, "Eric, don't you ever talk?"

"I feel so awkward," I said. "I don't fit in here."

Her questions pulled out shy feelings buried inside me. I talked on and on. She listened. Then she said, "I was shy, but the farm helped me. It can help you, too."

The pig started to have her first family. Becky ran to get Sue. Before they got back, however, I greeted six piglets. At lunch Becky announced, "Eric delivered six baby pigs!" People crowded around me for the story.

I felt so adept! Now I was a farmer. I had begun to fit in, thanks to a pig and my friend Becky.

PUBLISHING IDEAS

Share Aloud	Share in Writing
Organize a read-around. Take turns reading your narratives aloud within a small group. Allow time for your listeners to respond by sharing similar experiences.	Put your narrative in a notebook with a title such as "Important Moments." Add other narratives to preserve your memorable experiences. Share them with special friends.

CURRICULUM ·CONNECTION·

Writing Across the Curriculum   Mathematics

Many notable immigrants have been scientists and mathematicians. In these fields an important skill is solving problems in an orderly way. During this unit you practiced choosing appropriate kinds of order—a skill that can help you in science and math.

Writing to Learn

Think and Analyze ◆ Read this problem. Decide what steps you need to take to solve it. Decide in what order you will do the steps.

On Monday, Jane worked for six hours. During that time she answered the telephone and addressed 412 envelopes. Jane received $1.25 per hour. She also received four cents for each of the first 200 envelopes she addressed and six cents for each envelope above that number. How much did Jane earn?

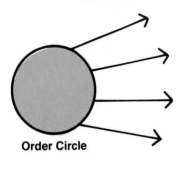

Order Circle

Write ◆ Explain how you solved the problem. Explain the steps, the order in which you took them, and why you did it that way.

Writing in Your Journal

At the beginning of this unit, you wrote what you knew about immigration to our country. During the unit you learned about immigrants who made special contributions, such as Albert Einstein, John J. Audubon, and E. I. DuPont. Now in your journal write about how you believe *you* can contribute positively to our nation's continued growth.

BOOKS TO ENJOY

Read More About It

Immigrant Kids   *by Russell Freedman*
What was it like to emigrate to the United States as a child?
How did kids adjust to new neighborhoods, new schools,
and a new language? This book recounts the experiences of
some typical immigrant kids.

Strangers in Their Own Land   *by Albert Prago*
Beginning with the arrival of the Spaniards in the New
World, the author traces the history of Mexican-Americans.
This is a detailed, moving account of the causes of problems
that many Chicanos face.

Book Report Idea   Letter to the Author

Did you ever enjoy a book so
much that you wanted to thank its
creator? A letter is one way to do
it. Such a letter can also serve as
your next book report.

Dear Author ♦ Begin by telling
the author what you liked most
about the book. Then ask questions you've wondered about:
Where did the plot idea come
from? Are the characters based on
real people? If the book had short-
comings, feel free to say that, too.

Post your letter in the classroom
for all to see. Then mail your letter
to the book's publisher. The publisher will forward the letter to the
author's home.

> *October 15, 1991*
> *Dear Ms. George,*
> *   I just finished
> reading your wonderful
> and exciting book Julie
> of the Wolves. Your
> descriptions of the Alaskan
> tundra made me feel as
> if I were there. To be
> honest, I didn't think
> at first that it was
> very realistic to show a
> girl becoming a member
> of a wolf pack. But as
> I read, I became con-
> vinced that the obser-
> vant Miyax could have
> managed it. Where
> did you get the idea*

UNIT REVIEW

Unit 3
Verbs   *pages 124–135*

A. Write each verb and label it *action* or *state-of-being*.

1. Last year Mom opened her new store on River Street.
2. She sells casual fashions for boys and girls.
3. A new business seemed risky at the time.
4. The store became a success almost immediately.

B. Write each verb or verb phrase. Underline any helping verbs.

5. My friends were soon shopping at Mom's store.
6. She has hired two sales assistants recently.
7. The casual clothes are affordable and fashionable.
8. My mother definitely has a flair for style.

C. Write each direct object. Write *whom* or *what* to show what question each answers.

9. The 1906 San Francisco earthquake ruined 500 square blocks.
10. Then the fire caused even more damage.
11. Reporters recently interviewed survivors of the earthquake.
12. These eyewitnesses recalled the victims and the events.

D. Write the sentences and underline the indirect objects.

13. The chance for a fresh start gave pioneers new hope.
14. Untamed lands brought settlers great challenges.
15. The settlers taught their children basic values.
16. They promised other Americans a future in the West.

E. Write the sentences. Underline each linking verb and label each predicate nominative and predicate adjective.

17. The colorful signs were expressions of their ideas.
18. The number of marchers grew larger.
19. The small group quickly became a crowd.

F. Write each verb and label it *transitive* or *intransitive*. If it is transitive, write its direct object.

20. The event was an impressive sight on television.
21. A delegation of children raised the flag for their country.
22. The scene produced strong emotions in onlookers.
23. The audience stood silently.
24. Cameras captured the poetry of the moment.

Synonyms   *pages 136–137*

G. Write each sentence, completing it with a synonym for the underlined word. Use a dictionary or thesaurus for help if necessary.

25. Carlos is <u>bright</u>; Hernando is _____.
26. Barbara is <u>skillful</u>; Alice is _____.
27. Bryan was <u>grateful</u>; Kate was _____.
28. Dennis <u>groaned</u>; Lisa _____.
29. Judy <u>invented</u> things; Eddie _____ things.

Dialogue   *pages 154–155*

H. Write what *you* think each statement shows about its speaker.

30. "You can't fool me," Brenda said, eyeing Pam intently. "You are planning a surprise party for me, aren't you?"
31. "I'm not afraid to make the delivery to that old house by myself!" Dave said. "I just thought you'd like to come along to see what it's like inside."

I. Write a brief dialogue for the characters in each of the following situations.

32. Jim wants his brother Wilfred to help him rake the yard so that Jim can go swimming with a friend. However, Wilfred has already finished his chores and plans to play tennis.
33. Christine tried out for the lead in the class play, but someone else got the part. Christine has now been asked to help with costumes and scenery. She discusses the matter with her grandmother.
34. Laura thinks that Emilio has the qualities to make a good student government president. She urges him to run for the office and offers to serve as his campaign manager.

Crossword Verbs

Copy and complete this crossword puzzle. (Hint: Each answer is a verb.)

Across
1. misstate
4. devote
6. foretell
7. be afraid
8. adjust a radio
9. require
12. rotate

Down
1. discover
2. loan
3. end
5. amuse
6. make believe
7. give food to
10. devour
11. plural of *is*

Verb Compounds

Write the word that can be used after each of the three words in the group to make a two-word verb like *go along*.

1. sum   catch   add   _ _
2. set   cast   blast   _ _ _
3. run   set   turn   _ _
4. put   shut   come   _ _ _ _
5. look   turn   scare   _ _
6. come   set   fall   _ _
7. look   come   set   _ _ _ _
8. go   stand   come   _ _
9. put   run   slow   _ _ _ _
10. turn   run   make   _ _ _ _
11. set   stand   turn   _ _ _
12. turn   set   come   _ _
13. come   bring   go   _ _ _ _ _ _
14. go   run   look   _ _ _ _ _
15. run   pull   go   _ _ _ _ _ _ _

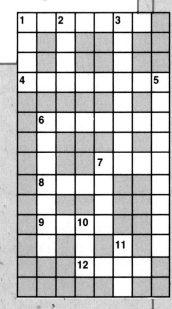

Unit 3 Extra Practice

1 Writing with Verbs

p. 124

A. Write the verb in each sentence.

1. The day begins.
2. Night is over.
3. The sun shines.
4. Forget about it.
5. Was she unhappy?
6. There he stayed.

B. Write the verb in each sentence. Then write *action verb* or *state-of-being verb* after it.

7. A narrow strip of land once connected North America and Siberia in Asia.
8. The first Americans traveled here from Asia.
9. These men, women, and children were hunters.
10. Imagine yourself with these people long ago.
11. You follow animal tracks along the "land bridge."
12. Eventually your group arrives in North America.
13. Game seems more plentiful here than in Asia.
14. Farther south you feel warmer temperatures.
15. The new land becomes your home.

C. This article contains fifteen verbs. Write the article. Then underline all of the verbs.

16. The first Americans came to North America thousands of years ago. **17.** Gradually they explored and settled most of the continent. **18.** Native Americans of the Northeast hunted and fished in the woodlands and rivers. **19.** In each village were many bark and pole houses. **20.** The Native Americans of the Great Plains pursued or followed the buffalo. **21.** Buffalo meat and skins provided them with food, clothing, and shelter. **22.** In the dry Southwest, Native Americans planted and harvested many crops. **23.** Each of their homes was a multifamily, hillside structure. **24.** The Native Americans of the Northwest caught salmon in the rivers and streams. **25.** They designed and constructed elaborate houses, boats, totem poles, and other wooden objects.

D. Rewrite the sentences below, substituting action verbs for linking verbs. Make all other necessary changes.

26. Cara is the originator of many hilarious jokes.
27. The cold lake was a shock to the bathers.
28. Her cough is a cause of conern to me.
29. He will always be a painter of landscapes.
30. This discussion will be of interest to you.
31. Who was the inventor of the phonograph?

2 Verb Phrases

p. 126

A. Write each sentence. Underline each main verb.

1. Have you ever heard of Bjarni Herjulfsson?
2. This Norse sailor might have sailed from Iceland to North America in the year 1000.
3. He had been searching for Greenland.
4. His ship, however, must have been blown off course.
5. The first European explorer may have reached our shores by mistake.
6. Norse explorer Eric the Red had settled in Greenland.
7. His son Leif Ericson had heard tales of land to the west.
8. He had led an expedition to Vinland in North America.
9. After a year's stay, his party did return to Greenland with timber and wild grapes.
10. He did settle in Brattahlid, Greenland.

B. Write each verb phrase after its sentence number. Underline the main verb twice. Underline each helping verb once.

11. Many Europeans had been thrilled by Columbus's discovery in 1492. **12.** Soon other navigators were exploring the new lands. **13.** One Italian explorer was named Amerigo Vespucci. **14.** By 1499 he had explored South America's northern shore. **15.** A German mapmaker, Martin Waldseemüller, must have admired Vespucci. **16.** Waldseemüller had used the name *America* for the first time in a geography book of 1507. **17.** At first the name was used only for South America. **18.** Later it was applied to the entire hemisphere. **19.** Amerigo Vespucci may have deserved his reputation as an explorer. **20.** Still, shouldn't the new land have been called *Columbia*?

C. Write helping verbs to complete the sentences.

21. _____ you imagine a "fountain of youth?"
22. Its water _____ keep you young forever.
23. By 1521 the Spanish explorer Ponce de León _____ _____ searching for the fountain for years.
24. Of course, Ponce de León _____ never find it.
25. He _____ found something good, though—Florida!

3 Verbs with Direct Objects

p. 128

A. Write the subject and the direct object in each sentence. Underline the direct object.

1. George and Martha Washington greatly expanded Mount Vernon. **2.** The beautiful gardens and elegant mansion reflected their excellent taste. **3.** However, a large estate requires constant care. **4.** War and government service kept the Washingtons away from their beautiful Virginia home. **5.** The Washingtons did spend their final years at Mount Vernon.

B. Write the direct object in each sentence. If a sentence has no direct object, write *none*.

6. Bushrod Washington inherited Mount Vernon from George Washington in 1802. **7.** He and his family, however, could not adequately maintain the huge estate. **8.** By 1850, Mount Vernon had crumbled into a state of disrepair. **9.** At that time the government did not actively preserve historical sites. **10.** Would the nation lose this great treasure? **11.** Fortunately, Ann Pamela Cunningham began her great crusade. **12.** For many years this energetic and resourceful woman worked toward one goal. **13.** She planned the restoration and preservation of the home of the Washingtons for the public benefit. **14.** For this purpose Cunningham formed the Mount Vernon Ladies' Association of the Union in 1853. **15.** The group soon purchased and restored 200 acres of the Washington estate. **16.** The group continues its work to this day. **17.** The present condition of Mount Vernon would please the Washingtons. **18.** Immaculate lawns and gardens surround the mansion. **19.** Many pieces of the original furniture have been returned to the house. **20.** Today the beauty of this great home can be enjoyed by all.

C. Write the verb and the direct object in each sentence. Underline the direct object.

21. Hernando de Soto explored the Mississippi region in 1540. **22.** After his death in 1542, his soldiers buried him in the Mississippi River. **23.** In 1699, Pierre le Moyne founded the first French settlement at old Biloxi. **24.** Then the French explored the area. **25.** They claimed much territory in Mississippi. **26.** After the French and Indian War in 1763, the French lost Mississippi to the English. **27.** The English ruled the area until the Revolutionary War. **28.** During the war, Spain seized control. **29.** Spain held the territory until 1798. **30.** The next two decades saw Mississippi as a territory of the United States. **31.** In 1817 the United States annexed Mississippi as its twentieth state. **32.** William Faulkner used his native Mississippi as the setting for his prize-winning novels.

4 Verbs with Indirect Objects   *p. 130*

A. Write the indirect object in each sentence.

1. Will you send us magnolias from Mississippi?
2. Guides show visitors the battlefield at Vicksburg.
3. The climate offers residents warm or mild winters.
4. Lakes and beaches give vacationers a treat.
5. Mississippi can offer you much enjoyment.

B. Write each sentence. Underline the direct object once and the indirect object twice.

6. The letter carrier handed Mom the letter.
7. Aunt Clara and Uncle Phil had sent their favorite niece and nephew an invitation to the ranch.
8. Dad bought Dana and Ray their plane tickets.
9. Mr. Heron gave the twins a ride to the airport.
10. Mom offered them books and magazines for the trip.
11. Dana and Ray waved their parents another good-bye.
12. The control tower gave the pilot clearance for takeoff.
13. The flight attendants showed the young people special attention during the flight.
14. After a while an attendant brought them lunch.
15. A first flight will give anyone a thrill.

C. Write the verb in each sentence. Then write whether each under-lined word is a direct object or an indirect object.

16. This fall the coach taught the <u>team</u> new <u>plays</u>.
17. Give the <u>players</u> a loud <u>cheer</u> now.
18. A bus brought the visiting <u>team</u> to the stadium.
19. The visiting team has fine <u>athletes</u> with good records and much enthusiasm.
20. The coaches gave the <u>players</u> final <u>instructions</u>.
21. The referee tossed a <u>coin</u> into the air.
22. Both teams eagerly awaited the <u>start</u> of the game.
23. The quarterback called the <u>signal</u> for the play.
24. Soon the halfback made a <u>touchdown</u> by running through the right side of the line.
25. Both teams treated the large <u>crowd</u> to an excellent game of football.
26. The crowd cheered the <u>players</u> to extraordinary feats.
27. At halftime the bands from both schools provided exciting <u>entertainment</u> for the fans of both teams.
28. The fans gained renewed <u>enthusiasm</u>.
29. Even the losing team played spectacular <u>football</u>.
30. Everyone had a wonderful <u>time</u>.

5 Predicate Nominatives and Predicate Adjectives

p. 132

A. Write each sentence and label the predicate nominative or predicate adjective in each.

1. Stone Mountain in Georgia has become famous. **2.** The side of the mountain is now a work of art. **3.** The carving on the mountain-side may well be the largest sculpture in the world. **4.** The task of the sculptors must have been extremely difficult. **5.** The figure of Robert E. Lee is the height of a nine-story building!

6. The Stone Mountain carving appears gigantic and spectacular. **7.** The figures in the sculpture are three men on horseback. **8.** The three men are Robert E. Lee, Stonewall Jackson, and Jefferson Davis. **9.** These men were great Southern leaders. **10.** Of the three figures on the carving, Robert E. Lee is largest. **11.** Georgia's Stone Mountain Park is an extraordinary place!

B. Write the verb or verb phrase in each sentence. Then write and label each direct object, predicate nominative, or predicate adjective.

> **EXAMPLE:** The third sculptor was he.
> **ANSWER:** was; he, predicate nominative

12. The entire carving is the size of a city block. **13.** At first glance, its proportions seem unbelievable to many observers. **14.** Yet the sculptors have not overlooked any details. **15.** The expressions on the leaders' faces appear noble and proud. **16.** Viewers can easily see buckles, fingers, and even strands of hair.

17. Gutzon Borglum began the work in the early 1920s. **18.** The rough figure of Lee is his contribution. **19.** Augustus Lukeman became the second sculptor. **20.** The designer for the present carving was he. **21.** Financial problems stopped the project in 1928. **22.** No sculptor carved figures there for thirty years. **23.** In 1958 the state of Georgia created the Stone Mountain Memorial Association. **24.** A recreational and educational park was the goal of this group. **25.** They selected the project's third and final sculptor, Walter Hahcock. **26.** Because of this group's dedication and hard work, Stone Mountain Park is both informative and interesting. **27.** Best of all, the dream of a completed carving became a reality in 1969!

C. Write each verb or verb phrase after its sentence number. Then label each linking verb. If a verb has a predicate nominative or predicate adjective, write and label it.

28. The name *Benedict Arnold* has become a synonym for *traitor*. **29.** Yet Benedict Arnold was at first a loyal patriot in the American cause. **30.** Early in the Revolution, Arnold was a great hero. **31.** With Ethan Allen, he captured Fort Ticonderoga from the British. **32.** In 1775, during the battle for Quebec, Arnold received a bullet wound in his knee. **33.** In 1777, Arnold did seem bitter about the promotion of other officers over him. **34.** Yet he remained loyal awhile. **35.** His leadership at the battle of Saratoga led to the American victory. **36.** Here he again received a battle wound for the American cause. **37.** This victory may well have been the turning point of the war. **38.** The reasons for Arnold's treasonous behavior toward the end of the war may never be completely clear. **39.** However, we should remember his accomplishments as well as his disgrace.

6 Transitive and Intransitive Verbs   *p. 134*

A. Write the transitive verb and its direct object in each sentence. Underline the direct object.

1. The state of Kentucky has gained great fame from horses. **2.** The Kentucky Derby at Churchill Downs in Louisville captures the world's attention every year. **3.** Many beautiful horse farms decorate the rolling hills around Lexington. **4.** This area produces the finest horses in the nation. **5.** The fertile land and mild climate form an ideal environment for horses. **6.** Many people visit Kentucky each year to see the horses.

B. Write each action verb. Then write whether it is transitive or intransitive.

7. Can we watch the cross-country horse race?
8. Look at those horses by the fence.
9. You can ride a pony or horse at the park.
10. Will you ride with me and the others now?
11. She raises thoroughbred horses.
12. Her trainer works hard.
13. He exercises the horses.
14. The horse ran alone in the paddock.
15. He rode the horse in the race.
16. We left the barn.
17. Watch me on this big gray stallion.

C. Write each verb and label it transitive or intransitive. If it is transitive, write its direct object.

18. Even before statehood in 1792, Kentuckians bred fine horses. **19.** Kentuckians have long supplied other states with horses for general use. **20.** Yet the state also produces thoroughbreds. **21.** A superior American horse of the nineteenth century was Lexington. **22.** He was named for his birthplace.

23. Today the Kentucky Horse Park in Lexington, Kentucky, celebrates the tradition of the horse. **24.** A large museum traces its history over the centuries. **25.** A farm tour shows the stages of horse training. **26.** A polo field and a steeplechase course are also popular attractions. **27.** You can even tour the park in a horse-drawn wagon.

UNIT FOUR

USING LANGUAGE
TO

PERSUADE

=== **PART ONE** ===

Unit Theme *Environments Around the World*

Language Awareness Verb Forms

=== **PART TWO** ===

Literature "Vaccination drives for kids will take place
around world" by Coretta Scott King

A Reason for Writing Persuading

Writing
IN YOUR JOURNAL

WRITER'S WARM-UP ◆ An environment includes all the surrounding conditions that affect the development of
living things. A city block, a suburban
street, a mountain village — there are countless
environments around the world. Which one would
you choose? Explore an ideal environment by
writing in your journal. Tell about at least ten
different aspects of the environment that have a
beneficial effect on people.

Make up a four-sentence story about hiking. Use all four of these verb forms in your story: *hike*, *hiked*, *have hiked*, and *are hiking*.

1 Principal Parts of Verbs

Verbs have different forms for different uses. Verbs have four basic forms, called their principal parts. Here are the principal parts of the verb *help*.

Present	Past	Past Participle	Present Participle
help	helped	(have) helped	(are) helping

Most verbs, like *help*, are regular verbs and form their past and past participle by adding *-ed* to the present form of the verb. The present participle is formed by adding *-ing* to the present. Use a form of the helping verb *have* with the past participle and a form of *be* with the present participle.

Some regular verbs change their spelling when *-ed* or *-ing* is added.

hope, hoped, hoping (drop final *e*)
step, stepped, stepping (double the final consonant)
dry, dried, drying (change final *y* to *i*)

About 130 verbs are called irregular verbs, since they do not form the past and the past participle by adding *-ed*. They change spellings in other ways. For help in spelling their different forms, use a dictionary. You will learn more about irregular verbs in Lesson 3.

> **Summary ◆** The **principal parts** of a verb are its basic forms. They are the present, the past, the past participle, and the present participle.

Guided Practice

Name the four principal parts of each verb.

1. work   **2.** hurry   **3.** scan   **4.** use   **5.** open

Practice

A. Write the four principal parts of each verb.

    6. seem   **7.** discover   **8.** create   **9.** clap   **10.** copy

B. Write each sentence, completing it with the principal part of the verb indicated in parentheses.

    11. United Nations organizations have (help, past participle) many people in times of great emergency.
    12. They (maintain, present) advisors in hundreds of areas.
    13. They have (carry, past participle) food by airplane to hungry people.
    14. They also (demonstrate, past) new agricultural techniques to farmers in developing countries.
    15. These organizations are (change, present participle) the world for the better.

C. Write the present participle or past participle of each verb.

    16. For over forty years the United Nations has (assist) people all over the world.
    17. Countries in every part of the world have (join) the UN.
    18. Member nations have (aid) others in times of famine and disaster.
    19. They have (provide) supplies and medicine.
    20. The UN World Health Organization is (strive) for improvements in medical care.
    21. The UN has (solve) many disputes between nations.
    22. It is continually (expand) its peacekeeping efforts.
    23. UN planners are (develop) even better programs for the future.
    24. Volunteers have (donate) time, money, and their expertise.
    25. Today the UN is (serve) people in need in many ways.

Apply • Think and Write

From Your Writing • Read what you wrote for the Writer's Warm-up. Find at least four regular verbs you used and write their principal parts.

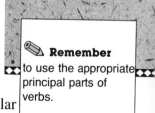

✎ **Remember** to use the appropriate principal parts of verbs.

GETTING
STARTED

What words could you use to complete each sentence?
_____ the piano.   I _____ the piano yesterday.
I _____ the piano next week.

2 Tenses of Verbs

The time expressed by a verb is called its tense. The six tenses of a verb are formed from its principal parts.

The **present tense** expresses an action taking place now.
■ Mrs. Wu's students <u>study</u> famous people.

The **past tense** expresses an action that took place in the past.
❚ Last week they <u>learned</u> about Albert Schweitzer and his hospital in Africa.

The **future tense** expresses an action that will occur in the future. It is formed by adding the helping verb *will* or *shall* to the present.
❚ This week they <u>will learn</u> more about Dr. Schweitzer and his many achievements.

The **present perfect tense** expresses an action that occurred at an indefinite time in the past and may still be going on. It is formed with the helping verb *have* or *has* and the past participle of the verb.
■ They <u>have learned</u> a great deal about him.

The **past perfect tense** expresses an action that occurred before another past action. It is formed with the helping verb *had* and the past participle.
❚ Before they studied about Schweitzer, they <u>had discussed</u> other humanitarians.

The **future perfect tense** expresses an action that will be completed before a definite time in the future. It is formed with *will have* or *shall have* and the past participle.
❚ By the end of the month, they <u>will have learned</u> even more about Schweitzer.

A list of all the forms of a verb, arranged by tense, is called a **conjugation**. Study the conjugation of the verb *talk* below. For conjugations of the irregular verbs *be*, *have*, and *do*, see page 676.

Conjugation of the Verb *Talk*		
Principal Parts: talk, talked, (have) talked, (are) talking		
Present Tense		
	Singular	**Plural**
First Person	I talk	we talk
Second Person	you talk	you talk
Third Person	he, she, it talks	they talk
Past Tense		
First Person	I talked	we talked
Second Person	you talked	you talked
Third Person	he, she, it talked	they talked
Future Tense		
First Person	I will (shall) talk	we will (shall) talk
Second Person	you will talk	you will talk
Third Person	he, she, it will talk	they will talk
Present Perfect Tense		
First Person	I have talked	we have talked
Second Person	you have talked	you have talked
Third Person	he, she, it has talked	they have talked
Past Perfect Tense		
First Person	I had talked	we had talked
Second Person	you had talked	you had talked
Third Person	he, she, it had talked	they had talked
Future Perfect Tense		
First Person	I will (shall) have talked	we will (shall) have talked
Second Person	you will have talked	you will have talked
Third Person	he, she, it will have talked	they will have talked

Summary ◆ The **tense** of a verb shows time.

Guided Practice

Name the tense of each verb.

1. walk
2. has used
3. cared
4. seems
5. had marked
6. will help
7. will have fixed
8. depended

Practice

A. Write the tense of each verb.

9. will try
10. discusses
11. wash
12. has enjoyed
13. had started

14. finished
15. have played
16. will have listened
17. crossed
18. shall have entered

B. Write the verb in each sentence. Then write its tense.

19. Albert Schweitzer accomplished many things in his life.
20. People around the world have admired those accomplishments.
21. By the age of thirty, he had achieved fame in several fields.
22. Since childhood he had studied music. 23. He soon mastered several instruments, including the organ. 24. The world still recognizes him as one of the greatest organists of all time. 25. Even earlier, Schweitzer had turned his attention to philosophy. 26. He devoted nine years to the study of the great philosophers of the past. 27. For the next sixty years, Schweitzer worked in the service of humanity. 28. People will remember his selfless devotion to others.

C. Write each sentence, completing it with the verb in the tense indicated in parentheses.

29. Schweitzer (base, past) his career on reverence for life.
30. Besides music and philosophy, he also (study, past perfect) medicine.
31. In 1913 he (establish, past) a medical facility in French Equatorial Africa, now Gabon.

32. Schweitzer (construct, past) a great hospital at Lambaréné.

33. He (research, past) many diseases, especially leprosy.

34. For centuries people (treat, past perfect) the victims of leprosy with fear and disdain.

35. Schweitzer (view, past) the disease differently.

36. He (pioneer, past) many new treatments for leprosy.

37. Today doctors (employ, present) many of Schweitzer's methods.

38. Thousands of people (benefit, future) from his work.

39. Schweitzer (contribute, present perfect) in other areas, too.

40. Earlier he (raise, past perfect) money for worthy causes.

41. In 1952 officials of the Nobel committee (award, past) Schweitzer the Nobel Peace Prize.

42. He (use, past) the prize money for his hospital.

43. Schweitzer (distinguish, past perfect) himself in other fields also.

44. He always (devote, past perfect) much of his time to literary studies.

45. Scholars (respect, present perfect) his interpretations of the great German poet Goethe.

46. Mrs. Wu's class (discover, future perfect) quite a bit about Schweitzer by the end of the week.

47. From the beginning, students (admire, past perfect) Schweitzer for his concern for humanity.

48. Since then they (learn, present perfect) many other interesting things about him.

D. Write a sentence of your own using each verb or verb phrase.

49. admires	**54.** developed
50. will have achieved	**55.** have improved
51. had used	**56.** changed
52. has triumphed	**57.** had learned
53. will help	**58.** shall continue

Apply • Think and Write

A Helpful Hero • Think of someone you know or have read about who has helped other people. Write a paragraph that tells about this person's accomplishments. Then underline each verb and write its tense.

✎ **Remember**
to use verb tenses carefully to show time.

Yesterday I _____ . I _____ today. Tomorrow I shall _____ .
Complete the sentences with above forms of these verbs: *sleep, eat, run, fly, ride.*

3 Irregular Verbs

Irregular verbs do not form their principal parts by adding *-ed*. However, many irregular verbs do follow other patterns.

Some irregular verbs form the past participle by adding *-n* to the past.

Present	Past	Past Participle	Present Participle
break	broke	(have) broken	(are) breaking
choose	chose	(have) chosen	(are) choosing
speak	spoke	(have) spoken	(are) speaking
steal	stole	(have) stolen	(are) stealing

Some form the past participle from the present.

draw	drew	(have) drawn	(are) drawing
drive	drove	(have) driven	(are) driving
eat	ate	(have) eaten	(are) eating
fall	fell	(have) fallen	(are) falling

Some have the same past and past participle.

catch	caught	(have) caught	(are) catching
have	had	(have) had	(are) having
leave	left	(have) left	(are) leaving
sleep	slept	(have) slept	(are) sleeping
tell	told	(have) told	(are) telling
think	thought	(have) thought	(are) thinking

Some have the same present, past, and past participle.

burst	burst	(have) burst	(are) bursting
cost	cost	(have) cost	(are) costing
spread	spread	(have) spread	(are) spreading
shut	shut	(have) shut	(are) shutting

Notice that some of the irregular verbs on the next page follow patterns, and others do not. Learn the forms of these verbs.

Irregular Verbs			
Present	**Past**	**Past Participle**	**Present Participle**
begin	began	(have) begun	(are) beginning
blow	blew	(have) blown	(are) blowing
bring	brought	(have) brought	(are) bringing
buy	bought	(have) bought	(are) buying
come	came	(have) come	(are) coming
do	did	(have) done	(are) doing
drink	drank	(have) drunk	(are) drinking
feel	felt	(have) felt	(are) feeling
find	found	(have) found	(are) finding
freeze	froze	(have) frozen	(are) freezing
fly	flew	(have) flown	(are) flying
get	got	(have) gotten, got	(are) getting
give	gave	(have) given	(are) giving
go	went	(have) gone	(are) going
hide	hid	(have) hidden	(are) hiding
hit	hit	(have) hit	(are) hitting
hold	held	(have) held	(are) holding
know	knew	(have) known	(are) knowing
make	made	(have) made	(are) making
ride	rode	(have) ridden	(are) riding
ring	rang	(have) rung	(are) ringing
run	ran	(have) run	(are) running
say	said	(have) said	(are) saying
see	saw	(have) seen	(are) seeing
sing	sang	(have) sung	(are) singing
stand	stood	(have) stood	(are) standing
swim	swam	(have) swum	(are) swimming
take	took	(have) taken	(are) taking
teach	taught	(have) taught	(are) teaching
throw	threw	(have) thrown	(are) throwing
wear	wore	(have) worn	(are) wearing
write	wrote	(have) written	(are) writing

Summary ✦ Some irregular verbs follow patterns when forming their principal parts. Others do not.

Guided Practice

Name the four principal parts of these verbs.

1. speak   **2.** cost   **3.** blow   **4.** stand   **5.** throw

Practice

A. Write the verb form in parentheses that correctly completes each sentence.

   6. Millions of people (took, taken) trips to America's national parks last year.
   7. The parks have (gave, given) visitors thrilling experiences for generations.
   8. Many people have (wrote, written) about the splendor of these wilderness areas.
   9. Most of them, however, have not (thinked, thought) about other important contributions of our national parks.
  10. The United States (got, gotten) its first park in 1872.
  11. Congress (maked, made) a vast northwestern wilderness area into Yellowstone National Park.
  12. The government (holded, held) the land for the use of all the people.
  13. Congress had (leaved, left) the land in this new park in its natural state.
  14. Its wild beauty has (drew, drawn) millions of people to it every year.
  15. Many have (fell, fallen) in love with this part of America.

B. Each sentence contains an incorrect form of an irregular verb. Write the correct verb.

  16. A desire for these special parks spreaded quickly.
  17. By 1916 national parks holded thousands of acres of land with natural wonders.
  18. In that year the government begun the National Park Service with a special act of Congress.
  19. The Park Service runned the national parks efficiently.
  20. Its rangers have teached a great many people about America's wilderness and natural resources.
  21. From the beginning the rangers have knowed the importance of these wilderness areas.
  22. The National Park Service gotten the public's help with conservation of these areas, too.
  23. The preservation of these wonderful wilderness lands catched the public's imagination from the very first.

24. Americans have sang the praises of their national parks as the best places for vacations.

25. Thousands of visitors have wrote about the foresight of the founders of the parks.

C. Write each sentence, completing it with the principal part of the verb indicated. Use *have* with the past participle and *are* with the present participle.

26. Before the establishment of national parks, many people (think, past) differently about their natural environment.

27. In the parks visitors (see, past) many of nature's greatest wonders.

28. Experiences in the parks (give, past participle) people new attitudes toward nature.

29. They (tell, past participle) others about their experiences.

30. The parks (bring, present participle) many people a greater appreciation of nature and their environment.

D. Write sentences about places you have visited or would like to visit. Use the principal parts of the verbs indicated.

31. buy, past
32. do, past participle
33. go, present participle
34. come, past
35. swim, present

36. drive, past
37. sleep, present participle
38. feel, past participle
39. wear, past
40. find, past participle

Apply • Think and Write

A True-False Test ♦ Construct a True-or-False Verb Test that includes at least ten items. Trade tests with a classmate.

Example:
1. <u>Costed</u> is the past participle of <u>cost</u>. T F
2. <u>Teach</u> is an irregular verb. T F
3. <u>Sang</u> is a present participle. T F

Pick an action such as running, reading, or swimming. Show that the action is in progress by completing this sentence with two words:
They _____ _____ right now.

4 Progressive and Emphatic Forms

You know that verbs have six basic tenses. Each tense also has a progressive form, which shows continuing action. The progressive form consists of a form of the verb *be* and the present participle of the verb. The form of *be* changes to show the tense. In the examples, progressive forms are used to show action in progress.

> They **are waiting** now. (present progressive)
> They **were waiting** yesterday. (past progressive)
> They **will be waiting** next week. (future progressive)
> They **have been waiting** an hour. (present perfect progressive)
> They **had been waiting** an hour when I arrived. (past perfect progressive)
> They **will have been waiting** for two hours when the park opens. (future perfect progressive)

The emphatic form of a verb is used to give emphasis or added force. It consists of the helping verb *do* and the present form of the verb. Only the present tense and the past tense have emphatic forms.

■ She **does call** every day.   He **did call** earlier.

When you wish to show action that continues, use a progressive form. When you wish to give special emphasis or show strong feeling, use an emphatic form.

> **Summary** ✦ The **progressive form** of a verb shows continuing action. The **emphatic form** of a verb shows emphasis or strong feeling.

Guided Practice

Tell whether each verb is progressive or emphatic. Then name the tense.

1. do speak   **2.** will be talking   **3.** did see   **4.** are finding

Practice

A. Write the verb in the form indicated.

5. we (discuss, past emphatic)
6. she (prepare, present perfect progressive)
7. they (move, future perfect progressive)
8. I (think, present emphatic)
9. you (report, future progressive)

B. Rewrite each sentence, changing the verb to the progressive form of the tense used.

10. Jean will work as a park ranger this summer.
11. She had wanted this career since childhood.
12. She has studied forestry in college for the past four years.
13. She also has worked in national parks during the summers.
14. Jean will have learned about many important topics.

C. Rewrite each sentence, changing the verb to the emphatic form of the tense used.

15. Jean enjoys her work in the outdoors.
16. She learned a great deal about conservation.
17. She also devoted many hours to the protection of wildlife.
18. Special projects take most of her time.
19. One project saves the homes of hundreds of wild animals.

D. Write a sentence, using each verb as indicated in parentheses.

20. work (present progressive)
21. visit (past emphatic)
22. erupt (present perfect progressive)
23. plan (future perfect progressive)
24. feel (present emphatic)

Apply • Think and Write

An Environmental Project • Write a brief description of a project you might do to help save a threatened wildlife species or to protect the environment. Use several progressive and emphatic verb forms in your description.

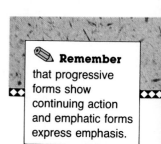

✎ **Remember**
that progressive forms show continuing action and emphatic forms express emphasis.

◆◆◆

5 Using Tenses Correctly

Shifts in tense can make writing confusing. Tenses should not be changed within a sentence or from one sentence to another in a paragraph unless the time changes.

When you write about actions in the past, use verbs in the past tense. When you write about actions in the present, use verbs in the present tense.

> **Today environmentalists <u>strive</u> for the cooperation of groups that <u>have</u> an interest in the environment.** (present)
>
> **People in many areas <u>wasted</u> natural resources and <u>destroyed</u> wildlife and forests. Early conservationists <u>called</u> attention to this problem.** (past)

When the time of the action changes, however, it is necessary to change the tenses of verbs. Notice the necessary shift in tense in the example sentence below.

>   **present**   **past**
> **We now <u>owe</u> much to the conservationists who <u>worked</u> so hard for the environment.**

Summary ◆ Do not shift tenses needlessly.

Guided Practice

Name the tense of each underlined verb. Tell which sentence contains a necessary shift in tense.

1. As long ago as the 1700s, people <u>protested</u> against those who <u>waste</u> natural resources.

2. Few early settlers <u>realized</u> that natural resources <u>will</u> <u>disappear</u> without conservation.

3. Some Americans <u>understood</u> that wildlife and wilderness areas <u>are</u> in danger.

Practice

A. Each sentence contains an unnecessary shift in tense. Write the tense of each underlined verb.

4. In the 1800s some Americans <u>discover</u> how others <u>wasted</u> natural resources.
5. John James Audubon <u>was</u> one person who <u>understands</u> the need for conservation.
6. Audubon <u>painted</u> North American birds and <u>writes</u> about the necessity of saving their habitats.
7. Another early conservationist <u>was</u> Julius Sterling Morton, who <u>originates</u> Arbor Day.
8. When loggers <u>removed</u> trees, Morton <u>replants</u> them.

The Granger Collection.

B. 9–13. Rewrite each sentence in **Practice A**. Change one verb in each sentence to avoid a needless shift in tense.

C. Write the paragraph below, correcting any needless shifts in tense. Use the past tense as the basic tense.

14. Rachel Carson was an American marine biologist, who writes in *The Sea Around Us* about the delicate balance of life in the seas and along the seashores. **15.** She emphasized and illustrates the interdependence of all living things. **16.** In 1962 her book *Silent Spring* brings to the attention of the public the dangers of chemical pesticides as they were then used. **17.** She shows how pesticides entered the food chain and poisoned many animals, including birds and fish. **18.** Her warnings led to changes in the use of pesticides in many countries and creates a more healthful environment.

Apply • Think and Write

Dictionary of Knowledge ◆ Read in the Dictionary of Knowledge about the different careers in environmental science. Choose one and write a brief job description. Work with a partner to correct any needless shifts in tense.

> ✎ **Remember**
> to use verbs in the same tense to show actions occurring at the same time.

What words could replace the underlined words in the sentences below?
The child was held by the mother.
The mother held the child.

6 Active and Passive Voice

In most sentences the subject performs the action. When the subject of a sentence performs the action, the verb is in the active voice.

■ Dr. Jonas Salk <u>developed</u> a polio vaccine.

When the subject receives the action, the verb is in the passive voice. A verb in the passive voice is a verb phrase made by using a form of *be* and a past participle.

■ A polio vaccine <u>was developed</u> by Dr. Jonas Salk.

Passive verbs often make writing wordy and weak. Active verbs are more direct and forceful. In most cases your writing will be better if you replace passive verbs with active verbs.

Passive: A Congressional gold medal <u>was received</u> by Salk.
Active: Salk <u>received</u> a Congressional gold medal.

The active voice should be used in most of your writing. The passive voice, however, is useful when the performer of an action is unknown or unimportant.

■ This deadly disease <u>has been feared</u> for centuries.

> **Summary** ♦ A verb is in the **active voice** when the subject performs the action. A verb is in the **passive voice** when the subject receives the action.

Guided Practice

Name each verb and identify the voice as active or passive.

1. This terrible disease can paralyze its victims.
2. The polio virus most often attacked children.
3. A weapon against the disease was sought by various researchers for years.

Practice

A. Write the verb in each sentence. Label it *active* or *passive*.

4. Work on Salk's project was begun in 1951.
5. Salk's group had undertaken an extremely difficult task.
6. Researchers recognized three different polio viruses.
7. An effective vaccine was needed for all three types.
8. After much hard work, the team achieved its goal.
9. The polio viruses in the trial vaccine had been killed.
10. Then the harmless viruses were injected into volunteers.
11. The vaccine stimulated the production of antibodies.
12. These antibodies protected the persons from the disease.
13. Much research was completed by Salk's team of scientists.

B. Rewrite the sentences, changing active verbs to passive verbs, and passive verbs to active verbs.

14. In 1953 a trial vaccine was announced by Salk.
15. The vaccine was given to Salk, his wife, and their three children by the scientists.
16. In 1954 a testing program was begun by the scientists.
17. That year 1,830,000 schoolchildren took the vaccine.
18. After this successful test, Salk received many honors.

C. Write two sentences for each of these verbs. In the first sentence, use the passive voice. In the second sentence, change the verb to the active voice.

EXAMPLE: Funds for research <u>were received</u> by Salk.
Salk <u>received</u> funds for research.

19. choose   21. discover   23. know
20. supply   22. try   24. gain

Apply • Think and Write

A Helpful Discovery • Imagine that you have just made a discovery that will help millions of people. Write a description of how you would feel and what you would think. With a partner, check your writing for the most effective use of active and passive voice. Make any necessary changes.

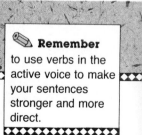

Remember to use verbs in the active voice to make your sentences stronger and more direct.

Is it possible to do these things? Why or why not?
Rise these rabbits. Raise up from your chair.
Set down and keep quiet. Sit the vase on that table.

7 Troublesome Verb Pairs

Certain pairs of verbs are frequently confused.

Sit, Set The verb *sit* means "to take a seat" or "to be in a place." Its principal parts are *sit*, *sat*, *sat*, *sitting*. It usually does not have a direct object.

■ **People sit in the park. They have sat there for hours.**

Set means "to put" or "to place." Its principal parts are *set*, *set*, *set*, *setting*. It usually has a direct object.

■ **Set the bench there.   Did they set it down?**

Lie, Lay The verb *lie* means "to rest" or "to recline." Its principal parts are *lie*, *lay*, *lain*, *lying*. It never has a direct object. Notice that *lay* is its past form.

▌**I will lie on the grass.   I lay there all afternoon.**
▌**My glasses are lying there.   They have lain there an hour.**

Lay means "to put down" or "to place." Its principal parts are *lay*, *laid*, *laid*, *laying*. It may have a direct object.

■ **Lay the blanket on the grass. He has already laid it there.**

Rise, Raise The verb *rise* means "to get up" or "to go up." Its principal parts are *rise*, *rose*, *risen*, *rising*. It never has a direct object.

■ **Water rises in the fountain.   The moon has risen.**

Raise means "to lift" or "to move higher." Its principal parts are *raise*, *raised*, *raised*, *raising*. It may have a direct object.

■ **The workers raised the window into place.**

> **Summary** ◆ Some verb pairs are often confused. Use *sit*, *set*, *lie*, *lay*, *rise*, and *raise* carefully in speaking and writing.

Guided Practice

Tell which verb correctly completes each sentence.

1. New buildings (raise, rise). **3.** (Set, Sit) the plans there.
2. (Lay, Lie) their foundations. **4.** He (sat, set) down.

Practice

A. Write the correct form of the verb in parentheses.

5. Many problems (lie, lay) before cities today.
6. Areas within many cities are (lying, laying) in ruins.
7. Some buildings have (lain, laid) idle for long periods.
8. Proposals for solutions have been (sit, set) in place.
9. Planners (sit, set) in many meetings about solutions for urban problems.
10. Proposals for zoos and parks (lie, lay) on officials' desks.
11. New proposals (lie, lay) the groundwork for great changes.
12. Officials (rise, raise) money for various projects.
13. New neighborhoods may (rise, raise) from ruins.
14. Expectations of city dwellers have (risen, raised) rapidly.

B. Write each sentence, completing it with the correct form of *sit*, *set*, *lie*, *lay*, *rise*, or *raise*.

15. A young architect has _____ a plan before the city council.
16. Council members _____ questions about this plan.
17. Funds for the project are _____ idle.
18. The plans _____ the foundation for a new development.
19. With this plan the neighborhood will _____ again.

C. Use each verb in a sentence. Use any form of the verb you wish.

20. sit **22.** lie **24.** rise
21. set **23.** lay **25.** raise

Apply • Think and Write

A Problem and Solution • What problem in your area would you most like to solve? Write a letter to your school newspaper describing your ideas for solving the problem. Use forms of troublesome verbs in your letter.

Remember to use forms of troublesome verbs carefully.

GETTING STARTED

What do these sayings mean? *Don't cry over spilt milk. A cat in gloves catches no mice. A penny saved is a penny earned.*

VOCABULARY ✦
Idioms

Idioms are expressions whose meanings cannot be understood by simply combining the meanings of the individual words. Look at the underlined words in the sentences below. What would these expressions mean if you took them literally, or word for word?

> Carmen is <u>throwing a party</u>.
> Have you <u>run across</u> Ted today?

Idioms occur often in everyday speech and writing. People who grow up speaking English hear them over and over again. Thus native speakers usually understand a large number of idioms. People who are learning English for the first time, however, usually find idioms challenging.

Idioms are not only important to understanding the language; they are also useful in writing and speaking. Idioms can help make writing more natural and can add color to both writing and speech. Choose your idioms carefully. If you are not sure what they mean, use a dictionary.

Building Your Vocabulary

Match the idioms in Column **A** with their meanings in Column **B**. Create sentences that include the idioms.

A	B
to lend a hand	to discourage
to cut something out	to fool; to trick
to pull someone's leg	to help
to throw cold water on	to search thoroughly
to leave no stone unturned	to stop doing something
to stick around	to accept or not accept
to take it or leave it	to wait

Make a list of idioms that would have a strange meaning if taken literally. Share your list with the class.

Practice

A. Rewrite each sentence. Replace the underlined idioms with words that would have clearer meanings to a new speaker of English.

1. The secretary <u>took down</u> notes at the meeting.
2. But he didn't <u>take into account</u> the speaker's fast speech.
3. "Please <u>take it easy</u>," the secretary asked the speaker.
4. The secretary was thinking that he should <u>take up</u> shorthand.
5. Suddenly the speaker <u>took off</u> in a <u>shower of words</u>.
6. The secretary then stood up, handed the speaker his pencil and paper, and said, "Here, you <u>take over</u>!"

B. Below are several idioms that name parts of the body. The meanings of the idioms are in parentheses. Write a sentence for each idiom.

Nose:	right under your nose (obvious)
	nose around (snoop)
Ears:	be all ears (listen closely)
	lend an ear (listen)
Feet:	drag your feet (be reluctant, hesitate)
	stand on your own two feet (be independent)
Hands:	on the other hand (from another point of view)
	have your hands full (be very busy)
Head:	lose your head (lose self-control)
	over your head (too difficult to understand)

LANGUAGE CORNER ◆ Word Meanings

Have you seen a **terrific** movie lately? Was it really scary? Or was it really enjoyable? *Terrific* once meant only "something causing great fear." *Terror* and *terrify* are related.

Find the meaning that the word *humor* had long ago.

This movie is terrific.

What do you mean?

How to Revise Sentences with Verbs

Using verb tenses correctly can make a difference in the effectiveness of your writing. Verb tenses are important because they tell a reader when actions are taking place. As you know, shifting verb tenses in a paragraph can confuse your reader. For example, read the paragraph below.

A small pond sits in a quiet park in my neighborhood. The pond was well hidden and not many people had discovered it. I went there often early in the evening to relax and think about my day. I have even made friends with a busy robin that has a nest in my favorite tree.

Can you tell whether the writer is talking about the present or the past time? Is the pond a place the writer visits now, or is it somewhere the writer used to go? These questions cannot be answered because the writer used both present and past verb tenses. Read the improved paragraph below and then answer the questions.

A small pond sits in a quiet park in my neighborhood. The pond is well hidden and not many people have discovered it. I go there often early in the evening to relax and think about my day. I have even made friends with a busy robin that has a nest in my favorite tree.

Remember, too, that using the active voice of verbs is another way to make your writing more effective. Try to use the active voice whenever possible as you do these activities.

The Grammar Game ◆ Focus on verb tense! Quickly write the past tense of each verb below. Then exchange papers with a classmate. Did you agree? If not, check with another classmate.

break	draw	sleep	freeze	hide	put
shake	say	cost	shut	throw	sink

Working Together

As you do activities **A** and **B**, choose the most appropriate verb tense and voice to make the group's writing clear and effective.

In Your Group
◆ Pay attention to all ideas.   ◆ Build on others' ideas.
◆ Summarize after each discussion.   ◆ Take turns recording suggestions.

A. Identify the tenses of the verbs in the sentences below. Then write the sentences, changing the verbs to a different tense and using the active voice where possible.

1. Two cattle ranches were owned by Theodore Roosevelt.
2. He had learned much about life in the wilderness.
3. Until his time, few people were interested in conservation.
4. Millions of acres of wilderness have been saved by President Roosevelt's conservation policies.
5. Because of his efforts, these areas remain wilderness.

B. Change all verbs in the paragraph below to tell about the past.

Theodore Roosevelt is called "Teddy" by his public. People often comment on Teddy's remarkable energy. Despite the demands of his busy days, he often swims, hikes, and rides horseback. With his stocky physique and burly appearance, he becomes a favorite subject of cartoonists, who like to draw him as a bear cub. Toymakers are producing stuffed animals known as "teddy bears."

WRITERS' CORNER ◆ Overused Verbs

Avoid using the same verbs repeatedly in your writing. Overused verbs can turn interesting sentences into boring ones.

My family camped in Voyageurs National Park last summer. We camped next to a remote lake in the wilderness. We camped there for a few days, and then we camped deep in a pine forest.

Rewrite these sentences, using the verb *camped* only once. Read what you wrote for the Writer's Warm-up. Did you overuse any verbs? If you did, can you change some of them to improve your writing?

TE RAHU RAHI
painting by Paul Gauguin, oil on canvas
jointly owned by The Cleveland Museum of Art and an anonymous collector, (75.263).

UNIT FOUR

USING LANGUAGE
TO

PERSUADE

=== **PART TWO** ===

Literature "Vaccination drives for kids will take place
around world" by Coretta Scott King

A Reason for Writing Persuading

CREATIVE
Writing

FINE ARTS ◆ Paul Gauguin has captured the
beauty and serenity of this scene for us to enjoy
forever. We can always look at the painting and
relax with the people gathered under the tree.
What memory of a favorite outdoor place of
beauty do you have? Write a description of it to
enjoy whenever you want to remind yourself of
that place.

CRITICAL THINKING ◆
A Strategy for Persuading

A CONCLUSION CHART

Persuading means getting someone to agree with you. One kind of persuasive writing is an editorial. Following this lesson, you will read an editorial by Coretta Scott King. Later you will write an editorial on a topic you feel strongly about. One topic Mrs. King feels strongly about is worldwide immunization. Here is part of her editorial about it.

> . . . vaccine-preventable diseases now claim the lives of 3 ½ million children every year and inflict permanent injury on millions more. . . . The supply of vaccines is now almost adequate to immunize every child on Earth at a cost of $5 per child. . . . The people of the wealthier nations have a moral obligation to redouble their financial and volunteer support of UNICEF, the United Nations International Children's Fund.

What facts does Mrs. King present? What does she conclude?

 Learning the Strategy

An active thinker draws conclusions. For example, suppose you are listening to a political debate. You evaluate the candidates' claims and promises. You draw your own conclusions. You can also draw conclusions about daily events. Imagine there is a new boy in your class. He doesn't speak to anyone and keeps to himself. Why do you think he is like that? What conclusion do you draw?

There are two important things to be aware of about drawing conclusions. One is that sometimes you don't have enough information to form a conclusion. If you reach a conclusion on the basis of too little information, you are *leaping* to a conclusion. The second is that people can draw different conclusions from the same information. That is why voters who have heard the same speeches can vote for opposing candidates.

It is up to you to decide if you have enough information to go on. You should be ready to change your conclusion if you get new information or new insights about old information. A conclusion chart can help. The one below shows a conclusion someone has reached about the new boy in your class.

Facts: He doesn't speak to anyone. He rarely smiles. He goes directly home after school.

My Conclusion: He doesn't like us.

Conclusion Check: Do I have all the facts? Are other conclusions possible?

Make your conclusion check. Then decide if you want to keep your conclusion, change it, or withhold judgment until you have more information. What conclusion would *you* reach about the new boy?

Using the Strategy

A. Suppose that movie stars Marla Marvelous and David Devine advertise Star Struck Shampoo with Formula X24. They recommend that you run right out and buy some. Make a conclusion chart. List the facts about Star Struck Shampoo. State your conclusion. Then evaluate your conclusion. Do you have all the facts you need? If not, tell what facts you want and how you might get them. Are other conclusions possible? Tell what they might be.

B. Make a conclusion chart about worldwide immunization. List the facts from the excerpt from Mrs. King's editorial. Write her conclusion or your own, if it is different from hers. Make a conclusion check. Do you have enough information to agree or disagree with her conclusion? Are other conclusions possible? Reevaluate your conclusion after you read the complete editorial.

Applying the Strategy

◆ How do you know if you should buy a new product?
◆ When might it be valuable to make a conclusion check?

Vaccination drives for kids will take place around world

By Coretta Scott King

In keeping with the theme, "Immunization: A Chance for Every Child," on Tuesday thousands of volunteers will celebrate World Health Day by taking part in massive vaccination drives on every continent.

These volunteers have mobilized a remarkable variety of resources -- everything from shopping bags to postage stamps and utility bills -- to promote the gospel of child immunization in developing nations. But much more remains to be done and they need our help.

As the newly-appointed good-will ambassador of UNICEF, Harry Belafonte has said his first priority will be to mobilize an international campaign to immunize millions of the world's children against polio, diphtheria, tuberculosis, measles, whooping cough and tetanus. These vaccine-preventable diseases now claim the lives of 3 1/2 million children every year and inflict permanent injury on millions more.

The most threatening of these diseases is measles, which accounts for more than half of all vaccine-preventable child deaths. Unlike the other diseases, however, only one dose of measles vaccine is needed, and a more heat-stable measles vaccine has been developed.

The other five vaccine-preventable diseases require multiple doses of refrigerated vaccine to be effective. Typically, 50 percent to 60 percent of the infants in a target area will be brought in for their first vaccinations; less than half will be brought back for the second and third. One survey of 81 immunization programs in developing nations found that the dropout rate between the first and third doses of diphtheria-pertussis-tetanus vaccine was almost 40 percent.

Despite the high mortality rate of children in developing nations from vaccine-preventable diseases, there is reason to hope that near-universal immunization can be achieved in the next five years.

A decade ago fewer than one in 20 children in developing nations received any vaccinations. Today, one out of four children are being vaccinated against measles and, according to UNICEF, two out of five of these children are being fully immunized against the other five diseases. These figures are expected to increase rapidly in the near future.

The supply of vaccines is now almost adequate to immunize every child on Earth at a cost of $5 per child. Even more encouraging, there has been a dramatic, worldwide improvement in political commitment to administer the vaccines even in nations torn by civil war such as El Salvador.

World support and cooperation eradicated small pox in 1977. The same can be done to other vaccine-preventable diseases if we rise to the challenge.

The people of the wealthier nations have a moral obligation to redouble their financial and volunteer support of UNICEF, the United Nations International Childrens Fund, as well as other agencies working for universal immunization.

We've got to recognize that the 3 1/2 million children who die of vaccine-preventable diseases every year are the brothers and sisters of our children in the same human family.

From *The Jersey Journal*, April 3, 1987.

In keeping with the theme, "Immunization: A Chance for Every Child," on Tuesday thousands of volunteers will celebrate World Health Day by taking part in massive vaccination drives on every continent.

These volunteers have mobilized a remarkable variety of re-sources—everything from shopping bags to postage stamps and utility bills—to promote the gospel of child immunization in developing nations. But much more remains to be done and they need our help.

As the newly-appointed goodwill ambassador of UNICEF, Harry Belafonte has said his first priority will be to mobilize an international campaign to immunize millions of the world's children against polio, diphtheria, tuberculosis, measles, whooping cough and tetanus. These vaccine-preventable diseases now claim the lives of 3 1/2 million children every year and inflict permanent injury on millions more.

The most threatening of these diseases is measles, which accounts for more than half of all vaccine-preventable child deaths. Unlike the other diseases, however, only one dose of measles vaccine is needed, and a more heat-stable measles vaccine has been developed.

The other five vaccine-preventable diseases require multiple doses of refrigerated vaccine to be effective. Typically, 50 percent to 60 percent of the infants in a target area will be brought in for their first vaccinations; less than half will be brought back for the second and third. One survey of 81 immunization programs in developing nations found that the dropout rate between the first and third doses of diphtheria-pertussis-tetanus vaccine was almost 40 percent.

Despite the high mortality rate of children in developing nations from vaccine-preventable diseases, there is reason to hope that near-universal immunization can be achieved in the next five years.

A decade ago fewer than one in 20 children in developing nations received any vaccinations. Today, one out of four children are being vaccinated against measles and, according to UNICEF, two out of five of these children are being fully immunized against the other five diseases. These figures are expected to increase rapidly in the near future.

The supply of vaccines is now almost adequate to immunize every child on Earth at a cost of $5 per child. Even more encouraging, there has been a dramatic, worldwide improvement in political commitment to administer the vaccines even in nations torn by civil war such as El Salvador.

World support and cooperation eradicated small pox in 1977. The same can be done to other vaccine-preventable diseases if we rise to the challenge.

The people of the wealthier nations have a moral obligation to redouble their financial and volunteer support of UNICEF, the United Nations International Childrens Fund, as well as other agencies working for universal immunization.

We've got to recognize that the 3 1/2 million children who die of vaccine-preventable diseases every year are the brothers and sisters of our children in the same human family.

Reader's Response

Why do you think some governments have not required vaccinations for every citizen?

Vaccination drives for kids will take place around world

Responding to Literature

1. Do you think Coretta Scott King's appeal will assist the vaccination drive? Why might her participation make a difference?

2. Create a slogan for the vaccination drive and put it on a poster. As the basis of your slogan, use one reason Mrs. King gave or use one reason of your own. Decorate your poster and display all the posters in your classroom.

3. If the UNICEF vaccination drive is successful in eliminating polio, diphtheria, tuberculosis, measles, whooping cough, and tetanus, what will be the consequences of its success? Explain.

Writing to Learn

Think and Conclude ♦ How could you persuade others to take action to improve the lives of children in your community? For example, would children benefit from having a playground or a library? What facts do you know? What conclusion can you draw from those facts? Make a conclusion chart like the one below for your topic.

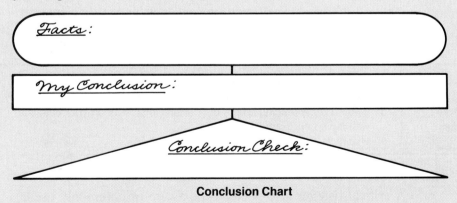

Facts:

My Conclusion:

Conclusion Check:

Conclusion Chart

Write ♦ Use the information from your chart in writing a paragraph. Persuade others to agree with your conclusion.

Tell about something you bought with great anticipation but were very disappointed with once you had the actual product. Why were you disappointed? What had you expected?

SPEAKING and LISTENING ◆
Critical Listening

Good listeners are critical listeners who evaluate the messages they hear. Every day, information comes to you from many different sources: television and radio, public speakers, newspapers and magazines, books, and films. To evaluate messages as a critical listener, you must be able to distinguish facts from opinions. A *fact* is information or knowledge that can be proved to be true. An *opinion* is someone's beliefs or thoughts about something. An opinion cannot be proved true or false; however, it can be supported with facts. Sometimes facts and opinions are used together in one message. To help you evaluate information that you hear, keep these guidelines in mind as you listen to a speaker.

Being a Critical Listener	**1.** Is the statement fact or opinion or both? **2.** Is the statement supported by facts or examples? **3.** Does the speaker give the sources for his or her facts? **4.** Are the sources reliable? Can they be checked or verified?

When you speak before an audience, remember that your listeners can also evaluate your messages with a critical ear. The guidelines below will help you present your appeal in a manner that is persuasive and effective.

Being an Effective Speaker	**1.** Present your information clearly and directly. **2.** Offer facts and examples to support your statements. **3.** If you are persuading others of your opinions, support your opinions with facts and examples. **4.** Use facts and examples that can be verified.

A critical listener also needs to be aware of commonly used propaganda techniques. Do you recognize any of the persuasive appeals presented on the next page?

Recognizing Propaganda Techniques

Propaganda is an organized effort to spread ideas about a person, product, or cause. It does not always contain accurate information. A critical listener is aware of and not misled by the propaganda techniques below.

Testimonial   Uses a famous personality to suggest that you should do, believe, or buy something because he or she claims to.

- **"All my fans love Fluffy Mush as much as I do."**

Transfer   Shows you something you have positive feelings about and tries to transfer those emotions to something else.

- **If you love the outdoors, you'll love Country Day air freshener.**

Bandwagon   Implies that you will be missing something if you don't "jump on the bandwagon" with everyone else.

- **Why be alone? Join your friends at Tiny's Turtle Races.**

Faulty Cause and Effect   Tries to convince you that one event causes another to happen. Usually there is no real connection.

- **Wearing Bells blue jeans changed my whole life!**

Either–or   Suggests that there are only two possible choices when, in fact, there are other alternatives.

- **If you don't vote for Proposition A, you are casting a vote for higher taxes.**

Mudslinging   Tells you why competitors or others are wrong, bad, or inferior without giving facts that you can verify.

- **Don't settle for second best. Buy your tapes at Scotty's.**

Loaded Words   Uses words that appeal to your emotions.

- **Tweedledee Action Park—land of excitement and adventure.**

Summary ✦ Critical listening requires that you distinguish facts from opinions in messages you receive from various sources. Effective speaking requires that you support your messages with facts. Recognizing common propaganda techniques can help you evaluate persuasive appeals.

Guided Practice

Tell whether each statement is a fact or an opinion.

1. Our candidate will make Beaville a better place to live.
2. Scientific tests show our Munchies are salt free.
3. Today's attendance at school was the highest all year.
4. I believe that our tennis rackets are far superior to others.
5. *Winkies* is the funniest movie you'll see this summer.

Practice

A. Write *fact* or *opinion* for each statement below.

6. Bran-O cereal has only 150 calories per ounce!
7. Anyone can tell you Dave's burgers are the best.
8. It's wrong to deny yourself the luxury of Heato socks.
9. "My voting record shows support for environmental concerns."
10. You need to get away from it all. Come to Fun City.

B. Write the name of the propaganda technique used in each message. Then write how you recognized each technique.

11. Wishing you were popular? Wear a Tiger jacket and watch new friends seek you out!
12. Yes, this is a business filled with false promises and hidden costs. But when you deal with Redd, Inc., you deal with people you can trust.
13. Who makes the guitar in Willy Flipp's masterful hands? We do, of course. He wouldn't use another. Should you?
14. Ride in comfort and style. Drive the new Zephyr sports car.
15. If you don't support a new athletic field, then you must be against sports.
16. Join up with the others who will be changing the course of history. Cast your ballot for me tomorrow.
17. Taste the freshness of spring when you drink Aqua bottled water.
18. Get rid of unsightly and disgusting lint on your clothes. End your embarrassment. Use Lintless Wonder Cleaner.

C. Working with a partner, find three statements of fact and three statements of opinion in a newspaper or magazine. Then try to verify the three facts either by checking them in a reference book or by observation.

D. 19–21. Write three brief paragraphs about one of the topics below. Use only facts in the first paragraph, use only opinions in the second paragraph, and mix facts and opinions in the third paragraph. Have a classmate identify the types of paragraphs as you read them aloud. Discuss with your partner which paragraph was the most convincing and why.

      sports   radio   travel   snow

E. Working with a small group of classmates, recall the different types of shows seen on television. Then discuss the questions.

- Which type of show contains more facts?
- Which type of show mixes facts and opinions?
- Do any shows use propaganda techniques? If so, which propaganda techniques are used?

F. Write a two-line advertisement for each item below. Use the propaganda technique indicated in parentheses.

    22. political candidate (bandwagon)
    23. skateboard (transfer)
    24. resort (loaded words)
    25. spinach (testimonial)

Apply • Think and Write

Dictionary of Knowledge • Read the facts that are given about Edward Jenner. Jenner, a British physician during the 1700s, was responsible for the first vaccination ever given. List three facts about his work that you could expect him to verify.

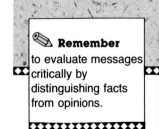

✎ **Remember**
to evaluate messages critically by distinguishing facts from opinions.

GETTING STARTED

Who is the most persuasive person you know? You needn't name him or her—but describe some methods the person uses to get you to change your mind on a subject.

WRITING ♦
Persuasive Strategies

A good persuasive strategy, a plan used to convince people of your opinion, begins with knowing your audience. Consider what is appropriate, appealing, and understandable to that audience and then build your argument, using one or more of these strategies.

Persuasive Strategies

Give a Precedent   Cite a precedent, a factual example from the past, that supports your view of the current situation. In general, positive precedents are more effective and appealing.

> **World support and cooperation eradicated smallpox in 1977.**

Respond to Objections   Anticipate opposing views and answer these objections in your statement.

> **Unlike the other diseases, however, only one dose of measles vaccine is needed, and a more heat-stable measles vaccine has been developed.**

Call for Fairness   Ask readers to see beyond their disagreements and consider what is fair and just.

> **We've got to recognize that the 3 1/2 million children who die of vaccine-preventable diseases every year are the brothers and sisters of our children in the same human family.**

Predict Results   Help readers to see the possible results that could occur from deciding or not deciding in your favor.

> **. . . there is reason to hope that near-universal immunization can be achieved in the next five years.**

Summary ♦ To convince readers of your opinion, use the persuasive strategies that are most appropriate to your audience and situation.

Guided Practice

Name the persuasive strategy used in each example below.

1. If people develop hobbies while young, they will have resources to help them relax and form new friendships later in life.
2. True, a hobby does require time; however, most people have some free time due to improved work conditions.
3. In the past, hobbies have led to extra income and even fame. Grandma Moses began painting at the age of seventy-six and went on to become one of America's most beloved artists.

Practice

A. Write *precedent, objection, fairness,* or *results* to identify the persuasive strategy used in each example below.

4. It is not fair to expect that your body can maintain good health without proper nutrition, exercise, and rest.
5. Students whose education included learning about health were able to make more intelligent decisions about what was good or not good for their physical well-being.
6. Exercises do not have to be boring or painful. Bicycling, swimming, and walking are enjoyable activities.
7. People in good health enjoy a more active life and are able to cope better with daily problems.

B. Write a two-line statement in support of each opinion below. Identify the persuasive strategy you use in each statement.

8. Hobbies can be beneficial to your health.
9. Regular checkups by a dentist are important.
10. Communities should use some of the money from taxes to provide health education to the public.

Apply ◆ Think and Write

Identifying Persuasive Strategies ◆ Find a letter to the editor in a newspaper or magazine about a topic that interests you. Copy the sentences that contain examples of the persuasive strategies studied in this lesson. After each sentence, write the type of persuasive strategy it illustrates.

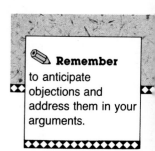

✎ **Remember**
to anticipate objections and address them in your arguments.

GETTING STARTED

Everybody knows that kids are great persuaders. How do you persuade someone? Share some of your secrets with classmates; maybe you will get some useful ideas, too.

WRITING ♦
Organizing an Argument

When you write to persuade readers of your opinion, it is useful to have a structure that will help you organize ideas and express yourself in the most effective way possible. If you are writing a single paragraph, you state your opinion in the topic sentence, give at least three reasons that support the opinion, and conclude with a sentence that restates the opinion. The chart below shows how to organize an argument, a presentation of several paragraphs intended to persuade.

Introduction	This **paragraph introduces** the main idea of your argument and catches the interest of the reader.
Body of Argument	These **paragraphs give reasons** that support your opinion, or main idea. They offer proof for the position you take.
Conclusion	This **paragraph restates** your main idea and urges readers to agree with you or to take action.

Notice that the structure of an argument is similar to that of a persuasive paragraph. The difference is that an argument develops reasons more fully in separate paragraphs.

It is usually a good idea to organize the reasons in your argument in order of importance, usually from least important to most important. However, the order can be reversed if you think that would be more effective.

Summary ♦ Organization is an important part of presenting an effective argument. Use paragraphs of introduction, support, and conclusion.

Guided Practice

Give a supporting reason or example for each main idea below.

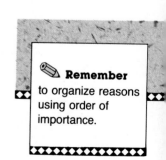

1. Pollution can cause harm to humans, animals, and plants.
2. Every plant and animal needs an appropriate place to live.
3. Dangerous insecticides should be banned from use.
4. Industrialized nations are the major polluters of the world.
5. Sensible laws should be passed to help end pollution.

Practice

A. Write a reason or an example that supports each main idea given.

   6. We must try to conserve our natural resources.
   7. Recycling saves our natural resources for further use and also reduces pollution.
   8. Everyday products, such as glass bottles and metal cans, should be recycled.
   9. Paper is another product that should be recycled.
   10. Plastic containers are particularly bad for the environment because they do not decompose.

B. Consider the topics below. Write a main idea that expresses an opinion about each topic.

   11. food for the future
   12. the control of diseases
   13. conserving wildlife
   14. communities
   15. tropical rain forests
   16. soil erosion
   17. ocean pollution
   18. conservation laws

C. Write at least three reasons or examples to support one of the main ideas you wrote for **Practice B**. List your reasons and examples in order of importance from least to most important.

Apply • Think and Write

Preparing an Argument • Practice taking the other side of an argument. Jot down notes for another equally convincing argument that opposes what you wrote for **Practice C**. Use the chart on page 216 as a guide.

> ✎ **Remember**
> to organize reasons using order of importance.

Focus on Opinions

Whenever you write, keep in mind the difference between a fact and an opinion. A **fact** is a statement that can be proved true by observation or research. An **opinion** states a personal belief or judgment. Even though you state an opinion forcefully and back it with strong evidence, you cannot prove its truth beyond any doubt.

In persuading an audience of something, you express your opinion. Coretta Scott King, for example, in her column on vaccination drives, wants to persuade readers that more still needs to be done in the fight against children's diseases in poor countries. That is her personal opinion, which she supports with several kinds of evidence.

- *A precedent, or previous example, showing that success is possible*: "World support and cooperation eradicated smallpox in 1977."
- *Statistics to show the need for more help:* "Typically, 50 percent to 60 percent of the infants in a target area will be brought in for their first vaccinations; less than half will be brought back for the second and third."
- *Facts showing how close we are to total success*: "The supply of vaccines is now almost adequate to immunize every child on Earth at a cost of $5 per child."

Whenever your writing involves persuasion, you will make it more convincing by using evidence to support your opinions. This evidence will usually be facts or examples. When readers are convinced of the truth of the evidence, they will tend to regard your opinions as accurate, well considered, and believable.

The Writer's Voice ♦ Does Coretta Scott King convince you that the wealthier nations have a moral obligation to promote immunization for all children worldwide? Why or why not?

Working Together

Support your opinions with facts or other evidence to be persuasive as your group works on activities **A** and **B**.

In Your Group
◆ Contribute your ideas. ◆ Agree or disagree in a pleasant way.
◆ Address people by name. ◆ Record the group's ideas.

A. Discuss the four numbered statements. Which ones support, and which ones do not support, the underlined opinion?

The ability to read and write is crucial in a democracy.

1. If a person cannot read, he or she cannot fully understand the issues in an election.
2. In the future, citizens will probably vote, perhaps by telephone, in elections conducted on television programs.
3. Thinking and writing are closely related; illiterates are unable to express or promote their own views effectively.
4. Friends can be found to read for you when necessary.

B. Suppose your group has been appointed to be an antipollution task force. You are concerned about air, water, and land pollution. Work together to write three statements that combine the group's opinions, followed by how-to advice. For example:

Litter is disgraceful. Posters can point out that even a single gum wrapper, properly disposed of, is a step toward improvement.

THESAURUS CORNER ◆ Word Choice

Verbs give sentences action. Your goal is to choose the right verbs to describe the actions. Use the Thesaurus and Thesaurus Index to replace each verb in dark type with a better synonym.

1. When my turn comes to speak, I will **solve** the false charges.
2. In my opinion, it is harder to **fashion** that box kite than it is to fly it.
3. I could just barely **see** the shape of Mr. Strell's argument through the haze of his words.

WRITING PROCESS
PERSUADING

Writing an Editorial

Newspapers contain many types of stories from news to sports. Most newspaper stories present facts, not opinions. Opinions appear in a special type of writing called the editorial. An editorial expresses the writer's or newspaper's position on an issue.

Reread Coretta Scott King's editorial. Mrs. King expressed her opinion that eradication of several childhood diseases is possible if wealthy nations would support worldwide vaccination programs. She supported her opinion with facts. She also used persuasive techniques. For example, she gave a precedent, the eradication of smallpox in 1977. She appealed to fairness by stating that wealthy nations have a moral obligation to help poorer nations.

> The people of the wealthier nations have a moral obligation to redouble their financial and volunteer support of UNICEF, the United Nations International Childrens Fund, as well as other agencies working for universal immunization.
>
> We've got to recognize that the 3 1/2 million children who die of vaccine-preventable diseases every year are the brothers and sisters of our children in the same human family.

Know Your Purpose and Audience

MY PURPOSE

In this lesson you will write an editorial on an issue you feel strongly about. Your purpose will be to persuade someone to agree with your opinion.

MY AUDIENCE

Your audience will be your classmates. Later you might read your editorial aloud or submit it to your school newspaper for publication.

1 Prewriting

Get ready to write your editorial by choosing a topic. Then use an idea-gathering strategy.

Choose Your Topic ♦ What current topics do you feel strongly about? What would you like to persuade others to do or believe? Choose a topic that you know thoroughly and that means something to you.

Think About It

Consider issues that relate especially to your school and your community. Is there a new school policy you disagree with? Is there a special program your community needs?

Talk About It

With your classmates brainstorm some possible topics for editorials. List the three topics you know most about. Of those, which do you feel most strongly about?

Topic Ideas

community issues
— library hours cut
— Drama Club funds cut
school issues
— weak pep club
— lack of locker space

Choose Your Strategy ◆ Here are two strategies to help you develop ideas. Read both and choose the one you wish to use.

PREWRITING IDEAS

CHOICE ONE

Looping

Looping is an idea-generating strategy. First write your topic. Then write anything that comes to mind about the topic for five minutes. Find the most important, or *center-of-gravity*, sentence. Copy it onto a second sheet.

Write nonstop on the second sheet for five minutes. Then copy the center-of-gravity sentence from that sheet onto a third sheet and make one more loop. Look for a main idea or thesis sentence. Underline it. It will become the focus of your editorial.

Model

There are about 30,000 taxpayers —Each will save a few cents by cutting the small drama budget —Other ways to save money — Cutting a popular program is an unnecessary, unwise way to lower taxes. Drama program important to many

CHOICE TWO

A Conclusion Chart

To build a persuasive argument, write your conclusion first. Above it, list supporting facts and arguments. Last, do a conclusion check.

Model

*Facts: Savings only 3 cents per taxpayer.
Precedents: Bowling was funded.
Appeal to fairness: Unfair to fund smaller group, not drama
Overcome objections: Other tax savings are possible
Explore consequences: teen mischief*

My Conclusion: Drama program funds should not be cut.

*Conclusion Check:
Have I listed the important facts? Will my arguments prevent other conclusions?*

2 Writing

Begin your editorial with a strong sentence to catch your readers' interest. Briefly state the problem and write your thesis, or conclusion sentence. Next, present supporting facts and persuasive arguments. In your concluding paragraph, suggest a solution. Try to make your readers want to get involved.

Sample First Draft ♦

To decrease taxes, the city wants to stop funding the drama program popular community programs should not be cut to lower taxes. Audiences beware!

The drama program is not only popular but also important. Many teenagers who might otherwise get into mischief participate.

The drama program's annule budget is $1,000. There are about 30,000 City Taxpayers. Thus, this funding cut would bring only a little per taxpayer! Other community programs, like the bowling league, have larger budgets. Only ten residents bowl more than thirty participated in drama. Hundreds attend performances.

The bowling league costs more, yet involves fewer people. To lower taxes, bowling should be cut, not drama. A better way to save some money might be to reduce city council mailings to taxpayers. However, we must keep the drama program!

3 Revising

Revise your draft editorial to clarify and strengthen it. This idea may help you.

As you read, review your purpose. Did you write an editorial to persuade your classmates on an issue you feel strongly about? Consider your audience. Will your classmates understand your arguments? Do you feel that most will be persuaded?

Focus: Have you supported your opinion with facts?

THEN   Share with a Partner

Read your editorial aloud to a partner and ask him or her to respond. Here are some guidelines you might use.

The Writer

Guidelines: Listen to your partner's responses. Does your partner raise objections you have not answered? Revise to answer new objections.

Sample questions:
- Have I persuaded you? Why or why not?
- What objections might readers raise to my opinion?
- **Focus question:** What other facts might support my opinion?

The Writer's Partner

Guidelines: Respond honestly, yet politely. Give specific suggestions.

Sample responses:
- I think some people would object to _____.
- You might add a fact about _____.

Revising Model ♦ Here is a sample draft of an editorial. Note the revising marks that show the writer's changes.

This sentence was moved for a stronger beginning.

A stronger supporting fact was added.

The writer caught this incorrect verb tense.

The writer's partner pointed out that this statement might anger bowlers who support the drama club.

Retain is a more precise verb than *keep*.

> To decrease taxes, the city wants to stop funding the drama program popular community programs should not be cut to lower taxes. ~~Audiences beware!~~

The drama program is not only popular but also important. Many teenagers who might otherwise get into mischief participate.

The drama program's annule budget is $1,000. There are about 30,000 City Taxpayers. Thus, this funding cut would bring only a little per taxpayer! *a savings of three cents* Other community programs, like the bowling league, have larger budgets. Only ten residents bowl more than thirty ~~participated~~ *participate* in drama. Hundreds attend performances.

The bowling league ~~costs~~ more, yet involves fewer people. ~~To lower taxes, bowling should be cut, not drama.~~ *The answer, however, is not to cut bowling. Bowling is important, too.* A better way to save some money might be to reduce ~~city~~ council mailings to taxpayers. However, we must ~~keep~~ *retain* the drama program!

Read the above editorial the way the writer has decided it *should* be. Then revise your own editorial.

Grammar Check ♦ To avoid confusing your readers, use consistent verb tenses.

Word Choice ♦ Some verbs like *keep* are imprecise and overused. A thesaurus is a good source of synonyms.

4 Proofreading

Now is the time to proofread for surface errors. An editorial that is correctly written is more persuasive.

Proofreading Model ♦ Here is the draft editorial about the community drama program. Proofreading changes appear in red.

<table>
<tr><th colspan="2">Proofreading Marks</th></tr>
<tr><td>capital letter</td><td>=</td></tr>
<tr><td>small letter</td><td>/</td></tr>
<tr><td>add comma</td><td>⋀</td></tr>
<tr><td>add period</td><td>⊙</td></tr>
<tr><td>indent paragraph</td><td>¶</td></tr>
<tr><td>check spelling</td><td>⬭</td></tr>
</table>

Proofreading Checklist

☐ Did I spell words correctly?

☐ Did I indent paragraphs?

☐ Did I use correct capitalization?

☐ Did I use correct punctuation?

☐ Did I type neatly or use my best handwriting?

To decrease taxes, the city wants to stop funding the drama program. popular community programs should not be cut to lower taxes. Audiences beware!

The drama program is not only popular but also important. Many teenagers who might otherwise get into mischief participate.

The drama program's *annual* annule budget is $1,000. There are about 30,000 City Taxpayers. Thus, this funding cut would bring only a little *a savings of three cents* per taxpayer! Other community programs, like the bowling league, have larger budgets. Only ten residents bowl, more than thirty participated *participate* in drama. Hundreds attend performances.

The bowling league costs more, yet involves fewer people. *The answer, however, is not to cut bowling* To lower taxes, bowling should be cut, not drama. *Bowling is important, too.* A better way to save some money might be to reduce city council mailings to taxpayers. However, we must keep *retain* the drama program!

PROOFREADING IDEA

Trading with a Partner

Sometimes it is easier to find someone else's mistakes. Find a partner and check each other's editorials. Put a pencil check in the margin where you find an error.

After proofreading, add a title and make a neat copy of your editorial.

5 Publishing

Try one of these ideas for sharing your editorial with others.

Keep the Drama Program

Audiences beware! To decrease taxes, the city wants to stop funding the drama program. Popular community programs should not be cut to lower taxes.

The drama program is not only popular but also important. Many teenagers who might otherwise get into mischief participate.

The drama program's annual budget is $1,000. There are about 30,000 city taxpayers. Thus, this funding cut would bring a savings of only three cents per taxpayer!

Other community programs, like the bowling league, have larger budgets. Only ten residents bowl. More than thirty participate in drama. Hundreds attend performances.

The bowling league costs more, yet involves fewer people. The answer, however, is not to cut bowling to lower taxes. Bowling is important, too. A better way to save some money might be to reduce city council mailings to taxpayers. However, we must retain the drama program!

PUBLISHING IDEAS

Share Aloud	Share in Writing
Read your editorial aloud to a small group. Ask the group to listen for propaganda techniques and persuasive strategies. Ask for comments about whether and why your editorial was persuasive.	Submit your editorial to the school newspaper for publication. If your school paper does not have a ''Letters to the Editor'' section, suggest that one be created so readers can respond to editorials.

CURRICULUM
·CONNECTION·

Writing Across the Curriculum   Health

Doctors and other health professionals recognize the influence of environment on physical and mental health. A similar awareness can help you safeguard and foster your own good health.

Writing to Learn

Think and Analyze ♦ Think about your community. What do you conclude is one improvement in the environment that would make it a more healthful place to live? At the bottom of your paper, write your conclusion. Then analyze your conclusion. Above your conclusion write facts, reasons, or examples that support it.

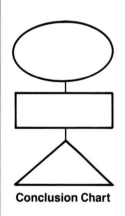

Conclusion Chart

Write ♦ Review your notes. Then write a persuasive argument that would lead a reader to draw the same conclusion you drew.

Writing in Your Journal

In the Writer's Warm-up you wrote about an ideal environment. Throughout this unit, you learned about a worldwide variety of environments. In your journal write what you believe is our planet's single most urgent environmental problem. Explain why you made this choice.

BOOKS TO ENJOY

Read More About It

Underground *by David Macaulay*
The ground beneath a city's streets is the subject of this superbly illustrated text. The detailed drawings of the intricate network of underground systems help us appreciate the complexity of urban environments.

Onion John *by Joseph Krumgold*
Onion John's environment, a hut of piled-up stones, isn't at all like the other suburban houses in town. Why then is Andy Rusch so interested in this old man and his strange surroundings? What should Andy do when his father refuses to let him go there? The answer for Andy is the key to growing up.

Newbery Award

Book Report Idea Book Sketch

Have you ever imagined that you were a character in a favorite book? A book sketch lets you act out this character's role. A sketch is a very brief play. A book sketch presents one important scene from a book. At least two of the main characters in the book should appear in the scene.

Choose Your Role ♦ After you choose the best scene to present, prepare and practice the dialogue with a classmate. After you present your sketch to the class, identify the title and author of the book.

UNIT REVIEW

Unit 4

Verbs   *pages 180–197*

A. Write the four principal parts of each verb.

1. shrug
2. try
3. wink
4. dance
5. protect
6. suppose
7. drip
8. employ

B. Write each verb and label its tense: *present, past, future, present perfect, past perfect,* or *future perfect.*

9. listen
10. displayed
11. had hated
12. will have used
13. will see
14. has liked
15. resulted
16. carves

C. Write the verb form in parentheses that correctly completes each sentence.

17. The voters (chosen, choose) the next President of the United States this November day.
18. The candidates have (flown, flew) back to their homes.
19. They (began, begun) their campaigns a year ago.
20. They (given, gave) their last speeches this morning.

D. Write whether each verb is progressive or emphatic. Then label its tense.

21. did say
22. will be calling
23. do think
24. does cost
25. were driving
26. have been using

E. Write the tense of each underlined verb. If there is a needless shift in tense in a sentence, change one verb.

27. The bus driver always <u>stopped</u> at the stop sign and then <u>continues</u>.
28. Most drivers <u>obey</u> the traffic signs they <u>see</u>.
29. Some cars now <u>have</u> air bags that <u>will protect</u> occupants in case of an accident.
30. Yesterday I <u>saw</u> a person who <u>needs</u> such protection.

F. Write the verb in each sentence. Label it *active* or *passive*.

31. This magazine brings you news of the world.

32. It is written by a staff of professionals.

33. I received the first issue in the mail last month.

34. A magazine of this quality was needed years ago.

G. Write the correct verb form in parentheses.

35. The key to our nation's future (lays, lies) in education.

36. New leaders will (rise, raise) from among today's youth.

37. Plans for the future have been (set, sit) in motion.

38. The foundation has already been (lain, laid).

Persuasive Strategies   *pages 214–215*

H. Write a sentence about each situation, explaining how you would correct the error in strategy.

39. Francis said to Lynn, "You don't believe that my position on a school dress code is both fair and right. I won't argue with you anymore. I hope your opposition plan backfires!"

40. Tracy uses a precedent to support her view. Her readers aren't sure, however, what the long-range effects of their decisions will be. Tracy ignores their concerns.

41. "The last time our class went on a trip, it was a disaster. But I'm certain there will be no problems on any future class trip," said the class president to the class.

42. Dwight tells his audience that his opponents' proposals can't possibly work. "Let's just forget about what they say," he adds. "Listen instead to what I am telling you."

Fact and Opinion   *pages 218–219*

I. Write *fact* or *opinion* for each statement.

43. Oxygen is a difficult word to spell.

44. Oxygen is a colorless, odorless, and tasteless gas.

45. Liquid oxygen is used in rocket fuel systems.

46. The two scientists who first isolated oxygen must have been brilliant.

47. Oxygen makes up about 90 percent of water.

CUMULATIVE REVIEW

UNIT 1: Sentences *pages 4–21*

A. Write and label each subject and verb.

1. A menu in computer language refers to programs or functions.
2. The workstation of the computer is the terminal.
3. The internal storage of information is called memory.
4. Information is stored on a floppy or hard disk.

B. Write *simple* or *compound* for each sentence.

5. Ann doesn't always use a computer, but she can operate one.
6. A word processor saves a writer time and effort.
7. Dan and Alicia looked high and low for their notes.
8. The notes were stored on a disk, or they were in a notebook.

UNIT 2: Nouns *pages 58–69*

C. Write each noun and label it *common* or *proper*.

9. The St. Lawrence and Great Lakes Waterway is the largest system of inland navigation in North America.
10. This waterway extends from the Atlantic Ocean to Duluth.
11. Ships can travel to ports in America and Canada.
12. The area from Montreal to Lake Ontario isn't a bottleneck.

D. Write the singular and plural possessive form of each noun.

13. woman   15. society   17. tooth
14. hero   16. witness   18. grandchild

E. Write the appositive in each sentence.

19. An almanac, a book published yearly, contains much data.
20. This almanac, a blend of fact and fun, is a reference book.
21. The almanac *Omni Future* is a space-age handbook.
22. That buyer's guide, a free publication, is helpful.

Unit 3: Verbs   *pages 124–135*

F. Write and label each direct object and indirect object.

23. Tell the class the topic of your report.
24. The teacher gave us a list of subjects.
25. Did you interview the witnesses to the incident?
26. They can give you valuable information.

G. Write the sentences. Underline each linking verb and label each predicate nominative and predicate adjective.

27. Flags are often oblong or square in shape.
28. Flag Day is not a legal holiday in the United States.
29. In early times a black flag became a symbol for piracy.
30. Its markings appeared especially sinister.

Unit 4: Verbs   *pages 180–197*

H. Write each verb and label its tense: *present, past, future, present perfect, past perfect,* or *future perfect.*

31. stayed   33. will have raced   35. have named
32. will see   34. approach   36. had timed

I. Write the correct form of the verb in parentheses.

37. The bear cub has not (ate, eaten) a thing all day.
38. The cub has (drank, drunk) some water from a nearby stream.
39. It (hidden, hid) in the brush until dark.
40. Some campers (went, gone) to another campsite.

J. Write whether each verb is progressive or emphatic. Then label its tense.

41. has been staying   43. does know   45. will be joining
42. was smiling   44. did object   46. do want

K. Write the correct form of the verb in parentheses.

47. (Lie, Lay) down your pen and listen.
48. Steam (rises, raises) from the radiator.
49. We have (sit, set) the desired temperature on the thermostat.

Verb Homophones

Homophones are words that sound alike. Write each pair of homophones. (Hint: The first word fits the definition; the second is a verb.)

1. a color: _ _ _ and _ _ _ _
2. not left: _ _ _ _ _ and _ _ _ _ _
3. an iron alloy: _ _ _ _ _ and _ _ _ _ _
4. not old: _ _ _ and _ _ _ _
5. by means of: _ _ _ _ _ _ _ and _ _ _ _ _
6. part of a chimney: _ _ _ _ and _ _ _ _
7. a coloring agent: _ _ _ and _ _ _
8. a number: _ _ _ _ _ and _ _ _
9. a flower necklace: _ _ _ and _ _ _
10. a metal: _ _ _ _ and _ _ _
11. not a whisper: _ _ _ _ _ and _ _ _ _ _ _ _
12. a wild pig: _ _ _ _ and _ _ _ _
13. a dog pest: _ _ _ _ and _ _ _ _
14. wonderful or large: _ _ _ _ _ and _ _ _ _ _
15. not there: _ _ _ _ and _ _ _ _
16. an onion relative: _ _ _ _ and _ _ _ _
17. large bodies of water: _ _ _ _ and _ _ _ _ _
18. a cut of meat: _ _ _ _ _ and _ _ _ _ _

Linked Verbs

Make verb chains with a partner or in a group. The first person names a verb. The second person must then say a verb that begins with the last letter of the first verb, and so on. The verbs must all be in the same tense as the first verb. A player who cannot name a verb is out.

EXAMPLE: grew, wrote, entertained, drank...

Unit 4 Extra Practice

1 Principal Parts of Verbs

p. 180

A. Each word below is either the past participle or the present participle of a regular verb. Write the word. Then write the present form next to it.

EXAMPLE: walking
ANSWER: walking, walk

1. sailed
2. crossing
3. spanning
4. covered
5. glided
6. rallying
7. ferrying
8. dried
9. clipping
10. mailed
11. reaching
12. creating
13. gripped
14. lapped
15. using

B. Write the four principal parts of each regular verb.

16. finish
17. change
18. probe
19. view
20. seem
21. turn
22. mix
23. knock
24. visit
25. step
26. design
27. open
28. push
29. lift
30. carry

C. Write the present or past participle of each verb.

31. She was (paint) her boat at the dock yesterday.
32. Lightning was (flicker) in the distance.
33. The stormy weather is (delay) their departure.
34. Have they (transport) all the supplies that we will need for the camping trip?
35. The campers were (devour) the small meal.
36. The little girl had (nibble) the bread.
37. The other children were (gulp) their sandwiches.
38. Earlier they had (gorge) themselves with cake.
39. They had (snack) while watching TV.
40. The hungry dogs were (gobble) their dinners.
41. Linda has (challenge) Charlene to a game of tick-tack-toe.

2 Tenses of Verbs

p. 182

A. Write the tense of each verb below.

1. will embark
2. floats
3. shall have docked
4. flowed
5. have changed
6. has navigated
7. had steered
8. announced
9. will have cleared
10. had departed

B. Write each underlined verb and its tense.

11. People <u>have traveled</u> by water for thousands of years. **12.** Before America's early settlers <u>had learned</u> to build roads, they <u>preferred</u> to go places by boat. **13.** That is why you <u>will find</u> most of America's older cities near water. **14.** In general, people <u>have founded</u> a city without access to water only after the advent of railroad service. **15.** If you <u>look</u> at pictures of early rivercraft, you <u>will see</u> that most had no sails. **16.** They <u>depended</u> on river currents for locomotion. **17.** Fortunately many of America's rivers <u>are</u> navigable. **18.** These rivers <u>have served</u> as great water highways for thousands of simple boats and their owners.

C. Write each sentence, changing the underlined verb to the tense indicated in parentheses.

EXAMPLE: He <u>sails</u> his boat on weekends. (future)
ANSWER: He will sail his boat on weekends.

19. People <u>move</u> goods by boat. (present perfect)
20. People <u>use</u> gondolas on the Merrimack. (past)
21. Many traders <u>depend</u> on boats. (present perfect)
22. The traders <u>ship</u> their wares by canoe. (past)
23. The boat <u>suits</u> only some rivers. (future)
24. Flat-bottomed boats <u>prevail</u>. (past perfect)
25. They <u>load</u> cotton onto flatboats. (present)
26. These boats <u>contain</u> large cargoes. (future)
27. "Cotton boxes" <u>clock</u> ten miles a day. (past)
28. Oars <u>propel</u> the boat downstream. (past perfect)
29. Long poles then <u>push</u> it upstream. (past)
30. Larger boats <u>float</u> on inland rivers. (future)

3 Irregular Verbs

A. Write the correct form of the verb in parentheses.

1. We have (began, begun) to move at last.
2. The canalboat (blew, blown) its whistle when we moved away from the pier.
3. We soon (drew, drawn) up our blankets.
4. We also (drank, drunk) hot tea to keep warm.
5. Everyone had (ate, eaten) breakfast already.
6. Several seagulls (flew, flown) overhead.
7. We had (went, gone) through two locks by noon.
8. How much has this trip (cost, costed) us?
9. They (buyed, bought) their tickets on board.
10. Have you (rode, ridden) on a canalboat before?
11. We have (saw, seen) the countryside this way.
12. I've (found, finded) I enjoy the slower pace.
13. We have (spoke, spoken) with several passengers.
14. They (rang, rung) a bell to announce meals.
15. How many photographs have you (took, taken)?
16. We (ran, run) twenty minutes ahead of schedule.

B. Write the past or past participle of the underlined verb to complete the answer to each question.

EXAMPLE: Have they <u>shut</u> the gates yet?
ANSWER: Yes, they shut them half an hour ago.

17. Did you <u>bring</u> a heavy sweater? No, I ____ only a windbreaker.
18. Have we <u>made</u> good time this morning? Yes, we have ____ excellent time.
19. Where did you <u>stand</u> to take that photograph? I ____ at the bow of the boat.
20. Did they <u>tell</u> you to bring warm clothing? Yes, they ____ me it would get chilly.
21. Have you ever <u>sung</u> the ballad about the Erie Canal? Yes, we ____ it just the other day.
22. Did you <u>sleep</u> on the boat last night? Yes, we ____ right on board.
23. What did you <u>say</u> you liked best about the trip? I ____ I liked the quiet and relaxing pace best.

4 Progressive and Emphatic Forms   *p. 190*

A. Write the indicated progressive form of each verb.

1. they (pack—present progressive)
2. you (stop—future progressive)
3. it (go—present perfect progressive)
4. she (drive—future perfect progressive)
5. you (begin—past progressive)
6. it (fall—past perfect progressive)
7. you (come—future progressive)
8. we (leave—present progressive)
9. he (carry—past perfect progressive)
10. we (blow—past progressive)

B. Write the sentences, changing each underlined verb to the progressive form of the tense used.

11. We <u>will move</u> to New Orleans next week. **12.** We <u>have planned</u> the move for months. **13.** Mom and Dad <u>had considered</u> several cities. **14.** Secretly I <u>hoped</u> they'd choose New Orleans. **15.** I <u>look</u> forward to living near the Mississippi River. **16.** Our class <u>has studied</u> the river this term. **17.** I <u>will have read</u> about its history for two months by the time we move. **18.** The Mississippi River delta constantly <u>changes</u> shape. **19.** The Mississippi River <u>has deposited</u> silt at its mouth for centuries. **20.** By the year 2000, people probably <u>will build</u> homes on the land that is now under water. **21.** In other parts of the delta, such as New Orleans, people <u>will fight</u> hard the river's efforts to reclaim the land. **22.** Some of New Orleans <u>occupies</u> land that is actually below sea level. **23.** People <u>have used</u> levees to contain the river for years. **24.** However, storms <u>will coax</u> the river over the tops of the levees again and again. **25.** I <u>have wondered</u> how the city has managed to thrive against such odds.

C. Rewrite each sentence, changing the verb to the emphatic form of the tense used.

26. I wonder about my family's life in New Orleans.
27. My classmates asked me about the restaurants.
28. I look forward to many visits from my friends.
29. They expect letters from me often.
30. We hope for new friends also.

5 Using Tenses Correctly

p. 192

A. Write the story. Change one verb in each sentence to avoid a needless shift in tense. Tell the story in the past tense. Underline the name in italics.

1. At first, steamboats traveled only on eastern rivers, but Nicholas and Lydia Roosevelt believe they were useful for the Ohio and Mississippi, too. **2.** The Roosevelts make a steamboat named the *New Orleans*, which proved their point. **3.** Lydia is expecting a baby when the *New Orleans* began its voyage in 1811, but she took the trip anyway. **4.** The boat stopped at Louisville, where Lydia has her baby. **5.** The trip from Pittsburgh to Louisville was smooth, but later many difficulties arise. **6.** Low water over the dangerous falls of the Ohio River stops them for a month. **7.** Then at Yellow Banks, Kentucky, the river is made wild by earthquakes, and tremors continued for weeks. **8.** The river was so changed that the pilot often gets lost. **9.** At last the Roosevelts reach Natchez, and the last part of the journey to New Orleans was uneventful. **10.** Their journey proves the value of steamboats on the Ohio and Mississippi rivers.

B. Write the passage below, correcting needless shifts in tense. Use the past as the base tense. One sentence is correct. Underline the title in italics.

11. In *Life on the Mississippi*, Mark Twain remarked, "I think a pilot's memory is about the most wonderful thing in the world." **12.** Pilots on the Mississippi River continued to sharpen their memories from the first day they take to the river. **13.** They lay up vast stores of knowledge with every run they made. **14.** Only after years of such study does a pilot really know the river. **15.** Eventually he knew where every passable channel is and where every sandbar lies. **16.** Yet a pilot also has to update his information constantly, for the river was forever changing. **17.** A severe drought often makes passable channels impassable. **18.** Pilots are paid handsomely for their great knowledge of the river. **19.** They were paid more than many lawyers make. **20.** Although they were treated like kings, they earn this royal treatment. **21.** However, their royal treatment does not last forever. **22.** Fierce competition from the railroads takes away shipping business from the riverboats. **23.** The era of the riverboat pilot comes to an end.

6 Active and Passive Voice

p. 194

A. Write the complete verb in each sentence. Label it *active* or *passive*.

1. The power of wind and current for transportation was replaced slowly by steam.
2. John Fitch adapted steam engines to boats.
3. He launched his first steamboat in 1787.
4. It was propelled by six paddles on each side.
5. A patent was obtained for his steamboat in 1791.
6. However, he won little support for his projects.
7. People mostly ignored his four steamboats.
8. John Fitch's name is known to few people today.
9. History has recorded Fitch as a tragic figure.

B. Write the passage below, changing each underlined verb from the passive voice to the active voice. Underline words in italics.

10. Work on steamboats was continued by Robert Fulton and Robert Livingston. 11. A partnership was formed by the two men. 12. Business sense, political influence, and money were supplied by Livingston. 13. Inventiveness and technical know-how were contributed by Fulton.

14. Fulton's boat was nicknamed *Fulton's Folly* by a scornful public. 15. Public awareness of the steamboat's potential was raised by Livingston through his political connections. 16. Scorn was changed to applause by the boat's successful trip from New York to Albany in 1807. 17. It was later given the more dignified name of the *Clermont* by Fulton. 18. The opening of the steamboat era has long been associated by people with Fulton. 19. Supportive backers are often needed by inventors for them to succeed.

C. Write the sentences, changing each verb from the passive to the active voice.

20. Ocean cargo was carried by clipper ships.
21. Clippers were partly replaced by the railroads.
22. The country was crossed more easily by trains.
23. The first oceangoing steamship was launched by John Stevens in 1809.
24. Clippers were displaced by steamers in the 1860s.

7 Troublesome Verb Pairs

p. 196

A. Write the correct form of the verb in parentheses.

1. Don't (sit, set) so near the edge of the boat.
2. It was all right when we (set, sat) here before.
3. (Sit, Set) your glasses in a safe place.
4. My best friend was (sitting, setting) beside me.
5. The pilot (set, sat) money aside for retirement.
6. He (raised, rose) several questions about the plan.
7. Steamboats still (raise, rise) sails sometimes.
8. The crew all (raised, rose) before dawn.
9. The river had (raised, risen) steadily for days.
10. Steamboats (raised, rose) the curtain on a new chapter in America's history.

B. Write the correct form of the verb in parentheses.

11. If you (lie, lay) still, you can hear the river.
12. Whose things are (laying, lying) on deck?
13. Our dog (laid, lay) down beside us.
14. She (lay, laid) out her things before packing.
15. He (lies, lays) awake for hours before a trip.
16. Please (lie, lay) the damp sails out on the grass.
17. We (lay, laid) the line in a neat coil on deck.
18. I can sleep only when I am (lying, laying) down.
19. She had just (lain, laid) the baby in its crib.
20. This rusty tool has (laid, lain) here awhile.

C. Write each sentence, completing it with the correct form of *lie* or *lay*.

21. We wanted to _____ out in the sun.
22. Did you _____ your umbrella on the shelf?
23. He fell asleep the minute he _____ down.
24. I have _____ the matter to rest.
25. She had _____ there for hours watching the stars.
26. He will _____ down awhile.
27. The fox _____ in the tall grass.
28. Your coat is _____ there.
29. It has _____ there a week.

Through water I drank
the deer stepped slow
without chinking a stone
slid into shadow.

—May Swenson

UNIT FIVE

USING LANGUAGE
TO

CREATE

=== **PART ONE** ===

Unit Theme *Famous American Poets*

Language Awareness Pronouns

=== **PART TWO** ===

Literature *Poetry*

A Reason for Writing Creating

WRITER'S WARM-UP ◆ Why do you think some people become poets? How have you reacted to the poetry experiences you have had? Perhaps you have read poetry in textbooks. Maybe you have chosen a book of poetry to read on your own. If you have ever tried to write a poem, you know that it requires skill. Write in your journal about what poetry means to you. Try to recall some poems you learned.

Writing
IN YOUR JOURNAL

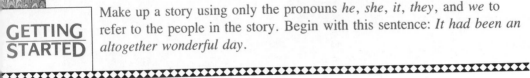

GETTING STARTED

Make up a story using only the pronouns *he*, *she*, *it*, *they*, and *we* to refer to the people in the story. Begin with this sentence: *It had been an altogether wonderful day.*

1 Writing with Pronouns

Pronouns are words that take the place of nouns. Use pronouns to avoid repeating nouns unnecessarily.

- Frank read about Emily Dickinson and ~~Emily Dickinsons's~~ ^{her} poetry.

- ~~Frank read the book~~ for ~~Frank's~~ report.
  ^{He}   ^{it}   ^{his}

The pronouns replacing nouns in the examples above are called **personal pronouns.** The chart below lists the personal pronouns.

	Singular	Plural
First Person (the speaker)	I, me my, mine	we, us our, ours
Second Person (person spoken to)	you your, yours	you your, yours
Third Person (person or thing spoken about)	she, her, hers he, him, his, it, its	they, them their, theirs

When you write, use pronouns to avoid using the same nouns again.

> **Summary** ♦ A **pronoun** takes the place of a noun or nouns. Use pronouns in your writing to avoid unnecessary repetition of nouns.

Guided Practice

Name each pronoun and tell its person and number.

1. Frank said he has just read a biography of the poet Emily Dickinson.

2. I read in my encyclopedia that Dickinson wrote over 1,700 poems.

3. Only seven of them were published while the poet lived.

Practice

A. Write each personal pronoun. Then write its person and number.

4. Jay said he used comparisons to express happiness in a poem.
5. Tiffany and Bella, you will select poems about the seasons.
6. This ballad was written by us, Alfredo and Rita Ortega.
7. The Wongs wrote this poem, and they added a refrain.
8. When Nina reads poetry, her foot taps to the rhythm.
9. Clarita, are the three story poems yours?
10. "Yes, the poems are mine," said Clarita.
11. "No, the poems are ours!" exclaimed Tommy and Mickey.
12. The students agreed that their favorite poems are limericks.
13. Ichino illustrated the poem that Yoko had sent him.

B. Choose from these pronouns to complete the paragraph about Carl Sandburg. Write the paragraph.

him   they   his   their   he

14. Carl Sandburg drew upon ＿＿ experiences as a laborer and journalist. **15.** ＿＿ was born in Illinois in 1878. **16.** Walt Whitman, another major American poet, influenced ＿＿ . **17.** Like Whitman, Sandburg wrote poems about ordinary people and ＿＿ lives. **18.** Later ＿＿ were published in volumes such as *The People, Yes*.

C. Rewrite the paragraph. Use pronouns in place of repetitive nouns.

19. Poetry can best be appreciated when poetry is read aloud. **20.** A poem can express strong feelings, or a poem can tell a story. **21.** Children are natural poets because children can express ideas easily in verse form. **22.** Although Sandburg and Sandburg's great ideal, Whitman, did not use rhyme, many poets do. **23.** Most poets do use strong rhythm in poets' poems.

Apply ◆ Think and Write

From Your Writing ◆ Read what you wrote for the Writer's Warm-up. Working with a partner, replace repetitive nouns with pronouns.

> ✎ **Remember**
> that pronouns can make your writing flow more smoothly.

GETTING STARTED

Play "Guess the Subject." Think of a sentence and replace the subject with a pronoun. Then say the sentence aloud and have a classmate try to guess the original subject. Example: *It (my pencil) is very dull.*

2 Pronouns and Antecedents

The word or words to which a pronoun refers is called its antecedent. Notice that an antecedent can come before or after a pronoun or even in a preceding sentence.

Langston Hughes often portrayed urban black life in his poetry.
After reading it, I memorized "*April Rain Song*."
Hughes's *operas* and *prose essays* are not as well-known. Have you read them?

Use a pronoun that agrees with its antecedent in number: a singular pronoun to refer to a singular antecedent, a plural pronoun to refer to a plural antecedent.

Singular: The *writer* was born in 1902, and he died in 1967.
Plural: Other poets read the *poems* and praised them highly.

Use a pronoun that agrees with its antecedent in gender.

Masculine: This collection by *Hughes* is his first book of poems.
Feminine: *Harriet Tubman* and her courage inspired Hughes.
Neuter: *Harlem* in the 1920s played host to its black writers.

Summary ♦ An **antecedent** is the word or words to which a pronoun refers. A pronoun agrees with its antecedent in number and gender. Use pronouns and antecedents to make clear references when you speak and write.

Guided Practice

Name each personal pronoun and its antecedent.

1. Nature is described in all its glory in the poem "In Time of Silver Rain."
2. Hughes talks about the renewal qualities of spring in his poem.
3. Carol and Wanda said that they enjoyed the poem.

Practice

A. Write the pronouns and their antecedents.

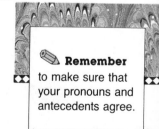

4. Gwendolyn Brooks is best known for her poetry.
5. Ann read the poems "Friend" and "The Explorer" and liked them.
6. Does the poet create images in your mind, Ann?
7. Brooks won a Pulitzer Prize. She was the first black woman to receive the award.
8. Walt Whitman said, "I understand the large hearts of heroes."
9. Whitman wrote that line in a poem of his.
10. Readers say the message applies to the world they know.
11. Whitman wrote *Leaves of Grass* and published it in 1855.
12. At that time the poet was not recognized for his genius.
13. Freedom and dignity are celebrated. They are powerful themes.

B. Write the sentences, completing them with pronouns that agree with the underlined antecedents.

14. The boys said _____ chose the poem "Mother to Son."
15. Nancy said _____ remembered the images of the crystal stair.
16. Does Jack prefer a poem that appeals to _____ emotions?
17. Paula was moved to write _____ own poem.
18. Sandburg wrote a poem about a father and _____ son.

C. Write a sentence using each pair of words. Be sure that the pronoun and its antecedent agree.

EXAMPLE: students, them
ANSWER: The students listened as the actor read them a poem.

19. poets, they
20. students, their
21. nature, it
22. Langston Hughes, he

23. people, their
24. poem, its
25. Gwendolyn Brooks, her
26. choice, it

Apply • Think and Write

Dictionary of Knowledge • Read about Langston Hughes in the Dictionary of Knowledge. Write several sentences about the poet or his poetry. Use pronouns and their antecedents in your sentences.

> ✎ **Remember**
> to make sure that your pronouns and antecedents agree.

Make up pairs of "have" or "have not" sentences like the following.

She has green eyes. Her eyes sparkle.

You have no shoes. Your feet are bare.

3 Possessive Pronouns

Like nouns, pronouns can show ownership, or possession. Pronouns that show possession are called possessive pronouns.

■ **Have you read Eric's poem? Have you read his poem?**

	Singular	**Plural**
First Person	my, mine	our, ours
Second Person	your, yours	your, yours
Third Person	his, her, hers, its	their, theirs

Some possessive pronouns are used like adjectives to modify, or describe, nouns. They are *my, your, his, her, its, our,* and *their*. Other possessive pronouns are used alone to replace nouns. They are *mine, yours, his, hers, ours,* and *theirs*.

Used to Modify Nouns

His rhymes are clever.

Used Alone

The first copy is his.

Possessive pronouns are often confused with contractions. A **contraction** is a shortened form of two words. An apostrophe replaces a letter or letters. A possessive pronoun has no apostrophe.

Possessive Pronouns	**Contractions**
its	it's (it is, it has)
your	you're (you are)
their	they're (they are)
theirs	there's (there is, there has)
I am happy about its appeal.	It's very appealing.
Your contrasts are effective.	You're the editor now.
It is their literary magazine.	They're pleased with it.
This one is theirs.	There's the new sponsor.

Summary ◆ A possessive pronoun shows ownership. Do not confuse possessive pronouns with contractions in your writing.

Guided Practice

Name each possessive pronoun.

1. The slave Phillis Wheatley had her poems published in 1773.
2. They were widely admired for their style and grace.
3. The finest verse tribute to General George Washington is hers.

Practice

A. Write each possessive pronoun. Then write whether it is used alone or with a noun.

4. Is this your poem?
5. Its details are precise.
6. Have you read his?
7. I revised mine earlier.
8. These are their drafts.
9. Listen carefully to hers.
10. Read its first line again.
11. Yours could be more vivid.
12. The challenge is ours.
13. Her repetition is effective.

B. Write possessive pronouns to replace the underlined words.

14. ''The clown of the typewriter'' is one of <u>e.e. cummings's</u> names.
15. <u>Your and my</u> library has a copy of his *Tulips and Chimneys*.
16. His verse is known for <u>the verse's</u> use of coined words.
17. Was the idea of writing the poet's name without capital letters <u>the poet's</u>?
18. On the other hand, was the idea <u>from his editors</u>?

C. Write the correct word to complete each sentence. Then label it *possessive pronoun* or *contraction*.

19. According to cummings, (its, it's) ''mudluscious'' in spring.
20. (Theirs, There's) magic in that poetry.
21. (Its, It's) lines depict a child's world vividly.
22. (Their, They're) images show the joy of children at play.
23. (Your, You're) correct with that interpretation.

Apply • Think and Write

Creating a Description • Write several sentences that give your impression of a scene. For example, you might describe the feelings you have when walking during a snowfall. Use possessive pronouns in your description.

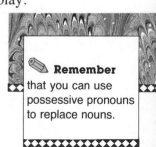

Remember that you can use possessive pronouns to replace nouns.

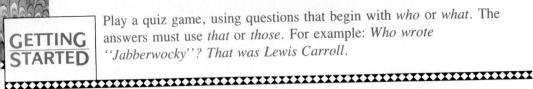

GETTING STARTED

Play a quiz game, using questions that begin with *who* or *what*. The answers must use *that* or *those*. For example: *Who wrote "Jabberwocky"? That was Lewis Carroll.*

4 Interrogative and Demonstrative Pronouns

Interrogative Pronouns A question may begin with *who, whose, whom, which,* or *what*. These words are called interrogative pronouns.

<u>Who</u> is Lucille Clifton?   <u>What</u> does she write?
<u>Whose</u> is this poem?   <u>Which</u> do you like best?
    <u>Whom</u> does she write about?

Demonstrative Pronouns The four demonstrative pronouns *this, that, these,* and *those* point out. *This* and *these* point to persons, places, or things nearby. *That* and *those* point to persons, places, or things farther away. *This* and *that* are singular; *these* and *those,* plural. A demonstrative pronoun must agree in number with its antecedent.

<u>This</u> is the newest *book*.   Are <u>these</u> the latest *changes*?
The book is about her *childhood*; <u>that</u> was a happy time.

Avoid saying or writing *this here* and *that there*.

■ This is my idea. (not *This here*)

When you write, use interrogative pronouns to begin questions and demonstrative pronouns to point out persons, places, or things.

> **Summary ◆** An **interrogative pronoun** asks a question. A **demonstrative pronoun** emphatically points out its antecedent.

Guided Practice

Name each interrogative pronoun and each demonstrative pronoun.

1. That is a poem by Lucille Clifton. Who has read it?
2. What does she write about in her poems?
3. Are these from her collection *An Ordinary Woman*?

Practice

A. Write and label each interrogative and demonstrative pronoun in these sentences about Robert Frost's poetry.

   4. Who has memorized "The Road Not Taken" by Robert Frost?

   5. This is a poem about making choices.

   6. Of the two roads, which appears more inviting?

   7. That is the road chosen by the speaker in the poem.

   8. What does the speaker in the poem regret?

   9. Those are the word pictures I like best in the poem.

  10. Whose are the watercolor illustrations of the scene?

  11. These were painted by Janice and Alex.

  12. Which is your favorite poem by Robert Frost?

  13. To whom was the choral reading of the poem presented?

B. Write each demonstrative pronoun and its antecedent.

  14. This is a poem about growing up by Lucille Clifton.

  15. That is a startling image in the poem "Still."

  16. *Good Times* appeared in 1969. That was her first book.

  17. These are experiences she remembers fondly.

  18. Are those Clifton's books of children's verse?

C. Write each sentence, completing it with the kind of pronoun indicated in parentheses.

  19. (Interrogative) is special about today?

  20. (Demonstrative) is the day I read "Nothing Gold Can Stay."

  21. Robert Frost wrote it, but (demonstrative) are my ideas for illustrating it.

  22. (Interrogative) is this folder of illustrated poems?

  23. Of the two drawings, (interrogative) do you prefer?

Apply • Think and Write

Creating Questions ♦ Write several questions you would like to ask a poet about a poem or poems. Use an interrogative or demonstrative pronoun in each question. Share your questions with a partner.

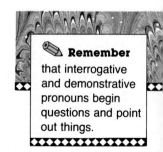

✎ **Remember** that interrogative and demonstrative pronouns begin questions and point out things.

Change the subject in this sentence to *she, he, it, we,* and *they: I saw myself reflected in the window.* What other word did you need to change as well? (Change the last word just for fun.)

5 Reflexive and Intensive Pronouns

Personal pronouns combined with *-self* or *-selves* are either reflexive or intensive pronouns. These two kinds of pronouns have the same forms but different uses. However, each pronoun must agree with its antecedent.

Singular: myself, yourself, himself, herself, itself
Plural: ourselves, yourselves, themselves

A reflexive pronoun reflects back to a noun or pronoun used earlier in the sentence, usually the subject. Generally it cannot be omitted without changing the meaning of the sentence.

Did *Anne Bradstreet* teach <u>herself</u> to write poetry?
The early *colonists* depended on <u>themselves</u>.

An intensive pronoun intensifies, or emphasizes, a noun or pronoun in the same sentence. Often it follows its antecedent immediately. An intensive pronoun can usually be omitted without changing the meaning of the sentence.

Bradstreet <u>herself</u> wrote those poems in 1650.
Her *husband* was <u>himself</u> governor of the colony for ten years.

Reflexive and intensive pronouns are always used with antecedents. Do not use them alone to replace personal pronouns.

■ Lee and <u>I</u> plan to read her poems. (not *Lee and myself*)
■ Did anyone read more than <u>you</u>? (not *yourself*)

Hisself, ourself, and *theirselves* are incorrect forms. Use *himself, ourselves,* and *themselves*.

■ They wrote these stanzas <u>themselves</u>. (not *theirselves*)

Summary ◆ A **reflexive pronoun** refers to a noun or pronoun in the same sentence, usually the subject. An **intensive pronoun** emphasizes another word in the sentence.

Guided Practice

Name each reflexive or intensive pronoun and its antecedent.

1. The Bradstreets found liberty for themselves in America.
2. Massachusetts itself was only a colony then.
3. You can discover for yourselves Bradstreet's poems, the first written in the American colonies.

Practice

A. In these sentences about Paul Laurence Dunbar, write and label each reflexive and intensive pronoun. Then write its antecedent.

4. Dunbar mastered the techniques of the great poets by himself.
5. The poems themselves picture black life.
6. Dunbar also used dialects himself in his performances.
7. His lyrical talent speaks for itself.
8. Dunbar discovered for himself the richness of folk materials.

B. Write the correct form of the pronoun.

9. My younger brother wrote that poem by (himself, hisself).
10. This is a secret between you and (me, myself).
11. My sisters (theirselves, themselves) like all kinds of poems.
12. Lisa and (myself, I) wrote a ballad that was set to music.
13. We write for (ourselves, ourself).

C. Write each sentence, completing it with the kind of pronoun indicated in parentheses.

14. Jane (intensive) often reads poetry aloud.
15. Nathan and Pete taught (reflexive) to read with feeling.
16. The technique (intensive) is not difficult.
17. You and I must train (reflexive) to use rhyme schemes.
18. I (intensive) have already started to practice.

Apply • Think and Write

Listening for Pronouns • Listen to your friends' conversations or to radio or TV ads. Then write examples of intensive and reflexive pronouns that you heard. Work with a partner and compare your examples.

✎ **Remember**
that intensive and reflexive pronouns need to agree with their antecedents.

Make up a chain story. Start with the sentence *Nobody wanted to leave*. Add sentences using words that contain *one*, *body*, or *thing* (*everyone*, *anybody*, *something*).

6 Indefinite Pronouns

A pronoun that does not always refer to a particular person, place, or thing is called an indefinite pronoun.

Common Indefinite Pronouns				
Singular			**Plural**	**Singular or Plural**
anybody	everyone	nothing	both	all
anyone	everything	one	few	any
anything	neither	somebody	many	most
each	nobody	someone	others	none
either	no one	something	several	some

Notice that some indefinite pronouns may be either singular or plural, depending on which word they refer to. They are singular when they refer to singular words and plural when they refer to plural words.

Singular: <u>Most</u> of the *rhythm* is regular. (*Rhythm* is singular.)
Plural: <u>Most</u> of the *images* are appealing. (*Images* is plural.)

When an indefinite pronoun is the antecedent of a personal pronoun, the two pronouns must agree.

<u>Either</u> of the boys could recite *his* own poem. (singular)
<u>Both</u> of the girls never referred to *their* texts. (plural)
Will <u>somebody</u> lend me *his* or *her* copy? (singular)

The use of *his or her* when the gender is unknown is often clumsy. If possible, rewrite the sentence.

■ Will somebody lend me a copy?

Summary ◆ An **indefinite pronoun** does not always refer to a particular person, place, or thing. Use indefinite pronouns in your writing when not referring to specific antecedents.

Guided Practice

Name each indefinite pronoun. Is it singular or plural?

1. Has anyone here read the poem ''The Hippopotamus'' by Ogden Nash?
2. Most of Nash's verse is quite humorous.
3. In *Bed Riddance*, many of the poems have clever rhymes.

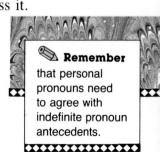

Practice

A. Write the indefinite pronoun in each sentence about Sara Teasdale. Then write *S* if it is singular or *P* if it is plural.

    4. Can anyone quote lines from Teasdale's ''Barter''?
    5. Somebody won a Pulitzer Prize for *Love Songs* in 1918.
    6. Some of my friends know it was the poet Sara Teasdale.
    7. All of the lyrics in the book are highly personal.
    8. In ''The Solitary,'' someone is happy and self-sufficient.

B. Choose the pronoun in parentheses that agrees with the indefinite pronoun. Write the sentences.

    9. Not many receive Pulitzer Prizes for (his, their) poetry.
  10. Both of these poets have won awards for (his, their) work.
  11. No one has won more prizes for (his, their) poetry than he.
  12. Others won awards for (her, their) fiction or drama, too.
  13. All of the winners receive $3,000 as (its, their) prize.

C. Write a different indefinite pronoun to complete each sentence.

  14. _____ of the winning poets is gifted.
  15. _____ are true geniuses, in the judges' opinion.
  16. _____ of them write short stories as well as poems.
  17. Has _____ read Marianne Moore's ''I May, I Might, I Must''?
  18. It says that _____ is impassable if you try to get across it.

Apply ◆ Think and Write

Summarizing a Survey ◆ Take a survey of your classmates' favorite poets and poems. Then write a summary of your findings, using several indefinite pronouns. Report your findings to the class. For example: *Everyone enjoys Ogden Nash's humorous verse.*

> ✎ **Remember**
> that personal pronouns need to agree with indefinite pronoun antecedents.

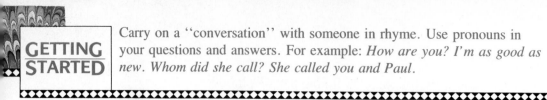

GETTING STARTED

Carry on a "conversation" with someone in rhyme. Use pronouns in your questions and answers. For example: *How are you? I'm as good as new. Whom did she call? She called you and Paul.*

7 Subject and Object Pronouns

Some pronouns have three different forms called cases: nominative, objective, and possessive. The way a pronoun is used in a sentence determines its case. A pronoun in the nominative case is called a **subject pronoun**; a pronoun in the objective case is called an **object pronoun**.

Subject Pronouns		Object Pronouns	
Singular	**Plural**	**Singular**	**Plural**
I	we	me	us
you	you	you	you
he, she, it	they	him, her, it	them
who	who	whom	whom
Use as subjects of verbs. I enjoy Maya Angelou's poems. Who creates images better?		Use as direct objects. The rhythm fascinates me. Whom did you choose?	
Use as predicate nominatives. It may be she or I.		Use as indirect objects. Dan gave me encouragement.	

Object pronouns are also used as the objects of prepositions: *Read your poem to us.*

> **Summary** ♦ Some pronouns change form to show case. Use the appropriate subject and object pronoun forms in your speaking and writing.

Guided Practice

Name each subject and object pronoun.

1. She won many awards.
2. I know it for a fact.
3. Who made the decision?
4. Are they or we the judges?
5. It gave her inspiration.
6. Whom did you see first?

Practice

A. Write each pronoun and label it *subject* or *object*.

    7. Is she the poet Maya Angelou?

    8. A student also of dance, drama, and music was she.

    9. Angelou's symbols in these poems surprised and pleased us.

    10. Who can interpret this passage?

    11. Jim gave them a clue to the meaning.

B. Write a pronoun to replace each underlined word or group of words. Label the pronoun *subject pronoun* or *object pronoun*.

    12. Maya Angelou and T. S. Eliot wrote plays as well as poetry.

    13. Has Angelou written more poetry or screenplays?

    14. Many have enjoyed her autobiographical novels.

    15. The librarian sent *I Know Why the Caged Bird Sings* to Ted.

    16. What person asked for the book after Ted?

C. Write the correct pronoun in parentheses. Label it *subject, predicate nominative, direct object,* or *indirect object.*

    17. Both T. S. Eliot and (she, her) were born in St. Louis.

    18. Of the two, (who, whom) later lived in London?

    19. The one often thought of as an English poet was (he, him).

    20. Lend (we, us) Eliot's humorous book of poems about cats.

    21. His descriptions of the cats amuse Jamie and (I, me).

D. Write a sentence using each word group correctly.

    22. Gerry and him   **24.** he and I   **26.** them and

    23. whom do you   **25.** were we   me

Apply • Think and Write

Creating Riddles • Create riddles, using as many subject and object pronouns as possible. For example: *What is it that, by losing an eye, has only a nose left? (Noise)*

✎ **Remember**
that subject and object pronouns can replace words in the subject and predicate.

Do these two sentences have different meanings? *She likes playing tennis more than him. She likes playing tennis more than he.* State the meaning of each sentence.

8 Special Pronoun Problems

You must often choose between subject and object pronouns. The simple tests below can help you make the correct choice easily.

If a pronoun is joined to a noun or another pronoun by *and* or *or*, test for the correct pronoun by leaving out the other element.

PROBLEM: Jill and (I, me) like the poem "Serenade."

WITHOUT OTHER ELEMENT: I like the poem "Serenade." (not *me*)

SOLUTION: Jill and I like the poem "Serenade." (subject)

To decide which pronoun is correct after *than* or *as*, supply the missing words that are understood after *than* or *as*.

PROBLEM: I know "A Psalm of Life" better than (she, her).

WITH ADDED WORDS: I know "A Psalm of Life" better than she does.

PROBLEM: It inspired her as much as (I, me).

WITH ADDED WORDS: It inspired her as much as it inspired me.

If a noun follows a pronoun as an appositive, test for the correct pronoun by leaving out the noun.

PROBLEM: (Us, We) boys enjoy Henry Wadsworth Longfellow's poems about American heroes.

WITHOUT NOUN: We enjoy Henry Wadsworth Longfellow's poems about American heroes.

SOLUTION: We boys enjoy Henry Wadsworth Longfellow's poems about American heroes.

Do not use an unnecessary pronoun after a noun.

That poet ~~he~~ wrote long narrative poems, too.

When you write, test for the correct pronoun form to avoid pronoun errors.

Summary ◆ Simple tests and guidelines can help you avoid many common pronoun errors.

Guided Practice

Name the correct pronoun in each sentence.

1. Don and (I, me) paraphrased Longfellow's "Paul Revere's Ride."
2. It gave (we, us) researchers a strong sense of history.
3. The American Revolution cost the British more than (we, us).

Practice

A. Write the correct pronouns in the sentences about Countee Cullen and James Weldon Johnson.

> **4.** Rita and (I, me) chose Cullen and Johnson for our project.
> **5.** Born in 1871, Johnson was older than (he, him).
> **6.** (We, us) students discovered *Copper Sun* by Countee Cullen.
> **7.** Only Jim and (I, me) read *God's Trombones* by Johnson.
> **8.** Their works give you and (I, me) a challenge.

B. Find the pronoun error and rewrite each sentence correctly.

> **9.** Eve Merriam she is a teacher as well as a poet.
> **10.** *It Doesn't Always Have to Rhyme* offers you and I choices.
> **11.** Us students imitated poems in *The Inner City Mother Goose*.
> **12.** I liked "Sing a Song of Subways" more than him.
> **13.** Our class and her met the poet at a lecture.

C. Write a sentence using each word group. Then rewrite the sentence, omitting the underlined word or words.

> **EXAMPLE:** as we <u>do</u>
> **ANSWER:** Do you appreciate Merriam's humor as much as we do?
> Do you appreciate Merriam's humor as much as we?

> **14.** as she <u>speaks</u>
> **15.** than <u>they gave</u> us
> **16.** as I <u>heard it</u>
> **17.** than we <u>know</u>
> **18.** as he <u>is clever</u>

Apply ◆ Think and Write

Comparing Poems ◆ Write a comparison of two poems you like to listen to or read aloud. Do they have many similarities, or do they have many differences? Use subject and object pronouns carefully in your comparison.

✎ **Remember**
that you can use simple tests to avoid pronoun errors.

GETTING STARTED

Members of the Fisher family have a way with words. What do they mean when they say that "something fishy's going on here"? That someone is "like a fish out of water"? That they have "other fish to fry"?

VOCABULARY ♦
Formal and Informal Language

Just as we dress differently for different occasions, we speak and write differently, too, depending on the *formality* of the situation. **Informal language** is the language of everyday speech and writing. It is the language used with friends and associates, in friendly letters, and in many newspaper and magazine articles. **Formal language**, on the other hand, is the language used on more serious occasions. Formal language is found in carefully written reports and essays, in legal documents, and in speeches given on solemn occasions.

In reality there are many different levels of formal and informal language, representing many different purposes and audiences. There are, however, certain characteristics that distinguish formal language from informal language. One major difference is in the use of **slang**— words or phrases used in common speech but not accepted in more formal English. For example, you might write to a friend "I had a blast in Washington," but in a letter to a senator you might write "I really enjoyed myself in Washington."

Another difference between formal and informal language is in the use of contractions and abbreviations. Contractions are rarely used in formal language, and only the most common abbreviations (such as *Mr.*, *Mrs.*, *Ms.*, and *Dr.*) are used. In formal usage, instead of writing "She's moving to Greene St.," you would write "She is moving to Greene Street."

Building Your Vocabulary

Choose more formal words and phrases to express those underlined in the sentences below.

1. The house looked kind of run-down.
2. The young boy blows his top at the drop of a hat.
3. The courtroom was a circus, and the judge was frazzled.
4. "If you ask me, that hot tip is all wet," said the private eye.
5. We're just waiting for you to give the go-ahead.

Practice

A. Rewrite the following sentences, substituting more formal language for the underlined words and expressions.

1. We thought the test was going to be <u>a cinch</u>.
2. That <u>kid</u> does nothing but <u>gripe</u> all day.
3. Rosa went home and <u>conked out</u> on the couch.
4. We earned <u>a bundle</u> mowing lawns during the summer.
5. David was quite <u>burned up</u> when he found out his brother had gotten <u>gunk</u> all over his bike.
6. The officer <u>nabbed</u> the thief <u>red-handed</u>.
7. Henry Ford and Thomas Edison <u>hit it off</u> from the beginning.
8. They became <u>pals</u> for life.
9. After three nights at the amusement park, we <u>were dead broke</u>.
10. I always <u>get cold feet</u> before I have to make a speech.

B. Rewrite the following sentences, spelling out all contractions and abbreviations.

11. They'll be here in less than an hr.
12. He'll graduate in Dec. of '92.
13. "'Twill be a long, cold night for us," declared the capt.
14. "What'll we do if we don't make it?" asked the mate.
15. "We'll swim the fifteen mi. ashore!" replied his cmdr.

LANGUAGE CORNER ◆ Eponyms

The fourth Earl of Sandwich, 1728-1792, often liked to spend long hours playing cards. Rather than interrupt his game for a meal, he often had a slice of meat between toast—which later became known as a *sandwich*.

For each meaning below, write the **eponym**—that is, the word that came from the name in parentheses.

to hypnotize (F. A. Mesmer)
food and grain (Ceres, goddess of agriculture)
whiskers on the sides of the face (A. E. Burnside)
a stuffed animal (Theodore Roosevelt)

How to Revise Sentences with Pronouns

By using pronouns correctly, you can make your writing clear. When you write, check the pronouns in your sentences to make sure you have not shifted from one personal pronoun to another unnecessarily. For example, read the sentences in example **1** below. Notice that the first sentence begins with the first person, *I*, but the sentence that follows shifts to the second person, *you*.

> **1.** I loved that poem about the sea. You could see the ocean very clearly in your imagination as you read.

There is no reason to shift to the pronoun *you*. The sentences would be less confusing if the writer used the pronoun *I* throughout.

> **2.** I loved that poem about the sea. I could see the ocean very clearly in my imagination as I read.

You should also avoid unnecessary shifts from an indefinite pronoun to the personal pronoun *you*. For example, read the sentences below. Notice that sentence **3** can be improved in more than one way, as shown in sentences **4** and **5**.

> **3.** When one closes one's eyes, you can smell the sea.
> **4.** When one closes one's eyes, one can smell the sea.
> **5.** When one closes one's eyes, he or she can smell the sea.

As you know, some indefinite pronouns may be either singular or plural, depending on the words they refer to. When you write, be especially careful with indefinite pronouns.

The Grammar Game ◆ Singular or plural? Quickly identify each indefinite pronoun.

one	everything	several	someone	all
both	nobody	most	neither	few

Working Together

As you work with your group on activities **A** and **B**, use pronouns correctly to make your writing clearer and easier to follow.

In Your Group

♦ Contribute your ideas.	♦ Look at others when they speak.
♦ Invite others to talk.	♦ Keep the group on the subject.

A. Tell what is wrong with each sentence below. Then write the sentences, correcting the errors that have been identified.

1. One must read carefully when you read poetry aloud.
2. Several of us wrote his or her poems about friends.
3. Someone wrote a poem about their vacation at the ocean.
4. As we listened, you could see the surf crashing on the shore.
5. When one writes, they have to concentrate on the subject.

B. Suppose your group is organizing a poetry reading. Write ten sentences about what you would do and what might happen. Include one of the groups of words below in each of your sentences.

6. everyone will be eligible
7. someone has
8. about birds in her backyard
9. for his great-grandmother
10. reads his poems
11. one begins
12. you should read
13. by yourself
14. we will begin
15. our best poems

WRITERS' CORNER ♦ Exact Information

Be careful not to use too many indefinite pronouns in a piece of writing. Overusing indefinite pronouns can make your writing vague and ineffective. Give exact information whenever possible.

VAGUE: Most of the items are mine, but a few belong to someone else.
EXACT: Most of the items are mine, but the pen and the keys belong to my sister.

Read what you wrote for the Writer's Warm-up. Did you use too many indefinite pronouns? Can you supply more exact information in place of some of the pronouns?

KINDRED SPIRITS
painting by Asher B. Durand
The New York Public Library, Astor, Lenox & Tilden Foundations.

USING LANGUAGE
TO

CREATE

=== **PART TWO** ===

Literature *Poetry*

A Reason for Writing Creating

CREATIVE
Writing

FINE ARTS ◆ Put yourself in this painting with the two men. What do you see? Smell? Hear? Feel? Write an article for a travel magazine. Your assignment is to entice visitors to the Hudson Valley in New York. Tell prospective tourists why they will want to travel there.

CREATIVE THINKING ◆
A Strategy for Creating

A QUESTION WHEEL

Creating is making up or expressing something new. Poets, for example, often see things in original ways. One kind of poem is a lyric poem, a poem that expresses the poet's own thoughts or ideas. After this lesson you will read some lyric poems, and later you will write one.

Have you ever had a troublesome time working at the computer? Did you wonder, "Who's in control here, the computer or me?" If so, you might enjoy these lines by the poet Gwendolyn Brooks.

> I am a human being.
> I am warm, I am wise.
> I have empathies for animals and
>   people.
>
> I conduct a computer.
> A computer does not conduct me.

In that same poem, Gwendolyn Brooks asks, "Who made it? Human beings made it." Poets often wonder and ask questions. Why are wondering and questioning useful ways of thinking?

Learning the Strategy

Wondering about things and asking questions can lead to learning and discovery. For example, why would you ask questions of a space-station inventor before deciding to go live there? Suppose a neighbor has hired you to do odd jobs. What questions might you ask before getting started? Suppose you want to improve your grade in science. How could wondering and questioning help you?

Have you ever noticed that some people ask a lot of questions, others very few? One reason may be that thinking up questions requires effort—especially if you are not in the habit.

Making a question wheel is one way to prompt yourself to generate questions. Write the topic in the hub and questions on the spokes. The more spokes, the more questions, the better. Mind-building is a little like body-building. Practice and repetitions pay off. Here, for example, is a question wheel about that job for a neighbor. What questions would you add?

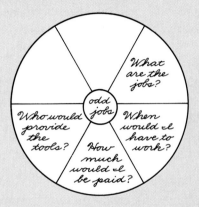

Using the Strategy

A. Do an experiment. Make a question wheel for your hardest school subject. Write the subject in the hub. Then think of questions about it that you could ask the teacher or other students. Write as many questions as you can think of. Resolve to ask three of those questions—or new ones if you think of any—during the coming week. Then decide if you learned anything—and what—by thinking up and asking the questions.

B. The poems you are about to read are on various topics. They include night, a fen or swamp, a computer, a firetruck, autumn, and the stars. Make a question wheel. Choose one of these topics for the hub. Write as many questions as you can about the topic on spokes. Then read the poems. See if the poets seemed to wonder about the same things you did.

Applying the Strategy

♦ Of course you can learn by getting an answer to a question. How do you learn by making up the question in the first place?

♦ Describe one time this week when you have wondered about something. Did you ask questions about it? Why or why not?

LITERATURE

In ancient Greece a lyric was a song sung to the music of a stringed instrument called a lyre. Today the lyric names a kind of brief, musical poem that expresses the poet's personal thoughts and feelings. Listen to these lyric poems for the thoughts and feelings the speakers express.

Acquainted with the Night

I have been one acquainted with the night.
I have walked out in rain—and back in rain.
I have outwalked the furthest city light.

I have looked down the saddest city lane.
I have passed by the watchman on his beat
And dropped my eyes, unwilling to explain.

I have stood still and stopped the sound of feet
When far away an interrupted cry
Came over houses from another street,

But not to call me back or say good-by;
And further still at an unearthly height,
One luminary clock against the sky

Proclaimed the time was neither wrong nor right.
I have been one acquainted with the night.
— *Robert Frost*

I May, I Might, I Must

If you will tell me why the fen
appears impassable, I then
will tell you why I think that I
can get across it if I try.
— *Marianne Moore*

The Great Figure

Among the rain
and lights
I saw the figure 5
in gold
on a red
firetruck
moving
tense
unheeded
to gong clangs
siren howls
and wheels rumbling
through the dark city.
— *William Carlos Williams*

Computer

A computer is a machine.
A machine is interesting.
A machine is useful.
I can study a computer.
I can use it.

Who made it?
Human beings made it.

I am a human being.
I am warm, I am wise.
I have empathies for animals and
    people.

I conduct a computer.
A computer does not conduct me.
— *Gwendolyn Brooks*

The morns are meeker than they were,
The nuts are getting brown;
The berry's cheek is plumper,
The rose is out of town.

The maple wears a gayer scarf,
The field a scarlet gown.
Lest I should be old-fashioned,
I'll put a trinket on.

— *Emily Dickinson*

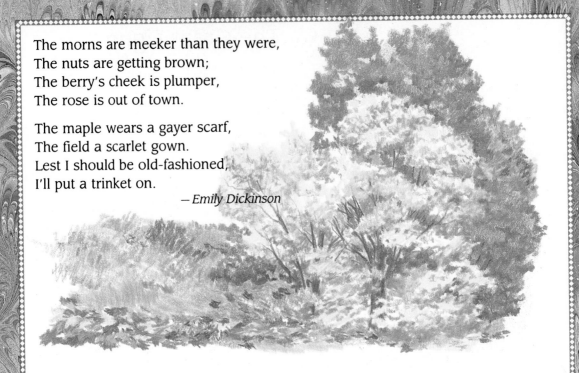

When I Heard the Learn'd Astronomer

When I heard the learn'd astronomer,
When the proofs, the figures, were ranged in columns before
    me,
When I was shown the charts and diagrams, to add, divide, and
    measure them,
When I sitting heard the astronomer where he lectured with
    much applause in the lecture-room,
How soon unaccountable I became tired and sick,
Till rising and gliding out I wander'd off by myself,
In the mystical moist night-air, and from time to time,
Look'd up in perfect silence at the stars.

— *Walt Whitman*

 Reader's Response

Which poem meant the most to you? Explain why.

Poetry

Responding to Literature

1. Respond to "Acquainted with the Night." Work with a small group to make a "night" collage. Use drawings, words from newspaper headlines, pictures, and small objects. One group member may present the collage to the class, telling why each piece was added.

2. In a class discussion, carry the comparison of humans and the computer a little further. Create two lists on the chalkboard to show how humans and computers are alike and different.

3. Julius Caesar was a Roman emperor who dreamed of conquering the world. He thought nothing could stop him. He said, "I came, I saw, I conquered." Compare that saying to the title of Marianne Moore's poem "I May, I Might, I Must." How does Caesar's quote help us better understand the poem?

Writing to Learn

Think and Question ♦ One way to unravel the meaning of a poem is to ask questions about it. Select one poem from this collection and ask questions about it.

Question Wheel

Write ♦ Read the poem and the questions aloud with a partner. Together find answers to the questions. Then try to summarize the poem's meaning in one sentence.

GETTING STARTED

Read aloud the poem "I May, I Might, I Must" on page 268. Read it once <u>without</u> pausing for the comma. Reread it, pausing this time. How does this comma make the meaning clear?

SPEAKING and LISTENING ◆
Reading Poetry Aloud

Each person who reads a poem aloud brings personal thoughts and feelings to the reading. Each reader also uses the poet's clues to sound and meaning. A poem's shape, the length of its lines, and its rhythm and rhyme are all clues for a poem's reader. Punctuation is an important clue as well.

When you read a poem aloud, let the poet's clues guide you to your own interpretation. Here are some guides to further help you.

Reading a Poem Aloud	1. Choose a poem you like, perhaps one that expresses experiences or feelings with which you can identify. 2. Read the poem silently and then aloud to listen to the sounds. 3. Try to identify the poem's speaker, which is usually "I" in lyric poems. The speaker could be the poet or an invented character. 4. Follow the poet's clues to discover the poem's complete thoughts, sounds, and images. Notice especially the pauses and end marks. If there is no punctuation at the end of a line, you could pause very briefly there—as if half a comma were inserted. 5. Note whether any parts of the poem are difficult for you. Can you better understand them by stating the thoughts in your own words? Would it help to look up unfamiliar words in a dictionary? 6. Think about how you can use your voice to interpret the poem's sound and meaning. Ask yourself, Which words would I like to stress? Where might I raise or lower my voice to add meaning? 7. Practice reading the poem aloud. When you read to an audience, read in a natural, expressive voice.
Being an Active Listener	1. Picture your own images for the poem as you listen. 2. Listen for the poem's sounds as well as for its meaning.

Summary ◆ Choose a poem you like and read it for the poet's clues to meaning. Try to identify the poem's speaker and the complete thoughts expressed. Note the poem's punctuation as one key to meaning. Work out difficult parts in a way that suits you. Use your voice to add your own interpretation to the words.

Guided Practice

The lines below are from Robert Frost's poem "Acquainted with the Night." What kind of person might the speaker of this poem be? How is the speaker feeling? Now become the speaker, and read the lines aloud. Pay attention to punctuation as a clue to sound and meaning.

> I have been one acquainted with the night.
> I have walked out in rain—and back in rain.
> I have outwalked the furthest city light.

Practice

A. Present an oral reading of the poem "Computer" on page 269. First listen as your teacher or a classmate reads the poem aloud. Then, with your class, discuss the questions below.

1. How does the poem's speaker feel about computers?
2. Notice the poem's complete thoughts, presented in very short sentences. How do these short sentences and many stops add to the poem's sound and meaning?
3. What kind of rhythm does this poem have? What kind of voice would you use to say this poem?

Now practice your reading of the poem. With a partner, take turns reading the poem. Discuss ways to improve your reading.

B. Work with a partner to present an oral reading of the poem "The Great Figure" on page 269. Make your own copies of the poem to mark with notes. Take turns reading the poem aloud in different ways to find places to pause or words to emphasize. Notice that the poem has only one complete thought, with each short line showing you one detail to observe in the whole picture. Mark your interpretations individually on your copies. Then take turns reading and listening. How are your readings different?

Apply ◆ Think and Write

Dictionary of Knowledge ◆ Read about Emily Dickinson. Make a copy of the poem that is included in the entry. Using the guides in this lesson, practice reading the poem aloud. When you are ready, read it to a friend or relative.

> **✎ Remember**
> to use the poet's clues and your own thoughts and feelings to read poetry aloud.

WRITING ♦
Poets Use Sound

Poets bring sound to poetry in a variety of ways that appeal to our senses. Listen to how this poet uses sound to help us see and hear a moving freight train on a winter morning.

—from **The Descent of Winter**

To freight cars in the air
all the slow
    clank, clank
    clank, clank
moving above the treetops
the
    wha, wha
of the hoarse whistle
    pah,   pah,   pah
    pah, pah, pah, pah, pah,
    piece and piece
    piece and piece
moving still trippingly
through the morningmist
long after the engine
has fought by
        and disappeared
in silence
        to the left

—William Carlos Williams

William Carlos Williams uses several sound devices to describe a moving freight train. He uses onomatopoeia, in which words sound like or imitate what they describe: *clank, clank*. He uses the device called alliteration, the repeating of beginning consonant sounds in words: p̲ah, p̲ah. He also adds sound through repetition—repeating words or phrases: *piece and piece*. Can you find other examples?

Traditionally, poets have used the sound of rhyme not only to please our ears but also to serve as an aid to memory. You may know these lines from the old rhyme that helps us remember how many days are in each month. It is written in a pattern called a **couplet**—two lines that rhyme, one after the other.

> Thirty days hath September
> April June, and November.

Poets also use rhyming sounds in other common patterns, such as the three-line stanza called the **tercet** and the four-line stanza called the **quatrain**. Robert Frost's poem "Acquainted with the Night," on page 268, includes four tercets. Which poems on pages 268–270 are written in rhymed quatrains?

Among the many ways poets bring sound to poetry, the most important one is rhythm. Sometimes poets use a regular pattern of rhythm, as Robert Frost does in "Acquainted with the Night." At other times, poets choose a freer, more irregular rhythm, as William Carlos Williams does to portray the sounds and movements of a train.

Summary ◆ Poets use sound devices such as **onomato-poeia**, **alliteration**, **repetition**, **rhyme**, and **rhythm**.

Responding to Poetry

1. William Carlos Williams describes a freight train's whistle with the invented words *wha, wha*. Think of another kind of whistle or a machine sound. Invent your own words to describe it.
2. Volunteer to say a poem you remember or choose a poem from pages 268–270. Ask your classmates to identify the sound devices.
3. People have always invented words to name animal sounds. With your class, list animal sounds you know, such as *baa* and *grrr*. Which sounds lend themselves to alliteration and repetition?

Apply ◆ Think and Write

Creative Writing ◆ Choose any sound device that you feel best expresses your own inner sense of music. Think of how you could use that element to describe something. Then write a few lines showing how you would begin a poem.

> ✏️ **Remember**
> that sound is one of the most important elements in poetry.

WRITING ♦
Poets Use Figures of Speech

In everyday life, people often use figurative language. You may have heard someone say, "It's as solid as a rock" or "This car's a lemon." People using figurative language do not mean to be taken in a literal sense, of course. Instead, they are making comparisons between different things that have some quality in common.

Many such comparisons have become stale and commonplace. Poets, however, search for fresh comparisons that stretch our imagination and help us see things in unusual ways. One figure of speech poets use to make comparisons is called a simile—a brief comparison that includes the word *like* or *as*. To what does poet Henry Wadsworth Longfellow compare the moon in this poem?

—from **Daylight and Moonlight**

> In broad daylight, and at noon,
> Yesterday I saw the moon
> Sailing high, but faint and white,
> As a school-boy's paper kite.
>
> *—Henry Wadsworth Longfellow*

Poets also use another kind of comparison called a metaphor, which says that one thing <u>is</u> another. A metaphor is usually introduced by the word *is* or *are*. Notice the metaphors used in "Dreams."

Dreams

> Hold fast to dreams
> For if dreams die
> Life is a broken-winged bird
> That cannot fly.
>
> Hold fast to dreams
> For when dreams go
> Life is a barren field
> Frozen with snow.
>
> *—Langston Hughes*

Poet Langston Hughes uses metaphors to help us see that life without dreams is "a broken-winged bird" and "a barren field." In these metaphors, the poet gives us images that help us see life more clearly. William Shakespeare has also given us a rich metaphor for life in his famous line, "All the world's a stage."

Another figure of speech poets use to stretch our imagination is personification—giving human characteristics to inanimate objects and other nonhuman things. We are using personification when we say that "the chair sits in the corner" or "the table groans with food." Notice how poet Carl Sandburg gives human qualities to the moon in this poem. What kind of person does the moon become?

I Sang

I sang to you and the moon
But only the moon remembers.
  I sang
O reckless free-hearted
        free-throated rhythms,
Even the moon remembers them
  And is kind to me.

          —*Carl Sandburg*

Summary ♦ Metaphor, **simile**, and **personification** are three figures of speech poets use to arouse our imagination.

Responding to Poetry

1. Langston Hughes gives us a picture of what may happen if we do not "hold fast to dreams." What other images can you think of for lost dreams?
2. Longfellow compared the moon to a kite. Have you heard that image before? To what else might you compare the moon?
3. What object in nature has been kind to you, as the moon was kind to one poet? How did you sense its kindness?

Apply ♦ Think and Write

Creative Writing ♦ Choose a figure of speech you would like to use in portraying something. Use it in the beginning lines of a poem.

✎ **Remember** that figures of speech help make your writing imaginative and colorful.

Focus on the Lyric Voice

The **lyric voice** is the voice poets use to express their thoughts and feelings. Of three voices—lyric, narrative, dramatic—that poets generally use in writing, the lyric voice is the most common.

The narrative voice is the voice poets use to tell a story or relate an event. The dramatic voice is a kind of mask poets put on when they wish to imagine themselves as other persons or things. The lyric voice is more personal. It invites the reader to observe the poets themselves —their actions, their feelings, their responses to life. The words *I* and *me* often appear in lyric poetry.

Listen to the lyric voice in these two poems.

Hope

Sometimes when I'm lonely,
Don't know why,
Keep thinkin' I won't be lonely
By and by.

—*Langston Hughes*

The Crossing

With stealthy wing
the hawk crossed over
the air I breathed
and sank in some cover.

Through water I drank
the deer stepped slow
without chinking a stone
slid into shadow.

The mountain's body ahead,
the same ground
I walked, hurried up
and out, away, and around

to where the distance stood.
It could not flee or hide.
It filled me. I filled it
and was satisfied.

—*May Swenson*

The Writer's Voice ♦ What feelings do Hughes and Swenson express? Besides feelings, what clues tell you the poets are speaking in the lyric voice? Swenson feels "filled" up by the mountain. What have you seen in nature that filled you with a strong, lasting impression?

Working Together

The lyric voice in poetry is a personal voice—often an "I"—that expresses feelings. As a group, complete activities **A** and **B**.

In Your Group
◆ Share ideas and opinions. ◆ Record all suggestions.
◆ Invite everyone to contribute. ◆ Stay on the job.

A. Make the Langston Hughes poem "Hope" into a song. Begin by having someone in your group copy the poem on a large sheet of paper or on the chalkboard. Discuss the poem. Your aim is to have the music fit the poem's feeling. Because the poem is short, you may want to repeat some words or lines. You may also want to add lines of your own. After deciding on the song's lyrics, melody, and rhythm, practice the song until it seems right. Then sing it for another group or for the class.

B. Some things appear in nature and are quickly gone, such as the hawk and deer in May Swenson's poem. Others remain, such as the mountain. Make two lists as shown below. Add at least five items to each list. Then discuss the items on the second list, "Lasting Things." Try to find one or two things on it about which everyone in the group has approximately the same feelings.

Fleeting Things	Lasting Things
hawk deer	mountain

THESAURUS CORNER ◆ Word Choice

Look up the word *nice* in the Thesaurus. Write three original sentences, using three synonyms for the word *nice*. Each sentence should express your feelings about a pleasant experience. Then write three more sentences, using three antonyms for *nice*. These sentences should express your feelings about an unpleasant event. Write in the first person, using such personal pronouns as *I, me,* and *my*. Be sure that every synonym and antonym you use fits the content of the sentence.

Writing a Poem

Writing a poem is one of the best ways to explore and express your feelings. In this unit, you have read Marianne Moore's ideas about things that seem impossible and Walt Whitman's ideas about the stars. Perhaps you empathized with William Carlos Williams's response to a fire truck or Emily Dickinson's response to autumn.

All of these are lyric poems, poems that express the poet's personal feelings. Written from the poet's own point of view, a lyric poem often includes the personal pronouns *I* and *me*. "I have been one acquainted with the night," wrote Robert Frost. Gwendolyn Brooks declared, "I conduct a computer. A computer does not conduct me."

Know Your Purpose and Audience

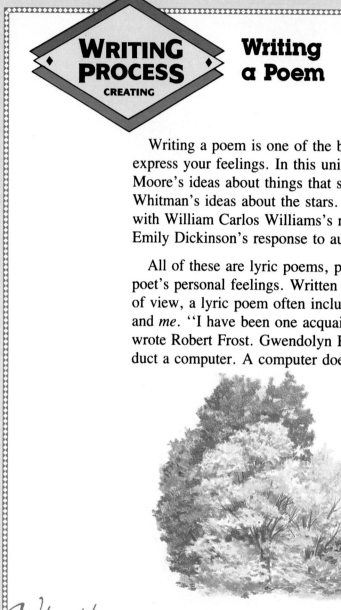

What's **MY PURPOSE**

In this lesson you will write a poem in the lyric voice. Your purpose will be to express your personal feelings about a topic.

Who's **MY AUDIENCE**

Your audience will be your classmates. Later you might tape-record your poems or create a poetry anthology.

1 Prewriting

First you need to choose a topic for your poem. Then you will need an idea-gathering strategy.

Choose Your Topic ◆ Fold a piece of paper to make two vertical columns. On one side write "I am ____." On the other side write "I wonder about ____." Then fill the columns with as many endings as you can to each sentence.

<table>
<tr><td>

Think About It

To complete the sentence "I am ____." consider how you relate to your family, your friends, and others you know. Then let your mind expand to recall all the things you wonder about.

</td><td>

Talk About It

Discuss your list with a partner, explaining the sentence endings you like best. Then circle the one about which you have the most vivid ideas or the strongest feelings.

</td></tr>
</table>

Topic Ideas

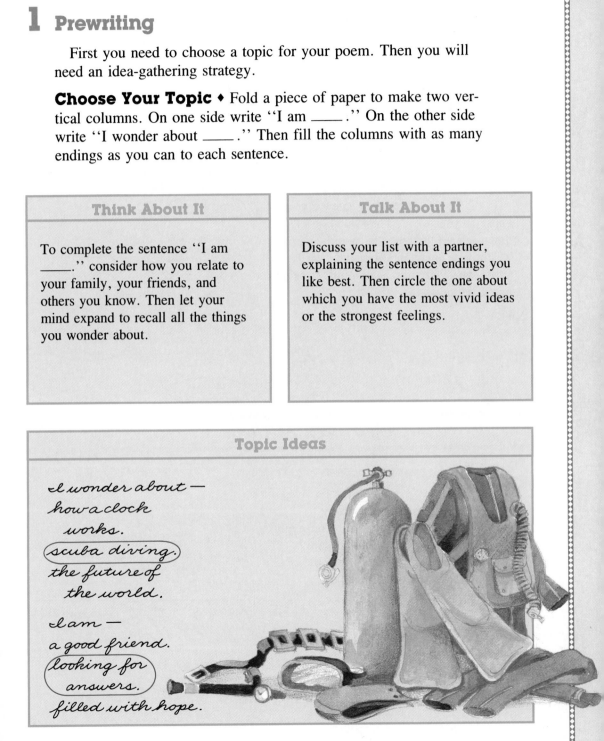

I wonder about —
how a clock
    works.
scuba diving.
the future of
    the world.

I am —
a good friend.
looking for
    answers.
filled with hope.

Choose Your Strategy ♦ Here are two strategies for gathering ideas about your topic. Read both and then use the one you think will work better for you.

PREWRITING IDEAS

CHOICE ONE

A Cluster Map

In the center, write the sentence you chose as your topic. Then quickly jot down related thoughts and feelings around it. Let your imagination wander freely. Write whatever springs to mind. Create as many subtopics as you like.

Model

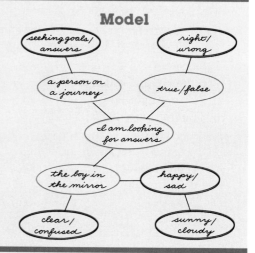

CHOICE TWO

A Question Wheel

Write your topic in the hub of a wheel. Then fill the wheel with as many questions as you can think of. You might use some of those questions in your poem. More likely, you will use the thoughts, ideas, and feelings your questions stimulate.

Model

WRITING PROCESS: Poem

2 Writing

You might begin with your original "I am ____" or "I wonder ____" sentence. Remember that a lyric poem expresses your personal feelings. In your prewriting notes, underline ideas that get to the heart of how you feel about your topic.

First get your most important ideas onto paper. Then have fun playing with the language and the sounds. Decide if you would like to try rhyme. Change or move words until the syllables form a metric pattern that sounds right. Consider using a bit of onomatopoeia or alliteration. Sharpen an image with a metaphor, a simile, or a bit of personification. You can get ideas by looking at the poems in this unit. Above all, however, please yourself.

Sample First Draft ♦

I am a Person looking for answers,
Who looks in the mirror and sees

a face,
sometimes happy, sometimes sad.
I am a person to who answers sometimes

seem as bright as a blue sky.
I am a person who sometimes sees

clouds of dout,
who sometimes loses his way.
in school, the answers are right

or wrong true or false
But what are the answers

3 Revising

Revising is "re-seeing." See your writing as your reader will see it; hear it as your reader will hear it. This idea may help.

REVISING IDEA

FIRST   Read to Yourself

As you read your poem aloud to yourself, think about your purpose. Have you written a lyric poem? Consider your audience. Will your classmates understand your poem? Does it say what *you* really feel? Do you like the images? Are you pleased with the sounds?

Focus: Have you used the lyric voice throughout? Have you clearly expressed your personal feelings about your topic?

THEN   Share with a Partner

Ask a partner to be your first audience. Read your poem aloud with expression. Ask your partner to respond. These guidelines may help you work together.

The Writer

Guidelines: Listen to your partner's responses. Did you make your meaning clear?

Sample questions:
- What image do you remember most clearly?
- **Focus question:** Did I make my feelings clear? What one word sums up my poem?

The Writer's Partner

Guidelines: A lyric poem is very personal. Be supportive and helpful rather than critical.

Sample responses:
- I especially liked the part where _____.
- I think your poem expresses a feeling of _____.

Revising Model ♦ This poem is being revised. The writer's changes are shown in blue.

Revising Marks	
delete	ℯ
add	∧
move	⟲

The writer added a detail to clarify meaning.

Joyful is a more precise and poetic word than *happy*.

The writer's partner noticed this pronoun error.

The writer decided to add alliteration to his simile.

I am a Person looking for answers,

Who looks in the mirror and sees

changing
a face,
∧

joyful
sometimes happy, sometimes sad.

whom
I am a person to who answers sometimes

sunny summer
seem as bright as a blue sky.

I am a person who sometimes sees

clouds of dout,

who sometimes loses his way.

in school, the answers are right

or wrong true or false

But what are the answers

Read the poem above the way the writer has decided it *should* be. Then revise your own poem.

Grammar Check ♦ A pronoun error, such as confusing *who* and *whom*, can ruin a poetic effect.

Word Choice ♦ Do you want a more precise or poetic word for an overused word such as *trip*? A thesaurus offers a choice of many synonyms.

Revising Checklist

☐ **Purpose:** Did I write a lyric poem?

☐ **Audience:** Will my classmates enjoy my poem?

☐ **Focus:** Did I use the lyric voice throughout? Did I clearly express my feelings about my topic?

4 Proofreading

Now check your poem for surface errors. In some poems, each line begins with a capital letter. If a line is too long, it continues onto a second, indented line. Poets do not always follow normal punctuation and capitalization rules. However, be sure that your line breaks, punctuation, and capitalization contribute to clarity and poetic effect.

Proofreading Model ◆ Here is the poem about the boy who is looking for answers. Proofreading changes have been added in red.

Proofreading Marks	
capital letter	=
small letter	/
add comma	⌄
add period	⊙
check spelling	⬭

Proofreading Checklist

- ☐ Did I spell words correctly?
- ☐ Did I use correct capitalization?
- ☐ Did I use correct punctuation?
- ☐ Did I type neatly or use my best handwriting?

I am a Person looking for answers,
Who looks in the mirror and sees
a face, *changing*
sometimes happy, *joyful* sometimes sad.
I am a person to who *whom* answers sometimes
seem as bright as a blue sky. *sunny summer*
I am a person who sometimes sees
clouds of doubt *doubt*,
who sometimes loses his way.
in school, the answers are right
or wrong, true or false.
But what are the answers

PROOFREADING IDEA

Spelling Check

Cut a window in a note card. Read through it to help you concentrate on the spelling of each single word.

Now proofread your poem, add a title, and make a neat copy.

5 Publishing

Here are two ways to share your poem with classmates.

Looking for Answers

I am a person looking for answers,
Who looks in the mirror and sees
   a changing face,
    sometimes joyful, sometimes sad.
I am a person to whom answers sometimes
    seem as bright as a sunny summer sky.
I am a person who sometimes sees
    clouds of doubt,
    who sometimes loses his way.
In school, the answers are right or wrong,
    true or false.
But what are the answers
    on the test of life?
I am a person on a journey
    to seek answers.
I am Jeffrey Hall.

PUBLISHING IDEAS

Share Aloud

Practice reading your poems clearly and with expression. Then make several "Poetry on Parade" tape recordings with about five poems, read by their writers, on each tape. Introduce each poem with the name of the poet and the title of the poem, if any. At the end of each tape, include a request for comments and letters to the poets. Lend the tapes to your school library. Make a copy to listen to in class.

Share in Writing

Find or draw pictures to accompany your poem or make a decorative border. Then, with classmates, make an anthology titled *Lyric Poems: Our Thoughts and Feelings*. Take turns reading the anthology in free time. Offer your responses and congratulations to the other poets.

CURRICULUM ·CONNECTION·

Writing Across the Curriculum Social Studies

Poets, historians, biographers—men and women in all fields wonder and ask questions. Asking questions is a strategy that can help you focus on what you want to find out about a topic.

Writing to Learn

Think and Question ◆ Look at the pictures of famous Americans below. Choose one you admire or would like to know more about. Make a question wheel. Write the person's name in the center. Fill the wheel with questions you would like to ask that person.

George Washington

Eleanor Roosevelt

Martin Luther King, Jr.

Question Wheel

Harriet Tubman

John Glenn, Jr.

Susan B. Anthony

Write ◆ At the library find a biography of the person you chose. Keep your question wheel nearby as you read. Take notes when you find answers to any of your questions.

Writing in Your Journal

In the Writer's Warm-up you wrote about what poetry means to you. Then you went on to read poems by Emily Dickinson, Langston Hughes, and others. Choose one poem or poet that you especially liked from this unit on American poets and poetry. In your journal write about your choice.

BOOKS TO ENJOY

Read More About It

The Poetry of Robert Frost
edited by Edward Connery Lathem
The surface meaning of a poem is only the beginning. With
each thoughtful rereading, the many poems in this collection are sure to grow in richness and meaning.

I'm Nobody! Who Are You? The Story of Emily
Dickinson   *by Edna Barth*
This informal biography traces the course of Emily Dickinson's life and her development as a poet. It includes quotations from letters and journals as well as a selection of her
better-known poems.

Book Report Idea   Poetry Reading on Tape

For your next book report, review a collection
of poems. You can choose a book of poems
by one poet or an anthology of
poems by different poets.

Pick Your Favorite Poem
Poetry is best when read aloud.
Include a few oral readings of
poems in your book report. You
might begin by taping your favorite poem from the book. Be sure
to read the poem with expression. Then give the title and author
and tell what you liked about the
work. You might want to quote
selected lines to make a point.
End your book report with one
or two more of the poems you
thought most effective.

Poems for Youth
by Emily Dickinson

Bronzeville Boys and Girls
by Gwendolyn Brooks

There Is No Rhyme for Silver
by Eve Merriam

Roofs of Gold
by Padraic Colum

UNIT REVIEW

Unit 5
Pronouns   *pages 244–259*

A. Write each personal pronoun. Then write its person and number.

1. Howard, you must have an opinion about their work.
2. Personally, I like his sculpture best.
3. Vicky finally chose mine because of its size.
4. Our art teacher encouraged us in every way.

B. Write the pronouns and their antecedents.

5. There is no other building like it anywhere.
6. The architect was famous for his unusual designs.
7. The mayor said, "I think this design is too unusual."
8. Style and grace are desirable; they are eye-catching.

C. Write each possessive pronoun. Then write whether it is used alone or with a noun.

9. Its origin is African.
10. Mine is Mexican.
11. The signature is hers.
12. It's important to its owner.

D. Write and label each interrogative and demonstrative pronoun.

13. Those are poisonous.
14. Whom did you ask?
15. Which are garter snakes?
16. These are quite harmless.

E. Write and label each reflexive or intensive pronoun and its antecedent.

17. The defendant threw himself on the mercy of the court.
18. The judge herself was impressed by his sincerity.
19. The jurors discussed the case among themselves.

F. Write each indefinite pronoun. Label it *singular* or *plural*.

20. Most of the songs were new.
21. Everything sounded great.
22. Few of us left our seats.
23. Most of the hour is up.

G. Write each pronoun and label it *subject* or *object*.

24. Who played the lead in the last school play?
25. Whom will they cast in the next production of *Annie*?
26. Maybe it will be she or I.
27. They will help us in rehearsals for the auditions.

H. Write the correct pronouns in the sentences.

28. At times, friendship offers her and (I, me) a challenge.
29. I can keep a secret better than (she, her).
30. (Us, We) friends are as close as sisters.
31. My parents and (they, them) get along well, too.

Formal and Informal Language   *pages 260–261*

I. Rewrite the following sentences, spelling out all contractions and abbreviations.

32. They're over an hr. late for the class picnic, and it's getting dark already.
33. The capt. said that we'll probably not have time to finish playing the games they've planned.
34. Who'd have thought that it would take them so long to walk the two-mi. trail?

Figures of Speech   *pages 276–277*

J. Read these lines taken from two poems. Then answer the questions below.

— *from* **When Moonlight Falls**
When moonlight falls on the water
It is like fingers touching the chords of a harp.
— *Hilda Conkling*

— *from* **An Indian Summer Day on the Prairie**
The sun is a smoldering fire,
That creeps through the high gray plain.
— *Vachel Lindsay*

35. What is an example of a simile?
36. What is an example of a metaphor?
37. What is one example of personification?

Unit 5 Challenge

Pronoun Who's Who

Figure out each pronoun from the clues. (Hint: Draw blanks for the letters and number each blank.)

1. I am a seven-letter indefinite pronoun.
   My 5, 6, 7 is a number.
   My 1, 2, 6 is the brother of a daughter.
   My 3, 4 is a personal pronoun for myself.
   My 3, 2, 5, 6 shines in the sky at night.
2. I am a five-letter demonstrative pronoun.
   My 4, 2, 3, 5 is worn on your foot.
   My 1, 3, 5, 4 are on your feet.
   My 2, 3, 4, 5 puts out fires.
   My 2, 3, 1 isn't cold.
3. I am a ten-letter reflexive-intensive pronoun.
   My 2, 3, 4 is the edge of your trousers.
   My 6, 7, 8, 9, 10 are tiny fantasy people.
   My 7, 6, 5, 10 is not more.
   My 8, 3, 5, 1 is a sleeveless jacket.
4. I am a seven-letter indefinite pronoun.
   My 4, 2, 1 is a number.
   My 5, 6, 7 is a feminine possessive pronoun.
   My 5, 6, 7, 2 is not there.
   My 3, 4 is a personal pronoun for a thing.

Pronoun Transformations

Change each of the following pronouns into another pronoun by adding one letter.

1. who	4. I	7. their
2. either	5. our	8. your
3. it	6. one	9. he

Unit 5 Extra Practice

1 Writing with Pronouns

A. Write the personal pronouns in each sentence.

1. Did he see us?
2. She didn't draw it.
3. I hope you do.
4. We lost him.
5. She gave him the job.
6. They saw me there.
7. You can ask us later.
8. May I talk to you now?

B. Thirteen of the underlined words in this article are personal pronouns. Write each underlined pronoun after its sentence number. Write *none* if a sentence has no underlined pronoun.

9. Years ago many American writers did at least part of their work in Europe. **10.** Some of them admired the long tradition of English literature. **11.** Others traveled to broaden their education. **12.** The American novelist Henry James wrote all his novels in Europe. **13.** He is famous for complex, psychological novels. **14.** Hilda Doolittle and Amy Lowell also wrote in England. **15.** They were poets called imagists. **16.** T.S. Eliot, who was born in Missouri, moved to London in 1914. **17.** Some of the most influential poems of our century are his. **18.** A native of Pennsylvania, Gertrude Stein spent her adult life in France. **19.** She helped many young American writers in their creative efforts. **20.** During the last fifty years, most of America's great writers have worked in the United States. **21.** They have made our nation a world literary center.

2 Pronouns and Antecedents

A. Write the correct pronoun and its antecedent in each sentence.

1. Did a member of the boys' travel club charge a call to (his, their) home telephone?
2. An aisle seat has (its, their) advantages.
3. Has Richard lost (his, their) boarding pass?
4. Ruth has (her, their) favorite travel story.
5. Our neighbors said (he, they) would meet us.

B. If the underlined pronoun agrees with its antecedent, write *correct*. If it does not, write the correct pronoun.

6. Can the Smiths bring <u>their</u> dog on board?
7. A person can easily make <u>their</u> seat recline.
8. Those students didn't even look at <u>her</u> books.
9. Parents should fasten <u>his</u> children's seat belts.
10. A passenger asked if <u>she</u> could have a pillow.
11. Many people can fit all <u>their</u> baggage under a seat.
12. Jo and Sue must wait <u>their</u> turn to be served.
13. That man left <u>his</u> briefcase under the seat.
14. A mother may get a bassinet for <u>their</u> baby.
15. Passengers can get a special meal if <u>they</u> request it.

C. Write a sentence using each pair of words. Be sure that the pronoun and its antecedent agree.

EXAMPLE: teacher, his
ANSWER: Our teacher went to Maine on his vacation.

16. actors, they
17. pilots, their
18. Paul, his
19. people, they
20. snack, it

21. company, its
22. student, her
23. traveler, he
24. father, his
25. flight attendants, they

3 Possessive Pronouns

p. 248

A. Write the possessive pronouns in each sentence.

1. I saw his equipment in my backyard.
2. Your fishing pole is older than mine.
3. Our farm is farther south than your cabin.
4. His sunglasses and her magazine are here.
5. Why is her hat in their closet?
6. Is that your towel or hers?
7. They left their dog at her kennel.
8. We keep ours at my grandparents' house.
9. I gave yours to her and his to Henry.
10. Mine is in your garage.
11. My mother cooked roast beef for our neighbors.

B. Write the correct word to complete each sentence. Then label it *possessive pronoun* or *contraction*.

12. Is (your, you're) report about Samuel Langhorne Clemens?
13. (Its, It's) true that he is better known by his pen name, Mark Twain. **14.** (Theirs, There's) much interest in his life, as it spanned a large part of the nineteenth century—1835 to 1910. **15.** (Your, You're) certain to enjoy his most famous novel *Adventures of Huckleberry Finn*. **16.** (Its, It's) effect on American literature has been great. **17.** In this novel Twain wrote language the way (its, it's) actually spoken. **18.** (Its, It's) natural, conversational style might not seem unusual today. **19.** Critics in (their, they're) reviews have said that Twain was the first American novelist to do it so well.
20. (Theirs, There's) much to be learned by studying Twain's writing style because it imitates ordinary speech.

4 Interrogative and Demonstrative Pronouns

p. 250

A. Write the interrogative pronoun in each sentence.

1. Whom did you ask about getting insurance for this sports car?
2. What is the price of this model?
3. Who can tell me about the special features of the white hatch-back with wire wheels?
4. Of these three models, which do you like best?
5. Whose was the late-model red convertible that we test-drove yesterday?
6. Whom should I ask for more information on the warranty and on the services you provide?
7. Who will make the arrangements for delivery of the car?

B. Write each sentence. Underline each demonstrative pronoun once and its antecedent twice.

8. Isn't this a poem by Gwendolyn Brooks?
9. Whose voice was that, anyway?
10. These are indeed fine pet otters!
11. What kind of snowshoes are those?
12. What a fine dinner this is!

C. Write each sentence, completing it with the kind of pronoun indicated in parentheses.

13. Are (demonstrative) your lost pigs?
14. (Demonstrative) is your invitation to the party tonight.
15. Under the circumstances, (interrogative) can I do?
16. (Demonstrative) are my parents, Mr. and Mrs. Gray.
17. Of Linda's three paintings, (interrogative) do you prefer?
18. In my opinion, (demonstrative) is the best computer on the market.
19. (Interrogative) of these flights to Los Angeles do you prefer?
20. Is (demonstrative) your book on the table?
21. (Interrogative) did you borrow yesterday?
22. Could (demonstrative) be one of the prizes?
23. (Interrogative) do you want me to tell her?
24. Is (demonstrative) the letter you are looking for?
25. (Demonstrative) is my favorite story.
26. (Interrogative) is your favorite?

5 Reflexive and Intensive Pronouns   *p. 252*

A. Write each sentence. Underline the reflexive pronoun once and its antecedent twice.

1. I haven't told you anything about myself yet.
2. Can the children help themselves to everything?
3. My little sister finished that entire puzzle by herself last night.
4. You must keep yourselves in good condition.
5. My book didn't get up and walk out by itself!

B. Write an appropriate reflexive pronoun to complete each sentence below.

EXAMPLE: We prided _____ on our thriftiness.
ANSWER: ourselves

6. We convinced _____ that we needed a new car.
7. He must read the owner's manual for _____ .
8. My parents bought for _____ a new car last month.
9. She likes to do the tune-up by _____ .
10. I want to check the gas mileage for _____ .

C. Write each sentence. Underline the intensive pronoun once and its antecedent twice.

11. Bruce himself hung up the campaign posters.
12. Marlene is herself a leader of the student council.
13. The class officers themselves could not improve the system.
14. The principal himself wrote letters of congratulation.
15. Frank himself admits that his speech was too long and dry.

D. Write each sentence, completing it with the kind of pronoun indicated in parentheses.

16. Margaret Fuller supported (reflexive) as a journalist.
17. This accomplishment (intensive) was remarkable for a woman in the early 1800s
18. Her father (intensive) saw to Margaret's early education.
19. Margaret distinguished (reflexive) in language studies.
20. She introduced (reflexive) to Boston's greatest thinkers.
21. She (intensive) edited *The Dial*, the country's first magazine of ideas.
22. Horace Greeley (intensive) hired her to write about the arts.
23. Margaret made (reflexive) famous through her reporting from Europe.
24. She involved (reflexive) with the Italian war for freedom.
25. The man she married was (intensive) an Italian count.

6 Indefinite Pronouns

p. 254

A. Write the indefinite pronoun in each sentence. Then label it *singular* or *plural*.

1. The doctors have not found anything wrong.
2. Neither of them came to our house last night.
3. Someone left a pen on that desk.
4. Only a few have answered the question correctly.
5. Both of the athletes broke records.
6. Many volunteered their help in the emergency.
7. Everyone must make up his or her own mind.
8. According to our records, nothing was lost.
9. Will the others help us with the scenery?
10. Is everything included in that price?

B. Write an indefinite pronoun that completes each sentence appropriately. Use no indefinite pronoun more than twice.

11. ____ of the uniforms was mine.
12. ____ will answer the telephone after 5:00 P.M.
13. I would like ____ of that pizza.
14. ____ of the candidates is qualified.
15. Has ____ been appointed as treasurer?
16. This tape recorder has ____ wrong with the rewind mechanism.
17. ____ of the pages were missing.
18. ____ remembered the recipe for the casserole.
19. Did ____ of the suits fit you?
20. Has ____ finished the problems for tomorrow?
21. ____ of the newspapers carried the story.
22. We could not find ____ of your records.
23. ____ of my friends belong to the school band.
24. Have you invited ____ to the victory celebration?
25. Only ____ of the phonographs is available today.

7 Subject and Object Pronouns   *p. 256*

A. Write a pronoun to replace each underlined word or group of words. Label the pronoun *subject pronoun* or *object pronoun*.

1. Has <u>Lou</u> ever been hiking in this area before?
2. <u>Ellen and I</u> knew the way.
3. We told <u>Lisa</u> to bring plenty of sunscreen.
4. It took <u>Lou and Bill</u> an hour to walk two miles.
5. They warned <u>Lisa and me</u> about blisters.
6. <u>Lou and Bill</u> wore tennis shoes.
7. <u>Which one of us</u> has the heaviest backpack?
8. To which one of you did <u>Bill</u> give my map of the park?
9. The most helpful person in the group is <u>Ellen</u>.
10. Please pass <u>Lou</u> the insect spray.
11. The parker ranger warned <u>Ellen and Lou</u> about insects.
12. <u>Bill</u> carried the compass and the canteen for me.

B. Write a sentence using each word group correctly.

13. Joe and her   15. she and I   17. whom did you
14. was they   16. them and us   18. Ellen and me

C. Write the correct pronoun in each sentence. Then label it *subject, predicate nominative, direct object,* or *indirect object.*

19. Ellen and (she, her) stopped to pick wild flowers.
20. It was (they, them) who spotted the oriole.
21. Give Lou and (he, him) a turn with the binoculars.
22. (Who, Whom) did you meet on the trail?
23. Lisa and (we, us) are ready for lunch.
24. Either (she, her) or Ellen brought extra rations.
25. Did (they, them) bring the water?
26. (Who, Whom) wants to hike again next weekend in another national park?

8 Special Pronoun Problems

p. 258

A. Write the correct pronoun in each sentence.

1. Our friends and (we, us) enjoy riding the subway.
2. You gave Karen and (I, me) the train schedule.
3. Dan and (I, me) get off here.
4. Those people and (he, him) tried to cut in line.
5. (We, Us) students can ride for half fare.

B. If a sentence below contains an error, rewrite the sentence correctly. If it does not, write *correct.*

6. Fred or her drives the station wagon to work.
7. Janet and me met them at the bus stop.
8. The driver lets us students off at the corner.
9. Did he tell you and they to bring exact change?
10. Those two people they're blocking the aisle.
11. Dad and us players sat together on the bus.
12. Do you and him live near the bus line?
13. Both Donna and her rode the whole way standing.

C. Write a sentence, using each word group correctly. Then rewrite the sentence, omitting the underlined word or words.

14. as she <u>spends</u>
15. than <u>he calls</u> me
16. than <u>they told</u> us

17. than they <u>enjoy it</u>
18. as <u>they gave</u> me
19. than <u>it took</u> her

UNIT SIX

USING LANGUAGE
TO

DESCRIBE

──────────── **PART ONE** ────────────

Unit Theme   *Early Air Travel*

Language Awareness   Adjectives

──────────── **PART TWO** ────────────

Literature   *North to the Orient*
        by Anne Morrow Lindbergh

A Reason for Writing   Describing

Writing
IN YOUR JOURNAL

WRITER'S WARM-UP ◆ What do you know about early air travel? Perhaps you have read about the Wright brothers at Kitty Hawk, North Carolina. You may have seen movies that feature airplanes in their early years. What must it have been like to fly one of those early airplanes? Write in your journal about early air travel. You might write about what you know or what you wonder about.

GETTING STARTED

Make a flying word chain. Use a word that describes a thing that can fly and begins with the same letter as the flying thing: *airmail airplane*, *billowy balloon*.

1 Writing with Adjectives

Adjectives are words that modify nouns or pronouns. *Modify* means "describe" or "limit." Adjectives answer these questions:

Which one?	How many? What kind?	How much?

■ <u>Each</u> engineer designed <u>several</u> <u>original</u> aircraft but had <u>no</u> success flying them.

Adjectives usually stand before the words they modify. Sometimes, however, they follow.

■ Airships, <u>real</u> and <u>imaginary</u>, are <u>fascinating</u>.

Notice how adjectives can change the meaning of a sentence.

The <u>foolish</u>, <u>absentminded</u> inventor designs <u>silly</u>, <u>useless</u> planes.
The <u>creative</u>, <u>brilliant</u> inventor designs <u>marvelous</u> <u>new</u> planes.

The articles *a*, *an*, and *the* are adjectives. *The* is called a **definite article** because it refers to specific persons, places, or things. *A* and *an* are **indefinite articles** because they refer to any person, place, or thing in general.

Name <u>the</u> first airplane. (a specific airplane)
Name <u>an</u> airplane or <u>a</u> helicopter. (any airplane or helicopter)

> **Summary** ◆ An **adjective** modifies a noun or pronoun. Use adjectives to add details to your writing.

Guided Practice

Name the adjectives in each sentence. Remember to include articles.

1. The brilliant Leonardo da Vinci lived in the sixteenth century.
2. He designed three different aircraft and the first parachute.
3. A glider, lightweight but large, was original, too.

Practice

A. Write the adjectives, including articles, in each sentence.

4. There is an old story about Daedalus, a great inventor, and Icarus, an only son. **5.** Daedalus had worked for the cruel King Minos of Crete but longed for a peaceful life in Athens. **6.** Minos refused to release him; therefore the clever Daedalus planned a strange escape. **7.** He built two ornithopters. **8.** The machines had movable wings with soft feathers and linen fastenings. **9.** Some wax held on the many feathers. **10.** Young Icarus flew behind Daedalus at a moderate height. **11.** Then the foolish boy became bold. **12.** He flew too near the hot sun, and the thin wax melted. **13.** Luckless Icarus fell into the deep blue sea.

B. Choose adjectives below that answer the questions in the blanks to complete the paragraph. Write the paragraph.

> **first   more   wealthy   eighteenth   real   same   hot   two**

In the (**14.** which one?) century (**15.** how many?) (**16.** what kind?) brothers in France sent up a balloon filled with (**17.** what kind?) air. Later Jacques Charles had even (**18.** how much?) success with a hydrogen balloon. In the (**19.** which one?) year Jean Pilatre de Rosier made the (**20.** which one?) (**21.** what kind?) flight in a balloon.

C. The sentences below contain the overworked adjective *good*. Rewrite the sentences, using more specific adjectives.

22. It was a good flight.
23. The wind was good.
24. The pilot seemed good.
25. She made a good takeoff.
26. We had good seats.
27. The visibility was good.
28. Our view of the sunset was especially good.

Apply • Think and Write

From Your Writing • Read what you wrote for the Writer's Warm-up. Change or add adjectives to create vivid word pictures.

✎ **Remember**
that adjectives help to create word pictures in your writing.

What things might you find at a World's Fair? Start your list with *Chinese kites*.

_____ lace, _____ pottery, _____ cars, _____ sardines

2 Proper and Demonstrative Adjectives

Proper Adjectives   An adjective formed from a proper noun is called a proper adjective.

MECHANICS "`;?!`"	Proper Nouns	Proper Adjectives
A proper adjective is always capitalized. For more information on capitalization, see pages 636–645.	America	American pilots
	Japan	Japanese children
	Canada	Canadian route
	April	April showers

Notice that some proper adjectives have the same form as the proper noun. If you are not sure about spelling, consult a dictionary.

Demonstrative Adjectives   When the words *this*, *these*, *that*, and *those* modify nouns, they are called demonstrative adjectives. A demonstrative adjective points out a specific person, place, or thing. *This* and *these* point out someone or something nearby. *That* and *those* point out someone or something farther away. Use *this* and *that* with singular nouns and *these* and *those* with plural nouns. Don't confuse demonstrative adjectives and demonstrative pronouns.

Demonstrative Adjectives	Demonstrative Pronouns
This plane was Lindbergh's.	This was the Lindbergh plane.
Those people are the Lindberghs.	Those are the Lindberghs.

> **Summary** ♦ A **proper adjective** is formed from a proper noun. A **demonstrative adjective** points out the noun it describes.

Guided Practice

Name the proper and demonstrative adjective in each sentence.

1. This American aviator is Charles Lindbergh.
2. He trained in those United States flying schools.
3. That headline tells of his Atlantic flight in 1927.

Practice

A. Write and label each proper and demonstrative adjective. If a sentence has no proper or demonstrative adjective, write *none*.

4. Lindbergh left this New York airport on May 20, 1927.
5. He landed at that Parisian airport on May 21, 1927.
6. This was the first transatlantic solo flight in history.
7. He won French and American awards for that flight.
8. Besides these awards, he was honored in many European cities.

B. Write each group of words. Use the correct adjective.

9. (this, these) solo flight
10. (this, that) plane over there
11. (that, those) Lindberghs
12. (that, this) one near me

C. Use the kind of adjective asked for in each blank to complete the paragraph. Use one adjective twice. Write the paragraph.

Oriental   those   that   **Mexican**   **American**

Lindbergh wrote *The Spirit of St. Louis* about (**13.** demonstrative) flight. He received a Pulitzer Prize for (**14.** demonstrative) book. Later he and his wife flew northern air routes to the Orient and visited many (**15.** proper) cities. They also flew (**16.** proper) air routes southward. His wife wrote about (**17.** demonstrative) flights. They were brave (**18.** proper) pilots.

D. Write proper adjectives to describe what the Lindberghs saw on their trips. Form each adjective from the proper noun.

19. They saw ancient ____ cities. (South America)
20. The Lindberghs viewed numerous ____ lakes. (Canada)
21. The Lindberghs visited ____ villages. (China)
22. They met many people in ____ countries. (Europe)
23. They made friends on their ____ trip. (Mexico)

Apply • Think and Write

Tour Description • Imagine that you are planning a world tour by air. At what cities would you stop? Write a brief description of your route. Include at least five proper adjectives and five demonstrative adjectives.

Remember that proper and demonstrative adjectives make your writing more precise.

3 Using Adjectives to Compare

Many adjectives change forms to show comparisons. There are three forms, called degrees of comparison.

Positive Degree: A turboprop plane is <u>fast</u>.
Comparative Degree: The 747 is <u>faster</u> than a turboprop plane.
Superlative Degree: The Concorde is the <u>fastest</u> of all.

To use comparative and superlative forms, learn the rules below.

Add -*er* and -*est* to the positive form of one-syllable and some two-syllable adjectives. Some spelling changes may occur.

Positive	Comparative	Superlative
old	older	oldest
big	bigger	biggest
busy	busier	busiest

Use *more* and *most* with some two-syllable adjectives and with adjectives of three or more syllables.

active	more active	most active
tedious	more tedious	most tedious
eager	more eager	most eager

If you are not sure how an adjective of two syllables forms its degrees of comparison, consult a dictionary.

Summary ♦ Many adjectives have three forms, or **degrees of comparison:** the positive, comparative, and superlative. Use the appropriate form to show comparisons when you write.

Guided Practice

Name the comparative and superlative forms of each adjective.

1. lively   **2.** flat   **3.** hungry   **4.** energetic   **5.** careful

The rules below will help you use adjectives correctly when you make comparisons.

Use the positive degree of an adjective to describe one person, place, or thing. **The Wright brothers' plane, *Flyer*, is <u>old</u>.**
Use the comparative degree to compare two persons, places, or things and with the phrase *of the two*. ***Flyer* is <u>older</u> than Lindbergh's plane.** **The Wrights' plane is the <u>older</u> of the two.**
Use the superlative degree to compare three or more. ***Flyer* is the <u>oldest</u> successfully flown airplane.**
Avoid double comparisons. Do not use both *-er* and *more* or *-est* and *most* to form the comparative or superlative degrees. **Which is the <u>biggest</u> airliner? (not <u>most</u> <u>biggest</u>)**
Put *less* or *least* before the positive degree of an adjective to make a comparison that means the opposite of *more* or *most*. **Flight speed is <u>more important</u> than comfort to them.** **Flight speed is <u>less important</u> than comfort to me.**
Use *than*, not *then*, when making comparisons. *Then* tells when. **This airport is busier <u>than</u> that one. (compares)** **We flew to Chicago and <u>then</u> to Newark. (tells when)**

Summary ♦ Use the **positive degree** to describe one person, place, or thing. Use the **comparative degree** to compare two. Use the **superlative degree** to compare three or more. Follow the rules of comparison when you write.

Guided Practice

Choose the correct word or words in parentheses.

6. A jet airplane is (faster, fastest) (than, then) a helicopter.
7. The (longest, most longest) runway is seven miles long.
8. This is the (larger, largest) of the two balloons.

Practice

A. Write whether each adjective is comparative or superlative.

   9. most gigantic   **11.** saddest   **13.** redder
   10. fussier   **12.** weaker

B. Write the correct form of each adjective in parentheses.

   14. The world's (large) balloon was built in Minnesota.
   15. The World Trade Center Helipad is the (high) landing pad.
   16. This large airport is (hectic) than that one.
   17. This flight was the (tedious) of the two.
   18. The Boeing 747 is the (heavy) airliner of all.

C. Rewrite each sentence, using *less* or *least*.

   19. Airline travel is more expensive than travel by ship.
   20. Flying is more comfortable than traveling by train.
   21. Air travel is the most interesting way to travel.

D. Write each sentence, using either *than* or *then*.

   22. *Flyer* flew for twelve seconds and _____ landed.
   23. The Wright brothers were more daring _____ most people.

E. If a sentence contains an error in adjective comparison, write the sentence correctly. If there is no error, write *correct*.

   24. Of all airports, the King Khalid Airport in Saudi Arabia is the greater in size.
   25. Compared with a helicopter, an airplane is fastest.
   26. What was the most earliest flight of an airship?
   27. Then the world's youngest pilot was only nine years old.
   28. Howard Hughes's *Spruce Goose* was the peculiarest plane; the eight-engine wooden craft flew only once.

Apply • Think and Write

Dictionary of Knowledge • The aviator and writer Amelia Earhart set several records in flying. Read about her in the Dictionary of Knowledge. Then use some superlative adjectives in a description of this outstanding person.

✎ **Remember** to use forms of adjectives to make interesting comparisons.

Take turns telling jokes. Then vote on these awards: Good Punch Line, Best Joke, Worst Joke, and Most Laughs.

4 Irregular Comparison of Adjectives

Some adjectives form their comparisons irregularly. Learn the irregular forms.

Positive	Comparative	Superlative
good, well	better	best
bad, ill	worse	worst
much, many	more	most
little	less	least
far	farther	farthest

> **Summary** ◆ Some adjectives have irregular forms in the comparative and superlative degrees. Use the appropriate forms when you speak and write.

Guided Practice

Name the comparative and superlative forms of each adjective.

1. many   **2.** bad   **3.** far   **4.** well   **5.** good

Practice

Write the correct form of each adjective in parentheses.

6. Early mail planes carried (little) mail than modern planes.
7. Of the three, that pilot has flown the (many) mail planes.
8. In 1927 the (good) cost of all for airmail was first determined.
9. Your letters can go the (far) distance by air.
10. Sending mail by ship was (bad) than by airplane.

Apply ◆ Think and Write

Describing Days ◆ Write a paragraph comparing your best day with your worst day last week.

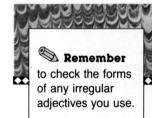

✎ **Remember**
to check the forms of any irregular adjectives you use.

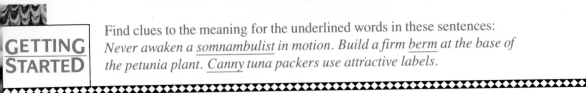

GETTING STARTED

Find clues to the meaning for the underlined words in these sentences:
Never awaken a somnambulist in motion. Build a firm berm at the base of the petunia plant. Canny tuna packers use attractive labels.

VOCABULARY ♦
Context Clues

English is a language rich with words. It has so many, in fact, that even the most educated person cannot hope to know them all. One way to learn new words is to use a dictionary. Another way is to use the *context*, or the words that surround an unknown word, to determine meaning.

Clues provided by context are called **context clues**. The chart below gives examples of different kinds of context clues.

Kind of Clue	Example
Direct definition	Amphibians *are airplanes that can take off from and land on ground or on water.*
Definition through description	The altimeter *indicated that the plane was 30,000 feet above the ground.*
Definition by apposition, or a synonym phrase set off by commas.	Early pilots needed great stamina, *or strength and endurance.*

Building Your Vocabulary

Tell whether each example gives a definition, description, or synonym for the underlined word. Then give the meaning of the word.

1. Gliders, or engineless planes, were among the first flying craft.
2. In 1909, Louis Blériot made the first international flight, from France to England.
3. The biplane, a popular early design, was a double-winged plane.
4. Designing planes took great mechanical and physical aptitude, or ability.
5. Early plane rides could be quite perilous. Many pilots were injured when their planes crashed.
6. Above all else, pilots in those days needed fortitude, which is the courage to face difficulty.

Practice

A. Write *definition*, *description*, or *synonym* to name the context clue given for each underlined word.

1. My grandfather once gave me a <u>discourse</u> on his early career as a pilot. It was quite a long speech.
2. He was an <u>aviator</u> who flew for the postal service.
3. "What kind of plane did you fly?" I <u>queried</u>, or asked.
4. His <u>rejoinder</u> was an answer I never expected.
5. I flew the <u>antiquated</u> flying cow, a plane no longer in use.
6. It was so named for its strange <u>oblong</u>, or rectangular, shape.
7. It had a <u>penchant</u>, an attraction, for landing in cow pastures.
8. But it had an <u>uncanny</u> ability, quite strange and mysterious, of missing the cows.
9. I never heard this tale's <u>finale</u>, though I'm sure it ended.
10. For I was dreaming happily <u>in the land of Nod</u>. I hope my grandfather wasn't offended!

B. Use the context clues to determine the meanings of the underlined words. Write the meanings.

11. <u>Aeronautics</u>, a relatively young science, has come a long way in recent years. Advances in flying have come year by year.
12. <u>Supersonic</u> jets can fly faster than the speed of sound.
13. Some <u>transport</u> planes can carry cargo as large as a helicopter.
14. <u>Commercial</u> planes are built for use in business.
15. Some special planes are used for <u>aerobatics</u>, the performance of stunts and tricks in the air.

LANGUAGE CORNER ◆ Word Origins

A *laconic* person is one who uses few words in speech or writing. *Laconic* comes from *Laconia*, a part of ancient Greece whose inhabitants were known for their brevity of speech. What places do the names below come from?

spaniel (literally, a dog from _____)
sardine (from an island in the Mediterranean Sea)
hamburger and frankfurter (cities in Germany)

How to Expand Sentences with Adjectives

You have been using adjectives with nouns to form descriptions. A vivid and exact adjective will give a clear description, whereas a vague and general one will add little information. When you write, choose exact adjectives to enliven your sentences and give your readers important information. For example, read these sentences.

1. Two brothers made history in 1903.
2. Two daring American brothers made aeronautical history in 1903.

Both sentences state a fact, but the adjectives *daring, American*, and *aeronautical* in sentence **2** give us much more information about the brothers and the kind of history they made.

One single, well-chosen adjective can make a difference in a sentence. When you choose adjectives, however, be careful not to repeat the same ones over and over. Overused adjectives can make a potentially interesting piece of writing boring. Substitute different adjectives for those you have used too often. For example, which sentence below would you rather read?

3. The little plane became a little spot as it flew over the sand dunes, but the little craft had remained aloft.
4. The tiny plane became a speck as it flew over the sand dunes, but the little craft had remained aloft.

Also try to avoid using too many common adjectives, such as *great, marvelous, wonderful,* and *terrific,* that do not add much real information. Use adjectives that add variety and exact detail instead.

The Grammar Game ♦ Create your own examples! Write at least four sentences, using the adjectives mentioned in the paragraph above at least once in each sentence. Then rewrite the sentences, replacing these adjectives.

Working Together

As your group expands sentences with adjectives in activities **A** and **B**, notice that your writing becomes more lively and informative.

In Your Group
◆ Listen carefully to each other. ◆ Respond to the ideas of others. ◆ Agree or disagree pleasantly. ◆ Stay on the job.

A. Write each noun below in a sentence, adding a pair of adjectives to describe the noun. Then write the sentence again, replacing the adjectives to change the description.

1. pilot	**5.** noise	**9.** idea
2. sandwich	**6.** spider	**10.** magazine
3. bridge	**7.** eyes	**11.** chair
4. glasses	**8.** sweater	**12.** storm

B. Imagine that your group is describing a ride on one of the first passenger planes. Rewrite this paragraph, adding adjectives to bring the experience to life.

    The plane lifted slowly off the ground. Inside, passengers huddled in their coats against the cold. Houses and trees swept along below, and people stretched to look down on the scene. Soon they were looking out over sky and clouds. "Flying is amazing," the passengers kept saying to themselves.

WRITERS' CORNER ◆ Overusing Adjectives

    Choose adjectives for nouns that need description. However, avoid stringing together too many adjectives to describe a noun and using adjectives that are unnecessary.

EXAMPLE: **The cold, wet, lashing rain had soaked us before we found shelter under a large, enormous oak tree.**

IMPROVED: **The cold, lashing rain had soaked us before we found shelter under an enormous oak tree.**

Read what you wrote for the Writer's Warm-up. Can you improve any sentences by using fewer, more effective adjectives?

FLYING MAN PATENT MODEL
sculpture by Reuban J. Spalding.

UNIT
SIX

USING LANGUAGE
TO

DESCRIBE

=== **PART TWO** ===

Literature *North to the Orient*
by Anne Morrow Lindbergh

A Reason for Writing Describing

CREATIVE
Writing

FINE ARTS ◆ Why are human beings so fascinated
with flying? Study the sculpture at the left. Then
put yourself in the place of the human form. Write
a poem about your experiences aloft.

CRITICAL THINKING ♦
A Strategy for Describing

AN ORDER CIRCLE

Describing is using details to paint word pictures. After this lesson you will read part of Anne Morrow Lindbergh's description of Canada as seen from the air, from her 1935 book *North to the Orient*. Later you will write firsthand descriptions of two places in your community.

There are many ways to describe something, and there are many ways to give order to a description. In the following passage, how has Anne Morrow Lindbergh organized her description of the flight over Canada?

Our first sight of the Mackenzie delta was twelve hours before. We had flown all night from Baker Lake. It never grew dark. For hours I watched a motionless sun set in a motionless cloud-bank . . . . Finally the sun set. Caught just below the horizon, it continued to light the sky with a strange green glow . . . . It was three o'clock in the morning when we finally found the settlement.

Phrases like "twelve hours before" give the reader a sense of the time order of events. What other words and phrases in the passage above help convey time order? When a writer gives order to information, it helps the reader understand and remember.

Learning the Strategy

Different topics or situations require different kinds of order. How, for example, would you arrange the tapes in a music store? Now suppose you are organizing some elementary school children for basketball teams. How would you group them? Then imagine you are going to write a report on early air travel. How would you organize the facts? Is there another kind of order that might be more interesting?

An order circle is one strategy for choosing a way to organize things or ideas. Inside a circle write a topic that needs organizing. On arrows write some kinds of order. Study the order circle. Then decide which kind of order works best for what you plan to organize. Below is an order circle for a tape collection. What other kinds of order might be considered?

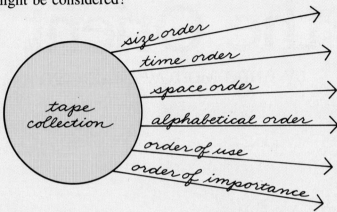

Using the Strategy

A. Do you have a collection—perhaps of books, old toys, stamps, or models? How might it be organized? Write the name of your collection inside an order circle. If you don't have a collection, imagine you plan to organize a postcard collection. Write some kinds of order on the arrows. Decide the kind of order you would use to organize your collection.

B. How would you organize a description of an airplane journey? What kind of order do you predict Anne Morrow Lindbergh used most in *North to the Orient*? Write the title inside an order circle. Write some kinds of order on the arrows. Predict the kind of order she used most. Then read to find out. You may find that the answer is not as simple as you think.

Applying the Strategy

♦ How did the order circle help you think about organizing your collection?
♦ What daily activity do you find most difficult to organize? How might choosing a kind of order help you?

from North to the Orient

by Anne Morrow Lindbergh

In 1931, Charles Lindbergh and his wife, Anne Morrow Lindbergh, charted a new Arctic route between North America and Asia in their plane, the Sirius. They flew north from New York across Canada and Alaska, along the coasts of Siberia and Japan, to Nanking, China. In the description below, they have left the small settlement of Baker Lake in Canada. They are flying north to the Eskimo village of Aklavik.

Our first sight of the Mackenzie delta was twelve hours before. We had flown all night from Baker Lake. It never grew dark. For hours I watched a motionless sun set in a motionless cloud-bank. For hours we skirted that gray, treeless coast, stretches on stretches of bleak land scattered with icy lakes. Always the same. Until I wondered, in spite of the vibration of the engine which hummed up through the soles of my feet, whether we were not motionless too. Were we caught, frozen into some timeless eternity there in the North? The world beneath had no reality that could be recognized, measured, and passed over. I knew that the white cloud-bank out to sea hung over the ice pack—that it marked, like the fiery ring around an enchanted castle, the outer circle of a frozen kingdom we could not enter. I knew from my husband's chart, handed back from time to time, that we followed the shore of Canada along Amundsen (ä´ mo͞on sən) Gulf to the Beaufort Sea. At one time we crossed a gray arm of coast which he pointed out as a tip of Victoria Island. "Victoria Island" — one of those pale pink lands which float off the top of the map — no, I could not believe it....

Finally the sun set. Caught just below the horizon, it continued to light the sky with a strange green glow, like that from a partial eclipse. We turned our backs on it and set our course southwest toward Aklavik (ə kläv´ ik). The land stretched out dark ahead of us.

We were both quite sleepy as we turned this corner of the flight. My husband, who had done all the flying, gave me the controls while he slept for short periods of a few minutes. Then he would fly again while I slept. During one of these naps I was jerked awake. Splutter—putt, putt, putt. The engine stopped. The nose of the ship dropped. We swayed forward. I could see my husband bent over the gas valves. Then the comforting splutter, splutter of the engine picking up again. One of the pontoon tanks had run dry. That was all. But I was stark awake by this time and wondering where we would land if the motor failed. I had been flying by compass and by that indistinct line, like the dregs of a wine bottle, that meant the horizon. Now I looked down at the ground below.

There, spread out for miles ahead, like so much tangled silver thread, were the meandering channels and watercourses worn by the Mackenzie River on the last slow lap of its journey to the Beaufort Sea. So many and so tortuous were the streams which made up this mammoth delta that I wondered how we would ever find the right bend in the right river, and Aklavik. Each circling stream had about the same course, the same number of tributary streams, some desultory and half choked with mud, others completely stopped at one end, making half-moon lakes—silver sickles of water.

As we came down lower and skimmed over the surface of one stream, we could not see across to another, for the banks were pine-covered. A strange sight in this treeless land, as though the great army of firs which had started out to accompany the Mackenzie River only a short distance had decided not to abandon her completely until she had safely reached the end of her journey, and had marched by her side even into this barren land, a thin phalanx of green.

It was three o'clock in the morning when we finally found the settlement—a big settlement for the North, about twenty or thirty houses, two churches, radio masts, and even another plane pulled up on the bank. At this hour it was so light that people ran out of their bungalows with cameras to take pictures.

As the roar of the motor died we heard for the first time that sound peculiar to the north, a bedlam of howling dogs. The term "howling dog" suggests back yards. This was the cry of a wild animal. And yet it was essentially the cry of resentment against the intruder—a strange bird which, roaring down the river, had broken the silence of their white night.

Library Link ♦ *Read more about the Lindberghs' pioneering flight in* North to the Orient *by Anne Morrow Lindbergh.*

Reader's Response

◆◆

Do you wish you had been with the Lindberghs on their historic flight to the Orient? Why or why not?

North to the Orient

Responding to Literature

1. Imagine that you had been sitting in Anne Morrow Lindbergh's seat when the engine stopped. What might you have thought? What might you have done? Write a journal entry about that experience.

2. How would you describe Anne Morrow Lindbergh? With your classmates, list words and phrases on the chalkboard that could be used to describe her. When the list is completed, choose three words or phrases that you would like people to use some-day to describe you. Select one of those choices. Write a paragraph to tell how you might someday earn that description.

Writing to Learn

Think and Plan ♦ Identify your favorite event in the selection from *North to the Orient*. What order did Mrs. Lindbergh use to tell about that event? Did she use space order, time order, or some other kind of order? Make an order circle. Investigate other kinds of order you could use to retell that event.

space order

(your favorite event from the selection)

time order

order of importance

Order Circle

Write ♦ Select an appropriate order and rewrite your favorite event from this selection. Compare your version with the original. Which do you prefer? Why?

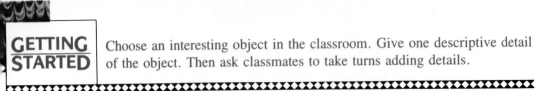

GETTING STARTED Choose an interesting object in the classroom. Give one descriptive detail of the object. Then ask classmates to take turns adding details.

SPEAKING and LISTENING ◆
Giving Descriptive Details

When you describe something, you should use the most vivid, accurate words possible. Such vivid descriptive details can help listeners picture what you are describing. With practice you can learn to use descriptive details effectively. The following guidelines will help you.

	Guidelines for Describing an Object
Giving a Description	1. Observe the object closely and carefully to collect complete details. Don't rely on your memory alone. 2. Identify the special characteristics it has. 3. Determine the overall impression you want to convey to listeners. Then select the details that support your purpose. 4. Choose precise words to create specific images for listeners. 5. If necessary, use gestures, drawings, or diagrams to clarify details.

When you listen to a description of an object, you should form a clear and complete impression of the object. These guidelines will help you become a better listener.

Being an Active Listener	1. Try to visualize the object as the speaker describes it. 2. Take notes if necessary. 3. Listen for precise descriptive details and ask questions if you don't understand the description.

Summary ◆ When describing an object, give precise descriptive details. Listen carefully to get a clear impression of the object.

Guided Practice

Give two specific details to describe each of the following.

1. an onion   **2.** a clock   **3.** a window   **4.** a student's desk

Practice

A. Choose an object in the classroom or any common object. List as many details as you can to give a precise, accurate description of the object.

B. Review your list of descriptive details for **Practice A**. Determine the overall impression of the object you would like to convey to a partner. Then select only those details that support your purpose. List these details.

C. Carefully observe your object again. Review your list of selected details for **Practice B**. Without naming the object, describe it precisely to a partner. Let your partner ask questions for clarification of details if necessary. Then see if your partner can identify the object. Have him or her tell which details helped most in identifying the object.

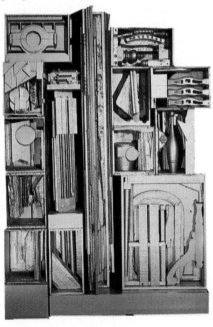

"Royal Tide-Dawn," 1960, Louise Nevelson. Wood painted gold, 91 x 63 x 10⅝". Photograph courtesy of the Pace Gallery.

Apply ◆ Think and Write

Dictionary of Knowledge ◆ Read about the outstanding features of Louise Nevelson's sculpture. Observe carefully her sculpture pictured above. Then tell a partner how this sculpture reflects those features.

Remember to give details that create specific images when describing an object.

Describe a familiar place. Use details that show how it sounds, looks, or feels. See if classmates can guess the place.

WRITING ◆
Sensory Details

To describe something effectively, use sensory details that show how it looks, sounds, smells, tastes, or feels. Details that appeal to the five senses are called sensory details. When you write, choose specific, colorful details that create vivid word pictures.

Notice how Anne Morrow Lindbergh appeals to the senses in the following excerpt from *North to the Orient*. Her precisely worded sensory details help the reader to experience that flight as she did.

> Our first sight of the Mackenzie delta was twelve hours before. We had flown all night from Baker Lake. It never grew dark. For hours I watched a motionless sun set in a motionless cloud-bank. For hours we skirted that gray, treeless coast, stretches on stretches of bleak land scattered with icy lakes. Always the same. Until I wondered, in spite of the vibration of the engine which hummed up through the soles of my feet, whether we were not motionless too . . . .

Lindbergh doesn't just say the scenery was impressive. She helps readers experience it through their senses with carefully chosen details. *Gray, treeless, motionless*, and *bleak* appeal to the sense of sight, and *icy*, to the sense of feeling. Did you notice how Lindbergh appeals to the senses of hearing and feeling in describing the engine's vibration, "which hummed up through the soles of my feet"?

> **Summary** ◆ Use **sensory details** to make your writing more specific and concrete.

Guided Practice

Name two sensory details that could describe each item below. Details may appeal to any sense you choose.

1. a sunset   **2.** a large lake   **3.** an airplane

Practice

A. Write two sentences that describe each item below. Appeal to the sense indicated in parentheses.

4. a secret hiding place (touch)
5. a wilderness lake at sunrise (hearing)
6. an ice-cream cone (taste)
7. a grove of orange trees with ripe fruit (smell)
8. lemonade on a hot day (taste)
9. pink flamingos wading in a lake (sight)
10. hot pavement beneath your feet (touch)
11. a busy city street (sight)
12. a freshly cooked meal (smell)
13. a jet plane taking off (hearing)

B. Draw five columns on a piece of paper. Label them *Sight, Hearing, Smell, Taste,* and *Touch.* Look at the picture below. List as many details about the picture as you can in each column.

Apply ◆ Think and Write

Writing Sensory Details ◆ Review your list of details for **Practice B.** Use details from the list to write five sentences—one for each sense—describing the picture. Be sure each sentence shows rather than merely tells what is being described.

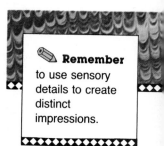

Remember to use sensory details to create distinct impressions.

GETTING STARTED

Describe a familiar place from left to right or from near to far, but name one detail out of place. See if anyone can identify the detail that is out of place.

WRITING ♦
Organizing a Descriptive Paragraph

After you have chosen the sensory details to include in a descriptive paragraph, you must organize them in a logical way. One way to organize a description is by space order. For example, you may describe a place from left to right, near to far, top to bottom, or inside to outside. Use any order that shows how the details in a scene relate to the whole.

Anne Morrow Lindbergh describes in space order her attempts to operate the radio and record messages in a cramped airplane.

> I managed, however, to do fairly well in an awkward-appearing position. My right hand took messages on a pad balanced on my left knee, while my left hand crossed over and controlled the dials at my right. An expert pianist sometimes looks like this, playing bass with his right hand and treble with his left, but an expert radio operator never should.

Notice how Lindbergh uses *left* and *right* and the image of the pianist with crossed hands to help the reader visualize the scene clearly.

Not all descriptions are organized in space order. Details may be arranged by order of impression to convey a dominant or overall impression of a scene.

> Brilliant October sunlight flooded the garden. Multicolored fish swam lazily in the reflecting pool, rising occasionally to catch insects. Red and yellow leaves blown by the wind rippled the surface of the pool.

The details in the paragraph above give a dominant impression of the garden.

Summary ♦ A descriptive paragraph may be organized by **space order** or by **order of impression**.

Guided Practice

State the kind of paragraph order suggested by each sentence beginning.

1. On the left of the runway lay . . .
2. The most memorable feature of the cabin was . . .
3. The most important sensation the navigator felt was . . .
4. Above the cloud cover gleamed . . .

Practice

A. Write the kind of paragraph order suggested by each sentence beginning.

5. A sudden yellow flash filled . . .
6. Just above the horizon, the sun grew . . .
7. The unrelenting noise of the engines became . . .
8. Farther away to the south, fog crept . . .
9. Close by the sandy bank lived . . .

B. Add one or more precise details to each sentence beginning in **Practice A**. Write your completed sentences.

C. Choose three of the following topics. For each topic you select, write three sentences that you could use to develop the topic into a descriptive paragraph. Each sentence group should use either space order or order of impression.

A recent school assembly
The way your classroom is arranged
Major attractions of a nearby vacation spot
A local historic landmark
The arrangement of books on your classroom shelves
A prominent land feature in your area

Apply • Think and Write

Organizing a Paragraph • Choose one of the topics you selected in **Practice C**. Expand your three sentences into a full descriptive paragraph. Organize your paragraph either by space order or order of impression. Remember to use sensory details to make your description more concrete.

✎ Remember
to use space order
or order of
impression in
descriptive
paragraphs.

Focus on Physical Viewpoint

When describing a scene, a writer has a certain angle of vision. He or she is ''standing'' (or ''sitting'') somewhere to observe the details being described. The writer's real or imagined location creates a **physical viewpoint.** Perhaps the writer is in the middle of the setting or above it or at the side. He or she may be close up or far away.

Notice the physical viewpoint in Anne Morrow Lindbergh's description in *North to the Orient,* which you read earlier.

Now I looked down at the ground below.
   There, spread out for miles ahead, like so much tangled silver thread, were the meandering channels and watercourses worn by the Mackenzie River on the last slow lap of its journey to the Beaufort Sea.

Lindbergh's story is true. Her physical viewpoint is that of a person in an airplane, looking down on the scene from a great height. If the river's channels look like ''tangled silver thread,'' we know that she must be very high indeed above the river. Now notice how the angle of vision changes as the plane descends.

   As we came down lower and skimmed over the surface of one stream, we could not see across to another, for the banks were pine-covered.

Here the many silver threads of streams are reduced to one, and the trees, previously unmentioned, become important. As the writer's perspective of the scene changes, the details change.

The Writer's Voice ◆ Suppose you were standing on the ground at Aklavik when the Lindberghs' plane landed. How would you describe the scene from that physical viewpoint?

Working Together

Physical viewpoint in description is the position from which a storyteller observes the scene. It frequently changes along with the action of the story. As a group, work on activities **A** and **B.**

In Your Group
◆ Invite everyone to talk.   ◆ Show appreciation to others.
◆ Record the group's ideas.   ◆ Offer help if needed.

A. Discuss the following sentences. Decide whether each physical viewpoint is *above, below, in the middle,* or *to the side* of the thing being described.

1. Across from the crowd, a biplane was taxiing for takeoff.
2. From an altitude of several hundred feet, the pilot could see the large features of the landscape clearly.
3. Spectators in small boats on the Hudson River were thrilled to see a small plane flying bravely above them.
4. From his seat near the center of the craft, Wilbur focused his attention on the controls to his left and right.

B. Working as a group, rewrite the sentences in activity **A** in the first person from the physical viewpoint of "Wilbur" who becomes "I." Retell all the events from his point of view. Between sentences **1** and **2,** add this sentence: "After many breathless moments, I finally got the aircraft off the ground."

THESAURUS CORNER ◆ Word Choice

Rewrite the paragraph below. Change it to first-person point of view. Use the Thesaurus and Thesaurus Index to replace each adjective in dark type with a better synonym.

His name is Eugene Ely, and the most **fetching** event of his life occurred on January 18, 1911. That morning he took off from an airfield twelve miles from where the battleship U.S.S. *Pennsylvania* was anchored. He would attempt to land his **elderly** Curtiss biplane on a 119-foot temporary wooden platform on its deck. Fifty feet from the ship, coming down in a **hasty** descent, he stopped the propeller. He almost overshot, but with **proficient** reflexes, he landed safely. It was a **glistening** day in naval aviation history.

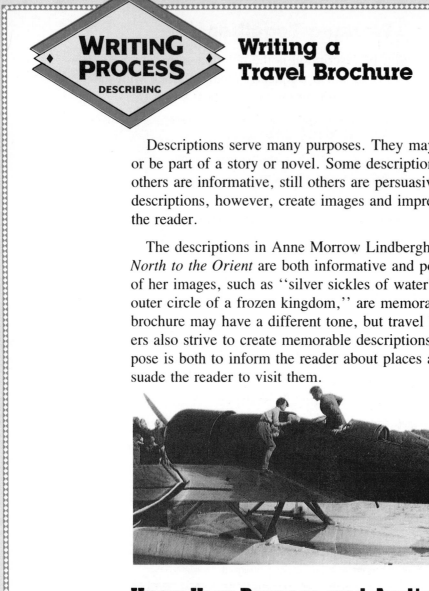

WRITING PROCESS

DESCRIBING

Writing a Travel Brochure

Descriptions serve many purposes. They may stand alone or be part of a story or novel. Some descriptions are poetic, others are informative, still others are persuasive. All descriptions, however, create images and impressions for the reader.

The descriptions in Anne Morrow Lindbergh's book *North to the Orient* are both informative and poetic. Many of her images, such as "silver sickles of water" and "the outer circle of a frozen kingdom," are memorable. A travel brochure may have a different tone, but travel brochure writers also strive to create memorable descriptions. Their purpose is both to inform the reader about places and to persuade the reader to visit them.

Know Your Purpose and Audience

What's
MY PURPOSE

In this lesson you will write a travel brochure about two places in your community. Your purpose is to write descriptions that will both inform and persuade your readers.

Who's
MY AUDIENCE

Your audience will be visitors or potential visitors of all ages. Later you might make a mock television commercial from your descriptions. You and your classmates might also present your brochures to your local chamber of commerce.

1 Prewriting

First choose as your topic two places of interest in your community. Then use a strategy to gather and organize your ideas.

Choose Your Topic ♦ Imagine that a friend or relative is coming to visit. You plan to give them a tour of your community. What are the most interesting places? Choose ones that you like; then you will be certain to interest others.

Think About It	Talk About It
Narrow your list to two places that may be near each other for a walking tour; are similar, such as an art museum and an art gallery; have physical beauty, such as a park and a lake; or have historical interest.	With your classmates brainstorm an exhaustive list of places in your community. Then each class member can scan the list for two places to include in a description.

Topic Ideas

the town hall and the
    police station
the zoo and the science
    museum
the two Victorian
mansions near the
train station
the town park and
Silver Lake

Choose Your Strategy ♦ Here are two strategies for planning a brochure. You might want to try one or both of them.

PREWRITING IDEAS

CHOICE ONE

Cubing

Just as a cube has six sides, cubing allows you to explore your topic from six perspectives. Get a piece of paper for each of your two places. Divide each sheet into six labeled squares. (The chart here tells what to do in each square.) Then write nonstop for three minutes about each place. Try to fill all six squares within the three minutes. Read your notes, looking for insights and details to use in your descriptions.

Model

Describe How does it look, sound, feel, etc.	**Compare** What is it simil to?
Associate What do you connect with it?	**Analyze** When/how wa created?
Argue What's good/bad about it?	**Apply** What can you there? Why w

CHOICE TWO

An Order Circle

Jot down facts and sensory details about your two places. Then make an order circle like this example. Add other kinds of order if you like. Study your order circle and decide which kind of order will work best for your description.

Model

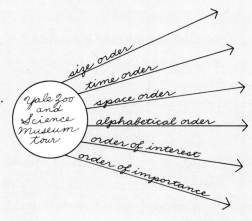

size order
time order
space order
alphabetical order
order of interest
order of importance

Yale Zoo and Science Museum tour

2 Writing

Use your prewriting notes as you organize and write your travel brochure. You might write four paragraphs. In the first paragraph introduce your community and the tour. Then write one paragraph about each of your two places. In your final paragraph urge readers to visit.

As you write, think about the power of a physical viewpoint. Remember how Anne Morrow Lindbergh gave her readers a sense of looking down on Canada from the air. In your brochure adopt one or more physical viewpoints toward the places you describe.

Sample First Draft ◆

A visit to Yale Iowa, is a treat you shouldn't miss! Here are two places you'll particularly enjoy.

Although small, Yale Zoo offers a fun-packed morning. Near the main gate are the Polar Bears. Sit on a bench and watch them splash about in their pool. Then move down the main path to the dolphin tank for the 11:00 show. Stand at the rail to watch the dolphins leap. End the morning with a picnic on the soft green field nearby.

After lunch take bus 4 to Yale Science Museum. Just inside, turn left to Dinosaur Hall. The mighty brontosaurus will make you feel tiny. Then proceed down the hall to the planetarium. Sit in the darkness as firey meteors explode in the sky above. Then climb aboard the spaceship in nearby Space Center. Listen in on mission control as you zoom past mars.

The city of Yale welcomes you please visit us soon!

3 Revising

Now reread your travel brochure and consider making changes to improve it. This idea may help you.

REVISING IDEA

FIRST   Read to Yourself

As you read, review your purpose. Did you write a description intended to inform and persuade potential visitors? Think about your audience. Will visitors of all ages want to visit the places you described? Listen to the sound of your writing. Consider how it will sound to a reader.

Focus: Have you written from one or more physical viewpoints?

THEN   Share with a Partner

Read your brochure to a partner. Then listen to his or her suggestions. These guidelines may help you work together.

The Writer

Guidelines: Read clearly. Listen to suggestions. Then make the changes *you* feel are important.

Sample questions:
- Did I include enough sensory details?
- Would my description make you want to visit?
- **Focus question:** Did I make my physical viewpoints clear?

The Writer's Partner

Guidelines: Listen carefully and give specific suggestions.

Sample responses:
- Could you add a detail about the sound of _____?
- I had trouble picturing where you were standing when you described _____.

Revising Model ◆ This draft of a travel brochure has been re-vised. The marks show the writer's changes.

The writer used a comparative adjective to clarify size.

The verb *meander* is more vivid than *move*.

The writer's partner suggested adding sound details.

This made the writer's physical viewpoint clearer.

A visit to Yale Iowa, is a treat you shouldn't miss! Here are two places you'll particularly enjoy.
Although small, *smaller than the zoo in Ames* Yale Zoo offers a fun-packed morning. Near the main gate are the Polar Bears. Sit on a bench and watch them splash about in their pool. Then ~~move~~ *meander* down the main path to the dolphin tank for the 11:00 show. Stand at the rail to watch the dolphins leap, *squeal, and chatter wildly.* End the morning with a picnic on the soft green field nearby.
After lunch take bus 4 to Yale Science Museum. Just inside, turn left to Dinosaur Hall. *if you stand next to* The mighty brontosaurus ~~will make you~~ *you'll* feel tiny. Then proceed down the hall to the planetarium. Sit in the darkness as firey meteors explode in the sky above. Then climb aboard the spaceship in nearby Space Center. Listen in on mission control as you zoom past mars.
The city of Yale welcomes you please visit us soon!

Read the revised brochure above as the writer wants it to be. Then revise your own travel brochure.

Revising Checklist

☐ **Purpose:** Did I write a travel brochure about local places? Did I write to inform and persuade visitors?

☐ **Audience:** Will visitors of all ages be able to picture the places I described? Will they be persuaded to visit?

☐ **Focus:** Have I written my descriptions from clear physical viewpoints?

Grammar Check ◆ A comparative adjective can help you show the relationship between two things.

Word Choice ◆ Do you want a more vivid word for a vague word like *move*? A thesaurus is a good source of vivid synonyms.

4 Proofreading

Now it is time to proofread your work. A brochure presented to the public must be correct.

Proofreading Model ♦ The travel brochure below has been proofread. The writer has made proofreading changes in red.

Proofreading Marks

capital letter	=
small letter	/
add comma	⌄
add period	⊙
indent paragraph	¶
check spelling	⬭

A visit to Yale, Iowa, is a treat you shouldn't miss! Here are two places you'll particularly enjoy.
   Although small, *smaller than the zoo in Ames* Yale Zoo offers a fun-packed morning. Near the main gate are the Polar Bears. Sit on a bench and watch them splash about in their pool. Then *meander* move down the main path to the dolphin tank for the 11:00 show. Stand at the rail to watch the dolphins leap, *squeal, and chatter wildly.* End the morning with a picnic on the soft green field nearby.
   After lunch take bus 4 to Yale Science Museum. Just inside, turn left to Dinosaur Hall. *if you stand next to* The mighty brontosaurus will make you *you'll* feel tiny. Then proceed down the hall to the planetarium. Sit in the darkness as *fiery* firey meteors explode in the sky above. Then climb aboard the spaceship in nearby Space Center. Listen in on mission control as you zoom past mars.
¶ The city of Yale welcomes you please visit us soon!

Proofreading Checklist

- ☐ Did I spell words correctly?
- ☐ Did I indent paragraphs?
- ☐ Did I use correct capitalization?
- ☐ Did I use correct punctuation?
- ☐ Did I type neatly or use my best handwriting?

PROOFREADING IDEA

Mechanics Check

   One quick way to catch errors is to focus on first letters. Is the first letter of a sentence or a quotation capitalized? Is the end punctuation of the preceding sentence correct? Are all words correctly capitalized or not capitalized? Is the first sound of each word correctly spelled?

   Now proofread your travel brochure, add a title, and make a neat copy.

5 Publishing

Here are two ways to share your travel brochure.

Visit Wonderful Yale, Iowa

A visit to Yale, Iowa, is a treat you shouldn't miss! Here are two places you'll particularly enjoy.

Although smaller than the zoo in Ames, Yale Zoo offers a fun-packed morning. Near the main gate are the polar bears. Sit on a bench and watch them splash about in their pool. Then meander down the main path to the dolphin tank for the 11:00 show. Stand at the rail to watch the dolphins leap, squeal, and chatter wildly. End the morning with a picnic on the soft green field nearby.

After lunch take bus 4 to Yale Science Museum. Just inside, turn left to Dinosaur Hall. You'll feel tiny if you stand next to the mighty brontosaurus. Then proceed down the hall to the planetarium. Sit in the darkness as fiery meteors explode in the sky above. Then climb aboard the spaceship in nearby Space Center. Listen in on mission control as you zoom past Mars.

The city of Yale welcomes you. Please visit us soon!

PUBLISHING IDEAS

Share Aloud	**Share in Writing**
Present a television commercial, using your brochure as a script. Add drawings, photos, or slogans. Ask classmates whether they would watch or zap your commercial if they had a remote-control device.	Illustrate your brochures and present them to your local chamber of commerce or a travel agency. Ask if the organization will forward any comments it receives from actual visitors to your area or from local residents.

Writing Across the Curriculum   Science

In this unit you chose a kind of order to organize your ideas. Futurists— scientists and others who predict the future—also choose ways of ordering their ideas. You can be a futurist, too.

Writing to Learn

Think and Predict ◆ Think of five important flight or space events that may happen before the year 3000. Choose a way to list these events in order. For example, make a time line (time order), a space map (space order), or a pyramid (order of importance).

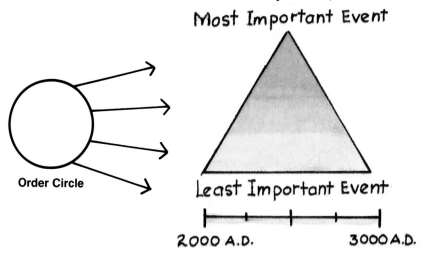

Most Important Event

Order Circle

Least Important Event

2000 A.D.   3000 A.D.

Write ◆ Use your list—your time line, space map, or pyramid—to write a prediction for the future of flight or space.

Writing in Your Journal

At the beginning of this unit, you wrote about early air travel. Then you went on to read more about the pioneers of flight. There is much more to know about early air travel. In your journal write questions you still have about the history of flight.

BOOKS TO ENJOY

Read More About It

The Second Mrs. Giaconda   by E. L. Konigsburg
This is a fictionalized account of the life and work of
Leonardo da Vinci as seen through the eyes of his assistant.
In these thirteen offbeat and exciting episodes, the great
genius achieves some of his greatest triumphs.

North to the Orient and **Listen! The Wind**
by Anne Morrow Lindbergh
A licensed pilot herself, Anne Morrow Lindbergh made
many long flights with her husband during the early 1930s
to chart new routes for airlines. In a sensitive and exciting
fashion, these books recreate those pioneering flights.

Book Report Idea   Book Tour

Reading a book is like going on a vacation.
Both readers and travelers see new
sights and meet new people. The
next time you report on a book
of fiction, pretend you are a
travel agent.

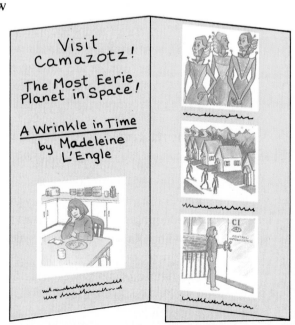

Create a Travel Brochure
A travel brochure pictures
points of interest at a particular
vacation spot. A travel brochure
book report should depict the
various settings in which the
main characters find themselves.
Include the main characters in
these sketches. Beneath each
picture on the brochure, include
a caption that describes the
settings and characters.

UNIT REVIEW

Unit 6
Adjectives   *pages 302–309*

A. Write the adjectives in each sentence. Include the articles.

  1. Washington, D.C., isn't just an ordinary city.
  2. The historical buildings and impressive monuments represent democracy.
  3. Long lines of eager tourists wait before the majestic Capitol.
  4. The glorious memorials to Jefferson and Lincoln are central attractions.
  5. Many museums, with free admissions and interesting tours, are educational and inspirational.
  6. Take a second look at the national capital, an extraordinary treasure.

B. Write and label each proper and demonstrative adjective.

  7. If you travel next summer, would you choose a European tour or an African safari?
  8. That travel agent recommends a tour of Spanish castles.
  9. Those travelers returned with Italian souvenirs.
  10. These tourists are staying at a hotel in the Tokyo area.
  11. Ask this person for directions to a Greek restaurant.
  12. Don't ignore the Egyptian pyramids or the Moroccan desert.

C. Write the correct form of each adjective in parentheses.

  13. Hawaii, often called the Big Island, is the (large) island of all the Hawaiian Islands.
  14. It is considered by many to be the (fascinating) island.
  15. Which is the (small) island in Hawaii?
  16. The black sand beaches are (extraordinary) than the tropical groves.
  17. These beaches seem (sunny) than those.
  18. Do you think the rain forest is (exotic) than the ancient volcano?

D. Write the correct comparative or superlative form of each adjective in parentheses.

19. One of the (bad) land weeds is barnyard grass.
20. At night an owl has (good) vision than an eagle.
21. Of the three animal trainers, Bárbara has the (much) experience with birds.
22. Which of the two bicyclists can ride the (far) distance?

Context Clues   *pages 310–311*

E. Use context clues to write definitions for the underlined words.

23. Andrew's cow is a <u>herbivorous</u> animal. Unlike Andrew's meat-eating cat, the cow is content to graze in the field.
24. Lillian is a <u>procrastinator</u>. She always delays doing her homework so that she scarcely has time to finish it.
25. The President of the United States is a <u>luminary</u>. Wherever he goes, he is recognized instantly.
26. The marble columns of the ancient temple had kept their <u>pristine</u> shine. Scientists were surprised at how fresh and new the columns still looked.

Sensory Details   *pages 324–325*

F. Write one or two sentences that describe each item below. Appeal to the sense indicated in parentheses.

27. a pizza parlor (smell)
28. a hard rainfall on the roof of a car (hearing)
29. brushing with toothpaste (taste)
30. a roadside vegetable stand (sight)

Proofreading

G. Proofread each sentence for correct capitals and punctuation. Write each sentence correctly.

31. Grant Wood an outstanding american painter painted an iowa farm couple
32. Wow This scene a painting by Diego Rivera is powerful
33. Well Georgia O'Keefe is my favorite painter
34. Her pictures of new mexico scenes are bold

·CUMULATIVE· REVIEW

UNIT 1: Sentences *pages 4–21*

A. Write and label each subject and verb.

1. The calendar year begins at midnight on December 31.
2. The earth rotates on its axis around the sun.
3. The rotation determines day and night.
4. The tilt of the earth's axis influences the seasons.

B. Write *simple* or *compound* for each sentence.

5. Great earthquakes usually begin with slight tremors, and the tremors rapidly increase.
6. The Richter scale indicates the magnitude of earthquakes.
7. Sensitive instruments record earthquakes around the world.
8. Seismologists are scientists, and they interpret the data.

UNIT 2: Nouns *pages 58–69*

C. Write each noun and label it *common* or *proper*.

9. The Globe Theater was a playhouse in London.
10. The plays of Shakespeare were often presented there.
11. This playwright and poet was born in Stratford-upon-Avon.
12. The historic theater was destroyed by fire.

D. Write the singular and plural possessive form of each noun.

13. territory   15. alumnus   17. bench
14. soprano   16. Smith   18. grandson

E. Write the appositive in each sentence.

19. The fifth largest planet, Earth, is a sphere.
20. Its outer shell, the crust, includes continents and oceans.
21. It is surrounded by the atmosphere, an envelope of gases.
22. Earth has one natural satellite, the moon.

UNIT 3: Verbs *pages 124–135*

F. Write and label each direct object and indirect object.

23. Alex threw the collie a stick or a branch.
24. The collie brought Alex and me his biscuit instead.
25. The dog showed us his new trick.
26. We fed him meat and cereal.

G. Write the sentences. Underline each linking verb and label each predicate nominative and predicate adjective.

27. Illinois is the birthplace of Ronald Reagan.
28. It became a state in 1818.
29. Its first settlers were resourceful.
30. The plains are fertile and treeless.

UNIT 4: Verbs *pages 180–198*

H. Write each verb and label its tense: *present, past, future, present perfect, past perfect,* or *future perfect.*

31. has washed   33. will move   35. worried
32. had named   34. munches   36. will have asked

I. Write the correct form of the verb in parentheses.

37. My neighbors (come, came) here a year ago from Korea.
38. They (rang, rung) our doorbell and introduced themselves.
39. I (taught, teached) them English.
40. They have (gone, went) to football games with me.

J. Write whether each verb is progressive or emphatic. Then label its tense.

41. does watch   43. has been closing   45. did appear
42. will be renting 44. do reveal   46. were cutting

K. Write the correct form of the verb in parentheses.

47. My sister has (set, sat) in front of the TV for an hour.
48. She has (laid, lain) all her work aside.
49. She (rose, raised) only once during that time.
50. Next time I shall (set, sit) the TV in my bedroom.

L. Write each possessive pronoun. Then write whether it is used alone or with a noun.

   51. Their machines are different.   **53.** Theirs is electric.

   52. His is a manual typewriter.   **54.** The new one is his gift.

M. Write and label each interrogative and demonstrative pronoun.

   55. That is an invitation.   **57.** With whom are you going?

   56. Who invited you?   **58.** This is a surprise.

N. Write and label each reflexive or intensive pronoun and its antecedent.

   59. The commuters packed themselves into a crowded bus.

   60. The bus itself was old and noisy.

   61. You yourself vowed never to ride in that bus.

   62. You know yourself better than anyone else does.

O. Write each indefinite pronoun. Label it *singular* or *plural*.

   63. Some of the lyrics seem very sad.

   64. No one will have a dry eye today after the performance.

   65. Many hum along or tap their feet to the music.

   66. Does anyone here sing harmony?

P. Write each pronoun and label it *subject* or *object*.

   67. Whom shall I call for an appointment?

   68. Did they prefer me or Kevin for the job?

   69. We recommended you and him for the promotion.

   70. The new inspectors will be he and I.

Q. Write the correct pronouns in parentheses.

   71. (Us, We) citizens have guaranteed constitutional rights.

   72. Our parents and (they, them) can vote in local, state, and national elections.

   73. The Constitution protects them as much as (we, us).

   74. You should cherish your freedom as much as (they, them) and (I, me).

Unit 6: Adjectives *pages 302–309*

R. Write the adjectives in each sentence. Include articles.

75. Doug read a recent report on the national population.
76. There has been a large increase in several states.
77. Certain other states have lost residents.
78. Substantial numbers are concentrated in the West.
79. The report showed that many Americans hold professional positions.

S. Write and label each proper and demonstrative adjective.

80. *Maine* originates from that ancient French province of the same name.
81. *Puerto Rico* is a Spanish word for "rich port."
82. *Alaska* is the Russian version of an Aleutian word.
83. The origins of these names are fascinating.

T. Write the correct adjective in parentheses.

84. Some sportscasters get (higher, highest) wages than athletes.
85. He's the (most youngest, youngest) winner in the league.
86. His pitching is (consistenter, more consistent) than ever.
87. His pitches are the (faster, fastest) in the league.

U. Write the correct comparative or superlative form of each adjective in parentheses.

88. What is the (bad) error you've ever made on a test?
89. Is your handwriting (good) now than it was last year?
90. Who has (little) energy, you or your brother?
91. Which member of the team has the (much) stamina of all?

Proofreading

V. Proofread each sentence for correct capitals and punctuation. Write each sentence correctly.

92. Emma Willard founded the first women's college in the united states in 1821
93. Well the erie canal made new york the chief atlantic port
94. Oops I almost threw away my swiss watch

LANGUAGE PUZZLERS

Unit 6 Challenge

Glad-Libs, Sad-Libs

Write this passage once as a Glad-Lib with cheery adjectives and once as a gloomy Sad-Lib. Make both the Glad-Lib and Sad-Lib as funny as possible. Include some comparative adjectives.

Last summer I had a _____ vacation at a _____ camp in the _____ mountains. _____ _____ kids shared my _____ bunkhouse, which was on top of the _____ hill with a _____ view of the _____ lake.

Swimming there was _____ because the lake was _____ and _____. We also took _____ _____ canoe trips and rode _____ horses. The food was _____, and especially _____. All in all I had the _____ summer vacation of my _____ life!

Adjective Anagrams

Unscramble the anagrams to find ten proper adjectives. (Hint: Each answer should be capitalized.)

1. in camera
2. rain at us
3. ant bite
4. in a din
5. dash in

6. his pans
7. shingle
8. gain type
9. ice hens
10. insane ploy

Make up anagrams for other proper adjectives. Have a friend unscramble them.

Unit 6 Extra Practice

1 Writing with Adjectives

p. 302

A. Write the adjectives, including articles, in each sentence.

1. A strong wind blew.
2. Buy new clothes.
3. Three girls arrived.
4. She looks thin.
5. Bring some money.
6. Eat this sandwich.
7. He was absent.
8. Powerful engines roared.
9. The class was not full.
10. More help is coming.

B. In the following article, eleven of the underlined words are adjectives. Write each adjective next to its sentence number.

11. Many Americans have written fine short stories. **12.** Edgar Allan Poe, brilliant and original, wrote tales of mystery and terror. **13.** He is the father of the modern detective novel. **14.** O. Henry is another popular short-story writer. **15.** His stories are known for careful plots and tricky endings. **16.** During the last century, Sarah Orne Jewett wrote sympathetic but humorous stories of New England life. **17.** Katherine Anne Porter's excellent stories often tell of her native Texas. **18.** Her superior style has made her famous. **19.** Many of the memorable characters in William Faulkner's stories appear also in his novels. **20.** Eudora Welty is another successful short-story writer. **21.** Her unusual tales often take place in small Mississippi towns.

C. Write the adjectives in each sentence. Next to each adjective, write *what kind*, *which one*, *how much*, or *how many* to show what question it answers. Do not write any articles.

22. This boy and two girls may go.
23. Good things come in small packages.
24. Every shower brought refreshing rain.
25. Last summer was hot and dry.
26. I like bread, fresh and hot from the oven.
27. Every cloud has a silver lining.
28. My big brother drank all the milk in the refrigerator.

D. The following paragraphs contain thirty adjectives. Write each adjective next to its sentence number. Do not write the articles *a* and *the*.

29. Humorous writing has always been popular in the United States. **30.** Mark Twain earned fame as a humorous writer in the last century. **31.** In recent years Dorothy Parker has gained a legendary reputation for witty stories. **32.** James Thurber's hilarious tales often described the misadventures of modern life. **33.** Ogden Nash created comical rhymes with peculiar words and incorrect grammar. **34.** The light verse of Phyllis McGinley treats the comic aspects of life with a certain seriousness.

35. Science fiction is another literary genre with a wide readership. **36.** Strange and eerie landscapes are the settings for much fiction by Ray Bradbury. **37.** Ursula K. LeGuin's fantastic novels are set on imaginary planets in the distant future. **38.** Isaac Asimov, a scientist, is a fine author. **39.** Asimov's scientific knowledge adds believability to the futuristic situations he creates. **40.** Arthur C. Clarke, outstanding writer and scientist, captured the modern imagination with the popular novel and film *2001: A Space Odyssey*.

2 Proper and Demonstrative Adjectives

p. 304

A. Write each proper adjective in this article next to its sentence number.

1. Many American writers have described interesting cultural influences in our land. **2.** Washington Irving wrote about the Dutch settlements of New York State. **3.** George Washington Cable told about the descendants of French and Spanish settlers in Louisiana. **4.** Ole Rölvaag described Norwegian farmers in the Dakotas. **5.** Edith Wharton's books often tell about wealthy Americans in European cities. **6.** Mary E. Wilkins Freeman wrote about the descendants of English settlers in the small towns of New England. **7.** William Saroyan's characters are often Armenian immigrants in California. **8.** In *Roots*, Alex Haley traced his ancestors from the Southern states to the African nation of Gambia. **9.** Saul Bellow's parents were Russian immigrants. **10.** In his novels he often explores Jewish culture in the United States.

B. Write each demonstrative adjective. Then write the noun it modifies.

11. There are thousands of fine books in this library.
12. That poetry is by Marianne Moore.
13. Did you read that story by Marjorie Kinnan Rawlings?
14. Both of these novels are by Edna Ferber.
15. A Broadway musical and a motion picture were made from this one book called *Show Boat*.
16. Did you find those sonnets by Edna St. Vincent Millay?
17. These poems by her show a great depth of feeling.
18. You may also enjoy this poetry by Sara Teasdale.
19. Those novels were written by John Steinbeck.
20. I enjoyed that story by Dorothy Canfield.
21. That novel by Gaston Leroux inspired many stage and screen versions of *The Phantom of the Opera*.

C. Write each sentence, completing it with the kind of adjective indicated in parentheses.

22. Was your grandmother a (proper) immigrant?
23. We studied (demonstrative) planet in science.
24. Have you ever eaten in a (proper) restaurant?
25. An (proper) tanker is now in the harbor.
26. Three (proper) students are visiting our city.
27. Include (demonstrative) tree in the photograph.
28. (Demonstrative) dogs and cats are my pets.
29. May I eat (demonstrative) carrots for lunch?
30. A (proper) author wrote (demonstrative) plays.
31. I really like (demonstrative) (proper) song.
32. (Demonstrative) is my favorite (proper) dish.

3 Using Adjectives to Compare
p. 306

A. Write each adjective. Then write its comparative and superlative forms.

1. bitter	6. fussy	11. small
2. graceful	7. sick	12. trustworthy
3. tan	8. stylish	13. great
4. thin	9. dirty	14. lovely
5. reliable	10. energetic	15. red

B. Write each adjective. Label it *comparative* or *superlative*. Then write its positive form after it.

EXAMPLE: wittier
ANSWER: wittier (comparative), witty

16. looser
17. flattest
18. fanciest
19. weaker

20. grimmest
21. steeper
22. slimmer
23. happiest

24. tanner
25. hungriest
26. saddest
27. wilder

C. Write the correct comparative or superlative form of each adjective in parentheses.

28. This was the (fast) ship in the nineteenth century.
29. Who had the (easy) Atlantic crossing of all?
30. This was the (clean) of the two old ships.
31. A room above deck was (spacious) than one below.
32. Food was (tasty) in first class than in third class.
33. First-class cabins were the (luxurious) of all.
34. One crossing was often (long) than another.
35. Were storms (frequent) than calm weather?
36. Steerage was (cheap) than third class.
37. Immigrants traveled steerage (much) of all.
38. A cabin was (desirable) than a dormitory.
39. A men's dorm was (terrible) than a family one.
40. Steerage quarters were the (dark) of all.
41. The quarters were the (filthy) they had seen.
42. The kosher kitchen was (tiny) than the galley.
43. Was one immigrant group (tolerant) than another?
44. The conveniences were the (crude) imaginable.

D. Rewrite each sentence. Use <u>less</u> or <u>least</u> to give it an opposite meaning.

45. Was dinner the most nutritious meal of all?
46. Was that voyage more tedious than the other?
47. Was happiness more frequent than misery?
48. A ship's berth was more comfortable than a bed.
49. That ship had the most satisfactory service of all.
50. Those were her most vivid memories.

E. Write each sentence, using either *than* or *then*.

51. Airline travel is more popular today _____ steamship travel.
52. Many travelers prefer to fly to a port and _____ take a cruise.
53. Isn't the food on a steamship better _____ the food on a plane?
54. I would rather eat at home and _____ travel.
55. Few restaurants prepare meals tastier _____ my mom's.

4 Irregular Comparison of Adjectives *p. 309*

A. Write the correct comparative or superlative form of each adjective in parentheses.

1. Jan and I plan to build a (good) clubhouse than last year's.
2. We picked the (far) tree from the garage.
3. The tree's sturdy fork was the (good) site we could find.
4. The new design has (many) new features than the old one.
5. We started building during the (bad) heat wave of the summer.
6. (Many) materials were donated by neighbors who were glad to have us clean out their basements and garages.
7. The roof needed (little) plywood than we had planned.
8. The old clubhouse had a (bad) view of the path than our new one does.
9. The (little) breeze made the treehouse sway.
10. Of the two windows, the (far) one was more troublesome to install.

B. Each sentence below contains an incorrect form of an adjective. Write the correct form.

11. Which of the two hikers can go the farthest distance?
12. The left field fence is far than the right.
13. Tom hit the ball over the fence many times than anyone else.
14. He is the good player on our team.
15. We have a best schedule than we had last year.
16. Our new coach has much enthusiasm than our old one.
17. The worse part about playing here is the condition of the field.
18. More teammates have already paid for the trip to the stadium.
19. My batting is bad than my fielding.
20. We have the little number of errors in the league.
21. Sally's fielding record is best than mine.

UNIT SEVEN

USING LANGUAGE
TO

RESEARCH

=== PART ONE ===

Unit Theme   *Interpreting Clues to the Past*

Language Awareness   Adverbs

=== PART TWO ===

Literature   "The Great Underground Army"
by Marjorie Jackson

A Reason for Writing   Researching

Writing
IN YOUR JOURNAL

WRITER'S WARM-UP ◆ Have you ever found an old object or tool and wondered who used it and why? How would you go about discovering the answers? Choose an object you use every day. What would those who uncover it 100 years from now think about it? Write about this discovery in your journal. Tell what was uncovered and what the discoverers thought about the object.

1 Writing with Adverbs

An adverb, like an adjective, modifies another word in a sentence. An adverb can modify or change the meaning of a verb, an adjective, or another adverb.

Archaeologists just rescued the treasures. (modifies verb)

Their discoveries were really important. (modifies adjective)

The treasures were unearthed very carefully. (modifies adverb)

Notice that the use of adverbs in the examples above makes the meaning of the sentences more exact.

In a sentence an adverb usually answers one of these questions about the word it modifies: *How? When? Where? How often? To what extent?*

How? They worked fast.   **When?** The digging began today.
How often? They seldom rested.   **Where?** The site is found nearby.
To what extent?   The workers have nearly completed the search.

The adverbs in each of the following sentences modifies a verb. An adverb that modifies a verb can come before or after the verb. It can also separate the parts of a verb phrase.

Now we *will uncover* a section of the ruins.
We *will uncover* a section of the ruins now.
We *will* now *uncover* a section of the ruins.

Notice that an adverb that modifies a verb can be located almost anywhere in a sentence. However, an adverb that modifies an adjective or another adverb usually comes directly before the word it modifies.

Adverb Modifying an Adjective
Many archaeological sites are quite magnificent.
Adverb Modifying Another Adverb
The pyramids in Egypt stand rather majestically.

As you may have noticed, many adverbs end in *-ly*. However, some adjectives also end in *-ly*. Some words can be used as either adverbs or adjectives.

Adverb: Scientists work <u>daily</u>. **Adjective:** All have <u>daily</u> tasks.
Adverb: They work <u>hard</u>. **Adjective:** Their job is <u>hard</u>.

Certain commonly used adverbs are frequently not recognized as adverbs because they do not end in *-ly*. Four of these adverbs are often used to begin questions: *how, when, where,* and *why*. More adverbs that do not end in *-ly* are shown in the chart below.

We are <u>almost</u> there.	He likes rocks <u>more</u>.
They had <u>already</u> left.	They <u>never</u> decay.
I will <u>also</u> look.	I do <u>not</u> agree.
He is <u>always</u> helpful.	They <u>often</u> dissolve.
Do you <u>ever</u> explore?	We <u>seldom</u> disagree.
Will this last <u>forever</u>?	Gems are <u>so</u> rare.
<u>Here</u> is the hill.	It is <u>still</u> early.
I <u>just</u> arrived.	<u>Then</u> we will rest.
We like that <u>least</u>.	We are <u>very</u> tired.
<u>Maybe</u> we will leave.	Are you done <u>yet</u>?

Summary ♦ An **adverb** modifies a verb, an adjective, or another adverb. Use adverbs to make your writing more vivid and exact.

Guided Practice

Name the adverb in each sentence. Tell what question is answered by the adverb.

1. The Roman city of Pompeii completely disappeared in A.D. 79.
2. A volcano, Mount Vesuvius, was nearby.
3. Mount Vesuvius erupted swiftly.
4. Ashes, dust, and cinders soon covered the town.
5. Is Pompeii buried today?

Practice

A. Write the adverb or adverbs in each sentence.

6. Mount Vesuvius erupted quite suddenly.
7. How did the citizens of Pompeii react?
8. They very quickly fled the city.
9. Pompeii lay quietly buried for centuries.
10. It was later discovered and excavations began.
11. Archaeologists have worked hard on its restoration.
12. Beautifully elaborate buildings were painstakingly restored.
13. A tour of ancient Roman homes is so impressive.
14. Many recovered treasures are always proudly displayed in the National Museum at Naples.
15. When will you visit the ruins of Pompeii?

B. Two words in each sentence end in *-ly*. One is an adverb. One is an adjective. Decide which word in the sentence is modified by each *-ly* word. Then write the adverb.

16. The lively city of Pompeii was fairly prosperous.
17. Princely houses gracefully lined the streets of the city.
18. The unexpected eruption of Mount Vesuvius buried the friendly city entirely.
19. The untimely ashes actually preserved the city.
20. Daily reports of objects discovered there were made readily available to the outside world.
21. Gradually we learned about the everyday habits and customs of these early Romans.
22. The stately sites revealed at Pompeii immediately fostered an interest in Roman history.
23. Lovely wall paintings were remarkably undisturbed by the effects of the volcanic eruption.
24. Fountains and lively statues as well as household goods were slowly unearthed.
25. Each year orderly crowds of tourists eagerly visit the streets and houses of old Pompeii.

C. Write each underlined adverb in the paragraph on the next page. Then write the word or words each adverb modifies. Label the word or words modified as *verb*, *adjective*, or *adverb*.

26. Easter Island is another <u>truly</u> incredible archaeological site. **27.** This South Pacific island is <u>justly</u> famous for its gigantic statues. **28.** Many of these statues weigh thirty tons, and some weigh <u>even</u> <u>more</u>. **29.** They are <u>very</u> tall and measure from twelve to twenty-five feet. **30.** The islanders <u>skillfully</u> made the statues from the rock of an extinct volcano. **31.** They <u>quite</u> <u>possibly</u> carved the statues using stone picks. **32.** <u>Somehow</u> the islanders placed the figures on raised platforms called *ahu*. **33.** Erecting such huge statues would present difficulties <u>even</u> <u>today</u>. **34.** <u>Maybe</u> scientists will unravel all the mysteries of Easter Island <u>eventually</u>.

D. Write each sentence. Complete it with an adverb from the chart on page 355.

    35. Of all possible careers, I have ____ liked the field of archaeology best.

    36. Divers ____ use metal detectors to uncover metal objects.

    37. Some people have ____ heard about underwater archaeology.

    38. Some of the methods used are ____ too different from those of land archaeology.

    39. Archaeologists have adapted to work in ____ any environment.

E. Write the groups of words below, using an adverb that answers the question in parentheses to complete each phrase.

    40. found objects (how often?)

    41. (to what extent?) gifted artist

    42. tossed the ball (where?)

    43. (how?) greeted a friend

    44. saw them (how often?)

    45. (to what extent?) won the race

    46. (how?) entered the museum

    47. was completed (when?)

    48. returned to work (when?)

    49. ran home (how?)

    50. pencil rolled (where?)

Apply • Think and Write

From Your Writing • Look at what you wrote for the Writer's Warm-up. Add or change some adverbs to make your sentences more vivid. Try to vary the locations of your adverbs.

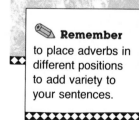

🖉 **Remember**
to place adverbs in different positions to add variety to your sentences.

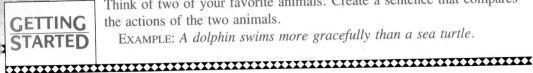

GETTING STARTED

Think of two of your favorite animals. Create a sentence that compares the actions of the two animals.

EXAMPLE: *A dolphin swims more gracefully than a sea turtle.*

2 Using Adverbs to Compare

Like adjectives, many adverbs can be used to show comparison. There are three forms, or degrees of comparison, of adverbs.

Positive Degree: I counted the objects <u>fast</u>.
Comparative Degree: He counted <u>faster</u>.
Superlative Degree: Rita counted <u>fastest</u> of all.

How to Form Comparative and Superlative Degrees

Add *-er* or *-est* to the positive form of most one-syllable adverbs.

soon	high	close
sooner	higher	closer
soonest	highest	closest

Put *more* or *most* before the positive form of most adverbs of two or more syllables.

clearly	easily	accurately
more clearly	more easily	more accurately
most clearly	most easily	most accurately

Become familiar with those adverbs that have irregular comparative and superlative forms.

well	badly	much	little
better	worse	more	less
best	worst	most	least

Use the comparative degree to compare two persons or things. Use the superlative to compare three or more.

Comparative: She arrived <u>earlier</u> than I did.
Superlative: Hanna arrived the <u>earliest</u> of all six students.

> **Summary** ♦ Many adverbs have three forms—the **positive,** the **comparative,** and the **superlative.**

Guided Practice

Name the comparative and superlative forms of each adverb.

1. near **2.** well **3.** much **4.** cheerfully **5.** boldly

Practice

A. Write the comparative and superlative forms of each adverb.

6. little **7.** promptly **8.** low **9.** deep **10.** carefully

B. Write the correct comparative or superlative form of each adverb in parentheses.

11. The history of China is reflected (vividly) of all through the story of its dynasties, or families of rulers.
12. Did any particular dynasty govern (well) than another?
13. The Shang dynasty's writing system lasted (long) of all its creations.
14. The Han family of rulers supported literature (vigorously) than the Ch'in family supported it.
15. I think the Ch'in dynasty contributed (much) to the culture of China than the Han dynasty did.
16. The first Ch'in emperor, Shih-huang-ti, worked (hard) than any other emperor to build the Great Wall of China.
17. It was (sturdily) built than other defensive structures.
18. Of all the ancient Chinese leaders, Shih-huang-ti governed the (forcefully) and brought about major changes in the land.
19. Archaeologists have discovered that Shih-huang-ti constructed one of the (completely) furnished burial vaults of all.

C. Write the comparative or the superlative form of the adverb in each phrase below. Write a sentence using the new phrase.

20. widely known **22.** was well suited **24.** did badly
21. arrived late **23.** walked straight

Apply ◆ Think and Write

Unearthing History ◆ Write a paragraph that describes taking part in an archaeological discovery. Use five examples of comparative and superlative degrees of adverbs.

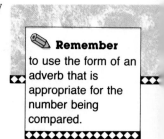

✎ **Remember** to use the form of an adverb that is appropriate for the number being compared.

3 Using Negatives Correctly

An affirmative sentence can be made negative by the use of just one negative word. Below are twelve commonly used negative words.

neither	nobody	not (n't)	barely
never	none	nothing	hardly
no	no one	nowhere	scarcely

Only one negative word is needed to make a sentence negative. If an extra negative word is added, the result is an error called a double negative.

Affirmative (right): I saw a skeleton of a mammoth.
Double Negative (wrong): I did <u>not</u> see <u>no</u> skeleton of a mammoth.
Negative (right): I did <u>not</u> see a skeleton of a mammoth.
Negative (right): I saw <u>no</u> skeleton of a mammoth.

You can use affirmative words to replace extra negative words.

Negatives: no   no one   nowhere   never
Affirmatives: any   anyone   anywhere   ever
Double negative (wrong): We <u>never</u> see <u>nothing</u> of interest.
Negative (right): We <u>never</u> see anything of interest.

Mistakes sometimes occur with *hardly, scarcely,* and *barely.* They are negatives and should not be used with other negatives.

Double Negative (wrong): I could <u>not hardly</u> believe their size.
Negative (right): I could <u>hardly</u> believe their size.

Many contractions include *n't* in place of the word *not.* Remember that *not* is a negative and should not be used with another negative.

Double Negative (wrong): <u>Aren't</u> there <u>no</u> mammoths alive today?
Negative (right): <u>Aren't</u> there any mammoths alive today?

> **Summary** ♦ A **double negative** is the incorrect use of two or more negative words in a sentence.

Guided Practice

Name the negative word in each sentence.

1. We could hardly wait to visit the museum at Rancho La Brea.
2. Doesn't the museum have over 240 kinds of animal remains?
3. No scientist will deny the value of studying these bone fossils.

Practice

A. Write the negative word in each sentence.

4. Isn't a fossil a plant or animal that has been preserved?
5. Tar in the pits of La Brea did not allow animals to escape.
6. Neither did it allow their bones to decay.
7. Nobody paid much attention to the bones for many years.
8. The animals never suspected the tar would trap them.

B. Write the correct word in parentheses.

9. The animals couldn't go (anywhere, nowhere) after being trapped.
10. Whole skeletons (are, aren't) hardly ever found.
11. Scientists don't (ever, never) fail to study the bones.
12. Scarcely (no one, anyone) thought mammoths would be so big.
13. There aren't (no, any) live mammoths in California today.

C. Write each sentence, correcting any double negatives you find. If a sentence is correct, write *correct*.

14. Neither of us hadn't seen a mammoth's ivory tusks before.
15. Didn't no one know that mammoths fed on grass?
16. Isn't the modern elephant related to the mammoth?
17. Nothing never remains of many animals except their fossils.
18. We hadn't barely seen everything when the museum closed.

Apply ◆ Think and Write

Formulating Rules ◆ Write five rules a zoo might have. Include several double negatives. Read your rules aloud and have a partner listen for and correct your double negatives.

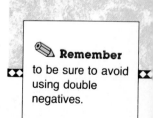

✎ **Remember** to be sure to avoid using double negatives.

4 Troublesome Adjectives and Adverbs

Certain adjectives and adverbs are often misused. The rules that follow will help you use these words correctly.

Good, Well; Bad, Badly *Good* and *bad* are adjectives. Use them only to modify nouns and pronouns. Be sure to use *good* and *bad* as predicate adjectives after linking verbs such as *be, feel, look, seem, appear, smell, sound,* and *taste.*

> That is a good goal.   It was not a bad decision.
> Eli felt good about it.   She looked bad. (not badly)

Well and *badly* are adverbs. Use them to modify verbs.

> ■ She works well with me. (not good)   I miss her badly. (not bad)

Well is an adjective when it is used to refer to a person's health.

> ■ Susanna was ill, but now she is well. (not good)

Real, Really; Sure, Surely *Really* and *surely* are adverbs. Use them to modify verbs, adjectives, and adverbs.

> **To modify an adverb:** We listened really intently. (not real)
> **To modify an adjective:** It was really fascinating. (not real)
> **To modify an adjective:** People are surely remarkable. (not sure)
> **To modify a verb:** They surely differ. (not sure)

Real and *sure* are adjectives. Use them to modify nouns and pronouns. Like *good* and *bad* they are used as predicate adjectives.

> It was a real opportunity.   Our winning was a sure thing.
> The trophy's silver was real.   I was sure of it.

Summary ◆ Do not replace an adverb with an adjective. Knowing the meanings of confusing adjectives and adverbs can help you choose the right ones to use.

Guided Practice

Tell which word should be used to complete each sentence.

1. Anthropologists study (real, really) people and their cultures.
2. They never speak (bad, badly) of the groups they research.
3. Their studies are (surely, sure) fascinating.
4. It is (well, good) to learn about other groups of people.

Practice

A. Write the correct adjective or adverb in each sentence.

5. Anthropologists must interact (well, good) with other people.
6. Interviews are conducted (really, real) frequently.
7. These scientists (surely, sure) ask many questions.
8. Is every group (sure, surely) of its values?
9. Do all societies feel (badly, bad) about loss?

B. Complete each sentence with one of the words below.

real   really   bad   badly   good   well

10. The studies of anthropologists are ____ varied.
11. Some feel ____ about researching and comparing languages.
12. Many investigate how ____ a person gets along with others.
13. Others question whether violence affects children ____ .
14. What area of behavior is of ____ interest to you?

C. Write each sentence, correcting any errors in the use of adjectives or adverbs.

15. Anthropologists work real tirelessly all around the world.
16. They need to stay good wherever they travel.
17. Margaret Mead was surely of her career choice.
18. She worked good with the islanders of the South Pacific.
19. Understanding other societies is a really challenge.

Apply ✦ Think and Write

Dictionary of Knowledge ✦ Read more about the science of anthropology in the Dictionary of Knowledge. Write a paragraph about anthropological research. Include four of the adjectives or adverbs from this lesson in your writing.

> ✎ **Remember**
> to recall the meanings of certain adjectives and similar adverbs to avoid misusing them.

GETTING STARTED

Here is one of the longest words in the English language
antidisestablishmentarianism
How many word parts—prefixes and suffixes—do you think it contains?

VOCABULARY ◆
Suffixes

A **suffix** is a word part added to the end of a base word. Some suffixes make nouns plural, and some suffixes change the tense of verbs.

■ **ladder + s = ladders**   **climb + ed = climbed**

Other suffixes change the meaning and the part of speech of the word to which they are added.

■ **When teachers <u>assign</u> homework, students have <u>assignments</u>.**

What suffix changed *assign*, a verb, into a noun?

The chart below lists suffixes that change the meaning and sometimes the part of speech of a word. Try to think of more words that could take each of these suffixes.

Suffix	Meaning and Part of Speech	Example
-en	become or cause to be; made of (verb, adjective)	soften
-ish	related to, having the qualities of (adjective)	childish
-ism	act of, devotion to (noun)	heroism
-ist	one who does, makes, or practices (noun)	pianist
-ment	act of; state of (noun)	amusement
-ness	state of; quality of (noun)	happiness

Building Your Vocabulary

Use the suffixes in the chart to form as many different words as you can by adding them to the words below.

bright	**colonial**	**black**	**small**	**establish**
nourish	**individual**	**develop**	**real**	**weak**

List other words you know to which these suffixes can be added.

Practice

A. Use the suffixes *-ment*, *-ness*, *-ist*, and *-ism* to form new words from the words listed below. Write the words.

1. enjoy	**6.** industrial	**11.** journal
2. critic	**7.** treat	**12.** fit
3. pave	**8.** commit	**13.** crooked
4. flute	**9.** bleak	**14.** manage
5. sore	**10.** canoe	**15.** motor

Choose five or more of the words you formed and write a paragraph that includes those words.

B. Add suffixes to the words in parentheses to complete the following sentences. Write the sentences.

16. A (botany) is a person who studies plant life.
17. Maria studies violin for her own (amuse).
18. The rain began to (slack), and the sky began to (bright).
19. He was a (bear) man with a (boy) face.
20. The medic's (calm) in the face of danger inspired us all.

C. Many words are formed with two or more suffixes. For example, *truthfulness* = *truth* + *-ful* + *-ness*. Write the base words and the suffixes that make up the words listed below.

childishness	**laughableness**	**brainlessness**
homelessness	**lovableness**	**quarrelsomeness**

LANGUAGE CORNER ♦ Back-formations

In this lesson you have added suffixes to base words to form new words. Sometimes words are formed in the opposite way—by subtracting a suffix from a word that already exists. For example, the verb *televise* was formed from the noun *television*.

What words were formed by subtracting suffixes from the words below?

donation   editor
burglar   escalator
jelly   ghostwriter

donation	**editor**	**burglar**
escalator	**jelly**	**ghostwriter**

How to Expand Sentences with Adverbs

In this unit, you have been using adverbs to modify verbs, adjectives, and other adverbs. Because adverbs tell *how, when, where,* or *to what extent,* they add important information to your writing. Notice how adverbs have been added in sentence **2** to expand the sentence and provide more information about how the archaeologist worked.

> **1.** The archaeologist cleaned the artifact.
> **2.** The archaeologist cleaned the artifact slowly and carefully.

Remember that an adverb placed at the beginning or end of a sentence has more emphasis than one placed in the middle.

> **3.** The archaeologist gently lifted the pottery from the rubble.
> **4.** Gently the archaeologist lifted the pottery from the rubble.

Changing the position of some adverbs, however, can change the meaning of the sentence. For example, the adverb *just* in sentence **5** tells when the statue was discovered. In sentence **6,** *just* means that no one else has found a statue.

> **5.** One scientist has just discovered a Mayan statue.
> **6.** Just one scientist has discovered a Mayan statue.

When you write, position adverbs where they will provide the kind of emphasis and meaning you want in your sentences. Remember also that overusing an adverb can make your sentences ineffective.

The Grammar Game ♦ How do *you* do it? The verbs below name common actions that are performed every day. Quickly write two or three adverbs to describe *how, when, where,* or *to what extent* you perform each action.

| smile | eat | write | run | sleep |
| dress | think | talk | wait | knock |

Working Together

As your group works on activities **A** and **B**, position adverbs to provide proper emphasis and meaning to your sentences.

In Your Group
♦ Ask relevant questions.   ♦ Help each other follow directions. ♦ Don't interrupt each other.   ♦ Help the group finish on time.

A. Add adverbs to expand the sentences below. Choose at least two adverbs that give different kinds of information to each sentence.

1. I moved from the edge of the cliff.
2. Kelly started her homework.
3. The rain stopped.
4. Joseph walked to school.
5. Everyone went to work.

B. Imagine that your group is working on the excavation of a Mayan city. Write this paragraph, adding adverbs to bring it to life.

> We arrived at the site. Dr. Sánchez explained the project and assigned tasks to each of us. We gathered our tools and went to work. Manuel and I talked as we began to dig. Manuel cried out. He had uncovered part of a small figurine and was lifting it from the dirt. We waved at Dr. Sánchez to come and look at what Manuel had found. We shall find more as we continue our work.

WRITERS' CORNER ♦ Word Choice

As you know, a carefully chosen adverb can add important detail to a sentence. However, choosing a more vivid and specific verb can sometimes make the addition of an adverb unnecessary.

EXAMPLE 1: Terry ran quickly across the field to catch the bus.
EXAMPLE 2: Terry raced across the field to catch the bus.

Read what you wrote for the Writer's Warm-up. Could you have used more specific verbs rather than adding adverbs to give detail to your sentences?

LIBRO DEI MORTI
Torino Museo Egizio/Art Resource.

USING LANGUAGE
TO

RESEARCH

PART TWO

Literature "The Great Underground Army"
by Marjorie Jackson

A Reason for Writing Researching

CREATIVE
Writing

FINE ARTS ◆ Many civilizations through the ages
have used various ways of communicating through
writing. How creative are you? Invent a new
alphabet. Then write a brief message with your
new alphabet. Share your code and ask a partner
to read your message and respond to it.

CREATIVE THINKING ♦
A Strategy for Researching

ANSWERING "WHAT IF?"

Researching is gathering information. Writing that is based on research does not need to be dull. After this lesson, you will read "The Great Underground Army," a research article that reads like a mystery. Later you will write a research report of your own.

"The Great Underground Army" tells about a strange discovery made by some villagers in northern China in 1974.

In the spring of 1974 villagers in the Shensi Province of northern China set out to dig an irrigation well in a nearby field. While digging the reddish soil of their Yellow River valley, the villagers made the most incredible find in recent archaeological history. They discovered the first figures of what we now know to be a lifesize army of over seven thousand soldiers, horses, and chariots, all made of clay. . . .

Like the villagers, archaeologists were both amazed and puzzled. What if the clay army was a mystery to be solved?

Learning the Strategy

Asking "what if" is a way of supposing. For example, what if—or suppose that—the clay army had been buried by someone long ago? Such a supposition suggests many follow-up questions. For example, who might have created the clay army? Why? Who might have buried it? Why? As soon as the clay army was discovered, scientists and historians began research to find answers.

The story of *Kon-Tiki*, which appeared on pages 78–82 of this book, is a good example of supposing. Thor Heyerdahl believed that ancient Peruvians had traveled by raft to the South Pacific. What led Heyerdahl to that belief? What "what if" questions might he have asked himself?

CREATIVE THINKING: Supposing

Sometimes you can use a "what if" question to help anticipate something you will read or view. For example, before watching a television special on polar exploration, you might wonder "What if *I* tried to go to the South Pole?" "What if" questions can help you think about actions you are considering. For instance, if you wanted to meet a new girl in your class, you could ask yourself "What if I went up to her and said hello?"

Asking follow-up questions can help you imagine or plan for the "what if" situation. The chart below shows some follow-up questions about the new girl. What questions might you add?

What if I say hello to the new girl?

What would she say back?	She'd probably say hello.
What if she isn't friendly?	I could be friendly anyway.

Using the Strategy

A. On a paper write "What if I could be anything I want to be when I grow up?" Then write three follow-up questions and your answers. You and your classmates might enjoy sharing some of your future dreams and plans.

B. Reread the passage from "The Great Underground Army" on page 370. On a piece of paper write "What if a lifesize clay army were found?" Write at least three follow-up questions. Then read "The Great Underground Army" to see if some or all of your questions are answered by the article.

Applying the Strategy

- How did you think of follow-up questions to the question about what you will be when you grow up?
- What is the difference between asking "what if" questions about past events and about future events?

The Great Underground Army

by Marjorie Jackson

In the spring of 1974 villagers in the Shensi Province of northern China set out to dig an irrigation well in a nearby field. While digging the reddish soil of their Yellow River valley, the villagers made the most incredible find in recent archaeological history. They discovered the first figures of what we now know to be a life-size army of over seven thousand soldiers, horses, and chariots, all made of clay and all guarding an emperor who died over two thousand years ago.

The clay warriors stood about six feet tall, fifteen to twenty feet underground, and were carefully arranged in battle formation, just as if they were alive. The spearmen—with real spears and shields—led the attack, while archers knelt on either side, their crossbows ready to be drawn. In the center of the brick-paved halls, infantrymen faced forward, waiting for the order to charge. Charioteers, somewhat taller than the foot soldiers, stood nearby in real chariots, ready to swing a team of four clay horses, hitched with leather harnesses and brass fittings, into action. The army's commanders were perhaps the most impressive, for in ancient Chinese art, rank was shown by size, and these warriors stood six feet, five inches tall.

Even more astonishing than the size and numbers of the clay figures was the fact that they were all different; no two soldiers and no two horses looked alike. Some of the soldiers wore armor and some belted robes; some had boots, some sandals, while others wore leggings. Some warriors had braided hair, some had hair pulled into a knot on top of their heads, some had beards or moustaches. Even the expressions on their faces were different—some stern and serious, some worried, some looking as if they were on the verge of a smile. The uniforms, faces, and hands of the soldiers had been brightly painted, as had been the horses, and chips of paint could still be seen.

When the well diggers found parts of this awesomely lifelike army in the earth, some figures were still standing, but many had fallen and were lying in crumbled heaps. Archaeologists were called to the scene, and excavation was begun at once. Many questions were raised: How had the huge army come to be buried in those peaceful fields, and who was the emperor it had guarded so faithfully over the centuries?

His name was Ch'in Shih-huang-ti (sher-hooang-dee), and he was only thirteen years old when he first came into power as King

Cheng of the state of Ch'in in 246 B.C. In those days China was divided into many states, each with its own ruler and each often at war with its neighbors, but the young King Cheng was determined to change that. It was said that he had the heart of a tiger and but two wishes in life: to join China's separate states into one kingdom, and to stay young forever.

King Cheng quickly learned to govern his people and command his army, and it wasn't long before he set out to control the rest of the country. For nearly twenty-five years he and his warriors waged fierce battles with neighboring states, and when the fighting stopped in 221 B.C., Cheng had conquered them all and become Ch'in Shih-huang-ti, First Emperor! For the first time in her long history, China was a unified nation, and it is said that she took her name China from Shih-huang's home state of Ch'in.

But Shih-huang didn't rest when his kingdom was united. Bands of roving tribesmen from Asia had always been a threat to the northern states of China, and the First Emperor was determined to put a stop to their raiding. In the past, each northern state had built its own small section of wall as protection; Shih-huang joined these sections together and extended the wall along the entire fifteen-hundred-mile northern boundary of China. Called the Great Wall, it was in some places wide enough for six horsemen to gallop abreast along the top as they patrolled the land; and it is still the longest fortification in the world. In fact, astronauts say that the Great Wall of China can be seen from their spaceships as they orbit the earth—the only man-made structure visible from outer space!

Shih-huang was a reformer as well. He wrote new laws, standardized tables of weights and measures, and organized the system of writing Chinese characters so that people all over China could use and understand the same written language. He built a vast network of roads throughout his entire kingdom, constructed canals for what would become the greatest inland water-communication system in the ancient world, and dug irrigation ditches, still used today, so his people could cultivate more of their land than ever before.

But in spite of all his power and success, Shih-huang was never content. Much of what he had done had been accomplished by force, and he had many enemies. Thousands, perhaps millions of men had died building the Great Wall; and their crushed bones,

LITERATURE: Article

buried beneath the heavy stones of the wall, gave it the name "the longest cemetery in the world."

Shih-huang was also afraid of anyone who thought differently than he did, or who openly opposed his rule. Because he felt that the teachings of the ancient philosopher, Confucius, supported the old form of government, he not only burned all of the Confucian books, but buried alive or beheaded over four hundred Confucian scholars who refused to accept his rule.

As Shih-huang grew older, his brave heart deserted him, and he grew more and more superstitious and afraid. He sent expeditions out to sea in search of a magic formula that would keep him young and powerful, but his captains returned home empty-handed. There were several attempts made on his life, and he began sleeping in a different room of the palace each night. Only his most trusted ministers knew where to find him. And he became increasingly worried about what would happen to him when he died.

This wasn't really a new worry—he had begun working on his tomb as soon as he was made King of Ch'in and, by the time he declared himself emperor, over seven hundred thousand workers were digging the vault and preparing the army that would protect him in the afterlife. It is said that each of the soldiers in the clay army was modeled after a living soldier in Shih-Huang's real army; the warriors supposedly were happy to pose for the sculptors, as it meant they wouldn't themselves be buried alive with their emperor, as had once been the custom!

When Shih-huang finally died (a natural death, despite his fears of assassination), he was buried under a man-made hill about the size of a five-story building. Mountains surrounded him on two sides, the temple of his ancestors protected him on the third, and under the open fields of the fourth was buried the amazing clay army that the frightened emperor had ordered built for his everlasting security.

Unfortunately, the clay warriors were not enough protection against grave robbers, and just four years after Shih-huang's death, the underground vault was broken into. Some of the weapons and valuables buried there were stolen, and the timbers that supported the roof over the army were burned. When the charred timbers collapsed, dirt and rocks buried the army, leaving the soldiers and horses silent and forgotten, until the well diggers' shovels found them two thousand years later.

These soldiers and horses, along with all of their equipment, are now being repaired and returned to their original positions—this time in a modern museum on the same site. When the work is finished, tourists and Chinese alike will be able to see Shih-huang's army of thousands standing in formation once more, just as it stood so long ago. And though the emperor Ch'in Shih-huang-ti didn't get his wish to be young forever, his name lives on even today.

Library Link ♦ *Read other historical articles in* Cricket, *a magazine for young people, found in your library.*

 ## Reader's Response

Would you like to have lived in China at the time the great underground army was being built? Why or why not?

The Great Underground Army

Responding to Literature

1. King Cheng was said to have the heart of a tiger. What does that comparison tell you about the young king?

2. Many fascinating facts were revealed in this article. Which fact most surprised you? Why?

3. What else would you like to know about King Cheng? Prepare five questions you would like to ask him. Work with a small group. Take turns asking questions and answering your class-mates' questions. When you answer, be sure to answer as King Cheng might have answered.

Writing to Learn

Think and Suppose ♦ Write three "what if" questions in response to the information given in "The Great Underground Army."

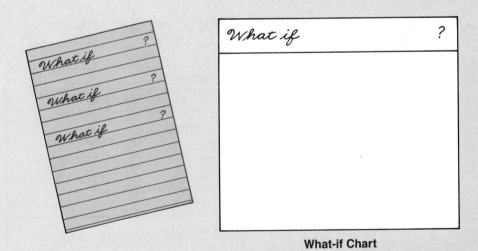

What-if Chart

Write ♦ Choose your favorite question of the three and write several follow-up questions for it. Then try to answer your questions. Write about what you suppose the answers would be.

GETTING STARTED Think of a topic you would like to report on. How could you capture listeners' attention in an opening sentence?

SPEAKING and LISTENING ♦ An Oral Report

In order to give a successful oral report, you must be able to organize material and present it an interesting way. Your report should have three main parts—an introduction, a body, and a conclusion. The introduction need not be long, but it should capture your listeners' attention. You might begin with an unusual fact or ask a question. The introduction should also give the main idea of the report.

The body of your report should contain most of the information—the details and examples that explain and support your main idea. Outline the material on note cards to help you remember the important points you wish to make. (See pages 596–597 for information on outlining.)

Your conclusion should summarize your main ideas in a memorable way and tie your report together. An apt quotation is often a fitting way to end a report.

These guidelines will help you present and listen to an oral report.

Giving a Report	1. Use note cards on which you include all necessary information. 2. Practice giving your report for friends or family and ask for suggestions for improvement. 3. Speak clearly and make eye contact with listeners. 4. Be sure your gestures look natural. 5. Use visual aids—charts, maps, drawings—to help your listeners understand your supporting details. 6. If you make an error, correct it without embarrassment. 7. Present your conclusion forcefully.
Being an Active Listener	1. Listen carefully for the main idea in the introduction and follow its development in the body. 2. Take notes, particularly if the topic is complex. 3. Mentally summarize the speaker's main points from time to time as you listen. 4. Afterward ask for clarification of a point if necessary.

> **Summary** ♦ Organize your oral report into an introduction, a body, and a conclusion and present it clearly. Listen carefully to understand the purpose and major points of a report.

Guided Practice

Tell whether each introductory statement would capture a listener's attention. If not, tell how you would improve the statement.

1. Archaeologists have uncovered in Peru the greatest ancient treasure ever discovered in the Western Hemisphere—the 1,500-year-old tomb of a Moche warrior priest.
2. What discovery could compare with the discovery of King Tutankhamen's tomb?
3. Archaeologists found some clues to an old civilization.
4. Archaeologists study the remains of past civilizations.

Practice

A. Write a brief introduction for an oral report. Include a startling statement, an unusual fact, or a question. Choose one of the topics below or select your own.

Our Student Government   How a Computer Helps Me Learn
The Benefits of Swimming   The Best Kind of Breakfast

B. Develop the introduction you wrote for **Practice A** into an oral report. Add a body that includes supporting details and examples. End with a strong conclusion. Present your report to a group of four or five classmates. Listen attentively to others' reports and ask questions on points that need clarification.

C. Select a brief article that interests you and read it aloud to a small group of classmates. Ask the listeners to state the main idea of the article and its most important points.

Apply ♦ Think and Write

Evaluating Oral Reports ♦ Write a list of questions you could use to evaluate oral reports. For example, did the speaker use visual aids? Use the questions to rate the oral reports you hear.

> **Remember**
> to prepare carefully and practice before presenting your oral report.

STUDY SKILLS ♦
Gathering Information

The first step in writing a research report is to choose a topic that interests you. The next step is to begin collecting information. A wide range of sources are at your disposal.

Personal Experiences   Firsthand information makes a report more reliable. Attend meetings or visit sites and museum exhibitions that relate to your topic. Use any personal information that you have.

Others' Experiences   Two methods for gathering firsthand information from others are interviews and surveys. Interview someone who has special knowledge about your topic. Be sure to take accurate notes or use a tape recorder. By conducting a survey, you can gather information from many people. Prepare a survey questionnaire. Conduct your survey by telephone, by mail, or in person.

Library Research   The library offers information on almost any topic. Use the card catalog to locate books and the *Readers' Guide to Periodical Literature* to locate magazine articles on your topic. Consult reference books. Encyclopedias have articles on most subjects. Atlases have maps and geographical information. Almanacs contain up-to-date facts and statistics on such topics as world events and population figures. (For more information on using the library, see pages 588–591.)

Nonprint Media   Don't overlook nonprint media, which can be excellent sources of information. They may be listed in the main card catalog or in a special catalog of their own. Microfilm and microfiche are used to store newspapers and some periodicals. Use cassette tapes and recordings of music, poetry, and plays. View films, filmstrips, slides, and videotapes that give instructions on how to do something or that document a subject. CD-ROM (compact disk read-only memory) is technology that stores a massive amount of information for reference on a single compact computer disk. Ask a librarian for help with these materials.

Summary ♦ When researching a report, gather information from your own and others' experiences, from books and magazines, and from nonprint media.

Guided Practice

Name a source you could use to find information on the topics listed below. Choose from these sources.

personal experience	survey	*Readers' Guide to*
encyclopedia	interview	*Periodical Literature*

1. expert firsthand knowledge about your subject
2. a general discussion of life in ancient China
3. a magazine article on recent excavations of Chinese tombs

Practice

A. List any source discussed in this lesson that you could use to find the following information.

    4. a map of China, showing the major cities
    5. opinions about China from recent visitors
    6. old newspaper articles on Chinese archaeological discoveries
    7. performances of modern Chinese opera
    8. the latest population statistics for China

B. Jody is writing a research report on ancient Chinese burial practices. Write *useful* or *not useful* to indicate whether each source below would likely contain information on Jody's topic.

    9. a visit to a museum exhibit about ancient Chinese culture
    10. a survey given to classmates
    11. books listed in the card catalog on burial practices
    12. a film about the last Chinese emperor

Apply ♦ Think and Write

Nonprint Media ♦ Make a list of nonprint media sources you might use in researching a report on Chinese drama. Then write a brief explanation about what kinds of information you would expect to find in these sources.

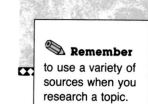

Remember
to use a variety of sources when you research a topic.

Imagine that an expert is telling you how to make something or perform a complicated task. You can't hope to remember all the details. What techniques could you use to help you retain the information until you use it?

STUDY SKILLS ♦
Taking Notes

As you gather information for a research report, you will read from various sources—encyclopedia articles, parts of nonfiction books, magazine articles. When you find details you want to include, you will need to take notes on index cards.

Your preliminary reading should help you determine a number of general divisions or topics you will cover. You can use these topics as headings for your note cards.

Each index card should contain a note on only one topic and from only one source. You may have several cards on the same topic but from different sources. This method helps you keep track of where each piece of information came from. It also enables you to arrange all note cards on the same topic together and to rearrange them in the order in which you will present the information.

The card below is for a report on the tomb of Ch'in Shih-huang-ti. Abbreviations and incomplete sentences are used to save space.

Main topic — *Appearance of Ch'in Shih-huang-ti's tomb*

Source — *Juliano, Treasures of China, p. 139*

Note — *Contains model of the universe—stars indicated by pearls on ceiling, rivers of quicksilver; rooms filled with treasures & guarded by crossbows.*

The following guidelines will help you take useful notes.
♦ Write the main topic at the top of the card.
♦ Write the author, title, and page numbers.
♦ For direct quotations, copy the exact words and put quotation marks around them. Name the person quoted.
♦ Write all other notes in your own words. Use brief phrases and abbreviations.

Summary ♦ Take notes in your own words on index cards for research reports.

Guided Practice

Using the note card on page 382, answer these questions.

1. What is the main topic on the card?
2. What information is given about the source?
3. Why are incomplete sentences used?

Practice

A. Write answers to these questions about taking notes.

    4. Why should you use index cards for taking notes?
    5. How many different topics can you include on one note card?
    6. What special rules should you follow when using direct quotations?
    7. Where on the index card should you place your main topic?

B. Read the paragraph from *The World Book Encyclopedia*. Take notes on the important facts in your own words. You do not need to write complete sentences.

Chinese painting was closely linked with the arts of poetry and *calligraphy* (fine handwriting) . . . . The Chinese traditionally considered calligraphy a branch of painting. During the 1200s, it became popular for painters to combine shanshui [landscapes of towering mountains and vast expanses of water] and other subjects with written inscriptions that formed part of the overall design. In many cases, these inscriptions consisted of a poem along with a description of the circumstances under which the painting was created.

Apply ♦ Think and Write

Taking Notes ♦ Look up a subject you are interested in in an encyclopedia. Take notes on the article in your own words.

✏️ **Remember**
⟨x⟩ to use brief phrases ⟨x⟩
when you take notes.

WRITING ◆
Paraphrasing

When you are taking notes for a research report, most of them should be written in your own words. Paraphrasing, or restating what you have read in your own words, can help you understand and remember the information.

As you prepare to paraphrase, first identify the important facts and ideas you want to include. In the following paragraph about Chinese inventions, this information is underlined.

> Many of the world's most important inventions, often assumed to have originated in Europe, began in China. Gunpowder, paper and printing, and the magnetic compass are three inventions, according to English philosopher Francis Bacon, that perhaps more than any others determined the nature of the postmedieval world. Scholars have determined that each of these inventions originated in China.

The underlined information should not be copied word for word unless you enclose it in quotation marks and give credit to its source. If you copy the material exactly without using quotation marks or giving credit, you are guilty of **plagiarism**. Simply rewrite the ideas in your own words. Notice how the following paraphrase compares with the original above.

> Gunpowder, paper and printing, and the magnetic compass—the three most important discoveries in shaping the modern world, according to Francis Bacon—all came from China.

Another way to put ideas in your own words is to summarize. When you **summarize**, you write only the main ideas in as few words as possible. Begin your summary by stating the main idea. Add supporting sentences to explain the most important details.

> **Summary** ◆ **Paraphrasing** is expressing in your own words ideas or information you have read.

Guided Practice

Paraphrase the following sentences.

1. Chinese navigators were using the magnetic compass to guide their ships by the 1100s.
2. Although the Chinese invented gunpowder, it was not used in weapons, except perhaps in rockets.
3. Paper was first made in China from the inner bark of the mulberry tree.

Practice

A. Paraphrase the following sentences by writing them in your own words.

4. The Chinese discovered that paper could also be made by pounding hemp rope into pulp.
5. A Chinese printer named Bi Sheng invented movable type around 1050.
6. Bi Sheng constructed separate pieces of clay type for each Chinese character.
7. This great Chinese invention did not make its way to Europe.
8. Printing with movable type was invented independently in Germany about 1440.

B. Write a paraphrase of the following paragraph from ''The Great Underground Army.''

Shih-huang was a reformer as well. He wrote new laws, standardized tables of weights and measures, and organized the system of writing Chinese characters so that people all over China could use and understand the same written language. He built a vast network of roads throughout his entire kingdom, constructed canals for what would become the greatest inland water-communication system in the ancient world, and dug irrigation ditches, still used today, so his people could cultivate more of their land than ever before.

Apply • Think and Write

Writing a Summary • Write a brief summary of the paragraph you paraphrased in **Practice B**. Write only the main ideas in as few words as possible.

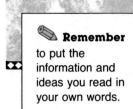

Remember to put the information and ideas you read in your own words.

Do you know how fireworks were developed? Give three possible
sources you could consult to find out.

WRITING ♦
Structuring and Documenting a Report

After you have completed your research, use your note cards to
help you structure your research report. Sort your note cards so that
all the information on each main topic is together. Then determine
the order in which you will present the information. (See page 596
for help with making an outline for your report.) Your report will
have three main parts: an introduction, a body, and a conclusion.

The **introduction** gives the subject and contains a thesis statement that tells the main idea you will develop. The introduction
may also state the purpose—to persuade or to inform, for example.
The introduction should be at least one paragraph.

The following paragraph is an introduction to a report on the
major achievements of the Ch'in dynasty.

> Perhaps in no other era of ancient history did so many achieve-
> ments occur so closely together as in the Ch'in dynasty (246–206
> B.C.). Among these achievements are the completion of the Great
> Wall, the building of a great transportation system on land and
> water, and remarkable advances in agriculture in a country having
> little cropland. These achievements have had a permanent influence
> on Chinese civilization.

The **body** of the report develops thoroughly each main topic of
your subject in at least one paragraph. Each paragraph has a topic
sentence that is developed with supporting sentences, using details
from your note cards. The following paragraph discusses the topic
of the Great Wall.

> The uniting of the various sections of the northern wall fit per-
> fectly with the emperor's policy of uniting the country. When all
> the various sections of the Great Wall had been connected,
> it extended over 1,500 miles along the entire northern boundary of
> China. Now a united China was safe from the invading tribes that
> had long threatened the northern states.

To end your report, you need a concluding paragraph. The **conclusion** restates or summarizes your main points in a different way.

It is remarkable how many landmark achievements of the Ch'in dynasty still remain. The Great Wall, the Magic Canal, and some irrigation ditches in use today all date from this era.

A research report ends with a **bibliography**, a list of all the sources of information that you used in preparing the report. A bibliography is important because it lets the reader know how many sources you have used and how up-to-date the information is. As you prepare your report, write an index card for each source showing the bibliographic information described below.

The sample bibliography entries show the forms for an encyclopedia article, a newspaper article, a book, and a magazine article. Notice that they are alphabetized according to the authors' last names (or by the names of the articles when there are no authors).

"China." The World Book Encyclopedia. 1988 ed.
"China Exhibit Captivates Crowds at World's Fair." New York Times 5 May 1982: A20.
Cotterell, Arthur. The First Emperor of China: The Greatest Archaeological Find of Our Time. New York: Holt, 1981.
Diggs, J. F. "China Unearths a 2200-Year-Old Tourist Lure." U.S. News and World Report 11 Jan. 1982: 62–63.

Use the following guidelines and the model entries above for help in writing your bibliography (unless your teacher gives you different instructions). Follow the models exactly for punctuation, spacing, and indention.

1. For a book, write the author's name (last name first), the title (underlined), place of publication, name of the publisher, and publication date.
2. For an encyclopedia article, list the author, if given. If not, write the title (in quotation marks), the name of the encyclopedia (underlined), and the year published.
3. For a magazine article, write the author's name, the title of the article (in quotation marks), the name of the magazine (underlined), the date, and the page numbers.

4. For a newspaper article, list the author's name, if given, the title (in quotation marks), the name of the newspaper (underlined), date, section number, and page number.

> **Summary** ◆ A **report** presents information that you have gathered and arranged in a well-organized form.

Guided Practice

Tell which part of a report each item is appropriate for—an introduction, a body, or a conclusion.

1. Systematic work on the Great Wall began about 221 B.C. and was completed about 204 B.C.
2. The Great Wall is a fortification in northern China that stretches from the Gulf of Chihli on the east to Gansu in the west, but it stands for much more than that to the Chinese people.
3. Thus the Great Wall symbolized not only national unity but gave a sense of order to the vast diversity within China.

Practice

A. Write which part of a research report each sentence belongs in—the introduction, body, or conclusion.

4. From earliest times, the Chinese have been concerned with repelling invaders and maintaining order and unity.
5. That people whose safety was threatened were concerned with the development of weapons is not surprising.
6. Therefore, of all early Chinese weapons, the rocket was probably the most important military invention.
7. A historical account published in 1044 praises the cross-bow as "indispensable."

B. Read these notes. Develop them into a paragraph for the body of a report on the uses of jade by the ancient Chinese.

8. used by ancient Chinese in place of gold
9. comes in many colors—dark green, white, red, black
10. carved into magnificent jewelry and utensils
11. buried with their dead

C. Prepare a bibliography entry for each of the following sources. Follow the forms shown in the model entries on page 387.

12. A book entitled A Traveler's Guide to Chinese History by Madge Huntington, published in New York by Holt in 1987.
13. An encyclopedia article entitled "Ch'in Dynasty" in The World Book Encyclopedia, 1984 edition.
14. A newspaper article entitled "A Fossil from the Land of Dragons" in the New York Times on June 14, 1988, section B, page 1.
15. A magazine article by Wen Ruitang entitled "Treasures from an Ancient Chinese Tomb" in Courier magazine in January of 1987 on pages 32–33.

D. Choose one of the topics below. Develop five bibliography entries for the topic, using sources in the library. Follow the forms shown in the model entries on page 387.

Chinese Porcelain   Development of Paper in China
Silk in Ancient China   Chinese Holidays

Apply • Think and Write

Dictionary of Knowledge • Read about the Great Wall of China and how it was extended by the first emperor. Make a list of facts from the entry that you could expand on for the body of a research report.

✎ **Remember**
to structure your research report carefully and give credit to your sources.

Focus on the Main Idea

Just as a paragraph expresses a main idea, so does a longer piece of writing. You may want to write a research report on China, for example, but China is a general subject, not a main idea. You must narrow the subject until it becomes a usable research topic. First, decide what would you like to find out more about. Are you intrigued by military affairs? Sports? Farming?

Let's say you have an interest in art. In that case, Chinese art is a possible topic. However, Chinese art is still too big a topic to be treated in a short research report. The inverted pyramid below shows how you might narrow it to a manageable size.

Chinese art from ancient times to the present
Chinese art before the twentieth century
Ancient Chinese sculpture
Shih-huang-ti's
tomb sculpture

After the narrowing is completed, you should be able to state the main idea for your research report in a single sentence.

♦ The lifesize statues in Shih-huang-ti's tomb are spectacular examples of ancient Chinese sculpture.

Once you have narrowed your topic, it is important to stick to the main idea. As you do your research and then write, remember that the main idea forms a boundary within which to work.

The Writer's Voice ♦ Develop an inverted pyramid for each of the following general subjects: automobiles, fashions, pop music, flowers, movies. Each main idea—the narrowed topic at the bottom—should be suitable for a short research report.

Working Together

When beginning a research report, your first task is to narrow a general subject. The main idea that results from this process is the basis for your report. As a group, complete activities **A** and **B**.

In Your Group

- ◆ Be sure people understand the task.
- ◆ Contribute your ideas.
- ◆ Agree or disagree in a pleasant way.
- ◆ Record all suggestions.

A. Narrow each of the following broad topics so that it is suitable for a research report. This report should be about the same length as Marjorie Jackson's "The Great Underground Army" (pages 372–376).

1. Airplanes
2. Cartoons
3. Astronomy
4. Careers
5. Local History
6. Women Writers

B. As a group, select one of the narrowed topics from activity **A**. Make a list of ideas that would help develop the topic. These ideas should all support the main idea of the research report.

THESAURUS CORNER ◆ Word Choice

Identify the sentence below that expresses the main idea being supported by the other sentences. Then complete each sentence with an appropriate synonym for either *usually* or *suddenly*. You may use either of these adverbs as well, but do not use the same synonym twice.

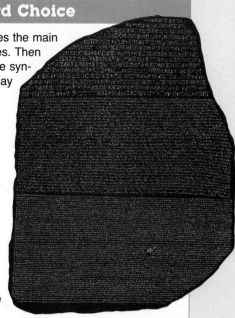

1. Advances in archaeology _____ come about through long, painstaking efforts.
2. But sometimes a new discovery will _____ focus attention on a field of study.
3. In 1806 the arrival of the Elgin Marbles in England _____ caused the British to take a great interest in ancient Greece.
4. Only a few years earlier the finding of the Rosetta Stone had _____ provided the key to Egyptian hieroglyphics.
5. Much more recently the discovery of the Dead Sea Scrolls aroused interest in the _____ quiet field of Biblical scholarship.

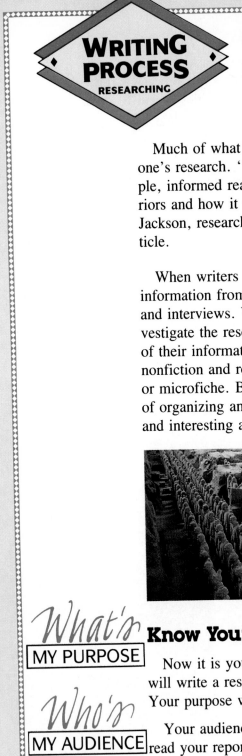

WRITING PROCESS
RESEARCHING

Writing a Research Report

Much of what you read in school is the result of some-one's research. "The Great Underground Army," for exam-ple, informed readers about Shih-huang's army of clay war-riors and how it was discovered. The author, Marjorie Jackson, researched the information in order to write her ar-ticle.

When writers do *primary research,* they collect their own information from personal experience, observation, surveys, and interviews. When they do *secondary research,* they in-vestigate the research done earlier by someone else. Much of their information comes from library materials, including nonfiction and reference books, periodicals, and microfilm or microfiche. Both kinds of research writers have the task of organizing and summarizing their information into clear and interesting articles or reports.

Know Your Purpose and Audience

What's
MY PURPOSE

Now it is your turn to research a subject you choose. You will write a research report based on secondary sources. Your purpose will be to inform.

Who's
MY AUDIENCE

Your audience will be your classmates. Later, you can read your reports aloud or collect them in a book.

1 Prewriting

First choose a topic and narrow it to fit the size of your report. Then gather information about your topic.

Choose Your Topic ◆ Choose a general subject that you like, such as music, aviation, art, or sports. Find a reference book on the subject and browse through it until you find a good research topic. Make a list, then choose the topic that interests you the most.

Think About It

To narrow your topic, look for one person, event, or detail that interests you. Which would you most like to learn about? Make sure there is information available on your topic.

Talk About It

With a partner, you might find books listing famous firsts or fascinating trivia in different fields. Discuss the topics that interest you the most.

Topic Ideas

Aviation

Wright Brothers
Kitty Hawk
glider tests
ballooning
first flight
(Mary Myers)
races
ultralights

Choose Your Strategy ♦ Read both strategies that follow.
Use the ideas you think will help you most.

PREWRITING IDEAS

CHOICE ONE

Answering "What If?"

Write a "what if" question about your topic. Then add several follow-up questions. Direct your research toward answering your questions.

Model

*What if a woman was a
pioneer of flight?*

*Who was she?   Mary Myers
When did she   late 1800's
fly?
What did she   balloons
fly?
Did she invent   steering
anything?   device
Did she make   1866 —
any unusual   ascended
flights?   4 miles*

CHOICE TWO

Taking Notes

As you read, take notes. Head each card with the main topic and source. Be sure to paraphrase, or restate the information carefully. If you do intend to use someone else's exact words, put them in quotation marks. When you have completed your research, put your notes in the order you will use in your report.

Model

Mary Myers

*Macmillan, High-Flying
Women, p. 137*

*first woman to solo balloon,
July 4, 1880; 1886 went up
4 miles without oxygen.*

2 Writing

Begin your report with an introduction that states the topic and your thesis, or claim about your topic. (Your thesis might be your proved supposition from your "what if" chart.) Try to catch the readers' interest in your introduction.

In the body, write a separate paragraph for each main idea that supports your thesis. Your notes will provide the details to support the topic sentence of the paragraph. Be sure to give proper credit if you use another writer's words or ideas.

Finish your report with a conclusion that restates your thesis and sums up the information.

Sample First Draft ◆

Most people know the name Amelia Earhart, yet hardly no one recognizes the name Mary Myers. However, Mary Myers name deserves recognition.

Mary and her husband, Carl, lived near little Falls, New York. Both did research on ballooning. On July 4 1880, Mary became the first woman to make a solo balloon flight.

Mary preformed similar flights in public for years. She called herself "Carlotta." In 1886, without any oxygen tanks, she asended to a height of four miles. She also developed new ballooning materials these included fabrics, basket materials, and a steering device, which she patented.

Mary Myers helped the field of Aviation a lot. Yet few people have heard her name. Someday perhaps the great "Carlotta" will have the recognition she deserves.

3 Revising

Revising means "seeing again." Try to read your report with new eyes, as a reader might. This idea may help you discover the changes and improvements you want to make.

REVISING IDEA

FIRST Read to Yourself

Read aloud to yourself, reviewing your purpose and your audience. Did your report give information based on secondary research? Will your classmates understand and be interested in your report? In the margin, put a light pencil check next to areas you think need more work.

Focus: Have you started with a clear thesis statement? Does your whole report support your thesis, or claim about your topic?

THEN Share with a Partner

Read your report aloud to a partner. Ask her or him to respond. The guidelines below may help you work together.

The Writer	The Writer's Partner
Guidelines: Listen to your partner's suggestions, but make only changes you agree with.	**Guidelines:** Be polite, but give specific suggestions.
Sample questions: • What is the strongest feature of this paper? • **Focus question:** Is my main idea clearly stated and supported?	**Sample responses:** • I think the strongest feature is ____. • I'd like to know more about ____. • This detail doesn't seem to support your thesis.

Revising Model ♦ The report below is being revised. Changes the writer wants to make are shown in blue.

The writer's partner heard this double negative.

The writer realized there was no clear thesis statement.

The next few details need their own topic sentence.

The word *contributed* is more precise than *helped*.

> Most people know the name Amelia Earhart,
> ^*anyone*
> yet hardly ~~no one~~ recognizes the name Mary
> Myers. However, Mary Myers name deserves
> *She was a pilot and researcher who was*
> recognition. ^*one of aviation's true pioneers.*
>
> Mary and her husband, Carl, lived near little
> Falls, New York. Both did research on ballooning.
> On July 4 1880, Mary became the first woman to
> make a solo balloon flight.
>
> Mary preformed similar flights in public for
> years. She called herself "Carlotta " In 1886,
> without any oxygen tanks, she asended to a height
> *Mary was more than just a performer,*
> of four miles. She also developed new ballooning
> *however.* ∧
> materials these included fabrics, basket materials,
> ~~and a~~ steering device, which she patented.
> *contributed ♦ to*
> Mary Myers ~~helped~~ the field of Aviation (a lot.)
> Yet few people have heard her name. Someday
> perhaps the great "Carlotta" will have the
> recognition she deserves.

Read the report above with the writer's changes. Then revise your own research report.

Grammar Check ♦ Double negatives can confuse readers. You can often find them by reading your sentences aloud.

Word Choice ♦ Do you want a more precise word for a word like *help*? A thesaurus can help you improve your word choice.

4 Proofreading

Now that your report says what you want it to say, it's time to proofread for surface errors.

Proofreading Model ♦ Here is the report about aviation pioneer Mary Myers. Proofreading changes have been added in red.

Proofreading Marks

capital letter	=
small letter	/
add comma	∧
add period	⊙
indent paragraph	¶
check spelling	⬭

Proofreading Checklist

- ☐ Did I spell words correctly?
- ☐ Did I indent paragraphs?
- ☐ Did I use correct capitalization?
- ☐ Did I use correct punctuation?
- ☐ Did I type neatly or use my best handwriting?

Most people know the name Amelia Earhart, yet hardly no one *anyone* recognizes the name Mary Myers. However, Mary *Myers's* Myers name deserves recognition. *She was a pilot and researcher who was one of aviation's true pioneers.*

Mary and her husband, Carl, lived near little Falls, New York. Both did research on ballooning. On July 4, 1880, Mary became the first woman to make a solo balloon flight.

Mary *performed* preformed similar flights in public for years. She called herself "Carlotta." In 1886, *Mary was more than just a performer, however.* without any oxygen tanks, she *ascended* asended to a height of four miles. She also developed new ballooning materials. these included fabrics, basket materials, and a steering device, which she patented.

Mary Myers helped *contributed to* the field of Aviation a lot. Yet few people have heard her name. Someday perhaps the great "Carlotta" will have the recognition she deserves.

PROOFREADING IDEA

Handwriting Check

Check that you have left a distinct space between separate words. Words and letters that are crowded are hard to read.

Now proofread your report, add a title, and make a neat copy.

5 Publishing

Make a bibliography for your report. List each source of information. Use the proper form for each entry. Attach your bibliography at the end of your report.

The Great "Carlotta"

Most people know the name Amelia Earhart, yet hardly anyone recognizes the name Mary Myers. However, Mary Myers's name deserves recognition. She was a pilot and researcher who was one of aviation's true pioneers.

Mary and her husband, Carl, lived near Little Falls, New York. Both did research on ballooning. On July 4, 1880, Mary became the first woman to make a solo balloon flight.

Mary performed similar flights in public for years. She called herself "Carlotta." In 1886, without any oxygen tanks, she ascended to a height of four miles.

Mary was more than just a performer, however. She also developed new ballooning materials. These include fabrics, basket materials, and a steering device, which she patented.

Mary Myers contributed a lot to the field of aviation. Yet few people have heard her name. Someday perhaps the great "Carlotta" will have the recognition she deserves.

PUBLISHING IDEAS

Share Aloud

Read your report aloud to the class or to a small group. Ask your listeners to say which fact they found most interesting.

Share in Writing

Alphabetize all the reports by topic, collect them in a notebook, and make an index. Take turns borrowing the notebook to read each other's reports. Have the class choose two reports to submit to a magazine for publication. Instructions for submissions are usually found on the staff page.

CURRICULUM
·CONNECTION·

Writing Across the Curriculum   Art

Art lovers often try to interpret a painting, guessing what the painter meant. You can do it, too. You can look at a painting and try to imagine what the painter intended to express.

Writing to Learn

Think and Suppose ◆ Here is a detail from a painting called *Still Music*. What if the artist could tell you about the painting? What do you think he would say? List at least three ideas.

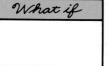

What-if Chart

Still Music, Ben Shahn. The Phillips Collection, Washington, D.C.

Write ◆ Write your interpretation of *Still Music*. Explain how the lines, colors, and shapes contribute to the meaning.

Writing in Your Journal

In the Writer's Warm-up you wrote about an object you use being discovered in the future. You went on to read about archaeologists, historians, and others who interpret clues to the past. In your journal write about something you think may happen in the future as a result of our knowledge of the past.

BOOKS TO ENJOY

Read More About It

Mysteries from the Past   *by Thomas G. Aylesworth*
This is the fascinating story of how archaeologists uncover
clues to ancient mysteries. The author includes the giant
statues of Easter Island and the lost "continent," Atlantis.

Diary of the Boy King Tut-Ankh-Amen
by June Reig
The discovery of King Tut's tomb, the major archaeological
discovery of this century, provided a detailed supply of
clues about a young Egyptian king. This intriguing fictionalized account of his life is based on that evidence.

Art and Archaeology   *by Shirley Glubok*
In this large-size book, Mrs. Glubok overviews important
archaeological findings such as the discovery of the tomb
of King Tutankhamen of Egypt. Each section is short and
illustrated with large, clear photographs.

Book Report Idea   Book Blurbs

Blurbs are brief descriptions that
often appear on the cover of a
book. The next time you really
enjoy a book, give a blurb report.
Begin by making a cover for the
book. The front of the cover
should list the title, author, and
a design that expresses the book's
theme. On the back cover, list at
least six blurbs. If the book is
fiction, write blurbs that address
different aspects of the book—
characters, setting, plot, theme,
and author's style.

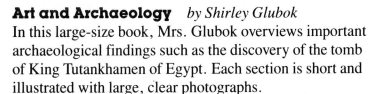

"Reckless young Kit and the
mysterious old Hannah form
a memorable friendship indeed!"

"Kit's trial for witchcraft is riveting!"

"Fine characterization and believable
dialogue make for superior reading."

"An arresting portrait of
Puritan New England!"

The Witch
of
Blackbird Pond

Elizabeth George Speare

UNIT REVIEW

Unit 7

Adverbs   *pages 354–361*

A. Write the adverb or adverbs in each sentence.

1. The friendly young couple gave fairly accurate directions to the tourist.
2. Greatly detailed directions would have confused him.
3. The strangely quiet streets suddenly became very congested.
4. Soon crowds poured hurriedly from the buses and subways.
5. Early shoppers were caught unexpectedly in a terrible traffic jam.
6. The tourist wisely sought shelter nearby in a restaurant.

B. Write the correct comparative or superlative form of each adverb in parentheses.

7. I can write (fast) with my right hand than with my left hand.
8. A southpaw pitches or writes (well) with his left hand than with his right hand.
9. Who writes (clearly) in your class?
10. My brother is (often) accused of having poor penmanship than I, perhaps unfairly.
11. He writes (frequently) than I do.
12. Ruth wrote the (forcefully) of all of us.

C. Write the correct word in parentheses.

13. Bill didn't take (no, any) jacket to the opening game of the World Series.
14. It (was, wasn't) hardly cold when Bill left the house in the early evening.
15. He hasn't (never, ever) misjudged the weather so badly.
16. He had never experienced (nothing, anything) like it.
17. Bill (couldn't, could) barely concentrate on the game because he felt so cold.
18. Bill's friend (was, wasn't) hardly able to enjoy the game either.

Adjectives and Adverbs   *pages 362–363*

D. Write the correct adjective or adverb in parentheses in each sentence.

19. The curators of the museum knew they had a (real, really) outstanding exhibit.
20. They felt (bad, badly) that some of the visitors could not get into the crowded museum.
21. Those disappointed visitors (sure, surely) missed a unique cultural experience.
22. The fortunate ones got to see a (good, well) representation of great artists' works.
23. In some cases, we were able to see how (good, well) the artists developed over the years.
24. Of course, none of these artists ever painted (bad, badly).
25. The (real, really) challenge for us was to concentrate on one painting at a time.
26. I wasn't (sure, surely) about the meanings behind some of the paintings.

Suffixes   *pages 364–365*

E. Use the following suffixes to form other words from the words listed below. Write the words.

-ment   **-ness**   **-ist**   **-ism**   **-en**   **-ish**

27. crisp	31. fiend	35. bewilder
28. commit	32. light	36. fresh
29. arson	33. organ	37. guitar
30. boy	34. tour	38. vandal

Main Idea   *pages 390–391*

F. Each of the following topics is too broad and unfocused for a research report. For each one, write two topics that are narrower and more suitable.

39. teen movies	43. dental hygiene
40. basketball	44. housing
41. careers	45. newspapers
42. fashions	46. electronics

LANGUAGE PUZZLERS

Unit 7 Challenge

Adjective-Adverb Links

Write the words defined. Five are adverbs, and one is an adjective. The boxed letters tell what these parts of speech do.

1. □ _ _ _ _ _   not strongly
2. _ □ _ _ _ _   in a frosty manner
3. _ _ □ _ _ _   excessively
4. _ _ _ □ _ _   without difficulty
5. _ _ _ _ □ _   hazardous
6. _ _ _ _ _ □   not quickly

Make a similar puzzle to share with a classmate.

Adverb Identifications

Identify each of the adverbs from the clues given.

1. the fourth letter of the alphabet + a nuisance
2. a preposition + the number after nine
3. a homophone for *two* + the opposite of day
4. a homophone for *four* + always
5. the fifth month + the second letter of the alphabet
6. a rodent + a possessive feminine pronoun
7. the opposite of *in* + neither front nor back
8. the opposite of *up* + a bridge between floors

Unit 7 Extra Practice

1 Writing with Adverbs

A. Write the adverb in each sentence.

1. We hurried out.
2. It moves backward.
3. They finally left.
4. Up she goes.
5. When may I leave?

6. She rarely talks.
7. How did it move?
8. Come with us tonight.
9. Can you run there?
10. We left it inside.

B. Twenty words are underlined in this article about the Washington Monument. Ten words are adverbs. Write the adverbs after their sentence numbers.

11. No one could ever say that the Washington Monument went up in record time. **12.** In 1783, Congress originally wanted a statue of the American president on horseback. **13.** A site for it was chosen eight years later. **14.** After Washington's death in 1799, plans for a memorial were again discussed. **15.** A plan for the 555-foot marble-faced obelisk was finally adopted in 1832. **16.** On July 4 in 1848, the cornerstone of the monument was ceremoniously placed. **17.** However, shortages of funds and political quarrels interrupted the work frequently during the 1850s and 1860s. **18.** The base was completed late in 1880. **19.** By 1884 the aluminum top had been carefully positioned. **20.** The first visitors happily entered the completed monument in 1888.

C. Write the sentences. Underline the adverbs in each.

21. Loudly and angrily the man shouted.
22. Jay dashed upstairs and called for me twice.
23. Will she ever fully understand?
24. By the end of the day, the librarian will have searched everywhere systematically.
25. Soon they had cautiously tested the chilly surf of Acadia National Park in Maine.
26. They seldom complete their chores early.

D. Two words in each sentence end in *-ly*. One is an adjective. One is an adverb. Write the adverb.

27. The daily news has not interested me lately.
28. The baby's curly hair was extremely wet.
29. We will pay for it easily in monthly payments.
30. She eagerly told us several lively stories.
31. The lizard's scaly skin was surprisingly cool.

E. Write the word or words each underlined adverb modifies. Label the word or words *verb*, *adjective*, or *adverb*.

32. Many people have <u>never</u> heard about the burning of the White House. **33.** This <u>very</u> unfortunate event occurred during the War of 1812. **34.** British soldiers entered Washington <u>rather</u> easily in August of 1814. **35.** The few American defenders were <u>completely</u> helpless. **36.** Alone in the White House, First Lady Dolley Madison could <u>clearly</u> see the flames of burning government buildings. **37.** She <u>also</u> knew her home would be next. **38.** However, she did not <u>just</u> flee in panic. **39.** In a <u>quite</u> orderly fashion, she gathered her husband's important presidential papers. **40.** A servant <u>then</u> carried them out of town safely. **41.** With a priceless portrait of George Washington under her arm, she <u>calmly</u> left the mansion.

F. Complete each sentence with an adverb.

42. Do you _____ have the measles?
43. We _____ ski together anymore.
44. I felt _____ sorry about your accident.
45. Jean _____ works late at night.
46. The Vitos _____ did find their lost dog.

2 Using Adverbs to Compare   *p. 358*

A. Write the comparative (C) or superlative (S) form of each adverb as indicated.

1. early (C)	**6.** recklessly (S)	**11.** straight (C)
2. wisely (S)	**7.** well (S)	**12.** abruptly (C)
3. soon (S)	**8.** hard (C)	**13.** badly (C)
4. hastily (S)	**9.** fearlessly (S)	**14.** deep (S)
5. near (C)	**10.** long (C)	**15.** silently (S)

B. Write the correct comparative or superlative form of each adverb in parentheses.

16. Wagons traveled (safely) of all when in groups.
17. Was the ox used (extensively) than the mule?
18. Wagon trains traveled (much) of all around 1850.
19. Was the prairie schooner chosen (often) than another kind of wagon for use in wagon trains?
20. Did the Conestoga wagon carry freight (easily) than the prairie schooner?
21. Wagons were (well) suited to plains than to mountains.
22. Some wagons were (sturdily) built than others.
23. Did that scout act (bravely) than the other?
24. They journeyed (fast) of all to Oregon.
25. Railroads moved people (rapidly) than wagons did.

C. Write the comparative or superlative form of the adverb in parentheses to complete each sentence correctly. Then label it *comparative* or *superlative*.

26. The latest space shuttle will not travel any (long) than the previous spacecraft.
27. Nor does it fly (fast) of all spaceships lauched from earth.
28. Still the shuttle is (well) suited for some kinds of space exploration than other spacecraft.
29. Primarily this is true because the shuttle can be used (often) than once, perhaps fifty times or more!
30. The powerful shuttle will work the (hard) of any spaceship.
31. Satellites can be launched (easily) from the shuttle than from the earth.
32. Technicians will be able to repair broken satellites (fast) from the shuttle than from the earth.

D. Write the comparative and superlative forms of the adverb in each phrase. Write a sentence using the phrase.

33. stayed long
34. dug deep
35. stood near
36. talked loudly
37. did badly
38. crept cautiously
39. heavily loaded
40. had come far
41. widely read
42. crudely constructed

3 Using Negatives Correctly

p. 360

A. Write the negative word in each sentence.

    1. Nineteenth-century America was in no way spared from the "modern" problem of heavy city traffic. **2.** Today's city traffic is nothing compared with that in the last century. **3.** A person was scarcely able to travel in a city without getting into an accident involving horses. **4.** Almost no one treated city horses properly. **5.** They were not given ample food and rest. **6.** So it is hardly surprising that they frequently bolted unpredictably. **7.** Drivers didn't hesitate to race their horses. **8.** Also, there was never a halt in the flow of traffic. **9.** Traffic lights had not been heard of. **10.** Nobody could cross a main street without being extremely careful.

B. Write the correct word in parentheses.

    11. She (had, hadn't) barely left the curb.
    12. There weren't (any, no) special traffic police.
    13. There (were, weren't) no crosswalks either.
    14. Couldn't (anybody, nobody) tell them to halt?
    15. Didn't they (ever, never) slow down?

C. Rewrite each sentence, correcting the double negative.

    16. There was hardly nowhere safe for pedestrians.
    17. A driver didn't never stop at a corner.
    18. He wouldn't yield the right of way to no one.
    19. Traffic couldn't barely move at all in snow.
    20. Horse-drawn snowplows weren't hardly effective.
    21. There was no pause in the traffic nowhere.
    22. Hasn't nobody mentioned the problem of parking?
    23. You can't hardly imagine the noisiness of horses.
    24. None weren't treated as badly as streetcar horses.
    25. She scarcely never crossed that busy street.
    26. Many people do not hardly regard lightning as a serious danger.
    27. Some still think that lightning does not strike twice in no one place.
    28. Most suburban houses do not have no lightning rods.
    29. Yet the dangers of lightning should not never be minimized.
    30. It's not never a good idea to be careless.

4 Troublesome Adjectives and Adverbs

p. 362

A. Write the correct adjective or adverb in each sentence.

1. Early America had very few (good, well) roads.
2. Horses tripped and were injured (bad, badly).
3. (Bad, Badly) patches of mud formed after rains.
4. Logs were laid across the road, forming a ribbed pattern (real, really) similar to corduroy cloth.
5. Corduroy was (sure, surely) better than dirt.
6. Logs seemed (good, well) for covering mud.
7. Corduroy roads were a (sure, surely) bet for bringing on motion sickness.
8. Plank roads would (sure, surely) be better.
9. Plank roads sounded (good, well) in theory.
10. Flat planks laid across a roadbed would (sure, surely) be less bumpy to ride on than logs.
11. The plank road at Syracuse was built (good, well)
12. After a while, planks needed repairs (bad, badly).
13. Plank roads had few (real, really) advantages.

B. Complete each sentence with one of the words below.

real   really   bad   badly   good   well

14. Newcomers were ____ sure their trip would be hard.
15. He felt ____ after jostling over the logs.
16. Despite feeling so ill, he looked ____ .
17. Horses and vehicles fared ____ on the crude roads.
18. ____ interest in improving roads developed in time.

C. Each sentence below contains one error. Write each sentence correctly.

19. Stagecoaches sounded really badly on corduroy roads.
20. It was well of the driver to avoid those ruts.
21. Reports of road conditions sure seemed unpromising.
22. You will not travel well if the roads are badly.
23. It was real hard to keep corduroy in good repair.
24. Logs rotted easily with real frequent rain.
25. Paved roads were sure a real improvement.

THE COWBOY
painting by Frederic Remington, 1902.
Amon Carter Museum, Fort Worth

USING LANGUAGE
TO

CLASSIFY

=== PART ONE ===

Unit Theme *The Arts in America*

Language Awareness Prepositions, Conjunctions,
and Interjections

=== PART TWO ===

Literature "Two Artists of the Old West"
by Elisabeth Godolphin

A Reason for Writing Classifying

Writing
IN YOUR JOURNAL

WRITER'S WARM-UP ◆ What do you
know about the arts? Perhaps you have
met an artist, a writer, or a musician.
You might plan to become involved in
some area of the arts someday. Which area
interests you the most—music, painting, film,
sculpture, architecture, literature? In your journal
write what you know about this field and why it
interests you more than other fields.

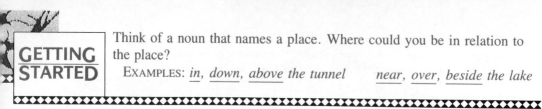

Think of a noun that names a place. Where could you be in relation to the place?

EXAMPLES: *in*, *down*, *above* the tunnel   *near*, *over*, *beside* the lake

1 Writing with Prepositions

Prepositions join words in a special way. They show how words in a sentence are related. In the sentence below, the underlined preposition <u>for</u> relates the noun *buildings* to the word *plans*.

■ An architect designs plans <u>for</u> buildings.

The noun or pronoun that follows a preposition is called the **object of the preposition**. A preposition, its object, and any words that modify the object make up a **prepositional phrase**.

Frank Lloyd Wright designed the ramp <u>inside</u> this *building*.
<u>By</u> *1905* he was America's most important architect.
Wright designed buildings <u>of</u> *steel*, *stone*, and *glass*.

In the examples above, the prepositional phrases are tinted. The prepositions are underlined, and the objects of the prepositions are in italics. Sometimes a preposition has two or more objects. These form a compound object.

Some words can be either prepositions or adverbs, depending on their use in sentences. You can tell the difference if you remember that prepositions always have objects and adverbs never do.

Preposition: Models of his buildings can be seen <u>inside</u> the museum.
Adverb: Models of his buildings can be seen <u>inside</u>.

Prepositional phrases can be used in different positions in sentences. This is a way of adding variety to your writing.

<u>Besides</u> an architect and an innovator, Wright was a teacher.
Wright was a teacher <u>besides</u> an architect and an innovator.

Become familiar with the prepositions shown on the next page.

Summary ♦ A **preposition** relates a noun or pronoun to another word in the sentence. Choose prepositions carefully to get the exact meaning you intend in your writing and speaking.

Prepositions in Prepositional Phrases

1.	aboard the bus	31.	in front of the camera
2.	about that time	32.	in spite of delays
3.	above the clouds	33.	inside his room
4.	according to Mark Twain	34.	instead of a movie
5.	across the street	35.	into the city
6.	after the dance	36.	like those painters
7.	against the tide	37.	near the center
8.	along the road	38.	of a book
9.	among three writers	39.	off the shelf
10.	around the corner	40.	on the stage
11.	at the studio	41.	out a back door
12.	because of lateness	42.	out of her sight
13.	before him or her	43.	outside your window
14.	behind the curtains	44.	over a cliff
15.	below the clouds	45.	past the time limit
16.	beneath the stairs	46.	since Saturday
17.	beside the barn	47.	through a tunnel
18.	besides Nina and Tony	48.	throughout the day
19.	between you and me	49.	till next season
20.	beyond the horizon	50.	to Miguel or Chen
21.	but (except) us	51.	toward the edge
22.	by candlelight	52.	under the rock
23.	concerning your health	53.	underneath the floor
24.	despite our help	54.	until tomorrow
25.	down the hill	55.	unto the end
26.	during the week	56.	up the chimney
27.	except modern jazz	57.	upon my lap
28.	for the people	58.	with tears and laughter
29.	from Nebraska	59.	within the limits
30.	in the theater	60.	without a trace

Guided Practice

Name the prepositions in the sentences.

1. Wright made important contributions to modern architecture.
2. He received recognition in Europe for his designs.
3. During his career of almost seventy years, Wright designed many imaginative structures.
4. Some consider him the greatest American architect of all time.

Practice

A. Write the preposition in each sentence.

    5. Wright trained with Louis Sullivan.
    6. Sullivan was a supporter of the modern skyscraper.
    7. Wright saw a relation between humans and the environment.
    8. He used natural materials throughout his homes.
    9. Among his favorite materials were stucco and wood.

B. Write the prepositional phrase in each sentence. Then underline each preposition and circle each object of the preposition.

    10. Wait for Chi and me.
    11. Let's go on a tour.
    12. Start from the beginning.
    13. See the houses by Wright.
    14. His homes mix with nature.

    15. They flow into the open.
    16. Look at their design.
    17. Many are in Chicago.
    18. Notice the use of wood.
    19. Learn about his designs.

C. Write the paragraph below. Select the preposition that best relates the words in each sentence.

    on   **among**   **of**   **after**   **with**

    The work required (**20.** ____) architects is (**21.** ____) the most varied of any profession. Architects also create drawings and models that show the buildings (**22.** ____) construction. They work (**23.** ____) building contractors and give advice (**24.** ____) costs.

D. Write the sentences. Add two prepositional phrases to each.

    EXAMPLE: The Guggenheim is unique.
    ANSWER: <u>Designed by Wright in 1943</u>, the Guggenheim is unique.

    25. The guide gave us a tour.
    26. The site is New York City.
    27. The museum is very modern.

    28. It is glass and concrete.
    29. Modern art is exhibited.
    30. The tour was enjoyable.

Apply • Think and Write

From Your Writing • Add variety and interest to the writing you did for the Writer's Warm-up. Rewrite several of your sentences so that they contain at least two prepositional phrases.

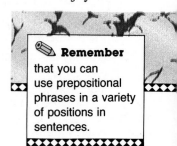

Remember that you can use prepositional phrases in a variety of positions in sentences.

Complete each movie title by adding a prepositional phrase.
Try to make your movie titles the big hits of the summer!

Day _____   Adventures _____   Creature _____

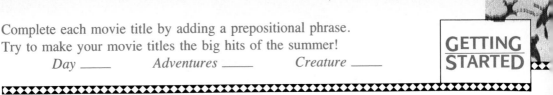

GETTING
STARTED

2 Prepositional Phrases as Modifiers

A prepositional phrase can be used as an adjective to modify a noun or a pronoun. A prepositional phrase that acts as an adjective is called an adjective phrase. Like adjectives, adjective phrases answer the questions *What kind? Which one? How much?* and *How many?*

An adjective and an adjective phrase in the sentences below are underlined. The words they modify are in italics. Notice that the adjective and the adjective phrase do the same work—they both modify the noun *arts*.

> **Adjective:** <u>American</u> *arts* are varied and unique.
> **Adjective phrase:** The *arts* <u>in America</u> are varied and unique.

An adjective phrase follows the noun or pronoun it modifies. More than one adjective phrase may modify a noun or pronoun.

> ▌ *Many* <u>of our friends</u> enjoy the theater.
>
> ▌ Theater is an art *form* <u>of great appeal</u> <u>with a long history</u>.

An adjective phrase may modify a noun used as an object of a preposition in the preceding prepositional phrase.

> ■ This lesson has *information* <u>about theater</u> <u>in America</u>.

Summary ◆ A **prepositional phrase** that modifies a noun or pronoun is an **adjective phrase.** You can add a variety of descriptive details to your writing by using adjective phrases.

Guided Practice

Name the adjective phrase or phrases in each sentence. Then tell which word each phrase modifies.

1. Theater is a branch of the performing arts.
2. It provides entertainment of great variety for everyone.
3. Theater requires the skills of many people with varied talents.

Adverb Phrases Not all prepositional phrases act as adjectives. Some prepositional phrases act as adverbs. They modify verbs, adjectives, and adverbs. Like adverbs, adverb phrases answer the questions *When? Where? How? How often?* and *To what extent?*

Compare the underlined adverb phrases in the examples below. Notice that they modify different parts of speech. The words modified are in italics.

> We *spent* the afternoon <u>at the theater</u>. (modifies verb)
> Some people arrived *late* <u>for the show</u>. (modifies adverb)
> The actors were *upset* <u>with the latecomers</u>. (modifies adjective)

Like adverbs, adverb phrases may be located almost anywhere in sentences. They can also be separated from the words they modify.

> The audience *applauded* <u>during the performance</u>.
> <u>During the performance</u> the audience *applauded*.

Sometimes a sentence contains both an adverb phrase and an adjective phrase.

> The stage was *lit* <u>with the warm glow</u> <u>of gaslight</u>.
>   adverb   adjective

Use prepositional phrases in place of adjectives and adverbs to add details and variety to your writing.

Summary ♦ A prepositional phrase that modifies a verb, an adjective, or an adverb is an **adverb phrase**. Use adverb phrases to create vivid word pictures in your reader's mind.

Guided Practice

Name the adverb phrase in each sentence. Then tell which word or words the phrase modifies.

4. Many think Eugene O'Neill was the best of American playwrights.
5. He experimented with various styles and dramatic devices.
6. His characters' lives were filled with tragedy.
7. Later in his career he received a Pultizer Prize.

Practice

A. Write the adjective phrase or phrases in each sentence. Then write the word each phrase modifies.

8. The trends of American theater have varied.
9. Tennessee Williams was another dramatist of renown.
10. His dramas contain intense portraits of character.
11. Arthur Miller also wrote plays of great popularity.
12. His plays are expressions of concern about issues.

B. Write the adverb phrase in each sentence. Then write the word or words each phrase modifies.

13. Notable black dramatists appeared later in the 1960s.
14. Among this group was Lorraine Hansberry.
15. The play *Raisin in the Sun* was written by her.
16. In this play human weaknesses are revealed.
17. According to the critics, it is outstanding.

C. Write the prepositional phrase or phrases in each sentence and identify each as an adjective phrase or an adverb phrase.

18. Today's dramatists in America are concerned with minorities.
19. Several of them write about the elderly.
20. Some explore the role of women in society.
21. Beth Henley and Maria Irene Fornes write about that issue.
22. The experiences of the physically challenged are another concern.

D. Write sentences using the prepositional phrases below. Identify each prepositional phrase as an adjective or adverb phrase.

23. between him and her
24. in front of the theater
25. for my friends
26. beside the lake
27. for dinner
28. about noon

Apply • Think and Write

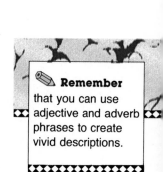

Space-Order Description • Write a detailed description of the inside or outside of a building, such as a theater. Use adjective phrases and adverb phrases to describe what you might see from top to bottom or from left to right.

> ✏ **Remember**
> that you can use adjective and adverb phrases to create vivid descriptions.

GETTING
STARTED

Complete this ad inviting tourists to visit a resort.
Use a word or word group for each blank.

Come to ____! Stay at ____ beside ____. Relax among ____ .

3 Using Prepositions Correctly

Prepositions show the relationships between words in sentences. Some prepositions are often misused. The chart below will help you use these prepositions correctly.

at	Indicates presence in a place **We were at the museum.**
to	Indicates motion toward a place **We went to an art museum.**
beside	Means "next to" or "at the side of" **Beside each painting was its title.**
besides	Means "in addition to" **Besides oil paintings, we saw watercolors.**
between	Used in discussing two people or objects **What is the difference between oils and watercolors?**
among	Used in discussing three or more **Who is your favorite artist among the painters?**
in	Indicates location within one place **Many masterpieces were in the museum.**
into	Indicates motion or change of location **We went into the museum to see them.**

When the object of a preposition is a pronoun, always use an object pronoun. Object pronouns are in the objective case.

My friend toured the museum with me. (not I)
For whom did she buy the art poster? (not who)

To see if you are using the right object pronoun as part of a compound object, say the pronoun alone with the preposition.

■ **American art is of special interest to Chun and me.** (not I)

Summary ♦ Mistakes in usage may occur in choosing a preposition or the object of a preposition.

418   USAGE: Prepositions

Guided Practice

Tell which word in parentheses correctly completes each sentence.

1. We went (in, into) the museum to see the exhibit.
2. My friend stood (besides, beside) me to buy a ticket.
3. I will share our adventure with Paolo and (he, him).

"The Beeches," Asher B. Durand. The Metropolitan Museum of Art, Bequest of Maria DeWitt Jesup, 1915. (15. 30. 59)

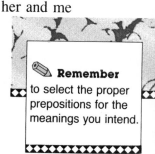

Practice

A. Write the correct word to complete each sentence.

We were (**4.** in, into) a room filled with early American portraits and landscapes. (**5.** Between, Among) you and me, I find landscapes more interesting. I noticed a portrait by John Copley (**6.** besides, beside) me. Then we walked (**7.** at, to) the cafeteria and had lunch. After lunch we went (**8.** in, into) a room of nineteenth-century art. Many masterpieces were (**9.** into, in) there. We were (**10.** among, between) the landscape paintings of the Hudson River School. I had gone (**11.** at, to) a lecture and learned about them. Choosing (**12.** among, between) any two of the landscapes is difficult. (**13.** Besides, Beside) the Hudson River painters, we also saw John James Audubon's wonderful paintings of birds. Mary Cassatt's paintings of mothers and children were displayed (**14.** besides, beside) the seascapes of Winslow Homer. Now we were (**15.** to, at) the end of the tour. We went (**16.** in, into) the souvenir shop. It was an enjoyable day for Carlos and (**17.** I, me). With (**18.** who, whom) would you like to visit a museum?

B. Write a sentence using each word group below.

19. shared among	**23.** sat at	**27.** between her and him
20. shared between	**24.** went to	**28.** with whom
21. beside the easel	**25.** walked in	**29.** among us
22. besides the easel	**26.** walked into	**30.** for her and me

Apply ◆ Think and Write

Dictionary of Knowledge ◆ Read about Winslow Homer and his paintings of the sea and seafolk. Write a description of how you, as a museum director, would position his paintings for display. Use at least four prepositions from page 418 in your writing.

✎ Remember to select the proper prepositions for the meanings you intend.

Supply a word with the same first letter to make related word pairs.

_____ *but hungry*   _____ *and softly*   _____ *or cheese*

In what ways are each completed pair alike?

4 Writing with Conjunctions

Conjunctions connect words that do the same kind of work in a sentence. *And*, *but*, *or*, and *nor* are the most frequently used conjunctions. They are called **coordinating conjunctions.**

Coordinating Conjunctions	
noun + noun	rhythm and music
noun + pronoun	Tina and her
pronoun + pronoun	you or I
adjective + adjective	graceful or awkward
verb + verb	hopped, skipped, and ran
adverb + adverb	quickly but carefully

Coordinating conjunctions can also connect groups of words.

> Isadora Duncan brought *new life* and *new forms* to modern dance.
> The dancer *did not trip*, nor *did she fall*.

Some conjunctions, such as *both . . . and*, *either . . . or*, *neither . . . nor*, work together in pairs. These pairs are called **correlative conjunctions**. Correlative conjunctions can connect either words or groups of words.

> Cynthia Gregory, a dancer, is not only *agile* but also *daring*.
> The audience likes both *her style* and *her form*.

Summary ♦ A **conjunction** joins words or groups of words in a sentence. Use conjunctions to combine ideas smoothly and concisely.

Guided Practice

Name the coordinating or correlative conjunction in each sentence.

1. Dancing involves rhythmical and patterned body movements.
2. Dance is not only the oldest but also the liveliest of the arts.
3. Neither music nor drama would have developed without dance.

Practice

A. Write each coordinating or correlative conjunction.

    4. You can either participate in dance or watch it.
    5. Theater dance is found on stage and screen.
    6. On stage both classical and modern dance steps are used.
    7. Dance steps are created or arranged by choreographers.
    8. Jerome Robbins steadily and clearly has established himself as one of America's foremost choreographers.

B. Write each conjunction and label it *coordinating* or *correlative*. Then write the words joined by the conjunction and the parts of speech of the words.

    9. Twyla Tharp both dances and choreographs.
    10. Good dancers must be innovative and disciplined.
    11. If they are determined, slowly but surely success will come.
    12. They must be prepared extensively or moderately for long tours.
    13. Dancers must not object to work nor travel.

C. Write the sentences, using a conjunction or a pair of conjunctions.

    14. The turkey trot _____ the bunny hug were new dances in 1900.
    15. In the 1920s people _____ swayed _____ jumped to the Charleston and the black bottom.
    16. Next the public danced furiously _____ happily to the Cuban rumba and other Latin-American dances.
    17. During the sixties rock and roll became popular _____ accepted.
    18. Today's rock music has produced _____ new sounds _____ unique dance variations.

D. Write three sentences using the following conjunctions.

    19. but   **20.** both. . . and   **21.** or

Apply • Think and Write

> **Remember**
> that using conjunctions can help you avoid short, choppy sentences.

Career Paragraph • Write a paragraph about a career in dancing. Use these word groups in your writing: far and wide, neither you nor I, both a dancer and a choreographer.

GETTING
STARTED

Repeat the sentence below several times but change the underlined word or words. See how many different emotions you can communicate.

EXAMPLES: *Wonderful! Is it time to go? Good grief! Is it time to go?*

5 Writing with Interjections

The interjection is a part of speech that expresses emotion. It may be a word, or two or more words. The other seven parts of speech work together to make a sentence function. The interjection has no grammatical relationship to any other words in a sentence. Some examples of interjections are shown in the chart below.

Interjections				
Ah	Goodness	Hooray	Oh, no	Ugh
Bravo	Great	Hush	Oops	Well
Brr	Help	Of course	Ouch	Whew
Dear me	Hey	Oh	Terrific	Wow

MECHANICS ";?!"

An interjection that expresses strong emotion is followed by an exclamation mark (!). An interjection that expresses mild emotion is followed by a comma. For more uses of the exclamation mark and the comma, see pages 648–657.

Interjections are used to indicate different feelings or degrees of emotions. An interjection may express intense or sudden emotion, or it may express moderate emotion.

Wow! I read a terrific book by Mark Twain.
Well, I'm glad you enjoyed it.

Notice in the examples above that an interjection may be part of a sentence or it may stand alone.

Summary ◆ An **interjection** expresses feeling or emotion. Use interjections to communicate a range of feelings.

Guided Practice

Name the interjection in each sentence.

1. Oh, was Mark Twain actually Samuel Langhorne Clemens?
2. Goodness! He was one of the masters of American literature!
3. Oh, no! I have lost my copy of *The Adventures of Tom Sawyer*.

Practice

A. Write the interjections in the sentences.

4. Oh, thank goodness! I found the book.
5. Wow, you really want to read Twain's book!
6. Well, his genius created some wonderful literature.
7. *The Adventures of Tom Sawyer* is filled with fun. Terrific!
8. Of course, Twain was a great humorist of the times.

B. Supply a different interjection for each sentence.

9. _____! I'm reading *The Good Earth* by Pearl S. Buck.
10. _____, like Mark Twain, her writing has regional details.
11. _____, she wrote moving novels about China.
12. _____! Buck lived in China for many years.
13. She urged better relations between the West and China. _____!
14. _____! You are reading *Invisible Man*, too!
15. _____! It was highly praised by James Baldwin.
16. _____, Ralph Ellison wrote this novel, of course.
17. _____, did you know he lectures on black culture and folklore?
18. _____! I have his book of essays and short stories, too.

C. Ten emotions are listed below. For each emotion, write a sentence that expresses the emotion. Include an appropriate interjection from the chart in each sentence.

19. joy
20. surprise
21. anger
22. delight
23. fear
24. disappointment
25. extreme fatigue
26. disgust
27. mild pain
28. sorrow

Apply • Think and Write

Conversations • Find a few conversational passages in a story. Rewrite each passage by adding appropriate interjections and punctuation. Read both versions aloud, and ask a classmate to comment on any difference in feeling.

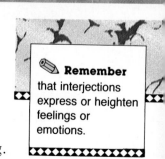

✎ **Remember** that interjections express or heighten feelings or emotions.

GETTING STARTED

Some words are terrifically talented and can do many things!
Back back down the hill with a back brace on your back.
Can you create a sentence using another talented word?

6 Words as Different Parts of Speech

A word such as *ouch* is easily identified as an interjection. How-ever, a word such as *work* can be used as different parts of speech. What part of speech *work* is depends on how it is used in a sen-tence. Look at the uses of *work* in the sentences below.

> The <u>work</u> of composers is to write music. (noun)
> Composers <u>work</u> hard to create music for everyone to enjoy. (verb)
> They must have disciplined <u>work</u> habits. (adjective)

Study the chart for more examples.

Some words that are usually nouns can be used as adjectives.
    Noun: Do you listen to all kinds of <u>music</u>?
Adjective: Would you like to work for a <u>music</u> shop?

Some pronouns can also be used as adjectives.
  Pronoun: These are very old. <u>Each</u> is a classic.
Adjective: <u>These</u> songs are very old. <u>Each</u> song is a classic.

Some adjectives can also function as adverbs.
Adjective: She placed her call with the <u>overseas</u> operator.
    Adverb: The composer traveled <u>overseas</u>.

Summary ✦ How a word is used in a sentence determines its part of speech.

Guided Practice

Tell what part of speech each underlined word is.

1. George Gershwin's music became a hit in <u>record</u> time.
2. I have a <u>record</u> of "Rhapsody in Blue."
3. <u>Jazz</u> bands like to play that tune.
4. It combines elements of <u>jazz</u> with classical music.
5. Many other musicians <u>record</u> his music.

Practice

A. Study the use of each underlined word in the sentences below. Then write the part of speech of the underlined word.

   6. Music is a wonderful form of <u>art</u>.
   7. The <u>art</u> world recognizes great composers.
   8. Aaron Copland is an <u>American</u>.
   9. He is a famous <u>American</u> composer.
 10. He is also well-known around the <u>world</u>.
 11. He has made many <u>world</u> tours as a conductor.
 12. His early <u>works</u> include *El Salón México* and *Rodeo*.
 13. He <u>works</u> very hard to blend many elements of music.
 14. We took an <u>early</u> train to the Copland concert.
 15. We arrived <u>early</u> to hear his works.
 16. Have you heard <u>this</u> music by him?
 17. <u>This</u> will always be a popular piece of music.

B. Write a sentence using each word as the part of speech shown in parentheses.

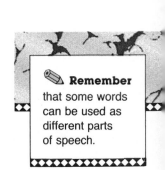

18. fast (adjective)	**24.** paper (adjective)
19. fast (adverb)	**25.** paper (noun)
20. iron (verb)	**26.** each (noun)
21. iron (noun)	**27.** each (adjective)
22. iron (adjective)	**28.** rose (verb)
23 paper (verb)	**29.** rose (noun)

C. Write ten sentences, using each of the following words as two different parts of speech. Then write the part of speech of each word.

30. question	**33.** open
31. light	**34.** those
32. left	**35.** farm

Apply ◆ Think and Write

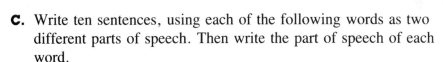

Song Titles ◆ Write titles for three different songs. Use the word *round* as a different part of speech in each song title. Read your titles aloud. Have a classmate identify the part of speech of *round* in each title.

✎ **Remember** that some words can be used as different parts of speech.

Can you tie a bow and bow to an audience? Can you lead parades and use lead pencils? Can you arrange items in rows and avoid quarrelsome rows? Create more "Can You..." pairs of your own.

VOCABULARY ♦
Homographs and Homophones

Homographs are words that are spelled alike but have different origins and meanings. The word *homograph* comes from two Greek roots—*homo*- meaning "same" and -*graph* meaning "write." Homographs often, but not always, have different pronunciations. The words *close* meaning "to shut" and *close* meaning "near" are homographs. *Band* meaning "narrow strip" and *band* meaning "group of musicians" are homographs.

Homophones are words that sound alike but have different origins, meanings, and spellings. The word part -*phone* comes from a Greek root meaning "sound." Homophones are often confused by writers. The words *their*, *there*, and *they're* are homophones: They're putting their books over there. The chart below shows four other troublesome homophones.

Homophone	Function	Example
whose	possessive form of *who*	Whose turn is it?
who's	contraction of *who is* or *who has*	Who's on first base?
your	possessive form of *you*	It's your turn now.
you're	contraction of *you are*	You're up next.

Building Your Vocabulary

Replace the incorrect words in these nonsense paragraphs with the correct homophones.

Their are many kinds of artists—sum who's paintings are shone inn galleries, and others who's music wee here and enjoy. Still others right, and wee enjoy they're thoughts and words. There talented people, awl rite.

Whose you're favorite artist? Your free two choose whichever won ewe like. Aisle choose won to.

Practice

A. Write the correct homophone to complete each sentence.

1. (Whose, Who's) elephant is that in the corner?
2. And (whose, who's) that on the elephant?
3. I think (your, you're) seeing things.
4. All I see is (your, you're) Bengal tiger!

B. Use each pair of homophones below in a sentence of your own.

EXAMPLE: baron, barren
ANSWER: The <u>baron</u> owned a <u>barren</u> piece of land.

5. medal, meddle	**7.** creek, creak	**9.** dual, duel
6. chute, shoot	**8.** foul, fowl	**10.** billed, build

C. Use pairs of homographs to complete the sentences below.

11. The _____ in her dress caused her to shed a _____ . (Clue: A <u>?</u> from a crocodile is large and salty.)
12. The _____ sang _____ in the fish choir. (Clue: <u>?</u> means low and deep in sound.)
13. The only _____ the detective found was a _____ bullet. (Clue: <u>?</u> is a very heavy metal.)
14. The clerk's job was to _____ everything that was said for the official _____ . (Clue: A <u>?</u> is usually played on a phonograph.)
15. He _____ the bandage around the _____ . (Clue: An electric clock does not have to be <u>?</u>)

LANGUAGE CORNER ◆ Word Meanings

Some homographs enter our language as new terms are needed. A recently formed homograph is a blend of *binary* and *digit*—**bit**, a term used in computer science.

Here are some clues that will help you find other meanings for *bit*.

A carpenter uses this bit.
This bit is found in a stable.
This bit is half of a quarter.
This bit is hardly anything.

How to Combine Sentences

You know that you can combine sentences that contain repeated information or related ideas. You have combined simple sentences to form compound sentences, and you have combined sentences with repeated subjects and predicates. Adjectives, adverbs, and prepositional phrases can also be used to join related sentences. For example, notice how sentence **2** joins the two predicate nouns *playwright* and *American* to form one strong, effective sentence.

> **1.** Eugene O'Neill was a playwright. He was an American.
> **2.** Eugene O'Neill was an American playwright.

In example **4** below, the prepositional phrase *by his plays* is used to combine the sentences in example **3**.

> **3.** Audiences were enthralled. They were enthralled by his plays.
> **4.** Audiences were enthralled by his plays.

Sometimes more than two sentences can be combined if they contain related information or ideas. Notice how the sentences in example **5** are combined by using adjectives and a prepositional phrase to form the single sentence in example **6**.

> **5.** O'Neill wrote many plays. They were written for the American stage. They were brilliant and insightful.
> **6.** O'Neill wrote many brilliant, insightful plays for the American stage.

The Grammar Game ♦ How would you combine them? Combine each pair of sentences below. Compare your new sentences with a classmate's. Did you combine them in the same way?

♦ O'Neill's father was famous. His father was an actor.
♦ O'Neill was dissatisfied. He left home at an early age. He traveled the world.

Working Together

Notice that your group's writing becomes more effective as you combine sentences in activities **A** and **B**.

In Your Group
◆ Encourage everyone to participate.   ◆ Listen to each other.
◆ Give additional ideas if needed.   ◆ Record the group's ideas.

A. Combine each pair of sentences below.

1. O'Neill was twenty-eight years old when his first play was staged. It was staged in 1916.

2. He was the first American dramatist to write tragedy. He wrote it consistently.

3. O'Neill's plays were daring. His plays were unusual. They often reflected his experiences at sea.

4. Audiences applauded loudly. They applauded energetically. They applauded for long periods of time.

B. Rewrite the following paragraph, combining sentences to make the paragraph read more smoothly and effectively.

Eugene O'Neill is a dramatist. He is considered to be America's greatest dramatist. He participated actively in many theater groups. He participated enthusiastically. His early plays were performed often. They were performed by the Provincetown Players and the Theater Guild. O'Neill won four Pulitzer Prizes. He won the Nobel Prize for literature in 1936.

WRITERS' CORNER ◆ Positioning Phrases

Check your writing to make sure prepositional phrases are placed as near as possible to the words they modify. An incorrectly placed phrase can sometimes completely change the meaning of a sentence.

EXAMPLE: In the lunchroom, Liah told us about the rehearsal.
CHANGE: Liah told us about the rehearsal in the lunchroom.

Read what you wrote for the Writer's Warm-up. Look carefully at the prepositional phrases you used. Are they correctly placed?

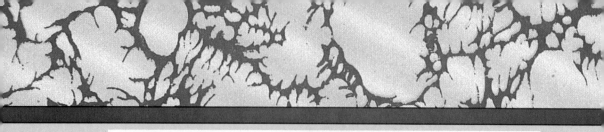

UNIT EIGHT

USING LANGUAGE
TO

CLASSIFY

=== **PART TWO** ===

Literature   "Two Artists of the Old West"
by Elisabeth Godolphin

A Reason for Writing   Classifying

CREATIVE
Writing

FINE ARTS ◆ The people in Mary Cassatt's painting seem to be enjoying the music. What are they
really thinking? What would they say to each other
if they could speak? Write a conversation between
the two. Tell what music they are playing and how
they feel about it.

CRITICAL THINKING ◆
A Strategy for Classifying

A CONCLUSION CHART

Classifying means sorting things into groups. It means putting together things that belong together. Comparing and contrasting are common ways of classifying information. After this lesson you will read "Two Artists of the Old West." In this article the author compares and contrasts the work of two outstanding American artists. Later you will write your own article comparing and contrasting two things.

Here is a passage from "Two Artists of the Old West" by Elisabeth Godolphin that contrasts the work of Frederic Remington and Charles Russell.

> Remington took his art more seriously than Russell. He even felt it necessary to destroy his paintings when they failed to meet his standards. Most art critics think that Remington's paintings are clearer and less cluttered than Russell's.

What conclusion does the author say critics have drawn about Remington and Russell? Do you think everyone would draw that conclusion? Should everyone draw the same conclusion?

Learning the Strategy

Different people can draw different conclusions from the same information. Suppose you read that your hometown baseball team won its last game because of good pitching. Statistics show that the losing team had a low batting average all season. Do you have to agree with the sportswriter's conclusion?

Often you need to know more facts before you can draw a conclusion. For example, suppose the first three integers in a series are 1, 2, 4. What three integers do you think complete the series? Do you have enough information to draw a conclusion?

CRITICAL THINKING: Drawing Conclusions

A conclusion chart can help you reach and check a conclusion. The chart below is about that winning baseball team.

Facts: The home team won the game. The pitching was excellent.

My Conclusion: The home team won because of a good pitching defense.

Conclusion Check: Do I have all the facts? Are other conclusions possible?

Make your conclusion check. Then decide if you want to keep your conclusion, change it, or withhold judgment until you have more information. What other conclusions are possible about why your team won the game?

Using the Strategy

A. What are you going to be when you grow up? Make a conclusion chart. List facts about your interests and abilities. Draw a conclusion about what you will be when you grow up. Then do a conclusion check. Do you have all the facts you need? Are other conclusions possible? If you like, write a prediction in your personal journal and save it to read again in the future.

B. Would you enjoy the paintings of Charles Russell and Frederic Remington? Make a conclusion chart. List the facts you have about your past experiences with art and about Russell and Remington. Draw a conclusion about whether you would enjoy their work. See if your conclusion is the same after you read "Two Artists of the Old West."

Applying the Strategy

♦ Did making a conclusion check alter your ideas about what you might be when you grow up? How?
♦ Is any conclusion ever completely "right" or "wrong"? If not, why draw conclusions?

Two Artists of the Old West

by Elisabeth Godolphin

In the days when much of America was still unsettled prairie and open plains, the American public was fascinated with the Western frontier. Two artists—Frederic Remington and Charles Russell—were particularly enchanted by the West. Remington and Russell lived during the same time, they saw similar sights, and they often painted the same subjects. But the two men viewed the West, and painted it, very differently.

If two people look at and draw the same thing, such as a tree, why are their drawings different? Shouldn't the tree look the same in both drawings? Not necessarily. Many factors influence the appearance of a piece of art. One of the most important is the artist's skill. Another is the way an artist looks at the subject. One artist might notice the different shades of green in the leaves and paint big blobs of color all over the page. Another artist might see the way the branches twist and turn and fill the page with braided tree limbs. The tree you recognize in one painting can look altogether different on the canvas of another artist.

Frederic Remington, like many people of his day, believed it was the United States' destiny to rule the lands once held by the Indians. This attitude affected the way he portrayed the cowboys, Indians, and soldiers in his paintings. In addition, although Remington loved the West, he had grown up in the East. This made his view of western life different from that of a true Westerner.

During his travels as a young man, Remington realized that the Old West would someday disappear, and he began to "record the

"The Cowboy," Frederic Remington, 1902. Amon Carter Museum, Fort Worth

facts." He journeyed all over the West with the Army, from Oregon to the dry Apache lands of the Southwest. Along the way, he set up his easel and painted, hoping to preserve the Wild West in pictures that "civilized" society could understand and enjoy.

Charles Russell was born into a Missouri farm family in 1864. A poor student but a good rider, Russell traveled to Montana when he was 15 and found work as a cowboy. He lived the cowboy life for 14 years, lodged with Indians for a time, and painted or sketched whenever he could. He had no formal art training, but he loved to paint.

By the end of his career as a cowboy, Russell was well-known for his art, especially in Montana. People commissioned, or hired, him to paint for them. He settled in Cascade, Montana, where he spent most of the rest of his life painting, drawing, and writing stories. Russell painted from his experience as a cowboy and a resident of the frontier. His art revealed his love of the West, its rivers, its mountains, and its inhabitants.

Many people cannot tell a Remington painting from a Russell without looking at the signature. It is easy to understand why. Both men portrayed the same subjects, including cowboys, Indians, and cavalrymen in action. Both painted their subjects to look realistic. Both spent a lot of time in the West. These two great painters of the West were also alike in how hard they worked on their paintings. Each tried to make his paintings as accurate as possible, paying attention to such details as the color of the beads in an Indian necklace.

But Remington and Russell differed from each other in important ways. Russell painted because he loved to paint, and doing so was fun for him. In later years, he was able to make a living from painting. Remington loved painting, too, but he also had a goal that Russell did not share. Remington's goal was to make great art out of Western subjects, and in the process, to record a way of life he saw was fading. Remington took his art more seriously than Russell. He even felt it necessary to destroy his paintings when they failed to meet his standards.

Most art critics think that Remington's paintings are clearer and less cluttered than Russell's. Remington's sculptures are considered more precise and artistic than Russell's. A closer look at how the two artists treated one of their favorite subjects—cowboys—sheds light on their differences as painters, and as observers of the Wild West.

In 1907, Charles Russell did a painting he called "A Quiet Day in Utica." The scene in the painting is anything but quiet, and it reveals Russell's sense of humor. The canvas is full of action—a dog gallops, horses buck, chickens squawk, and cowpokes laugh. Dust covers much of the foreground, allowing Russell to avoid painting precise details.

Russell's cowboys are not noble heroes who demand our admiration. Instead, they are rowdy, slightly reckless, ordinary human beings. They are almost faceless, too. This is probably because Russell had been a cowboy, and he might have felt silly glorifying the kind of life he himself had lived. Russell seems to have been a modest man, despite his success as an artist.

Frederic Remington's "The Cowboy" (1902) also shows action and drama, but all attention is focused on the rider and horse. The background hardly matters. The clarity and accuracy of the central figure are most important. The horse's muscles are precisely drawn and colored, as is the cowboy's balancing hand. Remington's rider is handsome and heroic. Even though the horse looks as though he may fall, the cowboy is relaxed and in control.

"A Quiet Day in Utica," Charles M. Russell; oil on canvas. Courtesy Sid Richardson Collection of Western Art, Forth Worth, Texas

Both artists painted the same subjects, but with such different results! Russell portrays a lively, funny scene of everyday life; Remington records for history a noble hero from the vanishing Old West. Studying the lives of these two artists helps us to see and to understand both the similarities and the differences in their art.

Library Link ◆ *If you enjoyed this article, you might enjoy reading other articles in* Cobblestone, *a magazine for young people. You can find it in your library.*

 Reader's Response

If you were studying art, would you choose either Russell or Remington as a teacher? Explain why or why not.

Two Artists of the Old West

Responding to Literature

1. If an artist came to your town to capture scenes showing the noble nature of the local people, to whom would you introduce the artist first?

2. Charles Russell had been a cowboy. How might his cowboy experiences have influenced his paintings?

3. If you could have heard Remington and Russell discuss painting, what might they have said? With a classmate, write a conversation that reveals each painter's personal ideas about painting the West. Decide which painter each of you will represent. Then read your conversation aloud to the class. Speak as though you were Russell or Remington.

Writing to Learn

Think and Conclude ✦ You have learned some facts about the art of the Old West in this article. You have probably also seen this kind of art before. Use these facts and your own experience to draw a conclusion. Tell whether you would like to learn more about this kind of art.

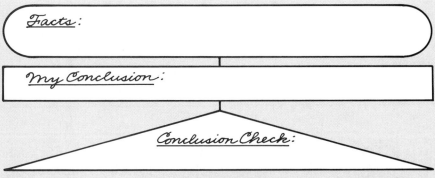

Facts:

My Conclusion:

Conclusion Check:

Conclusion Chart

Write ✦ Use the information from your conclusion chart in writing a paragraph. Tell how you feel about art that depicts the Old West.

Think of an object. Have your classmates ask questions that include the word *than* to guess the object. For example: "*Is it bigger than a desk? Does it make a noise louder than a mouse?*"

SPEAKING and LISTENING ◆
Listening for Comparisons

Can you remember a time when a friend asked you to describe something? You may have responded by explaining how that something was like or different from something else. If you did, you were using a comparison to help your friend understand.

When two subjects are compared in a discussion, each subject is made more understandable by showing how it is like or unlike the other. It is important to prepare for such a discussion so that you can contribute and respond to points as they are introduced. Make notes on the similarities and differences of the two subjects to be discussed. Use the guidelines below to help you actively participate in the discussion.

Making Comparisons	**1.** Provide your audience with the basic facts on both subjects before you point out similarities and differences. **2.** Find elements common to both subjects that can logically be compared. Give examples of the ways the subjects are alike or different. **3.** Summarize your conclusions at the end. Invite comments and questions from your listeners.
Listening for Comparisons	**1.** Listen attentively and thoughtfully. Decide whether the comparisons are logical. Do they compare equal things? **2.** Listen actively. Do you agree or disagree with the speaker's comparisons? Take notes for ideas or questions. **3.** If you have a question, ask it at the appropriate time—perhaps when the speaker asks for questions or at the end of the discussion.

Summary ◆ Before participating in a discussion that compares, identify the two subjects' similarities and differences. Prepare to give and listen for examples that illustrate likenesses and differences between the two subjects.

Guided Practice

Tell whether each student described below is following the guidelines for a discussion that compares. Explain your answers.

1. Cleo plans to present a comparison of two bands. She assumes everybody knows their music, so she doesn't play any of it.
2. Since Phil has just one question to ask about the subjects being compared, he daydreams till the discussion nears the end.
3. Lisa compares a dancer's movements with another dancer's costumes. She wonders why her listeners seem confused.

Practice

A. With a partner, take turns explaining whether or not you think the discussion guidelines are being followed in these examples.

4. Kei finishes his comparison and sits down immediately.
5. Dena doesn't agree with a comparison being made, so she jots it down and waits until the speaker invites comments.
6. Ralph says that, in his opinion, the differences are obvious. Then he wonders why he didn't convince anyone.
7. Paul asks a question as the speaker begins to summarize.
8. Dolores intends to ask a question, but she forgets it.

B. Study and take notes on the paintings by Remington and Russell on pages 435 and 437. Keep the guidelines in mind as you discuss these points of comparison.

9. How are the paintings similar in subject matter? How are they different in subject matter?
10. What is the feeling expressed in each painting? Do you think that the paintings are very similar or very different in feeling?
11. In your opinion, which artist had more talent? What details in the paintings did you compare to make your decision?

Apply • Think and Write

Comparing • Think about two of your favorite musical artists and decide if they are basically alike or different. Jot down your thoughts. Then write a brief paragraph that explains your viewpoint.

> ✎ **Remember**
> to find elements that can logically be compared.

What might happen if kids didn't go to school, if music didn't exist, if people didn't need to sleep? What interesting *if's* can you think of? Describe the results.

WRITING ◆
A Cause-and-Effect Paragraph

A cause is the reason something happens, and an effect is the result produced by the cause. A paragraph based on cause and effect can be organized in two ways.

One way to organize a cause-and-effect paragraph is to state the cause at the beginning. Then give supporting sentences that explain the effects resulting from the cause. Look at the example below.

> George Catlin, an obscure portrait painter, was impressed by some Native American chiefs who visited Philadelphia. Therefore, he decided to go west and paint scenes of Native American life. This decision would make him a famous artist.

As you can see, the chiefs' visit resulted in a new career for George Catlin. Also, notice that the word *therefore* acts as a signal to show the reader the cause-and-effect relationship.

Another way to organize a cause-and-effect paragraph is to give the effect first, followed by the causes. Look at this example from "Two Artists of the Old West."

> Russell's cowboys are not noble heroes who demand our admiration. Instead, they are rowdy, slightly reckless, ordinary human beings. . . . This is probably because Russell had been a cowboy, and he might have felt silly glorifying the kind of life he himself had lived.

Notice that the word *because* signals a cause-and-effect—or, in this instance, an effect-and-cause—relationship. Other words that act as signals include *therefore, since, as a result*, and *consequently*.

> **Summary** ◆ A **cause-and-effect paragraph** tells *what* happened and *why* it happened. It can be organized by stating either the cause or the effect first.

Guided Practice

Which sentences below show a cause-and-effect relationship?

1. In 1823, Catlin gave up his career as a lawyer and consequently became a painter.
2. George Catlin, an American painter and traveler, is famous for his paintings of Native Americans.
3. Catlin wanted to study North American Indian cultures, so he spent several summers among various Indian tribes.

National Museum of American Art, Smithsonian Institution. Gift of Mrs. Joseph Harrison, Jr.

Practice

A. Write the sentences that contain a cause-and-effect relationship. List any words that are used to signal cause and effect.

4. George Catlin returned to the East because he wanted to exhibit his paintings and sketches.
5. Easterners were curious about how the Sioux and other tribes lived, so they came to see Catlin's works.
6. George Catlin had little formal education and no training in art.
7. At that time, photography did not exist; as a result, Catlin's precise portrayals became works of great importance.
8. Today many of his paintings can be seen in the Smithsonian Institution in Washington, D.C.

B. For each cause, write two possible effects. For each effect, write two possible causes.

9. I have worked hard in school this year. (cause)
10. People have more time for leisure activities today. (effect)
11. Science has found cures for many diseases that were once considered fatal. (cause)
12. In some states, wearing seat belts is now required by law. (effect)

Apply • Think and Write

Dictionary of Knowledge • Read about *limners*, early American portrait painters, in the Dictionary of Knowledge. Write a paragraph explaining what caused these artists to be so popular in Colonial times.

> ✏ **Remember**
> that a signal word is often needed to make a cause-and-effect relationship clear.

In what ways are you different than you were two years ago? In what ways are you the same?

WRITING ◆
Comparison/Contrast Paragraphs

The words *comparison* and *contrast* are often used together. A comparison shows similarities between two things. A contrast points out differences. Comparisons and contrasts are useful in classifying, or grouping, things. Note, however, that the word *comparison* by itself is often used to mean both similarities and differences.

The chart below shows two different methods that writers use to organize a paragraph of comparison or a paragraph of contrast.

Ways to Compare and Contrast	
The Point-by-Point Method	**The Block Method**
AB _____ _____ ____ AB _____ _____ _____ AB _____ _____ _____ AB ____	A _____ _____ _____ _____ _____ B _____ _____ _____

Point-by-Point Method This method builds a paragraph with pairs of facts that illustrate similarities or differences. You describe one point about A and then the same point about B. In the example below, Elisabeth Godolphin compares the paintings of Remington and Russell.

Many people cannot tell a Remington painting from a Russell without looking at the signature. It is easy to understand why. Both men portrayed the same subjects, including cowboys, Indians, and cavalrymen in action. Both painted their subjects to look realistic. Both spent a lot of time in the West. These two great painters of the West were also alike in how hard they worked on their paintings. Each tried to make his paintings as accurate as possible, paying attention to such details as the color of the beads in an Indian necklace.

Block Method   The block method is useful in organizing and presenting more complex information. In the block method you tell all about topic A first. Then a transitional word or phrase is used to tell the reader, "Now here is how topic B is similar to or different from topic A." Then you tell all about topic B, in about the same amount of space you used on topic A. For example, the paragraph below explains the differences between the East and the West during the time Russell and Remington painted.

> Life in the West was very different from life in the East during the time Russell and Remington painted. The East had established communities with rather complex systems of government. Similarly, social activities of the East, such as entertaining visitors and attending the theater, were very formal. People in the East depended on carpenters to build their homes and on merchants to supply them with other necessities, such as food, clothing, and furniture. In contrast, the West, with its small, newly established communities, needed only simple forms of government. In a like manner, the West had simpler social activities, such as barn dances, cornhusking contests, and quilting bees. People in the West had to build their own homes, supply their own food, and make the most of their other necessities, such as clothing, candles, and tools.

In this paragraph, facts about life in the East are presented first. The transitional words *in contrast* act as a signal to inform the reader that now a new idea will be introduced—facts about life in the West. To present so much information point by point might be confusing to the reader. Here the block method contrasts the two subjects clearly.

Notice that both paragraphs begin by clearly stating the main idea; this tells the reader what will follow.

Summary ◆ To compare or contrast two things, first look for similarities or differences. Then use the point-by-point method or the block method to organize ideas.

Guided Practice

Which two sentences on page 446 tell the reader that a paragraph of comparison or contrast is being introduced?

1. Frontier people were very different from city people.
2. A desire for land caused many farmers to settle in the West.
3. The men and women who settled the West were alike in many ways.

Practice

A. Read the point-by-point paragraph of contrast below. Notice the transitional words between the first paired statements. Rewrite the paragraph, using the following transitional words where they are needed.

instead   **on the other hand**   **however**

The life of a cowboy in the days of the Western frontier was very different from the life of a modern cowboy. The early cowboy rode on horseback to tend cattle. In contrast, the cowboy of today uses a truck or even a helicopter to tend cattle. In the past a cowboy performed chores by hand. A cowboy today uses machines to help with tasks. The early cowboy led a lonely life, because the ranch was located far from town. A modern cowboy has good roads, automobiles, and trucks to travel to town. The cowboy of yesterday went on long overland trail drives to move cattle to a railroad station. The cowboy of today moves cattle in trucks.

B. Use the pairs of facts below to write a point-by-point paragraph of contrast. Add transitional words as needed. Begin with this sentence: *Watercolor painting differs from oil painting.*

4. Watercolor paintings are done on paper. Oil paintings can be done on many surfaces, including cardboard, canvas, and wood.
5. Watercolors dry faster than other paints, so the artist must work quickly to achieve different effects of color. Oil paint dries slowly, so the artist has more time to blend colors and make subjects appear more realistic.
6. Watercolor paint cracks if it is applied too thickly. Oil paint does not crack, even when it is applied thickly.

C. The facts below contain complex information. Is the point-by-point method or the block method the easier way to organize these facts? Demonstrate your answer by creating a paragraph of contrast from these facts. Begin your paragraph with this sentence: *Romanticism and realism are two very different styles of painting.*

7. The romantic style of painting reveals the imagination and emotions of artists.

8. The realistic style of painting shows artists' lifelike observations of life.

9. The romantic style frequently focuses on unusual events and faraway places.

10. Paintings done in the realistic style more often portray scenes from everyday life.

11. The romantic style of painting often uses nonrealistic colors to achieve a certain effect.

12. The realistic style of painting uses colors that accurately reflect what is observed.

National Gallery of Art.

The Metropolitan Museum of Art.

D. Select a topic that has two elements, such as winter and summer activities. Then write notes for a paragraph that will compare the two elements. Draft an introductory sentence for your paragraph. Be prepared to explain whether you would use the point-by-point or the block method of organization.

Apply ◆ Think and Write

Writing a Paragraph ◆ Recall your responses to the **Getting Started** exercise. Use the ways in which you are different or the ways in which you are the same to write a paragraph of comparison or contrast. Begin the paragraph with an introductory sentence.

✎ **Remember** to organize comparison/contrast paragraphs using the point-by-point or block method.

Focus on Comparisons

How did the author of "Two Artists of the Old West," which you read earlier, produce such a striking comparison of the two artists? What methods did she use? Here are some tips to keep in mind whenever you are comparing two subjects in your own writing.

1. *Begin with specific details about each subject.* From research and observation, make notes from which you can build your composition. The author of "Two Artists" seems to have made notes on each artist's *life, beliefs,* and *works of art.* She found both similarities and differences.

Remington	**Russell**
grew up in the East	A western cowboy at age 15
thought cowboys heroic	thought cowboys ordinary people
painted realistic detail	painted realistic detail

2. *Organize notes for paragraphs that clearly present similarities and differences.* In the notes above, you can see that both artists "painted realistic detail."
3. *Arrange paragraphs to create a clear, step-by-step comparison of your two subjects.* Read the following from "Two Artists."

   Remington and Russell lived during the same time, they saw similar sights. . . . But the two men viewed the West, and painted it, very differently.

The author then arranged her paragraphs to show how the men's lives, beliefs, and works differed—and were also alike. By the time you reach the summary, you fully understand the comparison.

The Writer's Voice ◆ Make notes for a comparison between two well-known sports figures or entertainers. List both similarities and differences.

Working Together

A comparison of two subjects should be based on careful observation or research or both. Point out differences as well as similarities as your group completes activities **A** and **B**.

In Your Group
♦ Encourage everyone to contribute. ♦ Don't interrupt each other.
♦ Share ideas and opinions. ♦ Record the group's ideas.

A. What are the similarities and differences between each pair of items? Compare your group's notes with those of other groups.

1. Painting and photography
2. Realistic and abstract art
3. Travelers to the West and people who lived in the West (1880s)
4. Cowboys in fact and cowboys in fiction

B. As a group, discuss some paired subjects (other than those in activity **A**) that could be developed effectively by comparison. Decide on one of the paired subjects and make notes on similarities and differences. Finally, write one or two sentences that accurately state the main idea of a report that could be written from the notes.

THESAURUS CORNER ♦ Word Choice

The special meanings of synonyms are compared in the Thesaurus. Rewrite the following paragraph. Fill in each blank with the most appropriate synonym for *get* or *good*. Then underline and label each preposition (prep), conjunction (conj), and interjection (interj).

You do not say, "I 'inherited' measles"; you say, "I _____ measles." The careful choice of words is essential to _____ writing. Through a written will, you might _____ a sizable art collection, but you would hardly 'corral' one from your uncle. Oh, you must _____ skill with words and become an exceptional writer.

"Lake McDonald" by Charles M. Russell
Amon Carter Museum, Fort Worth

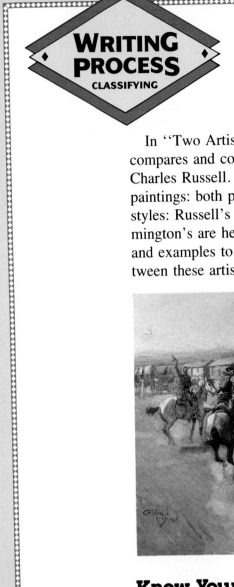

WRITING PROCESS
CLASSIFYING

Writing a Compare/Contrast Article

In "Two Artists of the Old West," Elisabeth Godolphin compares and contrasts the artists Frederic Remington and Charles Russell. She compares the subject matter of their paintings: both painted western scenes. She contrasts their styles: Russell's cowboys are ordinary people while Remington's are heroic. Godolphin presents specific details and examples to explain the similarities and differences between these artists.

"A Quiet Day in Utica," Charles M. Russell; oil on canvas. Courtesy Sid Richardson Collection of Western Art, Forth Worth, Texas

Know Your Purpose and Audience

In this lesson you will write an article. Your purpose will be to inform by comparing and contrasting two things or activities.

Your audience will be your classmates. After you have completed your article, you might read it aloud to the class. You and your classmates might also create a magazine for your school library.

1 Prewriting

Before beginning to write, choose a topic and gather your ideas for your compare-and-contrast article.

Choose Your Topic ◆ Make a list of pairs that interest you. Circle the pair you would most enjoy writing about. Choose your pair by considering the interesting likenesses and differences you could point out between the two.

Think About It	Talk About It
You might choose two holidays, games, animals, movies, or summer camps. Make sure you choose a topic that you like. Then you will be able to make it interesting for others.	Choose a partner and go over both lists. Talk about the possibilities for comparison and contrast that each pair offers. Then choose the topic that interests you both.

Topic Ideas

1. soccer and football
2. checkers and chess
3. dogs and fish as pets
4. Memorial Day and Labor Day

Choose Your Strategy ♦ Here are two strategies for gathering ideas. You might want to try using one or both of them.

PREWRITING IDEAS

CHOICE ONE

Listing

Write your two topics at the top of a sheet of paper. Then fold the paper to make two vertical columns. Label the columns ''Similarities'' and ''Differences.'' Then jot notes in both columns, listing as many comparisons and contrasts between the two topics as possible.

Model

Dogs and Fish

Similarities	*Differences*
Both interesting to watch	*Can't play with fish*
Both have to be fed	*Can't have dogs in most ap*
Both have many varieties	*Dogs' food and care expensi*

CHOICE TWO

A Conclusion Chart

Jot down facts about your pair of items. Read over your facts and then write a conclusion with which you might end your article. Finally, do a conclusion check to be sure your conclusion is sound.

Model

Facts About Dogs:
Can be played with
Need vet care
Expensive
Must go out

Facts About Fish:
Fun to watch
Easy to care for
Inexpensive
Must have water changed

My Conclusion: Both make good pets but have different requirements.

Conclusion Check:
Do I have enough facts?
Are other conclusions possible?

WRITING PROCESS: Compare/Contrast Article

2 Writing

Follow this diagram for help in developing your notes into a compare/contrast article. Use your conclusion sentence from your conclusion chart in the last paragraph.

Sample First Draft ◆

Dogs and fish make excellent pets. They have some similar qualities but they are also quite different.

Both are interesting animals to watch. Dogs like performing tricks, rolling down hills, or snapping at flies. Bright, colorful Tropical fish are fun to watch as they glide around. It's also fun to watch fish dart after each other and hide in the plants of the tank at the bottom.

You can play with a dog, but you have to be satisfied with just watching fish. Dogs are afectionite. Fish are not. On the other hand, fish are inexpensive and don't need medical care and room to roam as dogs do. Most landlords allow fish but don't allow dogs.

These are some things to think about before getting a dog or some fish both make fine pets but have very different qualities and living requirements.

	Point-by-Point Method	Block Method
Introduction	Identify the items. Tell main idea.	Identify the items. Tell main idea.
Paragraph 2	Compare (tell the likenesses).	Tell all about one item.
Paragraph 3	Contrast (tell the differences).	Tell all about the other item.
Conclusion	Sum up.	Sum up.

3 Revising

Revise your article to clarify meaning. The following idea may help you.

REVISING IDEA

FIRST Read to Yourself

As you read, review your purpose. Did you write an informative article about two things or activities? Consider your audience. Will your classmates enjoy your article? As you read aloud, listen to yourself. Are you stumbling over any words or sentences? Mark these parts for possible revision.

Focus: Did you compare and contrast? Did you tell the likenesses and differences of your two items?

THEN Share with a Partner

Test your writing on a partner. Read your article aloud and ask your partner to respond. These guidelines may help.

The Writer

Guidelines: Listen to your partner's suggestions. Make changes *you* feel are important.

Sample questions:
- Did I use specific facts and observations about both items?
- **Focus question:** Did I clarify the similarities *and* differences between the two things?

The Writer's Partner

Guidelines: Give suggestions that are specific enough to be really helpful.

Sample responses
- A detail you could add at this point is _____.
- You told a lot about the differences. Can you add more about similarities?

Revising Model ◆ Here is a compare/contrast article that is being revised. The marks show changes the writer wants to make.

Fascinating replaces the overused word *interesting*.

The writer's partner suggested making this detail more specific.

This prepositional phrase was moved to modify *plants*.

A cause-and-effect explanation strengthened the contrast.

> Dogs and fish make excellent pets. They have some similar qualities but they are also quite different.
>
> ~~Both~~ are ~~interesting~~ *fascinating* animals to watch. Dogs like performing tricks, rolling down hills, or snapping at flies. Bright, colorful Tropical fish are fun to watch as they glide around *through the water of their tank*. It's also fun to watch fish dart after each other and hide in the plants of the tank ⟨at the bottom⟩.
>
> You can play with a dog, but you have to be satisfied with just watching fish. Dogs are afectionite. Fish are not. On the other hand, fish are inexpensive and don't need medical care and room to roam as dogs do. Most landlords allow fish but don't allow dogs. *This happens because dogs sometimes bark* ∧ *or damage property.*
>
> These are some things to think about before getting a dog or some fish both make fine pets but have very different qualities and living requirements.

Read the compare/contrast article above the way the writer has decided it *should* be. Then revise your own article.

Grammar Check ◆ Placing prepositional phrases near the words they modify makes your meaning clearer.

Word Choice ◆ A thesaurus is a good source of synonyms for overused words like *interesting*.

Revising Checklist

☐ **Purpose:** Did I write an informative article about two things or activities?

☐ **Audience:** Will my classmates enjoy my article?

☐ **Focus:** Did I compare and contrast? Did I specify both likenesses and differences?

4 Proofreading

Proofreading for surface errors is a courtesy to your readers. Correct copy is easier to read and understand.

Proofreading Model ♦ Here is the article about dogs and fish. Proofreading changes appear in red.

Dogs and fish make excellent pets. They have some similar qualities but they are also quite different.

Both are ~~interesting~~ *fascinating* animals to watch. Dogs like performing tricks, rolling down hills, or snapping at flies. Bright, colorful Tropical fish are fun to watch as they glide around. *through the water of their tank* It's also fun to watch fish dart after each other and hide in the plants of the tank (at the bottom).

You can play with a dog, but you have to be satisfied with just watching fish. Dogs are ~~afectionite~~ *affectionate* Fish are not. On the other hand, fish are inexpensive and don't need medical care and room to roam as dogs do. Most landlords allow fish but don't allow dogs. *This happens because dogs sometimes bark or damage property.*

These are some things to think about before getting a dog or some fish both make fine pets but have very different qualities and living requirements.

PROOFREADING IDEA

Spelling Check

One trick for catching spelling errors is to read each sentence backwards. That way you can block out meaning and focus on correctness.

Now proofread your article, add a title, and make a neat copy.

5 Publishing

Here are two ways of sharing your compare/contrast article with others.

Dogs and Fish as Pets

Dogs and fish make excellent pets. They have some similar qualities, but they are also quite different.

Both are fascinating animals to watch. Dogs like performing tricks, rolling down hills, or snapping at flies. Bright, colorful tropical fish are fun to watch as they glide through the water of their tank. It's also fun to watch fish dart after each other and hide in the plants at the bottom of the tank.

You can play with a dog, but you have to be satisfied with just watching fish. Dogs are affectionate. Fish are not. On the other hand, fish are inexpensive and don't need medical care and room to roam as dogs do. Most landlords allow fish but don't allow dogs. This happens because dogs sometimes bark or damage property.

These are some things to think about before getting a dog or some fish. Both make fine pets but have very different qualities and living requirements.

PUBLISHING IDEAS

Share Aloud

Set up a read-around. Form small groups. Arrange chairs in a circle and read your compare/contrast article to the group. Ask your listeners to say if they would draw the same or a different conclusion from the facts you gave.

Share in Writing

With your classmates, make a magazine. Bind your articles together. Include an illustrated cover with a title such as *Alike and Different*, a table of contents, and an index. Include blank sheets at the back for readers' comments. Place your magazine in the school library.

Writing Across the Curriculum Literature

Do you and your friends all like exactly the same kinds of literature—books, movies, television, poetry? Who is right? Is it possible to decide what is "good" and what is "bad"?

Writing to Learn

Think and Evaluate ◆ Choose at least four books, stories, poems, movies, plays, or television shows that you have read or seen. At the bottom of your paper, classify them into two groups: those you have concluded were good and those you have concluded were just so-so or bad. Above your conclusion, list what you believe are some of the qualities of good and bad literature.

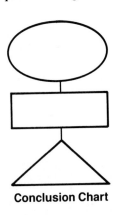

Conclusion Chart

Write ◆ Review your notes. Then write your opinion about whether it is possible to set standards for evaluating literature.

Writing in Your Journal

At the beginning of this unit, you wrote about a branch of the arts that interests you. You went on to read about leaders in the arts, such as the painter Mary Cassatt and the writer Ralph Ellison. In your journal explore your ideas about how the arts influence your life.

Read More About It

Cowboys of the Wild West   *by Russell Freedman*
If you are a fan of the romantic days of the Wild West, you should not miss this book. Through text and photographs you will learn fascinating details such as why the cowboy's boots were designed with pointed toes and high heels, and how cowboys treated themselves for minor injuries.

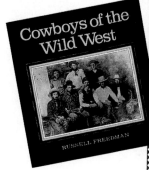

Lorraine Hansberry   *by Catherine Scheader*
Tragically short was the life of the brilliant black writer Lorraine Hansberry. There was time for many accomplishments, however, and they are recorded here for us.

Book Report Idea   Book Talk

TV talk-show hosts often interview authors about their new books. Presenting information in this way can boost a book's sales. You can boost the readership of a good book by giving a report in talk-show interview form.

Interview the Author
Pretending to be the author, show the book to your audience. Then tell a little bit about it. Another student, the show host, can ask questions to draw out more information. If the book is fiction, the host's questions should concern the setting, characters, and plot. Questions about nonfiction should focus on the main ideas of the book.

Unit 8

Prepositions   *pages 412–419*

A. Write the prepositional phrase in each sentence. Then underline each preposition and circle each object of the preposition.

1. Listen to this late-breaking news story.
2. An old water main burst beneath a busy city street.
3. Cascades of water covered the subway track below.
4. Subway service for morning commuters was disrupted.

B. Write the prepositional phrase or phrases in each sentence. Label each as an adjective phrase or an adverb phrase.

5. Pedro stuck to his original plan for a new magazine.
6. This school magazine will be distributed among the students.
7. According to Pedro, the magazine is the first of its kind.
8. Each issue of the magazine will center on a popular theme.

C. Write the correct word or words to complete each sentence.

9. Connie stayed (in, into) the same place backstage.
10. The drama coach stood (beside, besides) the director and (she, her).
11. Who (between, among) the three was the most absorbed in the play?
12. With (who, whom) did Connie stand (at, to) the rehearsal?

Conjunctions   *pages 420–421*

D. Write each conjunction and label it *coordinating* or *correlative*. Then write the word or words that are joined by the conjunction.

13. The music was neither loud nor soft.
14. Fred Astaire and Ginger Rogers danced gracefully.
15. They moved precisely but elegantly on stage.
16. They were not only dancers but also actors.

Interjections *pages 422–423*

E. Write the interjection in each sentence.

17. Aha! Glen wants to go to the same college his mother and father attended.

18. Well, I may go to an out-of-state college.

19. Dear me! I can't believe how much the cost of higher education has risen!

20. Karen's older sister won a four-year scholarship to study music! Bravo!

Words Used as Different Parts of Speech
pages 424–425

F. Write the part of speech of each underlined word.

21. Birds of a feather <u>flock</u> together.

22. A <u>flock</u> of geese is also known as a gaggle of geese.

23. The <u>early</u> bird catches the worm <u>early</u>.

24. <u>Few</u> would argue without a <u>few</u> facts.

Homophones and Homographs *pages 426–427*

G. Write the sentences, using the correct homophones.

25. Your my best friend.

26. Who's picture is this?

27. Who toad the car away?

28. I walk heavily on my heals.

H. Write the homographs and their parts of speech.

29. I paid a fair price for this lovely handmade quilt at a country fair.

30. Did the camel desert the traveler in the desert?

31. This striped tie will suit your suit perfectly.

32. What cost do you project for this project?

Comparison/Contrast Paragraphs *pages 444–447*

I. Select a topic that has two elements — such as records and tapes, guitars and banjos, or cross-country skiing and downhill skiing. Then write a paragraph comparing the two elements by showing their similarities. Use either the point-by-point method or the block method of organization.

CUMULATIVE REVIEW

UNIT 1: Sentences *pages 4–21*

A. Write and label each subject and verb.

1. Food contains fat, carbohydrates, water, proteins, vitamins, and minerals.
2. Sources of proteins include eggs, milk, fish, and meat.
3. High-quality proteins supply all the necessary amino acids.
4. We get water from all foods.

B. Write *simple* or *compound* for each sentence.

5. Carbohydrates include sugars and starches, and they provide energy to the body.
6. The best sources are grains, pasta, potatoes, and fruits.
7. Fats are the most concentrated source of energy in the diet.
8. They furnish calories, or they provide essential fatty acids.

UNIT 2: Nouns *pages 58–69*

C. Write each noun and label it *common* or *proper.*

9. The Federal Reserve System is a central banking system.
10. It monitors money and the growth of credit and prices.
11. Its Board of Governors is in Washington.
12. The Senate confirms its members.

D. Write the singular and plural possessive form of each noun.

13. Jefferson   15. burro   17. zookeeper
14. ditch   16. ox   18. university

E. Write the appositive in each sentence.

19. Mercury, the nearest planet to the sun, is the smallest.
20. The messenger of the gods, Mercury, is in Roman myths.
21. His Greek counterpart, Hermes, also wore winged sandals.
22. Quicksilver, or mercury, is a metallic element.

Unit 3: Verbs *pages 124–135*

F. Write and label each direct object and indirect object.

23. Include your full name and address in a business letter.
24. Don't write an angry, threatening, or pleading letter.
25. Give the recipient all the necessary information.
26. Show Mary or me the reply.

G. Write the sentences. Underline each linking verb and label each predicate nominative and predicate adjective.

27. Plato was a philosopher in ancient Greece.
28. He became a pupil and friend of Socrates.
29. His theories have been influential in Western civilization.
30. Plato's pupil Aristotle also grew famous and powerful.

Unit 4: Verbs *pages 180–198*

H. Write each verb and label its tense.

31. had dried   **33.** describe   **35.** rained   **37.** had timed
32. will have put **34.** has formed   **36.** will get   **38.** have eyed

I. Write the correct form of the verb in parentheses.

39. Yesterday a bird (bursted, burst) through our open window.
40. It (stealed, stole) a piece of bread.
41. This uninvited guest hasn't (broken, broke) anything yet.
42. Now it has (flown, flyed) far away.

J. Write whether each verb is progressive or emphatic. Then label its tense.

43. has been arguing   **45.** did scream   **47.** were farming
44. will be expecting   **46.** do know   **48.** does enjoy

K. Write the correct form of the verb in parentheses.

49. Two squirrels are (sitting, setting) in a tree.
50. I (rise, raise) to their chattering every morning.
51. A dog is (laying, lying) in the grass nearby.
52. We will (lay, lie) our blankets on the grass.

UNIT 5: Pronouns *pages 244–259*

L. Write each possessive pronoun. Then write whether it is used alone or with a noun.

53. Ours is an old house. **55.** Her house is modern.
54. Our plumbing is ancient. **56.** His is traditional.

M. Write and label each reflexive and intensive pronoun.

57. The truth itself sets you free. **59.** Can an eye see itself?
58. Do cats clean themselves? **60.** I myself can't see it.

N. Write the correct pronouns in parentheses.

61. (They, Them) wished (we, us) peace and prosperity.
62. (He, Him) and (I, me) appeared in a play together.
63. (Her, She) and her friend enjoyed it as much as (we, us).
64. The music inspired (we, us) listeners.

UNIT 6: Adjectives *pages 302–309*

O. Write the correct form of each adjective in parentheses.

65. Dad's eyesight is (bad) than mine.
66. He wore glasses at a (young) age than I.
67. Yet Dad was the (good) athlete in his class.
68. However, Mom is the (agile) member of our family.

UNIT 7: Adverbs *pages 354–363*

P. Write the comparative and superlative form of each adverb.

69. narrowly **71.** well **73.** little **75.** soon
70. often **72.** early **74.** much **76.** fast

Q. Write the correct word in parentheses.

77. Jan (can't, can) hardly wait to join the volleyball team.
78. She didn't see (no, any) reason for a delay.
79. I don't know (no one, anyone) who did better.
80. Doesn't she (ever, never) slow down?

R. Write the correct adjective or adverb in parentheses.

81. The pear tasted (good, well).

82. He sang (real, really) well.

83. My hat looks (bad, badly).

84. They (sure, surely) know.

Unit 8: Prepositions   *pages 412–419*

S. Write and label each adjective phrase and adverb phrase.

85. The last decade of the twentieth century will be a challenge.

86. A worldwide water shortage may occur during that time.

87. Scientists will struggle with air and water pollution.

88. Programs with different solutions will be implemented.

T. Write the word that correctly completes each sentence.

89. We were (at, to) the beach late in the afternoon.

90. Few bathers (beside, besides) us were swimming.

91. There was too much seaweed (in, into) the water.

92. (Among, Between) you and me, I prefer pools to beaches.

Conjunctions and Interjections   *pages 420–423*

U. Write each conjunction and label it *coordinating* or *correlative*.

93. The temperature of the water was either too hot or too cold.

94. We floated, swam, and dried off quickly.

95. Todd practiced his diving vigorously but cautiously.

96. He is not only a good swimmer but also a seasoned life-guard.

V. Write the interjection in each sentence.

97. I'm stuck here! Help!

98. Ugh! Look at the worms.

99. Well, I didn't expect it.

100. Terrific! The coast is clear.

Words Used as Different Parts of Speech
pages 424–425

W. Write the part of speech of each underlined word.

101. These do not belong with those books.

102. Don't leave your coats in the upstairs hall.

103. We have no upstairs in our beachhouse.

104. We'll fence in the yard with a metal fence.

Preposition Puzzler

Add two letters to each side of these letter combinations to make a preposition.

1. ain
2. nea
3. twe
4. rou
5. tho

6. th
7. wa
8. ce
9. ri
10. yo

be·st ag·nd

Pyramid Twister

Make a tongue-twister pyramid with prepositional phrases, without using any preposition twice. An example is shown below.

Tyler typed.
Tyler typed on the typewriter.
Tyler of Tulsa typed on the typewriter from Texas.
Tyler of Tulsa typed with temerity on the typewriter from Texas.

To find out how good your tongue twister is, ask a classmate to say the last line fast three times.

Unit 8 Extra Practice

1 Writing with Prepositions

A. Write the preposition in each sentence.

1. Into a hole it ran.
2. Look under the rock.
3. We live near you.
4. Stay in the truck.
5. Up the ramp it went.
6. Walk with us.
7. No one but Al came.
8. Many of them fell.
9. Wait until nightfall.
10. This is for you.
11. Work at a faster pace.
12. I come from Iowa.
13. Throw it to her.
14. I'll go after you.
15. Finish it by Thursday.
16. Keep off the grass.

B. In this article there are thirty prepositional phrases. Write each phrase after its sentence number. Underline each preposition once and each object twice.

EXAMPLE: Progress in women's rights was made slowly.

ANSWER: <u>in</u> women's <u>rights</u>

17. In 1898 an important event occurred at Seneca Falls in New York. **18.** It was the first American convention concerning women's rights. **19.** During the meeting an organizer, Elizabeth Cady Stanton, presented a women's bill of rights. **20.** In it she requested equal education, suffrage (the vote), and property rights for women. **21.** Stanton wanted equal rights with men. **22.** Colleges and professions like law and medicine were closed to women. **23.** Wives then could own no property and had few rights under the law. **24.** According to the law, a husband could control the earnings of his wife. **25.** Worst of all, women could not vote. **26.** In the following years some of the convention's aims were won. **27.** Largely through Stanton's efforts, property rights were soon obtained by women in New York. **28.** Despite great difficulties, the movement grew and grew. **29.** Unfair laws were changed in state after state because of the efforts of women like Elizabeth Cady Stanton. **30.** Among the women's goals, suffrage seemed farthest away. **31.** By 1900, however, women had won the vote in eleven states, mostly west of the Mississippi River.

2 Prepositional Phrases as Modifiers   *p. 415*

A. Write each adjective phrase after its sentence number. Then write the noun each phrase modifies.

EXAMPLE: A year for celebration was 1876.
ANSWER: for celebration, year

1. Americans from all the states celebrated their nation's centennial, or hundredth birthday. **2.** Philadelphia's six-month-long Centennial Exposition was a giant birthday party for the nation. **3.** This exposition was the first world's fair in American history. **4.** It celebrated the progressive nature of the American people. **5.** Eight million visitors to the fair saw more than 30,000 exhibits from the United States and foreign countries. **6.** However, exhibits of modern machinery and new inventions were the most popular. **7.** Alexander Graham Bell's telephone was an exhibit with many admirers. **8.** The American-built Corliss engine, the most powerful machine of its day, was also displayed. **9.** The power from this engine ran all the machinery in the exposition. **10.** The nation at its hundredth birthday was anticipating another century of freedom and progress.

B. Write each adverb phrase after its sentence number. Then write the word each phrase modifies.

11. After the Civil War, American cities grew quite rapidly. **12.** Their increasing populations were hungry for fresh meat. **13.** Texas alone had almost five million cattle at this time. **14.** In the late 1860s the cattle were driven north. **15.** The cowboy became important in American history and literature. **16.** Each day cowboys worked hard for only a dollar. **17.** They were parched in summer and lashed by winter winds. **18.** With patient skill they drove their herds north to the railroads. **19.** Along the thousand-mile Chisholm Trail, they traveled for two or three months. **20.** This famous trail ended in Kansas. **21.** At their destination the cowboys drove the cattle into pens or railroad cars. **22.** After their long drives, the cowboys were busy with roundups and other chores. **23.** In the 1880s, writers and artists immortalized the cowboys. **24.** By this time, however, the cowboy era was almost over. **25.** Natural disasters and over-grazed ranges had in a few short years made the long cattle drives unprofitable. **26.** Nevertheless, cowboy legend endures in song and story.

3 Using Prepositions Correctly
p. 418

A. Write each sentence, using the correct word in parentheses.

1. This summer we went (at, to) the amusement park.
2. Our family was vacationing (at, to) the seashore.
3. The fun house is right (beside, besides) the arcade.
4. Peggy would only ride the tilt-a-whirl, sitting (between, among) Joey and me.
5. (Beside, Besides) the candied apple, did you eat any supper?
6. I lost sight of Tom (between, among) the crowd members.
7. I caught up to him (beside, besides) the ferris wheel.
8. I followed him (in, into) the game room.
9. (Between, Among) the three of us we won seven prizes.
10. (In, Into) the car going home, we told Dad all about our adventures at the park.

B. Write each sentence, using the correct word in parentheses.

11. With (who, whom) did you go through the fun house?
12. The vampire character gave a scare to Tom and (I, me).
13. We couldn't help laughing when the bats flew past (we, us).
14. Karen went with Larry and (they, them) to get refreshments.
15. For Peggy and (he, him) the food was the best amusement.

4 Writing with Conjunctions
p. 420

A. Write each coordinating conjunction or correlative conjunction after its sentence number. Underline the correlative conjunctions.

1. The Homestead Act of 1862 opened America's plains and prairies to settlers. **2.** Any adult could file a claim and receive 160 acres of public land free. **3.** Homesteaders not only built houses but also planted crops. **4.** They lived on the land for five or more years, and then the land became their own. **5.** Most of the land had neither trees nor stones for buildings. **6.** Settlers either brought wood from the East or built houses from sod. **7.** Land on the prairies could be fertile or barren. **8.** Some settlers suffered not only from droughts but also from swarms of grasshoppers. **9.** Many homesteaders lasted the five years, but others gave up and moved on. **10.** Both American citizens and immigrants were eagerly waiting for any abandoned homesteads.

B. Write each coordinating and correlative conjunction. Then write and underline the words joined by the conjunctions.

11. A small but beautiful deer approached me.
12. Neither you nor I have been invited to the party.
13. Lydia plays the piano accurately and expressively.
14. Either this or that should be satisfactory.
15. We swam and skated after school today.
16. Not only the boys but also the girls will sing.
17. Bears move swiftly but quietly in the forest.

C. Supply a conjunction or a pair of conjunctions to complete each sentence. Write the sentence.

18. Horses _____ deer are Cindy's favorite animals.
19. Joel wants _____ a golden retriever _____ a cocker spaniel puppy.
20. Carol befriends _____ the chipmunks _____ every raccoon in the neighborhood.
21. Our neighbors' yard won an award for its elegant _____ economical landscape design.

5 Writing with Interjections

p. 422

A. Write each sentence. Then underline the interjection in each one.

1. "Whoa!" Sal shouted at the runaway horses.
2. The angry crowd yelled "Boo!"
3. "Hush! They'll hear us," whispered Annie.
4. Great! The whole house is painted at last.
5. Whew! It's going to be a hot day today.

B. Replace each interjection with a more appropriate one. Write the sentence.

6. Ugh! You sang beautifully.
7. Alas! I am so happy!
8. Bravo! That performance was terribly boring.
9. Whew! I lost my homework assignment.
10. Boo! What a delightful song.
11. Hooray! I just failed my mathematics quiz.
12. Great! I see a rat.

6 Using Words as Different Parts of Speech

p. 424

A. Write the part of speech of the underlined word in each sentence below.

1. You can have these books <u>but</u> not those.
2. Nothing <u>but</u> dust was in the little box.
3. People <u>like</u> your uncle are most admired.
4. They <u>like</u> traveling more than anything else in their retirement.
5. We can eat dinner <u>outside</u> again tonight.
6. A crowd gathered <u>outside</u> the stadium before the game.
7. Stop running <u>around</u> with those pointed sticks.
8. The children gathered <u>around</u> the new girl in the neighborhood.
9. Long <u>past</u> midnight we labored on.
10. Grandfather entertains us with wonderful stories about his <u>past</u>.
11. <u>Behind</u> us in the trees an animal growled loudly.
12. No matter how hard I work, I always fall <u>behind</u>.
13. The mouse made its nest <u>inside</u> the small cupboard in the pantry.
14. The detective considered the theft an <u>inside</u> job.
15. <u>Iron</u> your own shirts and handkerchiefs.
16. We dug up an old <u>iron</u> wheel.

B. Write a sentence using each word as the part of speech shown in parentheses.

17. water (verb)
18. water (noun)
19. steel (verb)
20. steel (adjective)
21. this (adjective)
22. this (pronoun)
23. love (adjective)
24. love (verb)

C. Write a sentence using each of the following words as two different parts of speech. Then label the parts of speech.

25. grate
26. walk
27. fan
28. plum
29. point
30. exercise

UNIT NINE

USING LANGUAGE
TO

IMAGINE

PART ONE

Unit Theme *Fantasy Worlds*

Language Awareness Verbals and Complex
Sentences

PART TWO

Literature *The Hobbit* by J.R.R. Tolkien

A Reason for Writing Imagining

Writing
IN YOUR JOURNAL

WRITER'S WARM-UP ◆ What fantasy
worlds have you encountered
in books and movies? How did those
worlds differ from our real world? What
is your favorite fantasy world? What did you like
about the characters? Write in your journal about
your favorite fantasy world. Describe it as well as
you can. Tell what aspects of it appeal to you the
most and why.

1 Participles and Participial Phrases

Verb forms that are used as adjectives, adverbs, or nouns are called **verbals**. A participle is a verbal used as an adjective.

There are two kinds of participles—the present participle and the past participle. The present participle ends in *ing*, and the past participle often ends in *ed*, *d*, *t*, *en*, or *n*.

■ Some fantasies are about <u>enchanting</u> and <u>forgotten</u> lands.

Do not confuse a participle used as an adjective with a participle used as the main verb in a verb phrase.

▌ Nina is <u>reading</u> a fantasy. (main verb)

▌ <u>Reading</u>, Nina enters a fantasy world. (participle used as adjective)

A participle can come before or after the noun or pronoun it modifies.

▌ This fantasy takes place in a <u>lost</u> world.

▌ The creatures <u>described</u> are not real.

> **Summary** ◆ A **participle** is a verb form used as an adjective. You can use participles to create interesting descriptions.

Guided Practice

Identify each participle. Tell whether it is present or past.

1. There is a growing interest in fantasy literature today.
2. Readers enjoy fantasy's inspired heroes and thrilling stories.
3. Fantasies may include talking animals, flying dragons, hidden lands, deformed monsters, rings stolen, and promises broken.

A participle can be expanded into a participial phrase by adding one or more adverbs as modifiers.

■ 1. Nina, reading rapidly, finished the fantasy in a week.

A participial phrase can also be formed by adding a prepositional phrase to the participle.

2. Niña, reading on the bus, finished the fantasy in a week.

In some participial phrases, the participle has a direct object.

3. A science fantasy called *Dragonsong* is Nina's favorite.

A participial phrase, like a participle, is used as an adjective. A participial phrase can come before or after the word it modifies.

4. Written by Anne McCaffrey, *Dragonsong* tells about the fantasy land of Pern.

5. *Dragonsong*, written by Anne McCaffrey, tells about Pern.

A **nonessential participial phrase** is not necessary to the meaning of the sentence but merely adds information. It is set off by commas, as in sentences **1** and **2** above. An **essential participial phrase** is necessary to the meaning of the sentence and is not set off by commas. See sentence **3**. Always use a comma after a participial phrase that begins a sentence, as in sentence **4**. See page 652.

Summary ✦ A **participial phrase** is a participle and its related words. It acts as an adjective. Participial phrases can add details to your writing.

Guided Practice

Identify the participial phrase in each sentence.

4. Creating an imaginary land, Anne McCaffrey tells of the battle between good and evil.
5. Strange animals called fire lizards live in Pern.
6. Borrowing from both the real world and from fantasy, McCaffrey invented a believable setting for her books.
7. Other authors, using similar techniques, also write fantasy.
8. Constantly growing in number, fantasy fans even have clubs.

Practice

A. Write the participial phrase in each sentence in this paragraph about another fantasy writer. Then underline each participle.

9. Using more traditional ideas of fantasy, Ursula Le Guin has written three novels. **10.** Her books, set in the land of Earthsea, are not based on science. **11.** The main character in her series is a magician named Ged. **12.** Noted for her large readership, Ursula Le Guin is a popular author of fantasy literature.

B. Write each sentence. Underline the participial phrase. Circle the word it modifies.

13. The fantasy book club members, applauding loudly, welcomed the speaker.
14. Having a large membership, the club puts out a newsletter.
15. Fantasies selected by the book critic are reviewed monthly.
16. Films based on fantasy novels are reviewed, too.
17. Sharing and exchanging books at meetings, members chat enthusiastically about their favorite fantasy novels.
18. Depending on your own taste in books, you too may start a fantasy book club in your school or community.

C. For each sentence write whether the participial phrase is essential or nonessential.

19. Bookstore owners, inspired by the popularity of fantasy, often set aside whole sections of their stores for fantasy.
20. A reader looking for a fantasy novel has a wide selection.
21. Fantasy series, often published as three books, are quite popular today.
22. Anyone bored by television will find fantasy novels a treat.
23. Why not spend an evening in a land called Pern or Earthsea?

Apply ◆ Think and Write

From Your Writing ◆ Read what you wrote for the Writer's Warm-up. Working with a partner, try to add some more vivid details by using participles and participial phrases.

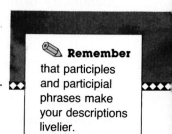

✎ **Remember** that participles and participial phrases make your descriptions livelier.

How many words that end in *ing* can you think of to complete these sentences?

_____ *is my favorite sport. I don't like* _____ .

GETTING
STARTED

2 Gerunds and Gerund Phrases

A gerund is a verbal ending in *ing* that is used as a noun. Like a noun, a gerund can be a subject, direct object, predicate nominative, or an object of a preposition.

> **Subject:** Writing brought Jonathan Swift fame.
> **Object of a Preposition:** He used a quill for writing.

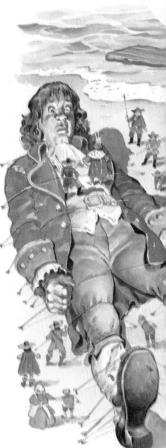

Both present participles and gerunds end in *ing*. To tell whether the word is a participle or a gerund, determine how the word is used in a sentence. When it is used as a noun, it is a gerund. When it is used as an adjective, it is a participle.

> **Gerund:** Traveling was Gulliver's greatest pleasure.
> **Participle:** *Gulliver's Travels* is about a traveling ship's doctor.

A gerund phrase is made up of a gerund and any direct object or modifiers it may have. The whole gerund phrase is used as a noun in a sentence.

> **Subject:** Writing *Gulliver's Travels* took Swift many years. (gerund with direct object, *Gulliver's Travels*)
> **Direct Object:** Readers have enjoyed the imaginative voyaging. (gerund with modifying adjectives, *the* and *imaginative*)
> **Predicate Nominative:** Gulliver's greatest pleasure was traveling to fantastic lands. (gerund with modifying prepositional phrase, *to fantastic lands*)
> **Object of Preposition:** Gulliver grew restless from staying home. (gerund with modifying adverb, *home*)

> **Summary** ♦ A **gerund** is a verb form ending in *ing* used as a noun. A **gerund phrase** is a gerund and its related words. A gerund phrase acts as a noun.

GRAMMAR: Gerunds and Gerund Phrases   **477**

Guided Practice

Name the gerund or gerund phrase in each sentence.

1. Sailing from England in 1699 marked the commencement of Gulliver's journey.
2. His first adventure was becoming shipwrecked in a storm.
3. Swimming to shore saved his life.
4. Upon awaking he found himself a captive of the Lilliputians.

Practice

A. Write the gerund or gerund phrase in each sentence. Then write whether it is used as a subject, direct object, predicate nominative, or object of a preposition.

5. Holding Gulliver as a prisoner was not hard for the six-inch-tall Lilliputians. 6. Hundreds of tiny ropes kept him from escaping. 7. The difficult part was moving their giant captive. 8. The pulling of Gulliver in a special wagon was finally accomplished by fifteen hundred Lilliputian horses, each about four and a half inches high. 9. Everyone in Lilliput enjoyed watching the spectacle.

B. Write original sentences, using the gerund phrases as indicated in parentheses.

10. looking for *Gulliver's Travels* (as a subject)
11. reading a fantasy novel (as a direct object)
12. writing a story (as an object of a preposition)
13. traveling around the world (as a subject)
14. having adventures (as a predicate nominative)

C. Complete each sentence with a gerund or gerund phrase.

15. _____ is fun. 17. I won for _____ .
16. I like _____ . 18. One sport is _____ .

Apply • Think and Write

Phrases for Signs • Make up ten signs, using a gerund or gerund phrase in each. Example: *Smoking in Public Is Prohibited.*

✏️ **Remember**
that you can use gerunds and gerund phrases to tell about action.

Can you finish these famous quotations?

"*To err is human, _____.*"   "*To be or not to __, _____.*"

◆◇◆

3 Infinitives and Infinitive Phrases

Like participles and gerunds, infinitives are a kind of verbal. An infinitive is formed with the word *to* and the basic form of the verb. Used as a noun, an infinitive can be a subject, direct object, predicate nominative, or object of a preposition.

> **Subject:** To entertain was Lewis Carroll's aim.
> **Direct Object:** Lewis Carroll wanted to entertain.

An infinitive can also be used as an adjective.

■ Wonderland is a hard place to forget. The one to ask is Alice.

Used as an adverb, an infinitive usually modifies a verb or an adjective.

To find out, read Carroll's fantasy *Alice in Wonderland*.
The book is fun to read. It is hard to put down.

In an infinitive, *to* is followed by a verb. In a prepositional phrase, *to* is followed by a noun or pronoun that is its object.

> **Infinitive:** Alice knew which door to open.
> **Prepositional Phrase:** It was the door to the garden.

> **Summary** ♦ An **infinitive** is the basic form of the verb preceded by *to*. It can be used as a noun, an adjective, or an adverb.

Guided Practice

Identify each infinitive. Be careful not to confuse an infinitive with a prepositional phrase.

1. Alice went into the rabbit hole and began to fall.
2. At the bottom of the tunnel, the White Rabbit led her to several locked doors.
3. Alice found a piece of cake to eat.

An infinitive can be combined with modifiers and objects to form an infinitive phrase. The entire infinitive phrase is used as a single part of speech. The phrases below act as nouns.

Subject: To follow the White Rabbit was Alice's aim.
(infinitive with direct object, *White Rabbit*)

Direct Object: Alice began to grow quickly.
(infinitive modified by adverb, *quickly*)

Predicate Nominative: Alice's goal was to fit through the tiny door. (infinitive modified by prepositional phrase, *through the tiny door*)

Object of Preposition: She had no alternative except to grow smaller. (infinitive modified by adjective, *smaller*)

An infinitive phrase can also be used as an adjective or adverb.

Adjective: Alice found a key to open the garden door.

Adverb: The White Rabbit rushed to visit the Duchess.

Adverb: He was eager to see her.

> **Summary** ◆ An **infinitive phrase** is an infinitive and its related words. An infinitive phrase acts as a noun, adjective, or adverb. Use infinitive phrases to add variety to your writing.

Guided Practice

Identify each infinitive phrase. Be careful not to confuse an infinitive phrase with a prepositional phrase.

4. Alice came to the Duchess's fantastic house.
5. Alice tried to quiet the Duchess's squalling baby.
6. To her amazement, it turned into a pig and ran into the forest.
7. Then the Duchess's Cheshire cat began to talk with Alice.
8. He was able to disappear at will.
9. The cat told Alice to go to the Mad Hatter's tea party.
10. At the tea party, Alice had to deal with very strange people.
11. The March Hare, the Mad Hatter, and the sleepy Dormouse were all too lazy to set the table correctly.
12. The Dormouse rudely began to fall asleep.
13. Alice used that moment to escape from the mad tea party.

Practice

A. Write each infinitive phrase in this paragraph about *Alice in Wonderland*. Write *none* if a sentence has no infinitive phrase.

14. Alice went to a garden of talking flowers. **15.** Gardeners with paint brushes were trying to paint the white roses red. **16.** The Queen's instructions were to plant red rose bushes. **17.** The gardeners were painting the roses to cover up their mistake. **18.** The Queen caught them, however, and gave an order to cut off their heads. **19.** To save the gardeners, Alice shoved them into a large flower pot. **20.** Then everyone began to play croquet. **21.** The Duchess, meanwhile, took Alice to the seaside to meet the Mock Turtle and the Gryphon. **22.** Later Alice was rushed to a courtroom for a trial. **23.** She was called before the King and Queen of Hearts to act as a witness.

B. Write the infinitive phrase in each sentence. Then write whether it is used as a noun, adjective, or adverb.

24. Lewis Carroll began *Alice in Wonderland* in 1862 to amuse three sisters—Lorina, Alice, and Edith Liddell.
25. To read *Alice in Wonderland* is a pleasure for adults as well as children.
26. Today it is possible to read the fantasy in forty languages.
27. *Alice in Wonderland* is a book to read over and over again.
28. Carroll later decided to write *Through the Looking Glass*.

C. Expand each infinitive into an infinitive phrase. Then write a sentence using your phrase as indicated in parentheses.

29. to travel (noun) **31.** to choose (noun) **33.** to go (adverb)
30. to visit (adverb) **32.** to try (adjective)

Apply ◆ Think and Write

A Paragraph of Preference ◆ In both *Alice in Wonderland* and *Gulliver's Travels*, size is important. Sometimes Alice grows into a giant; sometimes she shrinks to the size of a mouse. Gulliver is captured by six-inch-tall Lilliputians and later by giants. Explain in a paragraph whether you would prefer to be very small or very large. Include infinitives and infinitive phrases in your explanation.

Remember that you can use infinitives and infinitive phrases for variety.

GETTING STARTED

Lewis Carroll invented fantastic situations on purpose. This situation is fantastic, but it was not meant to be: *Howling at the fire alarm, Justin chased his dog.* What did the writer really mean?

4 Using Verbal Phrases Correctly

When you use a participial phrase, be sure there is a noun or pronoun in the sentence for the phrase to modify. A participial phrase that has no word it can logically modify in a sentence is called a **dangling modifier**.

Dangling: Looking for a fantasy, *Dragonsong* was discovered.
Corrected: Looking for a fantasy, Kim discovered *Dragonsong*.

Also be sure to place each participial phrase as closely as possible to the word it modifies. A participial phrase that is poorly placed is called a **misplaced modifier**.

Misplaced: Falling off the shelf, Jessica found *Alice in Wonderland*.
Corrected: Jessica found *Alice in Wonderland* falling off the shelf.

Another awkward use of a verbal is the split infinitive, caused by placing an adverb between the *to* and the verb. Although it is not necessarily wrong to split an infinitive, it is usually better to move the adverb or omit it.

Split Infinitive: I want to first read this.
Better: I want to read this first.

> **Summary** ♦ Good speakers and writers avoid dangling and misplaced modifiers. Be careful not to split infinitives unnecessarily.

Guided Practice

Correct or improve these sentences.

1. Talking to the author, the book became understandable.
2. Carlos expected to quickly finish the chapter.
3. We discussed the plot sitting around the table.

Practice

A. Rewrite the sentences, correcting dangling or misplaced participial phrases. If a sentence is correct, write *correct*.

4. Walking home from school, we stopped at the library.

5. Going into the library, my book was returned.

6. Wanting a fantasy novel, the card catalog was the first place to look.

7. Pushed behind some other books, Ema found *Mary Poppins*.

8. Regarded highly as a movie, *Mary Poppins* is also an entertaining book.

9. Looking for other fantasy novels, Nancy Bond's *The String in the Harp* was found.

10. Lying on a table, I saw the fantasy *Watership Down*.

11. Finding the perfect book, it was quickly picked up by Ema.

12. Wanting a fantasy novel for myself, some other books were looked at.

13. Displayed on a bookcase, I found *The Little Prince* by Antoine de Saint-Exupéry.

B. Rewrite each sentence to eliminate the split infinitives.

14. I hope to eventually see the Disney film *Fantasia*.

15. My grandparents went to first see it in the 1940s.

16. This fantasy film was to suddenly become a great artistic award winner for Walt Disney.

17. Disney's idea was to skillfully mix classical music with animated art.

Walt Disney Productions

18. Our local movie manager hopes to someday soon show the film.

Apply ◆ Think and Write

Dictionary of Knowledge ◆ Find out more about American artist and inventor Walt Disney in the Dictionary of Knowledge. Then write a paragraph about your favorite Disney creation. Include several participial phrases and infinitives.

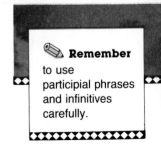

✎ **Remember** to use participial phrases and infinitives carefully.

GETTING STARTED
Can you finish these lines from famous songs?
"When you wish upon a star, . . ."   *"If I had a hammer, . . ."*
"If you're happy and you know it, . . ."   *"Oh, when the saints go . . ."*

5 Complex Sentences

A **clause** is a group of words that has a subject and a verb. An **independent clause** can stand alone as a simple sentence. Two or more independent clauses joined by a conjunction make up a compound sentence.

Independent Clause: My favorite fantasy is *Watership Down*.
Compound Sentence: *Watership Down* is a long book, but I read it quickly.

A **subordinate clause**, such as "when I read it," has a subject and a verb but cannot stand alone as a sentence. Subordinate clauses are introduced by such words as *since*, *because*, *when*, *if*, and *while*.

A sentence that has one independent clause and at least one subordinate clause is called a complex sentence. Subordinate clauses are underlined in the examples below.

> **MECHANICS ";?!"**
>
> Most subordinate clauses at the beginning or in the middle of sentences are set off by commas.

If you read it, you will like it.
The book, because it is about rabbits, is very unusual.
I even cried when I read it.

> **Summary ◆** A **complex sentence** has one independent clause and at least one subordinate clause. You can use complex sentences to show cause and effect when you speak and write.

Guided Practice

Tell whether each clause is independent or subordinate.

1. a British author, Richard Adams, wrote *Watership Down*
2. since it won the Carnegie Medal and the Guardian Award
3. if you enjoy reading fantasies about animals

Practice

A. Label each clause about *Watership Down*
independent or *subordinate*.

4. the main character is a rabbit named Hazel
5. because a rabbit called Fiver predicted disaster
6. Hazel led a group of rabbits to safe land
7. if Hazel could keep up the other rabbits' courage
8. since Hazel himself was frightened

B. Label each sentence *compound* or *complex*. For each
complex sentence, write the subordinate clause.

9. When Fiver made a prediction, he was usually right.
10. Fiver warned the others about a coming danger, but the Chief Rabbit didn't believe him.
11. Hazel did believe Fiver because Fiver had been right before.
12. Hazel decided to leave right away, and several followed.
13. While they were leaving, they were joined by Bigwig.
14. Hazel was glad to have Bigwig along since he was strong.
15. They came to another rabbit warren, and most of Hazel's band wanted to stay there.
16. Because he had bad feelings about the warren, Fiver did not want to stay there.
17. Although Hazel usually listened to Fiver, Hazel did not believe him this time.
18. Fiver proved to be right again because there was danger at the new warren.

C. Write a complex sentence for each subordinate clause.

19. since I met you
20. because I was afraid
21. when the match ended
22. if you knew me better
23. while I was learning to swim

Apply ◆ Think and Write

A Cooperative Story ◆ Have a partner write ten independent clauses that tell a story. You supply subordinate clauses for the sentences. Then write a second story. This time you write the independent clauses.

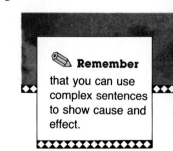

Remember
that you can use complex sentences to show cause and effect.

GETTING STARTED

How would you finish these sentences? *I am happiest when I . . . .*
They will join us after they . . . . Time was passing slowly until the . . . .

6 Adverb Clauses

A subordinate clause used as an adverb in a complex sentence is called an adverb clause. Like an adverb, an adverb clause may modify a verb, an adjective, or an adverb.

> *The Lord of the Rings* was written <u>while World War II raged</u>. (modifies verb)
>
> *The Hobbit* became more popular <u>than its author had expected</u>. (modifies adjective)
>
> *The Hobbit* was selling very well <u>before J.R.R. Tolkien finished writing *The Lord of the Rings*</u>. (modifies adverb)

MECHANICS ";?!"

When an adverb clause begins a sentence, it is followed by a comma. See page 652.
After he wrote *The Hobbit*, Tolkien wrote *The Lord of the Rings*.
Tolkien wrote *The Lord of the Rings* after he wrote *The Hobbit*.

Words that begin adverb clauses are called **subordinating conjunctions.** The most commonly used ones are listed below.

Subordinating Conjunctions				
after	as long as	if	though	whenever
although	as soon as	since	unless	where
as	because	so that	until	wherever
as if	before	than	when	while

Summary ♦ An **adverb clause** is a subordinate clause used as an adverb. Use subordinating conjunctions such as *after*, *before*, *as soon as*, *when*, and *while* in adverb clauses to show time sequence.

Guided Practice

Name the subordinating conjunctions in Getting Started above.

Practice

A. Write the paragraph, underlining each adverb clause. Add commas where needed.

  1. Although hobbits don't really exist they are well-known.
2. Tolkien invented these fantasy people when he wrote *The Hobbit*.
3. Tolkien wrote about them as if they were real. **4.** Because he described them so well we can imagine them easily. **5.** His bright-eyed hobbits are friendlier than the elves in his book are.

B. Combine each pair of sentences, using the subordinating conjunction in parentheses.

    EXAMPLE: Beau read *The Hobbit*. Ana had enjoyed it (because).
    ANSWER: Beau read *The Hobbit* because Ana had enjoyed it.

  6. Beau and Ana talked about the book. Beau read it (after).
  7. They liked the character Bilbo. He was brave (because).
  8. They were talking (as). They got an idea.
  9. Beau and Ana decided to make hobbit puppets. They could put on a play (so that).
  10. Beau made the Bilbo puppet. Ana made Gandalf (while).
  11. They were finished (when). They made other puppets, too.
  12. All the characters were made (as soon as). Ana and Beau wrote the script for the puppet show.
  13. They rehearsed the play. They were satisfied (until).
  14. Ana and Beau did the show for their families. They put on the play for their friends (before).
  15. The show was a hit (since). They put it on at school.

C. Change each simple sentence into a complex sentence by adding an adverb clause. Write the sentences.

    16. We went swimming.   **19.** I laughed.
    17. She got on the train.   **20.** Jan won.
    18. He will leave.

Apply ◆ Think and Write

Fictional Characters ◆ In a paragraph or two, tell about your favorite book character. Use several adverb clauses in your sentences.

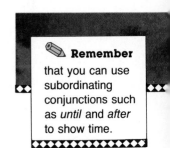

✎ **Remember**
that you can use subordinating conjunctions such as *until* and *after* to show time.

Make up some sayings like these.
"The gods help them that help themselves."—Aesop
"He that riseth late must trot all day."—Benjamin Franklin

7 Adjective Clauses

A subordinate clause that modifies a noun or pronoun is called an adjective clause. Adjective clauses are often introduced by relative pronouns. A **relative pronoun** relates the clause to the modified noun or pronoun. The relative pronouns *who*, *whom*, and *whose* refer to people; *which* refers to things; and *that* refers to people or things. Adjective clauses usually follow the words they modify.

> A fantasy that you will enjoy is *The Little Prince*.
>
> The story, which was written in French, is by Antoine de Saint-Exupéry.
>
> Katherine Woods, who knows French and English, translated it.

The words *when* and *where* may also begin adjective clauses.

> B-612 is the planet where the little prince lived.
> There came a time when he decided to visit Earth.

You can often combine two short sentences into one longer sentence that has an adjective clause.

> Onto B-612 blew a seed. It grew into a beautiful rose.
> Onto B-612 blew a seed, which grew into a beautiful rose.

A **nonessential clause** is an adjective clause that is not necessary to the meaning of the sentence but merely adds information. An **essential clause** is necessary, for without it the sentence would have a different meaning. Use commas to set off nonessential clauses; essential clauses are not set off.

The character whom the novel is about is a prince. (essential)
The little prince, who is the main character, is from a planet called B-612. (nonessential)

Summary ◆ An **adjective clause** is a subordinate clause that modifies a noun or pronoun. Two short sentences can often be combined into a sentence that has an adjective clause.

Guided Practice

Name each adjective clause. Then name the word the clause modifies.

1. The rose that grew on B-612 claimed to be the only rose in the universe.
2. The prince, who was no fool, doubted her claim.
3. She told him about the place where she had lived.
4. Yet she had come to B-612 as a seed, which couldn't know about the entire universe.
5. The prince, who wanted to know the truth, went to Earth.

Practice

A. Write each adjective clause and the word it modifies.

    6. On Earth the prince came to a rose garden, which was in bloom. **7.** The rose that was back on B-612 had been untruthful. **8.** The prince, who was a sensitive boy, cried. **9.** Then a wild fox, which had been hiding, talked to the boy. **10.** This very wise fox asked the prince, whom he liked, to tame him.

B. Write each sentence, punctuating the adjective clause correctly. Underline the relative pronoun or other introductory word in each adjective clause.

    11. The fox could not go to B-612 where the boy was born.
    12. The fox that the boy tamed told him a secret.
    13. There came a time when the prince grasped the secret.
    14. It was about the heart which can see better than the eyes.
    15. The prince who gained wisdom understood his special rose.

C. Use these adjective clauses in original sentences.

    16. which I wrote   **18.** where I live   **20.** when I'm
    17. who knows me   **19.** that I enjoy   happy

Apply • Think and Write

Cooperative Clauses • With a partner write five adjective clauses and five nouns or pronouns. Mix and match them in sentences.

✎ **Remember**
that you can use adjective clauses to add details to your sentences.

GETTING STARTED

Take turns leading this "Famous Person" game. Say: *"I'm thinking of a person who _____. The person is a _____ whom many admire. He/She is a person whose initials are _____."*

8 Relative Pronouns in Adjective Clauses

The relative pronouns *who*, *whom*, and *whose* introduce adjective clauses that refer to persons. To choose which of these pronouns to use, see how the pronoun is used in the clause.

Use *who* when the pronoun is the subject in the clause.

> **Joan Aiken, who wrote *Night Fall*, also wrote *Arabel's Raven*.**
> (*Who* is the subject of the verb *wrote*.)

Use *whom* when the pronoun is a direct object or an object of a preposition in the clause.

> **Aiken is a writer whom Jessica reads often.** (*Whom* is the direct object of the verb *reads*.)
> **Paula is a friend to whom Jessica gave a copy of *Night Fall*.**
> (*Whom* is the object of the preposition *to*.)

Use *whose* when the pronoun in the clause shows possession.

> **Paula is a reader whose favorite books are fantasies.**

> **Summary ◆** Use relative pronouns carefully in adjective clauses to make your meaning clear.

Guided Practice

Name the adjective clause in each sentence. Then tell how the relative pronoun is used in the clause: subject, direct object, or object of a preposition.

1. Joan Aiken, who had American parents, grew up and went to school in England.
2. She is an author whom fantasy readers appreciate.
3. Is she a writer with whom you are familiar?

Practice

A. Write the adjective clause in each sentence. Then write how the relative pronoun is used in the clause: subject, direct object, object of a preposition, or possessive.

4. Joan Aiken is the author who wrote "All You've Ever Wanted."
5. It is about a girl who is raised by her aunts.
6. Gertie is an aunt from whom she receives a wish in a poem on each birthday.
7. Aunt Gertie is a strange person whose wishes for her niece's birthday always come true.
8. Matilda is the name of the niece whom Gertie adores.

B. Write each sentence. Supply the correct relative pronoun: *who*, *whom*, or *whose*.

9. Gertie, _____ meant well, wished that her niece would make a new friend every day that year.
10. The friends _____ Matilda made numbered 365.
11. These were friends from _____ Matilda could not escape.
12. There are people _____ wishes seem harmless enough.
13. They should read about Matilda, _____ knew about wishes.

C. Use these adjective clauses in original sentences.

14. to whom I wrote
15. whom I resemble
16. who called me
17. whose hat was purple
18. with whom I left
19. whom you met yesterday
20. for whom we waited
21. whose record is missing
22. who was invited
23. who arrived late

Apply • Think and Write

Imagining • If you had the power to make wishes come true, what wishes would you make? For whom would you make them? Perhaps you would choose not to use your power. Write about what you would do. Include several sentences that contain adjective clauses with *who*, *whom*, and *whose*.

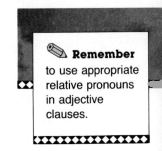

Remember to use appropriate relative pronouns in adjective clauses.

Use your imagination to complete these statements.

I wonder what _____ .   *Whoever arrives early _____ .*

9 Noun Clauses

A subordinate clause used as a noun is called a noun clause. Noun clauses can be used in the same ways as nouns in sentences.

> <u>Whoever made the rescue</u> was brave. (subject)
> I admire <u>whatever they do</u>. (direct object)
> This is <u>how they helped</u>. (predicate nominative)
> He is best remembered for <u>what he did for other people</u>. (object of preposition)

The following words often introduce noun clauses.

how	what	where	whichever	whom
if	whatever	whether	who	whomever
that	when	which	whoever	why

Some of the words that introduce noun clauses may also introduce other kinds of subordinate clauses. To determine the part of speech of a subordinate clause, first determine its use in the sentence.

> This is the fantasy <u>that I like best</u>. (adjective clause modifying *fantasy*)
> I didn't know <u>that Jack Finney wrote it</u>. (noun clause as direct object)

> **Summary** ♦ A **noun clause** is a subordinate clause used as a noun. You can use noun clauses to add information to your sentences.

Guided Practice

Name the noun clause in each sentence.

1. Do you know whether Jack Finney wrote ''Of Missing Persons''?
2. What he wrote is a short story with a fantasy setting.
3. I enjoy whatever Jack Finney writes.

Practice

A. Write *subject*, *direct object*, *predicate nominative*, or *object of a preposition* to show how each underlined noun clause is used in the sentence.

4. <u>What Finney wrote about in "Of Missing Persons"</u> is fantasy.
5. In the story, Charley Ewell believes <u>whatever he is told</u>.
6. <u>What he is told</u> is <u>that there is a planet called Verna</u>.
7. People go there to escape from <u>what they don't like here</u>.
8. Life on Verna is <u>how they would like life on Earth to be</u>.

B. Write the noun clause in each sentence. Then write how it is used in the sentence.

9. That Verna is light-years away from Earth does not matter. 10. The Acme Travel Bureau sends whoever it thinks should be rescued from Earth. 11. Acme is interested only in why you want to go to Verna. 12. You tell the travel agent why you want to leave Earth. 13. He takes care of how you get to Verna.

C. Write the sentences. Underline each subordinate clause and label it *noun*, *adjective*, or *adverb*.

14. Charley Ewell, who was a lonely man, wanted to go to Verna. 15. But he panicked when it was time to leave. 16. He did not believe that he would really go to Verna. 17. That he ended up being left behind was his own fault. 18. He would be one of those people who would always regret the mistake.

D. Use these noun clauses in original sentences.

19. that he hesitated   21. whoever asks
20. who was ready   22. what she saw

Apply • Think and Write

Creating a Setting ◆ Write a description of an ideal place you might like to escape to for a short while. Include several sentences that contain noun clauses.

✎ Remember that you can use noun clauses to add variety to your sentences.

GETTING STARTED

Which would you rather be called—*slender* or *scrawny*? *Thrifty* or *stingy*? *Carefree* or *reckless*? Think of some other word pairs that have about the same meanings but convey different "feelings."

VOCABULARY ♦
Denotation and Connotation

The exact meaning of a word is called its **denotation**. A dictionary contains the denotations of words. The positive or negative feeling associated with a word is called its **connotation**. Words often have about the same dictionary meaning, but the feelings they bring out often differ in some way. Consider the different feelings these two pairs of words suggest.

     youthful   childish   **curious   nosy**

While you might consider yourself *youthful*, you probably wouldn't consider yourself *childish*. And you would probably rather be known as *curious* than *nosy*. The words in each pair are synonyms. They have about the same *denotation*, but their *connotations* are very different.

The wrong connotations can give an unintended tone or meaning to language. The right connotations can reinforce your meaning and give your readers or listeners the impression you want to convey. To write or speak well, you must pay attention to the connotations as well as the denotations of words.

Building Your Vocabulary

Change the paragraph below. Choose synonyms from the list to replace the underlined words. You may use a dictionary to find the meanings of unfamiliar words.

arrogantly	**scheming**	**smirked**	**pushy**	**fat**
ill-behaved	**devoured**	**loafed**	**shack**	**grab**

The <u>mischievous</u> troll lived in a <u>small house</u> on the hill. He often <u>smiled</u> <u>confidently</u> as he <u>relaxed</u> in the forest. He was an <u>ambitious</u> troll, always <u>planning</u> ways to <u>take</u> his next meal. He was also <u>plump</u>, for he <u>ate</u> his meals twelve times a day.

Now compare the original paragraph with the new version. Notice how the connotations change the overall meaning of the paragraph.

Practice

A. Write the sentences. Use the words in parentheses that have the more positive connotations.

1. Our furniture is the (cheapest, least expensive) in town!
2. My (windblown, messy) hair needs combing.
3. The basketball player is a (tall, lanky) six feet four.
4. Margaret always trys to (scrimp, save) on her food bills.
5. We saw a (peculiar, unique) science-fiction movie.
6. The man (glowered, gazed) at us.
7. The teenagers were dressed (casually, sloppily).
8. The comedian had a most (unusual, bizarre) sense of humor.
9. He gave us a (cool, chilly) look and walked out of the room.
10. Those two kids have been known to (chatter, converse) all day.

B. Write the word from each group that has the most negative connotation.

11. skinny, thin, slender
12. task, challenge, chore
13. chuckle, snicker, laugh
14. serious, grim, somber
15. strange, wondrous, remarkable
16. curious, inquisitive, prying

C. Rewrite the sentences, replacing the underlined words with synonyms from the list. Label each sentence *more negative* or *more positive*.

| humble | grave | sound | overcast | lazy |

17. The day was cool and <u>gloomy</u>.
18. The tall and <u>dignified</u> scholar made an imposing sight.
19. The <u>noise</u> of their voices echoed through the room.
20. James has been <u>idle</u> all day.
21. Dr. Blake was a <u>meek</u> person.

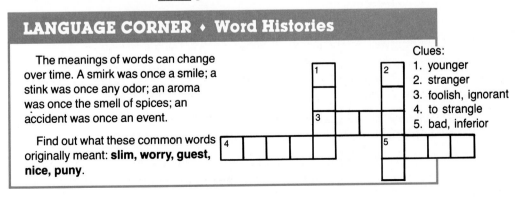

LANGUAGE CORNER ◆ Word Histories

The meanings of words can change over time. A smirk was once a smile; a stink was once any odor; an aroma was once the smell of spices; an accident was once an event.

Find out what these common words originally meant: **slim, worry, guest, nice, puny.**

Clues:
1. younger
2. stranger
3. foolish, ignorant
4. to strangle
5. bad, inferior

How to Combine Sentences

Sentence combining can improve your writing by making it smoother and less repetitious. Combining sentences with phrases and clauses can help you create more interesting sentences. Notice how the sentences in example **1** are combined with a verbal phrase to form the more effective sentence in example **2**.

1. Kim was reading the book again. Kim found new parts to enjoy.
2. Reading the book again, Kim found new parts to enjoy.

Sentences can also be combined to show time order. The two simple sentences in example **3** are combined in example **4** to form a complex sentence that clearly shows a sequence of events.

3. Kim finished the book. She gave it to Mark to read.
4. After Kim finished the book, she gave it to Mark to read.

Combining sentences can also help you avoid common errors in writing, such as sentence fragments. The information in a fragment is usually related to the sentence directly before or after it. In example **6**, the fragment in example **5** has been corrected by making it a subordinate clause and combining it with its companion sentence.

5. Kim read *The Hobbit*. Since she likes fantasies.
6. Kim read *The Hobbit*, since she likes fantasies.

The Grammar Game ◆ Try it yourself! Follow the directions given in parentheses to write a variety of strong sentences.

◆ School was over. Kim and her friends went to the library. (combine with the words *as soon as*)
◆ They ran most of the way. They were in a hurry. (combine with the word *because*)
◆ Mark and Rosa were browsing through the library. They found many interesting books. (combine with a verbal)

Working Together

As your group works on activities **A** and **B**, notice that combining sentences makes your writing smoother and more interesting to read.

In Your Group

♦ Keep on the subject.   ♦ Help the group reach agreement.

♦ Work quietly as you write.   ♦ Show appreciation for new ideas.

A. Combine each pair of sentences or fragments. Can your group combine some pairs in more than one way?

1. J.R.R. Tolkien was a scholar and a professor. He became famous for his fantasies.
2. Because Tolkien knew a great deal about the Middle Ages. His fantasies had a ring of truth to them.
3. Tolkien was creating entirely new places and characters. Tolkien gave readers a whole new world to explore.
4. People read his stories. They found themselves caught up in his strange world.

B. Rewrite the following paragraph, combining sentences as needed.

Lewis Carroll was writing almost a century before Tolkien. He also created wonderful fantasies. Carroll was a mathematician. His fantasy worlds were intricately logical. Speaking "nonsense." His characters made remarkable sense.

WRITERS' CORNER ♦ Choppy Sentences

Too many short, choppy sentences can cause your readers to lose interest in your writing. Combining sentences is an excellent way to solve this problem.

I read *Alice's Adventures in Wonderland* again. I loved reading it again. I understood it this time. I had read the book as a child. I had not understood much of it.

The writing in the paragraph above is choppy. Improve it by combining sentences. Then read what you wrote for the Writer's Warm-up. Is your writing choppy? If it is, can you improve it?

A MAD TEA PARTY
painting by Arthur Rackham
by kind permission of Barbara Edwards.

USING LANGUAGE
TO

IMAGINE

=== **PART TWO** ===

Literature   *The Hobbit* by J.R.R. Tolkien

A Reason for Writing   Imagining

CREATIVE
Writing

FINE ARTS ◆ Arthur Rackham painted this scene from Lewis Carroll's famous story about a little girl named Alice. Imagine for a moment that this is a scene from a television commercial. These zany characters are selling tea. Write the script for the commercial. What will the Mad Hatter, the dormouse, the rabbit, and Alice say about the tea?

CREATIVE THINKING ◆
A Strategy for Imagining

ANSWERING "WHAT IF?"

Imagining can be a way of making believe. After this lesson you will read part of a highly imaginative tale, *The Hobbit* by J.R.R. Tolkien. Later you will write your own imaginative story.

A hobbit is an imaginary creature living in a fantasy world created by the author. We don't know how Tolkien created his world. One way to create a fantasy world, however, is to ask some "what if" questions. For example, "What if there were a world of creatures almost, but not quite, human? What if one of them came upon a mountain with a magic door? Then . . ." Here is part of what happens in *The Hobbit*.

> The stars were coming out behind him in a pale sky barred with black when the hobbit crept through the enchanted door and stole into the Mountain. . . you can picture him coming to the end of the tunnel, an opening of much the same size and shape as the door above. Through it peeps the hobbit's little head. Before him lies the great bottommost cellar or dungeon-hall of the ancient dwarves right at the Mountain's root.

Here is another "what if" question. What if the hobbit enters that dungeon-hall? What might happen then?

Learning the Strategy

Asking "what if" is a way of supposing or imagining a situation. Sometimes, as in *The Hobbit*, your "what if" question may have to do with make-believe. Sometimes, however, "what if" questions can be about real life.

For example, you might ask yourself "What if I apply for an after-school job?" In chemistry class you might consider "What if I mix these two chemicals together?" After a tough day at school, you might think "What if I skip studying for that history test?" When you answer "what if" questions, you can imagine many possibilities.

Sometimes a series of follow-up questions can help. Look at the chart below about applying for a job. What other follow-up questions and answers might you add to this chart?

What if I apply for an after-school job?

What if they ask about prior experience?	*I'd say I have done odd jobs.*
	I'd say I'm very reliable.
When would I study?	*Before work and on weekends.*

Using the Strategy

A. What if tomorrow your favorite famous musician makes a surprise visit to your school? Use your imagination. Make a "what if" chart. Create and answer at least three follow-up questions. You might want to write a make-believe news article based on your suppositions about the situation.

B. Reread the excerpt from *The Hobbit* on the previous page. Make a chart. In the top box write "What if the hobbit goes into the dungeon-hall?" In the second box write at least three follow-up questions and your most imaginative answers to them. Then read to find out what happens in J.R.R. Tolkien's story.

Applying the Strategy

- How does answering "what if" questions make you use your imagination?
- When might asking and answering "what if" questions be useful to you during this coming week?

LITERATURE

from

The Hobbit

by J.R.R. Tolkien

Bilbo Baggins was a hobbit—a little person with a good-natured face, a fat stomach, and strong, furry feet that made shoes unnecessary. Like most hobbits, Bilbo had his own comfortable hobbit-hole in a hillside and never did anything adventurous or surprising. But one day, he suddenly left Bag-End, Underhill, for an unexpected adventure. Bilbo went off with Balin the dwarf and a dozen others to reclaim a great treasure made by the dwarves' ancestors and stolen by the dragon Smaug long ago.

Bilbo and the dwarves undertook a long journey to the dragon's lair in Lonely Mountain, where he was guarding the treasure. On the way, Bilbo found a magic ring that made him invisible. He would need the ring soon, when he fulfilled the dangerous task of being the dwarves' burglar. That night, while the dragon slept, Bilbo would go through a secret tunnel into the Mountain to steal some of the treasure, right under Smaug's nose.

The stars were coming out behind him in a pale sky barred with black when the hobbit crept through the enchanted door and stole into the Mountain. It was far easier going than he expected. This was no goblin entrance, or rough wood-elves' cave. It was a passage made by dwarves, at the height of their wealth and skill: straight as a ruler, smooth-floored and smooth-sided, going with a gentle never-varying slope direct—to some distant end in the blackness below.

After a while Balin bade Bilbo "Good luck!" and stopped where he could still see the faint outline of the door, and by a trick of the echoes of the tunnel hear the rustle of the whispering voices of the others just outside. Then the hobbit slipped on his ring, and warned by the echoes to take more than hobbit's care to make no sound, he crept noiselessly down, down, down into the dark. He was trembling with fear, but his little face was set and grim. Already he was a very different hobbit from the one that had run out without a pocket-handkerchief from Bag-End long ago. He had not had a pocket-handkerchief for ages. He loosened his dagger in its sheath, tightened his belt, and went on.

"Now you are in for it at last, Bilbo Baggins," he said to himself. "You went and put your foot right in it that night of the party, and now you have got to pull it out and pay for it! Dear me, what a fool I was and am!" said the least Tookish part of him. "I have absolutely no use for dragon-guarded treasures, and the whole lot could stay here forever, if only I could wake up and find this beastly tunnel was my own front-hall at home!"

He did not wake up of course, but went still on and on, till all sign of the door behind had faded away. He was altogether alone. Soon he thought it was beginning to feel warm. "Is that a kind of a glow I seem to see coming right ahead down there?" he thought.

It was. As he went forward it grew and grew, till there was no doubt about it. It was a red light steadily getting redder and redder. Also it was now undoubtedly hot in the tunnel. Wisps of vapour floated up and past him and he began to sweat. A sound, too, began to throb in his ears, a sort of bubbling like the noise of a large pot galloping on the fire, mixed with a rumble as of a gigantic tomcat purring. This grew to the unmistakable gurgling noise of some vast animal snoring in its sleep down there in the red glow in front of him.

It was at this point that Bilbo stopped. Going on from there was the bravest thing he ever did. The tremendous things that happened afterwards were as nothing compared to it. He fought the real battle in the tunnel alone, before he ever saw the vast danger that lay in wait. At any rate after a short halt go on he did; and you can picture him coming to the end of the tunnel, an opening of much the same size and shape as the door above. Through it peeps the hobbit's little head. Before him lies the great bottommost cellar or dungeon-hall of the ancient dwarves right at the Mountain's root. It is almost dark so that its vastness can only be dimly guessed, but rising from the near side of the rocky floor there is a great glow. The glow of Smaug!

There he lay, a vast red-golden dragon, fast asleep; a thrumming came from his jaws and nostrils, and wisps of smoke, but his fires were low in slumber. Beneath him, under all his limbs and his huge coiled tail, and about him on all sides stretching away across the unseen floors, lay countless piles of precious things, gold wrought and unwrought, gems and jewels, and silver red-stained in the ruddy light.

Smaug lay, with wings folded like an immeasurable bat, turned partly on one side, so that the hobbit could see his underparts and his long pale belly crusted with gems and fragments of gold from his long lying on his costly bed. Behind him where the walls were nearest could dimly be seen coats of mail, helms and axes, swords and spears hanging; and there in rows stood great jars and vessels filled with a wealth that could not be guessed.

To say that Bilbo's breath was taken away is no description at all. There are no words left to express his staggerment, since Men changed the language that they learned of elves in the days when all the world was wonderful. Bilbo had heard tell and sing of dragon-hoards before, but the splendour, the lust, the glory of such treasure had never yet come home to him. His heart was filled and pierced with enchantment and with the desire of dwarves; and he gazed motionless, almost forgetting the frightful guardian, at the gold beyond price and count.

He gazed for what seemed an age, before drawn almost against his will, he stole from the shadow of the doorway, across the floor to the nearest edge of the mounds of treasure. Above him the sleeping dragon lay, a dire menace even in his sleep. He grasped a great two-handled cup, as heavy as he could carry, and cast one fearful eye upwards. Smaug stirred a wing, opened a claw, the rumble of his snoring changed its note.

Then Bilbo fled. But the dragon did not wake—not yet—but shifted into other dreams of greed and violence, lying there in his stolen hall while the little hobbit toiled back up the long tunnel. His heart was beating and a more fevered shaking was in his legs than when he was going down, but still he clutched the cup, and his chief thought was: "I've done it! This will show them. 'More like a grocer than a burglar' indeed! Well, we'll hear no more of that."

Nor did he. Balin was overjoyed to see the hobbit again, and as delighted as he was surprised. He picked Bilbo up and carried him out into the open air. It was midnight and clouds had covered the stars, but Bilbo lay with his eyes shut, gasping and taking pleasure in the feel of the fresh air again, and hardly noticing the excitement of the dwarves, or how they praised him and patted him on the back and put themselves and all their families for generations to come at his service.

Library Link ♦ *Read more about Bilbo's suspense-filled journey in* The Hobbit *by J.R.R. Tolkien. You can find it in your library.*

Reader's Response

Would you like Bilbo to live next door to you? Why or why not?

LITERATURE: Fantasy

The Hobbit

Responding to Literature

1. Will Bilbo's life ever be the same? What do you think will happen to Bilbo now that he has demonstrated courage?

2. If a ring like Bilbo's—a ring that made its wearer invisible—could speak, what story would it tell? Work with a panel of five storytellers. One speaker begins the story while holding a ring. At a good place to change storytellers, the ring is handed on. The procedure is continued until the entire tale of the ring and its invisible wearer has been told.

3. Make a word picture of Bilbo. Draw a frame on a sheet of paper. Fill the frame with words that describe Bilbo. Make the words large or small or odd-shaped to indicate their importance in describing Bilbo. Share your work with the class.

Writing to Learn

Think and Suppose ◆ Ask three or more ''what if'' questions about Bilbo's adventure. Then choose your favorite question. Write follow-up questions to explore the topic further.

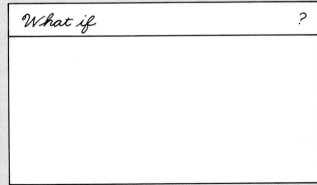

What if   **?**

What-if Chart

Write ◆ Trade papers with a partner. First write an answer to your partner's questions. Then discuss different ways each other's questions might have been answered.

GETTING STARTED What is the strangest, most intriguing place you have ever visited? Give clues that describe the place and have your classmates try to name it.

SPEAKING and LISTENING ◆
Brainstorming a Story Setting

Setting—the time and place in which a story happens—is an important element of a story. For example, try to imagine *The Hobbit* without its wonderful settings.

The technique of brainstorming is a helpful method to use in gathering ideas for a story setting. Brainstorming is a group activity that encourages the free flow of thought and the spontaneous contribution of ideas. All members of the group contribute ideas freely, and no ideas are criticized. In this way all the possible ideas and facts that each individual can contribute are discovered. Brainstorming sessions are usually brief, lasting only five or ten minutes. Use the brainstorming guidelines below for help as you and others generate ideas for a story setting.

As a Speaker	**1.** Help the group decide on the type of setting to be brainstormed. Should the setting be fantasy, realistic, or both? One person should record all the ideas. **2.** Contribute ideas as quickly as possible. Use your imagination and experience to help you think of story settings. Share your ideas, no matter how unusual they may seem. **3.** Do not make critical or judgmental comments. Instead, encourage others to offer more ideas for a setting.
As a Listener	**1.** Show interest by listening attentively as others explain and develop their ideas for a story setting. **2.** Be open and nonjudgmental as you listen to the suggestions of others for possible settings. **3.** As you listen to others contribute ideas for a setting, let your mind build on those suggestions and possibly create some additional ideas of your own to share.

Summary ◆ **Brainstorming** stimulates creative thought and generates ideas. During a brainstorming session, contribute ideas and listen to the ideas of others with an open mind.

Guided Practice

Explain why the behavior in each example below is not appropriate for a brainstorming session.

1. "Wait a minute or two," Jenn says. "I've almost got an idea."
2. "What a dumb setting for a story about seals!" said Serena.
3. Jason records only those ideas that he thinks are good.
4. While others are contributing ideas for a setting, Seth daydreams about his plans for the weekend.

Practice

A. Read each example below. With a partner take turns explaining why the behavior is or is not appropriate when brainstorming.

5. You think your ideas are silly, so you do not share them.
6. You explain your ideas briefly and as quickly as possible.
7. You listen and try to get more ideas from others' comments.
8. After contributing one idea, you decide that is enough.
9. You criticize those ideas that you do not agree with.

B. Work with a group of three to five students in a brainstorming session to develop a list of general features that could be part of a story setting. The list might include items such as buildings, plant life, and so on.

C. Working with your same group, choose several features from the list developed in **Practice B**. For each feature, brainstorm ideas for a fantasy setting. For instance, if your group chooses plant life, brainstorm ideas about the different kinds of plant life that might be good in a fantasy setting. See how many ideas your group can come up with. Keep trying even if you run out of ideas before time is up.

Apply ◆ Think and Write

A Fantasy Setting ◆ Use some of the ideas your group generated in **Practice C** to write a paragraph that describes a setting for a fantasy story you might write. Compare your ideas with those of someone else in your group by taking turns reading your paragraphs aloud.

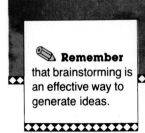

✎ **Remember**
that brainstorming is an effective way to generate ideas.

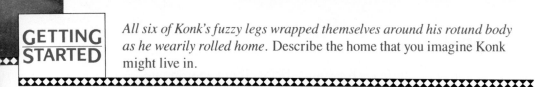
GETTING STARTED

All six of Konk's fuzzy legs wrapped themselves around his rotund body as he wearily rolled home. Describe the home that you imagine Konk might live in.

WRITING ♦
Character, Setting, and Plot

There are many different kinds of stories. However, most stories share three basic elements: character, setting, and plot.

Characters are the people or animals in a story. Readers get to know the characters through what the characters say and do and also from what the author tells about them. Most stories focus on one or two main characters. In *The Hobbit*, for instance, Bilbo Baggins is the main character because the action revolves around him. Sometimes minor characters are used to help develop a story. Tolkien uses Balin, a minor character, to show the reader how Bilbo, the main character, feels and how he changes.

Setting is the time and place in which the story happens. An entire story may take place in a setting as familiar as a living room. Other stories, like *The Hobbit*, take place in a variety of exotic settings. Writers always have good reasons for the settings they use. After all, where the characters in a story are placed determines what they can say and do. Bilbo, for example, could not have done his "bravest thing" without the terrifying setting of Smaug's dungeon-hall in which to become brave.

Plot is the story plan. It is the action, or the sequence of connected events. The plot may have a **conflict**, or a problem to be solved. Bilbo, for example, wants to be back home. Tolkien uses the plot to show how the shy Bilbo Baggins becomes an adventurer. Each action helps the story build to a **climax** — a high point of tension. In this segment you have read of *The Hobbit*, the turning point comes when Bilbo grasps the great two-handled cup and flees down the tunnel. His safe return to the dwarves is the plot's **resolution**, or what happens in the end.

> **Summary** ♦ The basic elements of a story are **character**, **setting**, and **plot**.

Guided Practice

Tell whether each sentence illustrates character, setting, or plot.

1. The ancient forest was shrouded in a cold, gray mist.
2. Ariel knelt down and suddenly saw the long-hidden entrance.
3. The black cloak enveloped her slight figure and long red hair.

Practice

A. Write whether each note below describes a fact about a character, a part of a setting, or an event in a plot.

4. The two hockey forwards came streaking down the ice with the puck passing between them.
5. The arena was crowded with fans, and the players on the bench were screaming.
6. Despite his skill and size, Norman felt alone against the coming players' attack.
7. Meanwhile, the clock was running out and the puck was shooting toward the opposing team's goal.

B. Each sentence below gives an idea for a character, a setting, or a plot for a story. Choose one idea and use that as the springboard for writing notes for the other two basic elements of a story. For example, if you choose sentence **8**, which describes a setting, write notes about character and plot, for that setting.

8. The moss-covered shelter was nestled among the tree branches.
9. She overcame her shyness and curiously peered into the room.
10. Their escape was suddenly blocked by a giant hand.

C. Explain to a classmate how the idea and your notes from **Practice B** could work together to create a story.

Apply ✦ Think and Write

Dictionary of Knowledge ✦ Read about the book *The Wonderful Wizard of Oz* by L. Frank Baum in the Dictionary of Knowledge. Write a brief paragraph, identifying the fantasy elements the author used in creating character, setting, and plot.

✎ **Remember** that the setting the characters are in determines what they can say and do.

GETTING STARTED

Explain why a certain place always makes you feel a particular way. How do you feel when you are in that place? What things do you see, hear, or smell that contribute to your feelings?

WRITING ♦
Creating Mood

A writer creates the mood, or atmosphere, in a story by using descriptive details. These details communicate a particular feeling to the reader. The mood in this passage from *The Hobbit*, for example, is one of suspense and fear.

> As he went forward it grew and grew, till there was no doubt about it. It was a red light steadily getting redder and redder. Also it was now undoubtedly hot in the tunnel. Wisps of vapour floated up and past him and he began to sweat. A sound, too, began to throb in his ears, a sort of bubbling like the noise of a large pot galloping on the fire, mixed with a rumble as of a gigantic tom-cat purring. This grew to the unmistakable gurgling noise of some vast animal snoring in its sleep down there in the red glow in front of him.

Tolkien creates a mood of increasing suspense and fear by using certain words to describe what Bilbo sees, hears, and feels. First, details such as "it grew and grew," "steadily getting redder and redder," and "now undoubtedly hot," begin to establish the fearful mood. Then Tolkien increases the suspense with descriptions such as "wisps of vapour floated up," and "he began to sweat." A sound is described as "a sort of bubbling" and "a rumble," but its source is not revealed. Bilbo and the reader are in the grip of the unknown — a state of suspense. Finally, Tolkien hints directly at what is causing Bilbo to feel such fear — "the...gurgling noise of some vast animal snoring."

The importance of mood can be illustrated through a retelling of the passage without the descriptive details used by Tolkien: *Bilbo walked down the tunnel. He saw a red light and heard a few noises. The noise seemed to come from a large animal.* Notice that this version does not communicate any feeling to the reader.

> **Summary** ♦ The **mood**, or general feeling, of a story is established through the use of descriptive details.

Guided Practice

Identify the mood created in each sentence.

1. She expected wonderful results from her hard work.
2. Sunshine sparkled on the hummingbird as it gaily gathered nectar.
3. "I can't believe you did that!" she said in astonishment.

Practice

A. Write a sentence that describes the mood in each example.

4. "Wow! The sunset is spectacular tonight," Felipe exclaimed.
5. The children gazed tenderly at the new baby.
6. She scrambled frantically to repair the torn air hose.
7. The welcome sounds of home lulled them to a peaceful rest.
8. With heads held high, we marched in our new band uniforms.

B. Identify the mood in the paragraph below. Then rewrite the paragraph, using different descriptive details to change the mood.

Anne skipped through the grounds of the State Fair, peeking into the gaily striped tents, catching the scents of the food, and delighting in the mixture of people and animal sounds. Just as she glanced up at the polished bell atop the "Test Your Strength" amusement, an eager person swung the mallet and rang the bell. Anne cheered and went her way.

C. Write three sentences that include descriptive details to explain the mood or feeling you get from observing the drawing below.

Apply ◆ Think and Write

Imagining ◆ Imagine the perfect place for you. What would it be like? How would it make you feel? Write a paragraph that describes your perfect place.

> ✏️ **Remember**
> that you can create different moods through the use of specific details.

Focus on Fantasy

Fiction is "something invented by the imagination." Some fiction is closely based on fact. Its characters and events resemble those in the real world. Other fiction—especially **fantasy**—has elements of fact but is not completely true to life. Fantasy such as Tolkien's *The Hobbit* introduces strange settings and fanciful characters. It creates an imaginary world. Notice how Tolkien, a master of fantasy, deals with setting, plot, and character.

Setting   Middle Earth, Tolkien's setting, has forests, mountains, rivers, towns, castles, birds, animals—all familiar parts of the world we know. Common physical laws, such as gravity and the passage of time, also apply. However, Tolkien's world has some bizarre features—trees that walk, animals that speak, and dragons that hoard stolen treasures in magical mountain caves.

Plot   *The Hobbit,* as you learned earlier, has a carefully constructed plot. Fantasy usually does. When characters are mythical and settings are exotic, the story line becomes especially important. A well-developed plot is essential.

Characters   Characters in fantasy can be wholly imaginative or essentially human. Some are a mixture of the two. Tolkien's Bilbo Baggins, for example, is an imaginary creature, a "hobbit": a small, quiet two-legged creature who loves breakfasts and a nice home. He feels the familiar human emotions of love, anger, fear. Yet he is distinctly different from "the Big People" in certain ways. His "neatly brushed feet" and his extraordinary "hobbit's care to make no sound" are fanciful traits that Tolkien invented.

The Writer's Voice ♦ Look back at the paragraph from *The Hobbit* on page 504 that begins, "It was at this point that Bilbo stopped." Which elements are true to life? Which are fanciful?

Working Together

Writers sometimes use common facts plus their creative imagination to create fantasy worlds. As a group complete activities **A** and **B**.

In Your Group
♦ Listen to each other. ♦ Agree or disagree pleasantly.
♦ Record the group's ideas. ♦ Help the group finish on time.

A. Discuss the statements below. Which ones are realistic? Which ones are fanciful? Be ready to explain.

1. "It's going to rain tomorrow," the old seagull said to Carla.
2. Bud was upset when he lost his album of old stamps.
3. The wizard tasted the elixir prepared by the Blue Nomads.

B. Read the realistic statements below. Discuss them with your group and decide on one of the statements to revise. Add fantasy elements to the statement of your choice. Try to include fanciful explanations of the "facts."

EXAMPLE: Cal goes nowhere unless he wears his red hat.
ANSWER: Cal is an alien posing as a human boy. His life-giving air tanks are concealed in his special red hat.

4. Claudia runs a prosperous ranch on the frontier; other ranchers visit her to seek advice.
5. No one could explain Jill's fear of the abandoned barn.
6. Phil, alone in his office, had been hearing unusual noises from outside all night long.

THESAURUS CORNER ♦ Word Choice

One reason that *The Hobbit*'s fantasy world rings true is that Tolkien uses precise words, even in his most imaginative flights of fancy. Recall the characters of Bilbo and Balin's dwarves. Which words below would they be unlikely to use in conversation? Use the Thesaurus and Thesaurus Index to find synonyms (from among the listed antonyms for the entry word) that seem more appropriate.

archetype query diminutive expedite

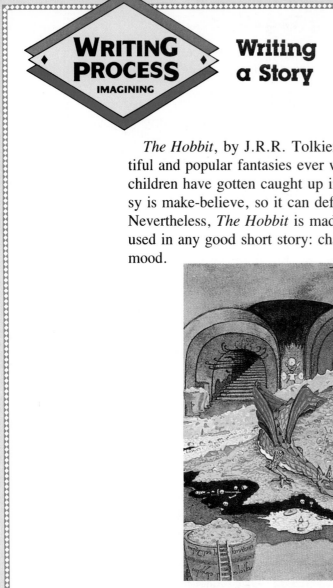

WRITING PROCESS
IMAGING

Writing a Story

The Hobbit, by J.R.R. Tolkien, is one of the most beautiful and popular fantasies ever written. Adults as well as children have gotten caught up in its special world. A fantasy is make-believe, so it can defy a lot of real-world rules. Nevertheless, *The Hobbit* is made up of the same elements used in any good short story: characters, plot, settings, and mood.

Know Your Purpose and Audience

MY PURPOSE

In this lesson you will write a fantasy story. Your purpose will be to entertain.

MY AUDIENCE

Your audience will be younger children. Later you can read your story aloud to a group of children. You might also publish an illustrated edition of your story for an elementary school library.

1 Prewriting

First you need to decide on a topic for your story. Then use an idea-gathering strategy as you get ready to write.

Choose Your Topic ◆ Begin by recalling the kinds of fantasy stories that you enjoyed as a child. Did you enjoy fairy tales with a mixture of human and magical characters? Did you enjoy tiny creatures who live in small places? Make a list of possible topics. Circle the most interesting.

Think About It

Recall all the most fantastic characters you ever met in stories. You might like talking dogs, robots, or monsters like Godzilla or King Kong. Choose a great character.

Talk About It

Talk with a partner about three of your favorite kinds of story characters. The discussion will help you recall events in stories and therefore get story ideas of your own.

Topic Ideas

Hansel and Gretel
Cinderella
talking horses
talking dog
Superman
King Kong

Choose Your Strategy ♦ How can you develop story ideas?
Here are two strategies that can help. Use the one you prefer.

PREWRITING IDEAS

CHOICE ONE

Nonstop Writing

Nonstop writing is a strategy for stimulating a flow of ideas. Head four sheets of paper *Characters, Setting, Plot,* and *Mood*. Write ideas nonstop for three minutes in each category. If you can't think of anything, write *blah, blah* or *I can't think of anything* until ideas flow again.

Model

Characters
There's this kid, Jay —
has a dog blah blah I can't
think of anything — the dog
always wanted to talk — very
smart — black with brown
spots — blah blah —

CHOICE TWO

Answering ''What If?''

Answering ''what if'' questions can help you develop plot ideas. Write *What if* (your fantasy situation) *happened?''* Write as many follow-up questions as you can think of. Then think of as many answers as you can. Choose the ideas you like best for your story.

Model

What if a boy's dog suddenly
learned to talk?

How could that   *Dog takes*
happen?   *speech lessons.*
   Lightning
   strikes.
   Go to school
What would   *with boy.*
dog do?   *Appear on TV.*
   It's wonderful.
What would   *It's a trick.*
people think?

2 Writing

Now begin to write your story. Most stories follow a pyramid-shaped pattern. To use the pattern, first introduce the main character, setting, and situation (A). Then build events (B) to an important or dramatic point (C), the climax. After the climax, let events fall (D) toward the final outcome, or resolution (E).

Sample First Draft ◆

When Jay woke up friday, he noticed the doghouse right away. It had obviously been struck by lightening in last night's storm. Jay was worried. Had Buster, his dog, lived? Jay looked into the house and sighed with releif. Since Buster looked fine, Jay started to leave for school.

"Wait for me!" Said a raspy voice.

Jay looked around wildly, wondering who had spoken

"Look down, Jay!" said the dog. "This is a joke, right?" Jay asked hopfully.

"No joke, Jay" answered Buster. "As you observe, I have gained the ability to speak. Something to do with the lightening bolt, I suspect. Now let's get going."

Usually, Buster stayed home. Jay went to school. Since the dog now talked however Jay agreed that Buster really ought to attend school. He wondered how his Teacher would feel about having a dog in class he soon learned the answer.

3 Revising

Now revise your fantasy story to improve it. How can you know what needs to be changed? This idea may help you.

REVISING IDEA

FIRST Read to Yourself

As you read your story aloud to yourself, review your purpose. Did you accomplish it? Is your story entertaining? Also think about your audience. Will younger children find it appealing?

Focus: Is your story a fantasy? Have you included elements of make-believe in your plot, characters, or settings?

THEN Share with a Partner

Choose a partner to listen as you read your story aloud. Ask your partner to pretend to be a young child. Remind him or her that the story is for young children. These guidelines may help.

The Writer

Guidelines: Read with expression. Then ask for your partner's suggestions.

Sample questions:
- Do you have suggestions about my plot, setting, characters, or mood?
- **Focus question:** What makes my story a fantasy?

The Writer's Partner

Guidelines: As you listen, think about what a young child might enjoy or be confused about. Offer helpful suggestions.

Sample responses:
- I think young children would really love the part where ___.
- Maybe you could add a detail about _____.

Revising Model ♦ Here is the beginning of a fantasy story. The writer's revisions are shown in blue.

Revising Marks

delete	ℯ
add	∧
move	⟲

Survived expresses the meaning more precisely than *lived*.

The writer wanted to emphasize the fantasy of the plot.

The writer's partner suggested this detail to clarify the dog's character.

The writer decided to form a complex sentence here.

When Jay woke up friday, he noticed the doghouse right away. It had obviously been struck by lightening in last night's storm. Jay was worried. Had Buster, his dog, ~~lived?~~ *survived?* Jay looked into the house and sighed with releif. Since Buster looked fine, Jay started to leave for school.

"Wait for me!" Said a raspy voice.

Jay looked around wildly, wondering who had spoken *The only living creature nearby was Buster.*

"Look down, Jay!" said the dog. "This is a joke, right?" Jay asked hopefully.

"No joke, Jay" answered Buster. "As you observe, I have gained the ability to speak. Something to do with the lightening bolt, I suspect. *It's time I got some education!* Now let's get going."

Usually, ⟲Buster stayed home.⟲ Jay went to *while* school. Since the dog now talked however Jay agreed that Buster really ought to attend school. He wondered how his Teacher would feel about having a dog in class he soon learned the answer.

Revising Checklist

☐ **Purpose:** Have I written an entertaining story?

☐ **Audience:** Will younger children find my story appealing?

☐ **Focus:** Have I written a fantasy? Have I included elements of make-believe in my plot, characters, or settings?

Read the story beginning above the way the writer has decided it *should* be. Then revise your own fantasy story.

Grammar Check ♦ Mixing simple, compound, and complex sentences can give your writing rhythm and variety.

Word Choice ♦ Precise words clarify meaning. You can often find the precise synonym you want in a thesaurus.

4 Proofreading

Now check your story for surface errors. Mistakes and sloppy handwriting can interfere with your readers' enjoyment.

Proofreading Model ◆ Here is the beginning of the talking dog fantasy. Proofreading corrections appear in red.

Proofreading Marks

capital letter	≡
small letter	/
add comma	⋀
add period	⊙
indent paragraph	¶
check spelling	⬭

Proofreading Checklist

☐ Did I spell words correctly?

☐ Did I indent paragraphs?

☐ Did I use correct capitalization?

☐ Did I use correct punctuation?

☐ Did I type neatly or use my best handwriting?

When Jay woke up friday, he noticed the doghouse right away. It had obviously been struck by lightening in last night's storm. Jay was worried. Had Buster, his dog, lived? *survived* Jay looked into the house and sighed with releif *relief* Since Buster looked fine, Jay started to leave for school.

"Wait for me!" Said a raspy voice.

Jay looked around wildly, wondering who had spoken⊙ *The only living creature nearby was Buster.*

"Look down, Jay!" said the dog. "This is a joke, right?" Jay asked hopfully. *hopefully*

"No joke, Jay," answered Buster. "As you observe, I have gained the ability to speak. Something to do with the lightening bolt, I suspect. Now let's get going." *It's time I got some education!*

Usually, Buster stayed home. Jay went to *while* school. Since the dog now talked, however, Jay agreed that Buster really ought to attend school. He wondered how his Teacher would feel about having a dog in class⊙he soon learned the answer.

PROOFREADING IDEA

Handwriting Check

Make sure your words don't begin neatly and then trail off illegibly. The end of each word should be formed as neatly as the beginning.

Now proofread your fantasy story, add a title, and make a neat copy.

5 Publishing

Here are two ways you might share your fantasy stories with some younger children.

Buster Goes to School

When Jay woke up Friday, he noticed the doghouse right away. It had obviously been struck by lightning in last night's storm. Jay was worried. Had Buster, his dog, survived? Jay looked into the house and sighed with relief. Since Buster looked fine, Jay started to leave for school.

"Wait for me!" said a raspy voice.

Jay looked around wildly, wondering who had spoken. The only living creature nearby was Buster.

"Look down, Jay!" said the dog.

"This is a joke, right?" Jay asked hopefully.

"No joke, Jay," answered Buster. "As you observe, I have gained the ability to speak. Something to do with the lightning bolt, I suspect. Now let's get going. It's time I got some education!"

Usually, while Jay went to school, Buster stayed home. Since the dog now talked, however, Jay agreed that Buster really ought to attend school. He wondered how his teacher would feel about having a dog in class. He soon learned the answer.

PUBLISHING IDEAS

Share Aloud	Share in Writing
Practice reading your story aloud. If possible, practice with a tape recorder so that you can listen to yourself. Then arrange a read-aloud session at an elementary school. Provide your listeners with paper and crayons and ask them to draw a scene from your story.	Bind your story between illustrated covers. In the back, add a sheet with your name, date, school, and class and an invitation for readers to send you their comments. Donate your story to an elementary school library.

CURRICULUM
◆CONNECTION◆

Writing Across the Curriculum   Music

Did you know that fantasies can be told in music as well as in words? Music lovers often guess about the story behind the music. You can do it, too.

Writing to Learn

Think and Suppose ◆ Scheherazade is a fairy tale character who had to tell stories to save her life. Find a recording of *Scheherazade* by Rimsky-Korsakov. What if the music were the voice of Scheherazade? What would she tell you? First, just listen to the music. Then as you listen again, write notes about the story that the music suggests to you.

What-if Chart

Write ◆ Briefly write the story that Rimsky-Korsakov's *Scheherazade* suggested to you.

Writing in Your Journal

At the beginning of this unit, you wrote about a favorite fantasy world. During the unit you read about Ann McCaffrey's *Dragonsong*, J.R.R. Tolkien's *The Hobbit*, and others. Choose your favorite fantasy setting or character from this unit. In your journal explain why it appeals to you.

BOOKS TO ENJOY

Read More About It

A Wizard of Earthsea   *by Ursula Le Guin*

Earthsea is a world of spells and charms. Young Ged shows promise of becoming a great wizard until he foolishly releases a nameless evil in the world. To save himself and his world, he must confront and overcome this evil.

The White Mountains   *by John Christopher*

Christopher's finely constructed fantasy world is Earth in the twenty-first century. In this world, machines called Tripods control human beings. Three boys rebel against their mechanical masters and join a band of freedom fighters.

The Grey King   *by Susan Cooper*

Bran, the son of King Arthur, has been sent forward in time to escape evil forces. In modern-day Wales, he meets young Will Stanton. The Arthurian world comes alive as Will and his friends ride against evil in a crucial battle.

Newbery Award

Book Report Idea   Fantasy Postcard

Imagine getting a postcard from a fantasy world. What picture might be on the front of the card? What message might the sender write on the back?

Send Your Message

Try giving a book report on a work of fantasy in the form of a large postcard. Pretend you are a main character in the story. On one side of the card, write about one of your adventures. On the other side, draw a scene that captures some aspect of the fantasy setting.

Unit 9

Verbals   *pages 474–483*

A. Write each participial phrase and the word it modifies.

1. At Hawk Mountain we observed a hawk soaring high above.
2. Many hawks, called birds of prey, can be seen in one day.
3. Observed by hawk watchers, the majestic birds fly south.
4. Watching through binoculars, we saw them gain altitude.

B. Write the gerund or gerund phrase in each sentence.

5. Flying is a delight.
6. My favorite pastime is watching birds in flight.
7. I never grow tired of seeing them.
8. Almost everyone enjoys observing an eagle.

C. Write the infinitive phrase in each sentence. Then write whether it is used as a noun, adjective, or adverb.

9. To travel deep into a jungle is the ultimate adventure.
10. They didn't go to find modern conveniences.
11. The Amazon is a place to explore natural treasures.
12. They quickly began to appreciate the beauty of the jungle.

D. Rewrite the sentences, correcting any dangling or misplaced participial phrase and split infinitive.

13. I hope to someday see the world.
14. Reading about faraway places, the world was explored.
15. Swinging from the vines, I can visualize monkeys.

Complex Sentences   *pages 484–493*

E. Label each sentence *compound* or *complex*.

16. While Dad and I were packing, Mom told us the news.
17. The bridge was washed out, and the road was closed.

18. We had to stay an extra day, but we made the best of it.

19. We didn't see the monument because we couldn't reach it.

F. Write each sentence. Underline the adverb clause and add commas where needed.

20. The actors spoke to each other as if there were no audience.

21. Whenever they joked we laughed along with them.

22. The play was better than I had expected.

23. Although the theater seats hundreds tickets were sold out.

G. Write each adjective clause and the noun it modifies.

24. Ben Franklin, who started as a printer, founded a magazine.

25. The skills that he acquired helped him in later life.

26. His prose style, which was lively, attracted attention.

27. The issues that he wrote about were political and social.

H. Write each adjective clause. Then write how the relative pronoun is used in the clause: subject, direct object, object of a preposition, or possessive.

28. Toni Morrison, who is a novelist, wrote *The Bluest Eye*.

29. She is an author with whom Americans have identified.

30. Isn't she a person whom you admire?

31. Morrison, whose style is poetic, is a keen observer.

I. Write each noun clause. Write how it is used in the sentence: subject, direct object, predicate nominative, or object of a preposition.

32. What the teacher talked about in class today is important.

33. What she said is that drugs are dangerous.

34. We know what drugs can do to us.

35. We learned about how young people can say "no" to drugs.

Denotation/Connotation   *pages 494–495*

J. Write each numbered word below and its synonym from the list. Circle the word in each pair with the more positive connotation.

speech   quick   misrepresent   scheme   quit   horrid

36. lie   **38.** tirade   **40.** plan

37. withdraw   **39.** bad   **41.** hasty

Conjunction Clues

Figure out five subordinating conjunctions from the clues below.

1. Change the *d* in raw pastry to *th*.
2. Take the *b* and an *s* from a freshwater fish.
3. Take the *s* from our closest star and add *til*.
4. Change the *t* to *l* in the opposite of black.
5. Take the *d* from the end of your arm and add a *t*.

Make up similar clues for some of the subordinating conjunctions below. Then ask a classmate to solve them.

after	because	unless	before
if	since	where	when

Skeletal Sayings

Only the vowels are missing from the six famous lines below. (Hint: Each contains at least one verbal.)

1. ntdwstnddvddwfll
2. tbrnttbthtsthqstn
3. prtngsschswtsrrw
4. rllngstngthrsnmss
5. tdrmthmpssbldrm
6. trrshmntfrgvdvn

Unit 9 Extra Practice

1 Participles and Participial Phrases *p. 474*

A. Write the participial phrase in each sentence. Underline each participle. Then write the word the phrase modifies.

1. Ranging in distance from 10 to 100 miles, bicycle road races are held the world over. **2.** Depending on the weather and terrain, speeds range from 20 to 30 miles per hour. **3.** Racers, pedaling hard throughout the race, need great endurance. **4.** Cars and trucks, creating hazards for bicyclists, also travel on the roads. **5.** However, official vehicles following or preceding the racers provide some protection. **6.** Growing in popularity, the criterium is a short course for road racers. **7.** The course, closed to other traffic, is often a city street or a street in a public park. **8.** Handling their bicycles skillfully, the participants race around the course 30 to 50 times.

9. Track races, differing greatly from road races, take place between two individuals or teams on hardwood oval indoor tracks. **10.** Measuring 333.3 meters, the tight little tracks are the sites for top international bicycle races. **11.** The sides of the track, steeply banked, provide a faster and safer surface. **12.** Mandated by official rules, track bikes have no brakes and just one gear. **13.** Noted for their intensity, track races test the riders' speed, endurance, and skill.

B. Write the participial phrase in each sentence. Then label the phrase *essential* or *nonessential*.

14. An indoor oval track called a velodrome is the place for bicycle track races.
15. The bicyclists, pedaling furiously, begin the race.
16. Spectators hoping for a lively race will not be disappointed.
17. Cyclocross, noted for roughness, is the third major type of bicycle race.
18. Covering 2,500 miles, the Tour de France is the world's most difficult bicycle race.
19. The winner, competing for twenty-five days, earns cycling's highest honor.

A. Write the gerund or gerund phrase in each sentence.

1. Tracing the history of hockey is fascinating. **2.** The early history of hockey is intertwined with the history of skating on ice. **3.** Skating on ice probably began in Scandinavia. **4.** Determining its exact origin is difficult. **5.** Before the discovery of iron, making skates from bone was common. **6.** The original purpose of skating was transportation. **7.** However, by the 1500s, northern Europeans enjoyed playing games on ice skates. **8.** Hitting a ball with a stick was the object of one medieval game played on ice.

9. Developing modern ice hockey was a Canadian achievement. **10.** The first hockey puck may have resulted from cutting a solid rubber ball in half. **11.** Moving flatly and stopping sooner were necessary. **12.** The flat surface slowed the skidding of the puck.

B. Write the gerund phrase in each sentence. Then write whether it is used as a subject, direct object, predicate nominative, or object of a preposition.

13. Studying word origins is often fascinating. **14.** A not uncommon practice is borrowing words from other languages. **15.** French shepherds used *hoquets*, or sticks with hooked necks, for controlling sheep. **16.** In their leisure time the shepherds enjoyed playing a ball game with the sticks. **17.** The changing of *hoquet* into *hockey* gave the game its present name.

18. Canadians first enjoyed playing modern ice hockey. **19.** Their favorite pastime is playing hockey. **20.** Fast, agile skating is important in ice hockey. **21.** Handling a hockey stick well takes skill. **22.** Great stamina is also required for playing on a hockey team.

C. Write original sentences, using the gerund phrases as indicated in parentheses.

23. finishing the book (as a subject)
24. skating with speed (as a direct object)
25. walking fast (as an object of a preposition)
26. talking too loud (as a predicate nominative)
27. running into the river (as a subject)
28. watching a hockey game (as an object of a preposition)

3 Infinitives and Infinitive Phrases   *p. 479*

A. Write each infinitive phrase. Write *none* if a sentence has no infinitive phrase.

1. Mildred "Babe" Didrikson liked to try every sport. **2.** To excel in sports was her greatest joy. **3.** America's great woman athlete had to practice hard.

4. Babe Didrikson was able to succeed in many sports. **5.** She led the Dallas Cyclones to three championships in women's basketball. **6.** In one game she herself managed to score 106 points! **7.** She was asked to tour the country on basketball, baseball, and billiards teams. **8.** Swimming, diving, handball, lacrosse, football, and even boxing were to her liking. **9.** She once said, "The best way to take athletics is to take them all." **10.** No one was surprised to see her accomplishments in the 1932 Olympics. **11.** Throwing the javelin and running hurdles seemed easy to her. **12.** Gold medals were awarded to Didrikson in these two events. **13.** Her performance in the high jump was good enough to win a silver medal.

B. Write the infinitive phrase in each sentence. Write whether it is used as a noun, adjective, or adverb.

14. After the Olympics, Babe Didrikson decided to dedicate herself to golf. **15.** To win seventeen amateur golf tournaments in a row gave her satisfaction. **16.** Didrikson later decided to become a professional golfer. **17.** Her goal was to play better. **18.** She wanted little except to win the tournament. **19.** As a professional golfer she was always sure to draw huge crowds. **20.** The Associated Press chose her to be woman athlete of the year five times. **21.** Her skill enabled women's golf to reach its present importance.

22. Babe Didrikson was an athlete to admire for many reasons. **23.** Fans gathered to watch her. **24.** They were anxious to see her. **25.** Her ability to excel in so many ways inspired everyone.

C. Expand each infinitive to an infinitive phrase. Then write a sentence using your phrase as indicated in parentheses.

26. to drive (noun)
27. to jump (adverb)
28. to go (adjective)

29. to win (noun)
30. to hope (adverb)
31. to achieve (adjective)

4 Using Verbal Phrases Correctly   *p. 482*

A. Rewrite the sentences, correcting dangling or misplaced participial phrases. If a sentence is correct, write *correct*.

1. Separated from birth, the school play was about twin brothers.
2. Wanting to get a good seat, I arrived early at the theater.
3. Thumbing through the program, one of the advertisements caught my attention.
4. Recommended highly by my father, I looked forward to seeing this play.
5. Dueling with so much energy, the actors knocked over several pieces of furniture.
6. Creeping around the room, the couch was between the two safecrackers.
7. Coming back to my seat after intermission, my coat was found on the floor.
8. Chased by three policemen, the baby carriage was jumped over by the convict.
9. Hidden behind the scenery, I couldn't see my cousin on the stage.
10. Applauding the curtain call, the actors beamed at the audience.

B. Rewrite each sentence to eliminate the split infinitives.

11. I decided to suddenly walk to my grandmother's house for lunch.
12. Jim agreed to reluctantly walk the three miles with me.
13. We convinced Paul and Matt to eventually join us.
14. I forgot to unfortunately tell Grandma we were coming.
15. The sun began to mercilessly bake us as we walked.
16. I felt bad that Grandma would have to unexpectedly feed us.
17. My friends began to annoyingly whine for something to drink.
18. I tried to patiently promise them Grandma's famous lemonade.
19. As we turned down her street, they began to excitedly run.
20. I tried to desperately cover my embarrassment when no one came to the door.
21. Disappointed, we started to slowly walk home.
22. Imagine our excitement when Grandma returned home and invited us to hungrily feast on her homemade treats!

5 Complex Sentences

p. 484

A. Label each clause below *independent* or *subordinate*.

   1. because Rube Goldberg drew it
   2. you will laugh
   3. while he drew the cartoons for hours
   4. many people enjoyed the crazy inventions
   5. because the complicated machines were hilarious
   6. if you can find any examples of his work
   7. he was a very successful cartoonist

B. Label each sentence *compound* or *complex*. For each complex sentence, write the subordinate clause.

   8. Although Rube Goldberg had an engineering degree, he always kidded our mechanical civilization. **9.** Read this description of his "automatic typewriter eraser," and enjoy a typically outlandish Goldberg invention.

   10. When an office worker enters an office, he trips over the feet of a window washer. **11.** Because the worker stumbles against a file cabinet, a pile of books falls off the cabinet. **12.** Since the books land on a desk in a certain way, they propel a sharp pen in the air. **13.** There is a loud bang when the pen punctures a big balloon. **14.** Behind the balloon is a bicycle where a trained monkey sits. **15.** When the monkey hears the bang, he begins to pedal. **16.** The rubber tire of the bicycle is directly over the typewriter, and it erases the mistake on the page. **17.** If this "eraser" seems impractical to you, perhaps you could invent a better one.

   18. When you look at Rube Goldberg's cartoons, you will see many ridiculous contraptions. **19.** These inventions, because they are absurd, are funny. **20.** We call something "Rube Goldberg" in manner if it is highly impractical.

C. Write a complex sentence for each subordinate clause.

   21. when the tennis match begins
   22. as the dog chases the cat
   23. while the bowling ball rolls down a ramp
   24. if the alarm clock goes off
   25. because the string is too short

A. Write the adverb clause in each sentence. Underline the subordinating conjunction.

1. When most people think of comic books, the name Superman comes to mind. **2.** Jerry Siegel created the idea for Superman when he was still in high school. **3.** Although Siegel wrote the script, Joe Schuster was the artist. **4.** At first no one would publish the comic strip because it was too "fantastic." **5.** As soon as it was published in 1938, it was an immediate success.

6. People can identify with Superman because he is also the rather ordinary Clark Kent. **7.** Superman could become a great deal weaker when he was exposed to the mysterious kryptonite. **8.** When the comic strip first appeared, Superman could only jump great distances. **9.** Later he was given the freedom of flight so that animated cartoons about him would be more effective. **10.** Since Superman was so popular, radio shows, TV shows, and movies have been based on him

B. Combine each pair of sentences, using the subordinating conjunction in parentheses.

EXAMPLE: Danger threatened (whenever). He was ready.
ANSWER: Whenever danger threatened, he was ready.

11. Superman is super. He can never lose (since).
12. He landed on earth as a baby (when). He was adopted by Ma and Pa Kent.
13. He came from Krypton (although). He looks human.
14. No one knew his identity (while). Some guessed it.
15. Superman was popular. He was powerful (because).

C. Change each simple sentence into a complex sentence by adding an adverb clause. Use the subordinating conjunction given in parentheses. Write the new sentence.

16. Dan likes Superman movies. (because)
17. Special effects make anything seem possible. (although)
18. Clark Kent seems foolish. (whenever)
19. Lois Lane laughs at him. (whenever)
20. Superman outwits the villains. (as soon as)

7 Adjective Clauses

A. Write each adjective clause and the word it modifies. A sentence may have more than one adjective clause.

1. This is the school where the cartoonist teaches.
2. The cartoonist, who was drawing rapidly, smiled.
3. The faces that appear in her cartoons are expressive.
4. A character who is angry will have eyebrows that slant inward and downward.
5. The angry character's mouth, which is always turned down, may be open to show teeth.
6. A character whose hair stands on end is frightened.
7. Eyes that are open very wide also indicate fear.

B. Write each sentence, punctuating the adjective clause(s) correctly. Underline the introductory word in each clause.

8. In cartoons a tear rests on the cheek of a character who is sad. 9. A very strong chin which indicates a strong will is a cartoon device that is often used. 10. A wrinkled forehead and diagonal eyebrows that slant outward indicate worry. 11. A figure who tugs at his collar appears worried, too. 12. A face that is happy will have a mouth that is turned up. 13. Characters who are in love have hearts over their heads. 14. A halo which indicates goodness is another device frequently used in cartoons.

C. Combine each pair of sentences by using an adjective clause. Use the relative pronoun given in parentheses. Add a comma before and after each clause.

EXAMPLE: His face is round. It looks young. (which)
ANSWER: His face, which looks young, is round.

15. That character is yawning. She is bored. (who)
16. A question mark is drawn over this character's head. It indicates puzzlement. (which)
17. This man is puzzled. He scratches his head. (who)
18. That girl is surprised. Her mouth is open. (whose)
19. This face looks crafty. It has shifty eyes. (which)
20. The eyes show emotions. They appear in cartoons. (which)

Extra Practice **535**

8 Relative Pronouns in Adjective Clauses

p. 490

A. Write the adjective clause in each sentence. Underline the relative pronoun.

1. I just saw the doctor whom you go to.
2. This story is about a boy who goes back in time.
3. A man whose daughter is a senator lives there.
4. The reporter who wrote that story won an award.
5. The actor whose hat blew off just laughed.

B. Write the adjective clause in each sentence. Then write how the relative pronoun is used in the clause: subject, direct object, object of a preposition, or possessive.

6. I met the writer who wrote that book.
7. The artist who illustrated the book was very good.
8. Do you know anyone from this part of the state whose book has been published?
9. The author who is signing autographs won the award.
10. Her editor, whose name is Kay Lee, is excellent.
11. She was the child for whom the book was originally written.

C. Write each sentence. Supply a correct relative pronoun: *who, whom,* or *whose*.

12. There are Americans of all races ____ have contributed to literature. 13. Richard Wright, ____ autobiography is *Black Boy*, is a very important writer. 14. Maya Angelou, ____tales are moving, writes of her childhood. 15. N. Scott Momaday, ____ writes fascinating stories, describes the ways of Native Americans. 16. Lawrence Yep and Maxine Hong Kingston, ____ are Chinese Americans, write about their experiences in San Francisco's Chinatown. 17. Ernesto Galarza, ____ wrote an autobiography, tells of his life in Mexico and the United States. 18. Nikki Giovanni and Gwendolyn Brooks are two black poets ____ you may have read. 19. Nicholasa Mohr, ____ is Puerto Rican, writes about her experiences in New York City. 20. Alex Haley, ____ best-seller was *Roots*, is another well-known writer. 21. Yoshiko Uchida, ____ stories tell of her childhood, lived in Japanese-American communities.

9 Noun Clauses

A. Write *subject*, *direct object*, *predicate nominative*, or *object of a preposition* to show how each underlined noun clause is used in the sentence.

1. I have described <u>what we saw at the lake</u>.
2. <u>That John never arrived</u> is certain.
3. The silver cup goes to <u>whoever wins the match</u>.
4. Tell the newspaper staff <u>why you came late</u>.
5. The question is <u>whether they will accept it</u>.
6. We should go by <u>whichever route is most scenic</u>.
7. My greatest concern is <u>how you will cross the ice</u>.
8. <u>Whomever you elect</u> must be a good speaker.
9. I don't know <u>that he even cares about the case</u>.
10. Tell the joke to <u>whoever will laugh</u>.

B. Write the noun clause in each sentence. Then write how it is used in the sentence.

11. That Mickey Mouse appeared in the first animated sound cartoon is not well-known. **12.** In 1928 he pleased whoever saw his films. **13.** Why Mickey was so popular is hard to say. **14.** The public's demand was that he appear in the daily comic strips. **15.** By 1930, Mickey was in the newspapers for whoever enjoyed his tricks. **16.** That Mickey earned many special awards is no surprise.

C. Write the sentences. Underline each subordinate clause and label it *noun*, *adjective*, or *adverb*.

17. Mickey Mouse, who was very mischievous at first, soon became well-mannered. **18.** This was a difference that led to the appearance of Donald Duck. **19.** That Donald became as popular as Mickey surprised many. **20.** People identified with Donald when he grew furious in frustrating situations. **21.** Animal characters with human failings are what people enjoy in comic strips.

D. Use each noun clause in an original sentence.

22. whatever you draw
23. what she made
24. who drew this cartoon
25. that he drew
26. what cartoonists do
27. whoever knows

Extra Practice **537**

UNIT TEN

MYTHOLOGY

═══════════ **PART ONE** ═══════════

Unit Theme *Mythology*

Language Awareness Subject-Verb Agreement

═══════════ **PART TWO** ═══════════

Literature "Athene's City" by Olivia Coolidge

Composition Mythology

Writing
IN YOUR JOURNAL

WRITER'S WARM-UP ◆ What do you know about mythology? You might have read some myths about gods and goddesses such as Zeus, Atlas, Minerva, or Athene. Why do you think that ancient people created myths? Do you think those stories still speak to us today? Write about myths in your journal. Tell what you know that makes myths different from legends and common folktales.

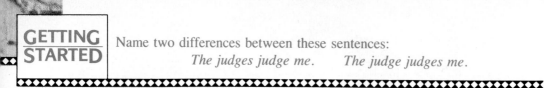
1 Making Subjects and Verbs Agree

Number means that a word is singular or plural. A verb and its subject must agree in number. Both must be singular, or both must be plural. The verb changes only in the third-person singular.

	Singular	Plural
First Person	I see	we see
Second Person	you see	you see
Third Person	he, she, it sees	they see

Use these rules of agreement when you speak and write.

If the subject is a singular noun or a third-person singular pronoun, use the present-tense verb ending in *-s* or *-es*.

Greek *culture* goes back thousands of years.

***It* interests people from all countries today.**

If the subject is a plural noun or any pronoun except a third-person singular pronoun, use the present-tense verb *not* ending in *-s* or *-es*.

Greek *myths* tell about powerful gods and goddesses.

***We* still read these stories.**

Rules for spelling present-tense verbs are on pages 633–634.

Summary ♦ A verb needs to agree with its subject in number. Check for subject and verb agreement when you write.

Guided Practice

Tell which verb agrees with the subject in each sentence.

1. The Greek city Athens (sit, sits) on a hill.
2. Its ancient buildings still (stand, stands).
3. This old city (remain, remains) the capital of modern Greece.

Practice

A. Complete each sentence about the ancient gods and goddesses. Write the verb that agrees with the subject.

4. The Greek gods (live, lives) on top of Mount Olympus.
5. Mount Olympus (lie, lies) in the north of Greece.
6. Zeus (rule, rules) the sky from Olympus with his wife, Hera.
7. She (sit, sits) on the throne with him.
8. The other gods (call, calls) Zeus "king."

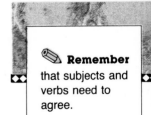

B. Write the correct present-tense form of the verb in parentheses.

9. The goddess Artemis (help) hunters.
10. Athene (give) wisdom to humans.
11. The arts (flourish) under Apollo's control.
12. Hephaestus, the god of fire, (work) at his forge.
13. He (make) armor of excellent quality.

C. Rewrite each sentence in the same tense, making the plural subject singular. Change the verb to agree.

EXAMPLE: The <u>gods</u> watch humans from Mount Olympus.
ANSWER: The <u>god</u> watches humans from Mount Olympus.

14. The <u>myths</u> tell us about ancient Greek beliefs.
15. The <u>crops</u> grow from a goddess's touch.
16. The <u>skies</u> thunder at Zeus's whim.
17. A sea god's <u>hands</u> reach for tiny ships.
18. The <u>humans</u> pass a goddess's test.

D. Use the third-person singular of each verb in a sentence. Use the spelling rules on page 633 if you need help.

19. reply	**21.** mix	**23.** like	**25.** ride	**27.** miss
20. echo	**22.** patch	**24.** send	**26.** rush	

Apply ♦ Think and Write

From Your Writing ♦ Read what you wrote for the Writer's Warm-up. List the subjects and verbs you used. Exchange papers with a partner and check to be sure each verb agrees with its subject.

> ✎ **Remember**
> that subjects and verbs need to agree.

Can you complete these proverbs?

Knowledge ____ power.   Every cloud ____ a silver lining.
When in Rome ____ as the Romans ____ .

2 Forms of *be, have,* and *do*

The forms of *be, have,* and *do,* which can be used as main verbs or as helping verbs, are irregular. Careful speakers and writers learn which forms to use for different subjects.

Forms of *be, have,* and *do*				
Singular	**Present**	**Past**	**Present**	**Present**
I	am	was	have	do
you	are	were	have	do
he, she, it (or a singular noun)	is	was	has	does
Plural				
we	are	were	have	do
you	are	were	have	do
they (or a plural noun)	are	were	have	do

The present- and past-tense forms of these verbs remain the same when they are combined with *n't* to form contractions.

■ you <u>aren't</u>   I <u>wasn't</u>   Hera <u>hasn't</u>   she <u>doesn't</u>   we <u>don't</u>

Break contractions into two words. Then make the verbs agree with their subjects: *doesn't (does not), don't (do not).*

> **Summary** ♦ The verbs *be, have,* and *do* have special singular and plural forms.

Guided Practice

Name the correct verb in parentheses.

1. The ancient Greek national festivals (was, were) called games.
2. The most important one (was, were) the Olympic Games.
3. Today we still (has, have) Olympics.

Practice

A. For each of these sentences about the Olympics, write the correct verb in parentheses.

4. Greek history (is, are) dated from the first Olympiad.
5. The Greek games (was, were) held every four years.
6. We (has, have) our Olympics every four years, too.
7. An Olympiad (is, are) the four years between games.
8. The first known Olympiad (was, were) begun in 776 B.C.
9. (Wasn't, Weren't) Olympia the site of the first games?
10. They (was, were) played to honor Zeus.
11. Garlands (was, were) awarded to the winners.
12. The games (has, have) brought about many achievements.
13. (Don't, Doesn't) you enjoy Olympic contests?

B. Rewrite each sentence in the same tense, making the underlined subject plural. Change the forms of *be*, *have*, or *do* to agree.

14. Does the modern athlete know about the first Olympics?
15. The footrace was the earliest sport.
16. The first wrestler was entered in 708 B.C.
17. Doesn't the field event interest you?
18. The opening ceremony has always appeared impressive.

C. Choose the correct forms of *be*, *have,* and *do* to complete the paragraph. Write the paragraph.

are	is	have	has	does

19. The pentathlon _____ remained part of the Olympic Games since 708 B.C. 20. _____ you ever seen a pentathlon? 21. In it each athlete _____ five different things. 22. One event _____ wrestling. 23. Other events _____ jumping, running, and discus and javelin throwing.

Apply ◆ Think and Write

Sports Introduction ◆ Imagine that you are introducing a new Olympic sport. Write the rules for the event. Also write a brief description of how the sport is played. Include the verbs *be*, *have*, and *do* in several of your sentences.

✎ **Remember** that *be, have,* and *do* have special forms.

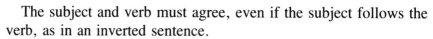

3 Special Problems of Agreement

Problems with agreement may occur when the noun just before a verb is not its subject. To avoid such errors, learn to identify the subject correctly.

Do not make the verb agree with a noun in a prepositional phrase. To check agreement when a prepositional phrase follows the subject, omit the prepositional phrase.

> **Myths about the goddess Athene (is, are) fascinating.**
> *Myths* <u>are</u> **fascinating. (The subject is the plural noun *myths*.)**

The subject and verb must agree, even if the subject follows the verb, as in an inverted sentence.

Normal Word Order: Olive *trees* <u>come</u> from the bounty of Athene.
Inverted Word Order: From the bounty of Athene <u>come</u> olive *trees*.

In speaking and in writing, be careful to avoid agreement errors when using the contraction for the verb *is* (*'s*) with the words *there*, *here*, or *where* to begin a sentence.

Incorrect: Where's the paintings of Athene?
  Correct: Where <u>are</u> the *paintings* of Athene? (*Paintings* is plural.)

> **Summary** ♦ Find the subject of a sentence and make the verb agree with it. Look for agreement between subjects and verbs whenever you are proofreading.

Guided Practice

Name the subject and choose the correct verb in each sentence.

1. Many tools for the farm (is, are) attributed to Athene.
2. There (is, are) musical instruments of her invention.
3. From Athene (come, comes) sailing ships, too.

Practice

A. Write the correct verb in parentheses for each of these sentences about the famous Parthenon of Athens.

4. There (was, were) an ancient temple dedicated to Athene.
5. On its ruins (stand, stands) the Parthenon.
6. Plans for the new temple (was, were) begun in 447 B.C.
7. In it (was, were) statues, including one of Athene.
8. On the east side (is, are) sculptures showing the birth of Athene.
9. On the west side (is, are) her fight with Poseidon.
10. The ruler of the seas (is, are) the god Poseidon.
11. Citizens of Athens (is, are) shown in a procession.
12. Here (is, are) their gift for Athene, a new robe.
13. Where (was, were) the statue of Athene?

B. Write *is* or *are* to complete each sentence.

14. There _____ many statues of Athene.
15. Usually on her head _____ a helmet.
16. A snake by her feet _____ common, too.
17. There _____ often a spear in her hand.
18. Owls with wide eyes _____ another symbol of the goddess.

C. Expand these word groups into sentences. Use present-tense verbs.

19. Buildings in America
20. Cities in this country
21. Statues of Lady Liberty
22. Here
23. A museum with many statues and paintings

Apply ◆ Think and Write

Creative Writing ◆ Imagine that you are a modern sculptor about to create a statue of someone important to you. The person can be real or imaginary. Describe your statue. What symbols would you use? What clothes would you put on the figure? Include an inverted sentence; a sentence beginning with *there*, *here*, or *where*; and a sentence with a subject followed by a prepositional phrase.

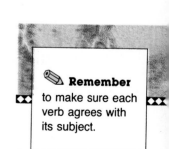

> ✎ **Remember**
> to make sure each verb agrees with its subject.

4 Agreement with Special Subjects

A collective noun, a noun that names a group, is often the subject of a sentence. See the examples in the box. Use a singular verb if the group acts together as a unit. Use a plural verb if the members of the group act as separate individuals.

family
crew
jury
crowd
group
team
class
band

| A *fleet* of ships <u>enters</u> the gulf near Athens.
| The *fleet* <u>enter</u> the gulf one at a time.

Words that refer to amounts (of money, time, measurement, or weight) usually take singular verbs when used as a single unit. When amounts are thought of as separate units, they take plural verbs.

| *Five dollars* <u>is</u> the price of this book. (a single sum)
| *Five dollars* <u>are</u> torn. (five separate bills)

Some nouns ending in *s* take singular verbs, but some take plural verbs, even though they are singular in meaning.

Singular: *news* <u>is</u>   *mathematics* <u>becomes</u>   *measles* <u>remains</u>
Plural: *pliers* <u>were</u>   *scissors* <u>cut</u>   *trousers* <u>have</u>

Titles, company names, and place-names take singular verbs, even if they are plural in form.

"Peanuts" <u>is</u>   *Smith Brothers* <u>sells</u>   the *United States* <u>was</u>

> **Summary** ♦ Special rules govern the verb forms used with collective nouns and with nouns that are plural in form but singular in meaning.

Guided Practice

Name the verb that correctly completes each sentence.

1. Our class (is, are) giving a Greek play.
2. Two weeks (gives, give) us little time to make the costumes.
3. Those scissors (is, are) extremely dull.

Practice

A. Write the correct verb in parentheses for each of these sentences about Greece.

4. Mathematics (was, were) changed by a Greek named Archimedes.
5. Trousers (was, were) not worn by the ancient Greeks; tunics were the fashion.
6. Greek economics (has, have) always been based on farming.
7. The news about this year's Greek festivals (is, are) exciting.

B. Complete each sentence with *is* or *are*. Write the sentences.

8. Greece is in southern Europe; the Netherlands _____ in northern Europe.
9. Athens _____ the capital of Greece.
10. Ten hours _____ the flight time from New York to Athens.
11. Two weeks _____ not long enough for a visit here.
12. *The Three Muses* _____ a sculpture based on Greek mythology.
13. Aristotle's *Poetics* _____ still read with interest today.

C. 14–18. Write two sentences for five of the following collective nouns. In the first sentence, refer to the whole group as a unit; in the second, refer to the individuals that make up the group.

EXAMPLE: A crowd is too large for this room.
            The crowd are all looking at the statues.

army	faculty	committee	team
troop	clan	jury	class
audience	swarm	group	family
band	club	crew	orchestra

Apply • Think and Write

Informative Letter ◆ Imagine that you have a Greek pen pal, who is planning to visit the United States. In a letter explain to your pen pal the amounts of money needed to buy certain things. Mention amounts of time needed to travel from place to place. Explain when it is appropriate to wear shorts, jeans, and trousers. Tell about American news, companies, movies, and anything else you think is important.

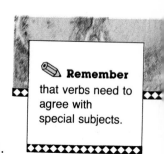

> ✎ **Remember**
> that verbs need to agree with special subjects.

GETTING STARTED

What cities have your class visited? *All of us have visited _____ . A few have visited _____ . One has visited _____ . Everyone has visited _____ . Most of us have visited _____ .*

5 Indefinite Pronouns as Subjects

Follow these rules when using an indefinite pronoun as the subject of a sentence.

Always use singular verbs with the following pronouns.

anybody	each	everyone	nobody	one
anyone	either	everything	no one	someone
anything	everybody	neither	nothing	something

Everyone admires art. **Each** of these goddesses is a Muse.

Always use plural verbs with these pronouns: *few, many, several, both, others.*

Several of our words come from *Muse.*
A few are *music, musician,* and *museum.*

These indefinite pronouns can be singular or plural: *all, any, most, none, some.* To tell whether the pronoun is singular or plural, look at the word it refers to.

Singular: **All** of the poem is addressed to a Muse. (*poem,* singular)

Plural: **All** of the poems are addressed to a Muse. (*poems,* plural)

Summary ◆ When an indefinite pronoun is the subject of a sentence, the pronoun and the verb need to agree in number. To ensure agreement, learn whether an indefinite pronoun is singular or plural.

Guided Practice

Tell whether each pronoun takes a singular or a plural verb.

1. everybody   **2.** few   **3.** everything   **4.** none   **5.** each

Practice

A. Write the correct word in parentheses for each of these sentences about English words that have come from mythology.

6. Do any of our words (comes, come) from ancient myths?
7. Nobody (was, were) stronger than Atlas.
8. Everything in the sky (was, were) held up by Atlas.
9. Today some of our map collections (is, are) called *atlases*.
10. Everyone (was, were) afraid of the god Pan's war cry.
11. Most of us (is, are) familiar with the word *panic*.
12. Anybody with good luck (has, have) *fortune*.
13. All of this luck (come, comes) from the goddess Fortuna.
14. Few (visits, visit) the god Vulcan in his forge in a mountain.
15. Many (knows, know) the heat and smoke of a *volcano*.
16. Both of the words *jovial* and *joviality* (is, are) derived from the name of the god Jove.
17. Everybody (uses, use) the time word *chronology*.
18. (Does, Do) anyone know Chronos, the god of time?
19. All of Echo's words (was, were) repetitions of the last words said to her; from her name comes *echo*.
20. One of our weekdays (is, are) named for the god Saturn.

B. Expand these word groups into sentences. Use present-tense verbs.

21. Several of the words
22. Either of the books
23. Something about her
24. Someone in this story
25. One out of five words

26. No one in this room
27. Each of these
28. Nothing in the world
29. Neither of us
30. Anything on this subject

Apply ♦ Think and Write

Borrowed Words ♦ Expand these word groups about borrowed words into sentences.

Both of the words *mused* and *musical*
Anyone who says "by Jove"
Others of our words from myths
Anything vulcanized

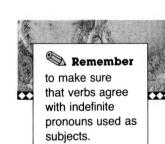

> ✎ **Remember**
> to make sure that verbs agree with indefinite pronouns used as subjects.

Some things are thought of as one thing. What other examples can you think of? *Macaroni and cheese is my favorite dish. Pins and needles is a strange feeling.*

6 Agreement with Compound Subjects

A compound subject may take a singular or a plural verb, depending on how the subjects are joined. Use these rules when you speak and write.

Use a plural verb with most subjects joined by *and*, whether the subjects are singular or plural. However, when two subjects joined by *and* are a unit, or name only one person or thing, use a singular verb.

> The Roman *gods* and Greek *gods* <u>were</u> similar. (both plural)
> Roman *Jupiter* and Greek *Zeus* <u>were</u> sky gods. (both singular)
> *King* of the gods and *lord* of the sky <u>was</u> he. (one person)
> <u>Was</u> *milk* and *honey* a favorite treat of the gods? (one unit)

Use a singular verb with singular subjects joined by *or* or *nor*, and a plural verb with plural subjects joined by *or* or *nor*.

> Either *Juno* or *Hera* <u>was</u> queen of the gods. (both singular)
> Neither *humans* nor lesser *gods* <u>were</u> safe from her. (both plural)

When a singular subject and a plural subject are joined by *or* or *nor*, make the verb agree with the nearer subject.

> Either *flowers* or a *baby* <u>was</u> usually shown with Juno or Hera.
> (The verb agrees with the nearer subject, *baby*.)

Summary ♦ Compound subjects joined by *and* use the plural form of the verb. Compound subjects joined by *or*, *either/or*, or *neither/nor* sometimes use the singular form of the verb and sometimes the plural.

Guided Practice

Tell whether each subject takes a singular or a plural verb.

1. A Roman or a Greek   **2.** Neither she nor they   **3.** He and I

Practice

A. The following sentences compare the Roman gods with Greek gods. For each sentence write the correct verb in parentheses.

4. Roman Minerva and Greek Athene (was, were) nearly the same.
5. The arts and wisdom (was, were) under their influence.
6. Either Mercury or Hermes (is, are) the gods' messenger.
7. Both the Romans and the Greeks (has, have) the god Apollo.
8. Either Venus or Aphrodite (is, are) the goddess of love.
9. Neither she nor the other goddesses (is, are) worshiped today.
10. The Roman goddess Ceres or the Greek goddess Demeter (makes, make) crops grow.
11. Both Athene and her Roman counterpart (was, were) protectors of olive groves.
12. The Roman sower of seed and tiller of land (is, are) Saturn.
13. Either Neptune or Poseidon (rules, rule) the sea.

B. Expand these word groups into sentences. Use present-tense verbs.

14. Mythology and history
15. Peanut butter and jelly
16. Either gods or goddesses
17. Both Zeus and Jupiter
18. Minerva or Athene
19. Peaches and cream
20. Rome and Athens
21. Neither he nor we
22. Either land or sea
23. Myths or a legend

Apply ♦ Think and Write

Dictionary of Knowledge ♦ Most ancient cultures around the world developed a mythology. Read about Norse mythology in the Dictionary of Knowledge. Then write several sentences that compare Norse myths with the myths of Rome and Greece. Use sentences with compound subjects to make your comparisons. Write your sentences in the present tense.

For example: Both Norse mythology and the Roman and Greek mythologies have a god of the sea.

✏ **Remember** to make sure your compound subjects and verbs agree.

GETTING STARTED

Use each word below as a "List Starter." What other words could you add to each list? Choose words that begin with the same few letters.

paralyze   superpower   antifreeze   contest

VOCABULARY ♦
Prefixes from Latin and Greek

A **prefix** is a word part added to the beginning of a base word or root. When a prefix is added, the meaning of a word changes, but its part of speech remains the same. *Prefix* is itself a word formed with a prefix: *pre-* "before" + "to fix." A prefix is something that is "fixed before" a word.

Most prefixes come from Latin, but many also come from Greek. Below are some often-used prefixes from these languages.

Latin		
Prefix	**Meaning**	**Example**
com-; con-; col-; cor-; co-	with, together	compare; conceal; collapse; correct; coexist
super-	over, above; extra; greater than others	superstructure; supersensitive; supermarket
trans-	over, through, across; beyond	transatlantic
Greek		
anti-	against, opposed to; preventing	antifreeze
dia-	through, across; between	dialogue
para-	at the side of, alongside; in a secondary capacity	paramedic

Building Your Vocabulary

You will notice that prefixes are often added to roots that are not English words in themselves. They become words that can stand alone when a prefix is attached. Use prefixes from the chart to form words with the roots below.

-fer	-ment	-sist	-lect
-site	-gress	-pose	-dote

Practice

A. Below is a list of roots and their meanings. Each of these roots can be joined with the prefix *trans-* or *anti-* to form a word. Attach the correct prefix and write the word.

    1. -cend (from Latin *scandere*, "to climb")
    2. -mit (from Latin *mittere*, "to send")
    3. -biotic (from Greek *bios*, "life")
    4. -port (from Latin *portare*, "to carry")
    5. -pathy (from Greek *pathos*, "feeling")
    6. -parent (from Latin *parere*, "to appear")
    7. -septic (from Greek *sepein*, "to cause to rot")

B. The prefix *com-* is somewhat like a chameleon. Its form changes depending on the word or root it is attached to. *Com-* may appear as *con-*, *col-*, *cor-*, or simply *co-*. Use the correct form of *com-* to form words from the following roots.

-mand	-ceal	-dition	-vince	-gratulate
-nect	-quest	-sider	-tain	-junction
-rupt	-lect	-equal	-mence	-rode

Can you find a pattern? Which words take which form of *com-*?

C. Add *super-* or *trans-* to each word below to form a new word. Write the meaning of the new word.

action	plant	highway
star	oceanic	power

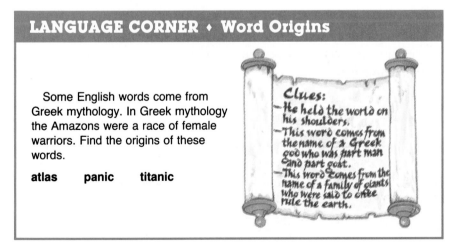

LANGUAGE CORNER ♦ Word Origins

Some English words come from Greek mythology. In Greek mythology the Amazons were a race of female warriors. Find the origins of these words.

atlas   **panic**   **titanic**

Clues:
- He held the world on his shoulders.
- This word comes from the name of a Greek god who was part man and part goat.
- This word comes from the name of a family of giants who were said to once rule the earth.

How to Combine Sentences

Combining sentences can sometimes cause problems in subject and verb agreement. For example, when you use a prepositional phrase to combine sentences, make sure the verb in your new sentence agrees with the subject and not with a noun in the prepositional phrase. Notice that when the two sentences in example **1** are combined in example **2**, the verb *are* still agrees with the plural subject *myths*, not with the singular noun *Greece*.

1. **Many myths are still told today. These myths are from ancient Greece.**
2. **Many myths from ancient Greece are still told today.**

When you use inverted word order in a sentence, make sure that the verb agrees with the subject and not with any noun that comes before the verb. In the combined sentence in example **4**, the plural verb agrees with the plural subject, regardless of their inverted positions in the sentence.

3. **Many familiar stories come from Greek mythology. From Greek mythology also come familiar characters.**
4. **From Greek mythology come many familiar stories and characters.**

Many combined sentences use compound subjects. Make sure that the verb in your combined sentence agrees with the compound subject as in example **6** below.

5. **These stories are based on a myth. This book is based on a myth.**
6. **These stories and this book are based on a myth.**

The Grammar Game ♦ Create your own combinations!
Write four pairs of sentences and then combine them in any way. Exchange papers with a partner and check for subject and verb agreement.

Working Together

Check subject and verb agreement to avoid errors in your writing as your group combines sentences in activities **A** and **B**.

In Your Group	
◆ Contribute your ideas.	◆ Respond to the ideas of others.
◆ Invite others to talk.	◆ Help the group stay on the job.

A. Combine each pair of sentences below. Can your group combine any of the sentence pairs in more than one way?

1. The experiences of Orpheus are described in a Greek myth. His fate is described in a Greek myth.
2. The musical talents of Orpheus enchant animals, trees, and stones. His talents are with the lyre.
3. His wife Eurydice is dead. To the underworld she is taken.
4. After her goes Orpheus. Orpheus is grieving.
5. His music moves the king and queen. His grief moves the king and queen of the underworld.

B. Use your knowledge of sentence combining to rewrite this paragraph.

    The king grants the request of Orpheus. The request is for the return of his wife. This is a great favor. On this is placed a single condition. Orpheus must not look back on Eurydice. He must not look back during the trip back to earth. Orpheus turns. He turns to Eurydice before reaching earth. She is lost to him. She is lost forever.

WRITERS' CORNER ◆ Sentence Variety

    Avoid using too many sentences of the same length in a paragraph. Too many short sentences are boring. Too many long sentences can be difficult to read. Varying the length of your sentences will make your writing more interesting to read and easier to follow. This paragraph, for example, uses sentences of different lengths.

Read what you wrote for the Writer's Warm-up. Did you use too many short or long sentences in your paragraphs? Can you improve any paragraphs by varying the length of your sentences?

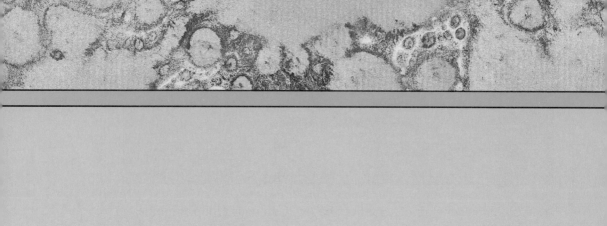

DIE ROSSE DES NEPTUN
painting by Walter Crane
Bayereische Staatsgemaldesammlungen, West Germany.

UNIT TEN

Mᴙᴛʜᴏʟᴏɢʏ

PART TWO

Literature "Athene's City" by Olivia Coolidge

Composition Mythology

CREATIVE
Writing

FINE ARTS ◆ Study the horses pulling Neptune from the sea. What would happen to a horse of Neptune's if it rushed from the sea and decided to stay on land? Is it possible for a horse of the sea to become a horse of the land? Write a story about the sea horse that strayed from the sea.

LITERATURE

from
Athene's City
by Olivia Coolidge

In the days when Greece was first being settled, Cecrops was king in Attica, a rugged, triangular little country, good mainly for goat farming and the culture of honey bees, and surrounded on two sides by the sea. Here Cecrops planned a city around a steep rock that jutted from the plain a few miles inland. Down on the shore were two fine harbors, while around spread fertile country watered by two streams. The gods, who were always interested in the affairs of men, approved the idea of Cecrops and gave the new city their blessing, foreseeing that it would become in time one of the famous cities of the world. For this reason there was great dispute among the gods as to which of them should be its special patron. Many claims were put forward by this god or by that, but at last, after much arguing, it became clear that the award should lie between Athene, goddess of wisdom, and the sea god, Poseidon. Between these two the gods decided to have a contest. Each should produce some marvel in the Attic land, and each should promise some gift to the city that was to come. The greater gift should win the city.

When the appointed day came, the judges ranged themselves on the rock, and the two gods came before them. Some say that the twelve judges chosen were the spirits of the Attic hills and rivers, and some maintain that they were twelve Olympian gods. Be that as it may, on one side stood Poseidon with flowing dark-blue beard and majestic stature, carrying in his hand the three-pronged trident with which he rules the waves. On the other side stood Athene, grey-eyed and serene, helmet on her golden head and spear in hand. At the word Poseidon raised his trident and struck the ground. Beneath the feet of the judges the whole earth was terribly shaken, and with a mighty rumbling sound it split apart before them. Then appeared the marvel, a salt spring four miles inland where no water had appeared before. To this Poseidon added his gift of sea power, promising the city a great empire, a mighty navy, famed shipwrights, and trading vessels which should make her name known in every corner of the sea.

The judges looked at one another as Poseidon spoke and nodded their heads in approval, thinking the gift indeed a great one and the salt spring and the earthquake fine symbols of Poseidon's power. Grey-eyed Athene said nothing, but smiled gently to herself as she laid aside her spear and quietly kneeling down appeared to plant something in the earth. Between her hands as she worked, there gradually unfolded a little tree, a bush rather, small and un-impressive, with grey-green leaves and grey-green berries about an inch in length. When it had grown to full size, Athene stood up and looked at the judges. That was all.

Poseidon glanced at the dusty looking bush that had grown so quietly. He looked at the hole that had gaped in the earth with the thunder of earthquake, and he threw back his head and laughed. Round the bay rumbled and re-echoed the laughter of the god like distant waves thundering on the rocks, while far out to sea in their deep, green caverns, the old sea gods, his subjects, sent a muffled answering roar. Presently as silence fell, the quiet voice of Athene spoke to the assembled gods.

"This little shrub is the olive, at the same time my marvel and my gift to the city," she said. "With these berries the poor man will flavor his coarse bread and goat's-milk cheese. With scented oil the rich man will deck himself for the feast. Oil poured to the gods shall be among their favorite offerings. With it the housewife will light her lamp and do her cooking, and the athlete will cleanse himself from dust and sweat. This is the ware merchants will carry in the ships Poseidon speaks of, to gain riches and renown for the city which sells what all men use. Moreover, I will make its people skilled in pottery, so that the jars in which the oil is carried shall themselves be a marvel, and the city shall flourish and be famous, not only in trade but in the arts."

She finished, and the judges cried out in surprise at the rich-ness of her dull-looking gift. They awarded the prize to Athene, who called the city Athens.

Library Link ◆ *Read about other mythological characters in* Greek Myths *by Olivia Coolidge. You can find it in your library.*

 Reader's Response

Which gift would you have chosen? Why?

Athene's City

Responding to Literature

1. If it were in your power to present any gift to the citizens of your community, what gift would you give? Explain your choice.

2. How did Poseidon's gift differ from Athene's gift? List the similarities and differences between the two offerings.

3. This myth told a story to explain how the olive tree came to Greece. What natural gift does your area have that is important to the people? Is it farmland? A body of water? A mineral below the ground? Make up a myth to explain how this gift was given to your people. Tell your myth to your classmates.

Writing to Learn

Think and Discover ◆ Athene displayed unique personality characteristics in this story. From her actions what did you learn about her intelligence, courage, and resourcefulness? Copy the chart below and list examples in each column.

Athene's qualities		
intelligence	*courage*	*resourcefulness*

Write ◆ Using the details from your chart, tell why Athene was a hero to her people.

GETTING STARTED | Who is your favorite storyteller? What techniques does the person use to make a story interesting?

SPEAKING and LISTENING ◆ The Oral Tradition

Imagine two scenes—in one, people gather around a campfire in ancient Greece; in the other, people gather in New York's Central Park for a festival. At the center of both scenes, you will find a storyteller and in both, eager listeners.

The oral tradition of sharing stories, passed down from generation to generation, is both extremely ancient and alive today. Why do certain stories survive and change and fascinate listeners from century to century?

Many tales try to explain the reason for something—how a city got its name or why the seasons change. Others teach the values of a certain society—for example, why honesty is a noble trait. However, the best stories also entertain. Storytellers of each century select, reshape, and retell the stories they find most appealing and appropriate for their audiences.

Follow these guidelines when you retell or listen to stories.

Telling a Story	**1.** Choose a story you enjoy and want to tell. Then practice telling your story to discover which parts to stress and which gestures and tone of voice to use. **2.** Picture each scene of the story in your mind for help in finding the best descriptive words. **3.** Apply your own creative judgment in changing details. Be able to justify any changes you make in the original story.
Listening Actively	**1.** Listen courteously and carefully for the basic story facts and for character development. **2.** Evaluate the storyteller's gestures and tone of voice. Did they make the story come alive or interfere with understanding?

> **Summary** ◆ Retell old stories clearly and creatively. Listen carefully for story facts and style of delivery.

Guided Practice

Tell whether each student below is following effective speaking and listening procedures for storytelling. Explain your answers.

1. Lee is thinking about tomorrow's test and fails to grasp the significance of a character's action.
2. Maury doesn't like certain details in the story she is retelling but hesitates to make any changes.
3. Mike is obviously enjoying relating his story to the group.

Practice

A. Discuss with a partner why you think each student below is or is not proceeding correctly.

4. Lenny knows the facts of his story, so he doesn't bother to practice telling it.
5. Wanda closes her eyes and visualizes her story because she wants just the right phrase to describe how a character looks.
6. Tony jots down examples of the storyteller's effective gestures and expressions and plans to adapt some of them himself.
7. After hearing a particularly amusing part of a story, Glen interrupts with details about a similar personal experience.
8. Gloria finds a good story to tell, but certain parts seem unclear. She reworks those parts to clarify and improve them.

B. Choose one storytelling idea below. Present it to a partner.

9. Create a brief scene that explains imaginatively how your community received its name.
10. Prepare a thundering speech for Poseidon in which he explains his gift to Athens and why he should win the contest.

C. Retell a favorite story to a group of classmates. Follow the guidelines on page 562.

Apply • Think and Write

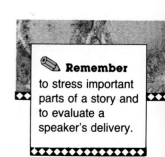

Remember to stress important parts of a story and to evaluate a speaker's delivery.

Comparing Familiar Stories ◆ Jot down a list of familiar stories often told in your family. Compare your list with lists of classmates to see how many stories appear on several lists.

GETTING STARTED Name a person you feel has done something amazing or heroic. Tell how that person went beyond ordinary efforts to accomplish something great.

WRITING ◆
Elements of a Myth

Myths have always fascinated people, and every country has its myths. Greek myths, in particular, have greatly influenced our language and our literature.

A myth is an ancient story, usually involving supernatural persons and events. Myths were first told in family or social gatherings. Thus their style is usually simple and easy to understand. Yet myths are rich and complex in meaning, which has kept them alive.

Scholars have found that myths from all over the world have certain characteristics. Many deal with common themes:

◆ an explanation of the earth's creation
◆ the dealings of gods with each other and with humans
◆ interpretations of natural events
◆ celebrations of the triumphs of heroes

A myth about the Greek god Zeus explains the thunderbolt and lightning; one of Apollo and Daphne, the origin of the laurel wreath. Other myths tell how the sun rises, how musical instruments were invented, and why the seasons change.

Characters in myths are memorable. The accomplishments of mythical heroes are comparable with those of today's heroes. Some heroes in myths are children of gods and goddesses and thus possess certain supernatural powers. Some heroes are humans who are assisted by gods and goddesses. To be a true hero, however, the character must possess extraordinary courage, perseverance, intelligence, strength, greatness of character, or leadership ability. The hero often must meet a challenge, go on a quest, or accomplish an almost impossible task. In contrast, an evil, arrogant, weak, or thoughtless character is punished dramatically.

> **Summary** ◆ **Myths** are ancient stories that share many common elements.

Guided Practice

Explain how each description illustrates a characteristic of myths.

1. The gods decide whether the goddess Athene or the god Poseidon will be allowed the honor of naming a city.
2. Arachne, an artistic weaver, courageously engages in a weaving contest with Athene and is turned into a spider upon losing.
3. The sun god Apollo, mourning the death of his son, refuses to come out; he leaves the sky covered with black clouds for days.

Practice

A. Write an explanation of what you think each description has in common with most myths.

4. Each day Eos, the rosy-fingered goddess of the dawn, ascends the sky in a chariot to announce the coming of the sun.
5. Icarus ignored his father's instructions about the dangerous invention. This mistake resulted in Icarus's tragic death.
6. A conflict arose between the Athenians and the people of Crete. Theseus, prince of Athens, journeyed to Crete to challenge his city's rivals.

B. Review the special qualities of characters in myths on page 564. Then create a character for a myth. Write a brief paragraph that describes the qualities of your character.

C. Think about the character you created in **Practice B** and the special characteristics of this person. Then write a simple myth with your character as the hero (or the villain).

Apply • Think and Write

Dictionary of Knowledge • Read the myth about Baucis and Philemon in the Dictionary of Knowledge. Assume you are preparing a script for a movie about the myth. List the facts needed for writing the script for these scenes.

1. In the small cottage
2. On top of the hill

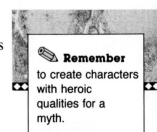

✎ **Remember**
to create characters with heroic qualities for a myth.

Focus on Your Growth as a Writer

You will recall from the Reading-Writing Connection (page 40) that keeping a journal is a good way to record thoughts, experiences, and insights for future use. You may see no immediate use for what you record, but in time you will find at least some of these entries to be valuable sources for your writing.

The more you challenge yourself—for example, by keeping a journal—the more you will develop as a writer. The suggestions below will help you solve your writing problems and evaluate your progress.

Vocabulary and Grammar   Words are the raw materials of writing. Grammar is the framework within which you shape those words. You must pay attention to both. Good writers are interested in words—their meanings, their placement, their power. The Thesaurus in this book is a useful tool in helping you express the exact shade of meaning you intend.

Reading and Imagination   Study the works of other writers. Think about what it is you admire about them. For a writer, reading *is* a very valuable kind of experience. Reading is also a spur to your imagination. It lets you think about things beyond your immediate surroundings. Equally important to your growth as a writer is regular practice. There is no substitute for the continuing effort of putting your thoughts into words.

Persistence   Good writing is hard work. Even professional authors cannot write perfect first drafts. Like you, they must keep at it—revising, improving, editing, proofreading.

The Writer's Voice ♦ What is your greatest strength as a writer? What is your greatest weakness? How do you think you can best correct your weakness?

Working Together

An interest in words, wide reading, and stick-to-itiveness are three important elements for growth as a writer. As a group, work on activities **A** and **B**.

In Your Group
◆ Contribute your ideas.   ◆ Work quietly as you write.
◆ Invite others to contribute.   ◆ Help the group reach agreement.

A. Writers often express the same concerns. Read the statements below, adding any that members of your group think are important. After discussing these difficulties that writers face, write a paragraph focusing on *one* of them. If possible, the group should also suggest a solution.

  1. ''I have no ideas for writing.''
  2. ''It isn't hard for me to start writing, but then everything bogs down.''
  3. ''I worry about what people will think of me if I write what I really believe and feel.''
  4. ''There's nothing I can write that hasn't been done before— and probably done better.''

B. Your group discussion in activity **A** may not have resulted in any instant solutions, but you probably see that others face problems similar to yours. Now write something on your own. It can be anything—a descriptive paragraph, a conversation, a news article, a poem. Share this writing with group members. You will gain both confidence and useful criticism.

THESAURUS CORNER ◆ Word Choice

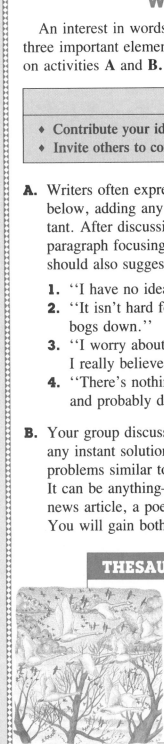

Close your eyes and imagine a scene involving each word below. Next, write the words in sentences about the scene. Then look in the Thesaurus to see if you can find a more exact synonym for each word. If you can, cross out the word below and use the synonym. If not, leave the original word.

move	live	do
go	keep	change

Writing Across the Curriculum   Drama

Gods, goddesses, and humans in myths portray distinct character and personality traits. Traits such as greed, curiosity, and playfulness are as much a part of life today as they were then. That is why many modern plays are based on ancient myths.

Writing to Learn

Think and Analyze ◆ List four of the major characters in Greek or Roman mythology. Beside each name, list that character's outstanding character or personality trait or traits.

Write ◆ Review your list of mythological characters. Then imagine that one of them appears in an episode of your favorite television series. Write an account of what might happen and why.

Writing in Your Journal

At the beginning of this unit, you wrote what you know about myths. Then you went on to learn a great deal more about Greek and Roman mythology. In your journal express your ideas about how a knowledge of ancient mythology might affect your life today or in the future.

Read More About It

The Children of Odin *by Padraic Colum*
In Norse mythology, Odin was supreme ruler of the world. The author presents the exploits of Odin and other Norse gods in a stirring yet lyrical fashion.

A Fair Wind for Troy *by Doris Gates*
Mythology, legend, and archaeology provide our only clues about the Trojan War, fought over 3,600 years ago. The author uses these sources to tell a splendid story of that war and show the role that Greek gods and goddesses played in the lives of mortals.

Book Report Idea   Classified Ad

Heroes in myth, fantasy, and other forms of fiction must often perform difficult tasks or go on dangerous quests. An amusing way to report on the activities of a fictional hero might be a help-wanted classified ad. As you probably know, classified ads for employment describe a job and its benefits. Such ads list the qualifications that the successful candidate should have.

Pick Your Hero ♦ Think about the hero of a book you have read recently. What did he or she have to do? What special qualifications would the person need? If you were advertising for such a hero, how would you word the ad? At the bottom of the ad, list the book's title and author so your classmates can find out more about the job.

> *Position Available*
> *— Monster Slayer —*
>
> *Powerful Greek king requires the services of a hero to kill the half-man, half-bull Minotaur. The right candidate must display great courage and physical strength. Must be willing to travel to the island of Crete. Rewards include gold, a royal marriage, and permanent hero status.*
>
> *For more information contact:*
> *King Aegeus of Athens*
> *The Way of Danger*
> *by Ian Serraillier*

Unit 10
Subject-Verb Agreement   *pages 540–551*

A. Write the verb that agrees with the subject of each sentence.

1. Modern-day heroes (appear, appears) down-to-earth.
2. An astronaut (return, returns) to everyday life after a mission.
3. Teachers (perform, performs) heroically at times.
4. Fire fighters (risk, risks) their lives daily on the job.
5. A student (look, looks) for role models.
6. Heroes (come, comes) from different walks of life.

B. Write the correct verb in parentheses.

7. (Doesn't, Don't) we have the tallest skyscraper in the world?
8. A skyline (is, are) the outline of buildings against the sky.
9. (Wasn't, Weren't) those birds skylarks?
10. The players (hasn't, haven't) hit a sky-high fly ball today.
11. Windows in roofs or ceilings (is, are) skylights.
12. Skylab (was, were) the first United States space station.

C. Write the subject of each sentence. Then write the correct verb.

13. Here (is, are) our nearest post office.
14. Maps of our city (is, are) available at this facility.
15. In the corner (stand, stands) the stamp machines.
16. Where (was, were) the stack of letters from my friends?
17. The people by the door (has, have) a long wait.
18. Behind the counter (was, were) only two clerks.

D. Write each sentence, completing it with *is* or *are*.

19. Thirty seconds _____ the length of many TV commercials.
20. The Mets _____ a New York baseball team.
21. The news _____ unexpectedly positive.
22. The lens on that camera _____ broken.
23. His trousers _____ quite unusual.

E. Write the indefinite pronoun in each sentence. Then write the correct verb in parentheses.

24. Both of my parents (has, have) jobs.
25. Most of their time during the work day (is, are) spent away from home.
26. Everybody (spends, spend) time together in the evening.
27. Something (is, are) always planned for weekends.
28. A few of our friends often (visits, visit) us.

F. Write the compound subject in each sentence. Then write the correct verb in parentheses.

29. Either a gully or a ravine (is, are) made by heavy rains.
30. (Was, Were) bread and butter Maggie's favorite afternoon snack?
31. Neither the cow nor the horses (was, were) in the barn.
32. Grapes and bananas (is, are) quite plentiful this year.
33. The mayor and the commissioners (agree, agrees) on recycling.

Prefixes from Latin and Greek   *pages 552–553*

G. Use the prefixes from the list below to form words from the numbered root words. Write the words.

trans-   **dia-**   **com-**   **con-**

34. -meter
35. -gram
36. -mit
37. -pose
38. -fer
39. -logue
40. -tend
41. -fuse
42. -mand

Proofreading

H. Write the correct form of each incorrect verb.

43. Isn't the stories in the same book?
44. There is our pictures on the front page of the school newspaper.
45. Two days weren't enough time to research the facts for my report.
46. The scissors has a broken blade.
47. An artist and a scholar were she.

UNIT 1: Sentences *pages 4–21*

A. Write *simple* or *compound* for each sentence.

   1. The chief agricultural crops of Florida are citrus fruits.
   2. Lemons and limes are citrus fruits.
   3. Some people prefer citrons, but I prefer lemons.
   4. It's much larger than a lemon, and it has a thicker rind.

UNIT 2: Nouns *pages 58–69*

B. Write each noun and label it *common* or *proper*.

   5. Australia, the smallest continent, has five mainland states.
   6. Austria, a republic, is at the crossroads of Europe.
   7. The capital of Texas is Austin.
   8. Jane Austen, an English novelist, wrote *Pride and Prejudice*.

C. Write the singular and plural possessive form of each noun.

   9. grass   11. headdress   13. Crawford
   10. artery   12. stepchild   14. attorney

UNIT 3: Verbs *pages 124–135*

D. Write and label each verb, direct object, and indirect object.

   15. Toula told her neighbor and me her policy.
   16. She follows proper instructions for new products.
   17. She keeps the sales receipts and the warranties.

E. Write the sentences. Underline each linking verb and label each predicate nominative and predicate adjective.

   18. Thomas Jefferson was a Democrat in 1800.
   19. Abraham Lincoln was a Republican in 1860.
   20. The two-party system became strong and competitive.
   21. Each party is powerful to this day.

UNIT 4: Verbs *pages 180–198*

F. Write each verb and label its tense.

22. will go   **24.** encourages   **26.** controlled
23. will have raised   **25.** had formed   **27.** has walked

UNIT 5: Pronouns *pages 244–259*

G. Write the sentences. Underline each possessive pronoun.

28. Their VCR is broken   **30.** Hers works perfectly well.
29. Theirs is not hooked up.   **31.** His TV reception is poor.

H. Write and label each reflexive and intensive pronoun.

32. I talked myself into it.   **34.** Can you yourself do it?
33. The job itself took an hour.   **35.** Ask yourself the question.

I. Write the correct pronoun in parentheses.

36. (Him, He) recognized (me, I) from the yearbook pictures.
37. (I, Me) remembered (they, them) also.
38. (They, Them) worked on the book as much as (we, us).
39. (We, Us) graduates had a memorable time.

UNIT 6: Adjectives *pages 302–309*

J. Write the correct form of each adjective in parentheses. Write the sentences.

40. Is this the (bad) joke you have ever heard?
41. Which of the two comedies do you think is (good)?
42. Isn't a clown the (funny) comedian?
43. Who is (tragic) than a weeping clown?

UNIT 7: Adverbs *pages 354–363*

K. Write the comparative and superlative forms of each adverb.

44. terribly   **46.** rarely   **48.** hard
45. low   **47.** slowly   **49.** well

L. Write the correct word in parentheses.

50. Stacey doesn't like that song (no more, anymore).
51. We didn't do (anything, nothing) to change her mind.
52. Why won't she go (anywhere, nowhere) it's playing?
53. Her new favorite (can, can't) barely measure up to it.

UNIT 8: Prepositions, Conjunctions, Interjections *412–425*

M. Write and label each adjective phrase and adverb phrase.

54. Atlas, a Greek giant, held the sky upon his shoulders.
55. The mythical island of Atlantis sank beneath the sea.
56. Athene was the goddess of war and wisdom.
57. She is typically represented in full armor.

N. Write each conjunction and label it *coordinating* or *correlative*.

58. The word *export* is not only a noun but also a verb.
59. Some words can function as adjectives, adverbs, and nouns.
60. The word *jingle* is either a noun or a verb.
61. It can mean "a short song" or "to make a clinking sound."

O. Write the interjection in each sentence.

62. So! He was the thief!   **64.** We did it. Hurrah!
63. Well, I'm speechless!   **65.** Oh, I suppose it is.

UNIT 9: Verbals *pages 473–483*

P. Write each participial phrase. Underline each participle.

66. Rubbing a magic lamp, Aladdin made a genie appear.
67. A genie, called a jinni in Arabic, is a mythical spirit.
68. Appearing in human or animal form, it does what is asked.
69. Called by Aladdin, the genie performed supernatural feats.

Q. Write the gerund or gerund phrase in each sentence.

70. You can save money by buying a generic product.
71. Economizing isn't easy, however.
72. Finding products without brand names may be difficult.
73. A common practice of manufacturers is using trademarks.

R. Write each infinitive phrase. Label it *noun, adjective,* or *adverb*.

74. To own her own tugboat is Marge's secret wish.
75. She will use it to tow cargo boats.
76. This small, powerful vessel is a boat to be proud of.

Complex Sentences   *pages 484–493*

S. Label each sentence *simple, compound,* or *complex*.

77. Clara Barton is a true hero, and many people praise her.
78. Barton, whose services were notable, was an army nurse.
79. She organized and promoted the American Red Cross.

T. Write the subordinate clause in each sentence. Then label it *adverb, adjective,* or *noun*.

80. Wherever the movie star goes, she is mobbed by her fans.
81. Katharine Hepburn, who is a living legend, is a great actress.
82. Her talents, which are considerable, are recorded on film.
83. I think that she is wonderful.

UNIT 10:   Subject-Verb Agreement   *pages 540–551*

U. Write the correct verb in parentheses.

84. A constellation (is, are) a group of stars.
85. (Doesn't, Don't) these stars have a recognizable shape?
86. I (haven't, hasn't) located the Big Dipper yet.

V. Complete each sentence with *is* or *are*. Write the sentences.

87. Two hours _____ a long time to wait for a train.
88. Six pennies _____ in my pocket.
89. The United Nations _____ a worldwide organization.
90. Our gym class _____ all talking about the tournament.

X. Write the subject of each sentence. Then write the correct verb.

91. Both of my friends (collect, collects) baseball cards.
92. (Was, Were) Mickey Mantle and Roger Maris rivals?
93. Neither the catcher nor the pitcher (was, were) in good form.
94. Most of their time (is, are) spent on the road.

State Facts Matchup

Play this trivia game about states. Match each subject with the correct predicate. Then write out each sentence.

Column A	Column B
1. Two states on the Canadian border	was part of the thirteen colonies.
2. Peanuts and cotton	was William Penn.
3. The founder of a northeastern state	are New York and Montana.
4. Neither the western states nor the Midwest	is a southern specialty.
5. Grits and red-eye gravy	connects New York and California.
6. Some of the Southwest	come from Georgia.
7. Some southwesterners	has its own flag.
8. Each of the states	borders Mexico.
9. One of the interstate highways	speak Spanish.

Word Dimensions

Make a new word out of each of the following words by adding a prefix.

pathetic	tension	sent	date
gram	sphere	weekly	noun
scope	meter	navigate	active
graph	circle	exist	marine
thesis	port	legal	polite

Unit 10 Extra Practice

1 Making Subjects and Verbs Agree *p. 540*

A. Write the present-tense verb form that agrees with a third-person singular subject.

1. blow	**6.** supply	**11.** echo
2. patch	**7.** match	**12.** annoy
3. buzz	**8.** mix	**13.** reply
4. notify	**9.** crush	**14.** miss
5. forego	**10.** rely	**15.** tax

B. Write the appropriate present-tense form of the verb in parentheses.

16. A worker (stand) near the roundhouse.

17. The train (slow) down as it nears the station.

18. Its whistle blows as it (approach).

19. She (rush) to catch the train every morning.

20. I (wait) for the train in the station.

21. The engineer (try) to arrive on schedule.

22. You (watch) for incoming trains from that area.

23. The loudspeaker (amplify) the conductor's words.

24. He (make) repairs on the tracks for one of the major railroads.

25. The conductor (cry) "All aboard!"

C. Rewrite each sentence in the same tense, making the plural subject singular. Change the verb to agree.

EXAMPLE: The late <u>passengers</u> hurry aboard.

ANSWER: The late passenger hurries aboard.

26. My <u>suitcases</u> fit on the rack above my seat.

27. The <u>railroads</u> employ many workers.

28. The <u>expresses</u> whizz by the local stops.

29. The <u>passengers</u> comply with smoking regulations.

30. The <u>cars</u> pitch from side to side when moving fast.

31. The <u>commuters</u> read the newspaper.

2 Forms of *be, have,* and *do*   *p. 542*

A. Write the correct verb in parentheses.

1. Early locomotives (was, were) powered by steam.
2. We (has, have) made drawings of some of them.
3. The cowcatcher (is, are) on the front.
4. We (is, are) also interested in old railroad cars.
5. Early cars (was, were) joined by chains.
6. Fortunately they (has, have) been replaced.
7. Link-and-pin couplings (does, do) work better.
8. I (has, have) seen early cars in museums.
9. (Don't, Doesn't) you enjoy looking at them?
10. They (is, are) shaped just like carriages.
11. A carriage (has, have) a tendency to overturn.
12. This later car design (does, do) much better.
13. (Wasn't, Weren't) early passengers afraid to ride on trains?
14. At first, accidents (was, were) quite common.
15. The train design (was, were) corrected.
16. I (is, am) not afraid to ride on trains.

B. Rewrite each sentence in the same tense, making the singular subject plural. Change the verb to agree.

EXAMPLE: The <u>man</u> hasn't left.
ANSWER: The men haven't left.

17. The car isn't clean.
18. The train is running.
19. The trip hasn't begun.
20. The engine doesn't work.
21. Does the rider know?
22. The track was new.

3 Special Problems of Agreement   *p. 544*

A. Write *was* or *were* to complete each sentence.

1. There _____ wood stoves on board for warmth.
2. There _____ a blanket for each passenger.
3. There _____ a plush carpet down the center aisle.
4. On the walls _____ fine mirrors and hangings.
5. Where _____ funds for those luxuries obtained?
6. There _____ a Chicago line willing to invest.
7. Here _____ the beginnings of today's Pullman cars.

B. This story about George Pullman is told in the present tense. Write the correct verb in parentheses.

8. A boy from the farm (begin, begins) work as a cabinetmaker in 1848. **9.** Designs of railroad cars (interest, interests) him. **10.** Passengers on an overnight trip (need, needs) to sleep. **11.** The energies of George Pullman (is, are) channeled into designing sleeping cars. **12.** Some railroaders in the Chicago area (is, are) intrigued by his ideas. **13.** The owners of one line (give, gives) him two cars. **14.** Each car (make, makes) ten sleeping sections. **15.** One of these sections (hold, holds) two berths. **16.** Curtains around a berth (give, gives) privacy. **17.** Berths by day (fold, folds) up to the ceiling. **18.** Not until 1858 (is, are) his sleeping cars tested publicly. **19.** In 1863 the artistry of Pullman and friend Ben Field (produce, produces) the famous sleeper *Pioneer*. **20.** One of the first delighted passengers (is, are) Mrs. Abraham Lincoln.

21. Only the first of many successes by Pullman (is, are) the patented *Pioneer*. **22.** The workers in his Palace Car Company (build, builds) the classic dining car in 1868. **23.** Later (follow, follows) the chair car and the vestibule car. **24.** Examples of Pullman's artistry (is, are) appreciated today in many restaurants and museums. **25.** In St. Louis's Transportation Museum (is, are) found several Pullman cars.

4 Agreement with Special Subjects   *p. 546*

A. Write the sentences. Underline the collective nouns. Write *was* or *were* to complete each sentence.

1. A train's crew ____ often widely scattered.
2. A team of robbers ____ able to overpower them.
3. The Reno gang ____ the first to rob a train.
4. The group ____ not all caught.
5. The most notorious clan of train robbers ____ headed by Jesse James.
6. A whole army of railroad detectives ____ not able to stop these "James Boys."
7. A crowd of civilians ____ the people who finally captured them.
8. Another infamous band ____ the Dalton gang.
9. The sheriff's posse ____ all expert gunslingers.
10. The jury ____ quick to make up their minds.

B. Write the correct verb in parentheses.

11. Mathematics (gives, give) some people a challenge.
12. The Netherlands (lies, lie) just north of Belgium.
13. Pliers (is, are) what you need to loosen that bolt.
14. Two hours (was, were) all it took to get to Omaha.
15. *Just So Stories* (is, are) her favorite book.
16. Lever Brothers (has, have) made soaps since 1895.
17. His Bermuda shorts (is, are) spotted with oil.
18. Twenty dollars (is, are) the fee for materials.
19. The United Nations (is, are) located in New York.
20. *The New York Times* (is, are) read nationwide.
21. Parker Brothers (makes, make) many board games.
22. Tweezers (is, are) what I use to remove splinters.
23. Economics (is, are) soon going to be required.
24. *Drums Along the Mohawk* (has, have) been televised.
25. Mumps (is, are) caused by a virus.
26. My family (travel, travels) together each summer.

5 Indefinite Pronouns as Subjects   *p. 548*

A. Write the correct word in parentheses.

1. Everyone in Chicago (seem, seems) to be in the station this morning.
2. No one in that group (has, have) been here before.
3. Several of the ticket windows (is, are) closed.
4. All of my patience (is, are) exhausted.
5. All of these gates (is, are) for northbound trains.
6. A few of these books (helps, help) pass the time.
7. (Is, Are) any of the newspaper interesting today?
8. One of these sections (contain, contains) advertisements and sports news.
9. Where (is, are) everything you brought?
10. None of the coffee sold here (is, are) very good.
11. Both of these tickets (cost, costs) the same.
12. (Has, Have) anything else gone wrong?
13. Most of the observation car (was, were) full.
14. Most of the window seats (was, were) taken.
15. Some of the cars (isn't, aren't) air-conditioned.
16. Some of the track (has, have) sharp curves.

B. Some of the sentences below contain verbs that do not agree with their subjects. Write the sentences correctly. If a sentence contains no error, write *correct*.

17. Only a few of us brings our own snacks.
18. Most of the riders buy something at the station.
19. Something about those children worries me.
20. Each of them look lost and scared.
21. Everybody on this line are going to Milwaukee.
22. Both of those windows sells tickets to Rockford.
23. Neither of those trains operate on Sunday.
24. Only one out of ten trains leave late.
25. Either of those seats are just fine.
26. Few of the times listed on that schedule is correct.

6 Agreement with Compound Subjects

p. 550

A. The sentences below contain compound subjects. Write each sentence with the correct verb in parentheses.

1. Either Charlie Chaplin or Buster Keaton (is, are) a good subject for your report.
2. Actor and stuntman (was, were) Keaton.
3. Neither Chaplin nor Keaton (was, were) successful in sound films.
4. Director and musician (was, were) Chaplin.
5. Neither Keaton nor the Keystone Cops (is, are) going to avoid that open manhole.
6. Abbot and Costello (was, were) popular in movies and television.
7. The Three Stooges and the Little Rascals (is, are) my favorites.
8. Neither Sam nor his friends (is, are) staying up to watch that old movie.

B. Complete each sentence, using a present-tense verb.

9. Neither Sis nor I
10. The ham and eggs
11. Walking and running
12. Room and board
13. Odds and ends
14. Neither Mom nor Dad
15. Either the twins or I
16. The stress and strain
17. Pen and ink
18. Breakfast and dinner

Acknowledgments continued from page ii.

permission of Harper & Row, Publishers, Inc. **Unit 8** 410: Amon Carter Museum, Forth Worth. 413: Brian J. Miller/Nawrocki Stock Photos. 417: Culver Pictures. 419: © The Metropolitan Museum of Art, Bequest of Maria DeWitt Jesup, 1915. (15.30.59). 421: © 1982 Jack Vartoogian. 425: The Bettmann Archive. 435: Amon Carter Museum, Fort Worth. 430: Virginia Museum of Fine Arts, Richmond. 437: Sid Richardson Collection of Western Art. 438: North Wind Picture Archives. 443: National Museum of American Art, Smithsonian Institution, Washington, DC. Gift of Mrs. Joseph Harrison, Jr., o/c 29 × 24″. (1985.66.149). 447: *l.* National Gallery of Art, Washington, D.C. Gift of the Avalon Foundation; *r,* © The Metropolitan Museum of Art, Purchase Alfred N. Punnett Fund & George D. Pratt gift. 1934. (34.92). 449: Amon Carter Museum, Forth Worth. 450: Sid Richardson Collection of Western Art. 454: Dan De Wilde for SB&G. 459: From *Cowboys of the Wild West* by Russell Freedman. Copyright © 1985 by Russell Freedman. Reprinted by permission of Clarion Books/Ticknor & Fields, a Houghton Mifflin company. **Unit 9** 483: Walt Disney Productions, Courtesy Kobal Collections. 498: By kind permission of Barbara Edwards, daughter of Arthur Rackham. 502, 505, 516: From *The Hobbit,* fiftieth anniversary edition, by J.R.R. Tolkien. Copyright © 1966 by J.R.R. Tolkien. Reprinted by permission of Houghton Mifflin Co. 520: Dan De Wilde for SB&G. 525: Reproduced by permission of Macmillan Publishing Company from *The Grey King* by Susan Cooper, cover illustration by David Wiesner. Text copyright © 1975 Susan Cooper. Cover illustration copyright © 1986 David Wiesner. **Unit 10** 541–544: The Granger Collection. 545: *t.* Phedon Salou/Shostal Associates; *b.* The Granger Collection. 547: Blumebild/H. Armstrong Roberts. 549: Culver Pictures. 551: *t.* The Granger Collection; *b.* © George Jones III/Photo Researchers, Inc. 556: Neue Pinakothek Munchen. 569: Illustration by Leo and Diane Dillon from *A Fair Wind for Troy* by Doris Gates. Illustration copyright © 1976 by Viking Penguin Inc. All rights reserved. Reprinted by permission of Viking Penguin, a division of Penguin Books, USA, Inc. **Back Matter** 592: Vasily Kandinsky, ''Calm,'' 1926. Collection of Solomon R. Guggenheim Museum, New York. Photo by Carmelo Guadagno. **Dictionary** 601: Dallas and John Heaton/TSW-Click/Chicago. 602: *l.* The American Red Cross; *r.* The Bettmann Archive. 603: *l.* Houghton Library, Harvard University; *r.* National Portrait Gallery, Smithsonian Institution, Washington DC. 604: *l.* Historical Pictures Service, Chicago; *r.* Jerry Blow for SB&G, 605: *l.* Dallas and John Heaton/TSW-Click/Chicago; *r.* Philadelphia Museum of Art; George W. Elkins Collection. 606: *l.* © Copyright Arnold Newman; *r.* The Johns Hopkins Institute of the History of Medicine. 607: Worcester Art Museum, Massachusetts. 608: *l.* Library of Congress. Courtesy of the Institute for Intercultural Studies, Inc; *r.* George Gerster/Comstock. 609: *l.* Private Collection, photograph by Charles Phillips; *r.* Werner Forman Archive. 610: Jimmy Rudnick/The Stock Market of NY. 611: *l.* Copyright 1939 Loew's Inc. Ren. 1966 Metro-Goldwyn-Mayer, Inc. Courtesy Kobal Collection; *r.* Department of Defense Still Media Depository. Every effort has been made to locate the original sources. If any errors have occurred the publisher can be notified and corrections will be made.

Permissions: We wish to thank the following authors, publishers, agents, corporations, and individuals for their permission to reprint copyrighted materials. Page 28: Excerpt from *Constance: A Story of Early Plymouth* by Patricia Clapp. Copyright © 1968 by Patricia Clapp. Used by permission of Lothrop, Lee & Shepard Books (a division of William Morrow & Co.) Page 78: "Westward Voyage" Copyright 1947 Time Inc. Reprinted by permission from *Time*. Page 80: "Word from a Raft" Copyright 1947 Time Inc. Reprinted by permission from *Time*. Page 82: "From Raft to Reef" Courtesy of *Newsweek* magazine Page 144: Excerpt from *Barrio Boy* by Ernesto Galarza. © 1971 by the University of Notre Dame Press, Notre Dame, IN. Reprinted by permission. Page 206: "Vaccination drives for kids will take place around world" by Coretta Scott King. Reprinted by permission of The New York Times Syndicate. © 1987 The New York Times Syndicate. Page 268: "Acquainted with the Night" by Robert Frost. Reprinted from *The Poetry of Robert Frost*. Edited by Edward Connery Lathem, by permission of Henry Holt & Co., Inc. Copyright 1928 by Holt, Rinehart & Winston, Inc., and renewed 1956 by Robert Frost. "I May, I Might, I Must" by Marianne Moore. From *Collected Poems* by Marianne Moore. Copyright © 1959 by Marianne Moore. Copyright renewed © 1987 by the Estate of Marianne Moore. All rights reserved. Used by permission of Viking Penguin, Inc. Page 269: "Computer" by Gwendolyn Brooks. © 1983 by Gwendolyn Brooks Blakely. Reprinted by permission of the author. "The Great Figure" by William Carlos Williams. From *Collected Poems 1909–1939* Volume I. Copyright 1938 by New Directions Publishing Corp. Reprinted by permission of New Directions Publishing Corp. Page 274: From "The Descent of Winter" by William Carlos Williams. From *Collected Poems 1909–1939* Volume I. Copyright 1938 by New Directions Publishing Corp. Reprinted by permission of New Directions Publishing Corp. Page 276: "Dreams" by Langston Hughes. Copyright 1932 by Alfred A. Knopf, Inc., and renewed 1960 by Langston Hughes. Reprinted from *The Dream Keepers and Other Poems* by Langston Hughes, by permission of the publisher. Page 278: "Hope" by Langston Hughes. Copyright 1942 by Alfred A. Knopf, Inc., and renewed 1970 by Arna Bontemps and George Houston Bass. Reprinted from *Selected Poems of Langston Hughes*, by permission of the publisher. Page 277: "I Sang" from *Chicago Poems* by Carl Sandburg. Copyright 1916 by Holt, Rinehart & Winston, Inc. Renewed 1944 by Carl Sandburg. Reprinted by permission of Harcourt Brace Jovanovich, Inc. Page 278: "The Crossing" from *To Mix with Time, New and Selected Poems* by May Swenson. © 1963 by May Swenson. Reprinted by permission of the author. Page 291: "When Moonlight Falls" by Hilda Conkling. Reprinted by kind permission of Elsa Kruuse. Page 318: Excerpt from *North to the Orient* by Anne Morrow Lindbergh. Copyright 1935, 1963 by Anne Morrow Lindbergh. Reprinted by permission of Harcourt Brace Jovanovich, Inc. Page 372: "The Great Underground Army" by Marjorie Jackson. © 1981 by Marjorie Jackson. This article first appeared in *Cricket* Magazine. Reprinted by permission of the author. Page 383: Excerpted from *The World Book Encyclopedia*. © 1988 World Book, Inc. Page 434: "Two Artists of the Old West" by Elisabeth Godolphin. Reprinted from November 1982 issue of *Cobblestone* Magazine. Page 502: Excerpt from *The Hobbit* by J.R.R. Tolkien. Copyright © 1966 by J.R.R. Tolkien. Reprinted by permission of Houghton Mifflin Co. and Unwin Hyman, Ltd. Page 558: "Athene's City" from *Greek Myths* by Olivia Coolidge. Copyright 1949. Renewed 1977 by Olivia E. Coolidge. Reprinted by permission of Houghton Mifflin Co. Page 592: Excerpt from "Wassily Kandinsky." Excerpted from *The World Book Encyclopedia*. © 1988 World Book, Inc. Page 594: Excerpt from "United States of America." *The World Almanac & Book of Facts*, 1988 edition, copyright © Newspaper Enterprise Association, Inc., 1987, New York, NY 10166.

WRITER'S REFERENCE BOOK

Study Skills Lessons

Study Habits

1. **Listen carefully in class.** Make sure you understand what your teacher wants you to do for homework.
2. **Have your homework materials ready.** You will need such items as textbooks, pens, and a notebook.
3. **Study in the same place every day.** You should try to find a quiet and comfortable place where people will not interrupt you. There should be good lighting, a comfortable chair, and a desk or table. Do not have the TV or radio on while studying.
4. **Plan your study time.** Develop a daily study schedule. First decide on the best time of the day for studying, and study at that same time every day. Then plan exactly when you will study each of your subjects. Work on your most difficult subject first, before you become tired. Include time for chores, or household tasks, and recreation. Write your study schedule, using the one shown below as a guide.
5. **Set a goal or purpose each time you study.** If, for example, you were going to have a science test, your goal would be to review and understand the material that would be tested. Keep that goal in mind when you study. If you do, you will concentrate better.

Study Schedule
3:30 to 4:00 P.M. — chores
4:00 to 5:00 P.M. — sports, trumpet practice
5:00 to 5:30 P.M. — study math
5:30 to 6:00 P.M. — study social studies
6:00 to 7:00 P.M. — dinner and free time
7:00 to 7:30 P.M. — study English
7:30 to 8:00 P.M. — study science
8:00 to 10:00 P.M. — hobbies, reading, TV

Practice

1. Using the study schedule you wrote for item **4** above, write a goal for today for each subject that you listed.
2. What benefits could result from planning your study time?

Test-taking Tips

Before a Test

1. Prepare for a test by studying regularly. Briefly review your notes and your textbook each night. Don't wait until the night before a test to begin studying.
2. Prepare for an essay, or composition, test by thinking about what questions on important ideas from the textbook might be on the test. Write answers to these questions.
3. Prepare for an objective, or short-answer, test by listing important information that you will probably have to know. Write key facts in your notebook.
4. Get plenty of sleep the night before a test so that you will be able to think clearly.

During a Test

1. Read or listen to the test directions carefully. Be sure you know what you are to do and where and how you are to mark your answers.
2. Plan your time. Quickly read all the test questions. Spend more time on the questions that are worth the most points. Don't spend too much time on any one question. Save time to check your answers.
3. Answer the easy questions first. If you have a choice of answers, narrow your choice by eliminating all answers you know are wrong.
4. Some tests you take may include analogy questions. An analogy compares two things and shows how they are related. To answer an analogy question, determine the relationship between the first pair of items. Then complete the analogy so that the second pair of items has the same relationship.

   EXAMPLE: Circle the letter of the correct answer.

   play : scene :: year:

   (a.) day   b. costume   c. time   d. drama

Practice

1. List some possible benefits of studying on a regular daily basis.
2. What should your strategy be when faced with a choice of answers?
3. How should you solve an analogy question?

Parts of a Book

Many textbooks and other nonfiction books have five parts that either provide you with information you need or tell you where to find it. These five parts are the title page, copyright page, table of contents, index, and glossary.

The **title page** tells the title, author, publisher's name, and place of publication. It appears at the front of the book. On its reverse side is the **copyright page**, which gives the date of publication.

The **table of contents** also appears in the front of a book. It gives a general view of what the book contains. Look at the following excerpt from the table of contents of an American history textbook. Like most textbooks, it is organized into units, chapters, and lessons. The unit title, "The American Revolution," names the general area of study. Each chapter, such as "Colonists Protest British Rule," covers a part of this broad topic. The lessons within a chapter focus on specific topics or events, such as "The Declaration of Independence."

At the back of a nonfiction book is the **index**, which lists in alphabetical order all the important topics covered. Some of these main topics are followed by subtopic listings. All listings have page references.

The index is a useful tool for finding a specfic topic or piece of information. For example, if you want to see how much information a book has on "freedom of the press," you should look for that heading in the index. If there is no such heading, think of a synonym or related heading, such as "freedom of expression." Looking for this heading may lead to the information you need. You should check all the index listings on a particular topic.

At the end of an index entry, you may see the words *See also* followed by another topic. This is a **cross-reference** to a topic in the index that will give you additional information.

Many textbooks also contain a glossary at the back. The **glossary** is an alphabetical list of all the important terms used in the book, along with their specialized meanings. The glossary indicates the pages where the words are introduced or defined and often gives the pronunciation of difficult words. When you encounter a term in your reading that you do not understand or know the specialized meaning of, you can look it up in the glossary. Note the example below.

Glossary of Terms

tax (taks). Money paid to a ruler or government and spent on providing government services. p. 183.

teak (tēk). A hard wood used in building ships and furniture. p. 505.

technology (tek nol′ ə jē). The knowledge and skill that people use to make things. p. 494.

tertiary (tur′ shē er′ ē). Third in order or type.

Practice

Use this textbook to complete these exercises.

1. In which unit can you learn about nouns?
2. Use the Table of Contents to write the title of one lesson on pronouns.
3. Use the Index to find the listing *Direct object*. Write the page number on which the lesson begins.
4. Write two subtopics from the Index listing *Commas*.
5. On what page does the Index begin?
6. In which part of this book would you look to find the meaning of an important term used in the book?

Using the Library

There are two basic steps to finding a book in the library. The first is to get information from the card catalog, a file cabinet that contains information on all the books in the library. The second step is to use that information to find the book on a library shelf.

Some libraries now have computer terminals in addition to the card catalog to help you locate books and information. The listings seen on a computer terminal contain the same information as the card catalog, but the information is stored in a computer. Sometimes the computer listing will also tell whether or not the book is currently on loan from the library.

The Card Catalog   The information cards are in alphabetical order. A **guide label** on each drawer shows the first letter or letters of the cards it contains. **Guide cards** within each drawer point out important topics.

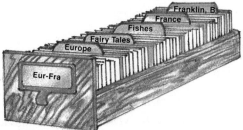

Suppose you are doing a report on Benjamin Franklin. Your teacher might recommend a book by Thomas Fleming on this subject. Because this is a nonfiction book, it has three cards in the catalog: a **title card**, an **author card**, and a **subject card**. (Fiction books have only title and author cards.) Each card gives the same information. Only the top line is different.

Look at the title, author, and subject cards shown below. The **call number** in the upper left-hand corner of each card matches the number on the spine or side of the book on the shelf. Use that number to find the book.

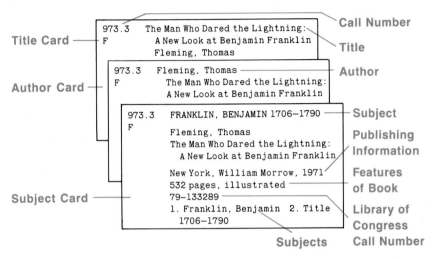

Title Card	Call Number
Author Card	Title
Subject Card	Author
	Subject
	Publishing Information
	Features of Book
	Library of Congress Call Number
	Subjects

973.3 F — The Man Who Dared the Lightning: A New Look at Benjamin Franklin — Fleming, Thomas

973.3 F — Fleming, Thomas — The Man Who Dared the Lightning: A New Look at Benjamin Franklin

973.3 F — FRANKLIN, BENJAMIN 1706–1790 — Fleming, Thomas — The Man Who Dared the Lightning: A New Look at Benjamin Franklin — New York, William Morrow, 1971 — 532 pages, illustrated — 79–133289 — 1. Franklin, Benjamin 1706–1790 2. Title

---

How to Find the Card You Need

1. A title card is filed under the first word of the title. If, however, the first word is *a, an*, or *the*, look up the second word.
2. For an author card, look up the author's last name.
3. All cards on the same subject will have the same subject heading. Under this heading you will find cards filed alphabetically by the authors' last names.
4. The first subject card may be a cross-reference card, which lists all other subject headings related to the topic. Look up these subject cards also.
5. If there is no subject heading for the topic you have in mind, think of related topics to look up.

Some books have special call numbers or listings.

Book Type: Call Number

1. **Fiction Book:** *F* + first letter of author's last name.
2. **Biography:** *B* or *92* + all or part of the last name of the person being written about.
3. **Reference Book:** *R* or *Ref* + call number.
4. **Short Story Collection:** *SC* + first letter of author's or editor's last name.
5. **Juvenile or Children's Book:** *J* + call number.

The Arrangement of Books The library is divided into several sections. Fiction, nonfiction, and reference books are grouped separately.

Nonfiction and reference books are arranged in numerical order by call numbers. The **Dewey decimal system** is a common method for assigning call numbers to books. All call numbers fall within ten subject areas.

Numbers	Subjects
000–099	**General Works** (reference works such as encyclopedias, atlases, almanacs)
100–199	**Philosophy** (includes psychology)
200–299	**Religion** (includes myths)
300–399	**Social Sciences** (includes education, government, folktales, fairy tales)
400–499	**Language** (includes the thesaurus, foreign language versions of the dictionary)
500–599	**Science** (includes mathematics, biology, chemistry, physics)
600–699	**Technology** (includes medicine, engineering, aviation, farming)
700–799	**The Arts** (includes painting, music, dance, theater, sports)
800–899	**Literature** (includes plays, poetry, essays, television scripts, but not fiction)
900–999	**History and Geography** (includes travel)

Each broad subject area is subdivided into more specific topics. For example, within the 900's the subdivision 970 is American history. Books about the Revolutionary period are in the further subdivision 973.3.

Each call number is followed by the initial of the author's last name. If there are several books with the same call number, they are shelved alphabetically.

Some libraries use the **Library of Congress system** to arrange books. It has a different combination of numbers and letters in its system of call numbers.

Practice

A. Write whether you would look for a title, author, or subject card to find each of the following. Then write the word under which the card is alphabetized.

1. A book of poems by Victor Hernandez Cruz
2. *The Dictionary of American Biography*
3. Books about the U.S. Constitutional Convention
4. Books about the sign language used by the deaf
5. *A View from the Rim: Willis Reed on Basketball*

B. For each book title, write the number range under which it would appear in the Dewey decimal system.

EXAMPLE: *Plays for American Holidays*
ANSWER: 800–899

6. *Religions of Asia*
7. *Travels Along the Nile River*
8. *Tall Tales from the Old West*
9. *Learning to Draw Horses and Dogs*
10. *Wildflowers of America*
11. *Information Please Almanac*
12. *Weather Forecasting*
13. *Speak French in Thirty Days*
14. *Build Your Own Computer*
15. *Ideals to Live By*

C. Go to the card catalog or computer terminal and write a title, author, and call number for each of the following.

16. A biography of Amelia Earhart
17. A book about modern ballet
18. A book of tall tales
19. A book about careers in aviation
20. A book of poems
21. A book about basketball
22. A collection of short stories
23. A book about conservation
24. A cookbook
25. A book about spaceflight

Encyclopedia

An **encyclopedia** is a collection of articles that give detailed information on many subjects. Encyclopedia articles are arranged in alphabetical order within books, or volumes. Guide words at the top of each page show the first and last entries on each page. Cross-references in an article (for example, **Expressionism** below) refer the reader to other related articles in the encyclopedia.

The first place to look for your topic in an encyclopedia is the index. In a multivolume encyclopedia, the index is usually the last volume. The index lists all entries in alphabetical order with their volume and page numbers. Read the article below from the *World Book Encyclopedia*.

Kandinsky, *kan DIHN skee,* **Wassily,** *VAS uh lee* (1866–1944), a Russian artist, is generally considered the first abstract painter. An abstract painting has no recognizable subject.

Kandinsky believed that painting — like music — is primarily a form of personal expression, rather than a way to tell a story or express an idea. His ideas on abstract painting appear in his book *On the Spiritual in Art* (1912). His paintings and theories made him a forerunner of the abstract expressionist movement that thrived in New York City during the 1940's and 1950's.

Kandinsky was born in Moscow and moved to Germany in 1896. He painted his first abstract pictures in 1910. In 1911, Kandinsky and the German artist Franz Marc founded an expressionist art movement that was called *Der Blaue Reiter* (The Blue Rider). See **Expressionism**.

From 1910 to about 1920, Kandinsky painted with bright, pure colors in a free, spontaneous style. *Little Pleasures, No. 174*, one of his works from this period, is reproduced in color in the **Painting** article. Kandinsky lived in Russia from 1914 to 1921 and then returned to Germany. He taught the theory of form at the Bauhaus school of design in Germany from 1922 to 1933 (see **Bauhaus**). During this period, Kandinsky painted carefully calculated abstract compositions of geometric shapes.   Gregory Battcock

Vasily Kandinsky. "Calm," 1926. Collection, Solomon R. Guggenheim Museum, New York.

Practice

1. List one reason why Kandinsky is considered an important painter in the history of art.
2. What is an abstract painting?
3. Where in the encyclopedia would you look to learn more about the Bauhaus school of design?

Atlas

An **atlas** is a book of maps. It may contain maps of cities, states, countries, and continents. Some atlases contain special maps, such as maps of altitude, climate, population, or even vegetation and mineral resources. Atlas maps are usually more detailed than those in encyclopedias. A **key** or **legend** explains the map's markings. The special map below shows average January temperatures. Notice the map key, or legend, labeled *The United States: Average January Temperatures*. Each color in the key represents a temperature range in degrees Fahrenheit (°F) and in degrees Celsius (°C).

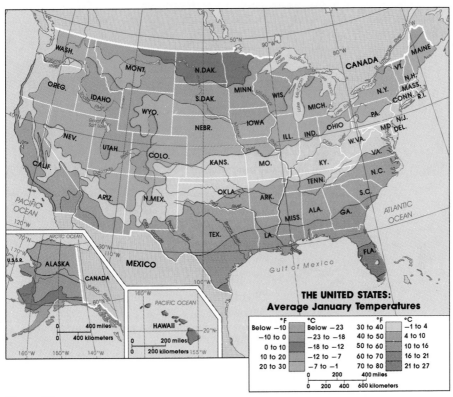

Practice

Use the map to answer **1** to **5**. Give both °F and °C.

1. What is Kentucky's average January temperature?
2. Which state — Utah or Rhode Island — is colder?
3. What is the temperature in the coldest part of Alaska?
4. What two states have the warmest January temperatures?
5. What state has the widest range of temperatures?

Almanac

Almanacs are published yearly and contain the latest facts and figures in chart, table, or list form. When you need to answer a specific question on current events, personalities, sports, population figures, or other topics, consult an almanac. Use the almanac index to locate a subject. The almanac article below gives key facts about the United States of America.

United States of America

People: Population (1986 est.): 240,856,000. Age distrib. (%): 0–14: 21.7; 15–59: 61.8; 60+: 16.5 Pop. density: 66 per sq. mi. **Urban** (1980): 79.2%.

Defense: 6.4% of GNP (1984).

Economy: Minerals: Coal, copper, lead, molybdenum, phosphates, uranium, bauxite, gold, iron, mercury, nickel, potash, silver, tungsten, zinc. **Crude oil reserves** (1985): 27 bin. bbls. **Arable land:** 21%. **Meat prod.** (1985): cattle: 105.4 min.; pigs: 52.2 min.; sheep: 9.9 min. **Fish catch** (1985): 2.8 min. metric tons. **Electricity prod.** (1985): 2,469 bln. kwh. **Crude steel prod.** (1985): 79.3 min. metric tons.

Finance: Gross national product (1985): $3,855 bln. **Per capita income** (1985): $13,451. **Imports** (1986): $387.0 bln.; partners: Can. 19%, Jap. 20%, Mex. 6%. **Exports** (1986): $217.3 bln; partners: Can. 22%, Jap. 10%, Mex. 6%, UK 5%. **Tourists** (1985): receipts $11 bln. **International reserves less gold** (Mar. 1987): $37.7 bln. **Gold:** 262.5 mln. oz. t. **Consumer prices** (change in 1986): 1.9%.

Transport: Railway traffic (1985): 15.5 bln. passenger-km; 1.3 bln. net ton-km. **Motor vehicles:** in use (1985): 130 mln. passenger cars, 39 mln. comm. vehicles. **Civil aviation** (1985): 478 bln. passenger-km; 11.5 bln. freight ton-km.

Communications: Television sets: 145 mln. in use (1985). **Radios:** 480 min. in use (1985). **Telephones in use** (1984): 134 mln. **Daily newspaper circ.** (1984): 267 per 1,000 pop.

Health: Life expectancy at birth (1986): 71.5 male; 78.5 female. Births (per 1,000 pop. 1985): 15.5 **Deaths** (per 1,000 pop. 1985): 8.7. **Natural increase** (1986): 6%. **Hospital beds** (1985): 1.3 mln. **Physicians** (1985): 527,900. **Infant mortality** (per 1,000 live births 1986): 10.4.

Major International Organizations: UN (GATT, IMF, WHO, FAO), OAS, NATO, OECD.

Education (1987): **Literacy:** 99%.

Practice

Use the almanac article to answer these questions.

1. Which of the following age groups in the United States is larger: 0–14 years or 60+ years?

2. By what percent did consumer prices change in 1986?

3. What are there more of in the U.S.: phones or TV's?

4. How many years more than the average male does the average female live in the United States?

5. What percent of the U.S. population is urban?

Readers' Guide

Periodicals are newspapers and magazines that are published at regular intervals, such as daily, weekly, or monthly. If you need magazine articles to complete research for a report, refer to the *Readers' Guide to Periodical Literature*. References to articles are arranged alphabetically by subject and by author. Large entries are divided by subheadings. Some entries have cross-references (marked *See* or *See also*) that refer to related articles. When you know what periodical you want, fill out a request form and the librarian will give you either the periodical itself or a reproduction of it from microfilm.

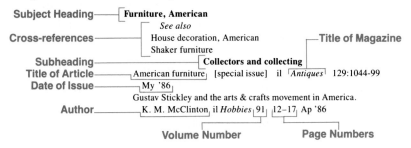

Abbreviations in the entry include *il* for *illustrated*, *My* for *May*, and *Ap* for *April*.

Practice

Use this *Readers' Guide* entry to answer the questions.

> **Uranus (Planet)**
> *See also*
> Space flight — Voyager flights
> **Atmosphere**
> A place called Uranus [Voyager mission] J. K. Beatty, il *Sky Telesc*
> 71:333–7 Ap '86
> **Photographs and photography**
> Uranus! J. Schefter. il *Pop Sci* 228:79–81+ My '86
> **Ring system**
> A place called Uranus [Voyager mission] J. K. Beatty. il *Sky Telesc*
> 71:333–7 Ap '86
> **Satellites**
> New moons [discoveries of Uranus' moons by S. Synnott] R. Schultz. il
> *Omni* 8:34+ My '86
> *Photographs and photography*
> Moons of Uranus [Voyager images] R. Schultz il *Omni* 8:92–9 My '86

1. Under which heading would you find general articles about the Voyager flights?
2. Which article is about photographs of Uranus's moons?
3. In what magazine does the article appear?
4. On what page does the article begin?

Outlining

An **outline** is a plan to follow when writing a composition, a speech, or a report. It organizes material in a logical way into main ideas, supporting ideas, and supporting details. While doing research, you will have compiled note cards to use in an outline.

Your note cards should be arranged so that all the information on each main idea or topic is together. Look over the main topics and decide on the order in which you will present them. Next, examine the cards for each main topic and decide which subtopics to include and in what order they should be presented. Rearrange the note cards accordingly. Finally, choose the supporting details to be used under each subtopic. Arrrange these details in order.

Now you are ready to turn your note cards into an outline. Each main idea or topic in your notes becomes a main topic of the outline. All main topics will be indicated by Roman numerals. Subtopics will be noted by letters, and supporting details will be indicated by Arabic numerals.

Decide whether to write a **sentence outline** or a **topic outline**. A sentence outline is written in full sentences. A topic outline is in words or phrases.

Follow the guidelines below for writing an outline.

How to Write an Outline

1. Center the title above the outline.
2. Every level of the outline must have at least two items (**I** and **II**, **A** and **B**, **1** and **2**).
3. Put a period after each numeral and letter.
4. Indent each new level of the outline.
5. All items of one kind (Roman numerals, capital letters, Arabic numerals) should line up with each other.
6. Capitalize the first word of each item.

Study the sample topic outline on the next page. Notice how it conforms to the rules in the chart above. All topic or sentence outlines have exactly the same structure. They follow the same pattern for lettering, numbering, and indenting.

Benjamin Franklin — Scientist and Inventor

I. Experiments with electricity
   A. Studied nature of electricity
   B. Discovered lightning equals electricity
   C. Invented lightning rod

II. Other scientific work
   A. Inventions
      1. Bifocal glasses
      2. Franklin stove
      3. Daylight saving time
   B. Scientific studies
      1. Charted Gulf Stream
      2. Worked on soil improvement

III. Importance as a scientist
   A. Scientific honors
   B. Writings translated into other languages
   C. What experts say about him

Practice

A. Refer to the same topic outline above to write the answers to the following questions.

   1. How many main topics are there?
   2. How many subtopics does the last main topic have?
   3. What main topic has both subtopics and details?
   4. How many details are included under the subtopic "Inventions"?
   5. What is the title of the report?

B. Choose a game, sport, or other activity that you know how to do well. Following the guidelines on page 596, prepare a topic outline on how to perform the activity. Use three or more main headings and appropriate subtopics and adequate supporting details in your outline.

Using a Dictionary

A dictionary can help you improve your skills in spelling, pronouncing, understanding, and using words. The entries below are from the Dictionary of Knowledge, which begins on page 600.

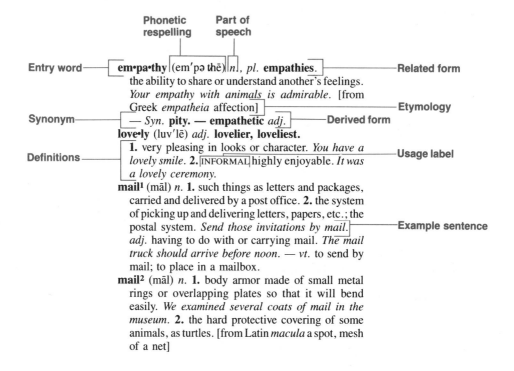

Entry word   This shows the spelling and syllable divisions of a word.

Phonetic respelling   This shows how a word is pronounced. It is given in symbols that stand for certain sounds. For example, the symbol ē stands for the long e sound heard in *keep*. The Pronunciation Key on page 600 tells the sound for each symbol. Stress marks (′) indicate syllables that are spoken with more force.

Part of speech   This label is abbreviated, such as *adv.* for adverb.

Related form   Plurals of nouns, principal parts of verbs, and comparatives and superlatives of adjectives and adverbs are shown when the spelling of a base word changes.

Etymology This is a word history, and it appears in brackets.

Synonym This is a word that has a similar meaning to the entry word. Its label is abbreviated *Syn.* Antonyms, labeled *Ant.,* are given for some entry words.

Derived forms These are related forms of the entry word that are made by adding a suffix to the base word that changes its part of speech.

Definitions The meanings are grouped by part of speech and numbered.

Usage label This label identifies a word or word meaning that is used only in certain situations.

Example sentence This shows a word in use and clarifies meaning.

Homographs These are words that are spelled alike but have different meanings and origins. They have separate entries followed by superscripts such as ^{1} and ^{2}.

Practice

A. Write the answer to each question, using the entries on page 598.

1. Which meaning of *lovely* is used only in informal speech?
2. Which entry words are homographs?
3. Which word derives from the Greek word for *affection*?
4. How many meanings are given for **mail**^{1} as a noun? As a verb?
5. Which syllable of *empathy* is spoken with most force?

B. Use the Dictionary of Knowledge to answer the questions below.

6. Which word means "terrible": *megalithic* or *dire*?
7. What part of speech is the word *pontoon*?
8. Which word is spelled incorrectly and how should it be spelled: *archaeological, buoyant, luminery, shipwright*?
9. What is the British spelling of the word *vapor*?
10. Which syllable is stressed in the word *belligerence*?

C. 11–13. Use the Dictionary of Knowledge to write a word quiz for classmates. Write three questions like those in **Practice B**.

Dictionary of Knowledge

This Dictionary of Knowledge has two kinds of entries, **word entries** and **encyclopedic entries**. Many of the word entries in this dictionary are taken from the literature pieces found throughout this book. You might use these entries to help you understand the meanings of words. You will use the encyclopedic entries in two "Apply" sections in each unit.

Word Entries ♦ These entries are just like the ones found in the ordinary dictionaries you are familiar with. Each entry includes such elements as pronunciation respellings, definitions, and example sentences.

Encyclopedic Entries ♦ These entries resemble encyclopedia articles. Each entry provides interesting information about a particular topic or person.

Abbreviations Used in This Dictionary

adj.	adjective	n.	noun	Syn.	Synonym
adv.	adverb	pl.	plural	vi.	intransitive verb
Ant.	Antonym	prep.	preposition	vt.	transitive verb
conj.	conjunction	pron.	pronoun		

Full pronunciation key* The pronunciation of each word is shown just after the word, in this way: **abbreviate** (ə brē′ vē āt).

The letters and signs used are pronounced as in the words below.

The mark ′ is placed after a syllable with a primary or heavy accent as in the example above.

The mark ′ after a syllable shows a secondary or lighter accent, as in **abbreviation** (ə brē′ vē ā′ shən).

SYMBOL	KEY WORDS	SYMBOL	KEY WORDS	SYMBOL	KEY WORDS	SYMBOL	KEY WORDS
a	ask, fat	ô	law, horn	o in collect		t	top, hat
ā	ape, date	oi	oil, point	u in focus		v	vat, have
ä	car, father	͝o͝o	look, pull	b	bed, dub	w	will, always
		o͞o	ooze, tool	d	did, had	y	yet, yard
e	elf, ten	yo͞o	unite, cure	f	fall, off	z	zebra, haze
er	berry, care	yo͞o	cute, few	g	get, dog		
ē	even, meet	ou	out, crowd	h	he, ahead		
				j	joy, jump	ch	chin, arch
		u	up, cut	k	kill, bake	ng	ring, singer
i	is, hit	ur	fur, fern	l	let, ball	sh	she, dash
ir	mirror, here			m	met, trim	th	thin, truth
ī	ice, fire	ə	a in ago	n	not, ton	th	then, father
			e in agent	p	put, tap	zh	s in pleasure
o	lot, pond		e in father	r	red, dear		
ō	open, go		i in unity	s	sell, pass	′	as in (ā′b'l)

*Pronunciation key adapted from *Webster's New World Dictionary, Basic School Edition*, Copyright © 1983 by Simon & Schuster, Inc. Reprinted by permission.

— A —

Ab•o•rig•i•nes   (ab′ ə rij′ ə nēz)

Aborigines are the first people known to have lived in any certain place. Australian Aborigines, for example, lived in Australia long before the arrival of European people.

Anthropologists believe that some aboriginal ways of life are similar to those of prehistoric people. Aborigines once lived by hunting animals, gathering roots and vegetables, and raising livestock.

Australian Aborigines are often termed "bushmen" because they live in Australia's harsh Outback, or sparsely settled bush country. The Aborigines there usually build their homes of thatch or use portable shelters, such as tents. Their skills at survival in the most arid regions are known worldwide. They can follow animal tracks for days when hunting and can locate underground plants that hold precious water during the dry season. The Australian Aborigines also have complex languages and social structures.

ale•wife   (āl′ wīf′) *n., pl.* **alewives. 1.** a woman who keeps an alehouse. *The alewife cooked a beef stew.* **2.** a species of food fish related to the shad.

an•thro•pol•o•gist   (an′ thrə pol′ ə jist) *n.* a person trained or expert in anthropology. *The anthropologists studied rare fossils.*

an•thro•pol•o•gy   (an′ thrə pol′ ə jē)

Anthropology is the study of human beings, both their physical and cultural characteristics. Some anthropologists study human physical development through the ages; others focus on similarities, differences, and achievements of various cultures.

A physical anthropologist might try to discover where American Indians came from by studying fossil remains of their prehistoric relatives in Asia. Similarities in such characteristics as bone structure and height allow scientists to trace people's migrations.

A cultural anthropologist might study the same question by comparing the tools, houses, or art (cultural things) of ancient tribes in Asia. Similarities among the groups analyzed might suggest that certain groups are specifically related.

Both kinds of anthropologists study various groups of people to determine their similarities and differences. Evidence and results of tests in the laboratories can then be exchanged on an international basis. Anthropology thus contributes to peaceful relations by providing understanding of different cultures around the world.

ar•chae•o•log•i•cal   (är′ kē ə läj′ i k′l) *adj.* of or having to do with archaeology, or the study of ancient times and ancient peoples. *She made important archaeological discoveries.* Also, **archeological.** — **archaeologically** *adv.*

ar•chae•ol•o•gist   (är′ kē ol′ ə jist) *n.* a person trained or expert in archaeology. *The archaeologists showed us the vases.* Also, **archeologist.**

a fat	er care	ī bite, fire	oi oil	u up	th thin	ə = a in ago
ā ape	ē even	o lot	oo look	ur fur	*th* then	e *in* agent
ä car, father	i hit	ō go	o͞o tool	ch chin	zh leisure	i *in* unity
e ten	ir here	ô law, horn	ou out	sh she	ŋ ring	o *in* collect
						u *in* focus

Dictionary of Knowledge

⎯⎯⎯⎯⎯ **B** ⎯⎯⎯⎯⎯

bal•sa (bôl′ sə) *n.* **1.** a tropical American tree that has very lightweight wood, used in making airplane models. **2.** a raft produced from this tree's wood. *The balsas of the ancient Peruvians were sturdy.*

bar•ri•o (bär′ ē ō) *n., pl.* **barrios.** a district or subdivision of a city or town, especially one with Spanish-speaking residents. *The festival in the barrio was fun.* [from Arabic *barri* rural]

Bar•ton, Cla•ra (bär′ t'n, klar′ ə) 1821–1912
The founder of the American Red Cross, Clara Barton, was known as the "Angel of the Battlefield." Barton earned this name during the Civil War. She had been working in the Patent Office in Washington, D.C., and had seen the suffering of soldiers wounded in battle or in need of food and supplies. Barton organized her own relief efforts. She treated wounded soldiers on the battlefields and led searches for missing soldiers.

As her fame grew, so did her power to help others. Many people rallied to her cause, and many lives were saved because of her immediate treatment of wounded soldiers. Soon an organization was needed, which Barton established on the model of the International Red Cross in Switzerland.

Bau•cis and Phi•le•mon (bô′ sis *and* fi lē′ mən)
A poor old wife named Baucis and her husband, Philemon, lived in a lowly thatched hut in a small village in the Phrygian countryside in Asia. They were farmers who could barely produce enough for their own needs. One day two wanderers seeking shelter found all the houses except theirs closed and locked against them. Baucis and Philemon welcomed the strangers and offered them food and rest.

As the couple laid out their best but humble food, they noticed that the pitcher always remained full, as if by magic. Then the aged couple realized that their guests were actually the gods Jupiter and Mercury in disguise.

The gods sent a flood, destroying all the surrounding houses, to punish the wicked neighbors for their lack of hospitality to strangers. The gods led Baucis and Philemon to the top of a hill. To the old couple's amazement, a stately temple appeared, and Jupiter appointed them as its attendants.

At their death many years later, Jupiter changed Philemon into an oak tree and Baucis into a linden tree so that they would always be together.

bed•lam (bed′ ləm) *n.* a place or condition of noise and confusion. *The game turned into a scene of bedlam.*

bel•lig•er•ence (bə lij′ər əns) *n.* an aggressive or warlike attitude, nature, or quality. *Their belligerence brought about a crisis.* — *Syn.* **hostility.** — *Ant.* **friendliness.**

buoy•ant (boi′ənt) *adj.* **1.** able to float or rise in liquid or air. *The small raft seems quite buoyant.* **2.** lively and cheerful. — **buoyantly** *adv.*

⎯⎯⎯⎯⎯ **C** ⎯⎯⎯⎯⎯

cav•al•ry•man (kav′'l rē mən) *n., pl.* **cavalrymen.** a soldier who fights on horseback. *The modern cavalryman often drives a vehicle.*

char (chär) *vt.* **charred, charring. 1.** to burn or scorch slightly. *The fire charred everything.* **2.** to change to charcoal by burning.

Dictionary of Knowledge

com·mit·ment (kə mit′ mənt) *n.* **1.** a serious promise or pledge. *He made a commitment to the Peace Corps.* **2.** official consignment as to a prison. **3.** a financial liability undertaken.

———————— **D** ————————

des·ul·to·ry (des′ ′l tôr′ē) *adj.* **1.** aimlessly passing from one subject or thing to another. *Their desultory conversation continued.* **2.** incidental. — *Syn.* **random**. — *Ant.* **purposeful**. — **desultorily** *adv.*

Dick·in·son, Em·i·ly (dik′in s′n, em′ ′l ē) 1830–1886

Emily Dickinson is recognized today as one of America's greatest poets. She was born and died in Amherst, Massachusetts, a small town with several universities nearby. There the "Belle of Amherst" lived what scholars call an uneventful life. However, her poems, which she wrote secretly, reveal her passionate intelligence and her doubts about traditional ways of thinking.

Only seven of her poems were published during her lifetime, all anonymously. Then after her death her family discovered nearly 1,800 poems in her desk, bureau, and boxes. They were left in packets tied with ribbons. The first volume of her poems was published four years after her death, and the poems have been acclaimed and republished ever since. Read the following poem by Emily Dickinson.

> To make a prairie it takes a clover
>   and one bee,
> And revery.
> The revery alone will do,
> If bees are few.

Emily Dickinson's papers, book, and desk. Courtesy of the Houghton Library, Harvard University.

dire (dīr) *adj.* **direr, direst. 1.** extreme or terrible. *She lived in dire poverty.* **2.** calling for quick action; urgent.

Dis·ney, Walt (diz′nē, wôlt′) 1901–1966

Born in Chicago, Walt Disney began his artistic career as a maker of advertising films in Midwestern cities. After 1919 he became interested in creating his own movie cartoons, and he moved to California in 1923.

There Disney produced and promoted cartoons. He became successful in 1928 when he created cartoons featuring Mickey Mouse. Disney used both sound and color creatively and introduced such wonderful characters as Donald Duck, Pluto, Dumbo, Bambi, and Goofy. His *Snow White and the Seven Dwarfs* was the first full-length cartoon film and became one of the most popular movies ever made.

Walt Disney portrait, Samuel Johnson Woolf, 1938 National Portrait Gallery, Smithsonian Institution, Washington, D.C.

Disney and his creations became world famous. His career ranged from making cartoons, television specials, and films to building the Disneyland amusement park in California and Walt Disney World in Florida.

———————— **E** ————————

Ear·hart, A·me·lia (er′härt, ə mēl′yə) 1898–1937

In 1932, Amelia Earhart became the first woman to fly an airplane solo across the Atlantic Ocean.

a	fat	er	care	ī	bite, fire	oi	oil	u	up	th	thin	ə = a *in* ago
ā	ape	ē	even	o	lot	oo	look	ur	fur	th	then	e *in* agent
ä	car, father	i	hit	ō	go	ōo	tool	ch	chin	zh	leisure	i *in* unity
e	ten	ir	here	ô	law, horn	ou	out	sh	she	ŋ	ring	o *in* collect
												u *in* focus

She was the first woman to fly solo from Hawaii to the United States mainland in 1935.

Her first record-setting flight was as the first woman passenger on a flight across the Atlantic. She then made flying her career and strove to set more records. Earhart was the first woman to receive the Distinguished Flying Cross. She wrote two books in which she described her experiences.

In 1937, Earhart was attempting a round-the-world flight when she and her copilot disappeared in the Pacific Ocean between New Guinea and Howland Island. Numerous books have been written to try to explain what happened to them, but no one has solved the mystery conclusively.

ea•sel (ē′z′l) *n.* an upright frame for holding an artist's canvas during work. *Jim worked at his easel all day long.*

eel (ēl) *n.* a snakelike fish with a long, slippery body.—*vi.* **eeled, eeling.** to move swiftly and smoothly like an eel. *She eeled past us.*

em•pa•thy (em′pə thē) *n., pl.* **empathies.** the ability to share or understand another's feelings. *Your empathy with animals is admirable.* [from Greek *empatheia* affection] — *Syn.* **pity.** — **empathetic** *adj.*

en•vi•ron•men•tal sci•ence
(in vī′rən men′t′l sī′əns)
There are dozens of very different careers available in the environmental sciences. In these careers, people work to protect living things by controlling pollution and the careless use of natural resources. Chemists, biologists, industrial and traffic engineers, oceanographers, agricultural researchers, and various kinds of technicians find jobs in the environmental sciences.

The problems of pollution and the efforts to protect the environment are being explored in many different ways. A chemist may travel with a biologist as they take samples of water from ponds to test for pollutants. Then both may work with technicians in the laboratory to complete the study or work with engineers to improve machines that detect the pollutants. In another area an industrial hygienist measures noise levels in a workplace.

Government agencies, such as the Environmental Protection Agency, employ hundreds of people — some of whom work to enforce environmental protection laws.

e•rad•i•cate (i rad′ə kāt) *vt.* **eradicated, eradicating.** to wipe out completely or remove at the source. *Doctors have eradicated smallpox.* [from Latin *e* - out + *radix* root] — *Syn.* **exterminate.** — **eradication** *n.*

——————————— **F** ———————————

fen (fen) *n.* a swamp or marshland. *Mosquitoes often breed in fens.*

fort•night (fôrt′nīt) *n.* a British word for a period of two weeks. *They spent a fortnight in the islands.*

——————————— **G** ———————————

Great Wall of Chi•na (grāt′ wôl′ uv chī′nə)
The Great Wall extends for hundreds of miles along China's northern borders. Work on the wall

began about 221 B.C., after Ch'in Shih-huang-ti, the first emperor, united the vast country under his rule. Each state had its own section of the wall, and Shih-huang joined these sections and extended them.

His forced laborers built nearly 1,200 miles of the wall's length as a defense against invaders. Watchtowers were built at regular intervals. In some places, six horses could trot along the top, side by side.

Later, during the Ming dynasty (1368–1644), the wall was repaired and extended, following courses of rivers and going up and down the sides of mountains and valleys.

Today the wall averages 25 feet in height and is 15 to 30 feet thick at the base. Since 1949, sections of the wall have been restored and are open to visitors. The Great Wall has become a major tourist attraction and is said to be visible to astronauts from outer space.

grin•go (griṅg′ gō) *n.* in Latin America, a foreigner, especially of English or American origin.

———————— **H** ————————

ham (ham) *n.* **1.** a type of pork meat. **2.** an awkward or showy actor. *Al is such a ham onstage.* **3.** an amateur radio operator. *Hams communicated news after the disastrous storm.*

helm (helm) *n.* **1.** the wheel or tiller by which a ship is steered. **2.** the position of a leader. *A new president has taken the helm.* **3.** a short form of *helmet*, a soldier's protective head covering. *The helms of the knights gleamed in the sun.*

Ho•mer, Wins•low (hō′mər, winz′lō) 1836–1910

Winslow Homer was an outstanding American painter and graphic artist, most famous for his realistic paintings of the sea. He was born in Boston and at eighteen was apprenticed to a lithographer, one who makes pictures or prints. By 1859 he was making a living as an illustrator for *Harper's Weekly* magazine in New York City. *Harper's* sent Homer to several battlefields of the Civil War so that he could illustrate what he saw at the front lines for magazine articles.

When he later began his oil paintings and watercolors, Homer focused on scenes of American country life. He lived in Europe for some time, after which there was a great transformation of his talent. His works became bolder and fresher of vision. In addition, he used color in more vigorous ways.

Finally Homer settled in Maine, and the sea, its sailors, and marine life became his chief subjects. *The Life Line, Eight Bells,* and *The Fog Warning* reflect his sensitive and powerful imagination, his eye for detail, and his bold sense of design.

Life Line, Winslow Homer, 1884
Philadelphia Museum of Art: George W. Elkins Collection

a fat	**er** care	**ī** bite, fire	**oi** oil	**u** up·	**th** thin	ə = a *in* ago
ā ape	**ē** even	**o** lot	**oo** look	**ur** fur	**th** then	e *in* agent
ä car, father	**i** hit	**ō** go	**ōō** tool	**ch** chin	**zh** leisure	i *in* unity
e ten	**ir** here	**ô** law, horn	**ou** out	**sh** she	**ṅg** ring	o *in* collect
						u *in* focus

Hughes, Lang·ston (hyo͞oz,′ laṅg′ stən) 1902–1967

Langston Hughes was a black writer, chiefly a poet, but he also wrote fiction, plays, and autobiographical sketches. He was a leader of the Harlem Renaissance, a flowering of black literature in the 1920s.

He settled in Harlem in New York City and wrote about the life of its people. There he began to experiment with writing forms and styles. He wrote of his early life in his first book of poems, *The Weary Blues*. Some of Hughes's poetry was influenced by jazz and blues rhythms. Many of his poems have been set to music. Hughes traveled widely, reading his poems in public in a highly dramatic style.

© Copyright Arnold Newman

I

im·mu·ni·za·tion (im′yə nə zā′shən) *n.* the act of giving protection from a certain disease, as by a vaccine. *Immunization against measles is very important for everyone.*

in·duc·tion (in duk′ shən) *n.* **1.** the act of bringing someone into a membership. *His induction into the army takes place soon.* **2.** the act of coming to a general conclusion based on particular facts; also, the conclusion reached. *The process of induction stimulated her.* — **inductive** *adj.*

in·fan·try·man (in′fən trē mən) *n., pl.* **infantrymen.** a soldier who fights on foot. *The infantryman trained diligently.*

J

Jen·ner, Ed·ward (jen′ər, ed′wərd) 1749–1823

Edward Jenner was an English doctor and naturalist who discovered vaccination for the prevention of smallpox. He received his M.D. degree in 1792 after many years of training with outstanding doctors and in English hospitals.

Jenner developed his ideas about vaccination slowly over many years. By the 1780s he was already researching a popular belief that some people who had had cowpox could later resist infection from smallpox, a related disease. He discovered that there were two types of cowpox, only one of which protected against smallpox.

In 1796, Jenner's research and strong belief in his own theories brought success. In May, Jenner innoculated a young boy with cowpox. Then in July he innoculated the boy with smallpox. The boy was protected against smallpox. Jenner published information about this vital discovery in 1798.

In 1802 he received recognition from his medical peers as well as funding for further research from the government. His successes led him to predict that vaccination would someday wipe out smallpox, which had taken heavy tolls on human life throughout history. The World Health Organization has announced that the disease is now believed to have been eradicated.

Edward Jenner portrait, John Rafael Smith, 1800. The Johns Hopkins Institute of the History of Medicine.

K

kir·tle (kur′ t'l) *n.* **1.** a man's tunic or coat. **2.** a woman's dress or skirt. — *vt.* **kirtled, kirtling.** to cover or enwrap, as in a kirtle. *She kirtled her skirt around her ankles.*

L

limn·er (lim′ər, lim′nər)

A limner was a traveling portrait painter in Colonial America. A limner painted people's portraits but usually did not sign the painting. Limners traveled from settlement to settlement in search of work for which they earned commissions — sums of money paid in advance for family or individual portraits.

Mrs. Elizabeth Freake and Baby Mary, artist unknown, c. 1671–1674. Worcester Art Museum, Worcester, Mass.

A limner was like the professional photographer today, though the limner seldom had formal training and did not try to make the subject dramatic in artistic ways. The limner aimed at producing a realistic, simple portrait, sometimes doing so in miniature, but usually working on a large canvas with oil paints.

Because they are direct and unadorned, the portraits by limners have unique power. *Mrs. Elizabeth Freake and Baby Mary* is a fine example of a limner's work. The paintings are also important historically because they show the clothing and furnishings of a particular period.

love·ly (luv′ lē) *adj.* **lovelier, loveliest. 1.** very pleasing in looks or character. *You have a lovely smile.* **2.** INFORMAL highly enjoyable. *It was a lovely ceremony.*

lu·mi·nar·y (l$\overline{oo}$′mə ner′ē) *n., pl.* **luminaries. 1.** a body that gives off light, such as the sun or moon. **2.** a famous or well-known person. *He is a luminary in political circles.* [from Latin *lumen* light] — *Syn.* **celebrity.**

M

mail[1] (māl) *n.* **1.** such things as letters and packages, carried and delivered by a post office. **2.** the system of picking up and delivering letters, papers, etc.; the postal system. *Send those invitations by mail.* — *adj.* having to do with or carrying mail. *The mail truck should arrive before noon.* — *vt.* to send by mail; to place in a mailbox.

mail[2] (māl) *n.* **1.** body armor made of small metal rings or overlapping plates so that it will bend easily. *We examined several coats of mail in the museum.* **2.** the hard protective covering of some animals, as turtles. [from Latin *macula* a spot, mesh of a net]

Mead, Mar·ga·ret (mēd,′ mär′ gər it) 1901–1978

Margaret Mead was one of the leading cultural anthropologists of her day, and her influence in that field is still strong. Mead was born in Philadelphia and earned a Ph.D. degree in anthropology from Columbia University. She became known as a tireless investigator of human culture and its effects on human character and personality.

Her first and perhaps most famous expedition was in 1928 to the central Pacific island of Samoa, where she lived for several years with native people and learned about their lives and beliefs. Her pioneering research in *Coming of Age in Samoa* compares the lives of Samoan adolescents with those of adolescents in Western countries. She also earned fame through her studies of child rearing, culture, and personality.

a fat	**er** care	**ī** bite, fire	**oi** oil	**u** up	**th** thin	ə = a *in* ago
ā ape	**ē** even	**o** lot	**oo** look	**ur** fur	**th** then	e *in* agent
ä car, father	**i** hit	**ō** go	**oo** tool	**ch** chin	**zh** leisure	i *in* unity
e ten	**ir** here	**ô** law, horn	**ou** out	**sh** she	**ng** ring	o *in* collect
						u *in* focus

Mead also lived and worked among the people of New Guinea and the island of Bali in the South Pacific. From 1940 onward she worked actively in programs concerning diet, mental health, and technological change. She was respected as a writer, lecturer, and thinker.

me•an•der   (mē an′ dər) *vi.* **1.** to wind back and forth along a course. *The river meandered across the plain.* **2.** to wander in an aimless or idle way. [from Greek *Maiandros* the name of a winding river in Asia Minor] — *Syn.* **wander**. — *Ant.* **march**. — **meandrous** *adj.*

meg•a•lith•ic   (meg′ ə lith′ ik) *adj.* **1.** like one of the huge stones used in prehistoric monuments. **2.** having to do with prehistoric monuments or with the times in which they were built. *We saw the megalithic structures of Stonehenge.* [from Greek *mega-* large + *lith* stone]

mer•ca•do   (mer kä′ dō) *n., pl.* **mercados.** a Spanish word meaning a market or public marketplace. *She browsed through the mercado.*

mo•bi•lize   (mō′ bə līz) *vt.* **mobilized, mobilizing.** to make or become organized or ready, as for war. *We mobilized all our resources and solved the problem.* — **mobilization** *n.*

mor•tal•i•ty   (môr tal′ə tē) *n., pl.* **mortalities. 1.** the condition of being certain to die sometime. **2.** the death of a large number of people, as from war or disease. **3.** the number of deaths in relation to the number of people, as in a certain place; the death rate. *The rate of mortality from many diseases is declining.* [from Latin *mortalis* mortal] — *Ant.* **immortality**.

Mound Build•ers   (mound′ bil′ dərz)

The term Mound Builders refers to the various tribes of American Indians who built huge earthworks — burial mounds, fortresses, and other structures — between approximately 1000 B.C. and A.D. 1700. These structures range from the simple patterns of dome-shaped hills in the United States to the pyramid-shaped mounds used as bases for temples and other important buildings in South America. Some are over 70 feet high and 275 feet in diameter.

Archaeologists believe that certain mounds served as homes for rulers; some, as temples for religious rites; and others, as burial places. Some mounds contain log or stone tombs. Other mounds were effigies (images) of sacred things. For example, the Great Serpent Mound in Ohio is an effigy of a wriggling snake.

Many similar structures still exist. Whatever their function, scientists agree that a high degree of social organization was required for people to have built them.

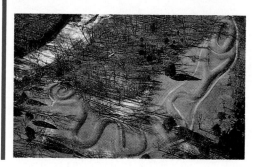

mys•ti•cal   (mis′ ti k′l) *adj.* **1.** having to do with spiritual things. **2.** secret, hidden, or mysterious. *The poet expressed mystical ideas in this poem.* — **mystically** *adv.*

——————————— **N** ———————————

Nev•el•son, Lou•ise   (nev′əl sən, loo wēz′) 1900–1988

Louise Nevelson, an internationally famous American sculptor, was born in Kiev, Russia, but her family settled in Maine in 1905. In her twenties, Nevelson studied several different art forms in New York. Then her travels in Mexico and South America influenced her early work in terra cotta (baked clay that is painted with a fine glaze).

Indian Chief, Louise Nevelson, 1955
Private collection. Photograph by Charles Phillips

In the 1950s, Nevelson began sculpting wood. These free-standing and wall-hung works brought her great acclaim. She collected fragments of old furniture and odds and ends and constructed huge walls or boxes of complex, abstract shapes. She usually painted them black, white, or gold. Her assemblages of framed boxes, shelves, and miscellaneous objects create an almost musical series of effects on viewers.

Nevelson also designed interiors of buildings, such as churches and public offices. Her works are displayed in museums all over the world.

Norse my•thol•o•gy   (nôrs′ mi thol′ə jē)
Norse mythology is also known as Scandinavian mythology. In this mythology there were many gods. In time, Odin became the most powerful and ruled as king of the gods and people from the beautiful Valhalla. He was the god of wisdom and of battle. The souls of slain heroes were carried to Valhalla on winged horses by the Valkyries, maidens in armor.

Odin's wife, Frigg, was the queen of the gods. She knew all things. One of their sons, Thor, was the god of thunder. He is often represented

as holding a thunderbolt with which he fought enemies and punished wrongdoers. Freya was the goddess of love, music, and flowers. In contrast, the clever Loki was the god of evil and mischief. He promoted quarrels, fraud, and deceit.

Norse gods and goddesses have characteristics similar to those of Greece and Rome. Like their Greek and Roman counterparts, the Norse gods had countless adventures concerning love, disputes, escapes, jealousy, war, and hidden treasures.

ob•nox•ious   (əb nok′ shəs) *adj.* annoying, unpleasant, or offensive. *Such obnoxious behavior is inexcusable.* — *Syn.* **hateful**. — **obnoxiously** *adv.*

a fat	er care	ī bite, fire	oi oil	u up	th thin	ə = a *in* ago
ā ape	ē even	o lot	oo look	ur fur	*th* then	e *in* agent
ä car, father	i hit	ō go	oo tool	ch chin	zh leisure	i *in* unity
e ten	ir here	ô law, horn	ou out	sh she	ng ring	o *in* collect u *in* focus

——————————— **P** ———————————

pha·lanx (fā′ laṇks) *n., pl.* **phalanxes. 1.** in ancient times, a group of soldiers in a very closely packed battle formation. *The phalanx advanced rapidly.* **2.** a massed group of individuals.

pon·toon (pon to͞on′) *n.* **1.** a small boat with a flat bottom. **2.** such a boat or other floating object used to hold up a temporary bridge, called a pontoon bridge. **3.** the float(s) on a seaplane. *The pilot checked the pontoons carefully.*

poth·er (poth′ ər) *n.* **1.** a choking cloud of smoke or dust. **2.** an uproar, commotion, fuss. *There was a pother of activity after the game.* — *vt.* to fuss or bother. *She pothered herself over small details.*

pro·claim (prō klām′) *vt.* **1.** to announce or otherwise make known publicly. *The senator proclaimed her victory in the election.* **2.** to praise or extol. [from Latin *pro-* before + *clamare* to cry out] — *Syn.* **announce.**

——————————— **R** ———————————

run·nel (run′ ′l) *n.* **1.** a small stream; little brook or rivulet. **2.** a small channel or watercourse. *Thin runnels of rainwater coursed down his face.*

——————————— **S** ———————————

shal·lop (shal′əp) *n.* a light, open boat fitted with oars or sails or both and used chiefly in shallow water. *The sailors came ashore in a shallop.*

ship·wright (ship′ rīt′) *n.* a person who builds and repairs ships. *The shipwrights finished the boat's hull.*

short·wave (shôrt′ wāv′) *n.* a radio wave 60 meters or less in length. *We picked up their signal on shortwave.*

Stat·ue of Lib·er·ty (stach′ o͞o uv lib′ ər tē)

The Statue of Liberty stands on Liberty Island in New York Harbor. It is a huge copper-clad statue, one of the largest ever made, of a woman wearing a crown and holding a torch in her upraised hand. The left arm holds a tablet bearing the date of the Declaration of Independence.

Officially named *Liberty Enlightening the World,* the statue was a gift from the French people on July 4, 1886.

During the great period of European immigration to America, the statue became a powerful symbol of people's hopes for freedom.

The Statue of Liberty was completely renovated in the mid 1980s, and a huge flotilla of ships and millions of people celebrated its centennial in 1986.

——————————— **T** ———————————

the·o·ret·i·cal (thē′ə ret′ i k′l) *adj.* **1.** of or constituting theory. **2.** limited to or based on theory; not practical or applied; hypothetical. *They studied about a theoretical landing on Mars.* — **theoretically** *adv.*

the·o·rize (thē′ə rīz) *vi.* **theorized, theorizing.** to form a theory or idea; to speculate. *He theorized about the future of the company.* — *Syn.* **imagine.** — **theorizer** *n.*

tor·tu·ous (tôr′ cho͞o wəs) *adj.* full of twists and turns; winding. *Hikers climbed the tortuous path.* — **tortuously** *adv.*

tri·dent (trīd′ ′nt) *n.* a spear with three prongs. *The god Poseidon lifted his trident.*

trin·ket (triṇ′ kit) *n.* **1.** a small ornament or piece of jewelry. *The child decorated her costume with trinkets.* **2.** a relatively worthless object. *Settlers traded trinkets for land.* [from Old French *trenchier* to cut]

——————————— **U** ———————————

un·in·tel·li·gi·ble (un′ in tel′ i jə b′l) *adj.* that cannot be understood. *The voices were completely unintelligible.* — **unintelligibly** *adv.*

u·til·i·ty (yo͞o til′ə tē) *n., pl.* **utilities. 1.** usefulness. **2.** something useful to the public, as the service of gas, water, etc.; also, a company that provides such a service: *also called* **public utility.** *How much does this utility charge for water?* — *adj.* useful or used in a number of different ways.

V

va•por or British **va•pour** (vā′pər) *n.* **1.** a thick mist or mass of tiny drops of water floating in the air, as steam or fog. *A cloud of vapor covered the mirror.* **2.** a gas formed when a substance that is usually liquid or solid is heated. — **vaporlike** *adj.*

verge (vʉrj) *n.* **1.** the edge, border, or brink. *They came to the verge of the forest.* **2.** the point at which something begins to happen. *The baby was on the verge of tears.* — *vi.* **verged, verging.** to come close to the edge or border; tend. *This idea verges on genius.*

W

The Won•der•ful Wiz•ard of Oz (wun′ dər fəl wiz′ərd uv oz′)

    The Wonderful Wizard of Oz was written in 1900 by L. Frank Baum, an author of children's books that have loving, adventurous characters. In the story a young girl named Dorothy is swept away in her house in Kansas by a cyclone. She and the house land in Oz, a fantasy land having many strange inhabitants, including a race of little friendly people.

    Dorothy learns that to get home to Kansas she must ask the Wizard of Oz in the Emerald City for help. Along the way to see him, she makes friends with a scarecrow who needs a brain, a tin man who needs a heart, and a lion who needs courage.

Copyright 1939 Loew's Incorporated
Ren. 1966 Metro-Goldwyn-Mayer Inc.

wrought (rôt) *adj.* **1.** formed or made. **2.** shaped by hammering or beating, as metals. *This gold flower is skillfully wrought.*

Y

Yea•ger, Charles (yā′gər, chärlz′) 1923–

    Charles "Chuck" Yeager is one of America's best-known test pilots. Yeager was born in West Virginia and had attended several military schools by the outbreak of World War II. When America entered the war in 1941, Yeager enlisted in the United States Army Air Force. He served as a fighter pilot in the air war over Europe.

    After the war he began flying experimental aircraft, including many early jets. In 1947 in a Bell X-1 rocket plane, he became the first person to fly faster than the speed of sound. He later established other flight records by test-piloting aircraft such as the Bell X-1A.

    Yeager's courage in dangerous situations and his knowledge of physical problems experienced in flight near the edge of space enabled him to make major contributions to America's space program. However, Yeager himself never flew in space.

a fat	**er** care	**ī** bite, fire	**oi** oil	**u** up	**th** thin	ə = a *in* ago
ā ape	**ē** even	**o** lot	**oo** look	**ʉr** fur	**th** then	e *in* agent
ä car, father	**i** hit	**ō** go	**ōō** tool	**ch** chin	**zh** leisure	i *in* unity
e ten	**ir** here	**ô** law, horn	**ou** out	**sh** she	**ŋ** ring	o *in* collect
							u *in* focus

Thesaurus

You will use this Thesaurus for the vocabulary lesson in Unit 1 and for the Thesaurus Corner in each Reading–Writing Connection in this book. You can also use the Thesaurus to find synonyms to make your writing more interesting.

Sample Entry

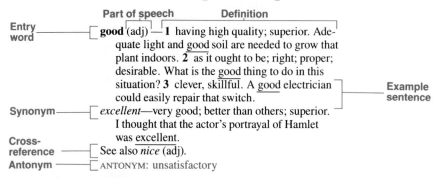

How to Use the Thesaurus Index

All entry words, synonyms, and antonyms are listed alphabetically in the Thesaurus Index on pages 612–616. Words in dark type are entry words, words in italic type are synonyms, and words in blue type are antonyms. A cross-reference (marked "See also") lists an entry that gives additional synonyms, related words, and antonyms. The page number tells where to find the word you are looking for.

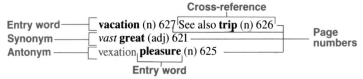

THESAURUS INDEX

A

abandon (v) **get** (v) 619
abandon (v) **keep** (v) 621
abhor **like** (v) 622
abominate **like** (v) 622
abruptly **suddenly** (adv) 626
absorbing **interesting** (adj) 621
abstain **eat** (v) 619
accomplish **do** (v) 618
accurate **right** (adj) 625
acquire **get** (v) 619
adapt **change** (v) 618
adept **good** (adj) 620

admire **like** (v) 622
advance **come** (v) 618
advance **go** (v) 620
advance **move** (v) 623
affliction pleasure (n) 625
agreeable **nice** (adj) 623
aid **help** (v) 621
alter **change** (v) 618
amiable **nice** (adj) 623
ancient **old** (adj) 623
annoyance pleasure (n) 625
answer (v) 617
antique **old** (adj) 623

Thesaurus

A

answer (v)—**1** to respond to; to write or speak in response to. Can you answer that question? **2** to move or act in response to. Michelle answered the telephone. **3** to find the solution to. I could not answer the last problem on the test.

react—to act in response. The crowd reacted to the announcement by cheering loudly.

refute—to show an opinion or claim to be incorrect or false; to prove wrong; to disprove. The witness refuted the testimony of the defendant.

reply—to answer by words or action; to answer; to respond. My friend replied that he would attend the picnic.

respond—to reply in words; to answer; to act in answer; to react. Volunteers responded to the needs of the community by helping out at the day-care center.

retort—to say in sharp or quick reply. "Leave me alone," he retorted.

solve—to find the answer to; to clear up. Daphne solved all ten algebra problems.

squelch [informal]—to cause to be silent; to crush; to put down or suppress. Our principal quickly squelched the rumor that was spreading through the school.

come back at [idiom]—to reply; to respond sharply. When I asked him where he had been for so long, he came back at me with a ridiculous story.

ANTONYMS: ask, inquire, interrogate, query (v), question (v), quiz (v)

B

bad (adj)—**1** not good; not as it ought to be. Yesterday was bad from start to finish for me. **2** causing harm; troublesome. Eating too much is bad for you.

contaminated—impure; polluted. The residents of the town were told not to drink the contaminated water.

harmful—causing pain, damage, or loss; injurious. Lack of sleep can have harmful effects.

mischievous—characterized by conduct that causes annoyance; naughty. The mischievous children threw snowballs at the stop sign.

noxious—very harmful; poisonous. The source of the noxious fumes was the leaky gas pipe.

poor—not satisfactory; not good in quality. The actor gave a poor performance in the play.

spoiled—bad or unfit for use; decayed; deteriorated. The spoiled milk tasted awful.

toxic—very harmful to health; poisonous. Are most household cleaning fluids toxic?

below par [idiom]—falling short of what is considered good; not satisfactory. Although he has almost completely recovered from the flu, he still feels below par.

ANTONYMS: beneficial, excellent, good (adj), healthful, pure, satisfactory, untainted

bright (adj)—**1** radiating or reflecting much light; shining. The bright headlights of the car were shining directly into my eyes. **2** intelligent; clever; quick-witted. Tyrone is a bright student.

brilliant—**1** shining brightly; glittering; sparkling. We viewed the brilliant sunset from the hilltop. **2** mentally keen or alert. The brilliant physicist discussed his theories with the professors.

dazzling—splendid or brilliant. The dazzling diamond necklace sparkled in the sunlight.

glistening—shining with a sparkling luster or light. A blanket of glistening snow covered the fields.

intelligent—showing or having understanding; able to learn and know. The intelligent student received an A on the test.

radiant—shining; beaming; sending out rays of heat or light. The radiant heat from the sun soon melted the ice from the sidewalk.

shimmering—shining with a soft trembling light. While I stood at the edge of the lake, I watched my shimmering reflection on the water.

brainy [informal]—clever; intelligent. Some brainy people enjoy solving difficult math problems.

sharp as a tack [idiom]—intelligent; quick-witted. That television commentator is sharp as a tack.

bright *(continued)*

ANTONYMS: drab (adj), dull (adj), faint (adj), ignorant, lackluster, pale (adj), subdued (adj)

C

change (v)—to make different; to modify; to alter. We changed our vacation plans several times before we left.

adapt—to make fit or suitable; to adjust. Some animals have adapted to living in city conditions.

alter—to make different; to change the appearance of. His suit had to be altered before he could wear it.

convert—to change in form, character, or function; to transform. The former ocean liner was converted into a floating museum.

fluctuate—to change continually; to vary irregularly; to vary. Prices on the stock exchange fluctuated wildly during the day.

modify—to change somewhat; to make partial changes in. The aircraft was modified to enable it to land on water.

transform—to change in appearance or form; to change in nature or character. In the fairy tale the frog was transformed into a handsome prince.

revamp [informal]—to make over; to take apart and put together in a new form. The revamped restaurant is reopening in October.

ANTONYMS: establish, fix (v), hold (v), keep (v), remain (v), set (v), stay (v)

come (v)—to approach; to move toward; to get near; to reach; to move into view. When you come to the second traffic light, turn left.

advance—to move or put forward; to push forward. The home football team advanced the ball quickly down the field.

appear—to come in sight; to become visible; to be seen. Dark clouds appeared on the horizon.

approach—to come near or nearer to; to move near. Please approach that busy intersection with caution.

arrive—to come to a place; to reach the end of a journey. She arrived in Los Angeles last Thursday.

emerge—to come into view; to come out; to come up. The submarine emerged from beneath the sea.

show up [informal]—to appear. Did Susan show up for the rehearsal yesterday?

blow in [slang]—to arrive. You'll never guess who just blew in.

ANTONYMS: depart, go, leave (v), quit, retreat (v), withdraw

copy (n)—a reproduction or imitation of an original work (as a painting or a dress); one of a series of reproductions of an original impression; a single specimen of a print, book, or such; something not genuine. Send me a copy of that map of Glacier National Park.

duplicate—either of two things that exactly resemble each other. Where is the duplicate of the license?

imitation—something that follows the pattern or example of something else; something produced as a copy. That artificial strawberry flavor was a poor imitation.

issue—an item or set of items published at one time. I just read the latest issue of my favorite magazine.

replica—any close reproduction of something, such as work of art. That is a replica of the Eiffel Tower.

ditto [informal]—a copy of something. Our science teacher gave us a ditto of the solar system.

phony [slang]—something not real or genuine; one that tries to deceive or mislead. As soon as he showed me the emerald, I knew that it was a phony.

dead ringer [idiom]—an exact likeness. She is a dead ringer for my Aunt Jane.

tenor [law]—an exact copy of a document. The trial will not proceed until the judge receives a tenor of the deed.

See also *picture* (n).

ANTONYMS: archetype, the genuine article, original (n), paradigm, prototype, the real McCoy, the real thing

D

do (v)—**1** to carry through to completion any work or action; to finish. The workers did the job in less than a day. **2** to be satisfactory or enough for. Just a little catsup on my hamburger will do. **3** to work out; to solve. I did the entire crossword puzzle by myself.

accomplish—to succeed in completing; to carry out, fulfill, or perform a plan or undertaking. My older sister will accomplish a goal by graduating from college next year.

decipher—to make out the meaning of something; to unravel or decode. Somehow I deciphered his nearly illegible handwriting.

perform—to go through and finish; to accomplish. In the talent show one of the eighth graders performed a very beautiful piano piece.

produce—to bring into existence by effort or labor; to create; to make from various materials; to manufacture. That factory produces home appliances.

suffice—to be enough; to be sufficient. A sweater will suffice in this kind of weather.

knock off [informal]—to do, especially in a hurried or routine way. I knocked off all of my chores in no time at all.

get by [slang]—to succeed with the least possible accomplishment or effort. The superior basketball team got by its little-known opponent without really playing hard.

See also *make* (v).

E

eat (v)—to chew and swallow food. What time do you usually eat supper?

consume—to eat or drink up, especially in great quantity. Jason consumed all of the mashed potatoes.

devour—to eat very hungrily or greedily. They devoured their lunches as if they were starving.

gorge—to devour; to stuff to capacity. We gorged ourselves on potato chips last night.

gulp—to swallow greedily or eagerly. I gulped the roll and butter quickly.

ingest—to take food into the body for digestion. The doctor asked whether the patient had recently ingested any unusual foods.

nibble—to bite gently; to eat little or lightly. Sharon devoured the mushrooms but nibbled the turnips.

snack [informal]—to eat a little food between meals. In the afternoon I snacked on bread and butter.

have a bite [idiom]—to eat something. Will you have a bite with me at noon?

ANTONYMS: abstain, famish, fast (v), starve

F

fast (adj)—moving, doing, or acting with speed; quick; swift. The fast train whizzed in a blur past the station.

expeditious—prompt and efficient; quick. I will show you an expeditious method of harvesting the berries from our blueberry bushes.

fleet—swiftly moving; rapid. The fleet horse galloped quickly away.

hasty—done or made in a hurry; hurried; quick. Tom made a hasty decision to quit his job.

quick—sudden and fast; swift. With a quick lunge she caught the plate before it hit the floor.

rapid—moving, doing, or acting with speed; swift; very quick. The rapid worker got the job done ahead of time.

speedy—acting, going, or moving with swift or rapid movement. My first ride in the speedy elevators of the Empire State Building was exciting.

swift—able to move very fast; moving very fast; fleet; speedy. The swift bird swooped down and then quickly up and away.

quick as lightning [idiom]—extremely fast. That tennis player's reflexes at the net are quick as lightning.

ANTONYMS: deliberate (adj), languorous, lethargic, slow (adj), sluggish

G

get (v)—**1** to come to have; to gain possession of; to obtain; to catch. I just got a new pair of shoes at the shopping mall. **2** to bring. Please get me the book on my desk.

acquire—to get by one's own actions or efforts; to come to have. The curator of

get *(continued)*

the art museum recently acquired a rare painting.

contract—to acquire, usually without choice. While on vacation Brian contracted pneumonia.

inherit—to receive after someone dies; to get as an heir. Her cousin inherited a large sum of money.

procure—to get by effort or care; to secure; to obtain. During the investigation a police detective procured an important piece of evidence.

receive—to take into one's hands or possession; to be given. I received your package in the mail today.

retrieve—to get again; to recover. Keith retrieved his golf ball from ankle-deep water in a pond near the seventeenth green.

corral [informal]—to collect; to gather. The coach corralled all of the team members before he himself boarded the bus.

come by [idiom]—to get possession of; to acquire. How did she come by such a large sum of money?

ANTONYMS: abandon (v), forego, forsake, give (v), relinquish, renounce, sacrifice (v)

go (v)—**1** to move along; to proceed. The truck carrying the huge load is going very slowly as it snakes around the sharply curving road. **2** to move away; to leave. Please go outside and see if there is any mail.

advance—to move or bring forward. That basketball team cannot advance the ball up the court when a pressing defense is applied.

cruise—to sail or travel about from place to place on business or pleasure. While on vacation last summer, our neighbor cruised to several tropical islands.

depart—to go away; to leave. The bus will depart in approximately fifteen mintues.

proceed—to go on after having stopped; to move forward; to continue; to progress. The jogger proceeded up and over the steep hill.

progress—to advance; to move forward; to go ahead. The workers who are putting in the new pipeline progressed about one hundred feet down the road.

travel—to go from one place to another; to journey. Ellen traveled to Alaska during her vacation this year.

mosey [informal]—to move along or away slowly. He just moseyed down the street as if he had all the time in the world.

make one's way [idiom]—to move ahead; to advance, especially in a profession or means of livelihood. Through hard work Jack made his way from store clerk to manager of his department.

See also *move* (v).

ANTONYMS: arrive, come, halt (v), remain (v), stay (v) stop (v)

good (adj)—**1** having high quality; superior. Adequate light and good soil are needed to grow that plant indoors. **2** as it ought to be; right; proper; desirable. What is the good thing to do in this situation? **3** clever, skillful. A good electrician could easily repair that switch.

adept—expert; very skillful. Glenn is an adept soccer player.

benevolent—desiring to promote the happiness of others; charitable; kindly. A benevolent individual donated the money necessary for the expansion of the youth center.

decent—right and proper. The decent thing to do would be to apologize.

excellent—very good; better than others; superior. I thought that the actor's portrayal of Hamlet was excellent.

gracious—kindly and pleasant; courteous. Being a gracious hostess, she made all of her guests feel welcome.

proficient—advanced in any science, art, or subject; expert. Maryann is obviously proficient in mathematics.

crack [informal]—excellent; very good. His enthusiasm for football helped him become a crack defensive player.

See also *nice* (adj).

ANTONYMS: bad (adj), cruel, improper, incompetent (adj), selfish, unsatisfactory

great (adj)—**1** large in amount, extent, size, or number; more than usual; much. Through the morning mist I can see a great mountain on the horizon. **2** important; remarkable; famous; high in rank. The film company produced a great motion picture.

distinguished—well-known; famous; celebrated. The distinguished scientist won numerous awards for her research.

eminent—above most others; outstanding; famous; noteworthy. During those times of extreme hardship, the eminent world leader was an inspiration to people everywhere.

enormous—very large; huge; immense; gigantic. An enormous boulder tumbled down the hillside and onto the road.

illustrious—very famous; outstanding; renowned. Winston Churchill was an illustrious British leader.

substantial—large; more than enough; large in degree or kind. Do you think there will be a substantial increase in the amount of wheat harvested this year?

vast—of great area; of immense extent; extensive; tremendous. A visit to the vast mountainous regions of the western United States is truly an unforgettable experience.

big-name [informal]—of top rank in popularity; notable. That hotel always gets the big-name entertainers.

ANTONYMS: diminutive (adj), inconsequential, inconsiderable, insignificant, little (adj), petty, trivial

H

help (v)—to give or do what is useful or needed; to relieve someone in trouble, want, or distress; to assist; to aid. Stranded motorists are often helped by the state police.

aid—to give support to; to assist; to help. As a volunteer at the hospital, Trena aids many patients.

assist—to help someone either when in need or when doing something; to give aid to. May I assist you in carrying those heavy boxes?

benefit—to do good to; to be good for. A good education benefits a person in countless ways.

contribute—to give help, money, or other support along with others; to give as a share. Tom and Stephen contributed much of their spare time to aid the fund drive.

encourage—to give courage, hope, or confidence to; to urge on; to support. Are you encouraged by your first-place finish in the track meet?

relieve—to reduce the pain or trouble of; to bring aid to; to help. The new highway has relieved traffic congestion in our town.

rescue—to save from capture, danger, or harm; to free. A lifeguard rescued the swimmer who had gone too far from shore.

go to bat for [idiom]—to help an individual, especially by speaking favorably about him or her. Will you go to bat for me at the meeting today?

ANTONYMS: discourage, frustrate, hinder, impede, obstruct, oppose, thwart

I

interesting (adj)—arousing interest or a feeling of wanting to know, see, do, or take part in; holding one's attention. Last night we saw an interesting television program.

absorbing—extremely interesting; fully occupying the attention; engrossing. That new paperback I was reading was so absorbing that I forgot to eat my lunch.

appealing—interesting, enjoyable, or attractive. That strawberry dessert looks most appealing to me.

enthralling—captivating; fascinating; charming. This mystery film is so enthralling that I do not want to miss a second of it.

fascinating—irresistibly attractive; charming; enchanting. The slides of your trip to Africa are fascinating.

stimulating—rousing to mental or physical action; inspiring; stirring. In our social studies class today, we had a stimulating discussion on current events.

striking—attracting attention; very noticeable; remarkable; impressive. Your blue and white sweater is striking.

fetching [informal]—charming; attractive. That is a fetching bonnet.

ANTONYMS: boring (adj), dull (adj), flat (adj), tedious, uninteresting

K

keep (v)—**1** to have for a long time; to continue to hold; to have and not let go of; to save. I will keep this ring for the rest of my life. **2** to hold back, to restrain; to

keep *(continued)*

prevent. Please keep the little child away from the hot oven.

impede—to stand in the way of; to obstruct; to hinder. The traffic flow on the highway was impeded while construction to add an extra lane took place.

preserve—to keep from change or harm; to keep safe. To be successful, athletes must preserve their health.

prevent—to stop or keep from. Please prevent your little sister from soiling her new outfit in that puddle.

restrain—to keep in check; to hold back; to keep within limits. The happy crowd was restrained from running onto the field after the game.

retain—to continue to hold or have; to keep. Even during the most difficult of economic times, that company retained all of its employees.

store—to stock or supply; to put away for later use. You should store canned foods for an emergency.

bottle up [informal]—to hold in; to keep back; to control. Why did he bottle up his anger over the injustice that was done to him?

ANTONYMS: abandon (v), discard (v), expedite, free (v), liberate, lose, release (v)

L

like   (v)—to be pleased with; to be satisfied with; to find congenial; to find agreeable. Of all the sports that Andrea takes part in, she likes swimming best.

admire—to regard with pleasure, wonder, and approval. I admire the dedication of the Olympic athletes.

appreciate—to think highly of; to recognize the quality or worth of; to value; to enjoy. Felicia appreciates a good book.

cherish—to hold dear, to treat with tenderness; to protect or aid. Parents cherish their children.

enjoy—to have or use with happiness; to take pleasure in. The tourists enjoyed their visit to New York.

prefer—to like better; to choose above another. Terry prefers ballet to opera.

savor—to enjoy the taste or smell of; to appreciate by taste or smell; to relish. My friend savored the delicious steak dinner.

treasure—to value highly; to prize; to cherish. The child treasured his model train.

get a kick out of [idiom]—to like; to enjoy. I get a kick out of that comedian.

ANTONYMS: abhor, abominate, detest, dislike (v), hate (v), loathe

live   (v)—**1** to be alive; to continue alive; to exist. Giant Sequoia trees live for thousands of years. **2** to occupy a home; to dwell. Jerry lives in an apartment on Fifteenth Street.

dwell—to live as a resident; to reside; to abide. They dwell in the suburbs.

exist—to continue to be; to have life; to live. We cannot exist without water to drink.

persist—to remain in existence; to last; to stay. Near the mountain's peak, the tiny plants persisted through long winters of bitter cold temperatures and icy winds.

reside—to live in or at a place permanently or continuously; to dwell. She resides in a new house on the other side of town.

survive—to live longer than; to outlive; to sustain the effects of something and continue to live; to outlast. Much of the citrus crop did not survive the outbreak of subfreezing weather.

roost [informal]—to lodge or stay for a period of time, usually in a temporary manner. Where did he roost on the night of the hurricane?

ANTONYMS: decline (v), depart, die (v), expire, fade (v), perish, wither

M

make   (v)—**1** to bring into being; to build, form, put together, or shape. Did you make that beautiful vase all by yourself? **2** to cause to; to force to. My parents made me mow the lawn today.

assemble—to put or fit together. We assembled the complicated jigsaw puzzle in about three days.

compel—to urge or drive with force; to force. Laura was compelled to stay up later than usual to finish writing her book report.

compose—to put together; to produce or arrange; to write or create. Who composed the music for that movie?

construct—to fit together, to put together; to build. During the past year a new bridge was constructed over the river.

fashion—to make, form, or shape. The sculptor fashioned a figure of a deer out of clay.

manufacture—to make by machine or by hand. A factory in our town manufactures clothing items.

bulldoze [informal]—to force insensitively or ruthlessly. Their boss bulldozed them into working overtime.

twist one's arm [idiom]—to force; to compel. Since you've twisted my arm with all of your pleading, I'll stay a bit longer.

See also *do* (v).

ANTONYMS: decimate, demolish, destroy, wreck (v)

move (v)—**1** to change or cause to change the position or place of; to put in motion; to keep in motion; to stir or shift. He moved the television set to the other side of the room. **2** to advance or proceed; to make progress. The remodeling of the library is moving quite nicely.

advance—to move or put forward; to push forward. Chess players usually think carefully before they advance their pieces.

budge—to cause to move something heavy or inert. I couldn't budge that large cabinet.

meander—to follow a winding or irregular course. When at the shopping mall, I often meander in and out of almost every store.

migrate—to move from one place in order to settle in another; to go from one region to another during the change in seasons. As the winter approaches, many birds migrate from colder areas to warmer ones.

progress—to advance; to move forward; to go ahead. Her recovery from pneumonia is progressing quite well.

relocate—to move to a different location. Because of an excellent job opportunity, he relocated to another part of the country.

travel—to go from one place to another; to journey. Last summer my cousin traveled to South America.

hit the road [idiom]—to travel or journey. I'll hit the road again before the week is over.

See also *go* (v).

ANTONYMS: discontinue, halt (v), stop (v)

N

nice (adj)—**1** good or pleasing; agreeable; satisfactory. The weather over the last few days has been very nice. **2** kind and thoughtful. Ms. Denton is a very nice person.

agreeable—pleasant; pleasing; giving pleasure. Watching a movie tonight sounds agreeable to me.

amiable—friendly and good-natured; pleasant and agreeable. A person with an amiable disposition does not get angry often.

enjoyable—that can be enjoyed or had or used with joy; giving joy. We spent an enjoyable afternoon playing tennis.

pleasant—that pleases; giving pleasure; agreeable; easy to get along with. It is difficult to concentrate on work on such a pleasant June day.

sympathetic—having or showing kind feelings toward others; compassionate; tender. I am sympathetic toward those who lose their pets.

warmhearted—kind; sympathetic; friendly. The warmhearted individual offered lodging to the motorists stranded in the snowstorm.

swell [slang]—very satisfactory; excellent. Everyone had a swell time at the dance the other night.

See also *good* (adj).

ANTONYMS: awful, dreadful, mean (adj), miserable, unfriendly, unkind, unpleasant

O

old (adj)—not young; having existed for some time; dating far back; belonging to the past. In a dusty trunk I found some old

old *(continued)*

photographs that dated from the last century.

ancient—of or belonging to times long past; of great age. In your history class have you studied about the pyramids of the <u>ancient</u> Egyptians?

antique—of times long ago; ancient; out-of-date. That <u>antique</u> furniture may be worth a fortune.

archaic—of, relating to, or characteristic of an earlier or more primitive time; no longer used in ordinary language. The word *dulcitude,* meaning "sweetness," is <u>archaic.</u>

elderly—beyond middle age; near old age. The <u>elderly</u> person in that photograph is my grandfather.

enduring—lasting; permanent; unchanging. We all hope for <u>enduring</u> peace throughout the world.

lifelong—lasting for one's entire life. The Jamisons are my parents' <u>lifelong</u> friends.

traditional—of tradition; of the handing down of beliefs, customs, and stories, conforming to customs or styles. Some of the <u>traditional</u> foods we have on Thanksgiving Day include turkey, stuffing, and cranberry sauce.

ANTONYMS: contemporary (adj), current (adj), modern, new (adj), recent, young (adj), youthful

P

picture (n)—**1** a painting, drawing, or photograph; a scene; an exact likeness. This book includes beautiful <u>pictures</u> of American wilderness areas. **2** a motion picture. There was a terrific <u>picture</u> on television last night.

illustration—a picture, diagram, or map used to decorate or explain something, especially in a printed work such as a book. That book is filled with colorful <u>illustrations.</u>

image—a copy or likeness; a picture in the mind. In my mind's eye are <u>images</u> of the places I have visited.

painting—something painted; a representation of a person, object, or scene in colors; a picture. I admire many of the <u>paintings</u> by the French artist Renoir.

photograph—a picture that is made with a camera. Some of my favorite <u>photographs</u> are those of glittering city skylines at night.

portrait—a picture of a person, especially of the face, as in a painting or photograph. Before the invention of the camera, a painted <u>portrait</u> was a way to leave a visual record for future generations.

sketch—a quickly done rough drawing representing the chief features of an object or scene. In some museums you can see delicate and detailed <u>sketches</u> by the French artist Toulouse-Lautrec.

movie [informal]—a motion picture. I think that most <u>movies</u> have their own individual styles and messages.

See also *copy* (n).

plan (n)—**1** a way of doing or making something that has been worked out beforehand; a way of proceeding; a method. We made careful <u>plans</u> for our vacation trip several months in advance. **2** a drawing or diagram that shows how something is arranged. Before planting a vegetable garden, draw a <u>plan</u> for it on paper.

blueprint—a photographic print in white on a blue background used especially for copying original drawings of building plans, mechanical drawings, and maps. The architect's <u>blueprints</u> for the new office building look extremely complicated.

design—a drawing, sketch, or plan made to serve as a pattern from which to work. Did you make the <u>design</u> for this beautiful blouse?

diagram—a sketch or drawing showing arrangements and relations of important parts of a thing. Science textbooks often include <u>diagrams</u> that illustrate important items.

layout—the arrangement or design or plan of something. This printed <u>layout</u> of the town includes every house and public building.

procedure—a way of carrying on any activity; a method of doing things. What is the <u>procedure</u> to follow in the event of a fire drill?

strategy—a careful method or plan. The <u>strategy</u> our coach has planned includes a strong defense.

course of action [idiom]—a method used to accomplish something. The heroic course of action executed by the firefighters during the blaze saved many lives.

pleasure (n)—a feeling of being pleased; delight; enjoyment; joy. I find great pleasure in simple pursuits, such as taking long walks.
delight—joy; great pleasure; delightfulness. It is always a delight to visit my grandmother.
elation—joy or pride; high spirits; exultant gladness. George was filled with elation when he scored a goal in the soccer game.
enjoyment—the state or act of enjoying; pleasure; joy; delight. Do you find more enjoyment in watching the sport or in participating in it?
happiness—the condition of being happy or contented; gladness. Gina was bursting with happiness when she received an A on the math test.
joy—a glad feeling; a strong feeling of pleasure; glad behavior; happiness. Doug was filled with joy when he sighted his brother at the airport.
jubilation—the act of rejoicing; the state of being filled with or of expressing great joy. Everyone in town was filled with jubilation when they were informed that no one had been injured by the tornado.
mirth—merry fun; being joyous; laughter; merriment; glee. Our surprise party was a time of mirth for everyone.
ANTONYMS: affliction, annoyance, distress (n), misery, sorrow (n), trouble (n), vexation

R

right (adj)—**1** agreeing with what is just, lawful, or good. It is right to tell the truth. **2** conforming to facts or truth; correct; true. All of my answers on the science test were right. **3** fitting; suitable; proper. Who in this store is the right person to see about a refund?
accurate—without mistakes or errors; exactly right; precisely correct. Make sure that all of the information asked for on the form you are filling out is accurate.

appropriate—right for the occasion; fitting; suitable; proper. I don't think slurping your soup is appropriate behavior with company at the dinner table.
correct—free from faults or mistakes; right; true. My teacher said that my composition was both interesting and grammatically correct.
fair—not favoring one more than any other; honest; just. It is not fair to have more members on one team than the other.
lawful—according to law; done as the law directs; allowed by law; rightful. In this state is it lawful to drive a car at age seventeen?
suitable—right for the occasion; fitting; appropriate; proper. I did not think that the blaring music in that film was suitable to the delicate subject matter.
OK [informal]—all right; approved; correct. Since you have finished your homework, it's OK to watch television.
ANTONYMS: erroneous, inappropriate, incorrect, unbecoming, unsatisfactory, unsuitable, wrong (adj)

S

see (v)—**1** to perceive, or be aware of, by use of the eyes; to look at. Did you see the magnificent fireworks display? **2** to form a mental picture of. The older man said that even now he could see himself in his teens.
discern—to see clearly; to perceive; to recognize or distinguish. I cannot discern the mountain peak through all of this fog.
glimpse—to catch a quick or brief view of. Did you glimpse our mayor as she drove by in the parade?
observe—to see and note; to notice; to carefully examine; to watch; to study. I observed from a distance what the electrician was doing.
view—to look at; to see; to behold, witness, or scan. Can we view the magnificent scenery from the lower elevation or should we go higher?
visualize—to form a mental picture of. I am visualizing the coat that Janice was wearing yesterday, but I cannot remember if it had a belt.

see *(continued)*

spot [informal]—to pick out; to detect or recognize. I spotted a tiny bird among the uppermost branches of that tree.

keep one's eye on [idiom]—to watch carefully; to look after. Please keep your eye on our luggage while I purchase the tickets.

ANTONYMS: disregard (v), ignore, overlook (v)

slow (adj)—taking longer than usual; taking a long time; not fast or quick. The slow truck barely made it to the top of the hill.

deliberate—slow, steady, and unhurried as though allowing time for decision on each individual action involved. A deliberate worker does a job carefully, without rushing.

gradual—moving, developing, or changing by fine, slight, or often imperceptible degrees. A gradual slope begins at this point in the road and continues for about five miles.

leisurely—taking plenty of time; without hurry; deliberate. I enjoy a leisurely vacation during which I can truly relax.

lumbering—ponderous or heavy and clumsy in movement. The lumbering freight train crawled across the long bridge.

sluggish—moving quite slowly; having little motion. The sluggish automobile limped into the service station.

tedious—long and tiring; irksome; boring. Trying to pair up socks that have just been washed is a tedious task.

as slow as molasses in January [idiom]—extremely slow. When it comes to cleaning his room, Tom is as slow as molasses in January.

ANTONYMS: fast (adj), hasty, hurried, prompt (adj), quick (adj), speedy, swift (adj)

suddenly (adv)—in a sudden manner; all at once; without preparation or warning. The torrential rain that had lasted all morning suddenly stopped.

abruptly—with sudden change; unexpectedly. The bus stopped abruptly to avoid a collision.

hastily—in a hasty manner; quickly; rashly. I hastily packed for the trip as soon as I received your call.

impetuously—rashly or with sudden feeling; hastily. She impetuously waved to her friend in the hall.

impulsively—suddenly or spontaneously; arising from a momentary impulse. He impulsively decided to buy the expensive jacket, even though he could not afford it.

startlingly—surprisingly; frighteningly. Hours before it was predicted to do so, the hurricane startlingly slammed ashore.

unexpectedly—without anticipation, advance warning, or preparation. To the amazement of her coworkers, she unexpectedly quit her job.

ANTONYMS: deliberately, gradually, slowly

T

trip (n)—the action of traveling about; a journey, voyage, or excursion. We went on a trip to Yellowstone National Park.

cruise—the act of sailing about from place to place on business or pleasure. Some people take cruises to forget about the stress of everyday life.

excursion—a trip, especially a short trip taken for pleasure or interest, often by a group of people. We went on an excursion to the Statue of Liberty.

expedition—a journey made for some special purpose. The latest expedition to climb Mount Everest was a success.

jaunt—a short journey or excursion, especially for pleasure. They went on a jaunt to the lake.

journey—a traveling from one place to another; a trip. A journey from Boston to Australia is a long one.

tour—the act of traveling around from place to place; a journey. When you go to Europe, will you be taking a group tour or traveling alone?

voyage—an act of journeying or traveling by water. The long voyage was a rough one because of continuous bad weather.

See also *vacation* (n).

U

usually (adv)—according to what is usual or what is commonly seen, used, or happening; commonly; customarily; ordinarily. I <u>usually</u> wake up at about seven o'clock in the morning.

commonly—occurring or appearing frequently; familiarly. Geese <u>commonly</u> appear in this area of the country.

customarily—commonly practiced, used, or observed; habitually; usually. The Fourth of July is <u>customarily</u> observed as a legal holiday in the United States.

generally—in most cases; usually. Stores in our town <u>generally</u> close at nine o'clock.

habitually—often done, seen, or used; usually; customarily. Tim <u>habitually</u> awakens early on Saturdays.

normally—in the normal way; regularly; generally; ordinarily. In this region forsythia bushes <u>normally</u> bloom in late March.

ordinarily—commonly; normally; regularly; usually. My neighbor <u>ordinarily</u> jogs every day, but the rain kept him indoors today.

regularly—in a regular manner; at regular times. All <u>regularly</u> scheduled classes at the college were cancelled yesterday because of the snowstorm.

for the most part [idiom]—in general; generally. My friends, <u>for the most part</u>, do not take the time to eat a nourishing breakfast.

ANTONYMS: infrequently, rarely, seldom (adv), uncommonly

V

vacation (n)—a time of rest and freedom from work; freedom from business, school, or other duties; a holiday. Does your family take a <u>vacation</u> every summer?

furlough—a leave of absence, especially for a soldier. Many of the soldiers on <u>furlough</u> purchased gifts for their families.

holiday—a day when one does not work; a day for enjoyment and pleasure. On <u>holidays</u> I keep busy with many hobbies.

leave—an authorized extended absence from duty or employment. Because of illness, Joyce was on <u>leave</u> from her job.

liberty—permission granted to a sailor to go ashore, usually for not more than forty-eight hours. The sailors on <u>liberty</u> in Hawaii had an enjoyable time.

recess—a time during which work stops, often for rest or relaxation. The teacher gave her class a brief <u>recess</u> after the test was over.

sabbatical leave—a leave of absence for a year or half a year given to college and university professors, commonly once in seven years, for study, travel, or rest. The French professor at the university went on <u>sabbatical leave</u> to Paris.

R & R [informal]—rest and recreation, usually used in the United States military. After strenuous duty overseas, the soldiers were happy to get some <u>R & R</u>.

See also *trip* (n).

ANTONYM: work (n)

Reports, Letters, Notes

Book Reports

A **book report** tells what a book is about and gives an opinion of it. It is usually divided into three main parts: an introduction, a body, and a conclusion. In the **introduction** identify the book by title and author. State whether it is fiction or nonfiction and give some information about the author.

In the **body** of the report, tell enough about the book so that your readers can decide whether or not they will find the book interesting. If the book is fiction, mention something about the setting, characters, and plot, but don't give away the ending.

In the **conclusion** of the report, give reasons that explain why you are either recommending or not recommending the book.

Read the sample book report below.

Introduction

Words by Heart is a novel by Ouida Sebestyen, a popular writer of the young adult novel. The author drew on her own family's experiences in a small Texas community to write this book.

Body

The novel is set in the early 1900s. It concerns a black family that has moved from a southern town "where everyone was black" to a western town "where no one was."

The plot of Words by Heart is exciting, but it is the characters who make this novel special. There are two main characters: Lena Sills and her father, Ben. Lena, maturing to adulthood, loves books. She is proud of being bright, but also a little ashamed of her pride. She also has a temper she cannot always control. Lena wants to be more like her father, a tower of strength. Ben can understand why his enemies act as they do, and he can forgive them. Because these characters seem real, you care about them.

Conclusion

I recommend Words by Heart to anyone who likes a novel with an exciting plot and an interesting setting. I especially recommend it to those who want to read about real and memorable characters.

Friendly Letters

A **friendly letter** is a personal letter. It is a good way to let a friend or relative know what you have been doing and how you feel. Less formal than a business letter, a friendly letter is similar to a conversation with a friend. Think of topics that will interest your reader. Include enough details to make your letter clear. If you are replying to a friend's letter, answer any questions he or she asked.

Study the five parts of the friendly letter below.

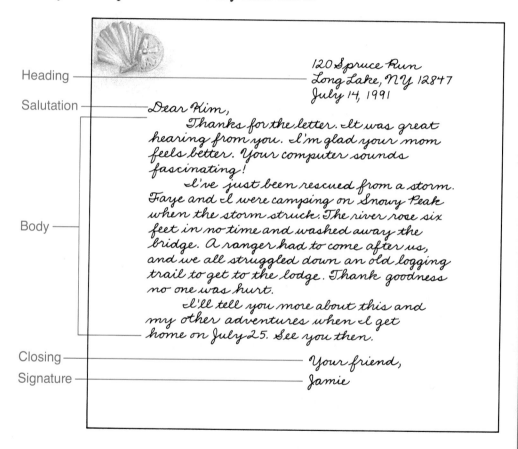

Heading

120 Spruce Run
Long Lake, NY 12847
July 14, 1991

Salutation

Dear Kim,

Body

Thanks for the letter. It was great hearing from you. I'm glad your mom feels better. Your computer sounds fascinating!

I've just been rescued from a storm. Faye and I were camping on Snowy Peak when the storm struck. The river rose six feet in no time and washed away the bridge. A ranger had to come after us, and we all struggled down an old logging trail to get to the lodge. Thank goodness no one was hurt.

I'll tell you more about this and my other adventures when I get home on July 25. See you then.

Closing

Your friend,

Signature

Jamie

Write your friendly letters as neatly as possible. Use blue or black ink on white or tinted paper. Notice in the letter above that Jamie has kept an equal margin on the top, the sides, and the bottom of the letter. Sometimes, in order to leave the necessary margin at the bottom, you have to continue a letter on a second page.

Social Notes

A **social note** is a short letter, such as a thank-you note or an invitation. There are many occasions when it is polite to write a social note. When you receive a gift, for example, a social note is a way to say thank you. You can also offer congratulations or express sympathy with a social note.

A social note follows a friendly letter form. It contains a heading, salutation, body, closing, and signature. Sometimes only the date is used in the heading.

A **bread-and-butter note** is one kind of social note. It is used to thank a host or hostess after staying overnight in his or her home. Always write a bread-and-butter note promptly after being entertained. Say something about your visit that shows genuine enjoyment or gratitude. Study the bread and butter note below.

January 17, 1991

Dear Mr. and Mrs. Carp,

Thank you very much for inviting me to spend the weekend with you and Al at your home. Your home is lovely, and it was fun skiing with Al on the slope at Crystal Mountain.

My bus arrived on time, and Mom was there to meet me. She couldn't believe how excited I was about skiing. I've already started saving for my own skis!

Once again, thank you for everything.

Yours truly,
David Green

An **invitation** should tell what event is planned and where and when the event will take place. When you receive an invitation, you may see the initials R.S.V.P. written at the bottom. This is an abbreviation for a French phrase meaning "please respond." Reply to such an invitation by writing a note of acceptance or regret. A note of regret should explain, if possible, why you will not be able to accept the invitation.

Business Letters

A **business letter** is briefer and more formal than a friendly letter. It should use correct business letter form and should be written in a clear and concise manner. Business letters may request information, place an order, or state a complaint.

Business letters have six parts. In addition to the five parts in the friendly letter, a business letter has an inside address — the name and address of the person or company to whom the letter is sent. Business letters should be typed neatly on 8½″ x 11″ paper. If you do not type, write the letter neatly in blue or black ink. Notice that a colon follows the salutation in a business letter. Study the example below.

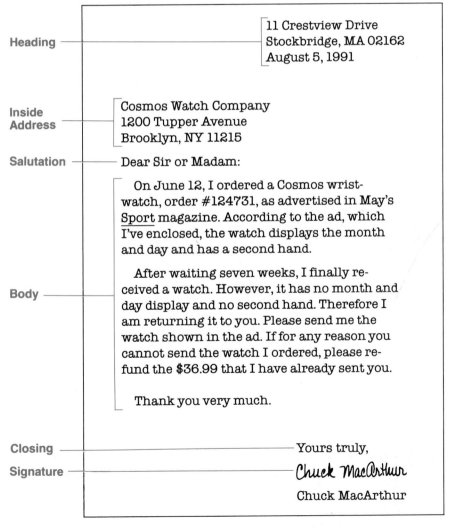

Heading

11 Crestview Drive
Stockbridge, MA 02162
August 5, 1991

Inside Address

Cosmos Watch Company
1200 Tupper Avenue
Brooklyn, NY 11215

Salutation

Dear Sir or Madam:

Body

On June 12, I ordered a Cosmos wristwatch, order #124731, as advertised in May's Sport magazine. According to the ad, which I've enclosed, the watch displays the month and day and has a second hand.

After waiting seven weeks, I finally received a watch. However, it has no month and day display and no second hand. Therefore I am returning it to you. Please send me the watch shown in the ad. If for any reason you cannot send the watch I ordered, please refund the $36.99 that I have already sent you.

Thank you very much.

Closing

Yours truly,

Signature

Chuck MacArthur

Chuck MacArthur

Preparing Letters for Mailing

When you finish writing any type of letter, make sure you fold it neatly. A business letter is usually folded in thirds by folding the bottom third up and the top third over it. Then you must address the envelope.

Every letter must contain a mailing address and a return address. The mailing address includes the receiver's name, street address, city, state, and ZIP code. The return address includes your name and complete address. Study the example below.

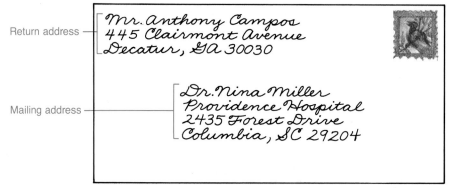

Return address —

Mr. Anthony Campos
445 Clairmont Avenue
Decatur, GA 30030

Mailing address —

Dr. Nina Miller
Providence Hospital
2435 Forest Drive
Columbia, SC 29204

Note the list of mailing abbreviations for the fifty states, the District of Columbia, Puerto Rico, and the Virgin Islands.

State	Abbr.	State	Abbr.
Alabama	AL	Nebraska	NE
Alaska	AK	Nevada	NV
Arizona	AZ	New Hampshire	NH
Arkansas	AR	New Jersey	NJ
California	CA	New Mexico	NM
Colorado	CO	New York	NY
Connecticut	CT	North Carolina	NC
Delaware	DE	North Dakota	ND
District of Columbia	DC	Ohio	OH
Florida	FL	Oklahoma	OK
Georgia	GA	Oregon	OR
Hawaii	HI	Pennsylvania	PA
Idaho	ID	Puerto Rico	PR
Illinois	IL	Rhode Island	RI
Indiana	IN	South Carolina	SC
Iowa	IA	South Dakota	SD
Kansas	KS	Tennessee	TN
Kentucky	KY	Texas	TX
Louisiana	LA	Utah	UT
Maine	ME	Vermont	VT
Maryland	MD	Virginia	VA
Massachusetts	MA	Virgin Islands	VI
Michigan	MI	Washington	WA
Minnesota	MN	West Virginia	WV
Mississippi	MS	Wisconsin	WI
Missouri	MO	Wyoming	WY
Montana	MT		

A Guide to Spelling

The English language has more than 250,000 words. This large number of words makes learning to spell a very challenging task. Because many English words have been borrowed from other languages, there is often more than one way to represent a sound in English.

As a result, learning to spell can be difficult. However, the following guidelines will help you to become a better speller.

♦ Look carefully at words when you read. Try to see each letter. Do this not only for new words but for familiar words, too.

♦ Pronounce words carefully when you speak. Some English words are not pronounced the way they are spelled. Frequently mispronunciation leads to misspelling. For example, a student who mispronounces *library* as *"liberry"* will probably also misspell the word.

♦ Use a dictionary to check the spelling of words. If you are not sure how a word begins, list all the logical possibilities. Then look up each possibility until you find the word. In addition to improving your spelling, the dictionary will help you use and pronounce words correctly.

♦ Maintain a list of personal spelling words in a notebook. If you are like most people, there are certain words that you misspell over and over. List these words alphabetically in your spelling notebook. Review them frequently.

♦ Learn to spell long or difficult words syllable by syllable. Since a syllable has only a few letters in it, it is easy to spell. Once you learn to spell each syllable, put them together.

♦ Use memory aids to help you remember the spelling of words that are especially troublesome. Usually, you will have to make a memory aid for each word that causes you trouble. For example, I *labor* in the *laboratory*.

Proofread all your writing carefully for spelling errors. During this stage of the writing process, it is necessary to reread all your words and correct any misspellings.

Rules for Spelling

Know the rules for spelling. Some of these rules are listed below. Learn these rules and use them when you write.

1. If a word ends in *e*, usually drop the *e* when you add a suffix that begins with a vowel.

VERBS lease leasing

2. If a word ends in a vowel and *y*, keep the *y* when you add a suffix.

NOUNS turkey turkeys **VERBS** pay paying

3. If a word ends in a consonant and *y*, change the *y* to *i* when you add a suffix unless the suffix begins with *i*.

NOUNS cherry cherries **VERBS** pry prying
ADJECTIVES muddy muddier muddiest

4. If a word ends in one vowel and one consonant and has one syllable or is stressed on the last syllable, double the last consonant when you add a suffix that begins with a vowel.

NOUNS swim swimmer **VERBS** refer referring

5. When you choose between *ie* and *ei*, use *ie* except after *c* or for a long *a* sound. (Exceptions: *leisure, either, seize, weird*)

thief shriek receive neighbors

6. The suffix *-s* can be added to most nouns and verbs. If a word ends in *s, ss, sh, ch, x*, or *zz* , add *-es*.

NOUNS bus buses **VERBS** hiss hisses
bush bushes punch punches
ax axes buzz buzzes

7. If a word ends in a single *f* or *fe*, usually change the *f* to *v* when you add *-s* or *-es*.

calf calves wife wives

8. The letter *q* is always followed by the letter *u* in English words.

quarter inquire request

Words Often Written

The words most often used by students in Grades 1 through 8 are, in alphabetical order, *a, all, and, be, but, for, go, had, have, he, I, in, is, it, like, me, my, of, on, said, she, so, that, the, then, there, they, to, was, we, went, when, with, would,* and *you.*

The list below contains words that were used most often in samples of writing done by students your age. Have you ever paid attention to the words *you* use most frequently?

1. able		26. kind
2. almost		27. knew
3. America		28. maturity
4. believe		29. may
5. black		30. maybe
6. blue		31. once
7. called		32. own
8. children		33. real
9. doing		34. remember
10. done		35. scared
11. eat		36. she's
12. end		37. since
13. enough		38. start
14. eyes		39. such
15. freedom		40. sure
16. game		41. teachers
17. hair		42. team
18. happened		43. today
19. having		44. together
20. he's		45. tried
21. hit		46. trip
22. hope		47. war
23. I've		48. whole
24. important		49. won't
25. keep		50. you're

Mechanics Lessons

Capitalizing Names and Titles

A proper noun names a particular person, place, or thing. It is always capitalized. A common noun is the general name of a person, place, or thing. It is not capitalized.

Capitalizing Proper Nouns
Capitalize the names of people. **Thelma F. Enriquez** **Ernest Washington, Sr.** **Linnea Hasagawa** **Jon A. Chase, Jr.** Middle initials and the abbreviations *Jr.* and *Sr.* should also be capitalized.
Capitalize titles or abbreviations that come before the names of people. **General Bernstein** **Professor West** **Dr. Stark** **Superintendent Smith** **Mr. Osato** **Captain Gray** **Chief Justice Rehnquist** **Dean Romera** **Senator Bentsen** Capitalize A.D. and B.C.; capitalize A.M. and P.M. Emperor Claudius I died in **A.D.** 54. The car wash opens at 8:00 **A.M.** and closes at 6:00 **P.M.**
Always capitalize the titles *President* and *Vice President* when referring to officials of the United States. The **President** was reelected. The **Vice President** is speaking. Do not capitalize other titles unless they appear before a person's name. Mr. John Stevens was the town's best <u>mayor</u>. At the dinner **Mayor** Stevens received an award.
Capitalize words showing family relationships when used as titles or as substitutes for a name. The first one to arrive was **Aunt** Elizabeth. The next visitor was **Grandfather**. I spent the summer with **Cousin** Nina. Do not capitalize such words when they are preceded by a possessive noun or pronoun. Ann's <u>aunt</u> arrived last. My <u>brother</u> is late. David's <u>father</u> is an excellent cook.

Practice

A. Write the following with correct capitals.

1. president jefferson
2. uncle bernard
3. 6:15 p.m.
4. 3 b.c.
5. 10:00 a.m.
6. dr. hoffman
7. judge donna ames
8. bret carle, jr.
9. aunt carol
10. mrs. fran m. lewis
11. a.d. 489
12. vice president adams

B. Write each sentence with correct capitals.

EXAMPLE: I bought the ticket from mr. gary green.
ANSWER: I bought the ticket from Mr. Gary Green.

13. The coin had ''33 b.c.''printed on it.
14. That's how mr. ford knew it was a fake.
15. The baby cried from 11:00 p.m. until 2:00 a.m.
16. aunt phyllis is president of her club.
17. Is mom working at uncle george's store?
18. The reporter spoke to senator thomas.
19. The vice president flew to Europe.
20. geoffrey chaucer, the poet, died in a.d. 1400.
21. gregory's uncle is a senator.
22. We heard alex fox, sr., speak on the radio.
23. I received a letter from alicia m. collins.

C. After each sentence number, write the words, initials, and abbreviations that should be capitalized.

24. mr. and mrs. richard t. sims, jr., and their daughter jill flew to Mexico City.
25. mrs. sims is known professionally as doctor sims.
26. She teaches at State College, which was founded by herbert n. davis.
27. The family arrived in Mexico at 11:30 a.m. and reached the hotel by 1:00 p.m.
28. They arrived on an exciting day because the president of the United States was making a tour of the city.
29. Jill's aunt would be joining them later on the trip.

Capitalizing Geographical Names

Capitalizing Proper Nouns			
Capitalize names of cities, states, countries, and continents.			
Cities:	Montreal, Chicago Calcutta, Melbourne	*States:*	Idaho, Delaware Hawaii, Michigan
Countries:	Peru, France China, Nigeria	*Continents:*	Europe, Africa Asia, Antarctica

Capitalize names of bodies of water and geographical features.

Bodies of Water: Black Sea, Missouri River

Geographical Features: Sahara Desert, Mt. Rainier

Do not capitalize *of* or *upon* with proper nouns.

Bay of Naples   Stratford-upon-Avon

Capitalize names of buildings, monuments, and bridges.

Buildings:	Empire State Building, Prudential Tower
Monuments:	Washington Monument, Lincoln Memorial
Bridges:	Brooklyn Bridge, Golden Gate Bridge

Capitalize names of streets and highways.

Streets:	Fifth Avenue, Wilshire Boulevard Riverside Drive, Losey Road
Highways:	Long Island Expressway, Route 65 Lincoln Highway, New York Thruway

---

Capitalize names of sections of the country.

the Atlantic Coast   the Southwest   New England

Do not capitalize directions of the compass.

Sally drove east from Toledo.
He lived west of Broadway.

Capitalize names of planets, stars, galaxies, and constellations.

Mars Sirius the Milky Way
Orion Jupiter Halley's Comet

Do not capitalize the words *sun* or *moon*. The word *earth* is generally not capitalized unless it is listed with other heavenly bodies.

The heat from the sun made us warm.
The moon shone brightly on the snow.
The earth is soft after the rain.

Practice

A. Write the following with correct capitals.

1. new orleans, louisiana
2. jupiter
3. luray caverns
4. massachusetts turnpike
5. midwest
6. isle of wight
7. the pacific coast
8. mediterranean sea
9. central america
10. the big dipper
11. paddington station
12. the white house
13. rocky mountains
14. statue of liberty

B. Write each sentence with correct capitals.

15. We spotted ursa minor in the night sky.
16. It is commonly called the little dipper.
17. Traffic was heavy on the hollywood freeway.
18. The marshall islands are in the pacific ocean.
19. A volcano called mauna loa is located in hawaii.
20. london bridge is now in lake havasu city, arizona.
21. Our history teacher said that the world's longest river is the nile.
22. America's pacific northwest is beautiful.
23. "An attraction in san francisco is the coit tower," said the travel agent.
24. Is australia a continent or an island?
25. The rio grande is the fifth largest river in north america.
26. Approximately every seventy-six years halley's comet can be seen.

C. After each sentence number, write the words that should be capitalized.

27. The Sims family liked mexico because it was so different from their home in austin, texas.
28. They visited the huge pyramid called the pyramid of the sun.
29. Jill learned that the yucatán peninsula separates the gulf of mexico from the caribbean sea.
30. One day the family went boating in the bay of campeche, east of veracruz.
31. Then they flew to mérida in the state of yucatán to visit the ruins at a place called chichén itzá.

Capitalizing Other Names

Capitalizing Proper Nouns

Capitalize names of clubs, organizations, businesses, and institutions.

Clubs: Girl Scouts, Automobile Club of America
Organizations: the American Medical Association
Businesses: Sandy's Auto Repair, Treadway Company
Institutions: Harvard University, Mercy Hospital

Do not capitalize words such as *school, college,* or *theater* unless they are part of a name.

Where do you go to college?
I attend Hunter College.

Capitalize brand names but do not capitalize the names of the products.

Delida yogurt — Lanolite lotion
Whitman soup — Sparkle soap

Capitalize the names of days, months, and holidays.

Saturday — April — New Year's Day
Monday — August — the Fourth of July

Do not capitalize names of seasons.

Everything looks beautiful in spring.
During the winter I ski a great deal.

Capitalize names of languages, races, and nationalities.

Languages: Hebrew, Portuguese, Greek
Races: Caucasian, Asian
Nationalities: American, Canadian, Irish

Do not capitalize names of school subjects except languages or specific courses that are followed by a number.

I love English, biology, and History II.
I also enjoy Russian and mathematics.

Capitalize names of historical events, periods, or documents.

Events: Spanish-American War, Battle of the Bulge
Periods: Middle Ages, Great Depression
Documents: Declaration of Independence, Bill of Rights

Capitalize the names of awards, prizes, and medals.

Academy Award — Nobel Prize
Purple Heart — Grammy Award
Caldecott Medal

Practice

A. Write each sentence with correct capitals.

1. The rios language school teaches spanish, french, and arabic.
2. The short stories have won the o. henry award.
3. For christmas Toby received chocho perfume.
4. Her russian grandparents spoke only yiddish.
5. On the first monday in june, Erica toured bennett college.
6. The treaty of versailles ended world war I.
7. Mom works for the capitol computer company.
8. The ice age is named for the glaciers of the time.
9. The pulitzer prize winners are named in april.
10. The mystic camera club was founded in 1949.
11. The australians wanted to visit the ford theater.
12. We are studying the industrial revolution in history class.
13. The schulz award is intended for college cartoonists.

B. After each sentence number, write the words that should be capitalized.

14. The aeromexico airlines flight to Mérida went smoothly and seemed to take only a short time.
15. The Simses flew on a hot thursday in july.
16. As they toured the Yucatán, they were glad they had brought their bronzy suntan lotion.
17. At Chichén Itzá they met tourists of many nationalities: german, french, and japanese, as well as mexican and american.
18. Everyone admired the ruins of structures that were built by the mayan people.
19. Dr. Sims met an instructor of hers from yale university.
20. He had been her professor in archaeology I.
21. He lent her a collection of poems by Pablo Neruda, the chilean poet who won the 1971 nobel prize for literature.
22. The professor and the Simses had dinner together on july 4 at the parador café.
23. The professor said that he was in Mexico for a meeting of the north american archaeological association.
24. Dr. Sims had studied spanish so that she was able to converse with many people on her travels through Mexico.

Capitalizing First Words and Certain Parts of Speech

Capitalizing First Words

Capitalize the first word of a sentence.
      Boys and girls played softball in the park.
      The games ended in a tie.

Capitalize the first word in a line of poetry.
      A bird came down the walk.
      He did not know I saw;
      He bit an angle-worm in halves
      And ate the fellow, raw.
          — Emily Dickinson
Not all poets use capital letters to begin lines of poetry. This is particularly true of modern poets.

Capitalize the first word of a direct quotation.
      Thad asked, "**W**hat is going on here?"
Do not capitalize the first word of an indirect quotation.
      Neil told him that nothing was going on.

Capitalize the first word in a letter salutation and the name or title of the person addressed.
      My dear **U**ncle **C**hris,   **D**ear **M**adam,   **D**ear **L**eslie,
      Dear **D**r. **B**rown,   **D**ear **S**ir,   **D**ear **G**randpa,
Capitalize only the first word in letter closings.
      Very truly yours,   **S**incerely yours,   **L**ove,
      Your friend,   **F**ondly,   **B**est wishes,

Capitalizing Certain Parts of Speech

Capitalize the pronoun *I*.
      These are the best strawberries **I** have ever eaten.
      Ted and **I** picked them this morning.

Capitalize proper adjectives.
      A **S**hakespearean sonnet ends with two rhyming lines.
      The **R**oman civilization was very advanced.
      What **E**uropean country would you like to visit?

A. Write each sentence with correct capitals.

1. she said, "it is too noisy here."
2. a baker's dozen includes thirteen items.
3. the letter closed with the words "as ever."
4. most of us cannot comprehend einsteinian theory.
5. when will i get my turn?
6. he and i are good friends.
7. homer is a famous greek poet.
8. pat said that he wanted to go.

B. Write each sentence, using capitals correctly. Some are lines of poetry.

9. i started early, took my dog,
   and visited the sea...
10. my african cousin and i toured California.
11. carol is studying newtonian physics.
12. joseph said that bavarian cream pie is his favorite.
13. "dear sir" is too formal in a friendly note.
14. Jean responded, "of course, you may go."
15. "the news is very good," he announced.

C. Write the letter, using correct capitals.

dear señorita michelle,
     this is the best time i have ever had. everything is great, especially the mexican food! my family and i will visit Costa Rica next. it will be our first central american stop. columbus named the country in 1502. we plan to travel by train while in Costa Rica. my mother wants to go to Limón, on the caribbean coast. we will begin our panamanian trip at colón.
     here are some lines from a poem i have just read.
     "i could not sleep for thinking of the sky,
     the unending sky, with all its million suns...."
i will write again soon to tell you more about this incredible trip.

     love,
     Jill

Capitalizing Other Titles

The titles of written works, movies, and works of art and music are capitalized in writing. This is true also for names of trains, ships, and all aircraft. Certain religious terms are also capitalized.

Capitalizing Other Titles

Capitalize the first word, the last word, and all important words in titles.

Books:	The Fighting Ground, Watership Down
Stories:	"The Secret Sharer"
Articles:	"Does TV Change the Way We Think?"
Poems:	"Jabberwocky," "El Dorado"
Magazines:	Newsweek, Popular Science
Plays:	The Glass Menagerie, My Fair Lady
Newspapers:	Los Angeles Times, The Sun
Movies:	Star Wars, The Black Stallion
Paintings:	The Night Watch, The Last Supper
Works of Music:	El Salón Mexico, "America"

Unimportant words, such as articles, coordinating conjunctions, and prepositions, are usually not capitalized unless they are the first or last word in the title.

> The Book of Lists, A Raisin in the Sun
> Porgy and Bess, "Word from a Raft"

Capitalize names of trains, ships, and all aircraft.

Orient Express	U.S.S. Enterprise
Concorde	Mayflower
Union Pacific	The Spirit of St. Louis

Capitalize words referring to the Deity, and names of holy books, religions, and denominations.

Deity:	God, Jehovah, Our Father
Holy Books:	the Bible, the Koran
Religions:	Judaism, Christianity, Buddhism
Denominations:	Catholic, Mormon, Protestant

Do not capitalize the word *god* when referring to deities in ancient mythologies.

> Ancient myths tell about gods and heroes.
> In Roman myths Vulcan was the god of fire.
> Minerva was the Roman goddess of wisdom.

Practice

A. Write the word groups with correct capitals.

    1. *peter and the wolf* (work of music)
    2. *by the seashore* (painting)
    3. *west side story* (play)
    4. *u.s. news and world report* (magazine)
    5. "the greatest city" (poem)
    6. *the spirit of st. louis* (aircraft)

B. Write each sentence with correct capitals.

    7. Jay read the article "garden pests."
    8. The *bhagavad-gita* is a sacred book of hinduism.
    9. Vermeer painted *young woman with a water jug*.
  10. Mozart composed *the magic flute*.
  11. They had a jewish prayer book.
  12. The *lake shore limited* chugged into Chicago.
  13. *the winter's tale* was first acted in 1611.
  14. Lee read *shōgun* in her new armchair.
  15. Ty saw the movie *e.t.* aboard the *queen elizabeth 2*.
  16. christians revere the new testament.

C. After each sentence number, write the words that should be capitalized.

  17. The Simses watched the freighter *palma* go through the Panama Canal.
  18. Then they traveled to Colón on a train nicknamed the *balboa bullet*.
  19. On the way Mr. Sims read *the star and herald* newspaper.
  20. Jill listened to "stayin' alive" on a tape of *saturday night fever*.
  21. She finished reading *ten little indians*.
  22. Then she picked up *travel* magazine.
  23. She read that Paul Gauguin, who painted *two tahitian women on the beach*, once visited Panama.
  24. Dr. Sims read her Spanish copy of the holy bible.
  25. The Simses were baptists.
  26. However, they went to a roman catholic church in Colón.

Writing Numbers

Writing Out Numbers

Write out numbers that are made up of fewer than three words.
 	
    I received **four** responses to my letter.
    About **eighty-six** actors tried out for ten roles.
    Over **638** people watched the parade.

Write out a number that begins a sentence or rewrite the sentence.
 	
    Two hundred forty-seven people were on the jet.
    The jet carried **247** people.

Write out ordinal numbers. Ordinal numbers are the names for numbers such as *first, fifth,* and *tenth.*
 	
    Carl King was **fourth** batter up.
    She is in the **twelfth** grade.

Write out approximate times of day.
 	
    The movie starts about **quarter** to **nine**.
    The race began at **4:27** P.M.

In dialogue write out all numbers except dates.   "On April **3, 1984,** ten thousand people visited the museum," said the guard.

Writing Numbers as Arabic Numerals
Write dates as numerals.   Bob was born on September **2, 1947**.

Write divisions of written material as numerals.
 	
    Chapter **8**   section **5**   paragraph **3**
    Item **4**   column **2**   line **16**

Write house numbers and room numbers as numerals.   Eli lives at **54** Third Street in the city.
When a numbered street is written out and hyphenated, the second word is not capitalized.   Tina lives at **101** Forty-third Street in Room **209**.

Practice

A. Write each sentence, using correct number forms.

1. Are you the new tenant in Room twenty-two?
2. I thought Chapter eight was the funniest.
3. Hillary came in 2nd in the competition.
4. On May twenty-eighth, we are having a barbecue.
5. "Only 9 people saw the play," she said sadly.
6. On June first, 80 guests came to the wedding.
7. Sal has a fever of one hundred three degrees.
8. Section two is on page four of the contract.
9. School starts at eight forty-five A.M.
10. Sonia lives at sixty-four East 12th Street.
11. "Waterville has over 900 families," Alexis said.
12. The dance is scheduled for October seven.
13. Dinner will be served about 6 o'clock.
14. John took 3rd place in the spelling bee.
15. Line ten of the poem rhymes with line eight.
16. 12 students volunteered to work on the posters for our class play.

B. Write the correct number form after each sentence number.

17. The Simses stayed in Rooms sixty and sixty-one of a hotel in Bogotá, Columbia.
18. Bogotá is more than two hundred ten miles from the Pacific Ocean.
19. It lies on a plateau more than eight thousand six hundred feet above sea level.
20. The family flew into Bogotá on July eighteenth at eleven fifty-two A.M.
21. After arriving, Jill wrote a note to her friend who lives at thirty 23rd Avenue.
22. Dr. Sims read Chapter fifteen of her book.
23. Mr. Sims read page two of the newspaper.
24. "The soccer team won the World Cup for the 2nd time," he said.
25. "Jill, did you know that Colombia produces more than 60,000,000 barrels of oil a year?" he asked.
26. That night they ate dinner in the hotel about 8.

End Marks

Periods   Use a period at the end of a declarative sentence. A declarative sentence makes a statement.

> Ohio has played an important role in the history
>   of the United States.
> Carol visited her friend in Columbus, Ohio.
> Columbus is an interesting city to visit.

Use a period at the end of an imperative sentence. An imperative sentence makes a command or a request.

> Don't walk on the grass. (command)
> Please speak more slowly. (request)

Use a period after abbreviations and initials. Use a period with A.M. and P.M.

> Gov. Peter G. Smith was elected on November 9.
> The play will start at 8:15 P.M. Thursday.
> Dr. Rios leaves at 6:15 A.M. daily.

Question Marks   Use a question mark at the end of an interrogative sentence. An interrogative sentence asks a question.

> Where is Victoria Falls located?
> Who would like to erase the board?

Exclamation Marks   Use an exclamation mark at the end of an exclamatory sentence. An exclamatory sentence expresses strong feeling.

> Wow! You can't possibly be serious!
> I was never so scared in my life!

Use an exclamation mark at the end of an imperative sentence that expresses strong feeling.

> Please don't move!
> Quick, look at that!

Summary ✦ **End marks** are punctuation marks that show where a sentence ends.

Practice

A. Write the sentences with the correct end marks.

1. Alan went camping over the weekend
2. Please bring us a menu
3. When are you going to do your homework I am ready to go to the meeting
4. Don't you dare speak to me that way
5. Be sure to take phone messages I am expecting an important call
6. Gee You look absolutely incredible
7. Where are you going on your vacation
8. Run for your life
9. Italy attracts tourists from all over the world Can you imagine seeing so many different people
10. The space creature is coming our way
11. Did you do exercises 2 and 3 on page 138
12. Should we take an umbrella It looks like rain
13. Please give me a hand with this I can't believe how heavy this package is
14. Elizabeth performed a perfect somersault, back flip, and cart-wheel
15. Will you help me You are a lifesaver
16. Remember to mail the letter
17. Did you enjoy the party
18. Goodness You frightened me
19. Will you answer the phone for me
20. My friend is coming to visit

B. Write the paragraph with the correct end marks.

There are some inventors who are familiar to everyone They include Thomas A Edison Does anybody need to ask what he invented Who knows, however, the name Alfred M. Butts Do not laugh, because he invented a game most people have played at least once You will be amazed to learn its name Think of a crossword game played with lettered tiles Does that sound familiar If not, think of the game called Scrabble It was invented in 1931 but was given the name Scrabble in 1948 I was astonished when I won two games in a row

Commas That Separate

Commas in a Series   Use a comma to separate items in a series. A series is made up of three or more items.

> Wendy received books, clothes, and an album. (words)
> Frisky sleeps on the rug, on the sofa, or among the plants. (phrases)
> I wrote, I studied, I passed the test. (clauses)

Do not use commas to separate items in a series when they are all connected by *and* or *or*.

> Carlos enjoys books about art and history and travel.
> Do you prefer bacon or ham or sausage?

Use a comma to separate two or more adjectives that come before a noun.

> The vase is a flawless, painted antique.
> Keith is a tall, slim, dark-haired man.

Do not use a comma between two adjectives if the adjectives are used together to express one idea made up of two closely related thoughts. Notice you would not pause between the two adjectives in the sentences below.

> Ricky bought a shiny new automobile.
> The toothpaste had a clean fresh scent.

Commas in Compound Sentences   Use a comma before the conjunction that joins the parts of a compound sentence.

> Cleavon drank water, but he was still thirsty.
> The sculpture exhibit closed early, and I had wanted very much to see it.

Do not use a comma before the conjunction in a short compound sentence or before a compound verb.

> Jill coughed and she sneezed.
> I went to the hardware store and bought nails.

> **Summary** ◆ Use a **comma** to separate items in a series and to separate compound sentences.

Practice

A. Write each sentence, adding commas where necessary.

1. Louis had a salad yogurt and a banana for lunch.
2. Our parakeet flew between the chairs over the cabinet and then out the window.
3. Steve studied hard and he passed the exam.
4. Molasses is thick dark and sticky.
5. I acted I sang and I danced in the school show.
6. She loved the sounds smells and colors of the woods after a spring shower.

B. Write each sentence, adding commas where necessary.

7. Kim sat in the back and she had to strain to hear the actors singers and orchestra.
8. Ed went to Anaheim Houston and Charleston.
9. We finished the scenery practiced the play and then went home.
10. Tennis golf and badminton are my favorite games.
11. That model is an expensive beautiful car.

C. Write the sentences, adding commas where necessary.

12. It looks like a huge hot-water bottle but it is not.
13. It is not attractive but it can make you look that way.
14. It is a portable bathtub and it is a very sensible invention.
15. This item was invented by a clever resourceful woman named Frances Allen.
16. She believed that travelers could use it after a long hot tiring trip.
17. All you have to do is attach the hoses to a water pipe step in zip up the bag and bathe!
18. Afterwards it can be emptied left to dry and then rolled up.
19. The tub can be carried in a backpack in a suitcase or under your arm.
20. It may seem like an unusual object but other inventors have worked on the idea.
21. It must be fun to carry your own tub around and you never have to call a plumber!

Commas After Introductory Words, Phrases, and Clauses

Introductory Words   Use a comma after words such as *yes, no, why,* and *well* at the beginning of a sentence.

> Yes, let's go to the movies tonight.
> Why, I haven't been to the movies in ages.
> Well, the show starts at 7:30 P.M.
> No, I think that is too early.

Introductory Phrases   Use a comma after a participial phrase at the beginning of a sentence.

> Waking up early, Victoria did a series of morning exercises and walked the dog.
> Arriving early at the theater, Paul waited for his friends in the lobby.
> Eating his breakfast, Rob ran to the school bus.

Introductory Clauses   Use a comma after an adverbial clause at the beginning of a sentence.

> When evening came, we put citronella lamps outside to fend off the mosquitoes.
> Wherever I went, people were helpful and polite.
> Although you expect to be very late, I will prepare and cook a wonderful dinner for you.

Do not use a comma before an adverbial clause that comes at the end of a sentence.

> Remember to keep your wallet in a safe place whenever you travel in a crowded area.
> Please take off your boots before you enter the house.
> Stay in the car while Gerald and I go to the bank.
> Jane and I listened to music after we ate dinner.

> **Summary** ◆ Use a comma after introductory words, phrases, and clauses.

Practice

A. Write each sentence, adding commas where necessary.

1. Involved in her reading Carmen did not see Todd.
2. When Pat raised her hand the teacher called on her.
3. Well I think we ought to discuss this further.
4. When the fire bell rang the students jumped up.
5. Having given his speech Chuck felt proud.
6. Yes you ought to try these African recipes.
7. Why the ingredients are easy to get.
8. Leaving the noisy disco Rick longed for quiet.
9. Astonished by the news Joni stared at us.
10. Where there's a will there's a way.

B. Write the sentences, adding commas where necessary.

11. Yes Samuel F.B. Morse was an interesting man.
12. After he graduated from Yale he became a painter.
13. Considered one of America's best artists he decided to become an inventor.
14. While he was sailing he made this decision.
15. No this was not an idle decision.
16. When he landed in America he had already sketched designs for his telegraph.
17. Having a lot of self-confidence Morse imagined he could do anything.
18. Well his initial attempts at telegraphy were not very successful.
19. Receiving help from the inventor Joseph Henry Samuel F.B. Morse worked out many technical problems.
20. If you have read about Morse keep in mind that he did not actually invent the telegraph.
21. Using his system people soon saw, however, that his was the best one available.
22. Having helped Morse so much Joseph Henry should have become equally famous.
23. Well Henry was to advise another ambitious inventor.
24. Whenever you use a telephone you should remember his name.
25. Yes it was the famous Alexander Graham Bell.

Commas with Interrupters

Appositives   Use commas to set off most appositives. Appositives explain the meaning of nouns that directly precede them. Appositives often include prepositional phrases.

> Ms. Ruiz, my teacher, comes from Puerto Rico.
> Carole ate spaghetti, one of her favorite dishes.
> Tama, our family dog, is a retriever.

Do not use commas with an appositive when it is part of a proper name or when it is needed to identify the noun it follows.

> her daughter Becky   Ethelred the Unready
> my friend Bob   Mary Queen of Scots

Nouns of Direct Address   Use commas to set off nouns of direct address. A noun of direct address is a person's name or a nonspecific name used by someone in conversation. It may be used anywhere in a sentence.

> Who was on the phone, Kristin?
> Pardon me, sir, you dropped your wallet.
> Tom, your mail has arrived.

Interrupters   Use commas to set off parenthetical expressions — interrupting words that are added to a sentence for emphasis or clarity.

> Stuart is the team's best player, in my opinion.
> After all, Juan did win first prize.
> We, however, chose not to attend.

Some common parenthetical expressions are in the chart below.

of course	for example	to tell the truth
after all	by the way	in my opinon
however	furthermore	on the other hand
mind you	besides	in addition
for instance	in fact	as I was saying

Summary ◆ Use commas with appositives, nouns of direct address, and interrupters.

Practice

A. Write each sentence, adding commas where necessary.

1. Waiter please bring our check now.
2. Marge one of my dearest friends works for them.
3. You my friend have the bluest eyes I have ever seen.
4. To tell the truth I wear contact lenses.
5. *Clipper* an airline magazine has good articles.
6. Okay John let's begin rehearsal.
7. Greg the hardest worker in our family has two jobs.
8. After all the plane does not arrive until nine.
9. By the way how far is it to the bus stop Tracy?
10. Hank the starting pitcher stepped up to the mound.
11. Rachel my friend wants to settle in Israel.
12. Leonardo da Vinci the artist was also an inventor.
13. It seems to me however that the plan will work.
14. Excuse me miss which way is the elevator?
15. On the other hand Manuel you did a fine job.

B. Write the sentences, adding commas where necessary.

16. Alexander Graham Bell the inventor of the telephone became world famous.
17. Before he became an inventor however he taught deaf-mutes people who cannot hear or speak.
18. He was born in Edinburgh the capital of Scotland.
19. However he is considered an American.
20. He came to the United States in 1871 in fact and taught at Boston University.
21. Joseph Henry the man who helped Morse encouraged Bell to develop his invention.
22. Bell followed his advice of course.
23. In March of 1876, he said to his assistant over the wires ''Mr. Watson please come here. I want you.''
24. In addition Bell invented other things.
25. He also invented the graphophone the forerunner of the phonograph.
26. He will always be remembered of course for the telephone the first device to successfully transmit speech over a wire.
27. Bell is one of America's most important scientists in my opinion.

Other Uses of Commas

Commas in Dates and Addresses   Use a comma to separate items in dates and addresses.

> Tuesday, June 27, 1991   April 3, 1775
> 90 Kent Court, Daly City, California 94015
> 41 Main Street, Branchville, New Jersey 07826

Use a comma after the last part of a date or an address when they are part of a sentence.

> On Thursday, June 2, 1991, Melissa graduated from the university and looked forward to beginning her career in the city.
> The address 10 East Tenth Street, New York, New York 10003, was clearly written on the envelope.
> On Monday, April 14, 1991, I sprained my ankle.

Write the ZIP code number a few spaces after the name of the state unless the ZIP code is included in an address in a sentence.

> Colorado Springs, Colorado   80915
> Provo, Utah   84601
> My new address is 2 Oak Street, Akron, Ohio 44310.
> My previous mailing address was 540 Doral Country Drive, Nashville, Tennessee 37221.

Do not use a comma between the month and the year if no specific day is given.

> February 1978   December 1988

Commas with Letter Parts   Commas are used with parts of a letter. Use a comma after the salutation of a friendly letter.

> Dear Aunt Beth,   Dear Evan,
> Dear Grandpa,   Dear Dina,

Use a comma after the closing of a friendly or a business letter.

> Regards,   Sincerely yours,
> Best wishes,   Very truly yours,

Summary ◆ Use a comma to separate items in dates and addresses. Use a comma with certain letter parts.

Practice

A. Write the phrases, adding commas where necessary.

1. Friday August 29
2. Sincerely yours
3. 4211 Avenue K Brooklyn New York 11230
4. Thursday January 19 1936
5. Dear Grandfather
6. 239 Brook Street Lynchburg Virginia 24501
7. Cordially yours

B. Write each sentence, adding commas where necessary.

8. Evelyn has lived at 18231 Abbott Lane Villa Park California for many years.
9. On July 6 1968 Larry went to Mexico City Mexico.
10. "Dear Sara" is probably not the right greeting for a letter to your doctor.
11. The address in the catalog was Lincoln Nebraska.
12. March 30 1853 was the birth date of Van Gogh.
13. On July 29 1890 this wonderful artist died.
14. A package arrived from Denver Colorado.
15. The McHugheses will soon move from Panama City Florida to Salt Lake City Utah.
16. Bob's first airplane trip was from Dallas Texas to Columbia South Carolina.
17. Saturday May 21 1983 was a great day in my life.

C. Write the sentences, adding commas where necessary.

18. In May 1876 the Centennial Exposition opened in Philadelphia Pennsylvania.
19. It was opened by President Ulysses Grant and Emperor Dom Pedro of Brazil.
20. On June 25 1876 the emperor asked Alexander Graham Bell to demonstrate the telephone.
21. Bell later gave a demonstration in Boston Massachusetts.
22. Thomas Edison, born on February 11 1847 in Milan Ohio was also at the exposition.

Quotation Marks

Direct Quotations   A direct quotation always begins with a capital letter. It is separated from the rest of the sentence by a comma. Use a comma *after* a quotation and *inside* the quotation marks if the quotation begins the sentence. Do not use a comma if the quotation ends with a question mark or an exclamation mark.

> "It is hot today," said Mark.   "There is no air!" Toni screamed.
> "Open the door," replied Nina.   Eli asked, "When can we leave?"

Use a comma *before* a quotation and *outside* quotation marks if the quotation ends a sentence. Periods are placed inside closing quotation marks. Question and exclamation marks go inside the quotation marks if they are part of the quotation. Otherwise place them outside the quotation marks.

> Mr. Liu said, "Please read Chapters 1–10."
> Hiro said, "Mr. Liu told us to read Chapters 1–10!"
> "Is the book interesting?" Hiro asked.
> Did you say, "Read Chapters 1–10"?

Do not use quotation marks with an indirect quotation.

> **Indirect:**   Ben said that he felt sick today.
>   He wished that he could rest today.
> **Direct:**   Ben said, "I feel sick today."
>   He replied, "I wish I could rest today."

Use single quotation marks around a quotation within a quotation.

> "Who said, 'I am hungry'?" asked Lisa.
> Tom explained, "When my sister saw the painting, she said,
>   'I like the colors of the trees and sky.' "

Quotation Marks with Titles   Use quotation marks to enclose titles of the following types of works:

> **Short stories:** "Reena"   **Chapters:** "Stress in Your Life"
> **Poems:** "Chicago"   **Songs:** "Tomorrow"

Summary ♦ Use **quotation marks** to enclose a person's exact words.

Practice

A. Write each sentence, adding quotation marks, commas, and capitals where necessary.

1. Mom said please help me clean out the garage.
2. Bryan said that Shelly did not come to the party.
3. who said I want to go home? asked Sue.
4. who will lend me money for lunch? asked Debbie.
5. The poem Trees was written by Joyce Kilmer.
6. Maria said that the chorus sings too loudly.
7. can Jennifer really recite French poetry? asked Al.
8. you'd better not do that again! cried Angie.
9. He asked who said I have been to the mountaintop?
10. Auld Lang Syne is a Scottish song.
11. The chapter is called Your Creative Child.
12. have you ever seen a better movie? asked Ricky.
13. Alan's favorite story is The Tell-Tale Heart by Edgar Allan Poe.
14. The song Loverly comes from *My Fair Lady*.
15. I watched that program on television said Jan.
16. Nan said Mrs. Smith has asked me to help her.

B. Write the paragraphs, adding quotation marks, commas, and capitals where necessary.

17. Steve was reading to Greg from a chapter called Inventions for the Home. Steve said to Greg the pressure cooker was invented in 1679.
18. you have got to be kidding! exclaimed Greg. I didn't realize it was invented so long ago he added.
19. my mom would say we have the original model remarked Steve. Steve continued did you know the electric toaster was invented in the 1920s? Then he said the can opener was invented in the 1860s.
20. what about other inventions outside the kitchen? Greg asked.
21. there is the phonograph Steve replied. yes, without it, we could not listen to records! Steve continued. can you imagine our lives without all these inventions? asked Steve.
22. who said necessity is the mother of invention? Greg asked.

Divided Quotations

Divided Quotations   A speaker's words may be divided into parts by other words. If the second part of the divided quotation is a separate sentence, begin it with a capital letter and enclose it in quotation marks.

> "Eat your spinach," said Dad. "It's good for you."
> "I don't like spinach," Chris said. "I would rather have broccoli."
> "How about some brussels sprouts?" asked Dad. "Green vege-tables are important in your diet."

Do not begin the second part of a divided quotation with a capital letter if that part is not a separate sentence. Put a comma after the first part of the quotation, and enclose that part with quotation marks. Begin the second part of the quotation with a small letter and enclose that part in quotation marks also.

> "Where is," said Marlene, "my new record?"
> "I didn't take it," Len cried, "so you must have lost it."
> "I remember now," replied Marlene, "that my friend bor-rowed it for the party."

Dialogue   A conversation between two people is a dialogue. Start a new paragraph each time another speaker begins talking. Do not put quotation marks around every sentence spoken by the same person. Put quotation marks around the entire uninterrupted speech. Read the following dialogue.

Hank said, "Would you help me study for the quiz? I'll bring the calculator and the peanuts."

"Sure," Amy replied, "but don't forget paper and pencils. I'll supply the raisins and beverages this time. Where would be a good place for us to meet and study?"

"I will meet you at my house," said Hank, "at 4:00 P.M. Don't worry, I will be on time. Amy, I really appreciate your helping me prepare for this history quiz."

Summary ◆ Sometimes a direct quotation is divided into two or more parts.

Practice

A. Write the sentences, adding quotation marks, commas, and capitals where necessary.

1. What asked Sue can I get Mom for her birthday?
2. I think said Dad that these muffins are great!
3. He is asleep said Li. Let's come back tomorrow.
4. How many more days asked Brian is it until my party?
5. Thanks for the book said Cary. it helped me a lot.
6. I studied for the history test last night responded Rita and I expect to do very well.

B. Write each quotation as a divided quotation.

7. "Did you ever visit Disney World?" asked Kelly.
8. Ilana said, "It's too bad you've got a cold and have to miss the picnic this Saturday."
9. Pete said, "I don't think their team has a chance."
10. "What did you learn about lasers?" asked Mrs. Lee.
11. Judy said, "The fair opens on Thursday night with a parade and free rides."
12. Kelly exclaimed, "The fair and its music and wonderful food are my favorite parts of summer!"
13. Rita asked, "What is the admission price?"
14. "Let's be sure to ride on the Ferris wheel," Judy remarked.
15. Bob exclaimed, "The weather should be beautiful."

C. Write the dialogue, adding quotation marks, commas, and capitals. Indent where necessary.

16. Lisa asked have you ever heard of Frederick Jones? 17. No, I haven't answered Robin. tell me about him. 18. He had a natural talent for making and fixing mechanical things Lisa replied. 19. Robin remarked he did everything. 20. You're right Lisa answered. In 1939 he invented the machine that hands you a ticket at the movie theater. 21. That is a handy gadget. what else did he invent? asked Robin. 22. Well Lisa continued think about frozen foods. 23. What do you mean? Robin asked. 24. Jones invented cooling units for trucks Lisa said. Food can be shipped all over the country she added because of his invention. 25. Robin said i must tell Ty about Mr. Jones.

Italics and Underlining

The titles of books, magazines, newspapers, movies, television shows, plays, paintings, and operas should be underlined in handwriting or in typing. The names of planes, trains, and ships should also be underlined in handwriting. In printed materials these titles and names appear in *italics*.

Books: *A Tale of Two Cities, Moby Dick*
Magazines: *Omni, Natural History*
Newspapers: *Rocky Mountain News*

Within a sentence, the title of a newspaper is underlined, but the word *the* before the title is not. The name of a city in a newspaper's title is usually underlined.

Movies: *The Sound of Music, American Graffiti*
Plays: *Julius Caesar, The Skin of Our Teeth*
Paintings: *Pool with Waterlilies*
Operas: *The Barber of Seville*
Ships: *Trieste II*
Television Shows: *The Bill Cosby Show*
Trains: *Orient Express,* the *Twentieth Century Limited*
Planes: *Concorde*

> **Summary** ♦ **Italics** are letters that lean to the right in printed material — *italics*. In writing, these words are underlined.

Practice

A. Write the following titles and names. Use underlining for italics or use quotation marks.

1. All's Well That Ends Well (play)
2. Family Ties (TV show)
3. The Adventures of Tom Sawyer (book)
4. Chicago Daily News (newspaper)
5. Savannah (ship)
6. Don Giovanni (opera)
7. Golden Arrow (train)
8. Goodbye, Mr. Chips (movie)
9. Young Woman with a Water Jug (painting)
10. The Marriage of Figaro (opera)

B. Write the sentences. Underline the titles that should be underlined.

11. Hector saw a listing in TV Guide for a movie called The Story of Louis Pasteur.
12. The Houston Chronicle said that this old film described how Pasteur developed a vaccine for rabies.
13. Hector, who wanted to be an inventor, watched the film, and then he listened to the opera Porgy and Bess.
14. He read Smithsonian, a magazine, while he listened.
15. He read about the Wright brothers and their historic first plane, Flyer.
16. Then he thought about how he was able to watch Casablanca, his favorite movie, because of the people who worked to invent television.
17. When the music finished, Hector skimmed through a library book called Weird and Wacky Inventions.
18. A picture in it reminded him of Charlie Chaplin's hilarious movie Modern Times.
19. Hector looked through another book called Inventions and Discoveries.
20. In it, he saw a reproduction of Rembrandt's painting The Anatomy Lesson.
21. Soon, Hector would be joining his friends to see the play Our Town.

Semicolons

A semicolon indicates a pause in an idea. The pause is longer than that indicated by a comma, but shorter and less important than that signaled by a period.

Use a semicolon to join independent clauses in a sentence when the clauses are not joined by a conjunction such as *and, but, or, nor, for,* or *yet.*

> **We intended to drive through northern New York; somehow
> we ended up in Vermont.**
> **Our vacation was very enjoyable and relaxing; needless to say,
> it ended much too soon.**

You could make two sentences out of each of the examples above. Separate sentences, however, would not show how closely related the ideas in the clauses are.

Commas may be used to separate very short independent clauses that are not joined by conjunctions.

> **I came, I saw, I conquered.**
> **We laughed together, we cried together, we grew up together.**

Use a semicolon to join independent clauses when the second clause begins with a word such as *however, for instance, for example, thus, that is, hence, moreover, furthermore, nevertheless, otherwise, therefore, besides, instead, consequently,* or *as a result.*

> **The rainstorm continued all weekend; consequently, we had to
> cancel our plans for a barbecue.**
> **The barbecue at the park was cancelled; however, everyone
> met at my house, and we had an indoor picnic.**

Use a semicolon between independent clauses of a sentence when there are commas within the clauses.

> **Dale paints, knits, and sews; and her sister crochets, weaves, and sings.**
> **My brother collects coins, old banks, and stamps; and I collect
> baseball cards, paperweights, and horse figurines.**

Summary ♦ Use a **semicolon** to connect two sentences that are closely related in thought.

Practice

A. Write each sentence, adding semicolons as needed.

EXAMPLE: The bus was late therefore, we did not arrive at school on time.

ANSWER: The bus was late; therefore, we did not arrive at school on time.

1. At the library, Devon went to the fiction section Yoko went to the reference room.
2. Saturn, the ringed planet, has been explored by satellite hence, scientists know a lot about it.
3. Generally, cameras are easy to use many of them are expensive as well.
4. A soft breeze blew in off the sunny, sparkling, blue bay and the hot, tanned bathers felt cooler and looked comfortable.
5. January beat the record for snow however, February is expected to be worse.
6. The storm had deposited several inches of snow as a result, conditions were just right for sledding.
7. I saw Tina, Evan, and Tim at the library and I met Miata, Samuel, and Carla at the pool.

B. Write the sentences, adding semicolons as needed.

8. We can be proud of American inventions produced over the years the list is long and impressive.
9. Some inventions came out of the United States in the early nineteenth century however, American inventive talent was really evident from the mid-1800s onward.
10. The late 1870s were very productive for America for example, the telephone, the phonograph, and the light bulb were invented in that period.
11. Some things have been around for a long time that is, they were invented in the United States earlier than you might think.
12. These are things people now use every day they include the rollfilm camera (1888), the zipper (1893), the safety razor (1895), and breakfast cereals (1900).
13. Many inventions have added comfort and convenience to our lives nevertheless, we take them for granted today.

Colons and Hyphens

Colons   Use a colon between the hour and the minute in time.

Time: 8:00 P.M.   12:41 A.M.

Use a colon after the salutation in a business letter.

Salutation: Madam: Gentlemen:

The phrases *as follows* or *the following* often appear in a sentence before a list. They signal that a list is to follow. Do not use a colon after a verb or a preposition. Either leave out the colon or reword the sentence.

Wrong: The winners are: Joe, Tia, and Otis.
Right: The winners are Joe, Tia, and Otis.
Right: The following people are the winners: Joe, Tia, and Otis.

Wrong: I am searching for: pencils, paper, and scissors.
Right: I am searching for pencils, paper, and scissors.
Right: I am searching for the following items: pencils, paper, and scissors.

Hyphens   Be sure to divide words correctly at the end of a line; that is, divide them only between syllables.

> Ms. Simmons said, "Believe it or not, you will really enjoy the home-work assignment."

Do not divide a word so that only one letter appears at the end or the beginning of a line. For example, *e-nough* is an incorrect division, as is *health-y*. One-syllable words cannot be divided.

Be sure to use a hyphen with compound numbers from twenty-one to ninety-nine and with fractions used as adjectives.

> sixty-six pages   two-thirds cup
> ninety-seven bells   three-fourths inch

Summary ◆ Use a **colon** between the hour and the minute in time, after the greeting of a business letter, and before a list of items. Use a **hyphen** to divide a word at the end of a line, with compound numbers, and with fractions.

Practice

A. Write each sentence, adding colons and hyphens.

1. Stir in the following ingredients one half cup of the zucchini, the eggplant, and the tomatoes.
2. Probably ninety nine people out of a hundred do not know the meanings of *fungo* and *aglet*.
3. Paul said he thought it was about time the candi dates discussed the important issues.
4. The following people are likely to be chosen Nan, Ty, and Bill.
5. Whenever you doubt the spelling or pronunci ation of a word, your dictionary can help.
6. The championship game between the two schools will begin at 245 P.M. this Friday.
7. Sue wrote the greeting "Dear Sir" in a letter in which she applied for a summer job.

B. Write the sentences, adding colons and hyphens where necessary.

8. It may surprise you to learn that the ancient Ro mans had a form of central heating.
9. Over 2,000 years ago they heated their public baths by cir culating hot air under the floors.
10. Today, of course, we use the following sources of ener gy gas, oil, and electricity.
11. Before it comes into a building, air can also be condi tioned as follows it can be cleaned, cooled, or warmed.
12. In the ancient world, archaeologists have made another sur prising discovery.
13. In a city in India, they found several ruins of lavato ries and drains as we know them today.
14. Europeans did not know about these things until many cen turies later.
15. Eventually inventors came to the rescue with the fol lowing items bathtubs, toilets, and sewage systems.
16. Housework was made easier, too, with the following inven tions the carpet sweeper, the vacuum cleaner, the washing machine, the dryer, and laundry detergent.
17. Quite a few of these items were invented less than ninety five years ago!

Diagraming Guide

Sentence Parts

A sentence diagram shows how the parts of a sentence work together. Using horizontal, vertical, and slanting lines, a sentence diagram shows the role of every word, phrase, and clause in a sentence. Learning to diagram sentences will strengthen your ability to recognize and use the many sentence parts you have studied.

Subjects and Verbs A sentence diagram begins with a horizontal line divided by a vertical line. A diagram shows that the subject and the verb are the two main sentence parts. Place the subject on the left of the dividing line and the verb on the right. Make sure the dividing line passes through and below the horizontal line.

Time flies.	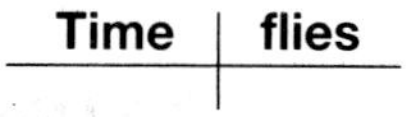	Rain was falling.	
Time	**flies**	**Rain**	**was falling**

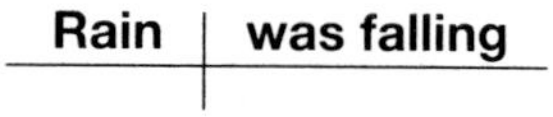

Notice that the entire verb phrase is written on the horizontal line.

The subject of an interrogative sentence often comes after the verb. In a diagram, however, place the subject before the verb. To show the subject of an imperative sentence, write *you* in parentheses in the subject place.

Can George dance?	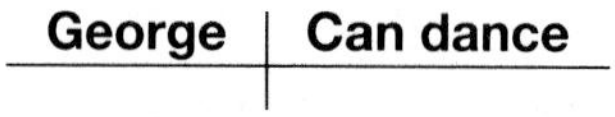	Run!	
George	**Can dance**	**(you)**	**Run**

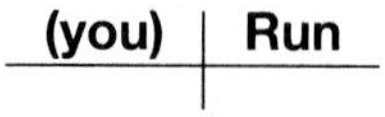

Notice that a sentence diagram shows the capital letters of a sentence but not the punctuation.

When a sentence has a compound subject or a compound verb, diagram them on separate horizontal lines. Write the conjunction that joins the subjects or verbs on a broken vertical line linking the horizontal lines.

Men and women sing.

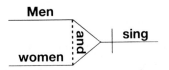

They walk, jog, or run.

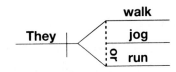

Adjectives and Adverbs   In a sentence diagram an adjective is written on a slanting line below the noun or pronoun it modifies. When more than one adjective modifies a word, each is written on its own line. The articles *a, an,* and *the* are also diagramed in this way.

The last bell rang.

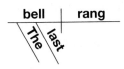

A huge white flag was flying.

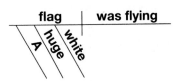

Adverbs are also diagramed on slanting lines. An adverb modifying a verb is placed below the verb. An adverb modifying an adjective or an adverb is placed on a slanting line attached to the word that is being modified.

She sang quite well.

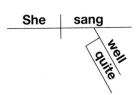

The very young child wept softly.

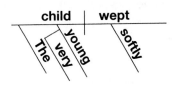

As you have seen, conjunctions are placed on broken lines between the words they join.

The small but brave dog barked loudly and angrily.

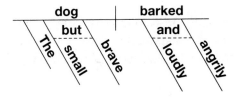

Here and There   The words *here* and *there* often begin sentences, but they are never subjects. Both can be adverbs that modify the verb. Diagram such adverbs on a slanting line below the verb.

Here is President Wilson.

There it lies.

President Wilson | is
\ *Here*

it | lies
\ *There*

There used as an introductory word is diagramed on a separate horizontal line above the subject.

There will be time.

There must be music.

There
_____
time | will be

There
_____
music | must be

Prepositional Phrases   A prepositional phrase is diagramed below the word it modifies. Write the preposition on a slanting line below the word modified. Then write the object of the preposition on a horizontal line connected to the slanting line.

The girls on our team run with great speed.

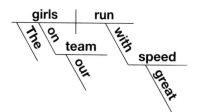

Often a prepositional phrase modifies the object of another preposition. In such a sentence, diagram the second phrase beneath the object it modifies.

The biology students hiked to the bottom of the canyon.

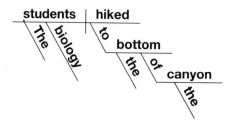

An adverb phrase does not always follow the verb it modifies. No matter where an adverb phrase appears in a sentence, diagram it below the word it modifies.

In the summer the Ausleys go to the mountains.

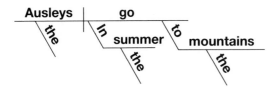

Other Sentence Parts A direct object appears on the horizontal line after the verb. It is separated from the verb by a short vertical line.

The workers uncovered several gold coins.

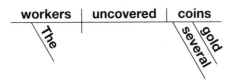

An indirect object appears on a horizontal line below the verb. A slanting line connects it to the verb.

Mrs. Egan showed us the movie.

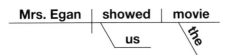

To diagram a predicate noun, a predicate pronoun, or a predicate adjective, write it on the horizontal line after the verb. It is separated from the verb by a line that slants toward the subject.

Janice is a big help.   She seems so mature.

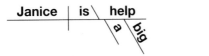   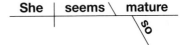

Practice

A. Diagram each sentence.

1. They will forget.
2. Think!
3. Can she wait?
4. It slipped!
5. I should finish.

6. Must they come?
7. Did you walk?
8. We might have won.
9. Answer!
10. Trucks have arrived.

B. Diagram each sentence. Remember to write each conjunction on a broken line.

11. Stay or go.
12. Leo or Tom called.
13. We ate and left.
14. May she and I start?
15. Cars and campers skidded.

C. Diagram each sentence. Write adjectives, adverbs, and introductory words correctly.

16. A large brown owl glided noiselessly overhead.
17. There were many serious problems.
18. The wise captain spoke firmly but calmly.
19. Here is a young and very beautiful fawn.
20. Did your doctor and his friends arrive late?

D. Diagram each sentence. Be sure to place each prepositional phrase below the word it modifies.

21. The helicopter landed on the top of the cliff.
22. In December we will go to France.
23. The man with the trumpet plays in a large band.
24. After a month of practice, we sang well.
25. Three of the boys dived from the high board.

E. Diagram each sentence. Be sure to show direct and indirect objects and predicate nouns, pronouns, and adjectives.

26. Did Eileen or Terry return the lost books?
27. Hank gave the audience his famous smile.
28. All of the children appear so polite.
29. Show Officer Graybar the exact location.
30. Henry was an excellent host.

F. Diagram each sentence. The sentences contain sentence parts and parts of speech you have studied.

31. At the back of your closet, you will find it.
32. Sleek and swift, the greyhound won the prize.
33. There is no excuse for such behavior.
34. Here is that card from your grandmother.
35. Slowly but steadily the old car crept uphill.

Compound and Complex Sentences

So far you have practiced diagraming simple sentences. You can use the same rules you have studied, however, to diagram more complicated sentences. In this section you will learn how to diagram compound sentences and complex sentences.

Compound Sentences   A compound sentence is formed from two or more independent clauses joined by a conjunction or a semicolon. To diagram a compound sentence, treat each independent clause as a simple sentence. Begin with the first clause of the compound sentence, writing its subject and verb on a horizontal line. Then add modifiers, phrases, and other sentence parts as you would in a simple sentence. Diagram the second clause of the sentence below the first clause. The verbs in the two clauses are joined by the conjunction as shown in the diagram below.

The sun feels hot, but the lake is too cold for a swim.

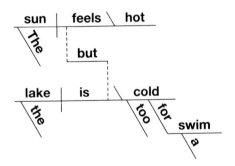

If a semicolon joins the two clauses of a compound sentence, use a broken line to join the two verbs. Put an *X* in parentheses on the horizontal line to show that there is no conjunction.

Len writes clever essays; he also writes funny stories.

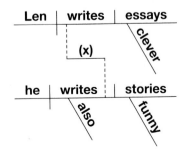

Complex Sentences   A complex sentence contains one independent clause and at least one subordinate clause. Diagram the independent clause first and the subordinate clause below it. An adjective clause usually begins with a relative pronoun, such as *who, whom, whose, which,* or *that,* and modifies a noun or pronoun in the independent clause. Use a broken line to connect the relative pronoun with the word the adjective clause modifies in the independent clause.

The woman whom you met is my teacher.
The boy who gave the party prepared the food.

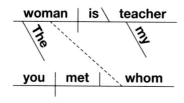

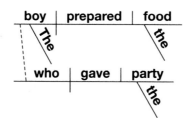

Notice that the relative pronoun has a function in its clause. It may be a subject, a direct object, a predicate pronoun, or a modifier.

A subordinate adverb clause is also diagramed below the independent clause. An adverb clause begins with a subordinating conjunction, such as *after, because, before, if, since,* or *when.* A slanting broken line connects the verbs in the two clauses. Write the subordinating conjunction on the broken line.

If you feel dizzy, we must call a doctor.

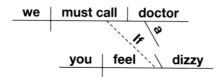

Practice

A. Diagram each compound sentence.

1. The party is on Friday, and we are invited.
2. Mike must leave now, or he will miss the bus.
3. The snow has stopped, but the walk is slippery.
4. I have done my part, and now you must finish.
5. The play is tomorrow, and I have no costume!

B. Diagram each complex sentence.

6. The money that you found is mine.
7. Since you like eggs, I made an omelet.
8. The person who made this table is my father.
9. Luckily no one was on the bridge when it fell.
10. If it had not rained, she would have been there.

C. Diagram each compound or complex sentence.

11. My family recently bought a computer, but I have not used it yet.
12. If you do not like this loud music, we can walk outside by the pool.
13. Their new home, which is near a state forest, is quite lovely.
14. Is the program that Mr. Conklin recommended so highly on television tonight?
15. Give me some better reasons, or I will not sign.

Glossary of Usage

Conjugation of the Verb *Be*

Principal Parts: be, was, (have) been, being

Present	Past	Future
I am	was	will (shall) be
she, he, it is	was	will be
we are	were	will (shall) be
you, they are	were	will be

Present Perfect	Past Perfect	Future Perfect
I, we have been	had been	will (shall) have been
she, he, it has been	had been	will have been
you, they have been	had been	will have been

Conjugation of the Verb *Have*

Principal Parts: have, had, (have) had, having

Present	Past	Future
I, we have	had	will (shall) have
you, they have	had	will have
she, he, it has	had	will have

Present Perfect	Past Perfect	Future Perfect
I, we have had	had had	will (shall) have had
you, they have had	had had	will have had
she, he, it has had	had had	will have had

Conjugation of the Verb *Do*

Principal Parts: do, did, (have) done, doing

Present	Past	Future
I, we do	did	will (shall) do
you, they do	did	will do
she, he, it does	did	will do

Present Perfect	Past Perfect	Future Perfect
I, we have done	had done	will (shall) have done
you, they have done	had done	will have done
she, he, it has done	had done	will have done

Usage Problems

a	An indefinite article used before a word beginning with a consonant sound
	Take <u>a</u> seat. This is <u>a</u> heavy package.
an	An indefinite article used before a word beginning with a vowel sound
	We reached <u>an</u> agreement. Give <u>an</u> honest answer.
accept	A verb that means "to receive" or "to agree to"
	Do they <u>accept</u> credit cards here?
except	As a preposition, means "excluding" or "but"
	We've looked everywhere <u>except</u> the attic.
advice	A noun that means "a recommendation regarding what to do"
	We followed her <u>advice</u> about where to stay.
advise	A verb that means "to recommend a course of action"
	The doctor <u>advised</u> me to get plenty of rest.
affect	A verb that means "to influence"
	The weather will <u>affect</u> our plans.
effect	Usually a noun that means "result"
	The <u>effect</u> of the storm was considerable.
	Also a verb that means "to bring about"
	They will <u>effect</u> a change in the agenda.
all ready	Means "completely prepared"
	We are <u>all ready</u> to leave.
already	An adverb that means "by now" or "by a given time"
	I have <u>already</u> had dinner.
all right	The preferred spelling. Do not use *alright*.
	Is it <u>all right</u> to leave my coat here?

all together	Means "everyone in the same place"
	Our family will be <u>all together</u> for Thanksgiving.
altogether	An adverb that means "completely"
	We were not <u>altogether</u> happy with the plan.
at	Indicates presence in a place
	They were <u>at</u> the beach.
to	Indicates motion toward a place
	They went <u>to</u> the lighthouse.
bad	An adjective used to modify a noun or a pronoun
	This is a <u>bad</u> picture. The milk smells <u>bad</u>.
badly	An adverb used to modify a verb
	The horse was injured <u>badly</u> in the fall.
beside	A preposition that means "next to" or "at the side of"
	She sat <u>beside</u> me on the bus.
besides	As a preposition, means "in addition to" or "other than"
	Who <u>besides</u> Tracy is going to the game?
between	A preposition used when speaking of two people or objects
	Lee and Kim split the cost <u>between</u> them.
among	A preposition used in discussing more than two
	The prize money was divided <u>among</u> ten people.
capital	Means "a city that serves as a seat of government"
	Raleigh is the <u>capital</u> of North Carolina.
capitol	Means "a building in which a state legislature meets"; when capitalized, means "the building in which the United States Congress meets"
	The dome of the state <u>capitol</u> can be seen for miles.
different from	*Different from* is generally preferred over *different than*.
	Monkeys are <u>different from</u> chimpanzees.

fewer	Refers to number; means "not as many"
	Jo sold <u>fewer</u> tickets than Pat.
less	Refers to size or degree; means "not as much"
	She also raised <u>less</u> money.
formerly	An adverb that means "at an earlier time"
	This building was <u>formerly</u> a school.
formally	An adverb that means "in accord with rules"
	The winner will be <u>formally</u> announced next week.
good	An adjective used to modify a noun or pronoun
	Jane wrote a <u>good</u> story. Mine is <u>good</u>, too.
well	An adverb used to modify a verb
	Pedro plays the piano <u>well</u>.
	An adjective when it refers to a person's health
	I did not feel <u>well</u> during the boat trip.
in	A preposition that means "inside" or "within"
	There was a message <u>in</u> the bottle.
into	A preposition that means "toward the inside"; indicates motion
	Do not toss the bottle <u>into</u> the ocean.
its	Possessive form of the pronoun *it*
	That company treats <u>its</u> employees well.
it's	Contraction of *it is* and *it has*
	<u>It's</u> convenient to get there from here.
lie	Means "to rest" or "to recline"; never has a direct object
	The cat likes to <u>lie</u> in the sun.
lay	Means "to put down" or "to place"; often has a direct object
	Please <u>lay</u> the toy on the shelf.
lose	A verb that means "to misplace" or "to suffer loss"
	Do not <u>lose</u> the keys to the car.
loose	An adjective that means "not tight" or "free"
	Wear <u>loose</u> clothing when you exercise.

principal	Means "the head of a school" or "chief, most important" Wheat is the <u>principal</u> crop of this region.
principle	Means "a basic rule or law" or "a rule of conduct" It is against her <u>principles</u> to lie.
rise	Means "to get up" or "to go up" After a heavy rain, the river always <u>rises.</u>
raise	Means "to lift" or "to move higher" Help us <u>raise</u> the mainsail.
shall, will	For the future and future perfect tenses, *shall* was once preferred with the first person (I <u>shall</u> try) and *will* was used with the second and third person (you, they <u>will</u> try). Today this distinction is not usually made, and *will* is acceptable with the first person also. I <u>will</u> be there by noon.
than	A conjunction often used when making comparisons My brother is older <u>than</u> I am.
then	An adverb that tells when Read the chapter; <u>then</u> answer the questions.
that, which	Relative pronouns used to introduce adjective clauses. *Which* refers to things; *that* refers to people or things. *That* is usually preferred in essential clauses (those not set off by commas); *which* is preferred in nonessential clauses (those set off by commas). The story <u>that</u> we read was a mystery. The story, <u>which</u> was written in 1845, is by Edgar Allan Poe.
their	Possessive form of the pronoun *they* <u>Their</u> team has won every game.
there	An adverb that tells where The car is over <u>there.</u> A word used with forms of the verb *be* to begin sentences <u>There</u> is no time to lose. An interjection <u>There</u>! That should stop the leak.
they're	Contraction of *they are* <u>They're</u> anxious to begin.

theirs	A possessive pronoun that can stand alone
	Our car is parked near <u>theirs.</u>
there's	Contraction of *there is* and *there has*
	<u>There's</u> a message for you by the phone.
to	A preposition that means "toward" or "against"
	Dad drove us <u>to</u> school today.
	A word used to begin an infinitive
	My sister is learning <u>to</u> drive.
too	An adverb that means "also"
	This box is empty, <u>too.</u>
	An adverb that means "very" or "excessively"
	It is <u>too</u> noisy in here.
two	Means "the number between one and three"
	Elena bought <u>two</u> tickets for the concert.
whose	Possessive form of the pronoun *who*
	<u>Whose</u> notebook is this?
who's	Contraction of *who is* and *who has*
	<u>Who's</u> your favorite short-story writer?
your	Possessive form of the pronoun *you*
	Don't forget <u>your</u> keys.
you're	Contraction of *you are*
	Let me know when <u>you're</u> ready.

Glossary of Terms

Active voice   A verb is in the active voice when the subject of a sentence performs the action. *page 194.*

Adjective   An adjective describes or modifies a noun or a pronoun. *pages 6, 302.*

Adjective clause   An adjective clause is a subordinate clause that modifies a noun or pronoun. *page 488.*

Adjective phrase   An adjective phrase is a prepositional phrase that modifies a noun or pronoun. *page 415.*

Adverb   An adverb modifies a verb, an adjective, or another adverb. *pages 6, 354.*

Adverb clause   An adverb clause is a subordinate clause used as an adverb in a complex sentence. *page 486.*

Adverb phrase   An adverb phrase is a prepositional phrase that modifies a verb, an adjective, or an adverb. *page 416.*

Alliteration   Alliteration is the repetition of an initial sound, usually a consonant. *page 274.*

Anecdote   An anecdote is a brief, interesting story. *page 150.*

Antecedent   An antecedent is the word or words to which a pronoun refers. A pronoun agrees with its antecedent in number and gender. *page 246.*

Antonyms   Antonyms are words with opposite meanings. *page 136.*

Appositive   An appositive is a word or group of words that follows a noun or pronoun and identifies or explains it. *page 68.*

Articles   The words *a*, *an*, and *the* are a special kind of adjective called articles. *page 302.*

Audience   The audience is the person or people you write for. *page 36.*

Bibliography   A bibliography is a list of all the sources of information used in preparing a report. *page 387.*

Cause-and-effect paragraph   A cause-and-effect paragraph tells what happened and why it happened. *page 442.*

Character   A character is a person or animal in a story. *page 510.*

Clause   A clause is a group of words that has a subject and a verb. *page 484.*

Climax   The climax is the highest point of tension in a story. *page 510.*

Clincher sentence   A clincher sentence summarizes or restates the main idea of the paragraph. *page 86.*

Collective noun   A collective noun is a noun that names a group. *page 546.*

Common noun   A common noun is the general name for a person, place, or thing. *page 60.*

Comparative degree   The comparative degree is the form of an adjective or adverb used to compare two persons, places, or things. *pages 307, 358.*

Complete predicate   A complete predicate is all the words in the predicate part of a sentence. It tells what the subject is or does. *page 8.*

Complete subject   A complete subject is all the words in the subject part of a sentence. It names someone or something. *page 8.*

Complex sentence   A complex sentence has one independent clause and at least one subordinate clause. *page 484.*

Compound   A compound is a word formed by connecting two or more smaller words. *page 70.*

Compound sentence   A compound sentence consists of two or more simple sentences joined with a conjunction or with a semicolon. *page 18.*

Compound subject   A compound subject is two or more simple subjects that have the same verb. *page 16.*

Compound verb   A compound verb is two or more verbs that have the same subject. *page 16.*

Conflict   Conflict is the problem to be solved in a story. *page 510.*

Conjugation   A conjugation is a list of all the forms of a verb, arranged by tense. *page 183.*

Conjunction   A conjunction joins words or groups of words in a sentence. *pages 6, 420.*

Connotation   A connotation is the positive or negative feeling associated with a word. *page 494.*

Context clue   A context clue is words that surround an unknown word and give a clue to its meaning. *page 310.*

Coordinating conjunctions   Coordinating conjunctions connect words or groups of words. *And*, *but*, *or*, and *nor* are coordinating conjunctions. *page 420.*

Correlative conjunctions Correlative conjunctions connect either words or groups of words. Examples are *both... and*, *either...or*, *neither...nor*. *page 420*.

Couplet A couplet is two lines of poetry that rhyme, one after the other. *page 275*.

Dangling modifier A dangling modifier is a participial phrase that has no word it can logically modify in a sentence. *page 482*.

Declarative sentence A declarative sentence makes a statement. It ends with a period. *page 4*.

Demonstrative adjective A demonstrative adjective points out the noun it describes. *page 304*.

Demonstrative pronoun A demonstrative pronoun emphatically points out its antecedent. *page 250*.

Denotation A denotation is the exact meaning of a word. *page 494*.

Dialogue Dialogue is the conversation between characters in a story. *page 154*.

Direct object A direct object receives the action of the verb. *page 128*.

Double negative A double negative is the incorrect use of two or more negative words in the same sentence. *page 360*.

Doublets Doublets are two words derived from the same source. *page 137*.

Emphatic form The emphatic form of a verb shows emphasis or strong feeling. *page 190*.

Essential clause An essential clause is an adjective clause that is necessary to the meaning of the sentence. *page 488*.

Essential participial phrase An essential participial phrase is necessary to the meaning of the sentence and is not set off by commas. *page 475*.

Exclamatory sentence An exclamatory sentence expresses strong feeling. It ends with an exclamation mark. *page 4*.

Explanatory paragraph An explanatory paragraph explains something or proves a point. *page 88*.

Formal language Formal language is the language used on more serious occasions, such as in reports, essays, legal documents, or speeches. *page 260*.

Future perfect tense The future perfect tense of a verb expresses an action that will be completed before a definite time in the future. *page 182*.

Future tense The future tense of a verb expresses an action that will occur in the future. *page 182*.

Gerund A gerund is a verb form ending in *-ing* that is used as a noun. *page 477*.

Gerund phrase A gerund phrase is a gerund and its related words. *page 477*.

Helping verb A helping verb is any of the other verbs besides the main verb in a verb phrase. *page 126*.

Homographs Homographs are words that are spelled alike but have different origins and meanings. *page 426*.

Homophones Homophones are words that sound alike but have different origins, meanings, and spellings. *page 426*.

Idiom An idiom is an expression whose meaning cannot be understood by simply combining the meanings of the individual words. *page 198*.

Imperative sentence An imperative sentence gives a command or makes a request. It ends with a period. *page 4*.

Indefinite pronoun An indefinite pronoun does not always refer to a particular person, place, or thing. *page 254*.

Independent clause An independent clause is a group of words that can stand alone as a simple sentence. *page 484*.

Indirect object An indirect object comes before the direct object and tells to whom or for whom the action of the verb is done. *page 130*.

Infinitive An infinitive is the basic form of the verb preceded by *to*. It can be used as a noun, an adjective, or an adverb. *page 479*.

Infinitive phrase An infinitive phrase is an infinitive and its related words. *page 479*.

Informal language Informal language is the language of everyday speech and writing. *page 260*.

Intensive pronoun An intensive pronoun emphasizes another word in the sentence. *page 252*.

Interjection An interjection is a word that expresses emotion or feeling. *pages 6, 422*.

Interrogative pronoun An interrogative pronoun is a pronoun that asks a question. *page 250*.

Interrogative sentence An interrogative sentence asks a question. It ends with a question mark. *page 4*.

Intransitive verb An intransitive verb is a verb that does not have a direct object. *page 134.*

Inverted word order In a sentence with inverted word order, the subject comes after the verb. *page 12.*

Irregular verb An irregular verb does not form its principal parts by adding *-ed. page 186.*

Linking verb A linking verb links the subject of a sentence with a word in the predicate. *page 132.*

Main verb A main verb is the most important verb in a verb phrase. *page 126.*

Metaphor A metaphor is a kind of comparison that says that one thing is another. *page 276.*

Mood Mood is the general feeling or atmosphere in a story. *page 512.*

Myths Myths are ancient stories that share many common elements. *page 564.*

Nonessential clause A nonessential clause is an adjective clause that is not necessary to the meaning of the sentence but merely adds information. *page 488.*

Nonessential participial phrase A nonessential participial phrase is not necessary to the meaning of the sentence but merely adds information. It is set off by commas. *page 475.*

Normal word order In a sentence with normal word order, the subject comes before the verb. *page 12.*

Noun A noun names a person, place, thing, or idea. *pages 6, 58.*

Noun clause A noun clause is a subordinate clause used as a noun. *page 492.*

Number Number means that a word is singular or plural. *page 540.*

Onomatopoeia Onomatopoeia is using words which sound alike or imitate what they describe. *page 274.*

Paragraph A paragraph is a group of related sentences about one main idea. *page 86.*

Paraphrasing Paraphrasing is expressing in your own words ideas or information you have read. *page 384.*

Participial phrase A participial phrase is a participle and its related words. It acts as an adjective. *page 475.*

Participle A participle is a verb form used as an adjective. *page 474.*

Passive voice A verb is in the passive voice when the subject of a sentence receives the action. *page 194.*

Past perfect tense The past perfect tense of a verb expresses an action that occurred before another past action. *page 182.*

Past tense The past tense of a verb expresses an action that took place in the past. *page 182.*

Personification Personification is giving human characteristics to inanimate objects and other nonhuman things. *page 277.*

Plagiarism Plagiarism is copying material exactly without using quotation marks or giving credit. *page 384.*

Plot The plot is the story plan. It is the action or sequence of events. *page 510.*

Point of view The point of view is the way a story gets told, either in the first person or the third person. *page 152.*

Positive degree The positive degree is the basic form of an adjective or adverb used to describe one person, place, or thing. *pages 307, 358.*

Possessive noun A possessive noun shows ownership. *page 66.*

Possessive pronoun A possessive pronoun shows ownership. Possessive pronouns are used to replace possessive nouns. *page 248.*

Predicate adjective A predicate adjective follows a linking verb and describes the subject of the sentence. *page 132.*

Predicate nominative A predicate nominative is a noun or pronoun that follows a linking verb and renames or identifies the subject of the sentence. *page 132.*

Prefix A prefix is a word part added to the beginning of a base word or root. *page 552.*

Preposition A preposition relates a noun or pronoun to another word in the sentence. *pages 6, 412.*

Prepositional phrase A prepositional phrase includes the preposition, its object, and any words that modify the object. *page 412.*

Present perfect tense The present perfect tense of a verb expresses an action that occurred at an indefinite time in the past and may still be going on. *page 182.*

Present tense The present tense of a verb expresses an action taking place now. *page 182.*

Prewriting   Prewriting is the stage in which writers gather ideas and get ready to write. *page Introduction 4.*

Principal parts   The principal parts of a verb are its basic forms. They are the present, the past, the past participle, and the present participle. *page 180.*

Progressive form   The progressive form of a verb shows continuing action. *page 190.*

Pronoun   A pronoun takes the place of a noun or nouns. *pages 6, 244.*

Proofreading   Proofreading is the stage in which writers look for and correct errors in their writing. *page Introduction 7.*

Proper adjective   A proper adjective is formed from a proper noun. *page 304.*

Proper noun   A proper noun names a particular person, place, or thing. *page 60.*

Publishing   Publishing is the stage in which writers share their writing with others. *page Introduction 7.*

Purpose   Purpose is your reason for writing. *page 36.*

Quatrain   A quatrain is a four-line stanza of poetry. *page 275.*

Reflexive pronoun   A reflexive pronoun refers to a noun or pronoun in the same sentence, usually the subject. *page 252.*

Relative pronoun   A relative pronoun relates an adjective clause to the modified noun or pronoun. *page 490.*

Resolution   The resolution is what happens at the end of a story. *page 510.*

Revising   Revising is the stage in which writers make changes to improve their writing. *page Introduction 6.*

Run-on sentence   A run-on sentence is two or more sentences separated by just a comma or no punctuation. *page 20.*

Sentence   A sentence is a group of words that expresses a complete thought. *page 4.*

Sentence fragment   A sentence fragment is part of a sentence written as if it were a sentence. *page 20.*

Setting   The setting is the time and place in which the story happens. *page 510.*

Simile   A simile is a kind of comparison that includes the word *like* or *as.* *page 276.*

Simple predicate   A simple predicate is the main word or words in the complete predicate of a sentence. It is always a verb. *page 10.*

Simple sentence   A simple sentence has one subject and one verb, either or both of which may be compound. *page 18.*

Simple subject   A simple subject is the main word or words in the complete subject of a sentence. *page 10.*

Slang   Slang is an expression used in informal language. *page 260.*

Split infinitive   A split infinitive is caused by placing an adverb between the *to* and the verb of an infinitive. *page 482.*

Subordinate clause   A subordinate clause has a subject and a verb but cannot stand alone as a sentence. *page 484.*

Subordinating conjunctions   Subordinating conjunctions are words that begin adverb clauses. *page 486.*

Suffix   A suffix is a word part added to the end of a base word. *page 364.*

Summarize   To summarize is to write only the main ideas in as few words as possible. *page 384.*

Superlative degree   The superlative degree is the form of an adjective or adverb used to compare three or more persons, places, or things. *pages 307, 358.*

Synonyms   Synonyms are words whose meanings are only slightly different. *page 136.*

Tense   The tense of a verb shows time. *page 183.*

Tercet   A tercet is a three-line stanza of poetry. *page 275.*

Thesaurus   A thesaurus is a book that contains a list of synonyms and sometimes antonyms. *page 22.*

Thesis statement   A thesis statement tells the main idea to be developed in a report. *page 386.*

Topic sentence   The topic sentence states the main idea of a paragraph. *page 86.*

Transitive verb   A transitive verb is a verb that has a direct object. *page 134.*

Verb   A verb expresses action or being. *pages 6, 124.*

Verb phrase   A verb phrase is made up of a main verb and one or more helping verbs. *page 126.*

Verbals   Verbals are verb forms that are used as adjectives, adverbs, or nouns. *page 474.*

Writing   Writing is the stage in which writers put their ideas on paper. *page Introduction 5.*

Index

Connections
between grammar and writing, *See* Grammar–Writing Connection.
between reading and writing, *See* Reading and Writing Connection.
Connotation, 494–495, 527
Constance: A Story of Early Plymouth, from, by Patricia Clapp, 28–33
Context clues, 310–311, 341
Contractions, 248–249, 542–543
Coolidge, Olivia, "Athene's City," 558–561
Cooperative learning, 25, 41, 73, 99, 139, 157, 201, 219, 263, 279, 313, 329, 367, 391, 429, 449, 497, 515, 555, 567
Coordinating conjunctions, 420–421, 460
Correlative conjunctions, 420–421, 460
Couplets, 274–275
Creating, A Strategy for, 266–267
Creating, Writing Process, 280–287
Creative Thinking. *See* Thinking Strategies.
Creative Writing, 27, 75, 141, 203, 265, 315, 369, 431, 499, 557
Critical Thinking. *See* Thinking Strategies.
"Crossing, The" by May Swenson, 278
Cubing, 332. *See also* Prewriting Strategies.
Curriculum Connection, 42, 108, 166, 228, 288, 338, 400, 458, 524, 568

Dates,
commas in, 629, 630, 631, 656–657
"Daylight and Moonlight," from, by Henry Wadsworth Longfellow, 276–277
Declarative sentences, 4–5, 12–15, 47
Definite article, 302–303
Demonstrative adjectives, 304–305, 340
Demonstrative pronouns, 250–251, 295–296
Denotation, 494–495, 527
"The Descent of Winter," from, by William Carlos Williams, 274
Describing, A Strategy for, 316–317
Describing, Writing Process, 330–337
Description
details for, 322–323
observe carefully, 322–323
words for the senses, 324–325, 326–327
visualize, 322–323
Descriptive paragraphs, 326–327
Details
in descriptive paragraphs, 324–325, 326–327
sensory, 324–325, 326–327, 341
specific words for, 322–323, 324–325, 326–327
in supporting sentences, 86–87, 88–89, 94–97
using to create mood, 512–513
writing with, 94–97, 324–325, 326–327
Dewey decimal system, 590–591
Diagraming, 668–675
Dialogue
punctuation of, 154–155, 642–643, 658–659, 660–661
writing, 154–155, 169

Dickinson, Emily, untitled poem, 270
Dictionary, 598–599. *See also* Thesaurus.
Dictionary of Knowledge, 600–611
using the, 11, 39, 67, 97, 127, 155, 193, 213, 247, 273, 308, 323, 363, 389, 419, 443, 483, 511, 551, 565
Different, from, 678
Direct objects, 128–129, 130–131, 256–257, 477–478
Discussions. *See* Listening; Speaking; Speaking and Listening.
Do
agreement of, with subject, 542–543, 578
in contractions, 542–543
emphatic forms of verbs, 190–191
as helping verb, 126–127, 190–191, 542–543
as main verb, 542–543
Double negatives, avoiding, 360–361, 402, 408
Doublets, 137
Drama. *See* Writing across the curriculum.
Drawing Conclusions, 204–205, 209, 222, 228, 432–433, 439, 452, 458. *See also* Thinking Skills.
"Dreams," by Langston Hughes, 276

Editing. *See* Proofreading; Revising.
Editorial
"Vaccination drives for kids will take place around world," by Coretta Scott King, 206–209
Elements of a story. *See* Myth; Story.
Emphatic forms of verbs, 190–191, 230
Encyclopedias, 380–381, 592
End marks, 4–5, 648–649
English, history of, 23, 71, 137, 199, 261, 311, 365, 427, 495, 553
Entry words. *See* Dictionary; Thesaurus.
Envelopes, addresses on, 632, 656–657
Eponyms, 261
Etymology, 23, 71, 137, 199, 261, 311, 365, 427, 495, 553
Exclamation marks
as end marks, 4–5, 648–649
after interjections, 422–423
Exclamatory sentence, 4–5, 47, 648–649

Fact and opinion, 210–213, 231
Fantasy
from *The Hobbit*, by J.R.R. Tolkien, 502–507
Fewer, less, 679
Fiction
from *Constance: A Story of Early Plymouth*, by Patricia Clapp, 28–31
See also Fantasy; Mythology.
Figurative language, 276–277, 291
Figures of speech, 276–277, 291
Fine Arts, 26–27, 74–75, 140–141, 202–203, 264–265, 314–315, 368–369, 430–431, 498–499, 556–557
First draft, sample, 103, 161, 223, 283, 333, 395, 453, 519
First-person point of view, 152–153